THE
CAPE BRETON FIDDLE
COMPANION

LIZ DOHERTY

Dedicated to Tic (1919-1995) and Emily Butler.
Thank you for giving me a Cape Breton home.

THE
CAPE BRETON FIDDLE
COMPANION

LIZ DOHERTY

Editorial Advisors

Fintan Vallely

Sheldon MacInnes

Paul MacDonald

Glenn Graham

Kate Dunlay

With Support From

Canada Research Chair In Musical Traditions, Cape Breton University
Celtic Colours International Festival, Cranford Publications,
Ulster University, The Arts Council /An Chomhairle Ealaíon

Cape Breton University Press recognizes the support of the Province of Nova Scotia and the support received for its publishing program from the Canada Council for the Arts Block Grants Program. We are pleased to work in partnership with these bodies to develop and promote our cultural resources.

With support from The Arts Council /An Chomhairle Ealaíon

Cover image: *Kitchen Party*, by Willam D. Roach, Chéticamp, NS.
Author photograph: Lorcan Doherty Photography.
Cover design: Cathy MacLean Design, Chéticamp, NS.
Layout: Mike Hunter, Port Hawkesbury and Sydney, NS.
Sheet music, front cover: "Trip to Mabou Ridge," by Dan Hughie MacEachern.
Sheet music, back cover: "Lonesome Eyes," by Jerry Holland. Courtesy of Fiddlesticks Music Publishing.
Music transcriptions: Paul Cranford, Cranford Publications.
First printed in Canada.

Library and Archives Canada Cataloguing in Publication

Doherty, Liz, author
    The Cape Breton fiddle companion / Liz Doherty.

Includes bibliographical references and index.
Issued in print and electronic formats.
ISBN 978-1-77206-024-9 (paperback).--ISBN 978-1-77206-025-6 (pdf).--
ISBN 978-1-77206-026-3 (epub).--ISBN 978-1-77206-027-0 (Kindle)

    1. Fiddling--Nova Scotia--Cape Breton Island--Encyclopedias.
2. Fiddle tunes--Nova Scotia--Cape Breton Island--Encyclopedias.
3. Fiddlers--Canada--Biography. I. Title.

ML863.7.N8D655 2015   787.2'1620097169   C2015-905908-9
                                                    C2015-905909-7

Cape Breton University Press
1250 Grand Lake Road
Sydney, NS B1P 6L2 CA
www.cbupress.ca

TABLE OF CONTENTS

Acknowledgements

There is an Irish proverb that reads *"ní neart go cur le chéile,"* or many hands make light work. *The Cape Breton Fiddle Companion* has been, from start to finish, a collaboration involving many people from both sides of the Atlantic Ocean. Since its inception, but most especially over the last few months, as the project inched toward the finish line, there was a whole community, albeit a scattered one, pulling together to make it happen. I feel particularly privileged to be enabled by that community to tell some of Cape Breton's music story for, no matter how much Cape Breton feels like my second home, I am conscious of the fact that I am absolutely an "outsider." This *Companion* is not the definitive overview of Cape Breton fiddle music but simply another contribution to the growing body of literature about this rich and unique culture.

The idea for the *Companion* came from the work of Fintan Vallely, who had compiled and edited *The Companion to Irish Traditional Music* in 1999, with a second, expanded edition published in 2011. Fintan has been on board since I suggested a Cape Breton version of the *Companion* – from teaching me how to use File Maker Pro to getting the red pen out and editing two complete drafts. A panel of Cape Breton advisors was also instated to oversee the full volume from a first draft stage: Sheldon MacInnes, Paul MacDonald, Glenn Graham and Kate Dunlay. Collectively their expertise covers pretty much all aspects of Cape Breton culture, from practitioner to academic; most importantly, each of them is passionate about Cape Breton music and their advice and guidance has been critical in shaping each and every entry in this book. Glenn took on this project in the midst of finishing his own PhD and Kate while busy teaching; Sheldon and Paul on many days have put in as many hours as me in checking details, reworking material, going back and digging some more – really, this whole project would not be anywhere near as complete without their immense knowledge of the Cape Breton music tradition.

There were many others whose input was invaluable for particular parts of the book. From day one, Paul Cranford has been unstinting in his generosity in sharing information, answering questions and providing new data and perspectives. A total star! Barbara Le Blanc and her team in Chéticamp – Charlie Dan Roach, Jean-Doris Le Blanc and Sally Ross – you are all amazing. To Wendy Bergfeldt and Barry Shears for the huge input into the media and bagpipe sections, respectively, I am indebted. And to all the others who helped with big sections of the material: Ken Donovan, Jim Watson, Lewis MacKinnon, Doug MacPhee, Chris McDonald, John Donald Cameron, Dan MacDonald, Frank MacInnis, Mark Wilson, Betty Matheson, Ron MacInnis, Ken Perlman, Burt Feintuch, Goiridh Dòmhnullach. Thanks also to Dave Mahalik, Rodney MacDonald, Mats Melin, Kinnon Beaton, Donnie Campbell, Andrea Beaton, Dawn Beaton, Margie Beaton, David Butler, Melody and Derrick Cameron, Sheumas MacNeil, Jackie Dunn MacIsaac, Margie Dunn, Cliff McGann, Ian McKinnon, Kinnon Beaton, Pat Chafe, Wendy MacIsaac, Marie Thompson, Ron Caplan, Chrissy

Crowley, Lisa Mitchell Brown, Daniel Neely, Mick Moloney, Roxanne O'Connell, Evelyn Osborne, Bridget O'Connell, Dale Gillis, Marlene MacInnes, Howie MacDonald, Susan MacLean, Barbara MacDonald Magone, Marie Thompson, Cheryl Smith, Lucy MacNeil, Sheumas MacNeil and all the Barra MacNeils, Jean and Columba MacNeil, Monica MacDougall, Marion MacLeod, Lois MacIsaac, Fr. Eugene Morris, Blair and Gerardette Brown, Donnie Campbell, Ian Hayes, Kimberley Fraser, Allie Bennett, John Pellerin, Joel Chiasson, Buddy MacDonald, Robert Deveaux, Jerry Holland Jr., Renie Fitzgerald, Mike Fitzgerald, Joanne Donovan and Chris White, Trish Donovan, Troy MacGillivray, Mac Morin, John Pellerin, Susan Beaton, Pat Phee, Trese MacNeil, Marie and Malcie MacPhee, Shauna Walters, Hilda Chiasson, Sarah Beck, Lisa MacIsaac, Lisa MacArthur, Shelly Campbell, Allan Dewar, Gaston Aucoin, Debbie Mullins, Tracey MacNeil, Eileen Forrester, Jim Morrow, Frances MacEachen, Wendell Ellis, Brenda Stubbert, Mario Colosimo, Lois Ferguson, Janine Randall, Harvey Beaton, David Greenberg, George Ruckert, Alan Snyder, Max MacDonald, Stephen MacDonald, Francis MacDonald, Bernadette MacNeil, Fred White, Dwayne Côté, Lorcan Doherty, John W. MacDonald, David Suff at Topic Records, Victor Maurice Faubert, Bill Aucoin, Flo Sampson, Ben Cheevers, Roberta Head, Sharon Quinn, Jane Arnold and Catherine Arseneau, Sheldon MacLeod Photography (Glace Bay). Those who had helped in earlier iterations of my Cape Breton research especially Allister MacGillivray, Joey Beaton, Dave MacIsaac, Denis Ryan, Mike and Marlene Denny and Máire O'Keefe. To all the institutions and organizations who have been incredibly helpful: The Beaton Institute, The Celtic Music Interpretive Centre, Highland Village Museum. A massive thanks also to Joella Foulds at Celtic Colours for her support from the start and to Richard MacKinnon and Heather Sparling at CBU for all of their help and guidance. To Mike Hunter at CBU for believing in the project and that it would come together – eventually! And for the wonderful front cover image – William (Bill) Roach.

Life (babies, jobs, house moves, etc.) meant that my original intention to write much of this book in Cape Breton did not come to be; most of it came together in Coounty Donegal and it was helped along in no small part by an amazing crew of friends and family who pitched in by doing everything from babysitting to counselling to proofreading! *Míle buíochas* to team Ireland Donegal: Anne Nelson (who was my right hand for so much of this project from start to finish), Deirdre Ní Theimhneáin, Keenan Barrett and Helena Foley, Una Daly, Warner Robinson, Louise Gallagher, Caoimhín MacAoidh, Seamus Maguire. In Derry at Ulster University: Cormac Newark, Paul Moore, Frank Lyons, Ailbhe Ó Corráin, Iseult Wilson, Billy Scampton, Karen Thompson, Catherine Russell, Sinead Grant, Caroline Elvin, Maggie Maguire, Aidan O'Donnell, Fionnuala Carlin; also in Derry: Gino Lupari, Frank Gallagher, Eibhlín Ní Dhochartaigh, Gearóid Ó hEára and all at Culturlann Uí Chanáin. In Cork: Tricia Harrington, Ann Burns. In Limerick: Mícheál Ó Súilleabháin, Mats Melin, Tony Langlois, Orfhlaith Ní Bhriain. In Dublin: Tom Sherlock, Rab Cherry, Martin Fanning, Rebecca Draisey-Collinshaw, Nicholas Carolan, Grace Toland and Danny Diamond at ITMA. And in Scotland, Louise Hunter, Lauren McColl, Fin Moore; and, in Amsterdam, Bairbre Scallan. To the Doherty family (especially my mother, Teresa, and sister Martina – not forgetting Nigel!), Woods family (especially

Granny Woods) and the Grants (Mary, Margaret and Joe) thank you for everything. And above all to my husband Jim for keeping everything together to let me get on with it (and for supplying coffee and chocolate in copius quantities!) – and to and our two lovely boys, Odhrán and Dallán … mammy's finished!!

I made my first visit to Cape Breton in April, 1992 – that trip changed my life. To all the amazing musicians who shared their music with me over the years, I thank you from the bottom of my heart. A number of those have since passed on – great music-loving friends like June Arnold and, sadly, too many great musicians. Among them are the very first Cape Breton players I had ever encountered: John Morris Rankin, Jerry Holland, Dougie MacDonald and Buddy MacMaster. I feel so fortunate to have had the opportunity to meet and play music with these – my musical heroes always. And finally, to the late Tic Butler and his wife, Emily – little did you know that when Denis Ryan landed with me at your door you were stuck with me for good! Thanks for everything.

Liz Doherty,
Buncrana, Co. Donegal

Using the Companion

Finding Information

Information is substantially in A-Z format. Exceptions to this are families, who are grouped together. Tune books, for the most part, are presented under the author/editor's name; otherwise, they appear alphabetically or in the "tune-books" article (e.g., *The Cape Breton Scottish Collection* can be found under "tune-books: Scotland"). Cross-references have been used throughout to guide the reader to connected articles.

Abbreviations

The convention adopted is to use abbreviations or acronyms for repeatedly used organizational and other titles. The most common of these are listed overleaf.

References

Where a published work is quoted or extensively drawn from in the writing of an article, bibliographic information is provided in abbreviated form and in square brackets at the end of the article; full references are provided in the Select Bibliography at the back of the book.

Contributors

Many people have contributed to the gathering of information for this book, particularly in relation to the articles on individuals. In addition, a number of people (in addition to the advisory panel) have made significant contribution to some of the more general articles. Their input is acknowledged at the end of the relevant articles by their initials. These contributors are: Wendy Bergfeldt (WB), Mats Melin (MM),

Glenn Graham (GG), Barbara Le Blanc (BLB), Jean-Doris Le Blanc (JDLB), Paul Mac-Donald (PMD), Sheldon MacInnes (SMI), Lewis MacKinnon (LMK), Charlie Dan Roach (CDR), Sally Ross (SR), Barry Shears (BS).

Index

The A-Z section of this book is in itself an index, but in order to facilitate the location of the many references to other key contributors to the tradition who are mentioned throughout, an index of such names is provided at the end of the book.

ABBREVIATIONS

Celtic Colours International Festival is referred to as **Celtic Colours.**
Colaiste na Gàidhlig / The Gaelic College is referred to as the **Gaelic College.**
Baile nan Gàidheal / Nova Scotia Highland Village is referred to as the **Highland Village**.

ACBC	*A Cape Breton Ceilidh* (book by Allister MacGillivray, 1988)
AHS	Antigonish Highland Society
AOH	Ancient Order of Hibernians
ATG	An Tulloch Gorm Society of Cape Breton
CARAS	Canadian Academy of Recording Arts and Sciences
CBC	Canadian Broadcasting Corporation
CBF	*The Cape Breton Fiddler* (book by Allister MacGillivray, 1981)
CBFA	Cape Breton Fiddlers' Association
CBM	Cape Breton's Magazine
CBMIC	Cape Breton Music Industry Cooperative
CBPMA	Cape Breton Professional Musicians' Association
CBU	Cape Breton University
CCA	Canadian Council for the Arts
CCB	Committee for Cape Breton
CFM	Comunn Feis Mhàbu
CFMA	Canadian Folk Music Awards
CIMA	Canadian Independent Music Association
CIRPA	Canadian Independent Record Production Association
CMIC	Celtic Music Interpretive Centre, Judique
CMPA	Canadian Music Publishers Association
CMRRA	Canadian Music Reproduction Rights Agency
CNSLC	Creative Nova Scotia Leadership Council
ECMA	East Coast Music Association; East Coast Music Awards
FACTOR	Foundation Assisting Canadian Talent on Recordings
MNS	Music Nova Scotia
MROC	Musicians' Rights Organization, Canada
NAFCo	North Atlantic Fiddle Convention
NSDCCH	Nova Scotia Department of Communities, Culture and Heritage
VCBF	*The Vanishing Cape Breton Fiddler* (CBC-TV documentary, 1971)

LIZ DOHERTY

A Note from the Editors

We have made every effort to properly identify and to acquire the permissions to publish images, facts and figures. That's not always an easy task and, though every effort has been made to obtain those important aspects for this publication of Dr. Doherty's research, we were not always successful. CBU Press understands and upholds its responsibilities in this regard to the best of our ability, and we sincerely regret any infringements in this area. Responsibility for the research and permissions, and for the opinions and theories expressed, rests with the author.

The scope of a project such as this is immense; the original outline included some 2,000 possible entries. Less than half of these are included in this present volume, and so some difficult decisions had to be made regarding inclusion criteria. The ambition of the book was to provide a broad overview of Cape Breton fiddle music as it exists in the early 21st century. As such, it was decided to foreground players who are particularly active in the public domain, generally those with commercially released recordings; in terms of historical players, those whose impact has significantly shaped today's tradition have also been included. This, of course, means that there are hundreds of great Cape Breton fiddle players who are not featured in individual articles in this book; many of them are referenced throughout and are listed in the index. It is also the ambition of this book to be expanded, over time, in an online capacity; this will allow for a more comprehensive approach. At the time of publication, the URL for the planned website will be

http://www.capebretonfiddlecompanion.com

A Timeline of Cape Breton Fiddle Music

— 1700-early 1900s —

This period is a formative one in terms of immigration and the transplanting of Gaelic culture from the Highlands and Islands of Scotland to Cape Breton Island, Nova Scotia. There is evidence of fiddle music, bagpiping, song and dance being practiced among the early settlers; from the 1820s evidence that the music was being passed on, informally and by "professors."

1700- A substantial body of Scottish fiddle music was published during this time, both traditional and newly composed tunes. This era included what came to be known as the "golden age" of Scottish fiddle music (ca. 1780-ca. 1820); among its chief exponents were such Gaelic-speaking fiddler-composers as Neil Gow and William Marshall.

1715-1758 Trained musicians from Europe engaged at Louisbourg.

1763 Cape Breton annexed to Nova Scotia.

1773-1850 Emigration from Scotland to Cape Breton, initially via the Nova Scotia mainland and Prince Edward Island and, from 1802, directly. An 1802 census records a population of 2,513 in Cape Breton; over the following decades some 30,000 Scots settled in Cape Breton.

1784 Colony of Cape Breton separated from Nova Scotia.

1815 Bishop Plessis in his diaries chastises musicians in the Little Bras d'Or area for their practices and behaviours.

1820 Cape Breton again annexed to Nova Scotia.

1845-1851 The Great Famine in Cape Breton.

1857 Congregation of the Sisters of Notre Dame (previously established in Cape Breton in the 1700s, teaching music to young women in French communities) arrived in Arichat and introduced the piano.

1861 Antigonish Highland Society formed; the Antigonish Highland Games were first held in 1863.

1865-1894 Fr. Kenneth MacDonald became parish priest in Mabou; led a robust campaign against alcohol consumption and associated events and activities, and gained notoriety for destroying fiddles.

1867 Canada formed, July 1.

1891 First known fiddle contest held in Glendale.

1892 Gaelic newspaper *Mac-Talla* founded in Sydney; continued until 1904.

1897 First Mabou Picnic held.

1890-1900 Square sets first introduced to Cape Breton from Boston.

ca. 1900 First dance halls appear in Cape Breton; pump organ (parlour reed organ) first used to accompany fiddle music.

ca. 1905   First Cape Breton tune appears in print, a pipe march by Archie A. Beaton of Mabou in David Glen's *Collection of Highland Bagpipe Music, Book 7*, published in Edinburgh, Scotland.

1914   First World War until 1918; pipers in the military receiving tuition in music literacy, a skill later passed on to fiddle players.

— 1920s —

Much Cape Breton fiddle music happening in Boston; the first commercial recordings featuring Cape Breton fiddlers are made in the U.S.; these are in 78 rpm record format. Fiddle contests are popular; radio is introduced; by now pianos have begun to be imported, often ordered through mail-order catalogue.

1920   The Sydney Gaelic Society is formed.

1926   Major fiddle contests held with regional heats around Cape Breton and finals held in Boston. Contests most popular in this decade, although continued to be so through the 1940s; after that they declined substantially although resurrected occasionally as late as the 1980s.

1928   First recordings of Cape Breton fiddlers Charlie MacKinnon and "Big" Dan Hughie MacEachern with the Columbia Scotch Band (also known as the Caledonia Scotch Band) in the U.S.

1929   CJCB Radio on air for the first time in Sydney; *Toronto Star* newspaper reports that bagpipes were still the popular instrument for dancing to in Cape Breton.

— 1930s —

Boston continues as a hotbed of activity for Cape Breton music and dance; Detroit also developing a busy Cape Breton scene. The first recordings of Cape Breton fiddlers made in Canada. Collecting of Gaelic language, song, storytelling begins in Cape Breton.

ca. 1930   Piano taking over from the pump organ as the accompanying instrument of choice; callers become a regular feature at dances.

1932   Pioneer Scottish fiddle recordings made in Canada by Colin J. Boyd of Antigonish, on the Brunswick label, with Bess Siddall MacDonald on piano.

1933   CBC Radio established (originally CRBC); in 1936 a regional production centre opens in Halifax.

1934   The Inverness Serenaders recorded for the Decca label in the U.S.

1935   Cape Breton fiddlers Dan J. Campbell, Angus Chisholm and Angus Allan Gillis, with Mrs. W.J. MacDonald on piano, record for Antigonish label Celtic Records, owned by Bernie MacIsaac, in Montréal. They were the first Cape Breton fiddlers to record in Canada. *Cottar's Saturday Night* radio show produced and broadcast nationwide until 1937; it featured Cape Breton fiddlers Tena Campbell and Jimmie MacLellan.

1936   Nova Scotia Club of Detroit formed; electricity comes to Cape Breton.

1937   John Lorne Campbell of Canna, Scotland, and his American wife, Margaret Fay Shaw, made first recording expedition to Cape Breton, collecting Gaelic songs.

1938   The Gaelic College of Arts and Crafts opens at St. Ann's.

1939   Second World War until 1945. Fiddler Dan R. MacDonald is stationed in Scotland with the Canadian Forces; acquires many published collections and establishes contact with booksellers; many tune books subsequently arrive in Cape Breton.

— 1940s—

Explosion of interest in published collections, now easily accessed from Scotland; repertoire of the fiddlers expands significantly as a result; increasing distinction between "dance" and "listening" players. The first collection of Cape Breton-composed tunes is published. Guitar becomes a regular addition to the fiddle-piano duo. Round and square dances become a popular social event; fiddlers expand into dance-band formations. Detroit becomes a new destination for Cape Breton migrants.

ca. 1940   First use of sound-amplification systems with fiddles; Winston Fitzgerald one of the first to use such a system.

1940   *The Cape Breton Collection of Scottish Melodies for the Violin*, by Gordon MacQuarrie is the first published collection of locally composed Cape Breton fiddle tunes (published in Medford, MA).

1940-1953 Much out-migration to Detroit-Windsor area.

1941   American collector Laura Boulton records fiddler Sandy MacLean; this is the first time a collector has focused on Cape Breton fiddle music; previous collectors concentrated on the Gaelic language, story telling and song.

1943-'44   Published articles about Cape Breton fiddlers by J. J. MacInnis in the *Eilean Cheap Breatann* edition of the Canadian-American Gael. Volume 2 published in 1948.

1943   CJFX Radio on air for the first time.

1948   CBI Sydney on air for the first time.

— 1950s —

Television is introduced. Cape Breton is linked to the mainland via the Canso Causeway. First Scottish Concert held. The Beaton Institute is founded; dance researchers Voyeur and Rhodes do work collecting in Cape Breton. Sydney and Halifax are developing active fiddle-music and dance scenes, as is Toronto. LPs replaced 78s. Discontent with the industry fiddlers move away from recording companies; in Boston home recordings become popular; domestic reel-to-reel tape machines coming on the market make this possible. Piano-accompaniment style evolving, taking on influences from other genres, much of this happening in Boston.

ca. 1950   The Five MacDonald Fiddlers (later the Five MacDonalds) formed in Detroit.

1953   Winston Fitzgerald became the first Canadian to record fiddle music on LP.

1954   CJCB-TV and later CBC-TV first broadcast in Nova Scotia.

1955   Canso Causeway opened linking Cape Breton and mainland Nova Scotia.

1957   The first Broad Cove Scottish Concert held. Cape Bretoniana and the College of Cape Breton Archives founded by Sr. Margaret Beaton; renamed the Beaton Institute after her death in 1975. Highland Village Society formed.

1959   The Mac label founded by Winston Fitzgerald, the first independent label for fiddle music in Cape Breton.

— 1960s —

Lively fiddle music and dance scene continues in the industrial east of Cape Breton; many people moved there from the western parts of the island for work. Few commercial recordings being released; however, home recordings popular and being widely disseminated; a number of fiddlers continue to get "into the books," sourcing new tunes from published collections and thus adding to the repertoire. John Allan Cameron, singing and playing fiddle tunes on guitar, is starting to make an impact at U.S. and Canadian Folk Festivals.

1960-'65 A spike in out-migration from Cape Breton to the Detroit-Windsor area.

1962 First Highland Village Day held; CJCB-TV broadcasts *Cape Breton Barndance* until 1969. First solo-piano album released by Alexander MacLean.

1963 Bill Lamey the first Cape Breton fiddler invited to perform in Scotland; cassette format introduced.

1964 First Big Pond Concert held.

1965-'66 Newport Folk Festival in the U.S. features Cape Breton artists, initially the North Shore Gaelic Singers, then fiddlers Angus Chisholm and Mike MacDougall.

1968 *Scottish Strings* radio show on CJFX with "Gus" MacKinnon; continues until 1981.

1969 The Cape Breton Gaelic Society formed.

— 1970s —

The start of the fiddle revival. Cape Breton identity being assumed and presented by fiddlers (replacing the "Scottish" label preferred until then). The first classes for fiddle music are organized; the Glendale Fiddle Festivals are established and the CBFA formed. Cape Breton fiddle presence on TV continues to grow; the Cape Breton Symphony Fiddlers group is formed. The first Cape Breton tune book since 1940 is published. Lots of events are held in recognition of the contribution of individual fiddlers; such events are organized by community groups or by the College of Cape Breton. Focused links with Scotland begin, supported also by the College, specifically the Continuing Education Department; this included visits to Cape Breton by Scottish groups such as na h-Òganaich and Boys of the Lough and local recordings by the BBC. Halifax has a growing Cape Breton music scene. A small number of individuals from the U.S. move to Cape Breton and make a significant contribution to cultural life.

1971 *The Vanishing Cape Breton Fiddler* documentary aired on CBC-TV; the local response to this ultimately leads to a revival of the fiddle music, shaping the scene for decades to come. CanCon broadcast quotas introduced. *MacTalla an Eilean/Island Echoes* first broadcast on CBC radio; this show continues in 2015.

1972 Committee for Cape Breton formed; later renamed the Cape Breton Fiddlers' Association. First formal classes of Cape Breton fiddle music taught by John MacDougall and Stan Chapman. *Ceilidh* show broadcast on CBC-TV, featuring Cape Breton fiddlers Winnie Chafe, Theresa MacLellan, Buddy MacMaster and Dan R. MacDonald. *Cape Breton's Magazine* first published. *Talent Cape Breton* show on CBC Radio. *The Scotia Sun* newspaper published a biography of a Cape Breton fiddler each week (until June 1973), mostly researched and written by John Gibson, Scotsman.

1973 The first Glendale Fiddlers' Festival held. The Gaelic Society of Cape Breton visits Scotland; fiddlers included in the touring group. Matinees start in the Doryman Tavern, Chéticamp.

1974	Sheldon MacInnes hosts *Celtic Serenade* on CJCB radio; Donnie Campbell takes over the role the next year; the show continues to be broadcast in 2015, with Campbell still presenting. *Cape Breton Talent Directory* published, complied by Doug MacPhee. Joe Cormier records for Rounder Records in the U.S., ending an extended hiatus in commercial fiddle-music recordings. Cape Breton Symphony Fiddlers formed as part of John Allan Cameron's TV show. First formal registering of Dan R. MacDonald's compositions to generate royalties. Earl V. Spielman's PhD thesis, the first to examine Cape Breton fiddle music. Sandy MacIntyre becomes the first Cape Breton fiddler to record, release and distribute his own album independently.
1975	*Highland Fling* radio show first broadcast hosted by Joey Beaton and later by Bob MacEachern; this continues in 2015 on The Hawk (CIGO FM). Dan Hughie MacEachern tune book published, the first to focus on the compositions of a single composer. Winnie Chafe participates in the first every Scottish concert held at Edinburgh Castle as official Scottish Ambassador for the Atlantic Provinces.
1976	*Inverness Oran* newspaper first published.
1978	Rounder Records released *The Beatons of Mabou* LP.
1979	Cranford Publications founded; *Archie Neil's Cape Breton* first broadcast on CBC.

— 1980s —

The first post-revival fiddlers emerging on the scene are beginning to make an impact locally, nationally and internationally; an expanding audience base encourages "listening" players to focus on their presentation skills. Academic interest in Cape Breton fiddle music and dance increasing among both locals and outsiders. Cape Breton music is "discovered" by Scottish fiddler Alasdair Fraser and piper Hamish Moore, leading to renewed contacts with Scotland; others from "away" begin exploring Cape Breton music in crossover contexts. Cassettes outselling vinyl; CD format introduced.

1981	*The Cape Breton Fiddler* book by Allister MacGillivray, published by College of Cape Breton Press.
1982	"The Cape Breton Concerto" composed by Daniel Goode for 6 Cape Breton fiddlers and symphonic band performed in Sydney and New York – the first such crossover with classical music. *Up Home Tonight* TV show, broadcast featuring many Cape Breton fiddlers and dancers; continued until 1989. Jerry Holland's influential *Master Cape Breton Fiddler* album released.
1983	Mary Janet MacDonald teaches Cape Breton step dance in Barra, Scotland; she is accompanied by a Scottish fiddler. "The Cape Breton Concerto."
1985	PhD thesis by Virginia Garrison on the teaching of Cape Breton fiddle music.
1986	*Traditional Celtic Music of Cape Breton Island* published by Kate Dunlay with David Reich; known locally as "the little blue book." Barbara Le Blanc completes the first doctoral thesis on Cape Breton dance. The Barra MacNeils formed. The Summertime Revue formed featuring Cape Breton fiddlers and dancers in a revue context; continued until 1998, revived in 2015. Winnie Chafe is the first Cape Breton fiddler to be recognized with an honorary doctorate (from St. FX).
1988	*A Cape Breton Ceilidh* book published by Allister MacGillivray. Winnie Chafe's album, *Echoes*, is the first in Cape Breton to appear in CD format.

1989   First pastoral airs concert held in Big Pond; Ian McKinnon's MA thesis on the recording industry in Cape Breton. Debut albums released by The Rankin Family and Buddy MacMaster. Music Nova Scotia formed. *A Tribute to Dan R. MacDonald*, a cassette recording, published by Cranford Publications, the first recording dedicated to the compositions of a single composer.

—1990s —

International interest in Cape Breton accelerates. Music industry takes notice as part of a wider "Celtic" music boom. Groups and individual fiddlers are signed to major labels and make significant impact on the music industry in Canada. International festival appearances and teaching, including in Scotland, where there is much interest in – and some resistance to - Cape Breton music. Lively local scene develops in terms of publishing, discourse. Celtic Colours International Festival is established and further development opportunities for the music explored.

1991   East Coast Music Association formed and the Maritime Music Awards re-named as ECMAs. *Am Bràighe* first published.

1992   Buddy MacMaster is the first Cape Bretoner to teach fiddle in Scotland, at Sabhal Mòr Ostaig.

1993   Balnain House Museum opened in Inverness, Scotland; it's Canada Room includes an exhibit of Cape Breton music collated by Allister MacGillivray and Sheldon MacInnes. Ashley MacIsaac releases a Christmas album, the first Cape Breton fiddler to enter this seasonal market; Francis MacDonald releases the first Cape Breton fiddle instructional video. Éigse na Laoi Festival at University College, Cork, Ireland, is dedicated to the music of Cape Breton.

1994   The Rankin Family win a Juno; two years later fiddler Ashley MacIsaac is the first Cape Breton fiddler to win this prestigious award.

1995   Ashley MacIsaac's collaboration with Gaelic singer, Mary Jane Lamond on "Sleepy Maggie" has unprecedented chart success.

1996   Ceilidh Trail School of Celtic Music founded in Inverness County; *Ceòlas* summer school founded in South Uist, Scotland, focusing on links with Cape Breton. The *Dun-Green Collection* published. PhD on Cape Breton fiddle music completed at University of Limerick, Ireland, by Liz Doherty.

1997   Celtic Colours International Festival founded.

1998   Beòlach formed; Rounder Records revives its 7000 series.

— 2000s —

Levelling off of some of the highs of the 1990s. Local infrastructure continues to develop to progress potential of fiddle music in terms of cultural tourism. Significant increase in academic activity focused on Cape Breton fiddle music, locally, nationally and internationally. In this decade the Cape Breton fiddle community tragically lost a number of key fiddlers in the 50-60 age group, something that is likely to have implications on the transmission of the tradition going forward.

2000   The first Irish-style public session is held weekly in Rollie's Wharf, North Sydney. Moves to alternative venue in 2013. *Fiddler* Magazine runs a special edition on Cape Breton.

2003   Celtic Colours Festival Volunteer Drive'ers Association formed.

2004   Red Shoe Pub opens in Mabou.

2005   The Big Fiddle is unveiled at the Sydney Marine Terminal. Cape Breton Live.com launched.

2006   Celtic Music Interpretive Centre opens in Judique. Centre for Cape Breton Studies established at Cape Breton University. Cape Breton fiddler Rodney MacDonald is Premier of Nova Scotia.

— 2010s —

New bands continue to emerge from Cape Breton; increased collaborations with Scottish, Irish and U.S. musicians facilitated through festival circuit. Skype teaching and online courses become available. Escalation in the alignment of Gaelic with the fiddle music labelling and branding; some concerns about the authenticity and sustainability of the tradition at the local level; Fèis Cape Breton is established.

2010   Còig formed. American folkolorist, Burt Feintuch publishes the award-winning *In the Blood: Cape Breton Conversations on Culture*, with photographer Gary Samson.

2012   Nuallan, a piping group specializing in the old Cape Breton dance-style piping is formed at the Gaelic College, underlining that institution's new policies foregrounding local Gaelic culture.

2013   Colaisde na Gàidhlig/The Gaelic College afforded the opportunity to use the "Royal" prefix as part of its name by Queen Elizabeth II; decides against this.

2014   A number of exponents of the old-style of fiddle music, including Buddy MacMaster, pass away. KitchenFest/Feis a' Chidsin launched by the Colaisde na Gàidhlig/The Gaelic College.

2015   Fèis Cheap Breatuinn established. Paul Cranford is honoured as patron of World Fiddle Day. Special square-dance tribute events held to recognize the significance of particular dances and dance halls. *The Vanishing Cape Breton Fiddler* documentary sequel is at an advanced stage of production.

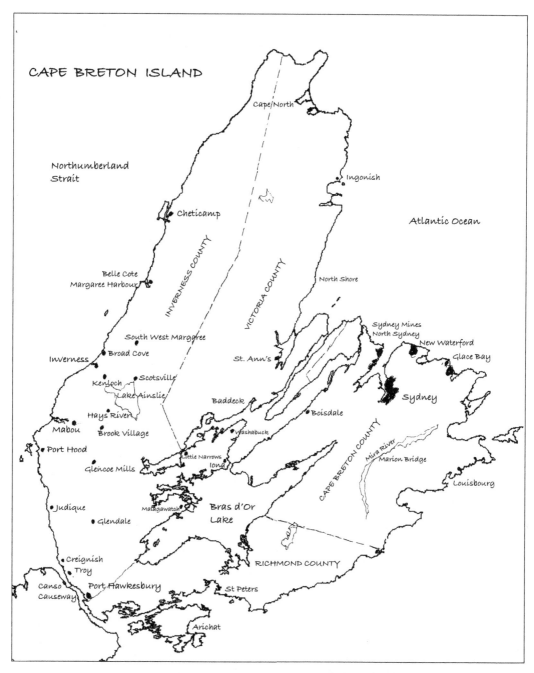

CAPE BRETON ISLAND

Northumberland Strait

Cape/North

Ingonish

Atlantic Ocean

Cheticamp

INVERNESS COUNTY

VICTORIA COUNTY

North Shore

Belle Cote
Margaree Harbour

Sydney Mines
North Sydney
New Waterford
Glace Bay

South West Margaree

St. Ann's

Inverness

Broad Cove

Kenloch   Scotsville
Lake Ainslie

Baddeck

Sydney

Boisdale

Hays River

Brook Village

Washabuck

Mabou

Little Narrows
Iona

CAPE BRETON COUNTY

Mira River
Marion Bridge

Port Hood

Glencoe Mills

Louisbourg

Judique

Mabagawatch

Bras d'Or
Lake

Glendale

Creignish
Troy

RICHMOND COUNTY

Canso
Causeway

Port Hawkesbury

St Peters

Arichat

Map provided by Mats Melin.

Introduction

The fiddle music of Cape Breton Island, Nova Scotia, has its own sound, artistic standards, performance practices and etiquette. A vibrant tradition, each of its elements is in flux as the music responds to and is modified by extra-musical social, economic, political and religious conditions. The Cape Breton fiddler of the 21st century is performing a music that was transplanted from the Highlands and Islands of Scotland in the 18th and early 19th centuries, adapted and evolved as it has passed down through several generations in the New World. Each of its exponents carries an inherited responsibility to maintain the music's integrity while also making it relevant for contemporary audiences, which today are as likely to be international as local. All the while, performers are exposed to the temptation of taking liberties, as technology, travel and artistic curiosity permit consideration of fresh, different sounds from diverse music traditions.

Exposure to influence from other musics is not new in the Cape Breton fiddle narrative, although, in the immediate aftermath of the first Scottish migration to Cape Breton, settlement patterns and isolation created an environment that enabled Gaelic language, song, story, music and dance to be maintained. Significantly, each of these elements, as they were transplanted and subsequently transmitted, were characterized by community and individual discrepencies – dialects and idolects (or personal variants) – which

contributed to a rich, cultural mosaic. Cape Breton classically demonstrates what later ethnomusicologists (Nettl and Myers 1976; Doherty 1996) regard as a "marginal survival"– nurturing old traditions and practices, in all of their variants, in a geographically peripheral enclave; meanwhile in the homeland, the original culture was changing. In the period following colonization of Cape Breton[1], back in Scotland a significant reorientation of fiddle-music sound and practice was championed by James Scott Skinner (1843-1927). His contribution endorsed an existing urban Scottish tradition that separated the music from the dance, moving it onto the concert platform and affording an increasingly prescriptive role to music literacy. While none of this appears to have immediately filtered across to Cape Breton (although future scholarship may reveal otherwise) there the older, dance-focused tradition was maintained as a cultural lifeline. That reality explains how Cape Breton could come to be somewhat romantically regarded as having enshrined a neglected, forgotten and unchanging tradition. Yet challenging such a belief is the fact that in Scotland itself, elements of the Highland tradition did survive despite being little recognized. Furthermore, in Cape Breton, out-migration to cities such as Boston, MA, and Detroit, MI, continuing Scottish immigration, and day-to-day interaction with other ethic groups worked against the island being completely isolated; in music terms, such factors influenced fiddle music from the earliest times, adding diversity to the aural palate. Such changes escalated after the turn of the 20th century as a result of increased out-migration, interaction between fiddlers and those musically literate bagpipers associated with the military during the two world wars, access to published tune collections, the advent of recording, then radio and, eventually, television and the logistical opening-up of the island through such as the construction of the Canso Causeway (1955), which linked Cape Breton to the North American mainland. Each of these factors contributed to the morphing of Highland Scottish fiddle music into today's unique, distinctive, Cape Breton sound, creating what is in no way a relic, but rather, a new voice of Scottish music.

Chief among its characteristics are the partnering of the fiddle with a distinctive piano style, a repertoire that has much locally composed music, and a connection with dance that continues to act as a template for style and performance practice. Recognition of the distinct character of Cape Breton fiddle music is not necessarily reflected in the corresponding labelling; from the 1920s and the birth of Scottish Catholic Societies throughout the island, the branding of the music and other elements of culture as "Scottish" began; this was reinforced from the late 1930s when the Gaelic College was established. By the 1970s fiddle music on the island was referred to, almost exclusively, as "Scottish" or "Scotch." It was only when challenged by a television documentary, which insinuated that the fiddle music was in danger of disappearing (*The Vanishing Cape Breton Fiddler*, 1971), that local ownership of the music began to be asserted. At first this was tentative – "Cape Breton Scottish fiddle"; this was gradually replaced by "Cape Breton fiddle" as confidence grew through a robust revivalist movement. The publication of such resources as *The Cape Breton Fiddler* (MacGillivray 1981), academic and media interest and output, and the introduction of formal teaching contexts which nurtured young emerging talent through the 1980s strengthened this confidence, rendering Cape Breton music

ideally positioned for access to the international stage during the Celtic boom of the 1990s. The impact of this continues to resonate within the tradition, despite the downturn in popularity of things Celtic from the start of the 21st century.

Today, Cape Breton music is recognized internationally as a distinct genre, and its exponents stand with confidence among peers from Scotland, Ireland, Canada, North America and Scandinavia, at festivals and at events around the world. As a result of this, Cape Breton Island has become a destination of choice in the cultural-tourism industry, with fiddle music now typically presented as part of the experience, this, in turn, bringing a new set of expectations and demands.

A resultant contemporary challenge is for players to retain the ethos of a grounding in their own tradition; in particular, to be mindful of the balance between the primacy of continuity with the inheritance from the past and seduction by the contemporary world's new sounds and ideas. Some scholars, describing these perspectives, respectively, as "vertical" (looking backward) and "horizontal" (looking outward) (Campbell and Hall 2006: 7), suggest that both are mutually exclusive.[2] But for the evolution of a music tradition, surely the very fulcrum, or key space, of creativity is most likely to be at the intersection between the vertical and the horizontal, the site from which the individual voice might emerge. The point at which such intersection occurs is determined by the balance of the old and the new; it is that middle ground between (to borrow the words of Gustav Mahler) "tending the flames" and "worshipping the ashes." Certainly, in the case of Cape Breton fiddle music, historically, the vertical perspective could be seen to dominate, with the inherited tradition, "the given note" (Heaney 1998: 36) being prioritized. Yet some space was always permitted for new and external elements (from the horizontal plane) to be absorbed, contributing to both the re-crafting of the music away from its Scottish origins and to maintenance of its relevance over time; as the 20th century progressed, external influences were increasingly embraced, yet always tempered by a solid connection with the inherited tradition. The outcome was a music sound, style and practice that allowed for – indeed was propelled by – individual discrepancies, unique takes on the shared tradition that contributed to the rich, mosaic-like tapestry of sound in newly imagined ways. Today's younger players are exposed to and have easy access to external influences to an unprecedented degree. They are also challenged by new audiences who have had other music experiences and who will bring different expectations to Cape Breton music, and find themselves faced with the lure of celebrity. Such performers may find that it is easier and more "hip" to look to the wider music world for reference, relegating traditions to the background. The other trend foregrounds the vertical, although, significantly, more in terms of branding than in the music itself. The strategic re-branding of the music as Gaelic might be interpreted cynically as an attempt to mask an increasingly pan-Celtic sound and performance-practice with an authentic veneer, or as a means of driving a wider language or cultural tourism agenda. A more positive interpretation might be that it is a reminder of the deeper historical, inherited dimensions of the music which will encourage contemporary learners and performers not to abandon the past to the seduction of the ever-widening world soundscape. Ultimately, however, in Cape Breton fiddle music, the divergence of the vertical and the horizontal has widened, with the result that the richness and variety of the earlier mosaic soundscape – the product of proportionate interaction of on-the-ground, individual and discrepant voices – has, increasingly, been replaced by a more homogenous sound and practice.

While certain stakeholders are confident that Cape Breton fiddle music is, at this point, in a robust state, others have a less positive impression. The outsider view recognizes that the tradition is, in fact, at a significant crossroads.

The last few years have seen the passing on of a number of many leading stylists, some of them at a young age and in tragic circumstances, and this has left gaps which may affect continuity in tradition and measured innovation. Indeed, some

of those who could logically have represented the benchmarks of style and practice for the next twenty to thirty years, to maintain equilibrium and to mentor the next generations, are no longer with us. Likewise, the ongoing drain of young people (in search of work, opportunity or adventure) away from Cape Breton means that only a small number of its music's players live on the island year-round; this is a challenge to keeping the music visible in the lives of the wider community for parts of the year – drawing people out to dances in the winter months, for example. Other challenges involve keeping the music alive at home, and ensuring that it is maintained locally through nurtured, functioning transmission processes; navigating a path that maintains the integrity of the music while making it relevant in contemporary social and economic circumstances; and, crucially, keeping alive the distinctive, individual voices within the overall music tradition both within Cape Breton itself and on stages around the world. Supporting the divergance of the outward-looking and the backward-looking ultimately creates a vacuum; most significantly, it removes the key creative space – that where the two approaches converge – from the narrative. Reframing the conversation, where the old and the new do not have to be mutually exclusive, may be of value going forward for Cape Breton fiddle music – incidentally it's most unique and, in my opinion, honest, label.

The Making of the Cape Breton Fiddle Companion

The idea for the Cape Breton Fiddle Companion came after more than a decade of reflection on my own position in relation to the Cape Breton fiddle music tradition. Having first visited Cape Breton in 1991 and completed my doctoral dissertation, "The Paradox of the Periphery: Evolution of the Cape Breton Fiddle Tradition c. 1928-1995" in 1996 (University of Limerick), my concerns were twofold. As a fiddle-player myself, but as an etic participant or "outsider," I questioned my understanding, interpretation and representation of a community that was not my own even though, from the outset, I had been welcomed into the it as both a musician and an academic. I was also concerned about the ethical issues necessary in ethnomusicological research and about how best I might give something back to the Cape Breton music community that had so generously resourced me.

The idea of devoting a dictionary or encyclopedia-style volume to the music of one country or region is by no means a new or novel one. The most obvious example is *The Encylopedia of Music in Canada* (1981; on-line 2001; enhanced digital format 2013). Europe has many examples, most profoundly *Enciclopédia da Música em Portugal no Século XX* [*Encyclopedia of Music in 20th Century Portugal*] (2010, 4 volumes) and, more recently, *The Encyclopedia of Music in Ireland* (2011). Genre-specific works include *The Rough Guide to Irish Music* (2001); however, it is *The Companion to Irish Traditional Music* edited by Fintan Vallely (Cork University Press, 1999 and 2011) that was the primary inspiration and model for *The Cape Breton Fiddle Companion*. Vallely, originally unconvinced about the A-Z format, admits to having soon "realized that the dictionary approach was a very sensible way to cover traditional music. In fact, it was becoming clear that the field was simply too vast to do it any other way" (Vallely 2000: 151). Not everyone agrees; in academic circles individuals have made persuasive arguments against low-level or positivistic musicology, which this type of project inevitably entails (Kerman 1985; Geertz 1973). However, if music in Cape Breton is to attain the level of critical insight and cultural debate which theorists require, the generation of an accessible *facto logy* about that music would seem to be demanded as an access point. Volumes such as the *Companion* would both focus the field of research and clarify issues by which our understanding of the role and meaning of music might be enriched. There is, of course, already a body of truly excellent scholarship on Cape Breton fiddle music. But it is limited in scale, is relatively recent and, to a large extent, is hidden in newspaper and magazine articles, liner

notes to recordings, tune-book introductions and academic dissertations. As such it is scattered in a way that makes a comprehensive roundup of information somewhat difficult to access. Futhermore, in terms of academic scholarship, recent work is often driven by ethnomusicological trends and theories; research to date has been somewhat clustered around a small number of themes, prioritizing contemporary rather than historical practice, while many interesting topics remain unexplored. The impetus driving *The Cape Breton Fiddle Companion* was to generate a corpus of facts about the history and contemporary practice of Cape Breton fiddle music through collating and synthesizing existing information and probing previously-neglected areas; it attempts to clarify, and dispel where appropriate, some of the woollier assumptions, habits, myths and lore which, as in any oral tradition, abound in the Cape Breton fiddle tradition. The book cannot, of course, be fully comprehensive but any absences should spark discussion, conversation and enquiry.

Structure

The *Cape Breton Fiddle Companion* borrows the alphabetic classification system of the encyclopedia and dictionary, but it should not be confused with either. Nor should it be considered to be an academic esoterica, for it is aimed at general readers – such as musicians, students, scholars and journalists. It aims to be an easy-access reference with bite-sized entries which give hard data, explanations and observations that encompass the Cape Breton fiddle music narrative, its history and contemporary practice. By presenting the data in A-Z form (rather than chronologically, thematically or conceptually) it hopes to encourage readers to explore and navigate the material in different ways, to effectively construct their own text. Although compiled from a single (and etic) perspective its material has been variously contributed by, informed by or resourced from exiting and new research from many musicians, scholars and Cape Breton music enthusiasts. It has aspired to a community consensus from the outset, a negotiated account, where the author's interpretation and subsequent presentation was checked and verified by the community, both individuals and, in the case of the complete draft manuscript, a panel of locally recognized authorities on the music tradition, all of whom are musicians themselves.

Rather than a set of discrete and logical steps or stages – planning, access, data collection, analysis, writing up, dissemination of the results – the research became a process as much as practice (Brewer 2000: 5), happening in a non-linear, non-sequential fashion. It assumed the air of an ongoing, open-ended conversation, the starting point of which was the author's original, early-1990s research. This has been reviewed with the advantage of time, now using a somewhat different critical lens, interrogating material afresh, updating and extending it and representing it in a new and accessible format. In assembling the *Companion*, reading and "doing" overlapped. Writing was started early, exposing gaps in information and highlighting areas which required further data collection, thus broadening the investigative process. Throughout, the volume of classification headings was in a state of flux, expanding as possible new entries emerged, and contracting as analysis allowed for the collating of individual entries into single units. The material itself was generated through various approaches: (i) collating and synthesizing existing information (both my own and from multiple other sources) (ii) probing previously neglected areas and (iii) generating new data using various ethnographic research processes. A triangulation method (Denzin 1970), routinely a feature of ethnography, was utilized; this allowed for the use of multiple methods (e.g., in-depth interviewing (in the field, by skype, by phone), participant observation, personal documents, desk research, surveys, musical transcription, etc.) in order to capture the breadth of the topic being explored.

Only two short site visits were possible, but several encounters with Cape Breton musicians visiting Ireland and Scotland also took place. Engaging the Cape Breton fiddle community in the conversation from the outset was a priority and multiple email and Facebook correspondences were initiated as ideas, theories, facts and figures started to be bounced back and forth across the Atlantic. As the corpus of material began to take shape, the challenge became increasingly about the interpretation and presentation of the data. Through this, the "writing and response" approach generated the most revealing insights as "insiders" responded to my early and often clumsy efforts. Honing the art of *précis* proved daunting in itself (and, indeed, was not always successful) given the bulk and complexity of the material collated. However, issues relating to the interpretation of the data have effectively dominated the process as I have attempted to bring coherence to the material as a whole.

The original classification occurred within three overarching themes: "people" (primarily musicians but also other key stakeholders), "music" (instruments, techniques, resources) and "other" (various topics such as festivals, events, venues and support agencies). Approaching the data under these three discrete, yet overlapping, headings kept the research reasonably focused and manageable; ultimately, all were amalgamated into a single alphabetical order. A timeline was devised to provide a chronological overview of the evolution of the music and its traditions, a bibliography was compiled to identify primary literary sources, and the Introduction offers an overview of the process of the *Companion's* assembly; the index lists, alphabetically, musicians and other stakeholders whose contribution to the tradition is noted throughout the book although (mostly due to issues of time and scale) not in individual entries.

The compiling of the *Cape Breton Fiddle Companion* has been, above all, a labour of love. However, on those days when, sitting in Co. Donegal, Cape Breton seemed very far away and this project more than a little overwhelming, the observations of D. H. Akenson (Akenson 1979) often came to mind – the reason a professional Irish historian should never attempt a local or regional history study [in this case, Cape Breton] is obvious: "there is scant professional credit in it [and] it is devilish hard work." Ultimately, though, I feel privileged to have been facilitated in undertaking the project and to have been supported along the way by so many members of the Cape Breton fiddle-music community. I hope this book will widen the field of view for future scholars of Cape Breton music, raise as many questions as it answers, and thus contribute to the ongoing conversation. Above all, it is a tribute to those who have carried and developed this wonderful music and shared it with so many of us around the world.

Liz Doherty

Notes

1. Undertaking this project it becomes clear that music traditions are no more exempt from political consequences than any other aspect of culture, and in this regard it must be said that the fiddle music of Cape Breton is, in the greatest part, that of immigrants sponsored by Imperial authorities who displaced and dispropertied the indigenous peoples – in this case the Mi'kmaq. Though profound and with consequences, that is a deeper and different subject which regrettably cannot be dealt with here. But in the course of these pages the author has striven to document indigenous people's contribution to and participation in fiddle music as well as that of other ethnic groups such as the Acadians.

2. "There is a profound difference between the two mental attitudes, which represent the different spirits of different ages, and which are very much in conflict."

A

Acadians. A population group descended from the original French settlers of Acadie, a colony in the 17th and 18th century that included present-day mainland Nova Scotia, New Brunswick, part of the Gaspé peninsula and part of the state of Maine. Acadie was a strategic territory coveted by both France and Britain. Consequently, the Acadians became victims of the colonial wars between the two superpowers. The British began deporting the Acadians in 1755, primarily to the thirteen Anglo-American colonies along the Atlantic seaboard but later to England and France. After the Treaty of Paris in 1763, many Acadians who survived the deportation years were able to obtain land in distant corners of Nova Scotia, New Brunswick and Prince Edward Island. Others were eventually able to make their way to Louisiana where they became known as Cajuns, a deformation of *Acadiens*. The publication of Henry Wadsworth Longfellow's epic poem, "Evangeline, A Tale of Acadie," in 1847, helped spark the beginning of an Acadian renaissance. In addition to an anthem and a flag, Acadians in the three Maritime Provinces were able to establish organizations and institutions that promoted their unique culture and heritage, including the French language. In the late 20th century, Acadians made significant achievements with regard to language and cultural rights as a minority group. Acadians throughout the Maritime Provinces are linked by the national CBC French-language radio and TV network. The Roman Catholic Church has also served as a cohesive force for the Acadians over the centuries, although to a lesser extent nowadays. In some Acadian areas, the co-operative movement has strengthened economic and cultural solidarity. In Nova Scotia, French-speaking Acadians form the majority in various communities, in the southwest corner of the province and in two main rural areas of Cape Breton Island—Chéticamp and Isle Madame; Chéticamp, in northern Cape Breton,

has a vibrant Acadian culture that has produced a number of world-class musicians and artists. There is also a large group of Acadians, many of whom have become assimilated into the English language, that live in the urban area of Sydney and surrounding towns. As a result of urbanization in recent generations, there is also a large population of Acadians in the capital city of Nova Scotia, Halifax. Like many other minority groups, being Acadian remains a complicated issue in the 21st century. Some Acadians no longer speak any French and have become fully assimilated into the wider community; of these, some have become "born-again" Acadians, passionate about re-engaging with their Acadian language and culture; others are bilingual; some speak three languages (standard French, any of the Acadian dialects and English); some come from families where some members speak French and others English.

music. Singing was always an essential part of early life in the Chéticamp area (settled ca. 1785 by Acadians returning from exile). The early repertoire was composed largely of songs brought from France by the first settlers of Acadie while other songs were no doubt composed in Acadie—songs that were transmitted orally from generation to generation. Sometimes, the fiddle would accompany the singers but, more often than not, songs were sung a cappella and sometimes accompanied by foot-tapping and hand-clapping. In the absence of a fiddler, women often performed mouth music or jigging so that participants could dance. The early Acadian settlers sang and played music to accompany daily life activities. Mothers would sing lullabies, men would sing to accompany gutting fish or mending nets while groups of singers would create the rhythm for milling frolics and other such activities. Outstanding singers would entertain in an a cappella style at house parties and/or weddings. Songs and later fiddle music were always part of the centuries-old traditions such as La Chandeleur, Le Mardi-Gras, La Mi-Carême, and in later years parish picnics and then community festivals. Dance was also an integral part of these social gatherings. In the 20th century, two Acadian scholars, Père

Anselme Chiasson and his cousin Père Daniel Boudreau, documented more than 500 of the old Acadian songs, Chansons d'Acadie, which are still sung as part of Acadian festivals, concerts and parties. Many have been recorded by local groups or individuals as well as by other Acadian or Canadian singers. The Church played both a positive and a negative role in the survival of the old song and dance repertoires. From a positive point of view, priests always encouraged the art of singing for their religious celebrations. The skills that were learned for religious ceremonies were transferred to secular singing; for example, the influence of Gregorian chants may be heard in the singing of some of the old songs. The nuns, Les Filles de Jésus, who looked after the education of the children from the beginning of the 20th century, also played a major role in teaching singing and playing musical instruments such as the piano, the organ and the violin. But the Church also impacted negatively on some aspects of the tradition. For many years, as was the case elsewhere in Cape Breton, there was a period when many forms of social entertainment, especially fiddle playing and dance, were discouraged by priests. Church moralists condemned forms of dance which they considered dangerous or evil. As in other Roman Catholic communities, they were also concerned about the social context within which dance gatherings took place. They feared that playing the "devil's instrument and music," abusing alcoholic beverages and being involved in close bodily contact were elements that would arouse and excite passions leading to sin. In the late 19th and early 20th centuries, public spaces began to take the place of private spaces for music and dance gatherings. For example, the annual two-day parish picnics were highlights of the calendar year; eventually, outdoor concerts and community festivals replaced these. Community and parish halls became favourite public places for music and dance evenings. As public places became more important for social encounters, Chéticamp's Doryman Tavern began holding a pub matinee in the 1970s, always with a resident house fiddler from the local area; this format was significantly different from the experience elsewhere on the island and appealed to fiddlers across Cape Breton. The Doryman on Saturday afternoons became a very important event for an audience familiar with and appreciative of the music; later, similar events began to be held in the neighbouring tavern, Le Gabriel. For several years Chéticamp was also known for what was one of the most comprehensive stockists of Cape Breton fiddle-music recordings, at Charlie's Downhome Music Store. Technological advances also influenced what music was being heard in Acadian communities. For example, around the 1930s gramophones arrived in the Chéticamp area. Early records that were particularly influential came from Québec. Residents began listening to such violin players as Joseph Allard and Joe Bouchard. This Québec influence might explain why the early fiddlers of the Acadian region had quite a distinct style from that of the Scottish and Irish fiddlers of Cape Breton; with modern communication, however, this distinction is no longer as prevalent. With the advent of radio in the area, country songs, both English and French, accompanied by the fiddle and guitar, became popular and were sung everywhere. Finally, the local Coopérative Radio Chéticamp (CKJM), founded in 1995, plays an important role by airing a mix of traditional and contemporary Acadian music, as well as fiddle tunes from all parts of Cape Breton.

musicians. The first prominent fiddler in the area was Padé LeBlanc (ca. 1855-1907) born to Paul and Angélique LeBlanc, who came into prominence in the late 1800s/early 1900s. The local "dean" of the fiddlers, "P'tit" Placide Odo (1879-1968), who always played unaccompanied, was highly admired for his impeccable timing and his controlled bowing. Considered by most as an Acadian-style, rather than a Scottish-style fiddler, he was the preferred player of his day at local dances, weddings and other events and festivities. Other fiddlers who were especially popular at picnics were Willie (à Sandy) Roach, his brothers Dan and Angus Roach and their cousin, Joe Aucoin. Acadian fiddlers from Cape Breton were also playing a significant role at the same time among the Cape Breton community in the Boston area. Alcide Aucoin, for example, was a member of the Inverness Serenaders, one of the first Cape Breton groups to record commercially. Later, Joe Cormier continued this Cape Breton-Acadian legacy in the Boston region, maintaining a high profile as a player and recording artist as a soloist, and with his group The Chéticamp Connection. There are many other fiddlers, guitarists and dancers from the Acadian communities who have been involved in the Cape Breton fiddle tradition among these are such as the Aucoin family of Sydney Mines, Alcide Aucoin, Marc Boudreau, Hilda Chiasson, Joel Chiasson, Joe Cormier, J. P. Cormier, Barbara Le Blanc, Didace LeBlanc, Donny LeBlanc, Paddy "Scotty" LeBlanc, Arthur Muise, Chester Delaney, Denis Harold Larade and Jason Roach. Fiddle player Robert Deveaux, a noted contemporary exponent of the Cape Breton style, includes many old French tunes in his repertoire and has begun research into this music, focusing on the unique style and practices of Chéticamp's Joseph Larade. *See* **individual entries; dance**.

style. Much discussion has been generated around the topic of the Cape Breton fiddle style and how it is interpreted by players of non-Scottish heritage. For instance, is there an Acadian style of playing Cape Breton fiddle music? Much of the discussion concerns matters of identity – something with which players themselves have clearly grappled. This is evidenced in their recording identities, such as was the case with Paddy "Scotty" LeBlanc who recorded *The Fiddling French Canadian Scot* in the 1950s. However, issues concerning stylistic discrepancies often highlight tempo as one area where distinctions might be evident. Acadian players are regarded as preferring a slightly faster tempo than would be typical of the larger cohort of Cape Breton players. Other conversations centre around accent, and reference language in much the same way as the "Gaelic" versus "English" discussion. For Acadian players learning to play Cape Breton-style fiddling since the 1970s, much of their learning environment has been similar to that of their Scottish-Cape Breton peers: listening to recordings (commercial

Joe Cormier. Courtesy of Mark Wilson.

and home recordings), radio, attending dances, concerts and other events and, increasingly, attending classes and workshops. Then, as in earlier times, much of the exposure to fiddle music came from players living in closest proximity (such as the Chisholms from the Margaree area) and those players whose music was accessible via the radio. The majority of players' own perception of the fiddle music is that it is Cape Breton music and does not indeed have a further, discrete ethnic stamp on it. In fact, while they may regard themselves as Acadian in other aspects of their lives, when it comes to the fiddle music they consider themselves simply as Cape Breton musicians.

It is important to note, nonetheless, that in a small number of fiddlers over the years, a more prominent French repertoire and style was maintained; Joseph Larade of Chéticamp, for instance, maintained a unique style of playing the fiddle while singing until the 1960s. Fiddlers of Acadian heritage have also contributed to the fiddle music tradition elsewhere on the island, most especially that of the Northside. Having returned to Cape Breton in 1785 from France, Saint-Pierre et Miquelon and the Magdalen Islands a number of Acadians settled in this area, Anglicized their names (e.g., Le Jeune to Young and Fortin to Fortune), and intermarried, in many cases with Irish settlers. While their music gave way to a more Irish, Scottish and, ultimately, Cape Breton style some French tunes did survive until well into the 20th century in the playing of such Northside fiddlers as Joe Confiant and Johnny Wilmot. (*With* BLB, JDLB, CDR, SR) [**Le Blanc 1986, 1997;**

MacGillivray 1981; Ross and Deveau 1992].

accent. The conscious addition of emphasis by way of rhythmic or melodic articulation or embellishment in order to highlight a particular note or beat. Accent, in fiddle playing, is realized primarily through the bowing (duration, pressure, pattern) and contributes to the swing or drive of the music. The choice to employ an accent at any given time is at the discretion of the individual player; certainly, in the past, choices made in relation to accent contributed to the distinctive style of individual fiddlers. Accent is also one of the factors that contributes to the identity of the Cape Breton style, as distinct from other fiddle styles. This is due to the fact that most Cape Breton fiddlers adhere to a fairly consistent pattern of stressed or emphasised beats in their interpretation of the basic metrical pulse of any given tune. *See* **bow-push accent; drive; style.**

accompaniment. The use of an additional instrument or instruments to harmonically and/or rhythmically augment a melodic performance; in Cape Breton, additional accompaniment in the form of foot-tapping also forms part of a typical fiddle-music performance. Accompaniment has been an integral part of the Cape Breton fiddle tradition from at least the end of the 19th century. In the U.S., record companies were chiefly responsible for dictating both what should be recorded and how it should be presented; typically, accompaniment (generally on piano) was mandatory. The first Cape Breton fiddlers to record commercially in Boston in 1928 played accompanied, in a dance-band configuration, with Dan Sullivan, an Irish-American piano player who had Nova Scotia connections. In recorded and in live performance contexts, instruments such as harmonica, banjo, guitar and double bass added further harmonic and/or rhythmic support to the fiddle tunes, while bones or clappers, drum kits and knitting needles were utilized from time to time as rhythmic accompaniment; drones were occasionally provided by Jew's harp or the kazoo-style comb-and-paper combination.

Pump organs and later pianos gradually became commonplace in Cape Breton, and by the mid-20th century, influenced by a range of other music traditions (such as Victorian parlour music and swing) which were experienced in diaspora communities and through emerging media, a new, distinctive piano style evolved to accompany the fiddle music. By the 1980s, with the addition of rock and pop influences as well as contemporary accompaniment practices used in related traditions, such as Irish, the Cape Breton piano sound had crystallized into something quite unique. As a wholly improvised, robust, syncopated piano style evolved, it influenced the fiddle playing, requiring compromise specifically in intonation and ornamentation. The fiddle-piano partnership that has been the predominant Cape Breton combination was frequently supplemented by the guitar from the mid-20th century; only in very rare instances, however, did the guitar replace the piano. While the fiddle-piano duo (with or without guitar) remains the staple instrumentation for square dances in presentational or listening contexts, it has, however, become increasingly common for larger groups of melody instruments (multiple fiddles, pipes and whistles, mainly) to perform together. Indeed, as the repertoire and arrangements become more "pan-Celtic" in style and approach in some contemporary configurations, it is the piano accompaniment stylings that remain as the strongest identifier of the discrete Cape Breton style. *See* **bands; guitar; piano; pump organ.**

accordion. A bellows-operated, free-reed instrument with both melody and accompaniment potential; two forms of the accordion exist – the button accordion and the piano accordion. On one side of the bellows there are rows of buttons (button accordion) or a keyboard (piano accordion) on which the melody is played; on the other side (of both variants) are buttons for bass notes and chords; the sound is created by pressing the buttons or keys, while manipulating the bellows in a push or pull motion; tempered steel reeds vibrate when air is forced through them via the bellows. On the button accordion a different note is generated on the push and pull, while on the piano accordion the same note is created when the bellows are moved in either direction; this is known as double action. While the accordion is a popular instrument in folk and traditional music in both Ireland (button and piano accordion) and Scotland (mostly piano accordion), it has had a limited presence in Cape Breton, where the fiddle as a melody instrument has dominated. However, evidence of the instrument in relation to Cape Breton dates from at least the 1920s. The piano accordion, invented by Bouton of Paris, in 1852, and greatly improved by the early decades of the 20th century, was popular among the ethnic populations in Sydney Mines and Whitney Pier, such as the Italians, Romanians and Ukrainians; Dave Mahalik of the Tom Fun Orchestra is a contemporary representative of such a tradition. The Inverness Serenaders, one of the early groups to record in Boston, for example, included an accordion player (Jim Aucoin). The instrument was also popular in the Northside area, particularly among the Newfoundland population; individuals, such as Leona O'Handley, married to Alex O'Handley of Barrachois Glen, one of a noted family of fiddlers and step dancers, played a few Cape Breton fiddle tunes on the accordion. Pockets of accordion players also existed, for example, in the Iona area and in Acadian communities. In Boston, Bill Lamey often included accordion player Billy Irwin in his band at dances. Both versions of the accordion (along with banjo) were popular among the old-time country music bands that flourished on the Northside, and later in the Sydney area, from around 1910-1960 where the music involved was a hybrid of Appalachian old-time and early country music. The most notable of these was Jerry's Hayshakers, which featured the piano accordion prominently. Fiddler, Jerry Toomey, from Sydney Mines (a neighbour of Irish-style fiddler, Billy Fortune, who had a significant influence on him), cut several records for the Copley label that included the accordion in an accompaniment setting; he also had weekly radio broadcasts while based in Boston and these could be picked up in Cape Breton. Although his band leaned toward a country, cowboy sound, they also featured Cape Breton tunes arranged in this manner. Their influence spawned many similar bands in the industrial area, including Sydney's Steel City Ramblers and The Tall Men. While it made an appearance on some of John Allan Cameron's TV shows in the 1970s it was not until the 1980s that the piano accordion was featured in the same circles as the fiddle music. One of the first to perform fiddle tunes on the instrument was Stewart MacNeil who introduced it to the line-up of the Barra MacNeils; MacNeil has also composed a number of tunes which have utilized the chromatic potential of the instrument. Today, a number of piano players occasionally play accordion, among them Mac Morin and Adam Young, while Betty Baldwin Muise and Laurie Simm are present-day button accordion players.

air. A slow and lyrical tune-type played for listening-only purposes and referred to variously as "air," "slow air," "pastoral air," "Gaelic air," "lament," "melody" and (in some printed Scottish collections) "solo." Many airs are instrumental versions of Gaelic songs; others have been composed with no such associations; marching airs have a slightly quicker metronome beat and more pronounced dotted rhythms. The air, although played at a slow tempo, is generally paced with a steady pulse maintained throughout. Typically too, the fiddle player is accompanied by piano; this is different from the practice of air playing in Ireland, for example, where airs tend to be performed unaccompanied and have no regular pulse or beat. As a tune-type, the air was cultivated by James Scott Skinner in the late-19th century, although earlier published sources include this tune-type (e.g., *The Skye Collection* (1887), *The Simon Fraser Collection* (1816) and others by George Jenkins (1793), Duncan MacIntyre (1794), William Morrisson (1812), John and Andrew Gow (ca. 1793) and William Christie (1820). Although some Cape Breton fiddle players such as Malcolm Beaton (1912-1953) and Sandy MacLean (1893-1982) were known to have slow airs in their repertoires, air playing was first afforded widespread recognition in the performances of Judique-born "Little" Jack MacDonald (1887-1969). Inspired by classical violinists such as Fritz Kreisler and Jascha Heifetz, whom he saw perform in Detroit, MacDonald re-imagined the air. A varied selection of airs was gradually discovered as fiddlers began to peruse the published collections becoming widely available after the 1940s. This coincided with a marked change in style evolving among fiddle players who favoured a clear and precise tone and a challenging technical dexterity, eventually leading to a division between "dance" and "listening" playing. As the divide between these contexts crystallized, more listening-to fiddlers came to include some airs in their solo repertoires for concerts, house parties, ceilidhs and recordings. Winston Fitzgerald adapted Irish song melodies and played them as airs, and local fiddler-composers such as Dan Hughie MacEachern and Elmer Briand began to compose new tunes of this type; Briand's "Beautiful Lake Ainslie" is a particularly well-known example. Encounters with Scottish fiddlers in Scotland, Cape Breton and its diaspora, such as Ron Gonella and Hector MacAndrew, further promoted interest in airs, and several players emerged as having a particular finesse for them, including Winnie Chafe, Lloyd MacDonald, Jerry Holland, Bobby MacNeil and Kyle MacNeil; some sought out classical-music instruction specifically in order to master air playing. Today, the majority of players have one or more airs within their repertoires.

air playing. The normal practice has been to play an air as the first in a group or medley that will also include such tune-types as march, strathspey and reel, but it has also become common today to hear the slow air played on its own. The tune type was prioritized in 1989 in a dedicated pastoral airs concert at St. Mary's Church, Big Pond, as part of that community's music festival; this has become an annual event. Other pastoral airs concerts have since been held in various other communities across the island. Many commercial recordings now typically include an air in the repertoire presented; a small number of recordings focus pre-dominantly or exclusively on this tune-type, such as Lloyd MacDonald's *Aires in Bloom* (2011) and Howie MacDonald's *Just Relax* (1998). The fact that the fiddle is typically accompanied by piano for the slow air likely accounts for the very definite beat with which it is generally played. An exception is in the playing of Dan Hughie MacEachern, who has composed original airs in which he indicates various metres, thus suggesting a degree of flexibility ("The Valleys of Mabou," for example, moves from common time through 3/4 and 2/4). "Little" Jack MacDonald also employed a degree of rubato in his rendition of certain airs, as did Winston Fitzgerald, the latter most notably when he performed unaccompanied; Lloyd MacDonald also maintained a degree of flexibility in the pulse of his airs. Other techniques adopted in the playing of slow airs that define their sound include the use of various forms, frequency and placement of vibrato, bow control, phrasing and tone quality. Slow airs have also become popular among piano players, some of whom – such as Mary Jessie MacDonald, Sheumas MacNeil, Mac Morin, Troy MacGillivray and Tracey MacNeil – are noted for the sensitivity with which they accompany the fiddle on these tunes as well as playing them as instrumental solos. *See* **repertoire.**

All Fired Up. A family band of three MacDonald brothers from Foot Cape, Inverness County. Kyle plays fiddle, mandolin and percussion, twin brother Keith plays bagpipes and guitar, and their older brother, Colin, plays piano, guitar, drums and is a step dancer. Both Kyle and Keith are members of the band Nuallan and all three brothers are on the staff of the Gaelic College.

Am Bràighe. (brae/higher ground). A quarterly tabloid-format bilingual magazine published in Mabou by Frances and Ron MacEachen, a sister and brother with Gaelic roots and experience in reporting, editing, publishing and marketing. *Am Bràighe* was launched in 1993 and continued until 2003, published initially by the Sandy Publishing Group in Mabou and later by Gaeltalk, MacEachen's own publishing company, based in Queensville. Over its ten years, the magazine had some 2,000 subscribers, approximately 60% of them from Nova Scotia and the remainder from outside the province. While much of the focus was the Gaelic language (through articles, interviews, and instruction by Jim Watson) a significant amount of related cultural content was on the interconnection and interdependence of all the elements of culture. Interviews with musicians, articles by scholars Kate Dunlay and John Shaw among others, and a tune transcription section by John Donald Cameron formed the music content; information was also provided on local events. As well as acknowledging and celebrating the local language and culture, *Am Bràighe* was a vehicle for exploring issues surrounding the tension between the cultural community and the music industry that was looking to Cape Breton in the 1990s in an unprecedented way. *Am Bràighe* has been digitized as part of the Nova Scotia Historical Newspapers Project, a project of Libraries Nova Scotia. [**Feintuch 2010**]. *See* **print media.**

amplification. Electronic mediation of music in order to render it clearly audible in large spaces or in otherwise noisy circumstances. Used with Cape Breton fiddle music, in performances it ideally creates the high-volume, "live" aesthetic (significantly different from acoustic performance) that has become part of the iconic dance-hall sound and is, increasingly, associated with other performance contexts such as pub gigs and, latterly, house parties. The technology used in amplifying Cape Breton fiddles is more or less standard, being shaped by function and, most significantly, local aesthetics; Cape Breton fiddlers appear to have a distinct sonic ideal that they aspire to, one which is different to that experienced in other traditions. Despite having been increasingly exposed to a variety of amplification options in the past decade, Cape Bretoners have, to date, showed a reluctance to abandon the entrenched preferences (of both performers and audiences) for high volume, highly compressed pickups. The preference for high volume in Cape Breton may link back to the prevalence of Highland Bagpipes, originally

the popular providers of dance music. Teams of two fiddles or the use of scordatura tuning were popular methods for increasing fiddle volume as this instrument gained in popularity. However, the need for amplification or "electrocuted music" as some fiddlers referred to it came about for various reasons. By the 1940s dance halls were much larger than before and the replacement of wooden walls and ceilings with Sheetrock as standard led to drastic changes in room acoustics. Audiences too became noisier. One of the first fiddlers to own a sound system in Cape Breton was Winston Fitzgerald in the 1940s; he used the De Armond model pickup which was placed on the belly or the back of the instrument, attached using an elastic band. While feedback and interrupted signal transmission would occur if consistent pressure was not maintained between the pickup and the instrument, this pickup did manage to reproduce the individual dynamics and tone of the player. This model became very popular in Cape Breton and was used right up until the 1990s. Following Fitzgerald's lead, it became common for fiddlers to have their own equipment that they would transport and set up at the dance halls on their circuit. It was not until the late 1990s that most venues installed in-house systems.

technology. By the 1990s virtually all Cape Breton fiddlers playing in public used transducers made by L. R. Baggs, a Californian company specializing in the amplification of acoustic instruments, and nearly all pianists used electronic keyboards. The latter is as a result of upright pianos in dance halls having fallen into disrepair, requiring tuning or, increasingly, in some venues, simply not being available. For fiddles, the L. R. Baggs pickup became the preferred option for players performing at dances allowing them to simply plug-and-go. This model was chosen even by musicians who had issues with its sound quality, simply because of its dependability, versatility and simplicity of use as well as it being an established convention and expected by the audience; it became both a status symbol and a security blanket of sorts for Cape Breton fiddlers, allowing them to play with a lighter touch while covering up any imperfections in details. The typical pickup sound is high-volume, highly compressed and quintessentially "electric"; it limits dynamics and promotes a homogenized tone, thus diminishing the all-important individual identity of Cape Breton fiddlers. A small number of Cape Breton engineers such as Paul MacDonald have worked hard to promote the alternative, a "natural" sound picked up by a microphone; he has made a number of recordings in an on-location, field-recording style, seeking conditions similar to typical Cape Breton homes in the 19th and early-20th century, which had tamarack or hardwood floors and walls of Douglas Fir or plaster, which created an excellent acoustic environment. Today, while attitudes relating to amplification choices are slow to change, there is evidence that an increasing number of fiddlers are beginning to experiment with condenser mics (DPAs) in concert settings. **[Hayes 2012, 2015].**

An Tulloch Gorm Society of Cape Breton (ATG). This was formed in 1985 to preserve and promote Cape Breton Celtic music and culture following discussion among a small group of enthusiasts who were almost exclusively non-musicians. The organization was driven and steered by a very active board of directors that included Dan MacDonald, John Gillis, Earle Morris, Larry Parks, Lorraine Ferguson, Joyce Keigan, Neil and Joan MacKenzie, Bill and Jean MacDonald, Hughie C. MacNeil, Bernie Landry, Jean Hill, Lloyd MacDonald and Courtney MacPherson. ATG operated on a membership basis, this advertised and available at "$5 plus an interest in the culture"; at its peak it incorporated a network of some fifty to sixty people who were kept informed of its activities though a regular newsletter. The organization began running projects in 1986 with a concert series initiated by Sheldon MacInnes and implemented in conjunction with the Extension and Community Affairs Department of Cape Breton University. This ran successfully for four years and introduced young, up-and-coming players from across Cape Breton to performance alongside well-known and established artists.

Highlights included performances by Howie MacDonald, John Morris Rankin, Dave MacIsaac and George MacInnis, as well as a "Next Generation" concert featuring students of Stan Chapman (Ashley MacIsaac, Natalie MacMaster, Jackie Dunn, Wendy MacIsaac, Glenn Graham), the Pellerin brothers, Dwayne Côté and students of Kyle MacNeil (Shawn MacDonald and Kent Lewis). ATG also ran monthly dances at the Brookshaven Recreation Centre in Prime Brook. As with the concert series, the dances introduced established and emerging artists to the industrial area of Cape Breton and regularly drew crowds from across the island. The most ambitious project ATG tackled was the Ben Eoin Fiddle and Folk Festival, an annual outdoor event that took place in mid-August on a local ski slope, outside of Sydney. This ran for twelve years until rendered unprofitable by rising costs and dwindling audiences. Over its years, however, the show featured a wide variety of talent, including guests from Scotland, Ireland, the U.S. and other parts of Canada. ATG's other activities included assisting a number of Cape Breton musicians to record and tour; sponsorship of research work such as Ian McKinnon's directory of recordings (which started as a project for the 1987 Canada Winter Games); running instructive events in various parts of the island at Ingonish, Chéticamp, Baddeck and St. Peter's; retail trading as a source and distribution outlet for recordings by local artists. By the 1990s, ATG had a huge inventory, managed by John Gillis, that included stock acquired from Bernie MacIsaac's Celtic Music Store in Antigonish, which closed in the mid-1980s. ATG was one of the first organizations to regularly pay performers beyond the going industry rate, recognizing that music-making was a business for which musicians should be paid a proper, sustaining wage. Volunteer-run, ATG was self-financed with occasional project support from CBU and the Nova Scotia Department of Tourism. It served a vital purpose in developing traditional music until it was wound up formally in 2000, overtaken by the growth of interest in Celtic culture by more fully resourced venues and organizations.

Ancient Order of Hibernians (AOH). America's oldest Irish Catholic Fraternal Organization, this was founded in Pennsylvania and New York City in 1836, and established divisions throughout Canada, including Cape Breton, in the 1880s. Originally founded to support Roman Catholic (RC) clergy and churches, the AOH widened its agenda to socially and economically support immigrants from Ireland. Its membership was open to RC males aged 16 or over who were Irish or of Irish descent. Mike Fitzgerald of Sydney was one of these in 1950, a committed promoter of Irish culture in Cape Breton, who served as the AOH's Canadian National Organizer for a number of years. St. Patrick's Church, Sydney (built in 1828), became the AOH base in Cape Breton in 1950; this became the site of historical projects rather than cultural, Irish-related ones. Activities of the Cape Breton chapter of the AOH included the erection of a granite monument engraved with shamrocks at Little Lorraine in 1949 to mark the 1834 shipwreck there of the immigrant vessel *Astrea* while en route from Limerick to Québec carrying 251 passengers, of whom only three survived. The Irish Benevolent Society replaced the AOH in Cape Breton in the 1960s. *See* **Irish Benevolent Society.**

Antigonish Highland Games. A series of events staged annually over a week in July by the Antigonish Highland Society (AHS) that was established to preserve Scottish culture and traditions. AHS was founded in 1861 as a development of a previous Society that had existed in Antigonish since 1836 and was originally named The Highland Society of the County of Sydney. The first Highland Games to be sponsored by the AHS were held in October 1863 and have since become AHS's signature event and a major tourist attraction. The primary focus of the Games is competition – in piping, drumming, pipe bands, Highland dance, athletics and other sporting activities (such as tug-of-war). The program also includes a range of cultural events such as a "clan day" and various ceilidhs and dances. The Antigonish Highland Games made a significant contribution to music

and culture; military-style pipers brought in to compete and to perform for dance competitions certainly had an impact on subsequent style and repertoire, for pipers and also for fiddlers, many of whom played both instruments. Over the years Cape Breton fiddlers have continued to engage with the Games at one of its key presentational events, "The Concert Under the Stars," which has featured numerous Cape Breton acts over the years. [**Gibson 2000**].

Apex Records. A Canadian record label owned by Compo Company Ltd., a Canadian firm established in the Montréal suburb of Lachine by Herbert S. Berliner in 1921. Apex was the longest-lasting of the Compo labels, surviving until the early 1970s, and at various stages released American and Canadian recordings for both Anglophone and Francophone communities; records pressed included those by such as Don Messer and His Islanders. The Apex catalogue also carried the commercial recordings of two Cape Breton artists, Bill Lamey (two 78s) and John Allan Cameron (two LPs, *Here Comes John Allan Cameron* [1968] and *The Minstrel of Cranberry Lane* [1969]). *See* **recording industry.**

ARC Records. A subsidiary of Arc Sound Co. Ltd. that was established in Toronto in 1958 by Philip G. Anderson and William R. Gilliland. At first a record distributor, Arc Sound began releasing its own recordings in 1959 and purchased the Precision Pressing Company in 1961. It released Cape Breton fiddler Joe MacIsaac's LP *The Sound of Cape Breton* in the 1960s, this most likely via a connection made through MacIsaac's appearances on the Don Messer Show. In 1969, ARC and its subsidiaries came under the control of a Canadian-owned holding company, the Ahed Music Corporation Ltd., Toronto, and operations were ceased in 1986. *See* **recording industry.**

archive. Different from a library (which focuses on published material) and a museum (which focuses on artefacts or physical objects), an archive is a repository for primary source materials (print, audio, visual, etc.) with a focus on unpublished original records. Archives historically occupy a physical space; today, the majority have – or are in the process of having – an on-line presence, immediately magnifying the potential for accessibility of material; some recent archival projects are accessible to the public only in an on-line capacity. The primary archive holding materials related to Cape Breton fiddle music (including print materials, photographs, commercial and non-commercial audio and audio-visual recordings) is the Beaton Institute at Cape Breton University, Sydney. The Celtic Music Interpretive Centre (CMIC) in Judique, opened in 2006, includes an archive; further materials are held at the Highland Village Museum, Iona, and at St. FX University. On-line archival projects – such as Gaelstream, initiated at St. FX University, and the Cape Breton "Unity in Diversity" site from the Beaton Institute – present significant audio and visual material in a hypertext format, focusing on the song and instrumental traditions, respectively; further material is available through such as the Nova Scotia Public Archives website and the Libraries of Nova Scotia digitization project which focuses on historical newspapers from the region. Archival material related to the Cape Breton fiddle tradition is also scattered at various universities and other institutions across Canada (e.g., Memorial University of Newfoundland and Labrador, the Museum of History, Ottawa, Nova Scotia Public Archives, Halifax), the U.S. (e.g., Smithsonian Institution, Washington, DC, the Library of Congress, Indiana University, Columbia University), Scotland (University of Glasgow) and Ireland (e.g., ITMA and the University of Limerick). *See* **Beaton Institute; Celtic Music Interpretive Centre; Highland Village Museum; St. FX.**

articulation. Refers to the way in which individual notes (both melody notes and embellishments) are connected; in fiddle playing, this is determined largely through the use of the bow. Notes may be attached to or separated from each other, creating a smooth (legato) effect or a more detached (staccato) one; most typically, a player will employ a variety of approaches in articulating any given tune.

Arts Nova Scotia. A provincial funding agency formed in 2012 as a result of the Arts Nova Scotia Act of 2011 during the premiership of Darrell Dexter. The previous administration's tourism and culture minister, Rodney MacDonald, in 2002 liquidated the Nova Scotia Arts Council (which had been in existence since 1996), citing among other reasons geographical/regional imbalances in distribution of awards funding and overall administrative costs. The Nova Scotia Arts and Culture Partnership Council replaced the Nova Scotia Arts Council with lower administrative costs and additional program dollars. With an initial budget of $2.4 million from the Department of Communities, Culture and Heritage, Arts Nova Scotia offers support to individual professional artists, organizations, producers and presenters, and manages awards like the Portia White Prize. Cape Breton music benefited from the first tranche of funding made available to individual artists in an award to fiddler and luthier Otis Tomas for his *Fiddletree* project.

Athole Collection of Scottish Dance Music. One of the principal sources for the older Cape Breton repertoire, this was compiled in 1884 by James Stewart Robertson (1823-1896) of Edradynate, Perthshire. He had studied fiddle under Duncan McKercher ("The Athole Paganini"), John McAlpine and William McLeish ("The Aberfeldy Paganini"). A founding member of the Edinburgh Highland Reel and Strathspey Society in 1881, Robertson was its first president, and died during its 1895-96 session. Remembered in obituaries as a lawyer, philanthropist and politician, his music was ignored by the press. Yet historically his memory endures on account of his editing and publishing of *The Athole Collection*, a work that arose out of his concern that public interest in Scottish fiddle music was waning. Considered by Francis Collinson to have encyclopaedic knowledge of Scottish dance music, the collection remains one of the standard books of Scottish fiddle music. Published by subscription by MacLachlan and Stewart of Edinburgh in two volumes, it carries a total of 870 strathspeys, reels, jigs, hornpipes and country dances arranged for piano. Its tunes are mainly paired as reel and strathspey with jigs, hornpipes and certain country-dances grouped in categories; tunes are ordered according to the key of the piano arrangements. The reprint of the collection in Edinburgh in 1961, with an introduction by Francis J. Collinson, made an impact in Cape Breton as a tremendous resource; but despite the fact that scholars and players were aware of it, access to the collection was difficult, and it remained one of the more expensive of the tune books until a further reprint was done by Balnain House, Inverness, in 1996. That edition was revised and republished in 2008 by The Highland Music Trust, omitting the rudimentary bass lines of the original but leaving the melody lines unaltered and the music grouped in keys – rendering it a valuable working volume for today's players. Notes on the sources of the tunes, were provided for this edition (by Charles Gore, compiler of *The Scottish Fiddle Music Index*); it also carries a foreword by the late Duke of Atholl and an introduction by the Scottish fiddler Alasdair Fraser. *See* **tune books.**

Aucoin family of Sydney Mines. A family of musicians with roots in the Acadian village of Chéticamp. **Gaston Aucoin** (1947-) is a fiddle player, guitar and mandolin player. His parents were musical; his father, Placide, played fiddle and accordion and his mother, Marie Therese, a singer, was active in church choirs. Among his siblings, all of them musical, his sister **Anna (Aucoin) MacDougall** is a noted piano player. He was among the fiddlers to play at the first Glendale Festival and has been actively involved in the CBFA since its inception. He married Claire O'Toole and, living in Sydney Mines, has a family of four, two of whom are well-known musicians.

Aucoin, Brent. (1983-). Fiddle and guitar. Sydney Mines and Millville, Cape Breton. Taught to play initially by his father, Gaston, he later took lessons from Allie Bennett. Other players such as Arthur Muise have also been a significant influence on his playing. Travelling to Fort McMurray, AB, to work in the oilfields for more than a decade, Aucoin's playing is limited to visits home when he plays the occasional concert and dance, often in ensemble with his father and sister. He has composed a small number of tunes, one of which is published in *The Cape Breton Fiddlers Collection* (2007) and has featured on commercial recordings by his sister Leanne.

Aucoin, Leanne. (1981-). Fiddle, piano, step dance, composition, teaching. Sydney Mines and Halifax. She began step dancing at an early age under the direction of Jean MacNeil and later began playing fiddle and piano, receiving lessons from Allie Bennett (fiddle) and Tracey Dares-MacNeil (piano). She has had numerous influences over the years, including her family and other players such as Howie MacDonald, Brenda Stubbert and Arthur Muise. She recorded *All Set* in 2006, a CD that features a track with her father, brother and aunt, Anna (Aucoin) MacDougall; this was nominated for an ECMA award in 2008. Known particularly for her playing of slower tunes, she is featured on *Failte: Airs and Waltzes*, released by Judique's CMIC in 2007; five of her compositions were published in the same year in Cranford's *The Cape Breton Fiddlers Collection*. A long-standing member of the Board and active worker in the CBFA, Aucoin is a regular teacher of fiddle and step dance at The Gaelic College in St. Ann's, Nova Scotia. A graduate of St. FX University, where she obtained a degree in Human Kinetics, she has taught Cape Breton fiddle and step-dance workshops in Ireland, at the University of Limerick, and at Scoil Samhraidh Willie Clancy, Milltown Malbay. Currently based in Halifax, she is a member of the folk band The Narrows, with Jon Goodman, Roy MacLaren, Colin Carrigan and Jessie Lewis, an ensemble that features uilleann pipes, flute and whistles, fiddles, banjo, guitar, piano and vocals; she also teachers Cape Breton step dance there.

Aucoin, Alcide. (1903-1963). Fiddle. Chéticamp, Cape Breton, and Boston, MA. The son of Jaques

Alcide Aucoin. Courtesy of Bill Aucoin.

Jim and Louise (LeFort) Aucoin he moved to Boston at the age of 19 where he secured employment at a shipyard in Quincy, MA. He played fiddle in clubs there up to four nights a week and at many house parties with other Cape Bretoners, such as Angus Chisholm, Winston Fitzgerald, Bill Lamey and Buddy MacMaster. Aucoin was one of the first Cape Breton fiddlers to record commercially; he was a member of The Inverness Serenaders in the 1930s and with them recorded six 78s for Decca; these discs include a number of solo sides from Aucoin, accompanied on piano by Elizabeth Maillet.

audiences. Cape Breton music may be experienced by audiences or listening contexts, such as concerts and ceilidhs, or in participatory contexts such as square dances, where the majority of those present engage kinesthetically with the music. Local Cape Breton audiences have an unusually close connection with the fiddle music, perhaps because of the primacy of participatory dance settings for many decades that fostered an intimate level of knowledge of the music or because many of those experiencing music, in a presentational setting would often be musicians or dancers themselves. This creates audiences that have a deep level of knowledge of the repertoire and style and who uses this knowledge to interact with the performer(s). This interaction may be manifest in spontaneous applause at points where a particularly popular tune is introduced into a medley, or at the point where a strathspey accelerates into

the reel (these often seem completely random to outsiders, leaving them somewhat bewildered); support is also demonstrated by whoops or calls of encouragement for the player to "drive 'er." It is also common for dancers within the audience to be sufficiently charged by the music to take to the floor or stage for a spontaneous display of step dancing.

tourist audiences. The romantic image of Cape Breton as an island of fiddlers and music in every home and public building is, as it is in Scotland and Ireland, a myth of course. There has indeed been a strategy in recent years to capitalize on fiddle music and dance for promoting cultural tourism, but it is still possible for visitors to certain parts of the island to experience very little of the local culture and, certainly, little that might be deemed authentic. While there are many notable institutions, projects and events which successfully allow tourism and culture to intersect to the benefit of all concerned (e.g., Celtic Colours, CMIC, the Baddeck Gathering Ceilidhs, The Red Shoe, Glenora Distillery Ceilidhs, etc.), in other instances the meeting of the insider and outsider has been less successful, and indeed considered by some to be detrimental to local cultural practice. This mostly concerns square dances. Despite the impression that these are spontaneous, inclusive affairs, such dances actually have a strict underlying etiquette that is observed by local participants; visitors, who often attend in groups, may miss the subtle nuances of the dance order and its responsiveness to the music and get caught up in the participatory element. In some cases, the increasing numbers of visitors have actually made local dancers less inclined to attend such dances, consequently depriving visitors of a true insight into the Cape Breton experience.

audience numbers and demographics. Cape Breton's population is largely made up of older people and children, with emigration continuing to drain the 20- to 60-year olds into urban centres such as Halifax, Toronto and out west, where work is plentiful; the audiences for Cape Breton fiddle music mirrors this. Until recently, Nova Scotia liquor laws prohibited those under 19 from attending venues where alcohol was sold;

thus a number of key music-performance venues were off-limits to the younger populace, who were restricted to "family" events where alcohol was not officially available; this law has recently been relaxed to allow under 19 to be present in licenced premised until 9pm, as long as food is being served. Local audiences for fiddle-music events tend to be small (fewer than 100), of an older age group and are highly experienced in and familiar with the music. The age profile may be a cause for concern in terms of the sustainability of the tradition, but the small numbers are not especially worrying for the venues – community halls, small pubs or private homes – lend themselves to select audiences of this size. However, a shift typically occurs in the summer months when Cape Bretoners "from away" return home for the holidays and the numbers at dances, concerts and ceilidhs swell; since the late 1990s there has been increasing visitor numbers. Outdoor community concerts, which had their heyday in the late 1980s/early 1990s, had the largest crowds; today the remaining concerts, such as Broad Cove and the CBFA's Fiddlers Festival, attract several hundred people. Established in 2014, KitchenFest!/Féis a' Chidsin!, held in June at the start of the tourist season, already has a following; Celtic Colours has reinvigorated audiences with its annual program of almost 300 performances and community events, drawing audiences in excess of 18,000 with a more or less stable 50-50 proportion of locals and visitors. At many formal concerts the audience profile is typical of Cape Breton, but the nightly Festival Club, an informal concert/dance event, has a predominantly younger audience and is generally filled to capacity at around 300 people.

international audiences for Cape Breton fiddle music. Since the early 20th century, documented evidence shows that Cape Breton music was both known and well received by audiences in diasporic contexts such as in Halifax, Boston, Detroit-Windsor and Toronto. From the 1960s onward, Cape Breton artists began appearing at popular folk festivals such as Newport and Mariposa. In the 1960s, the first organized performances of Cape Breton fiddlers in Scotland

Big Pond Scottish Concert, 1989. Photograph from The MacInnes Collection.

took place and soon after visits to Ireland had also begun to happen. However, it was the 1980s before regular international performing and touring opportunities emerged, first in the U.S. (e.g., at the Wolf Trap Folk Festivals in Washington, DC) and then, in the 1990s, increasingly in Scotland (e.g., Celtic Connections) and elsewhere in Europe. All of these festival appearances played a role in introducing Cape Breton music to new audiences. Prior to the 1990s it was difficult to access recordings of Cape Breton music abroad, mainly because little had been released on major international labels since the 1950s; live performances, following which the artists would sell their albums, was the only opportunity to purchase this material outside of Cape Breton. The establishment of Cranford Publications and *Cape Breton's Magazine* addressed international availability to some degree, through their mail-order services; with the advent of the Internet, new recording and distribution deals and increasing touring opportunities for Cape Breton fiddlers from the 1990s onward, access to Cape Breton music significantly increased for its growing international audience. Since then, the flow of international performers to the island has also dramatically increased (mainly through the establishment of Celtic Colours), bringing with it new and expanded audiences. **[Feintuch 2010; Ivakhiv 2005; Lavengood 2008]** *See* **Celtic music.**

aural transmission. The adjective "aural" relates to sounds perceived by the ear; in music contexts, where transmission (the passing on of the style and repertoire) occurs without the use of writing means the process engaged is correctly an aural one—what traditional musicians often refer to as learning or playing "by ear." *See* **ear players; oral tradition.**

awards. Since the 1970s there has been significant attention given to honouring fiddlers and other artists who have contributed to Cape Breton community and cultural life. This has generated various award systems that are non-competitive, and permit key stylists in the music to be recognized, and their artistic contribution celebrated locally, provincially and nationally; some Cape Bretoners have also been recognized internationally for their contributions to culture. The main awards and other accolades associated with Cape Breton fiddle music are (i) tributes and testimonials, (ii) industry awards, (iii) honorary degrees, (iv) government awards, (v) funded awards and prizes, (vi) awards for emerging musicians.

(i) tributes and testimonials. The 1970s saw the beginning of an effort by the wider Cape Breton community to recognize some of the island's key cultural figures, this coinciding with and contributing to a revival of the fiddle tradition. Tributes and testimonial events took many forms; some were concerts, while others involved a more formal meal and ceremony with speakers outlining the achievements of the guests of honour. Typically, the individual being honoured would receive a plaque or other token to mark the occasion. This concept was initiated by the Cape Breton Gaelic Society, which organized a series of annual concerts to celebrate and to recognize Gaelic bards. The idea was picked up and developed by other organizations and institutions (including CBU, the New Waterford Gaelic Society, An Tulloch Gorm Society of Cape Breton, CBFA and the Nova Scotia Highland Village Society) and remained popular, both in Cape Breton and throughout the diaspora, until the 1990s, when alternative systems of honouring artists were in-

troduced. Today, the practice of recognizing and honouring excellence and contribution of Cape Breton fiddlers has been continued by various community awards and by Celtic Colours, which regularly themes concerts around a particular player or group, living or deceased, as a means of honouring them. Cape Breton-style fiddlers such as Angus Chisholm, Colin J. Boyd and Hugh A. MacDonald have been inducted into the Nova Scotia Country Music Hall of Fame, established in 1997, while Buddy MacMaster was inducted into the Scottish Traditional Music Hall of Fame in 2006. In 2015 Winnie Chafe became the first woman honoured with the Lifetime Achievement Award from the Grand Masters National Fiddling Championships.

(ii) industry awards for Cape Breton fiddle music have been developed since the 1990s. A nomination for any of these is considered prestigious and will be proudly declared by artists in their promotional material. Winning such awards has proven to be advantageous in professional development for artists, bringing them a degree of national and international recognition within the industry. Showcase opportunities at the peripheral events surrounding awards ceremonies can themselves bring significant opportunities to emerging artists. Cape Bretoners who have collaborated with artists from other regions have also been nominated or have won awards in both Scotland and Ireland. At provincial and national levels in Canada, Cape Breton players have been successful in the major awards: East Coast Music Awards (ECMAs); Music Nova Scotia Music and Industry Awards (MNS); Canadian Folk Music Awards (CFMA) and Juno Awards. Other national awards bodies have also recognized Cape Breton fiddlers, e.g., The Cottars were nominated for a Gemini Award for achievements in Canadian TV in 2003; Natalie MacMaster won the Canadian Country Music Association Roots Artist of the Year in 2001; she also featured on an album with Yo-Yo Ma that won a Grammy; Cape Breton fiddlers signed to major labels have also picked up awards related to record sales; the Rankins, for example, won three SOCAN Awards. In 2014, Folk

Alliance International presented Buddy MacMaster with a Lifetime Achievement Award, the first Cape Breton fiddler to receive this accolade. *See* **Canadian Folk Music Awards, East Coast Music Awards, Juno Awards, Music Nova Scotia.**

(iii) **honorary awards and recognition**. Cape Breton fiddlers and others connected with the tradition have been the recipients of honorary degrees from a number of institutions. Honorary doctorates were conferred on Winnie Chafe (St. FX 1986, CBU 1995), Buddy MacMaster (St. FX 1995, CBU 1996), The Rankin Family (Acadia University 2010), John Allan Cameron (CBU 1998), The Barra MacNeils (CBU 2015) and Natalie MacMaster (Niagra University, NY, 2006, Trent University, ON, 2008; St.Thomas University, NB; Atlantic School of Theology and St. Mary's University, NS, 2013). Others who have received honorary doctorates whose contribution to the fiddle music and dance traditions forms part of their career profile include such as Fr. John Angus Rankin (St. FX 1983), Archie Neil Chisholm (CBU 1996), Allister MacGillivray (CBU 1997), Scott Macmillan (CBU 1997), Barbara Le Blanc (Acadia Univeristy 2004), Lloyd MacDonald (CBU 2012), Joella Foulds (CBU 2011) and Gordie Sampson (CBU and St. FX 2013).

(iv) **government awards, provincial and federal.** The contribution to the arts by various Cape Bretoners has been recognized by provincial and federal governments through the awarding of various honours such as the Order of Canada, the Order of Nova Scotia and various medals including the Queen's Jubilee Medal. In the U.S., in 1984, Joseph Cormier was honoured with an American Heritage Fellowship Award for his contribution to the preservation of Celtic music there, the first Cape Bretoner to receive such an accreditation; Natalie MacMaster received the Arts and Letters Award from the Canadian Association of New York in 2013. See **medals; Order of Canada; Order of Nova Scotia**.

(v) **funded awards and prizes.** Provincially based, these include such as the Community Arts and Culture Recognition Award and the Established Artists Recognition Awards, both made by the Creative Nova Scotia Leadership Council; in 2012, luthier, musician and composer, Otis Tomas became the first Cape Bretoner to receive the latter. The Portia White Prize is awarded annually by Arts Nova Scotia for cultural and artistic excellence on the part of a Nova Scotian artist who has attained professional status, mastery and recognition in a discipline. Named for Portia White, a world-renowned contralto, the prize consists of $18,000 and a certificate of recognition. In 2010, Gaelic singer Mary Jane Lamond of Glendale was the recipient, while composer, Scott Macmillan, received the award in 2014.

(vi) **awards for emerging musicians.** In addition to the above types of honours, which are bestowed on established artists, professional or semi-professional, there have been several initiatives established since the 1990s in order to recognize and encourage emerging musicians. These take the form of (a) local awards, (b) bursaries and (c) industry awards and showcases.

(a) **local awards.** Set up in memory of local supporters of Cape Breton music, the two relevant to the fiddle music are the Frank "Big Sampie" Sampson Award and the the Tic Butler Memorial Award, both of which offer financial supports to emerging young talent. See **Frank "Big Sampie" Sampson Award; Tic Butler Memorial Award.**

(b) **bursaries.** These awards, supporting students of Cape Breton fiddle music, are offered annually by the Gaelic College, CMIC and by independent organizations such as CBFA and the Festival Volunteer Drive'ers Association. Many of these support student fiddle players and typically range in value from $25-$500; recipients may be from Cape Breton or elsewhere. Among the bursaries available to Cape Breton fiddlers at the Gaelic College are the Mike MacDougall Memorial Bursary (sponsored by CBFA, awarded to a student who is one of their members); the Mary Johnson Boehl Music Bursary (for a Victoria County youth/student with primary interest in traditional Cape Breton or Celtic music); The Alexander Clark Norman Bursary (for a Nova Scotia Student studying Cape Breton Fiddle); and the Joe MacNeil Scholarship (for a young fiddle student to attend the Gaelc College summer school course). Other bursaries open to but not limited to fiddlers include the John Allan Cameron Bursary (five grants to students of any discipline, sponsored by the Celtic Colours Festival Volunteer Drive'ers Association); the Clan Donald Bursary (three stipends); the Brendan Patrick Lucey Bursary (for a U.S. student); the Gaelic College Foundation Bursary (for a live-in student at the youth sessions); the Major Sir Torquail Matheson Bursary (provided by the Winnipeg Foundation and available to any Canadian Student); the Skip Darcy Bursary (awarded to a student to further studies in any of the dance programs); and the Scots Bursary (awarded by The Scots North British Society to two students from the Halifax Regional Municipality). CMIC offers a bursary annually in memory of Jerry Holland for the Buddy MacMaster School of Fiddling.

(c) **industry awards and showcases.** A significant element of many provincial and national industry events is the programming of showcase opportunities around major award ceremonies, allowing younger, less established artists to perform before key stakeholders. Many of the award-giving organizations include a bespoke category for emerging professional musicians, and winning such an award has been an important career break through for young Cape Breton musicians in recent years. *See* **competition**.

(Below) Doug MacPhee receiving the Order of Canada, 2008. John W. MacDonald Photography.

(Right) Buddy MacMaster receives the Dr. Helen Creighton Lifetime Achievement Award at the ECMAs in 2006. The Canadian Press.

LIZ DOHERTY

B

back-string substitution. A melodic variation technique involving a note on the "back" or bass strings (G and D) being sounded in place of that same note in the melody line an octave or two above. Most commonly used in the A modes, it is generally found at the start of a phrase. Since an octave or two-octave span is typically involved between the notes being iterated, quite a jagged effect results in the contour of the melodic line. The technique may be further emphasized by adding either a double stop or an open string doubling to the lower note. **[Dunlay and Greenberg 1996; Dunlay with Reich 1986].**

back-stringers. Also referred to as "old back-stringers." A collective name for some popular traditional tunes where the melody for the first part of the tune is played on the G and D strings (the bass, "low" or "back" strings) and is thus in the lower register; the second part is played on the A and E strings (the treble, "high" or "front" strings), in a higher register. The contrast between the almost growling first part and the brighter second part made tunes that fit this pattern a favourite among step dancers, particularly those whose routines were created spontaneously in response to the music being played. The term was common among players until the mid-20th century; since then its usage greatly decreased and it is rarely used today.

bagpipe. Found in multiple variations in many cultures, universally the bagpipe is a reed instrument on which the melody is played on a chanter accompanied by one or more drones, the sound being activated by air pressure provided through a blowing pipe, via a bag reservoir, by the players lungs or a bellows. Early evidence pertaining to the existence of a form of pipes dates back to at least 1000 BCE in Roman society, and indeed earlier (ca. 2500 BCE) in Syria and ancient Egypt. Successive alterations were made to this simple reed pipe over the following centuries, including the addition of a blowpipe and drones. No accurate information exists regarding the arrival of the bagpipe in Scotland although theories point to either an Irish or a Roman connection with the instrument most likely making an appearance via England. The earliest depictions of the pipes in Scotland are at Melrose Abbey dating from 1136 and at Roslyn Chapel from 1440.

the instrument. Various forms of bagpipe exist in Scotland, roughly divided into Highland and Lowland categories. In the Highlands, as well as the popular Great Highland bagpipe, various forms of small pipe also existed, while in the Lowlands the popular forms were small pipes

The Old King's Reel

reel · traditional · arr: P.S.C

or border pipes. The Great Highland bagpipe has been the prominent bagpipe prevalent in Cape Breton; besides the full-size sets, three-quarter-size sets were also available (sometimes referred to as reel pipes), which were somewhat quieter; another member of this pipe family was the mouth-blown parlour or miniature pipes, used as practice sets with drone accompaniment. A few examples of the three-quarter size and parlour pipes were found in Cape Breton from the early 20th century, as were Irish uilleann pipes. A number of contemporary pipers also play forms of Scottish bellows-blown pipes, many of which originally were associated with the Lowlands. These are a very recent introduction dating back only to the early 1990s and to the visits of Hamish Moore, from Scotland. Another form of pipes occasionally found are the shuttle pipes, developed by John Walsh in Antigonish, and which resemble the French musette; the name refers to the mechanism employed to tune the instrument.

the Great Highland bagpipe (*píob mòr*) consists of a bag which acts as air reservoir, a blowpipe, a chanter with a double reed on which the melody is fingered, two tenor drones and one bass drone, each using a single reed; these have gradually been added to the instrument as it evolved. These drones each sound a continuous note, one octave apart and producing rudimentary harmony; the drones require frequent tuning. The chanter has a range of 9 notes that extends from one whole tone lower than the tonic, to one octave above it (G, A, B C D E F G' A'). The scale of the chanter is in the mixolydian mode, which includes a flattened 7th degree. More modern bagpipes with conical chanters do have the capacity to play tunes in other keys using C and F naturals, a feature of many of the more contemporary tunes often chosen by pipers (e.g., "Brenda Stubbert's Reel"). The bagpipe omits a continuous sound when air is passing through the chanter and has no capacity for creating dynamics, although the volume does decrease as the higher end of the range is employed.

small pipes. The Highland "small pipe" or "chamber pipe" is a mouth or bellows-blown in-strument that became increasingly popular from the 18th century, mainly since it was a much quieter instrument and could thus be played indoors for recreational purposes. It uses a parallel bore chanter and can be played in the key of A, B flat, C and D, thus making it possible to play along with other instruments. A major revival in Scotland of this instrument was instigated in the 1980s by a number of players such as Rab Wallace and Hamish Moore; Moore, who taught at The Gaelic College in the mid-1990s, introduced young Cape Breton pipers such as Ryan J. MacNeil, Ryan MacDonald, Rankin MacInnis and Angus and Kenneth MacKenzie to the instrument.

Lowland pipes may be mouth or bellows blown, with the latter being most common. "Border" pipes, popular in the Lowlands, were also in evidence in the Highlands; there, however, they were labelled "reel pipes." A quiet instrument used for dance music these reel pipes have three drones and a conical chanter in the key of A, which allows them to fit easily into performance contexts alongside other instruments. Developed in the 18th century, but almost extinct by the turn of the 20th, they were revived by Hamish Moore and have been embraced by a small number of Cape Breton's younger pipers.

uilleann pipes. The member of the bagpipe family typically associated with Ireland, the uilleann ("elbow" or "union") pipes is descended from the pastoral pipes common to Ireland, England and Scotland. Bellows blown, it has a chanter, three drones and keyed melody pipes or regulators that enable harmony notes to be sounded along with the melody line. The player performs while seated; typically the bag is held under the left arm, which applies pressure to it in order to generate the sound; air is pumped into this bag from a bellows attached near the elbow of the right arm. The chanter rests on the player's right knee, while the drones and regulators, fixed to a single stock, sit across the players lap behind the chanter. The scale of the uilleann pipes is D, E, F#, G, A, B, C# and the addition of keys to the chanter on some sets makes them partially or fully chromatic. The instrument has a range

Elizabeth (Liz) Maillet and Malcolm Gillis, Boston 1954. Courtesy of Janine Randall.

of two octaves and is generally tuned to concert pitch (although "flat" sets may also be found); this makes it easy to play along with fiddle (requiring no re-tuning or transposition) and piano. Historically, a small number of uilleann pipers have been noted in Cape Breton (e.g., Malcolm H. Gillis, b. 1856); John Burke (b. 1821), born in Ireland but who lived in Lingan for a period before moving on to the mainland, is listed in an early Census as being an "Irish Piper" by occupation. Uilleann pipes feature occasionally among contemporary players in band formats; Ryan MacNeil is the foremost player in Cape Breton and played uilleann pipes with the Barra MacNeils since the 1990s.

a chronology of piping in Cape Breton. Several place names across Cape Breton, such as Piper's Cove in Cape Breton County, Piper's Glen in Inverness County, Piper's Clearing and Piper's Brook in Victoria County, attest to the presence and recognition of piping on the Island during its settlement. As part of the substantial emigration of Scottish Highlanders to North America,

and specifically to Nova Scotia and Cape Breton between 1773 and 1850, a significant number of pipers relocated, to the extent that in the early 1800s, the east coast of Canada was believed to have been unsurpassed in the quality of its pipers, having probably the largest concentrations outside Scotland. Very little exists in the way of written records concerning these early-generation immigrant pipers, the majority of them being musically illiterate and with no active collecting or publishing interest, similar to those in contemporary Scotland. While data from the 1838 census identifies only 3 people who were professionally occupied as pipers, recent research by piping historian Barry Shears has uncovered further details surrounding 78 immigrant pipers from across the Highland and Islands, more than half of whom settled in Cape Breton in communities such as Washabuck, East Lake Ainslie, Ben Eoin, Inverness and French Road, and among whom were descendants of the great piping dynasties. Until almost the mid-20th century the piper in Cape Breton was effectively a community musician charged with supplying music for dances, weddings and funerals, and occasionally offering tuition; few, however, made their living exclusively as pipers but had to engage in other activities such as farming and lumbering in order to supplement their income. Documented evidence suggests that the pipes were more common in some areas than the fiddle, and even where both were present the older generations often preferred dancing to the pipes, with the piper sometimes performing in a seated position for long periods of time. Hereditary or intergenerational family-piping traditions evolved. Among the most notable of these were the MacIntyres of Perthshire who settled in Port Hood, the MacDougalls of Christmas Island and later Bay St. Lawrence, the MacKinnons of East Lake Ainslie, the MacDonnells of Kiltarlity who settled in Deepdale; the MacIntyres of French Road, the Jamiesons from Piper's Glen, later of Whitney Pier and Glace Bay, and the MacKinnons of East Lake Ainslie. While the piping tradition was male dominated, particularly as its association with the military increased, women did play an important role in the transmission process within families and communities and a number of female players were recognized around the island. In 1896 *The Casket*, in Antigonish, mentions "two or three young ladies in the parish [Margaree] who could play very sweetly on both the violin and bagpipes." Several female pipers were known in Cape Breton County, among them Annie Mac-Mullin, from Mira and later Glen Morrison, and "Little" Kate MacCormick (b. ca. 1872), both of whose families had immigrated from South Uist. The practice of dual musicianship, already evident in 18th-century Scotland, whereby a single individual was proficient on two instruments, typically pipes and fiddle, continued in Cape Breton. Pipe-making was also developed among second- and third-generation Scottish immigrants with a viable cottage industry in bagpipe-making peaking around the turn of the 20th century, after which time it became more prestigious to own a set of pipes acquired from Scotland. The isolation afforded by the geographical position of Cape Breton Island, patterns of settlement and limited interaction with the outside world allowed for the maintenance of a cultural environment that was reminiscent of that in the Old Country. As was the case with the fiddle tradition, old practices were maintained in Cape Breton, while back in Scotland, significant changes had impact on that same tradition, transforming it dramatically, with the older, solo piping tradition being replaced by the uniformity and regimented approach of the pipe band and the demands of competitions. Isolation, however, was never complete and, even from the time of the earliest settlement, interaction with the outside world existed; however, it wasn't until the early 20th century that external forces related to demographics, economic expansion and world events would reduce and eventually change the role of the community piper. These influences, specifically outward migration, relocation from rural locations to urban industrialized centres, the emerging prominence of an anglo-centric system of education and the role and experience of pipers during the two world wars impacted on the piping world. Some vestiges of the old ways

did, however, survive in Cape Breton until the late 20th century; last-minute documentation of that tradition, most notably the recording of Alex Currie by Barry Shears and others, brought renewed attention to the older style and repertoire that Currie had maintained. This fuelled a movement in Cape Breton that has seen an increasing number of pipers explore an alternative approach to that of the pipe band and competition; typically involving the pipers playing in a seated position, often playing for step dancers and in ensembles with other melody and accompaniment instruments, playing many fiddle tunes and modern pipe tunes, and using modern fingering techniques; this is increasingly referred to as "Cape Breton style" or "Gaelic" piping.

pipe bands. The army has been a major vehicle of change for bagpipe music both in Scotland and Canada, instigating a move from the solo piping tradition of the Highland clans towards an ensemble one, first as company pipers and later as pipe bands where pipes and drums were combined. In terms of performance practice and style this had significant implications; a homogeneous style of playing was, of necessity, promoted with a standardized approach to posture, fingering technique and repertoire being introduced. Not only an employment opportunity, pipers in the army also had time to practice and received often quite extensive training, which included music theory and literacy. Highland regiments were raised in Scotland since 1700s, and during the 18th and 19th centuries many of these units were stationed in mainland Nova Scotia and Cape Breton, including The Fraser Highlanders who embarked for Halifax in 1757 and six companies of the Black Watch, formed in 1786, who were sent to Cape Breton. In Canada, pipers who volunteered for service in the army received instruction in modern piping techniques from British army pipers. They passed on these new skills upon their return and swiftly and effectively the impact of this training across the wider piping community became apparent. By the mid-20th century the old-style community piper in Cape Breton had largely transitioned into the pipeband player. The 84th Regiment, Royal

Highland Emigrants was the first Highland regiment raised in the Americas. The first *Dominion of Canada Militia Act* became law in 1868, a year after the founding of Canada. In the absence of a regular army many of the smaller centres and rural areas were encouraged by government to establish one or more companies of riflemen for defence; in areas of Highland settlement these usually included a piper. The 94th Victoria Battalion Infantry, for example, was headquartered in Baddeck, where the musical requirement was supplied by various citizen bands, in particular the MacIntyre Pipe Band. During the First World War, some 26 of Canada's 260 Battalions were Highland units in that their members were primarily of Highland descent; most of these had pipe bands: the 85th Battalion, the 185th Cape Breton Highlanders and the 246th Battalion. During the Second World War, pipers once again were recruited, some who were also fiddlers, such as Duncan MacIntyre of French Road who served with the North Nova Scotia Highlanders, and "Red" Gordon MacQuarrie who served with the Cape Breton Highlanders. Post-war, the North Nova Scotia Highlanders, and the Cape Breton Highlanders were amalgamated to form the 1st and 2nd Battalions, Nova Scotia Highlanders and now have a combined battalion Pipe Band. In parallel with the emergence of brass bands, the first civilian pipe bands appeared in the late 1800s, largely instigated by non-Gaelic-speaking Scots who had settled in Nova Scotia, attracted by the potential in industrialization. Cape Breton's first civilian pipe band, the MacIntyre Pipe Band, was formed in the late 1890s, consisting of four brothers (Archie, Dan, Joe and Mickey) and several cousins from the French Road, descendants of South Uist emigrants who had arrived in 1826. The MacIntyre Pipe Band was assisted in its early band training by an immigrant Scot, Alexander "Sandy" Bowes, originally from Hamilton, Scotland, who moved to Cape Breton ca. 1898. The band played for events such as picnics, parades and fairs and is believed to have been associated with the 94th Regiment, Victoria Battalion local militia unit; it folded around 1940. Highland

Societies and Highland Games which began to appear in the Maritimes from the mid-1800s, gradually supplemented solo piping contests with pipe-band contests, providing further opportunities for performance for pipe bands.

transition. The major influences on the importation of "modern" Scottish piping were a handful of immigrant pipers who could read music and had pipe band experience at the turn of the last century. These pipers were Alexander "Sandy" Bowes in the Glace Bay/Louisbourg area (who settled there ca. 1896), David Manson, who was based in Halifax and who piped at the first Mabou Picnic in 1897, George Dey in Halifax, Sandy Russell, Inverness Town, PM John "Jock" Jamieson and William "Tug" Wilson, New Glasgow. The most influential of the pre-Second World War pipers were Pipe Major Kenneth MacKenzie Baillie (also a fiddler) and his wife, Catherine (MacLennan); pupils of the Baillies

Piper Danny MacIntyre with Fr. Stanley MacDonald, Parish Priest at St. Mary's Church, Big Pond. Photograph from The MacInnes Collection.

included Roddy Nicholson, a First World War veteran, who taught mostly at the Gaelic College and in Sydney. His students included Peter Morrison and Danny MacIntyre of Sydney, both of whom did a tremendous amount of teaching in the 1950s to 1970s. It was the mid-1950s before there was a concerted effort made to fully develop piping in Cape Breton in the modern Scottish form. The Gaelic College of Arts and Crafts, established at St. Ann's in 1938, emerged by the 1950s as a driving force for the importation of literate Scottish piping and modern Scottishness such as tartan and Highland dancing. Importing piping instructors from Scotland, including Seumas MacNeil, principal of the College of Piping in Glasgow, the emphasis was on a literate piping tradition; the approach was to denigrate existing local music tradition in the interests of "improvement" and thus to reinforce the modern style. The number of active pipe bands increased during this period, supported by performance and competitive opportunities at events such as mods and Highland games. By the 1960s pipers were rarely called on to play for dances, and opportunities to perform continued to decline; few ear-trained pipers remained and exponents of the older style were increasingly marginalized. Ironically, the decline in this old style of piping coincided with a marked increase in numbers learning to play, as tuition through institutions such as the Gaelic College became increasingly accessible, as did performance and competition opportunities. In the 1990s, a renewed interest in old-style piping was kindled. Local piper and academic Barry Shears (originally from Glace Bay, then living in Halifax) began drawing attention to the playing and performance practices of Alex Currie through his own performances, which included playing for step dancing and in an article published in *The Clansman* in 1986. Scottish piper, Hamish Moore, later became an advocate of the older style of playing as represented by Currie, flagging this back in Scotland in much the same way Alistair Fraser was already doing with Cape Breton fiddle music. Cape Breton pipers Paul MacNeil from Barra Glen and Jamie MacInnis from Big Pond, both in-

Nuallan at Celtic Colours 2012. Photo by Corey Katz. Courtesy of Celtic Colours International Festival.

volved in the Halifax Pipe Band, formed the Open Door Gang with Tracey Dares on piano and Dave MacIsaac on guitar, bringing the pipe tradition back into the same performance environment as the fiddle music and again relevant to the dance. Today in Cape Breton, while literate, competition-style piping still dominates, as is promoted by the Gaelic College and through its pipe bands, there is a viable tradition of solo pipers promoting what is referred to as the "Cape Breton style" of piping; indeed the Gaelic College in 2012 formed a piping ensemble, Nuallan, that focuses on this style. As with the fiddle music, the "Gaelic" label has been appropriated increasingly in recent times, so reference to this as the "Gaelic style" of piping are now becoming increasingly common. Many contemporary pipers play various forms of pipe other than, and as well as, the Highland bagpipes. Since the 1990s, bagpipes have featured alongside fiddles in various band formations, such as with Ashley MacIsaac, Natalie MacMaster, Slàinte Mhath and Beòlach, and Cape Breton pipers appear in Scottish-based bands like Dàimh and Seudan. The MacKenzie Brothers, Angus and Kenneth, are among this body of young pipers crossing between Cape Breton and Scotland. Celtic Colours provides regular opportunities for Cape Breton and Scottish pipers to collaborate, including at the annual Piper's Ceilidh. Piping in Cape Breton has also generated considerable academic interest from scholars including John

Gibson, Barry Shears and Scott Williams, and a select number of published books, tune collections and recordings are easily accessible.

the music. In the late Victorian period three categories of bagpipe music were recognized—big (*Ceòl mòr*), middling (*Ceòl meadhonach*) and little (*Ceòl beag*), this later (by 1875 in printed literature dealing with the bagpipe) being redefined into two, Ceòl Mòr and Ceòl Beag. Ceòl Mòr was the music known as *piobaireachd*, the classical music of the Great Highland bagpipe and involves a basic theme or *urlar* followed by a series of increasingly complex variations, concluding with a repeat of the theme itself. Often quite lengthy, the *piobaireachd* tunes – typically laments, marches or gathering/rallying tunes – were taught using a system of vocables known as *canntaireachd*. Several pipers played Ceòl Mòr in 19th-century Cape Breton. Ceòl Beag essentially includes all the rest of the bagpipe repertoire such as airs, marches, strathspeys, reels, hornpipes, jigs, clogs and waltzes; many examples of these tunes were composed in Cape Breton, supplementing the material handed down in both aural and literate forms from Scottish sources. Some Cape Breton pipers were noted for having extensive repertoires although this is challenged by some authorities (Alex Currie claimed to have learned 600 tunes from extended family; Joe Hughie MacIntyre of the French Road is alleged to have had more than 1,200 tunes). Alex Currie is also known to have been an impressive improviser. Also important was the fact that the older pipers learned their tunes in context in terms of source, history, etc. Women were important in passing on the music, often through jigging the tunes. A few early Cape Breton compositions by pipers Archie Beaton, Ranald Gillis and Malcolm Gillis were printed by Scottish music publishers in the early 20th century. As musical literacy became more prevalent, acquiring printed collections from Scotland became an important part of the tradition; some early-20th-century handwritten manuscripts containing previously unpublished tunes has recently been discovered in Nova Scotia. Of course, for the pipe band players, a different set of repertoire

criteria applied; newer pipers learned a handful of band tunes, usually marches and competition-style strathspeys and reels.

pipe-fiddle connections. Among the early generations of immigrants were a number of individuals who were proficient on both bagpipes and fiddles, and this practice of dual musicianship continued until well into the 20th century. In Barry Shears's publication, *Dance to the Piper, The Highland Bagpipe in Nova Scotia* (2008), a list of second- and third-generation pipers in Nova Scotia reveals that almost 20% of those identified, played both pipes and fiddle. In Cape Breton some of the best known examples of piper fiddlers include Malcolm H. Gillis (1856-1929) of South West Margaree, Rory "Shim" MacIsaac (b. 1855) of Ben Eoin, Annie MacKinnon of East Lake Ainslie, Sandy MacLean of Foot Cape, "Red" Gordon MacQuarrie (1897-1965) of Dunakin, Gordon Côté of St. Peter's, Rory (Roderick) MacDougall (1848-1936) from Christmas Island, later Bay St. Lawrence, and Francis MacDonald of Margaree, Sydney and Inverness. Fiddler/piper duos included Angus Campbell Beaton from Mabou Coal Mines who played with "Little" Mary MacDonald. While the transfer of repertoires and style was to be expected in these instances, a number of individual pipers were known to have had a significant influence on the fiddle tradition in Cape Breton. One of these was Pipe Major Kenneth MacKenzie Baillie, who taught a two-week camp with the militia each year, including to pipers who were also fiddlers such as Angus "the Ridge" MacDonald of Lower South River, Kenny Matherson of River Denys, Rory MacDougall of Ingonish, James D. Gillis of Inverness and several MacIntyres from Glace Bay. It is likely that he was the source of several Scottish pipe tunes from published collections that featured in the repertoire of the fiddlers. Perhaps the single most influential piper on the fiddle tradition from the mid-20th century was Sandy Boyd. He amassed a large collection of music books from Scotland and was in close contact with pipers there. Boyd introduced literally dozens of bagpipe tunes to fiddlers such as Angus Chisholm, Cameron Chisholm and Winston Fitzgerald, including marches by John MacColl and William Lawrie, reels by Peter MacLeod, and Donald MacLeod's "Crossing the Minch" – later called "MacNab's Hornpipe" by Winston Fitzgerald. Living an itinerant lifestyle he offered instruction in return for room and board for extended periods. Among those he taught were brothers Ken, Iain and Allan Mackenzie of St. Peter's, Rosemary, Myrna, Marion and Paul MacNeil of Barra Glen, and several pipers in Inverness, including brothers Harold and Jimmy MacDonnell and Rannie Kennedy. He introduced a lot of pipe tunes into the fiddler's repertoire; Cameron Chisholm, for instance, cites him as his greatest influence outside of his immediate family. Particular fiddle players were known for the influence of piping on their fiddle styles and repertoires. Bill Lamey, for instance, consciously emulated the ornaments and drones of the pipes; Theresa MacLellan is particularly associated with pipe marches; Donald Angus Beaton included a substantial number of piping tunes in his repertoire; Theresa (MacLean) Morrison, married a piper, played many pipe tunes and included piping influences in her style; and Mike MacDougall, Winston Fitzgerald and Angus Chisholm all included many pipe tunes in their repertoires. (*With BS*) **[Caplan 1988, 1989; 1998; Dickson 2006; Gibson 1998, 2000, 2002, 2005; MacGillivray 1988; Shears 1991, 2001, 2008; Williams 2000].**

Ballah, Moses Joseph "M. J." or "Mosey." (1892-1957). Radio producer and music director. North Sydney and Louisbourg. Of Lebanese heritage, Ballah was a graduate of St. FX and a classically trained vocalist. A vocal teacher, he was also a producer of variety, comedy and musical stage shows in Cape Breton. He was the musical director of the radio show, *Cottar's Saturday Night,* a prime time, weekly show that was broadcast across Canada during the 1930s and which featured Cape Breton fiddlers Tena Campbell and Jimmie MacLellan. **[Caplan 1988].** *See* **Cottar's Saturday Night.**

Balnain House Museum Project. Inverness, Scotland. The Museum of Highland and Scottish Island Music was located at Balnain House from 1993. It included a "Canada Room" in which was displayed an exhibition of photographs and ephemera documenting the story of the Cape Breton fiddle; it also included four 12-minutes videos documenting the Cape Breton tradition. The exhibit team members included: Senator Allan J. MacEachen, Sheldon MacInnes, Allister MacGillivray, Richard Lorway and Ken Donovan. In 1996 the heritage Georgian building was given over to the National Trust of Scotland, which ran the exhibition until 2000, since when it has been in storage.

bands. This performance format is now widely popular across all the Celtic regions and has been embraced by the Cape Breton fiddle community. While it has not replaced the more traditional fiddle-and-piano combination, particularly in dance contexts, it has, rather, developed around the fiddle-piano core as a viable alternative performance option in presentational contexts, one which younger players explore enthusiastically. Contrary to the general perception from both within and outside of Cape Breton, larger ensemble playing of this nature has, historically, always been part of the Cape Breton fiddle narrative in certain contexts. Indeed, in many ways, the evolution of ensemble playing gives a valuable overview of the history of the Cape Breton fiddle tradition since it reflects trends in out-migration, commercialization, and in transmission and revival, linking the music to the wider issue of identity as well as offering an insight into aesthetic preferences and practices over many decades.

twin fiddles. The practice of two fiddlers teaming up to play together – in unison and/or in octave harmony – dates to the early 20th century, initially done in order to create additional volume in the days before amplification. After the advent of sound systems, the "twin fiddles" practice was continued for aesthetic reasons, with the fiddles often being accompanied by piano and/or guitar. Popular twinnings of fiddlers with established reputations include: Bernie Ley and Joe MacDougall (who played with Joe Murphy and his Radio Swing Band and later as a duo), Dougald MacIntyre and Joe Smith, Joe Kennedy

Twin fiddles: Dougald MacIntyre and Joe Smith, 1904. 78-44-1794. Beaton Institute, CBU.

and John Alex "the big fiddler" MacDonald from Port Hood, Dan J. Campbell and Angus Allan Gillis, Malcolm Beaton and Sandy MacLean, Joe MacLean and Bill Lamey, John Campbell and Joe Cormier, Angus Joseph MacDonald and Donald Angus Beaton, Donald Angus and Kinnon Beaton, brothers Angus and Archie Neil Chisholm, and Donald and Theresa MacLellan who, accompanied by their sister, Marie, on piano recorded as The MacLellan Trio. The practice was revived in the 1990s by Willie Kennedy and Kenneth Joseph MacDonald, and recent popular duos include Glenn Graham and Rodney MacDonald. Twin fiddles form the core of melody instruments in groups such as the Barra MacNeils (Lucy and Kyle MacNeil), the Rankins (John Morris Rankin and Howie MacDonald) and Beòlach (Wendy MacIsaac and Mairi Rankin).

Cape Breton bands in the U.S. and Canada. Strong and reputable fiddle duos are a good basis for development into larger ensembles, and this has been a strong tendency among Cape Breton musicians since at least the 1920s. Such is the case with "Big" Dan Hughie MacEachern and Charlie MacKinnon, both of whom, while resident in Boston, formed the core of the Columbia Scotch Band and the Caledonia Scotch Band; they recorded in New York in 1928, marking the first appearance of Cape Breton musicians on commercial recordings. It is not surprising, perhaps, that instances of Cape Breton fiddlers being involved in a formal band context happened outside of their home ground; emigrant communities have traditionally prized their indigenous music style greatly, and Boston was home to a large, vibrant Cape Breton emigrant population. Also, Boston's substantial Irish emigrant population had a music life that centered round the dance band, a modernist iteration of the Irish *céilí* band. Given the interactions between these cultural groups, particularly around the Dudley Street area where much of the music and dance activity happened, it was inevitable that bands which drew on both Irish and Cape Breton musicians would form. The Inverness Serenaders, also formed in Boston, were popular at weekly dances held in the Dudley Street area during the 1930s and were also regularly heard on radio. This band, although modelled on the Irish dance bands of the day, was focused on Cape Breton repertoire and style. It involved three fiddles (Alick Gillis, Alcide Aucoin and Charlie MacKinnon), piano (Betty Maillet or Malcolm Gillis), accordion (Jim Aucoin), guitar and banjo (Paul Aucoin), and Hughie Young played clappers and step danced. From another Cape Breton emigrant community, this time in Detroit, a fiddle-dominated group, The Five MacDonald Fiddlers, emerged in the 1950s, representing the contemporary Cape Breton sound and practice. This band was significant in that it was not primarily a dance band but rather, a performance group, although the repertoire and style did not progress beyond the typical requirements of the Cape Breton step- and square-dance traditions.

While the U.S. experience of emigrant Cape Breton musicians encouraged them to foreground their own music traditions (albeit influenced in some instances by other emigrant traditions, such as the Irish in Boston), in some parts of Upper Canada, Cape Breton fiddlers tended to assimilate more fully into the host community's music practices, responding to new audiences, music tastes and expectations. Jimmie MacLellan in Sudbury, Ontario, for example, expanded his repertoire and style, developing what was to become a popular performing and recording act (Jimmie MacLellan and the Cosy Cotters), which included elements of his Cape Breton musical heritage fused with Down East music, swing, etc. In Cape Breton, where ensemble activity (beyond twin fiddles) was not common until the late 1950s, the Winston Fitzgerald Orchestra emerged as a hybrid formation; specifically created to cover all the requirements of the new, popular round and square dances, the fiddle-piano-guitar unit provided the tunes needed for the square-dance element of the event while wind, brass, percussion instruments and vocals took care of the music needed for the round dances such as waltzes and foxtrots, popular since the Second World War. Such a formation promoted a juxtaposition of styles and was not an attempt at fusion; and it was emulated by many other musicians in Cape Breton and remained popular until the 1960s, both in live settings and on radio.

multiple fiddles. In the early 1970s, a Cape Breton fiddle group, led by Winnie Chafe, appeared on the CTV *Ceilidh* show and, in 1974, John Allan Cameron's TV show led to the birth of the Cape Breton Symphony Fiddlers. This was the first of the Cape Breton bands to enjoy longevity maintaining a recording and touring career long after the TV show had ended its run; the Symphony continued to exist until the mid-1990s. A five-strong fiddle group which over the years included such highly esteemed players as Buddy MacMaster, Winston Scotty Fitzgerald and Jerry Holland, the Symphony was led by Scottish piano player Bobby Brown; it included an accompaniment section of bass and drums and later vocals. The idea of multiple fiddles performing in unison had gradually become part of the Cape Breton soundscape. In a dramatic expansion of the idea, over 100 fiddlers were assembled at the first Glen-

The Cape Breton Fiddlers' Association. Photo by Victor Maurice Faubert.

dale Fiddle Festival in 1973 to present a strong response to the implication of a CBC TV documentary that the Cape Breton fiddler was "vanishing." As part of the ensuing revival, massed fiddle groups became popular during the 1970s, appearing at every opportunity where showcasing of Cape Breton fiddle music was called for (e.g., to entertain Pope John Paul II, Queen Elizabeth II and at high profile international events such as Expo '86 and the Olympics) and became a standard finale for outdoor Scottish concerts. Fiddle groups presented students from the many music classes instigated at the time as part of the revival; the groups The Next Generation, Highland Classics and The Special Seven, for example, featured many of the student fiddlers of the day, including Natalie MacMaster and Ashley MacIsaac. In the 1980s, Amercian composer Daniel Goode wrote the *Cape Breton Concerto* for a fiddle group that included Kinnon Beaton, John Morris Rankin, Howie MacDonald and Donnie LeBlanc. Massed fiddle performance is maintained as part of the Cape Breton tradition today through the CBFA; this regularly features up to several dozen fiddlers in any given performance.

folk bands. Although Johnny Wilmot's recording of the 1960s which introduced tin-whistle, harmonica, guitar, bass and piano alongside the fiddle, might well be considered as Cape Breton's first foray into the territory of folk group it was the 1970s before the idea crystallized, inspired by Scottish group Na h-Òganaich, and no doubt influenced by Maritimes-based Irish bands such as Ryan's Fancy and Barley Bree, who were making occasional appearances on the Cape Breton scene and by U.S.-based Irish bands such as The Clancy Brothers and Tommy Makem. The Sons of Skye, a Big Pond-based band formed in 1974 and enjoyed a career lasting more than a decade presented a mix of Gaelic, English-language and Acadian songs, and traditional and contemporary tunes arranged to suit their instrumentation of fiddle, guitars, pipes, whistle and vocals. See crossover.

Irish influence. An Irish influence emerged again in the 1980s, seen in one of the most significant Cape Breton bands, the Barra MacNeils. Formed in 1986 by members of the MacNeil family from Sydney Mines, and gradually expanding over the years to include all six siblings, they were modelled on Irish bands such as The Chieftains and The Bothy Band that had been established in the late 1960s and 1970s, respectively. Ensemble playing of this nature had been developed by Seán Ó Riada (1931-1971), a classically and jazz-trained musician, who was interested in the possibilities of ensemble playing of traditional music, but did not favour the *céilí-* or dance-band models which were the only group formats in Irish music at the time (the former in Ireland, the latter in the U.S.). The primary function of such bands was to provide volume and rhythmic drive for dancers, this achieved by all musicians playing the melody line together at all times. Ó Riada was drawn to the possibilities inherent in more sophisticated ensemble arrangements, where, removed from the restrictions of the dance, the music could be interpreted and performed as an art form in its own right and on its own terms. His prototype was his experimental group Ceòltóirí Chualainn (a number of the members of which went on to form The Chieftains). The format involved a variety of melody instruments with harmonic and rhythmic accompaniment presenting a diverse repertoire of tune-types in new and interesting groupings. The music had carefully worked out arrangements, and introduced various layers and textures through changing combinations of instruments and the use of harmony and polyphony. The Barra MacNeils took inspiration for instrumentation, arrangement and presentation from this model as well as from Ceòltóirí Chualann's successors Planxty and the Bothy Band. In this way they introduced many new sounds and practices to Cape Breton music which ultimately became part of its tradition. This distinctive format became acceptable in Cape Breton for a variety of reasons. Most pertinent perhaps was that, ultimately, the MacNeils' sound still resonated as "Cape Breton," connected, no doubt, to the fact that their family roots included a long line of established fiddlers from the Washabuck area; furthermore, they foregrounded the wider Cape Breton culture through incorporating folk-style songs composed by Allister MacGillivray. The post-revival Cape Breton fiddle tradition – re-invigorated and proud of its newly claimed identity—was sufficiently strong to accept and embrace such change. In this way the Barra MacNeils played a significant role in paving the way for the rapid and massive changes that took place in Cape Breton music during the 1990s, making it and its fiddle music in particular the focus of a Celtic music "boom."

the Celtic boom. The period from the mid-1990s up to the 2000s was in many ways the "golden age" of Cape Breton fiddle music, when it peaked in popularity and commercial appeal throughout North America and in Europe. The Rankins, a family band from Mabou, Inverness County, led this stylistic wave performing harmonized songs that ranged from traditional Gaelic to contemporary compositions, Cape Breton-style fiddle-piano instrumental music and step dancing. Fiddlers Ashley MacIsaac and Natalie MacMaster built bands around themselves too, explored various fusion options and gave attention to the role of accompaniment in a reimagining of the presentation of Cape Breton fiddle music; the Newfoundland-Cape Breton band Rawlins Cross prioritized the bagpipes and introduced a Celtic rock element. Each of these ensembles played significant roles in embedding the concept of the band as a viable performance option within the Cape Breton music tradition. While these were the big, touring acts at the time, new bands were emerging on the local scene following this format as the new model; these included the fiddle-based Washabuck Connection and Dàl Riada, which followed the Rankins' lead in featuring Gaelic-language song. Elsewhere, Cape Breton fiddlers continuing to migrate to Halifax, Toronto and "out west," found themselves in demand to join various Celtic-flavoured folk and traditional bands.

Celtic Colours International Festival. The band format became properly validated as a viable and relevant Cape Breton performance option in 1997 following the establishment of Celtic Colours. The participation in this festival of bands from Scotland, Ireland, Shetland, Scandinavia, the U.S. and the provinces of Canada had a profound impact on Cape Breton fiddlers and, for the younger players, the band format came to be regarded as the norm, inevitably enticing them to explore it themselves. "The band" became a winning formula for securing invitations to participate in international festivals and was boosted further as the norm by the inclusion of band categories in the various award systems associated with Cape Breton music. By the turn of the 21st century, Cape Breton had a proliferation of its own bands, each striving to present a unique voice, it's own take on the model. Slàinte Mhath , which had been formed just prior to the first Celtic Colours festival, focused on instrumental material and generated a fresh and contemporary spin on previous Cape Breton bands' sound; Beòlach,

again focusing exclusively on the instrumental, combined twin fiddles and piano with pipes, and showcased the practice of choreographed step-dance routines as the Rankins had done previously; The Cottars combined vocals with a wide range of instruments, which included fiddle and piano, and also followed, to a degree, the Barra MacNeils' approach. Sprag Session and Còig are among the newer bands who represent a more pan-Celtic sound. The same band format has also been adopted in piping-led ensembles from The Open Door Gang and Rawlins Cross in the 1990s to Nuallan, a recent configuration established at the Gaelic College. While all of the Celtic Colours-era bands retain a (multiple) fiddle-piano and step-dance element, changes in the repertoire and arrangements nevertheless tend to lead them away from the quintessential Cape Breton dance-hall-linked sound toward something that is more generically Celtic flavored, more international, more hybrid and more homogeneous. From a Cape Breton viewpoint, the trend toward eclecticism in terms of repertoire and the emphasis on newly composed material – inspired not by the local soundscape but by the global – may appear daring and innovative. The impetus is on generating a unique sound, and, certainly at a local level, the bands have achieved this. From an international perspective these bands sit easily alongside their peers from Ireland, Scotland, the U.S. and Europe; they have the festival formula perfected and can easily secure invitations to the major events. However, the distinctive Cape Breton component is no longer immediately apparent in their playing, and in many instances it is the piano style alone which carries it, for neither the fiddling nor the tunes especially distinguish these bands as being from Cape Breton. It could be said that in their quest to be distinctive in Cape Breton, they have become the opposite on the international stage.

collaborations. The most recent trend unifying the Celtic music world involves collaboration, which by its nature necessitates the establishment of common ground. For over a decade, Cape Breton artists have been presented with a multitude of collaborative opportunities (by joining bands with international membership, engaging in bespoke collaborative projects at festivals and recording with musicians from other countries) which have generated the parity of esteem they now share with players from other related traditions. This also promotes homogenization in repertoire, style and approach, and contributes to a sense of pan-Celticism. [**Doherty 1996; Graham 2006; Hennessy 2008; Herdman 2008; Lavengood 2008; MacInnes 1997**].

banjo. A plucked, fretted lute where a thin skin diaphragm is stretched over a circular metal frame amplifying the sound of the strings. The instrument is believed to have evolved from various African and African-American prototypes. Four- and 5-stringed versions of the banjo are popular, each associated with specific music genres; the 5-stringed banjo, plucked and strummed with the fingers, is associated with Appalachian, old-time and bluegrass music, while the four-stringed versions (both the "plectrum" banjo, which is an identical 22-fret banjo, just like the 5-string instrument but without the fifth string and played with a plectrum, and the tenor banjo which has fewer frets [17 or 19], a shorter neck, is tuned in fifths and is played with a plectrum) is associated with vaudeville, Dixieland jazz, ragtime and swing, as well as Irish folk and traditional music. The first Irish banjo player to record commercially was James Wheeler, in the U.S. in 1916, for the Columbia label; as part of The Flanagan Brothers duo, Mick Flanagan recorded during the 1920s and 1930s as did others in the various dance bands popular in the U.S. at the time. Neil Nolan, a Boston-based banjo player originally from Prince Edward Island, recorded with Dan Sullivan's Shamrock Band; the collaboration with Sullivan led to him also being included in the line-up for the Caledonia and Columbia Scotch Bands, alongside Cape Breton fiddlers; these were recorded for 78s in 1928. In the 1930s The Inverness Serenaders also included a banjo player (Paul Aucoin). While the instrument was not widely used in Cape Breton, a few notable players were Packie Haley and Nellie Coakley, who were involved in the Northside Irish tradition of the 1920s and 1930s; Ed MacGillivray played banjo with Tena Campbell; and the Iona area had some banjo players, such as the "Lighthouse" MacLeans. The banjo was well known in Cape Breton's old-time tradition, especially in the 1960s, but was not really introduced to the Cape Breton fiddle scene until the 1970s when Paul Cranford, a 6-string banjo player, arrived from Toronto. He has since replaced the banjo with fiddle. A few fiddlers have dabbled with the instrument but it has had no major presence within the tradition.

Barn, The. *See* **Normaway Inn.**

barn dance. A type of social dance and accompanying tune, possibly derived from the schottische. It originated in America and was popular in Ireland, Scotland and England in the late 19th and early 20th centuries. In 4/4 time, the barndance is played at a relatively slow tempo and is characterized by a dotted rhythm and a specific pattern of three-quarter notes at the end of parts; in some respects it is a cross between a hornpipe and a march. There is no evidence to suggest that the barndance was ever a specific dance in Cape Breton, and barn dances only appear in the repertoire of Cape Breton fiddlers in rare instances. "Henry Ford's [Old] Barndance" has been recorded by Howie MacDonald on the CD *Live! West Mabou Hall* and on Dave MacIsaac's CD *From the Archives*, in both cases as a solo tune and not as part of a longer medley. Two barn dances, "McNamara's Band Barndance" and "Micheál Carr's Barndance" are to be found in *Jerry Holland's Second Collection* tune book, both of them from Irish sources. Cape Breton fiddlers Bernie Ley and Joe MacDougall feature on an LP titled *Barndance Music with Joe Murphy and his Band* (Rodeo), but the term barn dance here does not indicate the tune-type, for there are no tunes of this type on the recording; here the reference is most likely to a popular show format (heard on radio from the 1920s and seen on TV from the 1950s) in which a dance in a barn venue had a host, dancers and fiddlers who most typically played American old-time music.

Barra MacNeils, The. A Sydney Mines group named after their family's ancestral home on the isle of Barra in Scotland's Outer Hebrides. Formed in 1986, the band originally consisted of brothers Sheumas (1961-), Kyle (1963-), Stewart (1964-), later joined by their sister Lucy (1968-). In 2005, younger siblings Ryan and Boyd, previously members of another band, Slàinte Mhath, joined The Barra MacNeils (although Ryan left in 2013); bass player Jami Gatti has been a long-time member. Growing up in a rich Cape Breton culture (the MacNeil's mother, Jean, is a noted piano player, step dancer and teacher, one of the MacKenzies of Washabuck, a well-known family of musicians that includes fiddlers Carl and Hector), the MacNeils were also exposed to Irish music, which was popular in the Northside area around Sydney Mines, particularly that played by Robert Stubbert and Tommy Basker; they further explored Irish music on recordings by The Chieftains, Planxty and the Bothy Band. At a time when fiddles and pianos were the primary instruments in Cape Breton, the MacNeils experimented with tin whistle, accordion, flute, harp, bodhrán and uilleann pipes. Each of the MacNeils is also trained in classical music, the four older siblings being alumni of Mount Allison University, New Brunswick.

recordings. In 1986, the Barra MacNeils released their first eponymous album on their own independent label, Barra Music; two other independent releases followed: *Rock in the Stream* in 1989 and *Timeframe* in 1990. Polygram signed the group in 1993 and they released the pop-oriented *Closer to Paradise*, marked by a slight shift in musical direction and which brought them new audiences across Canada; this was followed by *The Traditional Album* in 1994 and the pop-oriented *The Question* in 1995. Back as an independent act, they released *Until Now* in 1997; 2 studio albums followed: *Racket in the Attic* (2001) and *All At Once* (2005), then the live *In Concert* (2009) and *In Session* (2009). Some recording was done in collaboration with other artists, such as *The Barra MacNeils with Symphony Nova Scotia* (2012) and *The Celtic Colours Sessions* (2012), with artists from Canada, Scotland and Ireland such as Ron

The Barra MacNeils.

Hynes, Matt Minglewood, Cathy Ann MacPhee, Tim Edey and the Black Family. A double CD, *The 20th Anniversary Collection Album*, was released in 2007. Many of the band's recordings have won awards (including ECMAs), gold certification (*Closer to Paradise* in 1993) and achieved chart success (*Closer to Paradise* at No. 10 on the Canadian country album charts; *The Question* peaking at 61 on the Canadian charts). The Barra MacNeils were the first Cape Breton traditional artists to explore the seasonal music market, originally with their St. Stephen's Day shows in Sydney, which gradually expanded into an annual nationwide tour taking up most of November and December. They have released three Christmas albums (1999, 2006, 2014) and a DVD, *A Cape Breton Christmas* (2005); two TV Christmas Specials are seasonal favourites across Canada and in the U.S. where they are played on Country Music Television (CMT) and on the Public Broadcasting Services network (PBS).

music. The Barra MacNeils perform songs and instrumental music, both traditional and contemporary, which reflects their heritage and preferences. The typical Cape Breton fiddle-and-piano combination is at the core of their sound, but they incorporate a range of instruments which demonstrates their versatility and their leaning toward Irish-style ensembles and arrangements. Stewart, Lucy and Kyle are the main vocalists, and the band is renowned for ensemble vocal harmonies. Their vocal repertoire includes both Gaelic and English languages, and covers traditional material, *puirt-a-beul*, and contemporary songs composed by Stewart and by other noted Cape Breton writers, such as Allister MacGillivray. The vocal material and delivery leans toward the folk tradition; this is further emphasized in live shows by the audience participation encouraged in sing-along, clap-along choruses. Step dancing, led by Lucy, is also part of their live performances. The Barra MacNeils have toured Canada, the U.S., the Caribbean and Europe and have any won many awards and accolades. They appeared as an opening act for Céline Dion in 1994 and with the Chieftains on Rita MacNeil's TV special (2000). Their song "The Island" was used in the CBC-TV movie *Island Love Song* (1987), in which the group sang and acted; they also appeared in Disney's *The Little Kidnappers* (1990) and their music is featured on the soundtrack for the movie *Men with Brooms* (2002). In 2015 the Barra MacNeils were recipients of honorary doctorates from CBU.

Basker, Tommy. (1923-1999). Harmonica, step dance, piano. Coxheath, Sydney. Thomas Joseph Basker was the son of Alexander (Alex) and Veronica (Gouthro) Basker. His father, from Mull River, Inverness County, was a harmonica player and step dancer who spoke some Gaelic; his mother, from Frenchvale, was of Acadian descent. Born in North Sydney, Tommy went to work in the coal mines at New Waterford in 1939 where he boarded with musicians Margaret and Doug MacPhee and befriended Mary Jessie Mac-Donald and her family. In the late 1960s, Basker moved to Hamilton, Ontario, before returning to Cape Breton in the early 1970s. He was well known for his interest in Irish traditional music as it was practised in Cape Breton's Northside by fiddlers such as a Joe Confiant, Johnny Wilmot and Robert Stubbert. Through recordings he was exposed to the music of Irish players such as James Morrison, O'Leary's Irish Minstrels, Dan Sullivan, the Hannifin Brothers, the Flanagan Brothers, Paddy Killoran and Michael Coleman. He visited Ireland a number of times during the 1990s, where he attended Scoil Samhraidh Willie Clancy in Milltown Malbay and recorded for

RTÉ and the Irish Traditional Music Archive. He recorded with Johnny Wilmot for a 78 rpm disc in 1952 (later re-issued as a CD) and an LP in the 1960s and, in 1994, he released *The Tin Sandwich,* a solo album of Scottish, Irish and Cape Breton tunes. While the harmonica, or mouth organ, was not in widespread use in Cape Breton it had, nonetheless, a steady, albeit limited presence within which Basker was highly regarded. He had a solid sense of timing that was influenced by his own Cape Breton step dancing, of which he was a particularly neat exponent. His playing had virtually no ornamentation, yet he rarely played single notes, rather making regular use of chords, and used throat rather than more contemporary tonguing-articulation techniques, emulating the drones and double stops of the older Cape Breton fiddlers. He began playing the piano late in life and carried a unique style that had elements of both Cape Breton and Irish styles, the latter influenced by the Irish-American player, Dan Sullivan on early 78s. A supporter of younger musicians, a mentor to many, and a great ambassador among visiting musicians, he was a regular participant in sessions with musicians such as Paul Cranford, Paul MacDonald, Jerry Holland, Otis Tomas and members of the MacNeil family of Sydney Mines, who collectively were responsible for introducing the concept of the session to Cape Breton. [**Mac-Gillivray 1988**].

Beaton Family of Mabou. One of the most highly regarded Cape Breton music families, the Beatons of Mabou were among the pioneer settlers of Cape Breton, with Alexander "Alasdair an Taillear" Beaton having arrived in the Mabou Coal Mines area from Lochaber, Scotland, in 1809. Fiddle music was passed down through the generations and the family name became synonymous with the Mabou Coal Mines style, one of the only distinct regional styles still recognized within Cape Breton fiddle music. Donald Angus Beaton was regarded as one of the great dance fiddlers; with his wife, Elizabeth (a MacEachen whose ancestor, Eoghan Dubh MacEachen, emigrated from Scotland in the 1800s and settled in Mabou), on piano and son Kinnon on fiddle they recorded *The Beatons of Mabou* LP in 1978, on Rounder; this has become one of the landmark recordings of Cape Breton fiddle music. In 2002, Smithsonian Folkways released *Cape Breton Fiddle and Piano Music: The Beaton Family of Mabou,* this time featuring three generations of the family, with Elizabeth on piano, her sons Kinnon and Joey, daughter Mary (Graham), daughter-in-law Betty Beaton, and a number of grandchildren, Andrea and Allison Beaton, and Glenn Graham and Rodney MacDonald. In 2014, Joey Beaton compiled and released a CD, *The Beatons of Mabou: Abounding in Tradition,* featuring much previously unreleased material. [**Feintuch 2004**].

— ≈ —

The Beaton Collection: Over 600 Cape Breton Fiddle Tunes. A tune compilation by Kinnon Beaton which includes 550 of his own compositions, 51 by his father, Donald Angus, and 16 by his daughter, Andrea, representing the compositions of three generations of a single family and as such, one of its kind in Cape Breton. It was published in 2000. In addition to the tunes of various types (airs, marches, strathspeys, reels, clogs and jigs), it contains a number of photographs of members of the extended Beaton family in performance.

— ≈ —

Beaton, Donald Angus. (1912-1982). Fiddle, composer. Born to parents Angus Ronald Beaton of McKinnon's Brook and Annie Bell Campbell of Black River, Donald Angus came from a strong music heritage on both sides of the family. His father was a fiddler and piper and was related to many of the "greats" of the Mabou Coal Mines area. His mother was of the well-known music family the Campbells of Glenora Falls. The Beaton family home was well known for music, and house parties or ceilidhs were a regular part of life when Donald Angus was growing up. Although never formally taught, he was encouraged in his music by family members and neighbours: Fr. Rory MacNeil sent a map of the fingerboard to help him

get started, while Allan Gillis taught him to sight-read when home on a visit from Minnesota. His first public performance was at a picnic in Glencoe Mills in 1924, at the age of twelve, encouraged by his father and Peter Campbell who were playing fiddles that day. In 1940 he married Elizabeth MacEachen and moved to Mabou, where they had a family of nine, many of whom went on to become noted musicians in their own right, as did their children in turn. Despite being a highly regarded exponent of the Cape Breton fiddle style, Donald Angus, as was typical of the time, did not make his living in this way, but rather worked at various times as a blacksmith, taxi driver and mail carrier. However, he played at weekly dances in Mabou, Brook Village, Strathlorne and Broad Cove, at concerts and various other formal and informal community events, including weddings, picnics and Pig 'n Whistles. He was in demand among migrant Cape Breton communities across Canada and in the U.S., and so travelled to perform in Windsor, Ontario, in Toronto, and in Brookline and Waltham, Massachusetts. He often teamed up with another fiddler to play, as was the practice before amplification became widely available in the 1960s. These fiddle partners included Sandy Donald Cameron and Angus Joseph MacDonald and, less regularly, Dan J. Campbell, Peter MacPhee, Danny Johnnie Ronald Beaton, Ronald Allan MacDonald and Malcolm Beaton. His piano accompanists over the years included

Beaton family: Kinnon and Andrea (fiddles) and Betty Lou (piano). Photo by Margie MacDonald.

Neil Finn, Danny MacEachen, his sister Janet and his son Joey, although his regular long-time accompanist was his wife, Elizabeth. Donald Angus Beaton is regarded as the outstanding 20th-century exponent of the Mabou Coal Mines style of playing, considered the epitome of the old Scottish sound as it was maintained in Cape Breton, characterized by a densely populated melody line with many discrete left-hand embellishments and bowing patterns such as flying spicatto. His music can be heard on a number of recordings, among them *A Musical Legacy* (1985), *Live at the House* (2008) and *The Beatons of Mabou* (1978). A composer, some of his tunes (including "Sandy MacIntyre's March," "The Mabou Jig," "Willie Fraser's Strathspey," "Over the Cabot Trail," "Joys of Mabou Mines" and "Memories of the late Rev. Donald Michael Rankin") are published in two collections, *Donald Angus Beaton's Cape Breton Scottish Violin Music* (1987) and *The Beaton Collection* (2000). The CMIC in Judique is continuing to document Beaton's contribution to Cape Breton music; to this end a DVD was released in 2009 (*Donald Angus Beaton, his Life and Music*), part of the the Donald Angus Beaton project, accessible online. Donald Angus Beaton was awarded the ECMA's "Stompin' Tom Award" in 2008. [**MacGillivray 1981**].

— ∽ —

Donald Angus Beaton's Cape Breton Scottish Violin Music. Compiled and edited by Donald Angus's son, Kinnon, this 26-page tune book was published in 1987, a few years after the tune-smith's death. Presented as "a remembrance of Donald Angus' music … a part of him that will live forever," it has 51 of his compositions: 11 strathspeys, 14 reels, 21 jigs, 4 marches, 1 clog and 1 lament, arranged by tune-type and by key. The pieces are named after people, places and events, with tune types indicated. The foreword, by Fr. John Angus Rankin, observes that Donald Angus's tunes "possess a soul that is characteristic of his Scottish ancestry and the influence and spirit he received from the land and environs of his birth, Mabou and Mabou Coal Mines."

It is dedicated to Elizabeth – Donald Angus' wife and lifelong accompanist – and carries notes, acknowledgements and a photograph of the composer.

— ∽ —

Beaton, Elizabeth. (1918-2011). Piano. Born Elizabeth MacEachen to parents Alexander "Sandy Hughie" and Elizabeth "Betty" (MacDonald) MacEachen, she was adopted as a child into the family of her uncle and aunt, Duncan and Mary (MacDonald) MacEachern, following the death of her parents. She first started to chord on the old-fashioned organ in 1918, soon becoming a popular accompanist to fiddlers at dances, weddings and house parties throughout Inverness County. She married Donald Angus Beaton, and with him had nine children, many of whom are highly regarded fiddlers, piano players and composers. A number of her grandchildren also are noted musicians and dancers. Elizabeth is featured on a number of recordings, mostly with members of her extended family.

Beaton, Joey (Joseph). (1948-). Piano, composer, researcher. He began playing the piano at the age of 13, and developed a distinct, robust style of accompaniment, which has led to him partnering with many fiddle players over the years, including his brother, Kinnon Beaton, John Morris Rankin, Buddy MacMaster and Ashley MacIsaac. He is featured on numerous recordings including those by Jerry Holland, Buddy MacMaster, Stephanie Wills, Brenda Stubbert and Karen Beaton. A noted composer of tunes he has published two books, *Mabou Music–Volume I* in 1980 (which contains eight of his own compositions) and *Tunes and Ties* in 1997. A passionate advocate for Cape Breton culture and tradition, he played a key role in the formation of the Cape Breton Fiddlers' Association in the 1970s. In 1993, as part of a research project for the Judique Centre (the precursor to the current CMIC), focusing on issues of change affecting the Cape Breton fiddle tradition at that time, he recorded interviews with key fiddlers and hosted a series of unique events where local communities were invited to gather to listen to and discuss recordings of fiddlers of the past. He developed and first presented the long-time radio program *Highland Fling* in 1975, and with Karen Beaton, has produced a summer series of family ceilidhs in Mabou. [**MacGillivray 1988**]

— ≈ —

Mabou Music by Joseph Beaton, Volume 1. This 1980, 12-page collection has 8 hand-scribed tunes: 3 jigs, 2 reels, and one each of slow strathspey, hornpipe and march all composed by "Scottish pianist and composer" Joseph (Joey) Beaton of Mabou, Cape Breton. There are 9 photographs (of the composer, of Mabou and of people for whom the tunes are named). Additional cultural information is provided by Rev. Hugh A. MacDonald in a 1977 poem about the Mabou Coal Mines area and it's music tradition, and a biography of Beaton. Acknowledgements and short commentary describe the tunes, among which is a comment by renowned Scottish violinists Hector MacAndrew on "The Gerhard Heinzman Piano" reel: "Here we have a tune of outstanding merit ... there is a spark of genius in the last two bars...."

— ≈ —

Tunes and Ties by Joey Beaton: Music from Mabou, Cape Breton. This 1997 collection has 14 compositions by piano player Joseph Beaton, dedicated to his mother, pianist Elizabeth Beaton. A biography of the composer has been written by Rev. Hugh A. MacDonald, and each tune is given a full page, including notes on dedication and on the composition process; some of the writing is by Joey Beaton, the remainder by Rev. MacDonald. The book has 6 jigs, 3 reels, 2 marches and one each of a strathspey, hornpipe and round dance; all of them (with the exception of the round dance "Autumn Leaves") have the tune-type referenced in the title, e.g., "Mary Elizabeth MacMaster's Strathspey," "Ray MacDonald's Reel."

— ≈ —

Beaton, Kinnon. (1956-). Fiddle, composer. Judique. A noted composer, and one of the most highly regarded dance-players on the island, he was inspired to take up the fiddle upon hearing his parents and his brother, Joey, perform on CJFX radio just before his twelveth birthday. He bought a tin fiddle at George Hunt's grocery store in 1968 and mastered his first tune, playing left-handed. Within the year he made his first public performance, at the Glendale concert. Dan R. MacDonald, a neighbour, taught him to read music, and he also played occasionally with John Morris Rankin, the only other young fiddler in the area at the time. Kinnon began playing at weddings to "spell off," or relieve, the main fiddler (often his father) and eventually took over some of Donald Angus's dances, accompanied on piano by either his mother or his brother, Joey. Influenced by his father, Kinnon plays close to what is referred to as the Mabou Coal Mines style, rich in embellishments and cuts and characterized by specific bowing patterns and techniques. He was often invited to play at dances in Cape Breton diaspora communities in Sudbury, Boston, Detroit and Windsor. In 1978 he married Betty-Lou MacMaster, sister of Buddy and a noted piano player, who has been his regular accompanist ever since; together they have two daughters, Andrea, a fiddler, piano player and composer, and Allison, a step dancer. Kinnon has taught workshops at the CMIC and at the Ceilidh Trail School of Music in Cape Breton, Fiddle Tunes in Port Townsend, Washington, and Ceòlas in South Uist, Scotland. A tunesmith, this began in his teenage years with "Jessie's Jig," and his ca. 700 tunes to date mark him as one of the most prolific Cape Breton composers. Some of this work is published in two collections: *Kinnon Beaton–105 Original Fiddle Tunes* (2010) and *100 Original Fiddle Tunes* (2003). Kinnon's commercial recordings include *Cape Breton Fiddle 1* (1982), *Cape Breton Fiddle 2* (1984), *Sprig of Ivy* (1989), *Saturday Night Lively* (2000), *Eoghan Dubh* (2003) and *Tunesmith* (2010); he released *Cape Breton Fiddle Compilation* (2004), with Betty-Lou Beaton, and *Kinnon and Andrea Beaton* (2007) with his daughter. He is featured on the 1978 Rounder LP *The Beatons of Mabou* with his parents and brother, Joey, and on the 2002 Smithsonian Folkways album *The Beaton Family of Mabou*, as well as on *The Heart of Cape Breton: Fiddle Music Recorded Live along the Ceilidh Trail* (2002). Kinnon's business skills led him to run his own menswear store in Port Hawkesbury until his relocation to Judique, and to responsibility as director of music and operations at the CMIC from 2006-2009. There his achievements included working closely with Buddy MacMaster on progressing what was to become The Buddy MacMaster School of Fiddling, which now happens annually. [**MacGillivray 1981**].

— ∾ —

Beaton's Collection of Cape Breton Scottish Violin Music. Volume 1. 100 Compositions by Kinnon Beaton. Strathspeys, Marches, Clogs, Reels, Jigs. A tune-book published in 1984, compiled and edited by Kinnon Beaton, Port Hawkesbury. This 42-page collection has 100 tunes composed by Beaton, plus a tune named in his honour – "Kinnon Beaton's Jig" – composed by Dan R. MacDonald. It has 39 jigs, 35 reels, 16 strathspeys, 10 marches and one Clog, all arranged by tune-type and key; tunes are listed alphabetically in their categories.

— ∾ —

Cape Breton Fiddler Kinnon Beaton's 100 Original Fiddle Tunes. Published in 2003 this collection of 6 marches, 2 airs and clogs, 6 strathspeys, 36 reels and 48 jigs is a companion book to Beaton's *Eoghan Dubh* CD. Its 60 pages include 4 with colour photographs of people for whom Kinnon has composed tunes; front and back cover photographs are provided by Gary Sampson and Burt Feintuch (Smithsonian Folkways Recordings). A contents page lists tunes as they are presented in the collection, by type and alphabetically by title, with a short introduction by the composer. Except for two tunes ("The One O'Clock Reel" and "The Fifty-fifty Jig"), made in collaboration with his daughter and wife, respectively, the tunes were all composed by Kinnon between 2001 and 2003.

— ∾ —

105 Fiddle Tunes by Cape Breton Fiddler/ Composer Kinnon Beaton. This 2010 collection has 105 pieces in its 43 pages: 44 jigs, 35 reels, 11 marches, 4 laments/airs, 2 clogs, 4 strathspeys and 5 waltzes. All the tunes – which include popular pieces like the reel "Carona"– are dated, and are grouped by type. Their titles are also given in an alphabetic index, a display which, as Beaton says in his introduction is "a representation of places, relatives, occasions, events, friends, musicians and supporters." While the composer invites readers to interpret the tunes as they see fit, declaring that it is "interesting to hear other musicians' interpretations and expressions of my tunes by adding their own grace notes, flavour, stamp, sound and so on," he adds that it is "even more rewarding" is to "hear the correct notes being used as well ... the composer's notes, the musicians' expression!"

— ∾ —

Beaton, Betty Lou (MacMaster). (1943-). Piano. Born in Judique, she was brought up in an environment of music, and learned to play in the early 1950s on an upright piano purchased by mail order from Eaton's. She began playing the piano at the age of 5, learning mostly by ear with a few classical lessons along the way. At 14, she started playing dances with her brother, Buddy MacMaster, and has been accompanying fiddlers for dances and concerts ever since. She married Kinnon Beaton in 1978, and the two have been music partners for many years. A teacher of her instrument, she has taught at the Ceilidh Trail School of Music, Cape Breton, at Fiddle Tunes in Port Townsend in Washington, and at Ceòlas in South Uist, Scotland. She has accompanied fiddlers on numerous recordings, including Kinnon on all of his albums, and is featured on the Smithsonian Folkways recordings, *Cape Breton Fiddle and Piano Music–The Beaton Family of Mabou* (2004) and *The Heart of Cape Breton: Fiddle Music Recorded Live along the Ceilidh Trail* (2002); she is featured on all of the self-titled albums by her brother Buddy MacMaster and niece Natalie MacMaster, and alongside Mac Morin on his piano album. Her daughters have followed her in music, with Andrea being a fiddler, piano player and composer, and Allison a step dancer.

Beaton, Andrea. (1979-). Fiddle, piano, step dance, composer, teacher. Born and raised in Port Hawkesbury, later based in Judique and, since 2011, in Montréal, she has a rich music pedigree from both sides of her family, from the Beatons on her father, Kinnon's, side, and from the MacMasters, on her mother, Betty-Lou's, side. Although surrounded by music at home, and afforded the opportunity to take lessons from Stephanie Wills in Creignish from a young age, it was only when she was at university in PEI that Andrea began to connect with Cape Breton fiddle music in earnest. Practising intensively, she spent hours on the phone checking with home that she had learned the correct versions of tunes, composing new material and expanding her repertoire. While her style has elements of both the Beatons and the MacMasters, she is also influenced by fiddlers such as John Morris Rankin, Howie MacDonald and various PEI musicians such as the Chiassons; she also has an impressive repertoire of Irish tunes. Andrea is one of a small number of contemporary Cape Breton fiddlers to have made music her full-time career, occasionally supplementing this with seasonal work or arts projects. In 2008, for example, she was the lead interviewer on an extensive collection project for Judique's CMIC and she has also worked as a co-producer and host for Cape Breton Live Internet radio. She has recorded five solo albums to date as well as a duet album with her father, Kinnon (2007). She is featured on various compilation albums, including the Smithsonian Folkways, *Cape Breton Fiddle and Piano Music–The Beaton Family of Mabou* (2004). Andrea has performed with various Cape Breton, American, Scottish and Irish musicians, spending several months living in Scotland, in fact her musical collaborations from that period are captured on her live CD, the *Tap Sessions* (2006). While the roots of her music are solidly within the Cape Breton tradition, she is open to exploring new soundscapes; her recordings feature various accompanists and instrumental combinations; on her 2012 recording, *Little Black Book*, she eschews the standard Cape Breton piano accompaniment in favour of guitar and cello, and she also sings occasionally (e.g., on *Branches*, 2009). She is regarded as one of the stronger dance players of her age-group, but prefers the concert stage. A composer, she is constantly creating new tunes, some 40 of which she has recorded; a printed collection of these—*Tunes from the Albums*—was published in 2008. Andrea Beaton has been honoured by various ECMA nominations (e.g., for *License to Drive 'Er* and *Cuts*), and she won the Instrumental Recording of the Year category for her *Branches* CD in 2010. Now living in Montréal, she is a member of the all-female Panache Quartet with Franco-Americaine fiddler Donna Hébert, Southern-style fiddler Jane Rothfield and Québéqoise fiddler Veronique Plasse; they released a video, *In Concert*, in 2014.

— ≈ —

Andrea Beaton: Tunes from the Albums. A 62-page tune-book published in 2008 and specifically designed to fit into a fiddle case. It has 46 tunes, all of which have been recorded either by Beaton herself, on her albums *License to Drive 'er* (2002, 13 tunes), *Cuts* (2004, 16 tunes), *The Tap Sessions* (2006, 3 tunes) and *Kinnon and Andrea Beaton* (2007, 6 tunes), or recorded by other Cape Bretoners such as Kinnon and Betty Lou Beaton, Glenn Graham, and by Timothy Chiasson of PEI. Included are 16 reels, 14 jigs, 9 strathspeys, 6 marches and one clog. One of the pieces – "Brent Chiasson's" – appears in both strathspey and reel settings; another – "Exit 120 Strathspey" – is notated in both standard and high-bass settings. 44 of the tunes are composed by Beaton and 4 were made in collaboration with other musicians: one each with guitarist Gordie Sampson and PEI fiddler Kevin Chiasson, and two with fiddler, Glenn Graham. Tunes are presented one per page with titles and music notes and indexed album/track data, and are grouped accord-

Joey Beaton presenting a tape collection to the Beaton Institute. L-R Robert (Bob) Morgan, Richard MacKinnon, John Cotton and Joey Beaton. Photograph from The MacInnes Collection.

ing to source album; a second index groups the tunes by key. The melodies are named mostly after family, friends and events, and the production is illustrated by photographs. As a personal collection of copyright material based on the compiler's own recordings, the work represents a fresh, contemporary approach to the publishing of tunes.

— ∼ —

Beaton Institute. A regional archive mandated to preserve the social, economic, political and cultural history of Cape Breton Island. Located at CBU in Sydney, the Beaton Institute also houses the University's operational records. The facilities include a reading room, vault, specialized collections rooms, offices and work room. The archive was established in 1957 by Sister Margaret Beaton (Mother St. Margaret of Scotland), librarian at Xavier Junior College. Sister Beaton identified the need to collect and preserve historically significant documents, community oral histories and musical recordings for future scholars. By 1966 it was apparent that the concept of collecting should be formalized, and so the Cape Breton Collection (at that time named Cape Bretoniana and the College of Cape Breton Archives) developed into a full-time operation, moving to various locations in Sydney (MacDonald Arts Building, Sydney, and later to the MacLeod Building at George and Pitt Street). In 1975, in response to the growth of the collection and increase in the frequency of donations, Cape Bretoniana expanded to include two main divisions: the archives and institute library, and ethnic studies, folklore and social and cultural history of Cape Breton Island. That same year the archive was renamed in Sr. Margaret Beaton's honour after her tragic death in a car accident. In 1979, the Institute, along with the rest of the Sydney campus, moved to Grand Lake Road, where it was located in the Information and Communications Centre; in 1998 it was relocated to its current premises in the Student, Culture and Heritage Centre. The Beaton Institute collection includes some 3,200 manuscript collections, 250,000 images, and 3,000 sound recordings, 2,500 video cassettes and film reels, 1,500 reference books, 3,000 maps and plans. A substantial portion of the holdings reflects the musical and cultural heritage of Cape Breton Island; for example, the Celtic Music Collection includes more than 1,000 recordings, both commercial and noncommercial, of Cape Breton fiddlers. In addition, it houses collections of tune books – many of them donated by individual fiddlers – photographs and ephemera also related to the fiddle-music tradition. Recent acquisitions include recordings from local CBC radio programming and the Rodeo Records Collection, which includes the earliest commercial Cape Breton recordings, from the Celtic Music label; it also includes masters from associated labels such as Banff, Melbourne, Caprice, Canadian Calvacade and Citadel, which represents, not only the history of Cape Breton fiddling, but of Canadian fiddling in general.

Beaton Sisters, The. Dawn (1981-) and **Margie** (1984-) Beaton were raised in South West Mabou. Their family tree includes many noted musicians and step dancers, including Mary Janet MacDonald (aunt), Minnie (aunt) and Natalie MacMaster (cousin), Fr. Francis and Janet Cameron (cousins), and Donald *Mór* Cameron (great-grandfather); their paternal grandmother was Maggie Ann Cameron Beaton, a respected step dancer also known for jigging tunes, while their maternal grandfather, John F. MacIsaac, was a house fiddler

The Beaton Sisters, Dawn and Margie. Photograph by David MacVicar.

and always on hand to help them with their music. Although their parents (Loretta and Donald Alex Beaton) were not players themselves, they got both girls involved in music from an early age. Supported by a family structure, and with Margie inheriting her uncle Elias MacIsaac's fiddle, after his death at a young age, the sisters began to take weekly lessons, Dawn from Stan Chapman at An Drochaid Museum in Mabou and Margie from Stephanie Wills in Creignish. They were also regulars at the Gaelic College summer courses, where they studied with Sandy MacIntyre. The local parish priest in Mabou, fiddler Fr. Angus Morris, encouraged them and provided much insight into the Mabou fiddle sound and piping stylings. As teenagers, they appeared on Mary Janet MacDonald's instructional step-dance video *A Family Tradition* (1997), and they went on to become a noted step-dance duo. In 2008, they were recipients of the Frank "Big Sampie" Sampson Award, which helped them record their first album, *A Taste of Gaelic*. The Beaton Sisters won an ECMA for Roots/Traditional Group of the Year in 2010 and have since built a steady international touring profile performing at such

as Festival Interceltique de Lorient (2009), in England, Ireland, Brazil and China as part of the Clipper Round the World Race (2009-2010), and at the North Atlantic Fiddle Convention in Ireland (2012). Collaborations with other artists include a project with Scotland's four-person step-dance troupe Dannsa, performing in primary schools around the Scottish Highlands. The Beaton Sisters Band formalizes the sisters' music partnership, with Dawn and Margie playing fiddle and step dancing; Margie also plays piano and they are joined by Jason Roach from Chéticamp on piano and Kenneth MacKenzie from Mabou on pipes and fiddle. Professionally, the sisters both work closely with the music tradition; both graduates of St. FX, Dawn has been involved with Celtic Colours since 2009 and in 2013 was appointed artistic director; Margie currently works with The Gaelic College as director of marketing/design.

Beaton, Alexander J. (b. 1837). Fiddle. Mabou Coal Mines, Inverness County. One of the earliest known fiddlers in Cape Breton and a grandson of a pioneer settler of Mabou Coal Mines, he came from a music family which included his mother, Mary MacDonald, a dance teacher in MacKinnon's Brook and his brother Angus (1823-1899), a noted fiddle player. Alexander's significant contribution to the Cape Breton music tradition is that in his later years he taught fiddle and dance to Mary "Hughie" MacDonald and members of her family who then continued that style for a further generation. [**MacGillivray 1981**].

Beaton, Ambrose. (1890-1984). Fiddle, bagpipes, piano, composer, collector. Black River, Inverness County, and South Rockwood, Munroe County, MI. One of the early multi-instrumentalists to emerge from Cape Breton (he also played harp and organ), his music was passed down to him through his family by his father, one of the island's first musically literate fiddlers, and his uncle, the piper "Professor" Archie Beaton from Mabou Coal Mines. Known for his settings of certain tunes and for some of his own compositions, he spent much of his life from the 1920s in Michigan, where he was involved in the Cape Breton community, and where he was known both as a player and for his collection of home recordings, which he amassed up to the 1970s. [**MacGillivray 1981**].

Beaton, Andrea. *See* **Beaton family of Mabou.**

Beaton, Betty-Lou. *See* **Beaton family of Mabou.**

Beaton, Dawn. *See* **Beaton sisters.**

Beaton, Donald Angus. *See* **Beaton family of Mabou.**

Beaton, Donald John "the Tailor." (1856-1919). Fiddle. Mabou Coal Mines, Inverness County. One of the earliest Cape Breton Scottish fiddlers known to have received formal music training – in his case from a professor from Edinburgh – and thus musically literate, he held one of the first collections of fiddle books on the island. Living a semi-itinerant lifestyle, he was a significant figure in disseminating tunes and techniques, and he influenced many fiddlers of his time. [**MacGillivray 1981**].

Beaton, Elizabeth. *See* **Beaton family of Mabou.**

Beaton, Harvey. (1962-). Step dance, piano, teacher. Port Hastings, Cape Breton, and Dartmouth, NS. Considered to be one of the finest Cape Breton step dancers of his generation, Harvey Beaton grew up in a cultural environment of music and dance in Port Hastings, Cape Breton. His mother, Marie MacDonald, was from Troy and featured at local concerts where she danced solos and in eight-hand reel sets, although Harvey never saw her perform in public. All of his mother's siblings could dance, and her father, Duncan Francis MacDonald, was a fiddler. Harvey's cousins, one of whom is Howie MacDonald, played music, and parties were common in the home; at these, fiddlers such as Donnie "Dougald" MacDonald from Queensville would perform. Harvey mastered his first steps at home, taught by his mother, but began attending lessons with Minnie MacMaster and Geraldine MacIsaac in Creignish at the age of fourteen. His first public performance was in 1976 at a Halloween masquerade in Glendale, with Carl MacKenzie on fiddle; this was followed

by a concert at the Glendale Hall the next year. He became a regular participant in square dances in Glencoe Mills where Buddy MacMaster and Betty Lou Beaton played, and at Cameron and Maybelle Chisholm's Brook Village dances where he was often encouraged to perform a few solo steps. He cites Minnie MacMaster, Margaret Dunn and Willie Fraser as key influences as his style evolved. In 1977, while still a teenager himself, Harvey began to teach step dance in Port Hastings with more than seventy students taking his classes at one point. He has gone on to lead workshops in the United States, Canada and Europe. In 1991 he travelled to Inverness, Scotland, to perform and teach alongside fiddler Sandy MacIntyre, a visit which marks an important moment in the "rediscovery" of Cape Breton traditions in Scotland. Beaton's performances sparked a debate on the dances origins, possible influences, maintenance and its existence or non-existence in Scotland, leading ultimately to a renewed focus on step dance there. This interest was supported by further visits over the following years, specifically to offer tuition. Since 1992, he taught for several years at Sabhal Mór Ostaig on the Isle of Skye with Buddy MacMaster and was a regular teacher and performer at Ceòlas, the Gaelic-music summer school in the Hebrides. Beaton was part of the Cape Breton contingent that travelled to Cork, Ireland, for Éigse na Laoi in 1993 and he also performed on RTÉ-TV's traditional music program, *The Pure Drop*. Harvey Beaton's style has been described as being "neat," "old style," "effortless" and "close to the floor"; certain steps and certain movements have been attributed to him. As a piano accompanist he has played with many Cape Breton fiddlers. [**MacGillivray 1988**].

Beaton, Joey. *See* **Beaton family of Mabou.**

Beaton, Johnny Ranald. (1862-1928). Fiddle. Mabou Coal Mines, Inverness County, Cape Breton. A member of a large musical family Johnny Ranald Beaton was an influential player, known for his correctness and his penchant for playing in keys (such as the flat keys) which were not common in Cape Breton at the time. He was one of the players invited to perform at the first Mabou Picnic, in 1897. [**MacGillivray 1981**].

Beaton, Karen (MacLean). Fiddle, teacher. East Lake Ainslie and Mabou, Inverness County. The daughter of fiddler D. J. MacLean, she has been playing the fiddle since her teenage years, first taking lessons from John MacDougall at the Fire Hall in Scotsville, and later with Winnie Chafe; she also completed a year of classical training with Peter Dunn of Halifax. She competed successfully in various competitions across Nova Scotia and won many awards, including the Angus Chisholm Memorial Trophy in the 1980s. Along with pianist Joey Beaton (of the Mabou Beaton family) she has performed at concerts, ceilidhs and dances, and together they organized and hosted an annual summer ceilidh series in Mabou for several years. She also played weekly at Baddeck's Telegraph House Inn and Dining Room. A music teacher in the Mabou area, Karen has organized informal music-sharing and learning gatherings, such as that for local fiddlers at the hall in Scotsville. She has recorded four CDs since 2000, on which she is accompanied by Joey Beaton on piano: *Route 19*, *How Sweet the Sound*, *Once Upon a Time* and *Helping Hands*. A strong slow air player, she has also composed tunes, a number of which are performed on her albums. In 2001 she released a video, *From Mabou to Medicine Hat*, which documents her teaching and performances in the Alberta region.

Beaton, Kinnon. *See* **Beaton family of Mabou.**

Beaton, Malcolm. (1912-1953). Fiddle. Strath-lorne, Inverness County, Cape Breton. Coming from a musical family and influenced by local fiddle player Sandy MacLean, he was among the early fiddlers to become interested in printed collections such as *Kerr's* and *The Skye Collection*. He was also one of the first players to be featured regularly on radio, playing live in duet with his brother Neil Archie on the CJFX Radio show, *Kismuil Castle*. [**MacGillivray 1981**].

Beaton, Margie. *See* Beaton Sisters.

Beaton, Neil. (1967-). Fiddle. Vancouver, BC, Judique, Cape Breton, and Edmonton, AB. Born in Vancouver, he studied Suzuki-method violin in elementary school there and, later, took instruction in Cape Breton fiddle style from John Mac-Dougall in Mabou when his family moved back to Cape Breton. There he had lots of exposure to the local fiddle music and cites Buddy MacMaster and Stan Chapman as major influences; Fr. Colonel MacLeod (the parish priest in Creignish), Archie A. MacNeil, John Lewis MacDonald and Hughie D. MacDonald were other key influences on his earlier music. He played his first concert in Judique at the age of 11 accompanied on piano by Anna Mae MacEachern. In the early 1990s he played often with Stephanie Wills and was the resident fiddler at the Normaway Inn in Margaree during the summer season of 1993. He was a fiddle instructor at the Ceilidh Trail School of Celtic Music in Inverness, and is featured on its 1999 CD release. Accompanied by Angus Beaton on piano, he was the first "house" fiddler hired to play for the West Mabou Square Dances when they re-started in the 1990s. Other performance highlights include an episode of *Up Home Tonight* (ATV) and a performance with a group of Cape Breton fiddlers for the 1984 papal visit to Halifax. After some 14 years in Judique he moved west to Edmonton, which is still his home. Prior to dropping out of public performance there he played occasionally with Charlie Chiasson, a Chéticamp fiddler based in Calgary, on the local pub scene along with guitarist Bill Doucet from Ingonish, and for a time with the Bat McGra Celtic rock group.

Beck, Sarah. (1974-). Fiddle, piano, composer. Williams Lake, BC, and North Shore, Cape Breton. Fiddle and piano. Born to parents Reg and Joan Beck, she was exposed to a range of fiddle styles, including that of Cape Breton's, while growing up in Western Canada. However, it was not until she moved to the island in 2002 that she became immersed in the local music. She is married to Paul Cranford, and together they are regular participants in the weekly sessions held on the Northside and are members of the group Rocky Shore. She has featured on albums including *Celtic Colours Vol. IX* and *The Fiddletree* (2011) and has composed tunes including "Wildfire" and "Dougie's Favourite Key."

Bennett, Allie. (1956-). Fiddle, guitar, bass, composer. Sydney Mines and North Sydney, Cape Breton, and Dartmouth, NS. A multi-instrumentalist, and involved in the music industry since the 1970s, he administers a private music school, teaching fiddle and guitar in addition to working as a studio and touring musician. Bennett grew up listening to recordings as well as to his father and brother playing guitar and mandolin; family friends and influences included Winston Fitzgerald and John Allan Cameron, who provided him with many opportunities within the music industry, both as a performer and a producer. As a studio musician he has contributed to some 125 album projects, recording with (among many others) John Allan Cameron, Rita MacNeil, The Rankins, The Barra MacNeils, Mary Jane Lamond, Natalie MacMaster, Bruce Guthro, Dave Gunning, Howie MacDonald, Ashley MacIsaac, Raylene Rankin and Stan Rogers. He was musical director for the 1995 ECMAs and was band leader for the 1997 and 1998 editions of the *Cape Breton Summertime Revue,* and the 2000 and 2001 productions of Howie MacDonald's *Howie's Celtic Brew;* in 2003 he was musical director of *The Rise And Follies Of Cape Breton–The Second Coming.* He has toured Canada, the U.S., Britain, Sweden, Australia and Germany, and released his first solo fiddle album, *It's About Time*, in 2004. This has some of his own compositions, including "Laurel's Reel," which has been recorded by Irish artists such as Fiddlesticks and North Cregg. He received the ECMA Musician's Achievement Award in 2005 and, in 2011, another ECMA for his co-production of Dave Gunning's *A Tribute to John Allan Cameron* in the Roots/Traditional Solo Recording of the Year category. His second CD, *Full Circle* (2013), features five of his own compositions, tunes popularized by the legendary Winston Fitzgerald, and three vocal tracks; on

this he collaborates with a host of local musicians including Mario Colosimo, Brian Talbot, Stephen Muise, Kimberley Fraser, Dave MacIsaac, Fred Lavery and Dave Gunning.

Benoit family. Jarvis (1924-2008) was born in Trenton, NS, to Charles and Gladys (DesLaurier) Benoit. He began his performing at the age of five, busking with harmonica in Watertown, Massachusetts. In the 1930s he took up the fiddle, playing traditional Scottish, Irish, French and Maritimes tunes as well as hot jazz and swing. Throughout the 1940s and 1950s he was prominent in Cape Breton music circles in the U.S., where he performed in concerts and at dances; in 1951, after five years of heading his own band, The Acadian Playboys, he played for seven years with orchestra leader Fulbert Boudreau. They toured a sophisticated blend of traditional and "swing time" music around Cape Breton and mainland Nova Scotia, during which time Jarvis guested on radio station CJFX in Antigonish. In 1957, with the relocation of his family to Halifax, he retired from a full-time music profession until 1972. With his son **Louis**, Andrew Russell (banjo and guitar), Kevin Roach (guitar/dobro) and bassist John MacMillan he then recorded an LP, *Jarvis Benoit*, with Solar. As The Jarvis Benoit Quartet the group achieved regional and national popularity, featuring at festivals across the country, on multiple TV and radio shows (including *Up Home Tonight*), and in collaboration with major symphony orchestras. A second LP, *The Jarvis Benoit Quartet,* followed in 1981, and Benoit was later featured on the soundtrack of two films: *Just One Big Mess: The Halifax Explosion, 1917* (1991) and *Buried on Sunday* (1992). An Acadian fiddler, Benoit was known for his blending of styles—French, Cape Breton, Irish, bluegrass, swing, classical—and for having an extensive repertoire. He was regarded as a Cape Breton fiddler off-island, particularly in Halifax. His son, Louis, is an important figure in the contemporary Cape Breton scene in Halifax; he plays mandolin and guitar, along with fiddler-guitarist Dave MacIsaac, on a weekly basis at the Old Triangle Pub in the city.

Beòlach. From the Gaelic word meaning "lively youth," this group was formed following an impromptu music session at the 1998 Celtic Colours. Originally a six-piece band until drummer/percussionist Matthew Foulds left, its members are Wendy MacIsaac (fiddle, piano, step dance), Mairi Rankin (fiddle, step dance), Patrick Gillis (guitar), Ryan J. MacNeil (pipes, whistles) and Mac Morin (piano, accordion, step dance). Beòlach is heavily influenced by contemporary Scottish and Irish music and music practices and is similar to many of the current internationally-touring bands in instrumentation, repertoire and arrangements; however, they foreground a unique Cape Breton identity in their twin-fiddle and piano combinations and step-dance routines as performed by Morin, MacIsaac and Rankin. Despite the absence of vocals, Beòlach is both dynamic and entertaining and, popular in North America and Europe, has performed at major festivals such as Celtic Connections, the Vancouver Folk Festival and at the Tønder Festival, Denmark. The band has two albums, *Beòlach* (2001) and *Variations* (2004), and was twice nominated for an ECMA and for a CFMA for Best Instrumental Artist. Today the band only occasionally comes together, mostly for festival performances.

Bergfeldt, Wendy. Radio producer and host. Mozart, SK, and Sydney River, Cape Breton. Having started working for the University of Saskatchewan's campus radio in Saskatoon, Bergfeldt was later employed at CBC Saskatchewan (Regina) and CBC North (LaRonge) as a writer/broadcaster and summer replacement host, and later hired as a summer replacement studio director for six weeks at CBC Cape Breton in 1989. Although she had no family connections with Cape Breton, she had previously experienced Cape Breton music through the media of radio, records and television; taking up a 6-month post as an announcer-operator, she moved permanently to Cape Breton the following year. While she was primarily associated with news and current affairs departments, she was increasingly drawn to music. When Brian Sutcliffe left CBC Cape Breton in 1988 there was a

gap and it was clear that both audiences and musicians wanted access to the airwaves. The regional shows *Atlantic Airwaves,* produced in Halifax by Glenn Meisner, and Brian Sutcliffe's new show *Weekend Mornings* needed a Cape Breton contributor; under the mentorship of producers Bill Doyle in Sydney and Glenn Meisner in Halifax, Bergfeldt filled that gap, helping to rebuild the capacity at CBC Cape Breton to record music and create programming. She went on to become the host and producer of *Island Echoes* (1993-present) and *Mainstreet Cape Breton* (1996-present). As part of *The Mainstreet Sessions* that run concurrent to Celtic Colours Bergfeldt interviews musicians and produces live performances, which are recorded for airplay later. Bergfeldt has produced commercial recordings, including one for the CBFA on their 25th anniversary and with Féis an Eilein, Còmhla Cruinn: *Gathered Together–A Cape Breton Gaelic Celebration.* She has acted as a field producer for BBC Scotland on several Cape Breton musical and cultural productions and was a current affairs columnist for BBC Scotland from 1997-2004. She was also vice-chair of the ECMA from 1999-2005. Bergfeldt's work with the CBC in Cape Breton informed much of the 2011 senior honors thesis by Elizabeth Cusick Hazeltin (Univeristy of North Carolina School of Journalism and Mass Communication): *The Water's Width: Community Media's Relation to Place, Community and Identity in the Isle of Skye in Scotland and Cape Breton Island in Nova Scotia.* She has also been nominated for both ECMA and MNS awards. In 2015 Bergfeldt completed her Master of Arts degree at Athabasca University, for which she completed a dissertation titled *Tuned in: Radio, Ritual and Resistance–Cape Breton's Traditional Music, 1973-1998.* See **CBC, Island Echoes.**

Big Fiddle, The; also **The Big Ceilidh Fiddle** (Fidheal Mhor a' Ceilidh). The world's largest fiddle, it has been displayed on the docks at the Sydney Marine Terminal since January 2005. It was commissioned for the Joan Harris Cruise Pavillion following consultation on what the public thought would be a fitting symbol to represent

Cape Breton Island and its cultural associations with music, culture, hospitality and the sea. Crafted by artist-welder Cyril Hearn and costing ca. $100,000, the fiddle, complete with strings and bow, is 16.5 metres high by 4.5 metres wide, weighs 10 tonnes and was constructed almost entirely from steel at the site of the former Sydney Steel Plant; its size is such in order to fit with the magnitude of cruise liners docking in Sydney Harbour. Hector MacNeil, of Gaelic studies at CBU, advised on the naming of the sculpture, and fiddler Kinnon Beaton was commissioned to compose a "Sydney Ports Medley" consisting of a march, strathspey and reel, each named in honour of individuals who were involved in developing cruise-ship facilities in Sydney. The fiddle does encourage passengers on visiting vessels to disembark and explore the locality; in the period since its installation there has been a significant increase in tourism. [**Mulley MacDonald 2007**].

Big Pond Concert, The. This annual celebration of music and community, modelled on the Inverness County Broad Cove Concert, began in July, 1964. Originally located on Morrison's field, near St. Mary's church, it moved, after the first year, to MacIntyre's farm, located west of the church. Twenty-one fiddlers from across Cape Breton were featured in the initial Big Pond concert, including Dan Joe MacInnis, whose involvement was of appeal to the visiting fiddlers. By 1967, the organizing committee of community volunteers showcased the event over several days to celebrate Canada's centennial. In 1979, the concert was extended to a two-day program, although it did revert back to a one-day event within a few years. Over the years and in keeping with the times in music, different titles were affixed to describe the concert: Scotch, Scottish, Cape Breton, Folk and Festival; the Annual Big Pond Summer Concert label prevailed through the 1980s. The festival idea was introduced in 1989 to mark the 25th anniversary, and a homecoming feature was added to attract native sons and daughters living away back home to celebrate the summer festivities. The day-long concert at MacIntyre's farm remained a highlight that year, while other attractions were

The Boisdale Trio. Courtesy of Mark Wilson.

added—a pastoral airs concert, family and school reunions, special sporting activities, seniors day, and so on. As the location was so near the industrial area of Sydney and surrounding towns, including New Waterford and Glace Bay, the Big Pond Concert maintained a progressive stance; as early as the 1970s, the program introduced international groups and acts like Scotland's Na h-Òganaich, followed by others like Capercaillie and Ossian. Soloists from Scotland and Ireland, such as Alasdair Fraser, Denis Ryan and Dr. Angus MacDonald, performed at the concert. Dance troops representing the multicultural side of the Sydney area performed – Ukrainian, Lebanese, and Polish dancers were always popular. Regional artists like Newfoundland's Dick Nolan, Harry Hibbs and PEI's Angèle Arsenault were featured. Rita MacNeil was a major attraction in the 1989 program with her first solo concert in the outdoors. At the core of the music on stage, however, have always been Cape Breton fiddlers, step dancers and Gaelic singers. This was the case through to the 50th anniversary celebration, which took place in 2014. Typically the Big Pond event attracted substantial audiences, with up to several thousand attending in some years. Like some other outdoor summer events, however, it had ceased as a major "outdoor" attraction by the early 2000s, although it does continue to the present day on a smaller scale in the community hall. The Concert was managed for much of its history by a voluntary committee, under the leadership of Jackie MacNeil. It has served as a backdrop to several multimedia productions for TV and film; in 1991 it was accorded an award by Tourist Industry Association of Nova Scotia. [**MacInnes 1997**].

blending. *See* **crossover.**

Boes, Joan (MacDonald). *See* **MacDonald siblings of Foot Cape, New Waterford and Detroit.**

Boisdale Trio, The. Fiddlers Joe Peter MacLean and Paul Wukitch joined with piano player Janet Cameron to form the Boisdale Trio in the 1990s. The group is featured on Joe Peter's Rounder release from 2005, *Back of Boisdale*.

bones. A concussion idiophone made from two animal rib bones and articulated in a clicking pattern by one or two hands. These were made popular by travelling minstrel shows from the 1830s onward, and could be easily home-made. The term used in Cape Breton and Canada is "clappers," originating as the clapper in a bell. *See* **clappers.**

Boot Records Ltd. A country-music label formed in 1971 in Toronto by renowned artist Stompin' Tom Connors and his manager, Jury Krytiuk. At first an outlet for Connors's own recordings, Boot soon began to add other Canadian country and bluegrass artists to its catalogue. Cape Breton musicians Dave MacIsaac, Carl MacKenzie and Mike MacDougall appeared on the label on the 1979 LP *Atlantic Folk Festival* and Jerry Holland's iconic *Master Cape Breton Fiddler* was released in 1982. Boot issued albums until the mid-1980s.

Borggreen, Jørn. (1937-). A former professor of physics from Denmark and involved in the Danish-Cape Breton Society between 2003 and 2005, Borggreen first visited Cape Breton in 1997, attracted initially by the landscape and the music. Already a contra-dance caller with an interest in dance history, he became involved in the Cape Breton square-dance tradition and embarked on extensive research through fieldtrips to the island

from 2000 onward. His 2002 publication *Right to the Helm: Cape Breton Square Dances* is currently in its fourth edition. Informed by personal field recordings, interviews and desk research, this booklet gives a general introduction to the square-dance tradition and a comprehensive overview of variants found on the island. Borggreen was a square-dance instructor at the Cape Breton Summer Dance School held at the Gaelic College, St. Ann's, in 2005 as well as at Cape Breton dance workshops held in Denmark (2014). He has presented papers on the subject at conferences and events in Denmark and in Ireland.

Boston. Located some 1,200 km (750 miles) from Cape Breton Island, this city was one of the first popular destinations for out-migration from the island from as early as the 17th and 18th centuries, when Boston and New England conducted trade with the Acadians. Boston's Peter Faneuil was known to have supplied strings, violins and music books to the settlement at the Fortress of Louisbourg; indeed, in the early 1700s there was a tavern named The Cape Breton Tavern in Boston. Members of Cape Breton's Irish population were among the first to emigrate there from Cape Breton in the first quarter of the 19th century. Although Cape Breton had been a destination for Irish immigrants during Cape Breton's colonial time, the establishment of Irish communities in Boston changed this, and the Irish then bypassed Cape Breton or used it simply as a stopover en route to New England. Many Irish, already settled in Cape Breton, relocated, including miners from Sydney Mines (1785-1820); many of these found themselves working as labourers, building up Roxbury and the foundations of Dudley Street. Irish families, settled in Richmond County (such as the Dorans and other Co. Wexford families) also left for Boston; Irish Cove, for example, home to more than a dozen Irish families, saw many leave for that city, among them members of the Cash family. Scottish Cape Bretoners followed suit from the early 19th century, and while some were located in Bedford, Gloucester and other ports connected to the fishing industry, many men and women headed for the city. Between 1840 and 1870 the first stop for many was the notorious Irish ghetto on Ann Street known as "the Black Sea," although many of the women left immediately, seeking domestic work in the big houses of Brookline and Cambridge. By the 1880s, "the Boston States" was the popular destination for young Cape Bretoners; Ann Street had been cleaned up by this time and both the Irish and the Cape Bretoners moved toward Watertown and Waltham, where many worked in a watch factory, and to the suburbs of Brookline, Brighton and Dorchester, taking up employment as carpenters, labourers, factory workers and domestics. Typically, they settled near each other, creating Cape Breton community clusters in the urban area. They socialized in dance halls on the streets of Dudley Square; this area, originally a centre of commerce, was laid out as early as 1632; by the 1950s it had developed a tightly-knit, working class, Irish-American community who lived alongside Canadians and small Jewish and Italian communities. A common practice among Cape Bretoners in Boston was to return to Cape Breton when a child was born, raise him/her there but return to the U.S. before the child was 21 years old in order to retain citizenship; this ensured that migration to and from the city continued in an on-going chain. This was reinforced by working Boston Cape Bretoners travelling home "from away" each summer at vacation time. Direct emigration to Boston declined steeply with the rise of economic opportunity offered by Western Canada, and it is now only occasionally that younger musicians relocate there.

Displaced Cape Bretoners, often connected by family and community ties, were drawn together by their shared Cape Breton identity; music and dance traditions thrived in this environment. It was out of Boston that the first Cape Breton recording artists emerged: "Big" Dan Hughie MacEachern and Charlie MacKinnon with the Columbia Scotch Band and the Caledonia Scotch Band, followed by the Inverness Serenaders with Alick Gillis and Alcide Aucoin. Gordon MacQuarrie's *The Cape Breton Collection* (1940)

Bill Lamey, "Big" Dan Hughie MacEachern and "Little" Jack MacDonald, Boston. Courstesy of Mary Lamey.

was published in this area too, at Medford, Massachusetts. Numerous Cape Bretoners visited over the years to perform at dances and other events. Scottish Gaelic was also a living language, supported by the Gaelic Club; as recently as the 1980s there was still a Gaelic choir in Needham, Massachusetts, associated with a local Presbyterian church. The Cape Breton community played a significant role in the fiddle contests that became popular in Boston from the 1920s. Dance itself was hugely popular for several decades in the area, providing performance opportunities for fiddlers, and Cape Breton fiddlers were prominent on radio during that era; house parties abounded and, significantly, during the 1950s and 1960s in particular, valuable home recordings were made, which contributed much to the dissemination and transmission of the fiddle music. Some private collections of these "home recordings" have been donated to the library at Boston College. It was also in Boston – where exposure to other music styles and traditions was possible – that the distinctive piano stylings associated with Cape Breton were developed.

dance halls. From the 1920s through to the 1960s Cape Breton musicians played in Boston dance halls, such as at the Orange Hall in Brookline. The greatest hub of activity, however, was in the Dudley Square area of Roxbury, home to five popular dance halls: The Inter-colonial, Hibernian, Rose Croix, Dudley Street Opera House and Winslow Hall, which housed both Irish and Cape Breton dances. In one of these, the Rose Croix, dances were run by Cape Bretoner Bill Lamey after he moved there in 1953, his events having a regular couple of hundred participants. On many weekends the major Cape Breton fiddlers played there, such as "Little" Jack MacDonald, Winston Fitzgerald and Angus Chisholm; piano players were often women, among them Anna Mae Rankin MacEachern, Lila MacIsaac, Mary Kennedy, Mary Eleanor "Gacie" Muise and Mary Jessie MacDonald. The popular Grenville café was owned by Joe MacPherson from Big Pond; other Nova Scotians organized dances in the Oak Square Bungalow in Brighton and at Circle Hall in Somerville. Ralph MacGillivray from Antigonish ran dances in all of Dudley Street's great halls, at which some of the finest musicians played. Alick Gillis and The Inverness Serenaders were regulars in the years before Gillis started up his own Dudley Street dances. Most of the players and dancers were from the Maritimes, although the dances also attracted Americans and Irish Americans; many met their future marriage partners at these socials, at which there might be 400-600 young women. The dances were "called," giving the term "Boston sets" which was brought back to Cape Breton. When MacGillivray moved back home in 1934 he brought the dance craze with him, running dances in Antigonish on an outdoors platform billed "The Casino by the Sea." Solo step dancers were feted, among them Mary Jessie Mac Donald, who recalled that on the first night she danced in 1932 people threw dollar bills at her. Alick and Malcolm Gillis, Angus Allan Gillis, Dave MacNeil, Catherine Graham, Alcide Aucoin and Veronica Steele Morgan were among the participants in that "golden age." Some, like Bill Lamey, also broadcast on WVOM radio. The Irish and Cape Breton music communities in Boston overlapped to a considerable degree: the shared dance halls led to dances such as the quadrille being introduced to Cape Breton; dance bands were formed that employed musicians from both traditions; house parties and sessions, many of which were recorded for posterity, often included Cape Breton and Irish players.

recent times. Lasting until into the 1960s, the heyday of Cape Breton music began to decline somewhat in Boston during the 1970s, although some prominent figures – in particular John Campbell and Joe Cormier—ensured that the music maintained a strong profile beyond that. Another "master" fiddler to emerge from the Boston area was Jerry Holland, from Brockton, MA, although he left to settle in Cape Breton around that time. Cape Breton music continued in the dance halls and, from the 1970s, once again became widely available on commercial recordings, many of these released on the American Rounder label. Folk and Celtic music festivals such as that hosted by Boston College presented younger Cape Breton artists in their programming. The Boston Scottish Fiddle Club included Cape Breton music as part of its repertoire and, as a consequence of activities initiated in the 1990s both in Boston and in Cape Breton, a new participatory market for Cape Breton fiddle music, piano and step dance created a demand for teaching workshops in the Boston area, which catered not only to those with Cape Breton connections but to a wider demographic. Today, the primary sites for Cape Breton fiddle music are the Canadian American Club ("the CA") in Watertown and the French American Victory Club ("the French club") in Waltham; there are also occasional house parties, weddings and other private events. While the French club is, historically, widely representative of all the Maritime traditions and is allegedly the site of the oldest continuous quadrille tradition in New England, the CA was something of a stronghold of Boston Cape Breton music and hosted regular dances, featuring Boston-based and visiting Cape Breton musicians; it has recently been re-energized and continues to host regular Cape Breton music gatherings. While the Cape Breton population in Boston is an aging one, some second- and third-generation Cape Bretoners are active performers: Doug Lamey, fiddle player and grandson of Bill Lamey, was raised in Boston, although he now lives in Cape Breton; Cliff MacGann is a guitar player and academic who has carried out much research on the music of fiddler-composer, Dan R. MacDonald; Janine Randall, a piano player, who founded the Ceilidh Trail School of Celtic Music in Inverness County in 1996 is also Boston-based. Cape Breton fiddlers continue to visit Boston for occasional performances; fiddler Kimberley Fraser spent a number of years there while attending Berklee's jazz-music program; a number of scholars of Cape Breton music have emerged from the Boston area (e.g., Dorchak, Dunlay, Feintuch, McGann, Randall, Sommers Smith) and there has been some academic focus on the story of Cape Breton music in the city. (*With* **PMD**) [**Burill 1992; Feintuch 2002; Ferrel 1999; Gedutis 2004; Graham 2006; MacDonald 2000**].

Boucher, Gillian. (1981-). Fiddle, step dance, composer, teacher. Though her roots are firmly in Cape Breton traditions, her music interests are quite eclectic (from Irish, to Scottish, to Eastern European), resulting in a sound, a repertoire and a versatility that is quite distinctive. Growing up in Broad Cove, Inverness County, she was introduced to music and step dancing from the age of six; she was taught step dancing by Mary Janet MacDonald, Maureen Fraser and Rodney MacDonald, and fiddle by Stan Chapman and Cameron Chisholm; she also attended summer courses at The Gaelic College, St. Ann's. She became interested in Irish music after attending Green Linnet's Gala in the Catskills, and was influenced by many Irish American performers, particularly by fiddler Brendan Mulvihill, who was a regular visitor to Cape Breton and who presented her with a fiddle on her sixteenth birthday. Her improvisatory skills were developed through several years collaborating with New Zealand guitarist, Andrew White; their duo was later joined by New Zealand-born, London-based harmonica player, Brendan Power. Boucher's debut fiddle album, *Elemental*, was released in 2008, a recording which earned her a MNS award in 2009 for Roots Traditional Recording of the Year and an ECMA nomination in the same category. In 2012

she brought together The Celtic Umbrella Ensemble, a collaboration of Nova Scotia musicians that has included Cassie and Maggie MacDonald and Mary Beth Carty. In 2013, *Attuned*, a duo album with guitarist Seph Peters, was released, which, while having a more traditional repertoire, reflects her free interpretation of the Cape Breton sound by moving away from the typical fiddle-piano instrumentation; this album garnered both MNS and CFMA nominations. She has taught fiddle internationally, including with two well-established teaching resources in Scotland (Adult Learning Project, in Edinburgh, and The Glasgow Fiddle Workshop); in 2012 she launched an online, distance-education program *Learn Celtic Fiddle* for Irish, Scottish and Cape Breton styles, this reflecting her diversity of stylistic experience.

Boudreau, Marc. (1985-). Fiddle, step dance. He grew up in the Acadian community of Chéticamp. There he learned to step dance before taking up the fiddle in the early 1990s. The first recipient of the Tic Butler Music Award, which acknowledges young emerging artists, he released his debut album, *Steppin' It Up*, in June 2008, featuring Dave MacIsaac on guitar and Joel Chiasson on piano. In 2012 his second CD, *Live at the Doryman Pub* was released, featuring Howie MacDonald and Hilda Chiasson on piano and Chris Babineau on guitar.

Boulton, Laura. (1899-1980). A renowned American ethnomusicologist whose work is honoured by the namesake Laura Boulton Foundation in New York City, which administers research support awarded through Indiana University. In 1941, initially working alongside Helen Creighton, she made field recordings of Cape Breton music and song as part of a commission by the Canadian government and the newly formed National Film Board of Canada to collect the folk music of various cultural groups across Canada. The outcome was to be a series of twelve film documentaries representing these cultures, to be presented to lecture audiences and university groups throughout the U.S. As part of this project, Boulton recorded the only archival-quality music of Cape Breton fiddler, Sandy MacLean, of Foot Cape. In 2002-2003, supported by the Laura Boulton Research Fellowship, Kathleen Lavengood, a graduate student at Indiana University, researched the MacLean recordings and published the outcome as *A Journey Through Time and Tradition: Laura Boulton's Discovery of Cape Breton Fiddler Sandy MacLean* (Resound: A Quarterly of the Archives of Traditional Music, 2003, Vol. 22, No. 3/4). The original Boulton field tapes from the Canadian field expedition are held at The Smithsonian Institution and Library of Congress in Washington DC, with copies at the Canadian Museum of History; much of the material, although simply labelled "Scottish music" on 20, 7-inch reels, is from Cape Breton. Much of Boulton's work (although not the Cape Breton component) is documented in her autobiography, *The Music Hunter: The Autobiography of a Career* from 1969. [**Boulton 1969; Lavengood 2003**]. *See* **MacLean, Sandy; Lavengood, Kathleen Elizabeth.**

bow. As an instrument accessory, the bow originated in the Byzantine Empire and was introduced to Europe in the 11th century, where it gained widespread usage. Evolving in length, shape and curvature, it was in Europe that the bow, as it is known today, was developed by Francois Tourte (1747-1835) and Wilhelm Cramer (1745-1799), mainly to suit the development of the violin as a solo, virtuoso instrument. A concave bow became standard, and the length settled at around 75cm/30 in. 50-200 strands of horse-tail hair about 1-cm wide were attached to a moveable "frog," allowing for the tension on the hair to be controlled by means of an end-piece screw. The bow was now held between the thumb and fingertips, allowing for greater wrist flexibility.

grip. The standard violin bow grip evolved as the bow itself was developed with the earlier practice of grasping the bow with the full hand being replaced, by the late 18th century, with a lighter touch, holding the bow at the frog, and between the thumb and fingertips. In most folk fiddle traditions this standard bow hold is flexible, as fiddlers often settle on a grip that allows them

to find the balance point that will allow them to articulate the sound, volume and/or ornaments essential in determining their personal style. In Cape Breton there has long been an awareness and appreciation of classical music, even where opportunities to participate directly in this type of music were limited; as a result many Cape Breton fiddlers, past and present, grip their bows in what may be considered a standard, classical music fashion. However, many variants are also found; notably, Jerry Holland gripped the bow using only one and sometimes two fingers, along with the thumb; other fiddlers such as Howie MacDonald and Dougie MacDonald imitated this hold.

application. While the approach to bow hold may be fairly standard, the *amount* of bow used and the part of the bow applied to the strings, are the primary factors that influence the overall sound, and there is much personal choice in this matter. For the majority of Cape Breton players today, the full length of the bow is regularly utilized; however, in keeping with 18th-century Scottish fiddle-music practices, many older players tended to use only part of the bow. Viewing the bow as being in three sections – (i) bottom (near the frog) (ii) middle and (iii) middle-to-tip – some among the older players focused on the middle-to-tip sections (e.g., Willie Kennedy, Alex Francis MacKay, Theresa MacLellan and Mary MacDonald) while others (e.g., Sandy MacLean) preferred to use the entire bow length. More recently, players such as Jerry Holland, John Morris Rankin and Buddy MacMaster continued to emphasize the middle-to-tip, but with more use of the upper part of the middle section and, for particular points of accentuation, would use the entire length. Others such as Natalie MacMaster and Ashley MacIsaac make more consistent use of the whole bow.

bow-push accent. A fundamental aspect of the basic accentual pattern within Cape Breton fiddling and one of the elements that contributes significantly to the quintessential Cape Breton sound. The term was coined by David Greenberg and first described in *The DunGreen Collection* (1996). It is achieved by applying extra pressure to the bow at the start of a note (although not in a marked or pointed fashion) and then relaxing this pressure within the same bow-stroke motion in a contact>pressure>relax pattern. The aim is to create dynamic within a single note and, by applying this regularly throughout a tune, a sense of pulse is generated. The "bow-push accent" is applied to the primary accented tones of a measure (beats 1 and 4 of a bar in 6/8 or beats 1 and 5 of a bar in 4/4). These typically happen on a down-bow and are further identified by the foot-tapping pattern employed by the fiddler, marking the points where the main beat occurs. Since many of the tunes played in Cape Breton utilize long notes at these points in a tune, the articulation of the bow-push accent is especially noticeable. Cape Breton fiddlers also "push" the bow in this manner when playing grace-notes. [**Dunlay and Greenberg 1996**]. *See* **accent; bowing style.**

bowing style. The use of the bow within the Cape Breton fiddle tradition is fundamental in shaping aspects of the music "sound" such as articulation, accentuation and phrasing, thus generating the rhythmic "lift" or "drive" of the music. Bowing continues to be a spontaneous rather than a fixed form and varies from one individual to the next; however, descriptors are occasionally found identifying and distinguishing between somewhat generic bowing styles (e.g., light versus heavy or Scottish-influenced versus Irish-influenced). The basic Cape Breton bowing pattern involves regularly alternating down and up bow strokes (down-bow, up-bow); the strong beat of each bar generally coincides with the down-bow. While equal pressure is applied in both down and up directions, this is combined with a specific, bow-generated accent (the "bow-push accent"); the impulse thus created is a major contributor to the distinct Cape Breton sound, one which sets it apart from contemporary Scottish, Irish and other related styles. The prevalence of this single-stroke bowing style and related accentual pattern can be traced back to 18th-century Scotland, where Neil Gow was highly regarded for his powerful bow-hand, and specifically for his powerful execution of the up-bow. That style of bowing was less favourably regarded by later Scottish music commentators (such as James Hunter), who referred to it, specifically in relation to strathspey playing, as "hack-bowing" or "hacking." While the single-stroke approach can be considered the basis of the Cape Breton fiddlers' bowing style, and is applied across all tune-types, there are a number of specific bowing patterns at their disposal, which they may or may not choose to integrate into their playing, thus adding complexity and variety to the basic sound. These include: slur, double up-bow, up-driven bow and flying spicatto, fat-flat stroke and whip-bow. The Cape Breton fiddler also employs specific bowed ornaments such as the "cut" and "crushed bow-stroke," while the bow-push accent affects the overall metrical impulse of the tune. [**Doherty 1996; Dunlay and Greenberg 1996; Graham 2006; Hunter 1979**]. *See* **bow-push accent; crushed bow-stroke; cut; double up-bow; fat-flat stroke; flying spicatto; slur; up-driven bow; whip-bow.**

Boyd, Colin J. "Collie." (1891-1975). Fiddle. Lakevale, Antigonish County, NS. Born to parents Alan R. and Eunice (MacGillivray) Boyd, his family roots were in Arisaig, Scotland; from there his ancestors emigrated to Nova Scotia in the late 18th century. Colin's father played fiddle and Jew's harp, and spoke and sang in Gaelic, the language of the Boyd household; on his mother's side, his uncle Hughie MacGillivray was a fiddle player who encouraged Collie to take up the fiddle at the age of twelve, which he chose over the bagpipes, with which he had previously dabbled. Soon he was playing at local events such as dances, weddings and concerts, performing jigs, reels and also polkas, which were popular on mainland Nova Scotia at the time. In search of work, he moved to Cobalt, Ontario in 1909 and later lived in Boston from 1911 to 1916, and again in the 1920s. In these urban centres he expanded his music experience, attending concerts by leading violinist such as Heifetz, taking classical music lessons to develop his technique, and following a series of tutorials from a New York music school to improve his music literacy. In Boston he met and befriended Dan

"The Ridge" MacDonald of Mabou, a fiddler he held in high regard and who was the source of the tune "The Little Burnt Potato," which later became Boyd's trademark. He is perhaps best known as the pioneer of Scottish violin-music recording in Canada having recorded the first known 78s (for Brunswick in 1932). Later, in 1935, he recorded two 78s for Bernie MacIsaac on the Antigonish-based Celtic label, travelling to Montréal with Hugh A. MacDonald, "the Polka King," who also made two recordings during that trip. Over the next few years Boyd continued to record, for Brunswick, Columbia and Celtic, releasing a total of seven discs that featured Bess Siddall MacDonald on piano. He made his only LP at the age of 72, with selections recorded in Halifax. A further LP, with his old 78 tracks, was posthumously released in 1979 by Shanachie as *Colin J. Boyd: Pioneer Scottish Fiddler*. Boyd's music taste and repertoire was typical of mainland Nova Scotia at the time and somewhat different to that of the Cape Breton fiddle community. His speciality became hornpipes, and he also favoured slow airs, although he rarely played these in public. His recordings were influential, and he was admired among his contemporaries, for example by Dan R. MacDonald and the piper, Sandy Boyd. He was inducted into the Nova Scotia Country Music Hall of Fame in 2002 and, along with Hugh A. MacDonald, his contribution to music was recognized at the 2006 Antigonish Highland Games by a plaque from the Provincial Department of Tourism, Culture and Heritage. [**MacGillivray 1981**]. *See* **Brunswick.**

Boyd, Sandy. (1907-1982). Bagpipes. One of the most influential Scottish pipers of the post-Second World War period. Originally from Scotland he moved to Canada in 1942 and spent a number of years as pipe major with the Pictou Highlanders; he later became known as a travelling musician and spent much time in Cape Breton where he taught many pipers and introduced note reading and several published collections to the fiddle-music community. *See* **bagpipe.**

Briand, Elmer. (1922-1991). Fiddle, composer. L'Ardoise, Richmond County and Halifax, NS. Although of Acadian descent, Elmer Briand grew up in a home where he was exposed to Scottish culture with his father, George P. Briand, a piper, and his mother, Nora Bona, a Gaelic speaker. Several neighbouring fiddlers, including "Johnny" Alex Thibeau, Willie Mombourquette, Charlie Sampson and Johnny MacDonald, encouraged Elmer to start playing at the age of 12. In 1936 the family moved to Halifax, where he became acquainted with many Inverness County fiddlers. He learned from Charlie MacKinnon and Roddy "The Plumber" MacDonald, who encouraged him to read music. He studied many fiddlers, focusing particularly on bowing styles, and developed his own sound. Between 1938 and 1942 he was with the Merchant Navy, always travelling with his fiddle and providing entertainment for his colleagues. Torpedoed off Russia, he returned to Halifax where he formed a dance band – Elmer Briand and his Cabot Trail Boys – which was frequently featured on CHNS and CJCH radio and on TV. His versatility as a musician led to invitations to perform with other artists such as Hank Snow, Hank the Yodelling Ranger and Pop Brown and His Merry Makers. Elmer composed music for Don Messer and made three guest appearances on his TV shows as well as featuring in a film. Like many other Cape Breton fiddlers at the time, Briand took part in the contest circuit, and in 1962 was placed in the top ten at the Shelburne Fiddle Contest. A founding member of the Cape Breton Club in Halifax, he was also a popular composer and has contributed a significant body of tunes to the Cape Breton repertoire; some of these – such as "Beautiful Lake Ainslie" and "The Chéticamp Jig" – are regarded as classics. Some 50 of his compositions were published in 1980 as *Fiddle Tunes, A Collection of Elmer Briand's Musical Compositions, Cape Breton Style*, among them slow airs, waltzes, clogs, strathspeys, reels and jigs. His music is recorded on two Celtic Records LPs from the 1960s: *The Cape Breton Fiddle of Elmer Briand* and *Elmer Briand & His Cape Breton Fiddle*. [**MacGillivray 1981**].

Fiddle Tunes, A Collection of Elmer Briand's Musical Compositions, Cape Breton Style. Original and consisting of Slow Airs, Waltzes, Clogs, Strathspeys, Reels, Jigs. This 1980 collection compiled and edited by Elmer Briand has 51 tunes: 20 jigs, 11 waltzes, 9 reels, 4 strathspeys, 3 airs after 3 hornpipe/ clogs and 1 march. 47 of these are composed by Briand himself, including what is probably his best-known piece and which has become a Cape Breton classic, the air "Beautiful Lake Ainslie." One reel – "Don Leo Rankin" – is a joint effort with Dan R. MacDonald, and three others are by Peter Briand ("Peter's Jig"), Wilfred Prosper ("Elmer Briand's Jig") and Francis E. (Bert) MacDonald ("Francis E. (Bert) MacDonald's Jig"). The collection includes an index and a preface; tunes are presented in handwritten form and are not ordered after any particular fashion. The collection was published by George LeFort who grew up in Cape Breton but lived for years in Toronto, where he was a strong supporter of Cape Breton fiddle music.

– ≈ –

Broad Cove Scottish Concert, The Annual. The first outdoor concert ever held in Cape Breton (August 7, 1957) at Broad Cove, Inverness County, in celebration of the centenary of the construction of St. Margaret's Church. Organized by a parish committee under the guidance of Fr. Michael MacAdam, the parish priest, the event featured Gaelic singing, fiddle music and step dancing, and followed an outdoor mass celebrated by bishops, priests and deacons, and a meal; the altar doubled as both stage and platform. Performers were selected by local Gaelic teacher, Katie Florence Kennedy, and included fiddlers Donald Angus Beaton, Cameron Chisholm, Angus Allan Gillis and Theresa MacLellan; Gaelic singers Lauchie Dan N. MacLellan, Donald Ronald Dan MacDonald, Neil Gillis, Alex MacIsaac and Danny MacDougall; and step dancers Willie Fraser, Minnie MacMaster and Fr. Angus Alex MacDonnell;

much of the program was given over to piping. Thousands of people attended the first event and subsequently the Broad Cove Scottish Concert has been held annually, on the last Sunday of July. The longest-running of all the island's concerts and, as the major fund-raiser for its local parish and held on the grounds of the Church, it continues to be community-sponsored. Beginning at 3 p.m., it runs for approximately seven hours and can feature as many as 70 performers. It is usually followed by a square dance at a local hall; a popular house party has also become a regular occurrence, post-concert. Broad Cove has always taken a wide view of Cape Breton culture, with fiddle music, dance, piping, Gaelic song and story included in the programme. In more recent times a further change has been the adoption of a "headline" act; in 2013 this was Nashville-based, Big Pond singer-songwriter Gordie Sampson. The MC is also considered important, for many years being, variously, Archie Neil Chisholm, Archie Dan MacLellan and Jake MacDonald. The concert has also been the site of presentation of significant awards for contribution to Cape Breton culture.

Brook Village. The location of a regular summertime square dance held on Monday nights in the community hall; occasional dances are held at other times of the year, such as at Halloween. The original hall was burned in 1939 and re-opened in 1945. [**Addison 2001**] .

Brown, Bobby (1941-2011). Piano, piano accordion. Scotland and Ontario. A leading proponent of Scottish country dance and traditional Scottish music throughout Britain and North America for more than 50 years through his work with The Scottish Accent and the Cape Breton Symphony Fiddlers, of which he was musical director. Born in Dennyloanhead, Falkirk, Scotland, he grew up in a musical family. His mother, Jean Day, was widely known in Scotland as a concert soprano, who often performed with Harry Lauder and Will Fyffe. His father was a fiddler, and several uncles were pipers and drummers. As a child he played the mouth organ and had lessons on piano; later he made his career playing both piano and piano accordion. In 1957, Bobby Brown immigrated to Canada, first to Winnipeg, then to Windsor, Ontario, where he joined fellow expatriates Stan Hamilton and Bobby Frew in their dance band The Clansman, later The Flying Scotsmen. In 1973, he became involved with the Cape Breton Symphony Fiddlers, which had been formed as part of the CBC-TV program *The John Allan Cameron Show*, assuming the roles of piano player, musical director and manager during that group's twenty-year history. This group toured Ireland, Scotland, Germany and Canada and recorded a number of LPs, several released on Brown's own label, Brownrigg. As a performer and producer Brown has worked with many other Scottish and Canadian artists, including Andy Stewart, Hamish Imlach, Rita MacNeil, Edith Butler, the Rankins and Ashley MacIsaac. For his encyclopedic knowledge of Scottish music and in recognition of his work in this field, he received the Scroll of Honor from the Royal Scottish Country Dance Society in Edinburgh in 2004. He was also honored posthumously by the RSCDS London, Ontario, and the NAAFC in Scotland.

Brownrigg Productions. A music production company formed in 1979 in Toronto by Scottish immigrant, Bobby Brown. It produced albums for The Cape Breton Symphony Fiddlers and a Scottish country-dance band, The Scottish Accent, two ensembles with which he was involved. Brownrigg also leased rights for several popular Scottish albums by such as Jimmy Shand, Jim MacLeod, Ron Gonnella and the Edinburgh Military Tattoo, manufacturing and marketing the LPs in Canada. The Cape Breton Symphony released several albums on the Brownrigg label: *Canada on Tour* (1982), *The Cape Breton Symphony Fiddle, Volume 1* (1977, 1982 on cassette), *The Cape Breton Symphony Fiddle, Volume 2* (ca. 1978, 1982 on casssette) and *The Great Cape Breton Fiddle Co.* (1992 on cassette, 1995 on CD). Compilation albums were: *Pure Cape Breton: A Souvenir Album* (ca. 1982, 1986 on cassette) and *Through the Years with Bobby Brown and the Cape*

Breton Symphony Fiddlers (2008). Various tracks from these Cape Breton Symphony Fiddlers albums were included on other LPs, including anthologies such as *A Salute to Scotland* (ca. 1983, 1986 on cassette) and *Ready ... And!* (Teacher's Association of Canada, re-released on CD in 2010). *See* **Cape Breton Symphony Fiddlers.**

Brunswick Recording. In 1932 in Montréal this record label issued the first known recording of Scottish fiddle music made in Canada. The performer was Colin J. Boyd from Antigonish County who recorded two 78s which were released in the U.S. as part of the label's *Songs from Dixie* series. One of the premier labels in North America and Britain, with a strong international reputation in classical and popular music, Brunswick issued its first Canadian material as the Brunswick-Balke-Collender Company in 1916. It was taken over by Warner Brothers in 1930, then by the new American Record Corporation (ARC), which renamed it the Brunswick Radio Corporation. In 1940, however, following ARC's purchase by Columbia, the Brunswick label was discontinued. Decca acquired and revived it in 1943 with its "80,000" series, following which it was developed as a Rock label from the 1950s until the 1970s, when it disappeared. *See* **recording industry.**

bunch dance. An informal dance held when a crowd would gather at a house or other location, such as a bridge, to dance. Typically, the crowd or "bunch" would move to different locations to engage in this type of activity, which was popular in the early decades of the 20th century, before halls were used to host dances.

bursary. A valuable form of economic support for the aesthetic and professional development of musicianship. Typically for smaller sums of money, to cover specialist tuition, a dozen or so of these are offered annually by various organizations and institutions as a key part of encouragement offered to Cape Breton musicians, and are particularly valuable to younger players. *See* **awards.**

C

Caledonia Scotch Band. A 1920s, Boston ensemble including Cape Breton fiddlers "Big" Dan Hughie MacEachern (Glenora) and Charlie MacKinnon (Lake Ainslie). The band had the same membership as the Columbia Scotch Band, both of them assembled by Boston-based Irish-American piano player Dan Sullivan, for one of Columbia Records' competition-style talent auditions; with Neil Nolan from PEI on banjo and Sullivan on piano, the sound of these musicians, under both of their ensemble titles, was modelled on the Irish dance bands of the day. They recorded three 78s in New York, in April 1928, which were released on Columbia's "F" (foreign music) catalogue. On two of these they were called The Caledonia Scotch Band and play "The Campbell's are Coming," "The Kilties Tartan" and "The Braes of Glencoe" (37029-F), and "Caledonia Farewell," "Miss Drummond of Perth" and "The Mason's Apron" (37022-F). On the other disc they are The Columbia Scotch Band, playing the tunes "Jerome's Farewell" and "Lord MacDonald's Reel" (37017-F). These recordings are significant in that they represent the first known commercial recording of Cape Breton fiddlers. Musically, however, the sound is more Irish than Scottish or Cape Breton, which might be expected under the leadership of Dan Sullivan. *See* **Columbia Records.**

caller. The role assigned to an individual to "call" or "prompt" the social or square dances. On stage alongside the musicians, the caller or prompter effectively managed the dance, ensuring that the correct number of dancers were assigned to each set and were aware of the movements required of them at any given time. Prompters first appeared in Cape Breton around the 1930s and developed their own narrative or relied on books such as *Dick's Quadrille Call-Book and Ball-Room Prompter* (1878, 1923), which they purchased by mail order. The vocabulary used by the caller contains many stock phrases, but such calls may have different meanings depending on location; some calls are considered fillers or patter and their inclusion/non-inclusion is at the discretion of the individual caller. Some used an approach that was virtually a sung line following the fiddle tune; others were known as flamboyant characters who would step dance on stage whilst prompting; some fiddlers themselves would call a set when necessary. Although callers were considered an integral part of the square dance experience they rarely received any recompense for their contribution at dances. Yet their contribution was immense: "a good prompter was 40% of your band; some of them you could dance to without the music!" (Cormier 2001). When square dancing enjoyed renewed popularity in the Scottish communities in Cape Breton from the 1970s as part of the wider fiddle music revival, the role of the prompter was not reinstated; this is something now regarded by some as regrettable since the dances have, in some instances, become somewhat less organized; recent discussion has centred around the need for introducing a floor manager to control the size and make-up of sets. Interestingly, within the Acadian communities the role of the caller was and is maintained, and the variety, order and distinctiveness of the individual square sets in that area has is evident as a result. Jørn Borggreen's publication *Right to the Helm* (2002) documents several square dance variants, most of which he attributes to individual callers in Cape Breton and among its diaspora such as: Bernie MacDonald (Baddeck), Wendell MacPhee (Baddeck), Mike Hughes (Baddeck), Keith Bain (Big Bras d'Or), Norman MacEachern (Wilmington, MA), John R. Fitzgerald (Cape North), Hector MacDougall (Cape North), Donnie Morrisson (Sydney); others are John Alex MacMullin MacNeil (Rear Boisdale), Peter MacKay (Scotsville), Johnny Stamper, Owen Dan Gillis, Danny Hector MacEachern, Joe MacDougall, Dan Joe Cameron (north side Lake Ainslie), Danny Guthro, Danny Fraser, Tupper MacAskill, Mike MacNeil, Mike Fitzgerald, Burton MacIntyre. [**Borggreen 2002**].*See* **dance.**

Cameron brothers: **John Allan** and **John Donald**. Glencoe Station, Inverness County. Sons to Daniel L. Cameron and Katie Anne (Catherine) MacDonald, they were absorbed in music from an early age. Their mother's brother was fiddler-composer Dan R. MacDonald; her father Johnny MacDonald, played fiddle and his brother Angus "The Carpenter" MacDonald was a noted step dancer; she herself played fiddle. On their father's side, the Camerons, originally from Lochaber, Scotland, included musicians, such as his cousin, Danny, a fiddle player from Craigmore, Cape Breton. The Cameron children were all musical: John Allan (guitar, fiddle, song), John Donald (fiddle, song), Marie and Jessie Ann (piano, song), Alex Dan and D. A. (step dance), and Cyril (guitar). In 1945 the family moved to Glencoe Station. They listened to music regularly on the radio, especially on CJFX; they also had a gramophone and listened to records of fiddle music. John Donald's and John Allan's first live music experience was of fiddler "Little" Johnny MacIsaac of River Center. Both began playing in 1951, when their father purchased a $25 fiddle at Hughie John MacIntyre's store in Port Hawkesbury. Their mother, who had not played for some years, taught them their first tune, "The Balkan Hills." A year later, influenced by Finlay and Colin Nicholson who were playing as a guitar and fiddle duo, John Allan switched to guitar, while John Donald continued with the fiddle. Avid musicians, they played with John Willie Campbell and listened to locals such as "Red" Johnny Campbell, a note reader and considered by their father to be a "complete" player. The brothers' first public engagement for a dance at the Dunmore School in 1953 led to a busy schedule of playing together for school dances, concerts, house parties and weddings until John Allan's entry to the seminary in 1957. Though the Cameron brothers' mother Katie Anne was an ear player, their father thought they should read music and arranged for "Red" Johnny Campbell to teach them; he gave them a copy of Cole's *One Thousand Fiddle Tunes* and, later, their uncle, Dan R. MacDonald, shared books he had acquired in Scotland. John Donald became

interested in the written note and the published collections and subsequently amassed a wide and unique repertoire.

Cameron, John Donald. (1937-). Fiddler, composer, teacher, collector, writer. Glencoe Station and Judique, Cape Breton. He played first in a successful duet with his brother, guitarist John Allan, until the latter's entry to the seminary in 1957, then with guitarist Jerry MacNeil, a neighbour who had grown up learning music alongside the Camerons. In 1958 he went to work in the banking sector in Nova Scotia, Newfoundland and Québec, in each location playing with various bands. He returned to Nova Scotia in 1974 (briefly to Cape Breton, then to Dartmouth), the year in which John Allan's TV show began in Montréal, and joined his featured fiddle group, The Cape Breton Symphony, for which he selected the music that piano player, Bobby Brown, then arranged. He continued with The Symphony, playing on their several recordings and sharing in their international reputation. A respected authority on Cape Breton music, particularly regarded for his knowledge of tune names and sources, John Donald was responsible for collating and publishing the compositions of his uncle, Dan R. MacDonald, as *The Heather Hill Collection* (1990) and *The Trip to Windsor Collection* (1994); many tunes from these have come to be regarded as standards. John Donald is also featured on his brother's 1968 LP album, *Here Comes John Allan Cameron* (RCA Victor). His extensive knowledge underpinned his writing of a column on aspects of Cape Breton fiddle music for the Gaelic cultural quarterly *Am Bràighe* (1997-1998); he continues to teach fiddle and organize local concerts, and he runs a music store in Port Hawkesbury. [**MacGillivray 1981**].

Cameron, John Allan. (1938-2006). 12-string guitar, voice. Glencoe Station and Pickering, ON. One of Canada's leading folk singers, he first played fiddle, but in 1952 was given a guitar and began picking out fiddle and pipe melodies rather than chords; thus he was one of the first in Canada to play dance tunes in this manner on guitar. In the 1950s he and his brother were in demand in Inverness County as a guitar/fiddle

John Donald and John Allan Cameron. Courtesy of Paul MacDonald.

duet, playing at school dances, weddings, concerts and house parties; John Allan also accompanied other fiddlers such as John Willie Campbell and Dan Hughie MacEachern. While a student at St. FX he played with a group, The Cavaliers, as well as being involved in the local radio station CJFX. Following a short time teaching in London, ON, and having decided against joining the priesthood, he adopted a music career, he adopted a music career in 1968 after sharing the stage at the Mariposa Folk Festival with Joan Baez, Bob Dylan and Joni Mitchell, and with Johnny Cash, Kris Kristofferson, Pentangle, Van Morrison and James Taylor at the Newport Folk Festival. The first Cape Bretoner to break into that scene, he thus introduced wider audiences to Cape Breton, Scottish and Irish music on guitar and established himself as one of Canada's leading folk singers and entertainers.

media and honours. Beginning as a regular performer on the *Singalong Jubilee* TV show (1961-1974), he went on to host his own national-media series, *The John Allan Cameron Show* on CTV (1975-1976) and on CBC (1979-1981); The Cape Breton Symphony Fiddlers (an ensemble of top Cape Breton fiddlers) grew out of this series, a group with which he recorded and toured occasionally over the course of its twenty years. Between 1968 and 1996, Cameron recorded 10 original albums, the first, *Here Comes John Allan Cameron*, released in 1968 and the last, *Glencoe Station*, in 1996; his debut album was re-released

on CD format, remixed and remastered in 2012. His popularity was due both to his ability to perform fiddle and pipe tunes on guitar and his rendering of traditional songs such as 'The Four Marys" and "There was an Old Woman from Mabou"; he was also a pioneer in recording *puirt-a-beul* from Cape Breton. John Allan was a driving force in bringing the music and song of Cape Breton to national and international attention, for example, by performing with symphony orchestras in Edmonton, AB, and London, ON, and at the Grand Ole Opry, Nashville, in 1970. He was the first Cape Breton artist to pick up on professional opportunities presented by the folk revival of the 1960s and 1970s, opening doors for later generations of his region's musicians; he entered the mainstream without compromising the integrity of his music heritage. A consummate showman, and described variously as "a national treasure" and "the godfather of Celtic music in Canada," John Allan Cameron, often dressed in full kilt and associated paraphernalia, was an influential ambassador for Cape Breton music. He was the chieftain of the Fergus Scottish Festival and Highland Games in Ontario from 1985 to 2006, he was honoured with an ECMA Lifetime Achievement Award in 1995, and with an honorary doctor of letters from CBU, Sydney, in 1998. He acted as honorary chairman of the 1998, Celtic Colours and of the 1999 Fiddles of the World Festival in Halifax, and was invested into the Order of Canada in 2003. Before his death, many tribute concerts were held in recognition of Cameron's contribution to Cape Breton music; fiddler Sandy MacIntyre produced a 40-track compilation CD, featuring artists who performed with or were influenced by Cameron: *Yes! Let's Hear it for John Allan Cameron!* (Scotsmarket 2006). [**Historica Canada 2015; MacDonald 2012; McDonald 2012**]. *See* **Cameron, Stuart.**

Cameron family of Belle Côte. With family connections to such as the renowned Rankin and Beaton families, Lawrence Cameron is a piano player and teacher. A music education graduate from Acadia University, he has taught music both in public and private schools. His daughter, Rose, is a piano player and son, Douglas Cameron (1991-), plays piano and fiddle. Douglas is a regular concert and dance player and has also performed in Scotland, Ireland and France. He released his first, self-titled CD in 2010. Both father and son are actively involved with the CBFA.

Cameron family of Boisdale. Angus Finlay and Sera (Beaton) Cameron moved from South West Mabou to North Sydney and then to Boisdale in the late 1930s, and it was in this community that they raised their family, listening to recordings and experiencing live fiddle music from Inverness County whenever possible. Angus was a Gaelic singer and mouth-organ player and he became involved in organizing fiddle concerts and dances in the local Boisdale hall. Many of the major stylists of the day – including Winston Fitzgerald, Angus Chisholm, Joe MacLean, Dan J. Campbell, Angus Allan Gillis, Bill Lamey and Buddy MacMaster – came to perform, and the Cameron home became a popular ceilidh house; this continued as some of the children began to express an interest in playing, with Francis taking up the fiddle, and Janet the piano. Janet has performed and recorded for more than 20 years as a member of The Boisdale Trio and is a regular accompanist with the CBFA.

    Cameron, Fr. Francis. (1934-). Fiddle. Mabou. Francis began playing fiddle at the age of 12 and, inspired by Winston Fitzgerald, to whom he listened regularly on the radio, he taught himself the standard tunes of the day. He was also exposed often to live playing at parish concerts organized by his father, where Inverness County fiddlers, in particular, were often featured; he also attended regular dances in the local hall. Later, Francis learned to read by taking piano lessons in high school; he also became interested in the tone of the instrument, that of classical violinists and of Scottish players such as Hector MacAndrew. Fiddle music continued to be a constant in his life even as he attended St. FX and later joined the priesthood. His first parish work was in New Waterford, where he heard Mary MacDonald and Duncan MacQuarrie; later he is stationed in Guysborough County on mainland Nova Scotia. In the 1970s, he became the priest at Mabou where the Glebe House became a regular gathering place for local fiddlers such as Willie Kennedy, Sandy Cameron, Kenneth Joseph MacDonald, Flora MacLellan and Gregory Campbell, with Danny MacEachern or Joey Beaton on piano. Later he was stationed back in Boisdale, where he played with local musicians Joe Peter MacLean, Paul Wuckitch and Janet Cameron. Cape Breton fiddle music has been woven into the fabric of Fr. Cameron's entire life and parish work as a priest; for instance, he often played at weddings at which he had just performed the ceremony; this gave him strong views on keeping the fiddle music integrated with the wider community. He was a keen supporter of the CBFA, with which he still performs; he has played an important role in encouraging younger players promoting awareness of historical as well as contemporary sounds and practices. Fr. Cameron is featured on Rounder's North American Series *Traditional Fiddle Music of Cape Breton, Volume 3: Bras d'Or House*, with his sister, Janet, on piano. He is celebrated by one of John Campbell's compositions, the tune "Fr. Francis Cameron." [**MacGillivray 1981; Wilson and MacLean 2008**].

Cameron, Derrick. (1969-). Guitar, singer. Mabou. Growing up in a farming community, Derrick Cameron's awareness of the music tradition around him was reinforced by his father's interest in listening to recordings. He took guitar lessons as a boy, but only began accompanying fiddle tunes when he started dating, and later married, step dancer and fiddler, Melody Warner, at the age of 20. Their home came to be a popular for house sessions among such players as Willie Kennedy, Kenneth Joseph MacDonald, Fr. Angus Morris, Joey Beaton, Karen Beaton, Mac Morin, Bonnie Jean MacDonald and Mairi Rankin. This music-making, in an informal, intergenerational setting, would serve as the inspiration for a music-mentoring program that was developed and coordinated by Derrick and Melody and delivered under the auspices of Commun Féis

Mhàbu (CFM) from 2005 to 2011. Through organized house sessions young performers were brought together with established players; later they were given opportunities to perform at community concerts, dances and events in Mabou, at the Gaelic College, St. Ann's, the CMIC, the Red Shoe, the Baddeck Gathering Ceilidhs and at Celtic Colours, with the young players sharing the stage with their mentors. Derrick served as both vice chair and chair of CFM from 2004 to 2014. A dairy farmer by profession, he performs mostly locally with Melody as a duo, with fiddle, guitar, step dance and song; occasional off-island performances have brought them to the U.S. (Washington Irish Folk Festival, Maine, Massachusetts and Connecticut) and to Scotland (NAFCo, 2010). *See* **Cameron, Melody**.

Cameron, Douglas. *See* **Cameron family of Belle Cote.**

Cameron, John Allan. *See* **Cameron brothers.**

Cameron, John Donald. *See* **Cameron brothers.**

Cameron, Lawrence. *See* **Cameron family of Belle Cote.**

Cameron, Melody (Warner). (1969-). Step dance, fiddle, composer. River Bourgeois and Mabou. She was exposed to music on both sides of the family; her father, Norman Warner Jr., was of Irish and Scottish heritage with a family background of pipers, fiddlers, step dancers and Gaelic speakers. On her mother's side, her grandparents, Roderick and Viola Touesnard, were of Acadian descent; their home, where Melody spent a lot of time, hosted many kitchen parties. Encouraged by her father and grandfather, both step dancers, Melody began dancing at a very early age and as a teenager was performing synchronized step dance routines with her sister, Kelly, as The Warner Sisters. Popular at Cape Breton festivals and events through the 1980s, they performed on the CBC-TV show *Up Home Tonight* and on the Channel 4 Documentary *Down Home* (1985), presented by Shetland fiddler, Aly Bain. In 1998, Melody worked as a choreographer for the Rankins and in 2005 she and her sister performed their synchronized step-dance routine on The Rankin Sisters' *Home*

for Christmas program on Bravo! TV. A fiddler also, Melody took up the instrument at the age of 13, taught by Howie MacDonald at Loch Lomond Hall, and later by Gordon Côté, Stephanie Wills and Kinnon Beaton. Melody and her husband, guitarist and singer, Derrick Cameron, have released three albums, which include some of her own compositions: *Looking Forward, Looking Back* (2002), *When There's Music...* (2004) and *Sincerely* (2010). She and Derrick were featured in a 2006 TV documentary (*And They Danced*, Genuine Pictures) on Canada's Bravo! Network, and were the founders of the group, Triskele, which performed at Canadian and U.S. music festivals. She also continues to perform often as a step dancer, solo or, on occasion, with her sister, Kelly (Warner) MacLennan, and her nieces and nephews. *See* **Cameron, Derrick**.

Cameron, Stuart. (1972-). Guitar, singer. Pickering and Toronto, ON. The son of John Allan and Angela Cameron he grew up with Cape Breton music, exposed to fiddlers such as Dave MacIsaac and Allie Bennett. His first performance, at the age of 4, was at the Gaelic Mod at St Ann's, Cape Breton, where he wore a kilt and sang Gaelic songs taught to him by his great-grandmother, Mary MacInnes. His life as a professional musician has been largely performing, touring and recording in the pop and rock genres with The Heartbroken, Matthew Good, Crash Test Dummies and Amanda Marshall. Yet he spent a number of years in the mid-1990s living in Cape Breton, when he was a member of Ashley MacIsaac's band and is featured on the 1997 recording *Hi, How Are You Today?* He continues to play with Cape Breton fiddler Sandy MacIntyre in Toronto. Also a prominent figure in the Fergus Scottish Festival and Highland Games at Fergus, Ontario, he took over as its "Chieftain of the Games" after his father's death in 2006. *See* **Cameron brothers**.

Campbell family. Glenora Falls, Inverness County. One of the foremost families of Cape Breton fiddlers, the Campbell ancestry can be traced back to one John Campbell, who emigrated from Argyll, Scotland, in 1816, and was himself a fiddle player. Dan J. Campbell, a great-grandson of John, was one of the first Cape Breton fiddlers to record; several other fiddlers are numbered among his ancestors, including his grandmother's uncle, John MacInnis, who settled in Mabou Ridge, and who was reputedly one of the best players to come from Scotland. Among Dan J.'s own children are many noted exponents of Cape Breton fiddle, among them John and Donald. [**Ruckert 2009**].

Campbell, Dan J. (ca. 1895-1981). Fiddle. The son of John A. Campbell (1855-1919) and Annie MacDonald, originally from Mull River, Dan J. is one of the major names in the Cape Breton fiddle tradition. He took up the fiddle at the age of ten in a family home known for music; his father played the fiddle and greatly valued the printed collections as sources of interesting material. The home also had an organ, making it a popular gathering-place for local musicians; regular visitors included Donald Beaton, Ronald MacDougall, John Beaton and Donald Allan MacLellan. Dan J.'s brother, Angus (1892-1922), also played the fiddle; his sister Catherine, a pianist, studied music in Antigonish and helped both brothers develop note-reading skills. Dan J. became highly regarded as an exponent of the old Scottish repertoire and style, often performing with fiddlers Sandy MacLean or Angus Allan Gillis; his recording of "The Old Time Wedding Reels" in duet with Angus Allan Gillis is considered part of the Cape Breton fiddle-music canon. Sydney writer J. J. MacInnis referred to him as "undoubtedly one of Inverness's best violin players. He possesses a very correct ear and is a very pleasing performer of Scottish national melodies and dance music" (MacInnis, 1943-1944). Campbell was one of the first Cape Breton fiddlers to make a commercial recording in Canada when, with Angus Chisholm and Angus Allan Gillis, in 1935 he travelled to Montréal to record two 78s for the Antigonish label, Celtic Music, accompanied by Mrs. Bess Siddall MacDonald on piano. The instrument on which Dan J. recorded these was found at the family home in 1995 by his daughter Mary Louise in a box labelled "The broken violin of Dan J. Campbell—Pioneer Records, 1935." It was a Stradivarius model violin, made in Czechoslovakia, and purchased by Dan

J. from a neighbour who got it in a pawn shop in Western Canada; it had been damaged in 1955. It was restored by John MacDougall of Kenloch and placed on display in Inverness in 1995 to mark the 100th anniversary of Dan J.'s birth and the 60th of his recordings. Dan J.'s wife, Mary Magdalene (MacLellan), was also a musician, and as a pianist often accompanied him; she too had a strong musical pedigree. Her sister Jessie (MacLellan) Munroe from Loch Lomond played piano and her niece was Deanie Munroe Beaton, a noted piper. Brothers John Alex MacLellan played fiddle and saxophone while Roddie, Charlie and Joe played fiddle, and Wilfred played piano. Of Dan J. and Mary Magdalene's 10 children, several became noted exponents of Cape Breton fiddle and/or piano. [**MacGillivray 1981**].

Campbell, John. (1929-2010). Fiddle, composer. Glenora Falls and Watertown, MA. Inspired by a rich home environment of music, John and his brothers Donald and Alex took up the fiddle, while a number of their sisters played piano. They were influenced by the style and values of their father in particular, and other noted players of the day such as Winston Fitzgerald and Buddy MacMaster. John's first public performance, at a wedding in Glenora Falls in 1947, established him as a dance player, and through the early 1950s he performed at Neily's Hall in Harbourview accompanied by his sister Ann on piano and John Allan Cameron on guitar. In 1956 he moved to Hamilton, Ontario, where he worked in the mines for four years. Back in Cape Breton, he married Beatrice MacDonnell of Port Hood in 1962 and the following year they settled in the Boston area. John played regularly for dances in the Orange Hall in Brookline, the French Club in Waltham and the Rose Croix, as well as at the Canadian American Club and at frequent house parties. His popularity there led to invitations from other displaced communities of Cape Bretoners, particularly in Detroit. Self-employed, Campbell ran a furnace-repair business that allowed him to return to Cape Breton each summer to play a busy dance circuit around Inverness County. John Campbell was particularly noted for his timing and drive, qualities important in a dance

Sandy MacIntyre's Trip to Boston

reel

John Campbell, 1929-2010

© Estate of John Campbell.

player, and he was held in high regard also as a fiddle-music teacher. He ran classes in the Boston area, both privately and through the Canadian American Club, for many years, and became a regular instructor at the summer courses held at the Gaelic College in Cape Breton. As a composer within the Cape Breton idiom he made tunes, such as "Sandy MacIntyre's Trip to Boston," which have come to be regarded as classics. Many of his 450 original compositions have been edited by one of his fiddle students, George Ruckert, and published by Mel Bay in *John Campbell: A Cape Breton Legacy* (2009). He released several albums, including a compilation CD *John Campbell - Cape Breton Violin Music* (as part of Rounder's North American Fiddle Music series) which includes the music from his 1976 Rounder LP plus tracks from his independent releases from the 1980s. [**MacGillivray 1981; Ruckert 2009**].

— ∼ —

John Campbell – A Cape Breton Legacy. Transcribed with a written introduction by George Ruckert. This 2009 collection of 348 tunes from the repertoire of Inverness County-born and Boston-based fiddler John Campbell includes both his own compositions and a more general Cape Breton repertoire of tunes from Scottish, Irish, American

and other audio and printed sources. It is in two sections: (i) *John Campbell's Compositions* and (ii) *Cape Breton Legacy* (referred to throughout the volume as *John Campbell's Cape Breton Book*). There are 59 of his own pieces, divided by tune type: 20 jigs, 33 reels, 6 strathspeys and one each of slow strathspey and hornpipe. The *Legacy* music has 289 tunes, among them 114 reels, 70 jigs, 59 strathspeys, 26 hornpipes, 8 marches, 8 airs, 2 waltzes and 2 Scottish country dances. Besides Campbell's own compositions, a further 56 tunes are credited to composers from Scotland, Shetland, America and Cape Breton from the 18th century right through to the early 21st. The balance of the music is, by implication, traditional, but a significant number of both jigs and hornpipes appear to be of Irish origin. The composers referenced are: Dan Hughie MacEachern, Dan R. MacDonald, James Fraser, Joe Kennedy, Charles Sharpe, Carl MacKenzie, William Morrison, Neil Gow, Peter MacPhee, Johnny MacLean, J. Scott Skinner, A. McAlpin, William Martin, Nathaniel Gow, Peter Milne, Jerry Holland, J. Murdoch Henderson, Alexander Walker, Johnny MacDonald, E. P. Christie, Pipe Major Angus MacDonald, Frank Livingstone, Clem

Titus, T. Densmore, Robert MacIntosh, William Marshall, Elmer Briand, Zeke Backus, Ann Campbell, Tom Anderson, John Mc Coll and Donald Campbell. While most of these are represented by a single tune, sometimes two, a few have more substantial contributions: Scott Skinner (9), Dan R. MacDonald (7) and Dan Hughie MacEachern (5). The book carries acknowledgements, introduction, a biography of John Campbell, a narrative on Cape Breton style and tradition, notes on the tunes and on tune types, and on John Campbell's compositions. A Campbell family tree, discography and sources locate Campbell in Canadian music, and an index of tunes eases referencing. Occasional information highlights issues of form or technique, and indicates also that John's father was a source of many of his tunes and a huge inspiration to him. Illustrated with two dozen photographs, this collection was created by Campbell along with George Ruckert (sarod player, fiddler and academic based in Boston), and as such is one of the few Cape Breton tune collections to involve an "outsider" to its tradition.

— ∾ —

Campbell, Donald. (1934-). Fiddler, composer. Glenora Falls and Blenheim, ON. Although Dan J. Campbell did not particularly wish for his children to play music, Don took up the fiddle at about the age of 9, assisted by his sister, Ann. He and his brothers practiced in secret, or with no hair on the bow in order to be silent. He eased into the public domain as a player, however, performing at the occasional wedding and concert and played his first square dance at the age of seventeen. He worked in Sudbury, Ontario, and in Vancouver, but returned to Cape Breton to play a regular circuit with a three-piece band, often six nights a week. In 1958 he moved to Wallaceburg, Ontario, where his future wife, Marguerite MacLeod, of North Sydney, was teaching school. A violin and piano player, she had studied in her home locality under Prof. James MacDonald and was able to assist Don in note reading; he later took lessons himself from MacDonald to extend his technical skill base. The Campbells lived between Ontario and Cape Breton, and while in Sydney in 1962-1963 Don was a regular on the CJCB Radio show, *Cape Breton Round Up*, along with his brother-in-law, John MacLeod; he also appeared regularly on *The Cape Breton Ceilidh* TV show with Winston Fitzgerald. A tune composer, he wrote "The Whycocomagh Reel," and in Ontario he was successful in fiddle contests, once reaching the semi-final of the North American Old Time Fiddle Championships, at Shelburne. Though he never recorded commercially, he was highly regarded as a Cape Breton fiddler and was profiled by John Gibson in No. 18 of the 1970s *Scotia Sun* series. [**MacGillivray 1981**].

Campbell, Dan J. *See* **Campbell family.**

Campbell, Donald. *See* **Campbell family.**

Campbell, Donald. (ca. 1789-1878). Possibly The earliest documented Scottish fiddle player in Cape Breton, he left Scotland to settle at Lynch's River. He is said to have utilized various high-bass tunings, and to have presented himself as both a dance player and a listening player, illustrating that such a distinction was in effect from the time of the earliest settlers. Local lore suggests that he inherited his music from the fairies, something which (in Ireland also) implies emphasis on the surreal or artistic. [**MacGillivray 1981**].

Campbell, Donnie. (1954-). Guitar, mandolin, singer, radio host and producer, collector. Sydney. Born to parents Dan J. and Margaret (MacInnis) Campbell, and into a musical family; his mother was a singer, as was her father; his grandfather, Michael played the fiddle, and his father's uncles Neil R. and John R. MacIsaac played the bagpipes. Largely self taught, Donnie Campbell cites Archie Thomas, Charlie MacKinnon and John Allan Cameron as his early influences. A singer in church and school choirs, his first stage appearance was at the Highland Village Concert in Iona at the age of fourteen. Although he spent a short spell as a full-time musician after university, most of his working life was spent with Nova Scotia Power. He sings Scottish, Irish, Cape Breton and Canadian folk repertoire and style, playing in clubs and at concerts, dances and ceilidhs; as well as being a soloist, he has also performed with bands such as Miller's Jug and with singer-songwriter, Buddy MacDonald. He is featured on various compilations, such as *Big Pond the Album*, *Failte: Traditions* (CMIC), *Celtic Colours Volume XI*, and with St. Theresa's Folk Choir; he has released two solo CDs and has performed on CJCB-TV and CBC-TV and on various local, Maritimes and national radio programs. Donnie Campbell has hosted *Celtic Serenade*, a program of Gaelic, traditional and folk music from Cape Breton, Ireland and Scotland on CJCB Radio, Sydney, for more than 40 years, and as such is the longest-running host of a single radio show in Canada. His contribution to Cape Breton music has been recognized in many ways through awards (e.g., the Tic Butler Memorial Award in 2006) and with a special anniversary event in 1994 to mark 20 years of his radio show. *See **Celtic Serenade**.*

Campbell, James P. (1863-1942). Fiddle. Red Islands, Cape Breton County. He learned to play the fiddle while working in the Boston area, developing a somewhat eclectic style and repertoire that gained him second place in an early (1926) North Sydney fiddle contest. [**MacGillivray 1981**].

Campbell, John. *See **Campbell family**.*

Campbell, John Willie. (b. 1928). Fiddle. Glencoe, Inverness County. Born to parents Tom and Mary Kate (MacEachern) Campbell, John Willie grew up in a music environment where several family members and relatives – including his paternal grandfather, his father, uncles Angus and Dan Campbell and John Hughie MacEachern, brothers Joe, Dougald and Alex and cousin, Archie Campbell – played fiddle. As was common at the time, he was not formally taught to play, but rather was guided and encouraged by those around him, both family and members of the wider community, in this instance fiddlers such as John Joe MacInnis, Robert MacLeod, Donald Angus MacLean, Archie Campbell and John Hughie MacEachern. During the 1930s he played at house

parties, school dances, church picnics and box socials around the Glencoe area. In 1953 he moved to Sydney, returning there after a short sojourn in Toronto, during which time he befriended Cape Breton's Irish-style fiddler, Johnny Wilmot. John Willie Campbell was known for his old-style playing, particularly his penchant for using high-bass tuning for more than 30 tunes, and for his timing, which was regarded as ideal for step dancing. He was regularly heard on CJCB and CJFX radio and also featured on the Topic LP *Cape Breton Scottish Fiddle, The Music of Cape Breton Vol. 2* (1978). [**MacGillivray 1981**].

Campbell, Shelly. (1981-). Fiddle, step dance, piano, teacher. West Bay Road. She was taught first by Gertie Coffin in Port Hawkesbury, then guided by Stephanie Wills in exploring style and repertoire. Encouragement from local community members kept her focused, among these fiddler Theresa MacLellan, who drove her school bus. Influential too were Alex Francis MacKay and the MacDonald family from Kingsville, particularly Sandy, Johnny, Jeff and their uncle, Donnie "Dougald" MacDonald; at the many house parties held at the MacDonald home she had an opportunity to play with and to hear others. A primary school and Gaelic teacher, Campbell plays for concerts and dances around Inverness County, most often with accompanist Allan Dewar and, on occasion, with such as Sandy MacDonald, Joel Chiasson, Troy MacGillivray, Kenneth MacKenzie and Andrea Beaton. She has taught fiddle at Ceòlas in Scotland and offers classes at home during the winter months. A board member of the CMIC in Judique, she is actively involved in promoting engagement with the Gaelic language and favours the older sounds, traditions and practices in Cape Breton fiddle. A tunes composer, she is featured on several albums, including Kinnon Beaton's *Tunesmith (2010)*, and Kenneth MacKenzie's *Piob is Fidheal (2011)*, as well as on various compilation CDs and the 2008 DVD *Tribute to Jerry Holland*.

Campbell, Tena. (1899-1949). Fiddle. Grand Mira, Cape Breton County. Encouraged by her father, Joseph, and brothers who played fiddle, she took up that instrument at the age of seven, inspired also by local musicians Rory MacDonald, John Stephen Currie and others who were regular visitors to the home. At school in Sydney she took formal lessons from Prof. James MacDonald, and later teamed up with pianist, Gertie Boutilier, to play a regular spot at the Saturday night dances at the Hillcoat Academy, Marion Bridge. The duo was popular, and played twice a week at venues as far away as Christmas Island, Iona, Bras d'Or and locally at the Navy League at Whitney Pier, the Institute for the Blind and the Old League of the Cross. Winning fiddle contests in the 1930s led to her broadcasting on local radio as often as six times a week. She was a regular on the popular *Cottar's Saturday Night* show from 1935 to 1937, and she also played *Celtic Ceilidh*, another Sydney radio show which could be heard on the trans-Canada hook-up. During the 1930s and 1940s she teamed up with pianist, Beattie Wallace for dance playing, travelling by bus and train to Johnstown, St. Peter's, Port Hawkesbury, Mulgrave and Antigonish and, for one long-term residency, at East Bay, where they played over 15 years for $4 a night. They also played regularly in Sydney, where at Carpenters Hall and St. Theresa's Hall they were joined by banjoist Ed McGillivary and fiddler Sandy MacInnis. At the Lyceum, she and Bessie McKinnon played with Peter Dominic for dancing, with Rod McIsaac as prompter, and she was a featured artist with Joe Murphy and his Band, often flown to Boston to play square dances there. Tena Campbell had a driving rhythm that compelled dancing and she came to be associated with particular tunes such as "Lord MacDonald's Reel." A petite woman, she was regarded as a very strong and vigorous player whose fingers left indents on the fingerboard of her fiddle. Her versatility as a fiddler created multiple, diverse opportunities for her, enabling her to build a reputation at a time when female fiddlers were in the minority. Her "great skill and dexterity" were noted by J. J. MacInnis in the 1943-1944 publication *Eilean Cheap Breatann* and in her time she was honoured by a song titled "Queen of the Bow,"

set to the melody of "The Inverness Gathering." **[MacGillivray 1981; MacInnes, 1943-1944].**

Canada Council for the Arts (CCA). Created by an *Act* of Parliament in 1957 to foster and promote the study, enjoyment and production of works in the arts, and to operate at arm's length from government, the CCA provides funding to individual professional artists and arts organizations through a peer assessment process. It awards fellowships and prizes and conducts research, communications and arts promotion activities to further support, promote and celebrate the arts. Initial funding for programs came from an endowment fund of CAD$100 million derived from the death duties of Nova Scotia industrialists Sir James Dunn and Izaak Walton Killam. The CCA began receiving annual allocations from Parliament in the late 1960s, and currently this is the major source of its resources. In its first year the CCA funded 29 arts organizations, most of them repertoire companies in the performing arts, and two individual artists. In 2013-2014 it awarded 5,811 grants to artists and arts organizations across Canada, totalling $142.1 million; of this, $4.3 million was allocated to the arts in Nova Scotia. Requests from practitioners of the various forms of traditional Celtic music, including fiddlers, are relatively rare; however, a number of Cape Breton musicians have been recipients of CCA support, with awards ranging from $700 to $18,200. Under the CCA's Music Section, travel grants and grants to individuals are available, as is support for professional development and composition, for production projects (including recording), and for national and international touring. The CCA's Audience and Market Development Office also offers travel grants that enable musicians to travel when selected for showcases at contact events. Cape Breton musicians receiving such support have included: Beòlach, Jerry Holland, Dave MacIsaac, The Cottars, Buddy MacMaster, Slàinte Mhath , Mary Jane Lamond, Troy MacGillivray and The Beaton Sisters.

Canadian Academy of Recording Arts and Sciences (CARAS). An umbrella, not-for-profit organization founded in 1975 to promote and celebrate Canadian music and artists. It operates as a membership program where various industry-related opportunities are available to its members. It is also linked to the JUNO Awards, MusiCounts (a music education program) and the Canadian Music Hall of Fame (founded 1978). Only a small number of Cape Breton fiddlers are associated with CARAS. *See* **awards; Juno awards**.

Canadian Broadcasting Corporation. *See* **CBC**.

Canadian Family Herald. A weekly magazine first issued on November 29, 1851, by D. McDougall. The *Herald* was a family publication devoted to agriculture, art, science and literature, with no political writing; it ceased publication in 1968. Initially costing a dollar a year, the magazine's focus was rural Canada. Its music content concentrated on Canadian songs, regularly publishing song lyrics, but its biggest impact on Cape Breton music was related to the advertisements it carried with many instruments, especially pianos, ordered via its mail-order services. The Beaton family of Mabou, for instance, ordered their Gerard Heinzman piano from Toronto through this magazine.

Canadian Folk Music Awards (CFMA). These are made at an annual ceremony held each November in recognition of achievements by Canadian musicians in traditional and contemporary folk music, and in other "roots" genres. The program was created in 2005 by a group of independent-label representatives, folk-music presenters, artists and enthusiasts, who felt that contemporary Canadian music awards had a restricted view of the traditional/folk/roots genres; it now offers 19 individual awards categories. Nominations are made by the artist or their representative. As in the Juno Awards, the judging process uses a two-stage elimination model, with a jury drawn from the folk music community. Cape Breton musicians (including fiddlers and singers) have featured among the award winners since 2005 (e.g., J. P. Cormier, Chrissy Crowley, Mary Jane Lamond and Wendy MacIsaac and Còig). *See* **awards.**

Canadian Independent Music Association (CIMA). Known from 1975 to 2009 as CIRPA, this is a trade organization that is the collective voice of independent music businesses in English-speaking Canada. Its members are Canadian-owned companies and representatives of Canadian-owned companies involved in every aspect of the music, sound recording and music-related industries. Its mandate is the long-term development of the sector and to raise the profile of independent Canadian music nationally and internationally. CIMA deals with areas such as culture-industry policies and programs, intellectual property and copyright law, tax laws and tariffs, international export and trade development programs and professional development. At home and abroad it operates outgoing and incoming trade missions, marketing campaigns and education programs, and takes export marketing initiatives at international conferences and trade shows, assisting the independent sector to identify, develop and expand business-to-business opportunities and business partnerships in the international marketplace. Chief among CIMA strategies has been the creation and provision of "The Canada Stand" at international trade shows. Through the services provided by this presence, Canadian independent labels and companies are helped to build strategic alliances in major markets and establish new contacts and networks, to strengthen relations with existing contacts, to access new sales territories and new distribution networks, to license product, to export/import finished goods and to gain a better understanding of international markets; in 1978, this was brought to MIDEM in France and has since been supported at POPKOMM in Berlin (since 1996) and at SXSW in Texas (since 2005). CIMA also directly participates in world trade shows and festivals including Music Matters in Hong Kong, CMJ in New York, and WOMEX in Europe. Other key activities over the years have included the formation and funding of FACTOR in 1982, the initiation of the Canadian Music Industry Database and the publication of various reports such as *The Investor's Guide to the Music Industry in*

Canada and *The Copyright Handbook*. The Cape Breton Music Industry Co-operative and Music Nova Scotia are both members of CIMA.

Canadian Independent Record Production Association (CIRPA). Known since 2009 as the **Canadian Independent Music Association (CIMA).**

Canadian Music Publishers Association (CMPA). Now known as **Canadian Musical Reproduction Rights Agency Ltd. (CMRRA).**

Canadian Musical Reproduction Rights Agency Ltd. (CMRRA). A music-licensing agency based in Toronto that was founded in 1975 as a non-profit organization to represent Canadian music publishers and music copyright owners; on their behalf, it issues licenses authorizing the reproduction of musical works in Canada. These licenses authorize the reproduction of music on CDs and cassettes ("mechanical" licensing) and in films, TV programs and other audio-visual productions ("synchronization" licensing). Licensees pay royalties relating to such licenses to CMRRA which, in turn, distributes the proceeds to its publisher members. The publisher then passes on the song- or melody-writer's portion of such revenues to the writer/composer involved. Membership is open to any music publisher or copyright owner dealing with the Canadian use of the reproduction rights in its music. Many of the best-known Cape Breton fiddle players have tunes registered with CMRRA, among these are Dan R. MacDonald, John Morris Rankin, Jerry Holland, Brenda Stubbert, Otis Tomas, Natalie MacMaster and Ashley MacIsaac.

Canadian Radio Broadcasting Commission, The (CRBC). Canada's first public broadcaster, this government agency was established by Parliament in 1932 with the objective of setting up a radio network to broadcast Canadian-produced programmes across the country. As in other countries, this was seen as primarily necessary for the maintenance of national integrity and communications; it was also seen as important to challenge the influence of cultural intrusion over the airwaves from U.S. broadcasters all along Canada's southern border. CRBC was superseded in 1936 by the Canadian Broadcasting Corporation (CBC). *See* **CBC**.

CanCon (Canadian-Content Quota). A regulatory system whereby a certain percentage of music played on public radio and TV must be Canadian. In an effort to develop the Canadian music industry, perceived as being undermined by American and British music, a quota system was introduced in the early 1970s. Under this, the Canadian Radio-Television and Telecommunications Commission's legislation (1971) specified 30% Canadian content on the AM frequency and, in 1975, also on FM. These "CanCon" quotas thus established exposure opportunities for Canadian artists, but were challenged by private broadcasters who questioned the control over the material available to them for airplay. Furthermore, individual licensing commitments required broadcasters to invest in Canadian talent through supporting local musical events and funding "homegrown" albums of emerging talent. Initially voluntary, after 2005, this system became mandatory, and in order to qualify for radio-broadcasting license renewals, radio stations now must play a minimum number of "Canadian" recordings to satisfy CanCon requirements. To qualify as Canadian, recordings are stamped with a MAPL (music, artists, production, lyrics) designation where at least two out of these four criteria must be met. The percentage varies according to format (AM, FM, CBC), but all radio stations must now ensure that 35% of the music they air each week is Canadian. In addition, commercial radio stations must ensure that 35% of the music aired between 6 a.m. and 6 p.m., Monday through Friday, is Canadian. Ethnic radio stations must ensure that at least 7% of the music they air each week during ethnic programming periods is Canadian; French-language radio stations must ensure that at least 65% of their music overall is in French, and at least 55% of that aired from 6 a.m. to 6 p.m., Monday through Friday, is in French. Equally, private TV stations and networks (e.g., CTV, Global) and ethnic TV stations must achieve a yearly Canadian content level; this may be up to 60%. CanCon legislation does not yet apply to the Internet. Canada's entry in 2012 to the Trans-Pacific Partnership, a multilateral Free Trade Agreement, now raises the prospect of the loss of the protective CanCon quota requirements. *See* **FACTOR**.

Cape Breton Fiddler. (a) Generic name used since the 1970s to refer to a fiddle player from the region playing in that style of music which, post-revival, came to be labelled "Cape Breton fiddle music." Previously an exponent of this music was typically referred to in Cape Breton as a "violinist" while the term "fiddler" was reserved for individuals of lesser technical ability and musicianship; the qualifier "Cape Breton" was added from the 1970s onward. Before that the violinist was referred to as Scottish (sometimes Scotch), an acknowledgement of the Highland Scottish origins of the fiddle music style and repertoire. Toward the end of the 20th century the fashion was to use to the term Celtic to describe fiddlers and fiddle music; in the past decade the trend has again changed, now in favour of the label Gaelic. **(b)** *The Cape Breton Fiddler* is a significant publication from 1981 by Allister MacGillivray, the first non-tune book related to the Cape Breton fiddle tradition. It includes biographies of 93 fiddlers and a substantial index of others, and includes fiddlers from Cape Breton and its diaspora as well as other Cape Breton-style fiddlers from mainland Nova Scotia. Based on personal fieldwork and existing documentation in newspapers and magazines, MacGillivray's work on early Cape Breton fiddlers (those deceased pre-1981) represents, in many cases, the definitive overview of their music based on existing written accounts and, where available, audio recordings. Only those early fiddlers who had a significant public profile are included in this Companion; in such cases, only a brief overview is given and article-end references guide the reader to the original publication. Other fiddlers who continued to be active as recording artists after the publication of MacGillivray's book are included here, with their information updated as appropriate. MacGillivray's 1988 book, *A Cape Breton Ceilidh* (Sea Cape Music Ltd.), deals with piano players, step dancers and pipers, again in a series of biographies, and is referenced in this *Companion* as is appropriate. [**Caplan 1981; MacGillivray 1981, 1988, 1997**].

Cape Breton Fiddlers' Association (CBFA). As an organization and associated performance group, it was originally set up as "The Committee for Cape Breton" (CCB) in 1972 as an organizing committee for the first festival of fiddle music, a response to the CBC-TV documentary *The Vanishing Cape Breton Fiddler.* The association was responsible for a number of key initiatives which resulted in the consolidation and revival of the Cape Breton fiddle tradition, chief among them being the Cape Breton Fiddle Festivals held in Glendale (1973, '75, '77, '79) which, in many ways, refuted the claims of the *VCBF* and proved that the Cape Breton fiddler was alive and well. A highlight of the Glendale events came to be the finale, where all the fiddlers in attendance (often upward of 100) joined forces to perform several tune selections under the baton of Fr. John Angus Rankin, the local parish priest (who co-directed the festival with Joey Beaton). The CCB scheduled rehearsals for these finales throughout the year and they became an important part of the fiddlers' social calendar, allowing them an opportunity to meet and play tunes together. The establishment of group classes to ensure the transmission of the fiddle tradition was another significant venture. Individual classes in fiddle music had already been offered in the Sydney area by Prof. James MacDonald; however, it was 1972 when John MacDougall was hired to teach groups of people in a number of locations around Inverness County, with classes being offered free of charge. Within a year, 240 students in the Inverness area were attending; later, Stan Chapman from Antigonish also began to offer group teaching in association with the CCB. An important part of the CCB's engagement with the previously fragmented fiddle community was the publication of a newsletter,

The Cape Breton Fiddlers Association 40th Anniversary celebrations. Courtesy of the Cape Breton Fiddlers Association.

begun in October 1973, which carried information on births, deaths, marriages, music events and old and new tune transcriptions. Edited and compiled by Frank MacInnis, the publication aimed to "act as a unifying force so that all those with an appreciation of Scottish music will be able to maintain a closer link with each other and that the good spirit arising from the Glendale Festival will continue to flourish and grow" (Newsletter no. 1, October, 1973); the newsletter, *Fiddlers' Info*, continues to be published today with the same mandate. The CCB also encouraged the documentation of the fiddle tradition in various ways. In 1974, *Weekend* magazine committed to coverage of the 1975 festival, and in that year the CCB produced a 30-page newspaper, *Fiddlers to the Fore*, written by local writer and Gaelic culture specialist, John Gibson. In 1977, the Belvedere Tobacco Company sponsored the Fiddlers Festival and created a printed brochure that included a history of the fiddlers' movement. A 42-page newspaper, *Highland Heritage*, with both original and reprinted articles, was also published by John Gibson and Joey Beaton. In 1975, the CCB conducted a survey among the Cape Breton fiddlers and the wider community to gather information

and opinions on the fiddle tradition and related activities. In 1976, the committee was invited to provide music for Queen Elizabeth II in Halifax at the Olympic Games in Canada celebrations. A small group then travelled to Montréal to perform as part of the Cultural Olympics, sponsored there by the federal government; the contingent included John Morris Rankin, Greg Smith, Stan Chapman, Sandy MacInnis, Theresa MacLellan, Buddy MacMaster, Donald Angus Beaton, Fr. Francis Cameron and Joey Beaton. The early CCB involved: Frank MacInnis, Fr. Eugene Morris, Fr. John Angus Rankin, Rod Chisholm, Judge Hugh J. MacPherson, Archie Neil Chisholm, Joey Beaton, Anne Marie MacDonald, Jeannette Beaton and Burton MacIntyre. In 1979 the committee registered with the Nova Scotia Registry of Joint Stocks, in order to aid in their application for grants, and was re-named "The Cape Breton Fiddlers Association." After 1981, the Glendale Fiddle Festivals moved to different locations (Iona, Sydney), finally settling at the Gaelic College, St. Ann's. Since 1982, the Fiddlers' Festival has become an annual 2-day affair.

The CBFA continues to play a significant role in the maintaining of Cape Breton fiddle music on the island; through it, the sense of a "community" of fiddlers has remained constant since the 1970s. It provides an important forum for fiddlers of all ages and levels to be involved; for some, less inclined toward the spotlight, it is an ideal way to perform, where there is safety in numbers. For younger, emerging players, it is an early performance opportunity; for all, it is a chance to learn new tunes and to share repertoire. The CBFA has also undertaken a number of special projects, including performance tours (e.g., to Scotland, PEI, Glengarry, ON, Boston, MA), the publication of a tune book, *The Cape Breton Fiddlers Collection* (Cranford 2007), and high-profile performances at Celtic Colours. Current membership of the organization exceeds 500; the organization is administered by Betty Matheson and a team of directors that includes Leanne Aucoin, Janet Cameron, Bob MacEachern, Isabel MacGillivray, Frank MacInnis, Burton MacIntyre, Mary MacNeil, Fr. Eugene Morris, Eddie Rogers, Trina Samson, Pauline Davis, Blair Mombourquette, Julia MacKenzie, Steve MacNeil and Lawrence Cameron. The CBFA's massed fiddle group was directed variously by Stan Chapman, Joey Beaton, Fr. Angus Morris and Carl MacKenzie in the past; current directors are Eddie Rogers, Dara Smith MacDonald and Leanne Aucoin. [**MacInnis in Cranford 2007; Thompson 2003, 2006**].

— ∼ —

Cape Breton Fiddlers Collection, The. Published in 2007 as Vol. 7 of **The Cape Breton Musical Heritage** series, and edited by Paul Cranford, this is a compilation of 267 melodies arranged from the repertoires of past and present members and friends of the CBFA. 120 pages display tunes in broad tune-type categories: (a) marches, strathspeys and reels (with hornpipes, slow strathspeys, quickstep and piping repertoire), (b) jigs, (c) slow airs, laments and other melodies (such as two-step and waltz). These are numbered and arranged within categories according to key, the rationale being to "allow users to create their own medleys." There are 89 reels, 83 jigs, 39 strathspeys and 25 marches, only a small

number of which have previously appeared in print. The music represents that which has been played by the CBFA members over its first quarter-century history, representing, as Jody Stecher comments in *Fiddler Magazine*, "a kind of palimpsest of various moments in its history" (2008). The collection includes an editor's preface and a "Response to *The Vanishing Cape Breton Fiddler*," by Frank MacInnis, which includes a short overview of contributions made to the CBFA by off-island fiddlers such as those from Prince Edward Island, Glengarry, ON, Scotland, Ireland, etc. There is a brief explanation of arrangements and symbols provided and notes are given for certain tunes to highlight, for example, unusual structures, previous publications or recordings, alternative titles or melodic variations. An alphabetical index to tunes is given, and chords to all are supplied by Allie Bennett. The cover and in-text photographs are by Herb Rosenberg and David Gillis.

composers represented. Of the 114 composers indexed, seventeen are 18th- and 19th-century Scottish and one is Irish (Tony Smith), while the rest are either Cape Bretoners or friends of the CBFA; a quarter of the composers are female. It is noted that some of the island's more prolific composers have not included previously published tunes here in order to avoid duplication, making the roll call of names all the more impressive for its scale. Those whose tunes are included are: Brent Aucoin (1), Leanne Aucoin (5), Michael Barron(10), Andrea Beaton (3), Elizabeth Beaton (1), Joey Beaton (2), Kinnon Beaton (3), Allie Bennett (4), Melanie Bonnell (1), Jennifer Bowman (3), Elmer Briand (7), Peter Briand (1), Lawrence Cameron (1), Mac Campbell (3), Ann Campbell Brown (1), Kevin Chiasson (1), Aubrey Chapman (1), Stan Chapman (2), Cameron Chisholm (2), Maybelle Chisholm (1), Gordon Côté (2), P. S. Cranford (97), Lee Cremo (2), Joe Doucette (4), Marcel Doucet (1), Kate Dunlay (1), Jackie

Dunn (1), Ray Ellis (4), Laurne Fraser (1), Murray Gallant (1), Jim Gaskins (1), Kyle Gillis (1), Danny Graham (2), Glenn Graham (3), Colin Grant (1), David Greenberg (2), Jerry Holland (4), Bill Lamey (1), Charlie MacCuspic (1), Anita MacDonald (1), Bill MacDonald (1), Dan R. MacDonald (8), Dougie MacDonald (1), Howie MacDonald (1), Rev. Hugh A. MacDonald (1), Rodney MacDonald (2), William MacDonald (1), Joan MacDonald Boes (1), Annie Mae MacEachern (2), Donna MacEachern Frizzell (1), Sandy MacInnis (2), Sandy MacIntyre (3), Ashley MacIsaac (1), Wendy MacIsaac (1), Carl MacKenzie (4), Hector MacKenzie (3), Maynard MacKenzie (10), Jacinta MacKinnon (1), Shawn MacKinnon (1), Stanley MacKinnon (5), Phillip MacLeod (1), Gordon MacLean (3), Joe MacLean (1), Johnny Washabuck MacLean (1), Susan MacLean (1), Donald MacLellan (1), Rannie MacLellan (4), Natalie MacMaster (2), Archie A. MacNeil (1), Jean MacNeil (2), Joe MacNeil (1), Lucy MacNeil (2), McKayla MacNeil (1), Ryan MacNeil (1), Stewart MacNeil (3), Doug MacPhee (1), Ian R. MacPhee (2), Margaret MacPhee (3), Peter MacPhee (1), Allison Mombourquette (3), Fr. Angus Morris (1), Theresa Morrison (5), Hugh Murray (1), Larry Parks (1), Rosemary Poirier (2), Wilfred Prosper (2), John Morris Rankin (1), Mairi Rankin (1), Andrew Ritchie (1), Jennifer Roland (2), Harry Slaunwhite (3), Johnny Steele (1), Brenda Stubbert (1), Otis Thomas (2), Johnny White (1), Johnny Wilmot (1). As modern compositions, the majority of tunes in the collection are in copyright.

— ∼ —

Cape Breton Island. (French: Île du Cap-Breton – formerly Île Royale; Scottish Gaelic: Ceap Breatainn or Eilean Cheap Bhreatainn; Mi'qmaw: Únama'ki). The most easterly region of Nova Scotia, the name most likely corresponds to the word *Breton*, the French adjective referring to the Atlantic province of Brittany, in reference to some of the early colonial settlers. Cape Breton Island has been linked to mainland Nova Scotia by road only since 1955, when the Canso Causeway was built. The 10,311 km² (3,981 m²) island accounts for 18.7% of the total area of Nova Scotia. The island is located east-northeast of the mainland, with its northern and western coasts fronting on the Gulf of Saint Lawrence; its western coast also forms the eastern limits of the Northumberland Strait. The eastern and southern coasts front the Atlantic Ocean; its eastern coast also forms the western limits of the Cabot Strait. Its landmass slopes upward from south to north, culminating in the Highlands of its northern cape. One of the world's largest saltwater lakes, Bras d'Or, dominates the centre of the island. The island is divided into four of Nova Scotia's eighteen counties: Cape Breton, Inverness, Richmond and Victoria. The majority of the population (ca. 75%) is located in the Cape Breton Regional Municipality (CBRM) which includes all of Cape Breton County and is often referred to as "Industrial Cape Breton"; this area, with its long history of coal mining and steel manufacturing, was Nova Scotia's industrial heartland throughout much of the 20th century.

history. The indigenous settlers of Cape Breton were ancestors of the Mi'kmaq, the Aboriginal population at the time the first European settlers arrived. Legend has it that Prince Henry Sinclair, Earl of Orkney, explored Cape Breton and Nova Scotia waters in the late 14th century, but the first of the colonial explorers is acknowledged to have been John Cabot (in 1497), followed (ca. 1521) by Portuguese fishermen who established a colony on the island. During the Anglo-French war (1627-1629), a Scottish-led colony was established at Baleine. The French ultimately overruled the British, renaming the territory Île Royale and establishing the first permanent settlements at what are now Englishtown and St. Peter's. These were abandoned in 1659 and remained so until 1713, when Louisbourg and its associated communities were established. Louisbourg was captured by the British in 1745 and again in 1758; however, Île Royale remained part of New France until it was ceded to Great Britain under the Treaty of Paris (1763). As part of Nova Scotia (which included New Brunswick, mainland Nova Scotia, PEI [formerly St. John's Island] and Newfoundland), it was governed out of Halifax until 1784; then, as part of a re-structuring of the colony, Cape Breton became independent, with Sydney established as its capital. In 1820 it merged with Nova Scotia once again.

population. Cape Breton's population at the time of the 2011 census was 135,974, representing approximately 15% of the provincial population, which had declined by roughly 4.4% since the previous census in 2006, largely due to poor economic conditions resulting in a population drain, particularly of young people. Cape Breton has many ethnic groups, including Mi'kmaq, Acadian, Scottish, Irish, English and others; the early 20th century saw an influx of Loyalists from the U.S., Italians and Eastern Europeans, who mostly settled in the eastern part of the island around the Industrial region. The Scottish Gaels, with a large influx of immigrants arriving mainly in the late-18th and early-to-mid-19th centuries, came to outnumber other immigrant groups and have continued to make up the largest portion of the island's population.

economy. Cape Breton's fluctuating economic fortunes have been mainly linked to coal mining and, later, steel manufacturing; as mines in the western part of the island closed down, a population shift from rural to urban centres on the east of the island became common from the late 19th century onward, as did out-migration, which has been part of the Cape Breton experience from the earliest days of settlement. Cities such as Boston were early sites for displaced Cape Bretoners, but gradually the flow of migration moved farther west, through Detroit and Toronto; more recently it is to Alberta, where work in industry surrounding the oil sands development, especially around Fort McMurray, is plentiful. With the coal and steel industries in disarray in the 1960s, private ownership abandoned the enterprises. To offset potential social and economic calamity, the federal and provincial government intervened, taking over the mines and phasing them out through creating the government Crown Cape Breton Development Corporation (DEVCO)

and later Enterprise Cape Breton Corporation (ECBC). In 2014, ECBC was dismantled and its programs and services absorbed into the federal Atlantic Canada Opportunities Agency (ACOA). In the 1960s, the Nova Scotia government took over the steel mill until it was finally closed in 2000. DEVCO and ECBC were left to work with community stakeholders in diversifying the economy, which remained in dire circumstances. Tourism has been a key factor in turning the economic tide, boosted by recent 21st-century accolades from *National Geographic* and *Travel and Leisure* magazines, which ranked it as among the world's top destinations; recent major new initiatives such as the development of high-end golf facilities in Inverness County have added to the tourism and leisure-market potential. Culture has also been harnessed to attract tourists, especially music, with Celtic Colours most prominent; this extends the annual tourist season into October and generates an annual revenue of some CAD$8 million for the local economy. Kitchenfest!/Féis a' Chidsin!, established by The Gaelic College in 2014, now happens in June, this expanding the tourist season further. (*With* **GG**) [**Bickerton 2013; Feintuch 2010; Graham 2006; Higgins 1993; Johnson 2007; Morgan 2000, 2009**].

culture. Virtually all the art forms are found in Cape Breton, and many internationally regarded artists such as the writer Alistair MacLeod (1936-2014) and singer Rita MacNeil (1944-2013) are associated with the island. Popular mainstream culture dominated local arts once radio and later TV became available, but this also inspired a generic Cape Breton "singer-songwriter" practice since the 1970s; however, strong cultural traditions associated with individual ethnic groups survived on the island, such as Acadian song and Mi'kmaw drumming. The dominant ethnic culture, however, was Scottish, the result of pioneer settlers bringing with them their own cultural resources, which played a large part in directing their lives. Scottish immigrants may have abandoned "the old land," but they retained their culture and traditions, and so language, music, song, dance, storytelling and superstition were elevated to a new level of importance, serving initially as a nostalgic reminder of the old home, and the old ways. Culture was also highly relevant in retaining Scottish identity, first to distinguish Scots from the other ethnic groups on the island and, secondly, to assert their Scottishness, thus proving that geographical relocation alone could not weaken this; and so Highland ways were nurtured in their new Cape Breton environment. With regard to the Gaelic language and song, various sources testify to their presence in early Cape Breton life. Where fiddle music is concerned, occasional information may be gleaned from social and historical accounts of pioneer life. Unfortunately, however, no aural evidence of the music was available until the late 1920s. This makes the issue of determining the nature of music change prior to 1928 (when the first commercial recording of a Cape Breton fiddler was made) quite nebulous. Given the predominance of Highland Scottish settlers in Cape Breton in such isolation, it can be reasoned that existing music practices and other aspects of culture could flourish; however, the impact from the outset of the conditions of its New World location should never be underestimated. The music transplanted to Cape Breton was that typical of the 18th-century Highland Scottish fiddler, the era known as the "golden age" of Scottish fiddle music, with well-known exponents including such as Niel Gow (1727-1807) and William Marshall (1748-1833). Paradoxically, while this music style and repertoire, closely related to the dance tradition, was becoming embedded in its new Cape Breton environment, it was undergoing massive change back in Scotland. *See* **Scotland.**

a new voice in Scottish music. Cape Breton has always had significant out-migration (certainly from the late 17th century) and thus has been exposed to the influences brought home by those "from away." Serial emigration accelerated in the 20th century with substantial diasporic communities becoming established in Boston, Halifax, Detroit and Toronto. Interaction with other music communities and audiences inevitably influenced the sound and practices of the Cape

Breton fiddlers. In Boston, for example, the first such fiddlers to record did so in the context of an Irish dance-band format; later, the piano stylings of other genres experienced in such urban melting pots influenced the development of the idiosyncratic Cape Breton piano sound. The quadrilles popular in the Irish dance halls came to dominate the Cape Breton social dance scene there. Such influences gradually filtered through to Cape Breton itself and, coinciding with other societal changes such as the advent of radio and the accessibility of pianos via mail order, gradually influenced the existing fiddle tradition, not as it had in Scotland, but rather shaped by its own unique conditions. Between 1930 and 1960, a significant evolution of the Cape Breton fiddle style and sound effectively resulted in a Cape Breton fiddle music emerging as new voice in Scottish music.

Cape Breton identity. Fiddlers (generally referred to as violinists until the 1970s), as with all Cape Bretoners of Highland Scottish descent, were aware and proud of their heritage and were generally identified as Scottish or, sometimes, Scotch. Fiddlers of merit from other ethnic backgrounds were encouraged (often by industry personnel) to adjust their names to highlight the Scottish connection; thus, recordings from the 1950s onward announce Winston "Scotty" Fitzgerald and Paddy "Scotty" LeBlanc. The "Cape Breton-Scottish" tag later came to replace the previous "Scottish" tag as it referred to fiddle players and their music; this new label became widespread in the period following the *Vanishing Cape Breton Fiddler* (1971), which, by suggesting that this tradition was in danger of disappearing, provoked a revival, part of which involved a re-branding of identity. As Cape Breton fiddlers began to engage with contemporary Scotland on a regular basis from the late 1980s, and became players on the international Celtic market in the 1990s, a new, discrete Cape Breton label came to be uniformly adopted. However, by the turn of the century the term Celtic was being increasingly used to describe local fiddle players and their music. Since the 1970s, the term Gaelic has been associated with fiddle (and pipe) music, used initially by scholars rather than practitioners. In the past decade this label has increasingly been appropriated by the players themselves, perhaps as a means to reinforce the roots of their tradition in Gaelic culture. However, the term "Gaelic fiddle music" presents many challenges relating to music-linguistic connections, identity, inclusiveness and authenticity, all of which should be addressed. [**Doherty 1996; Feintuch 2010; Graham 2006**].

Cape Breton Live. CapeBretonLive.com started life as an Internet radio show; it was established in 2005 by Natalie MacMaster and her husband, fiddle player Donnell Leahy, in order to make live performances of Cape Breton fiddle music available on the web. A five-week pilot series was launched in 2005 with the first live audio broadcast airing in September, featuring Natalie and Buddy MacMaster, with Betty Lou Beaton on piano and Dave MacIsaac on guitar. Glenn Graham and Andrea Beaton were hired as hosts, recording cultural commentary to help contextualize the performances. A lack of funding resources led to the project being discontinued in 2008; however, an archive of more than 50 shows, recorded live in various venues across Cape Breton, from halls, to pubs, to kitchens, remained; two CDs featuring material from these shows are available: *Cape Breton Live: Take 01* and *Cape Breton Live: Take 02*. Since 2014, the CMIC has taken over Cape Breton Live and a new series of recordings started; these are now available for online streaming on a subscription basis through the CMIC website.

Cape Breton Music Industry Cooperative (CBMIC). A not-for-profit organization run by a volunteer board of directors developed to grow and support Cape Breton's music industry. The focus is on building a structure in Cape Breton to provide knowledge, advice, training and support for local artists throughout their music careers. The vision is to create an internationally recognized Cape Breton music industry that is economically and culturally sustainable. Since 2008 the CBMIC has been involved with the Cape Breton Music Export Program in association with

Enterprise Cape Breton Corporation (ECBC) and it also administers the Cape Breton International Music Export Program (IMEP), which was created in 2010, funded in part by the Government of Canada. This program supports artists endeavouring to develop new markets outside of Canada by providing developmental costs such as attendance at international music-industry conferences and showcases like the ECMA International Program, Nova Scotia Music Week, and Celtic Colours International Buyers and Media Program. CBMIC activities to date include the SoundBites Concert Series and, in partnership with Celtic Colours, a showcase of export-ready artists at the ECMA Week; this is aimed at improving profile and marketability by exposing them to global music-industry guests. In 2011, as part of Celtic Connections in Glasgow, Scotland, the province of Nova Scotia was highlighted at the Showcase Scotland presentation, which attracted some 200 international delegates, most of them festival and talent buyers; CBMIC took part in this and in other industry events across the U.K. CBMIC's board of directors has a number of musicians, including representatives of the local fiddle community.

Cape Breton Musical Heritage Series. Collective title for a series of publications issued by Cranford Publications, Englishtown, Cape Breton. Described by the publisher as "Melodies from Cape Breton, Irish, Scottish and Other Sources" and "Music for a Continuing Tradition," since 1988, there have been nine volumes of notated music, each compiled by Paul Cranford. These have over 2,000 distinct melodies, about half of them Scottish with the rest a mixture of tunes composed in Cape Breton, with others both Irish and North American in origin. In order of publication, the books in the series are: *Jerry Holland's Collection of Fiddle Tunes*, *Brenda Stubbert's Collection of Fiddle Tunes*, *The Lighthouse Collection of Newly Composed Fiddle Tunes*, *Winston Fitzgerald: A Collection of Fiddle Tunes*, *Jerry Holland: The Second Collection*, *Brenda Stubbert–The Second Collection*, *The Cape Breton Fiddlers' Collection,*

The Cape Breton Scottish Collection and *The Cape Breton Highland Collection*. Some of the volumes (notably the first of Jerry Holland's music) have been revised and reprinted a number of times. The books in this collection all have a musician-friendly, A4-portrait layout with lay-flat perfect binding; different colours on the covers distinguish between each volume. The collections carry photographs, comment on style and technique, scales and modes, as well as historical information and data on individual tunes; after volume 4, all editions show chords. A master index of all the tunes included in the series is provided on Cranford's website. Three further volumes are planned. *See* **Cranford, Paul; Cranford Publications**.

Cape Breton Post, The. For many years the only daily newspaper published on Cape Breton Island. Based in Sydney, NS, it exists as a continuation of more than 100 years of various publications that, through different amalgamations (including *The Record* and *The Post*), ended up as the current *Cape Breton Post*. It is owned by the Montréal-based Transcontinental Media Inc. While covering the main location, national and international news stories, *The Post* has, over the years, also supported the local arts and cultural scene through interviews with local artists and musicians, reviewing books, recordings and shows and including information on tours and upcoming events. In recent years, however, there has gradually ceased to be a regular reporter assigned to arts and culture and happenings within that scene; providing information on music now falls mainly to a number of regular or semi-regular columnists who report on various aspects of the music industry; these include Ken Chishom, Dan MacDonald, Laura Jean Grant and Rannie Gillis. *See* **print media**.

Cape Breton Professional Musicians Association, The (CBPMA). A musicians' union, this is a constituent unit of the American Federation of Musicians of the United States and Canada (AFM). As the largest organization of its kind in the world, AFM represents the interests of some

100,000 professional musicians across a range of genres (including alternative rock, classical, pop, gospel, jazz, country, folk, rock, big band, reggae, contemporary and Christian). The CBPMA (Local 355) was chartered on March 7, 1966. Its mandate is to protect the rights of musicians in live performance and on recorded material; it provides benefit programs to stimulate careers; it lobbies for legislation and public awareness that protect musicians' interests and monitors payment rates and working conditions for its members. The CBPMA also runs a local and federation booking/referral service, and through the larger organization there is access to an international on-line referral service, franchized booking agents, on-line resources, default claims, a pension fund, contracts information, insurance and liability information, travel insurance and immigration assistance service. Membership of the CBPMA is open to full- and part-time professional musicians. Despite the fact that a fiddler, Bernie Ley, was one of its founder members, the organization has not, however, fully connected with the local fiddle community, even though the professionalisation of the sector has increased since the 1990s.

Cape Breton Store and Tearoom, The. Located on Barrington Street, Halifax, in 1997-1998 this venue carried the invitation: "Come in for God's sake, the tea's on." It was run by Joanne Donovan, a native of Big Pond, opened in her awareness that there was no regular meeting place for the large Cape Breton community living in Halifax. Loosely modelled on Rita MacNeil's renowned Tea Room and Gift Shop in Big Pond, the store offered Cape Breton hospitality, arts, crafts and

Courtesy of Joanne Donovan.

music. With a small stage and an upright piano, in-house music sessions were hosted regularly, some scheduled, others impromptu. Musicians such as Dwyane Côté, Howie MacDonald, Ashley MacIsaac, Dave MacIsaac, John Feguson, Tracey Dares, Paul MacNeil, Hilda Chiasson, J. P. Cormier, John Allan Cameron, Slàinte Mhath and Kilt performed there; Mairi Rankin was the resident fiddler. Highlights included televised interviews and performances by Ashley MacIsaac and Howie MacDonald during the 1998 ECMAs and the presentation ceremony for an industry "Gold" CD to Paddy Moloney of The Chieftains for their *Fire in the Kitchen* album, which featured several Cape Breton fiddlers; Moloney later presented a Gold album to Donovan for her contribution to sales and support of the project.

Cape Breton Summertime Revue. *See* **Shows**.

Cape Breton Symphony Fiddlers. Formed in 1974, the Cape Breton Symphony (later renamed the Cape Breton Symphony Fiddlers) was originally a feature on *The John Allan Cameron Show*, a CTV series that showcased contemporary folk music; the group was named by the show's producer, Bill Langstroth. The show was recorded in Montréal between 1974 and 1975 (and ran as a repeat for a few years after); later, it aired out

The Cape Breton Symphony Fiddlers. L-R John Donald Cameron, Buddy MacMaster, Bobby Brown (piano), Sandy MacIntyre, Wilfred Gillis. Courtesy of the Bobby Brown Collection.

of Halifax during 1979-1980 on CBC-TV before a live audience. The show ran to 26 episodes per season; originally, the Cape Breton Symphony had a single slot per show; later, this was increased to two. A precedent for this type of ensemble already existed in Cape Breton music: the CBC TV show *Ceilidh* had introduced "The Cape Breton Fiddlers" in 1973, a group that included fiddlers such as Winnie Chafe, Theresa MacLellan, Buddy MacMaster, Dan R. MacDonald and, for a time, Sandy MacIntyre. Doug MacPhee was the piano player. "The Symphony" had four fiddlers: Winston Fitzgerald, Wilfred Gillis, John Donald Cameron and Jerry Holland; Angus Chisholm was included in the early shows. This group was accompanied by a band with piano, accordion, guitar, drums and bass. Bobby Brown, a Scottish country dance accordionist and piano player, originally from Falkirk, Scotland, was appointed by the producers as arranger and musical director of the group. From the outset, the concept, practice and production challenged the fiddlers involved. Emphasis was placed on strict ensemble playing in order to achieve a coherent unison string effect and players were expected to adhere to a given notated setting of the tune; medleys of tunes were constructed using frequent modulations rather than maintaining a single tonal area; the busy, syncopated piano stylings typical of Cape Breton were replaced by a more streamlined chording style; introductions, harmonies and various arrangements and textures were utilized; rhythms and chordal patterns were regulated by the provision of detailed chord charts. The result was a highly-polished, slick ensemble where Cape Breton tunes – often including new compositions by fiddlers such as Dan R. MacDonald – were showcased, albeit presented in a way that was somewhat unfamiliar to Cape Breton audiences. The Cape Breton Symphony Fiddlers continued their career as touring ensemble until 2003 under the management of Bobby Brown. The line-up changed over the years, with Brown and John Donald Cameron being the only two members involved for the full duration of the band's existence. Others who joined or replaced the original members included Buddy MacMaster, Sandy MacIntyre, Gordon Côté, Dave MacIsaac and Jerry Pizzarello at various points; while John Allan Cameron and occasionally others such as Dave MacIsaac and Allie Bennett provided accompaniment from time to time, for the majority of performances the back-up band was Brown's Scottish dance band, The Scottish Accent. The Symphony's recordings were released on labels such as Glencoe (John Allan Cameron's company), Brownrigg and Lismore, and they feature also on two compilations. The albums became less fiddle-centred over the years, with vocal and other instrument-led tracks reflecting the variety that the group had in its live performances. Typically, the live stage show included dance, vocals, comedy routines and fiddle solos alongside the arranged, rehearsed ensemble fiddle pieces; this was advertised as a "Scottish Fiddle and Variety Show." "Timour the Tartar" remained their signature tune, and this was used to close all of their performances. The Symphony was never especially popular in Cape Breton; however, the group did make a valuable contribution in terms of drawing attention to Cape Breton music nationally and internationally. Through it, Cape Breton fiddlers – who had previously been little known outside of Nova Scotia and its out-migration centres – were now seen on Canadian national television on popular shows such as *The Tommy Hunter Show* and *The Ronnie Prophet Show;* the Symphony also featured at the Shelburne Fiddle Contest. Bobby Brown's connections in Scotland led to the group touring there and in Ireland and Germany several times during the 1970s-1990s. Tunes written in their honour include "The Cape Breton Visit" and "The Cape Breton Return to Shetland" (both by Shetland fiddler Willie Hunter), and "Cape Breton Fiddle Magic" (by Ian Powrie). In Ireland, in particular, for many who became fans of Cape Breton music the point of introduction was the Cape Breton Symphony albums; the impact that this group had internationally cannot be underestimated. [Graham 2006]. *See* **Cameron brothers; Brown, Bobby; Brownrigg**.

Cape Breton Talent Directory. The first of its kind in Cape Breton, this was a 1974 initiative by Doug MacPhee to support the professional development of Cape Breton musicians. It carried names and contact details of musicians, singers, equipment rental agencies, set designers, square-dance callers and various halls and venues. Funded by DEVCO and the Industrial Cape Breton Board of Trade, its emphasis was on industrial Cape Breton and Inverness County. The musicians covered included 54 Scottish fiddlers, 20 of whom were in the Sydney area, and 31 piano players. There were 67 dance bands, 53 of them in Industrial Cape Breton, including The Blue Barrons, The Civil Intervention Band, Grin and Barrett, Miller's Jug, The Savoys, The Trade Winds Orchestra and the Yachts Men. Four of these bands were led by well-known Scottish fiddlers: Marie and Theresa MacLellan, The Rankin Orchestra (led by twelve-year-old John Morris Rankin), Winnie Chafe and Co., and Lee Cremo's Orchestra. Another category designated "Country and Old Time" included nine Cape Breton fiddlers, among them exponents of the local Cape Breton style, such as Lee Cremo.

Cape Breton University (CBU). Cape Breton's only post-secondary degree-granting institution. The university is enabled by the *Cape Breton University Act* passed by the Nova Scotia House of Assembly; it is an ordinary (full) member of the Association of Universities and Colleges of Canada (AUCC), the Association of Canadian Community Colleges (ACCC) and Association of Atlantic Universities (AAU), as well as an Associate Member of the Association of Commonwealth Universities (ACU). In 1951, St. Francis Xavier University, Sydney Campus (or Xavier Junior College or "Little X"), opened in downtown Sydney as a satellite campus of St. Francis Xavier University of Antigonish. In 1968, the Nova Scotia Eastern Institute of Technology (NSEIT), which focused on business technology and trades, opened just outside of Sydney. The amalgamation of both of these institutions led to the establishment of the College of Cape Breton (CCB), in 1974. In 1980, the former NSEIT campus on Grand Lake Road was expanded as the two institutions consolidated at this location. The Government of Nova Scotia granted CCB a charter for granting university degrees in 1982, which saw the institution rename itself as the University College of Cape Breton (UCCB) – the first university college in Canada. It became a public degree-granting institution, and retained technical and vocational programs from the former NSEIT together with programs in the liberal arts and sciences. In 2004, UCCB transferred its trades and technology programs to the Nova Scotia Community College (NSCC). In 2005, through the *University College of Cape Breton Act*, the name Cape Breton University (CBU) was adopted. In 2014, CBU had 4 faculties – School of Arts and Social Sciences, Shannon School of Business, School of Professional Studies and School of Science and Technology – and one affiliated college, Unama'ki College which specializes in Mi'kmaw history, culture and education. CBU is also home to the Beaton Institute (established as Cape Bretoniana in 1957), an archive which houses a substantial collection of Cape Breton fiddle music and associated documentation. The Beaton Institute continues to play a significant role in the development of Celtic music research and teaching at CBU. In 2006, the Centre for Cape Breton Studies was established.

Continuing Education (CE) was perhaps the strongest arm at CBU in the promotion of Celtic music beginning in the 1970s through until the mid-1990s. Under the leadership of its director Dr. Ora McManus CE produced and delivered a series of research projects, short talks, videos and workshops to support teaching and instruction in Celtic music and dance. Connections between Cape Breton and Scotland were a feature. A battery of initiatives and programs were introduced and led by program director Sheldon MacInnes, including a series of tribute programs to outstanding Cape Breton musicians like John Allan Cameron (1979), Dan Hughie MacEachern (1980), Buddy MacMaster (1982) and Fr. Eugene Morris (1989); social and working sessions with Gaelic-language advocates, media specialists and entre-

preneurs from the Scottish islands and highly acclaimed concerts at CBU and the Gaelic College were held during 1982-1986, several of which were recorded for local and regional CBC radio. Specialized summer courses were conducted with, among others, Scottish historian Dr. Jim Hunter (1981) and ethnomusicologist Dr. Liz Doherty, from Ireland (1996). Furthermore, non-credit courses in Cape Breton fiddle music were also sponsored by CE. Networking and promotion for multi-media initiatives that included Cape Breton segments for TV documentaries were actively supported through CE, like those produced at MITV, CTV and BBC, including: *Down Home–The Far Travelled Fiddler* (1986), *The World Celts* (1987), *The Blood is Strong* (1986), *Way Out West–The Final Fling* (1998). Similar assistance was given to Scottish touring groups like Boys of the Lough (1983), Battlefield Band (1985), Capercaillie (1985) and Ossian (1989), as well as performers in *The Road to the Isles* program: Finley J. MacDonald (narrator), Dr. Angus MacDonald (piper), Kathleen MacDonald (Gaelic vocalist) and Rhonda MacKay (harpist).

Active partnerships evolved to include The Gaelic Society of Cape Breton, An Tulloch Gorm Society and Dance Nova Scotia. Partnerships expanded into local concerts like the *Working Man Concert* (1991) in Big Pond, featuring Rita MacNeil, and the *Dancer's Dream* in Mabou (1997). Some of the proceeds from the former helped to establish a CBU scholarship program. Other activities were important to CE, including the awarding of honorary degrees to noted local musicians from the mid-1990s, including John Allan Cameron (1995) as was assistance in the production of LPs including *Gaileagan Mabou* (1989) and *Celtic Music of Cape Breton* (1985). The 1987 International Conference on Gaelic Language and Culture, organized by CE, was a significant contributor to the 1991 founding of the Gaelic Language Council of Nova Scotia. Also important to CE's goals were participation in the Cape Breton Festival held in Cork, Ireland, in 1993, acquiring *The Finlay Walker Collection* (a series paintings of Cape Breton rural Gaels by artist Ellison Robertson), and participation in the development of the Balnain/Cape Breton exhibit at Canada House, Inverness, Scotland. Media coverage for all of these programs, activities and initiatives was widespread through radio, TV and print. Support funding was received from the public as well as the private sector. By the late 1990s, however, the successful effort by Celtic Colours was well established at the community level and the focus at CBU was now on academic courses and research in Celtic music. Several academic departments participated in the development and delivery of courses that addressed Celtic music and related disciplines in the Scottish, Canadian and Cape Breton context, including credit courses in instructional fiddle, Cape Breton style; Winnie Chafe acted as associate professor of Celtic Studies for 1999-2000.

Cape Breton Studies. In 2004, Dr. Richard MacKinnon, folklorist, was awarded the prestigious Tier One Canada Research Chair in Intangible Culture. This opened opportunities for further program growth and capital expansion at CBU dedicated to support research and teaching in Celtic music and related disciplines, including the development of a state-of-the-art performance, digitization and recording centre. Shortly thereafter, a folklore studies major, the only one in the Maritimes, was developed alongside a Bachelor of Arts Community Studies in Music, with a focus on traditional music. Well-known Cape Breton fiddle music teachers, such as Kyle MacNeil from The Barra MacNeils and Stan Chapman, teach a variety of fiddle music courses for this program. Further strategic hires at the university at this time included 2 Tier Two Canada Research Chairs (CRC): Dr. Heather Sparling, (CRC in Musical Traditions), and Dr. Marcia Ostashewski, (CRC in Communities and Cultures); other posts were filled by Dr. Christopher McDonald, ethnomusicologist, who is currently working on a study of accompaniment within the Cape Breton fiddle tradition, and Dr. Ian Brodie, folkorist and specialist on oral narrative traditions. In 2006, the Center for Cape Breton Studies was formally established at the university. Meanwhile, ongoing research and collecting at the time resulted in

several exciting projects like the static exhibit at the Sydney Ports, highlighting early Cape Breton fiddle music, and the *Highland Legacy* DVD.

In addition, a short educational DVD, *Donald Angus Beaton: His Life and Music, A Music Documentary*, was produced by the CMIC in collaboration with the Centre for Cape Breton Studies. In 2009, the Centre released the book and accompanying CD *Guthan Prìseil: Guthan agus Òrain Gàidheil Cheap Breatainn / Voices and Songs of the Cape Breton Gael*, collected by Ann Landin. The Centre also collaborated with a community group to release *Lauchie Gillis, Songs of the Mira Volume 2* (2009), a collection of archival recordings of Gaelic songs. Today the Center for Cape Breton Studies engages in partnerships with community groups, the Beaton Institute archives, the university's publishing arm (CBU Press) and has an excellent team of faculty across several disciplines like ethnomusicology, folklore, and history to support teaching and research in Cape Breton and other related musics. [**Feintuch, 2010**].

Cape Breton's Magazine. A most important medium in promoting Cape Breton music and culture, this was established in 1972 by American Ron Caplan, who had recently moved to the island; Bonnie Thomson was his assistant. It began with a unique large-format (roughly tabloid) size, with up to 100 or more newsprint pages bound in a glossy cover. Four numbered issues were published each year; none were dated. The magazine encapsulated Cape Breton life and culture, past, present and future: an expression of a culture that was in transition; its masthead declared it to be "devoted to the history, natural history and future of Cape Breton Island." All of the articles were based on interviews with local people, many of them conducted by Caplan himself, transcribed verbatim and with no editorial. Articles were eclectic and quirky (e.g., "How to Make an Ax Handle," "How to Make Alexander Graham Bell's Winged-Cell Tetrahedron Kite," "The First Priest and the Indians," "Remembering Those Rum-running Days," "Evidence of Early Man on Cape Breton," "How we buried our Dead," "The 1929

Earthquake: Two Memories," "The Great Famine in Cape Breton 1845-51," "Joe Delaney and His Scarecrows," "The Four Lives of the Micmac Copper Pot"). The magazine, which was styled after the U.S. magazine *Foxfire* (started in 1966), also included many original photographs, book reviews, folklore and folktales, poems, tunes and recipes. In all, there were 74 issues of *Cape Breton's Magazine* published, if somewhat irregularly, up until its last edition, in 1998. Material from the publication is housed in the NS Public Archives, Halifax; the entire series is housed in the Beaton Institute and the entire catalogue can also be accessed online at capebretonsmagazine.com.

fiddle music and fiddlers. From the outset, *Cape Breton's Magazine* documented and profiled many aspects of the Cape Breton fiddle-music tradition. Four of its covers featured Cape Breton musicians: Lee Cremo (1), Sandy MacLean (29), Jerry Holland and Paul Cranford (48) and Estwood Davidson (54). The magazine carried several features specifically on the fiddle tradition, and others on dance, bagpipes, song, other instruments and ceilidhs (almost 50 in total over the full catalogue). In issue no. 38 (1985), the first transcriptions of tunes by Paul Cranford were included and, with that edition, the magazine issued the first of a series of commercial recordings, *Mike MacDougall's Tape for Fr. Hector;* this was followed by *Cape Breton Fiddlers on Early LPs* (1986) and by *Winston Fitzgerald: House Parties and 78s* (1987). Under the associated Breton Books imprint, publisher Ron Caplan has featured selected interviews from *Cape Breton's Magazine* in book form. One of these, *Talking Cape Breton Music–Conversations with People Who Love and Make the Music,* is dedicated to the fiddle-music tradition. In 2013, Breton Books published *Ten Nights Without Sleep,* by Dave Mahalik, an insider's perspective on Celtic Colours.

Caplan, Ron. (1945-). Publisher, writer. Pittsburgh, PA, and Wreck Cove, Cape Breton. Born and raised in the U.S., Ronald Caplan moved to Canada in 1971, one of a number of Americans who were to make Cape Breton their home in the 1970s and, ultimately, make a significant contribution to the local community and culture. He founded *Cape Breton's Magazine* in 1972, for which he interviewed and photographed people from all over Cape Breton, thus documenting a varied and vibrant culture. Caplan later founded the Breton Books imprint; this continues today, although the magazine ceased publication in 1998. Caplan was invested with an Order of Canada in 2010 in recognition of his contribution to the culture of Cape Breton Island through publishing.

Casket, The. Canada's oldest continuing weekly newspaper, established in 1852, it is the community newspaper for Antigonish town and county. Originally with four pages, half in English and half in Gaelic, it was started in Antigonish by John Boyd, a Pictou County school teacher. Idealistically envisioned as "a guardian of liberty," the paper bore the motto "Liberty the choicest gem of the Old World, and the fairest flower of the New," and its title suggested a treasure box or a container of precious things. Today a paid weekly newspaper, it reaches households in Antigonish, Guysborough, Inverness and Richmond counties; in 2013 it extended to an online edition, progressive at the time for a community newspaper; in 2012 it was purchared by Brace Capital Ltd., owners of Halifax's daily newspaper, the *Chronicle Herald.* Reflecting – and promoting – its social remit, *The Casket,* like other local and regional presses, is a vital source of information on music, dance and other cultural and artistic activities through advertising, previews, review and reporting. In the past it has carried advertising for instruments, and for music books available otherwise only in the U.S., as well as event notices, opinion, and musicians' obituaries. *See* **print media**.

CBC (Canadian Broadcasting Corporation). A crown corporation responsible to, but independent of, the Canadian government, it was inaugurated in 1936, successor to the CRBC, with various regional production centres, including Halifax. Its function is to broadcast Canadian-produced programs, but it also made a number of acetate disc recordings of historic interest (such as speeches); these were not catalogued or archived until 1959. The network decided in 1945 to record artists for distribution to affiliate radio stations in an attempt to increase Canadian content in broadcasting; Cape Breton fiddlers Winnie Chafe and Buddy MacMaster were among the first to be recorded to this end. In 1947, Radio Canada International (RCI) was set up to provide recordings of Canadian performances to foreign audiences, but in 1966, in response to growing demand for distinctly Canadian music performances, CBC began issuing its recordings commercially. With the expansion of telecommunications after the Second World War, CBC-TV was established by the corporation in 1954. *See* **Canadian Radio Broadcasting Commission; CBC Radio; CBC-TV.**

CBC Radio. The CBC Radio Broadcasting Commission (CRBC) was formed in 1932 and supported a series of small production centers in many locations across the country, distributing programs to private stations. CBC Radio took over from the CRBC in 1936, with Halifax as a regional production centre. The network expanded dramatically in April 1939, which enabled it to be heard throughout the Maritimes. It maintained two networks, Dominion (which included one CBC station in Toronto and 34 private affiliate stations) and the Trans Canada Network (which provided programming to CBC-owned and operated stations). In 1948, CBI Sydney went on the air producing local newscasts and providing programming to the network and regional services; based in Sydney, its reach did not service the whole island; still, it played an important role in encouraging local programming – specifically fiddle music – during the 1970s particularly. CBC produced a number of programs during the 1950s and 1960s which were popular and hugely influential across the country, among them *Don Messer's Jubilee*. However, the advent of television in 1954 impacted negatively on the popularity of radio and eventually forced a revival campaign in the late 1960s and early 1970s, which emphasized local programming. From this, several significant programs featuring Cape Breton fiddle music were produced. *Mac Talla an Eilean* (*Island Echoes*) was first aired on May 8, 1971, for 15 minutes, an outcome of a campaign to encourage CBC to broadcast a Gaelic program in order to build on connections already made with the BBC in Scotland; this show continues today (now as *Island Echoes*), hosted by Wendy Bergfeldt, and is broadcast on Saturday evenings for one hour. Perhaps the most significant CBC program for Cape Breton fiddle music during the 1970s and 1980s was *Talent Cape Breton*, a showcase of local musicians. The program helped launch the professional careers of many Cape Breton artists by introducing their music to regional and national audiences. The program was the brainchild of CBC Cape Breton station manager Bert Wilson (brother-in-law to Ray "Mac" MacDonald.) He wanted a show that would highlight the variety of talent that was emerging on the island. All genres, including fiddle music, were represented. Twice a year producer Brian Sutcliffe would hold open auditions, and from that process was able to plan his season's recording sessions. At its height, *Talent Cape Breton* recorded over 100 artists every year, sharing much of the tape with regional and national shows across the CBC network. Out of that success, CBC Cape Breton created a specialty program mandated to highlight Cape Breton's Scottish culture exclusively. *Archie Neil's Cape Breton* (1979-1983) focused not only on fiddle music, but storytelling and other elements of the oral tradition that host Archie Neil Chisholm deftly translated into a radio format. The show recreated a ceilidh atmosphere and was recorded at Archie Neil's home in Margaree Forks. The show was so successful that in its final season it became a national show, heard by Canadians from coast to coast. CBC was also responsible for a number of special broadcasts such as the New Year's Eve live ceilidhs broadcast for four consecutive years from 1976-1977 to 1980-1981. Brian Sutcliffe produced the broadcast for all of Canada from the Confederation Room in the old Isle Royal Hotel in Sydney. These 90-minute shows featured musicians such as the Sons of Skye, Carl MacKenzie, Winnie Chafe and Doug MacPhee. In 1978, the first ever trans-Atlantic Ceilidh was produced jointly by BBC Scotland and CBC Sydney, and featured the Sons of Skye, with Gaelic songs by Fr. Allan MacMillan and stories by Joe Neil MacNeil and Donald MacEachern from the Gaelic Society of Cape Breton. While CBC certainly made a valuable contribution to the Cape Breton fiddle tradition, providing exposure to the fiddle players and to key events, there were some challenges to be overcome, especially since, after the cancellation of *Talent Cape Breton*, Halifax was the choice location for recording live shows rather than Sydney. Furthermore, radio transmitters in Antigonish and Guysborough on the mainland broadcast only the Halifax service to those areas and to parts of southern Cape Breton, including Inverness County. However, a number of individuals who worked for the CBC were significant in maintaining positive relations with the fiddle community and worked tirelessly to achieve satisfactory levels of engagement. Throughout the 1970s and 1980s, Brian Sutcliffe produced virtually every music and variety show on the air. Later, Joella Foulds, a long-time host of CBC Cape Breton's *Information Morning* program, highlighted a wide variety of cultural activities on the island. At the regional level, Natalie MacMaster and Max MacDonald hosted *Atlantic Airwaves* and the *Kitchen Party*, respectively. While both shows were produced in Halifax by Glenn Meisner in the late 1990s and early 2000s, each had a distinctly Cape Breton flavour and were often heard by listeners as "local" productions. On CBC Radio One, Cape Breton, Wendy Bergfeldt continues to host *Mainstreet Cape Breton*, which highlights local talent through interviews and live recording sessions. Since 1997, her live *Mainstreet Sessions* runs concurrent to the Celtic Colours Festival and is broadcast the same day it is recorded. These programs are offered online nationally and internationally throughout the season. She also often produces shows featuring Cape Breton performers in partnership with other broadcasters, including the BBC, which air in the U.K. and other international media markets. *See* **Bergfeldt, Wendy;** *Island Echoes;* **radio**.

CBC-TV. The dominant TV provider in Eastern Canada, from the outset its primary objective was to combat the cultural intrusion of broadcasting from the U.S.; thus, when CBC-TV's new production centre opened in Halifax in 1954, the focus was on recording and reflecting the society of the Maritimes. An entertainment and documentary programming schedule was developed to target a mix of national, regional and local audiences. One of the network's success stories was *Don Messer's Jubilee*, broadcast nationwide from 1957 to 1969. This show presented New Brunswick fiddler Don Messer with a professional back-up band; various guests were then introduced. This show set new standards, both in fiddle-playing and in how it was presented. While its direct impact on Cape Breton fiddle music was limited (indeed, the only Cape Breton fiddlers invited to appear on the show were Bernie Ley and Joe MacDougall, Winston Fitzgerald and Jerry Holland) it did influence developments within the tradition. Likely it was the slick performance style and ensemble presentation used on *Don Messer's Jubilee* that influenced the formation of such fiddle bands as that formed for the *Ceilidh* show and The Cape Breton Symphony Fiddlers, both in the 1970s. CBC also invested in the production of documentaries and live broadcasts which focused on various aspects of Maritime life, all of which are relevant to music in society. Early shows included *Heritage* (1954 to 1986) and *Country Calendar* (1952), which expanded in 1967 to include a fishery element called *Fisherman's Log;* this became *Land and Sea* in 1970, and continues today. For these and other shows, such as *Telescope, 20-20, Take Thirty* and *Here and There*, filming crews from Halifax often found themselves in Cape Breton seeking rural coverage for special features on topics like the Cabot Trail populace, the Gaelic College, Alexander Graham Bell and the *Bluenose*. It was perhaps inevitable, therefore, that the focus of transition and decline in Maritime life would note the Cape Breton fiddle tradition. Thus, in 1971, CBC-TV produced the documentary *The Vanishing Cape Breton Fiddler*, which suggested that the Cape Breton fiddle tradition was in danger of disappearing since it was not being handed down to current generations. This provoked fiddle-music enthusiasts who, in their quest to refute these claims, set in motion a revival that has had significant consequences down to the present day. CBC-TV later broadcast two documentaries produced by Ron MacInnis, who had been the writer and commentator on the VCBF, showing his efforts in the 1980s to mount a show with the CBFA. In 2001, a 10-minute documentary was presented on the CBC-TV show *Country Canada–The Fate of the Fiddle,* produced by Marie Thompson; this was expanded in 2002 to a half-hour show, *The Wakeup Call.* CBC itself joined in the resurgence of interest in the Cape Breton fiddle tradition and, from 1972 to 1974, produced *Ceilidh.* Initially presented by John Allan Cameron, this show achieved a primetime, Saturday slot on CBC-TV's national network, just prior to the high-ratings *Hockey Night in Canada.* In 1979, Cameron returned with his own *John Allan Cameron Show* (which had previously had a successful season on CTV, Montréal), featuring the Cape Breton Symphony Fiddlers, a show produced in Halifax until 1981. During the 1970s, local producers at CBC-TV Sydney undertook to seek out talent and create opportunities for established and emerging artists and also invested considerable time and money scouting Cape Breton in search of talent. Fred Martin and Peter MacNeil, who had worked on shows such as *Don Messer's Jubilee* and *Singalong Jubilee,* were particularly interested in the Cape Breton story and travelled in 1975 to Scotland to record with Alasdair Gillies. They also spent at least three weeks in Cape Breton each summer recording various concerts, including the Glendale Fiddler's Festivals; these were broadcast as 2 one-hour TV shows: *In Your Footsteps* and *A Heritage Remembered.* In 1977, their other recordings were edited into five weekly programs titled *Showcase.* In addition to national network programs from 1972 CBC-TV's local Sydney station not only broadcast local news and entertainment programming to the island, but, eventually, also featured local artists. Cape Breton fiddle players occasionally appear on mainstream TV broadcasting, but a number of programs and documentaries have specifically been produced to profile them, including "specials" such as those celebrating the likes of the Barra MacNeils and Natalie MacMaster. (*With* **WB**). [**Harper 2002**] *See* **Ceilidh; John Allan Cameron Show; television; Vanishing Cape Breton Fiddler.**

ceilidh. Coming from the Gaelic word meaning "to visit," a ceilidh refers to a social gathering typically involving informal entertainment (music, song, dance, storytelling) and conversation, and with refreshments being served. In earlier times, the ceilidh house was an educational institution, though lacking the formalities of official schools. To maintain learning, people came together in each other's homes to create, reproduce, transmit and celebrate their cultural inheritance. A ceilidh is a private event to which people are invited; the entertainment is programmed to a degree, where the host (a key participant requiring a skill set) or nominated person keeps the entertainment flowing, ensuring that all the artists present have a chance to perform.

house ceilidh. A house ceilidh might be planned around a specific event or celebration such as the day after a wedding, the return of an emigrant for a vacation, following a local concert, or to mark special days of celebration (New Years, birthdays). The ceilidh, until the late 20th century, happened exclusively in a home environment, and particular homes became known as popular venues for this type of event. This was often connected to the fact that they had a resident artist/ performer (instrumentalist and/or vocalist) – either a family member or a travelling musician who had arrived for an extended stay; as pump organs, and later pianos, became popular, the houses where these instruments were available became popular for ceilidhs. Ceilidhs might have upward of 50 people in attendance, many of them travelling long distances to attend. A supper – usually an extensive spread – would be served a few hours into the festivities. *See* **house party; house session; kitchen racket.**

public ceilidh. For many visitors to Cape Breton, however, the house ceilidhs, where arguably much of the finest music and dance took place, was somewhat elusive; it operated on a local invite system and thus was beyond the reach of "outsiders." Visitors were often aware of the fact that they were somehow missing out on a vibrant strand of the culture: a "hidden" Cape Breton, so to speak, where the authentic Cape Breton experience existed, and to which as outsiders they were not privy. The public ceilidh in Cape Breton is a response to the identified needs of tourists seeking culture; this represents a compromise between the house ceilidh and the more formal presentational concert and the participatory square-dance contexts. As such, the ceilidh is a semi formal concert. A typical ceilidh might last for a couple of hours, a small admission fee is charged and a light supper may be served. A host fiddler will play, talk to the audience and offer some historical and social background to the music and dance; there may or may not be an opportunity for participation in the form of a square set. Typically, besides the house musicians, other local guests are featured; occasionally, a visiting musician may be invited to perform. This type of ceilidh is intended to be more intimate than a concert, allowing the audience to get some sense of the "real" tradition. For the artists involved, these commercial, tourist-oriented ceilidhs offer a regular, seasonal source of income and a public platform on which younger, emerging musicians can hone their craft. Ceilidhs of this type abound during the summer season and are regular fixtures in the Cape Breton cultural calendar. Among the most established are those held in Baddeck (Baddeck Gathering Ceilidhs), Inverness (Inverness Firehall Ceilidhs), Port Hood (Dockside Ceilidh and Chestico Museum), North Sydney (Ferry Terminal Dockside Ceilidhs), Glendale (Kitchen Ceilidhs at the Fr. John Angus Rankin Cultural Centre), Mabou (Summer Ceilidh Series at An Droichead/The Bridge Museum and the Tuesday Ceilidhs at the Community Hall), St. Ann's (The Gaelic College), Port Hawkesbury (Creamery) and Judique (Judique Community Centre and the CMIC, the latter the only venue which maintains weekly, year-round ceilidhs). A second type of public ceilidh that has become popular since the 1980s, takes the form of the Irish-style session

and tends to be referred to as such; the session, distinguished by its ensemble participation, may be found in a small number of venues (including pubs, gastro-pubs and community halls) around the island, having started originally at house or private ceilidhs in the Northside area. [**Doherty 1996; Feintuch 2010; Graham 2006; Lavengood 2008; MacInnes 1997; Newton 2015**]; *See* **concert; matinee; session**.

Ceilidh. **(a)** A 1972-1974 CBC-TV show featuring Cape Breton and, later, Scottish musicians. Screened in a prime-time Saturday slot on CBC-TV's national network just prior to the high-ratings *Hockey Night in Canada*, it was produced by Charlie Reynolds, who had previously worked on *The Vanishing Cape Breton Fiddler. Ceilidh* was initially a regional, hour-long production hosted by a kilted John Allan Cameron, who introduced a variety of guest musicians, singers and dancers. He was replaced, however, by Scotsman Alasdair Gillies, and increasingly the guests were from overseas. Some prominent Cape Breton fiddlers were involved, among them Winnie Chafe, Buddy MacMaster, Dan R. MacDonald, Theresa MacLellan, John Campbell and Cameron Chisholm. They were encouraged to perform in an ensemble context, under the direction of Winnie Chafe, and to work out groups of tunes that were timed and rehearsed—something that was quite new to the players at the time. The show was discontinued after a couple of seasons. *See* **CBC-TV**.

(b) A popular and influential radio show presented by Ray "Mac" MacDonald on CJFX through the 1980s and 1990s; it continued after his retirement in 1999 with other hosts such as Jon Matthews; Barry MacKinnon has been the presenter for several years. The show has become a weekly rather than a nightly show and is broadcast on Sunday evenings on air and online. *Ceilidh* is also referred to colloquially as as "CJFX Ceilidh" and "Celtic Ceilidh."

Ceilidh Trail School of Celtic Music, The. This was founded in 1996 by Janine Randall, a piano player from Boston, MA, whose parents were both musicians from Cape Breton. Inspired by the story of Fr. McDwyer, who had capitalized on the cultural tourism potential of Glencolumcille (a small, Irish-speaking region in southwest Donegal, Ireland) by foregrounding indigenous cultural activities, she brought her business training and acumen to bear on developing a music school as an alternative to the Gaelic College at St. Ann's. She established this on the tourism-designated "Ceilidh Trail," in a property outside of Inverness town purchased from the local council and parish on condition that it be developed as a cultural centre. Randall used her own funds to renovate the building into a five-room teaching site and, with Jerry Holland as musical director for the first year of the project, she developed a program of instruction in fiddle, piano, guitar and step dance. This represented a "first" for Cape Breton in that, alongside established Cape Breton artists, she invited teachers from Scotland, Ireland and the U.S. to become involved. The school's first year was hugely ambitious, and featured tutors Buddy MacMaster, Natalie MacMaster, Jerry Holland, Brenda Stubbert, Tracey Dares, Dave MacIsaac, Hilda Chiasson, Harvey Beaton, Melody Warner Cameron, Ashley MacIsaac, Gordon Côté, Allan Dewar, John Pellerin, Mary Jessie Gillis, Joel Chiasson, Gordie Sampson, Mary Janet MacDonald, J. P. Cormier, Stephanie Wills, Richard Wood, John McCusker, Brendan Mulvihill, Jesse Smith, James Kelly, Zan McLeod, Donna Long, Dermot McLaughlin, Liz Doherty and Máire O'Keeffe. In time, the student numbers stabilized and, over the following summers, the school adopted a more intensive approach, prioritizing the Cape Breton element of the tuition and consequently gaining a strong international profile. The Ceilidh Trail School has been cited as a model for other teaching programs, notably the Southern Hemisphere School of Scottish Fiddle, founded in New Zealand by Australian fiddle player, Catherine Fraser. In 2007, when Randall retired from the project, the venue moved to the Inverness Academy; Jerry Holland was designated co-director between 2007 and 2009, along with Roberta Head. Head continued the school after Holland died in 2009; his son,

Jerry Holland Jr. became co-director. The school was discontinued the following year. *See* **music schools**.

Celtic Colours International Festival. Established in 1997, and now the largest annual festival in Cape Breton, Celtic Colours was conceived by Joella Foulds and Max MacDonald. The organizers' plan was to create a festival in Cape Breton of similar scope and standard as the Celtic Connections Festival in Glagow, yet which would be integrated into the predominately rural and dispersed Cape Breton society as opposed to the big-city event it was in Scotland. Celtic Colours is a non-profit organization registered under the *Societies Act* of Nova Scotia, overseen by a board of directors and managed by a small, year-round core staff. From April, this team expands to include term and box office staff, and finally, close to the event, festival volunteers are recruited and trained. The festival has won culture and tourism awards, and has come to be cited as a prime example of a successful cultural tourism event. It has also been used as a model for the development of festivals in other parts of the world, such as the Blas Festival in Scotland and Cape Cod Celtic in the U.S.

growth. Celtic Colours' mission is to promote, celebrate and develop Cape Breton music in a way that builds cultural and economic relationships. Festival programming is guided by its mission statement's artistic vision, and begins with the selection of artists based upon the criteria of excellence and Celtic origin. It takes place over nine days each October in multiple venues, all over Cape Breton Island, ranging in size from a 2,000-seat arena to 120-seat community halls and in schools. The festival has grown steadily since its inception, beginning with 26 performances and 22 workshops hosted in 25 community groups. By 2013, this had grown to 46 performances and 234 other cultural events hosted by 115 community groups. Ticket sales were 11,770 in 1997. By 2013, this had increased to 18,753, or 84% of the available tickets. The major growth has been in community events (square dances, sessions and suppers) and educational programs. Allowing for year-to-year fluctuation, typically the audience is 45% local with the balance from off-island – including all regions of Canada, the U.S. and over 20 other countries. Celtic Colours visitors contribute more than $8 million to the Cape Breton economy annually which, due to the decentralization of events, is spread widely throughout the island among tourism, hospitality, service and retail sectors, and constitutes important revenue streams for the largely rural communities. Close to 500 performers participate in Celtic Colours each year, 75% of them from Cape Breton. A wide variety of not-for-profit community groups host events and provide the 1,700 volunteers who each contribute in the region of 37 hours of work. An important part of this is transporting artists; this is the responsibility of the Volunteer Drive'ers Association, who also manage merchandising of artists' CDs and host a number of awards and bursaries.

participation. A themed approach to the programming was adopted in 2009. In that year it was "The Irish are Coming," with other foci in subsequent years including "Appalachian and Cajun Connections" and "Nordic Links." Concerts are also themed, and typically feature several acts. Major international artists who have performed over the years, include: Capercaillie, Blazin' Fiddles, Alasdair Fraser, Phil Cunningham and Aly Bain, from Scotland; The Chieftains, Sharon Shannon, Altan, and Bumblebees, from Ireland; Carlos Nunez from Galicia; Väsen from Sweden; and Harald Haugaard from Denmark. Opportunities for collaborative creation are encouraged, and often emerge from the artist-in-residence program, which each year since 2001 has featured a Cape Breton artist and an international artist. The festival also has a couple of "special projects" each year, which have included commissions such as *Suite Silver Dart* by Scott Macmillan and *The Fiddletree Project* by Otis Tomas. A youth outreach program engages with schools presenting educational programs and performances at all grade levels. This was developed in spite of several years in which provincial education policy discouraged non-curriculum activities in schools. Other youth outreach activities over the years have included a showcase called The Archie Neil Youth Stage. Another event, the International Festival Presenters and Media Program, facilitates international delegates to attend the festival with a view to inviting Cape Breton performers to participate in their own events abroad. Regarded as the heart and soul of Celtic Colours is the Festival Club, which is held nightly at The Gaelic College in St. Ann's. Here artists and audiences connect after the formal concerts. A four-hour event hosted by singer-songwriter Buddy MacDonald, musicians perform solo, with their bands, and in spontaneous collaborations. A backstage green room, open to artists only, provides a creative stimulus out of which have come several new bands, including Beòlach. The seeds of many new artistic collaborations have happened as a result of late-night sessions at the Festival Club.

other activities. During the festival itself, beginning in 2011, several shows are streamed live to the Internet. CBC hosts a daily live radio show from Baddeck throughout the festival featuring artists performing and interviewing with host Wendy Bergfeldt. In 2011, a book was produced to celebrate the festival's 15th anniversary: The *Celtic Colours Collection* features compositions, both songs and tunes, that were created by festival artists either as a result of, or inspired by, the festival. Annual compilation CDs featuring artists from each years program were produced from the early years. In 2013, ten concerts were recorded in multi-track and a compilation CD of live music from the festival was produced for the first time. In 2014, a series of video podcasts devised by Celtic Colours in association with CBU was presented on the festival website offering further contextual insights into Cape Breton culture via interviews with local fiddlers and other artists. Also in 2014, *Ten Nights Without Sleep*, a book of stories and experiences from the early days of Celtic Colours, was published by author and staff member Dave Mahalik. **[Ivakhiv 2005; Mahalik 2014].** *See* **Festival Volunteer Drive'ers Association.**

―❧―

The Celtic Colours Collection. Tunes and Songs Celebrating the First 15 years of Cape Breton's Annual festival. Published in 2011, this book has 112 pages with 60 new tunes and 22 songs, all of which were composed as part of, or in response to, experiences at Celtic Colours. The 45 composers are, variously, from Cape Breton, Scotland, Ireland, England and Shetland, and include many of the best-known names in music, among them Andrea Beaton, Dawn Beaton, Kinnon Beaton, Margie Beaton, Rose Cousins, Paul Cranford, Phil Cunningham, Rachel Davis, Goiridh Dòmhnallach, Archie Fisher, David Francey, Colin Grant, John Grant, Martin Green, Dave Gunning, Corrina Hewat, Jerry Holland, James Keeleghan, Nuala Kennedy, Daniel Lapp, Catriona MacDonald, Dougie MacDonald, Steven MacDougall, Fiona MacGillivray, Troy MacGillivray, Wendy MacIsaac, Kenneth MacKenzie, Rosie MacKenzie, Dougie MacLean, John MacLean, Scott Macmillan, Ryan J. MacNeil, Catriona McKay, Carmel Mikol, David Milligan, Malcolm Munro, Brian Ó hEadhra, Aidan O'Rourke, Karine Polwart, Jason Roach, Gordie Sampson, Carleton Stone, Chris Stout, Brenda Stubbert, Otis Tomas and Lori Watson. The introduction is by Joella Foulds, artistic director of Celtic Colours, the foreword is by Paul Cranford, and there is a composer listing and an alphabetical list of tune titles. Biographical data is given for composers, and contextual festival information by Dawn Beaton, Dave Mahalik, Joella Foulds and Paul Cranford is interspersed among the tunes along with archive photographs.

―❧―

Celtic music. The 1990s gave rise to a commercial phenomenon that was dubbed "Celtic music," effectively folk and traditional musics from countries (and their diasporas) that could, by reasons underpinned by language and heritage, be marketed collectively under a single label; as the term generated a viable commodity the legitimacy criteria became increasingly nebulous and, in many ways, is indeed a misnomer in relation to the music traditions it supposedly reflects. "Celtic" had rarely been used by musicians in Cape Breton up until this time, although it had appeared in relation to specific businesses such as the Celtic Music Store and the Celtic record label in Antigonish (indeed, others used it too although spelled with a "K" (e.g., Keltic Lodge, Keltic Motors). In the 1990s, however, as the Celtic fashion infiltrated Cape Breton as it did elsewhere, and as the flow of music traffic between Cape Breton and other Celtic music centres significantly increased, the term was appropriated in various contexts. For events (e.g., Celtic Colours) and activities such as fiddle programs (e.g., Ceilidh Trail School of Celtic Music), the addition of the word Celtic increased marketability; similarly, the use of the term helped position Cape Breton music securely alongside long-recognized music traditions. Around 2000, a new hybrid dance form was developed in Cape Breton, referred to as Celtic step dance, this involving a fusion of Cape Breton step dance, Irish and Highland dance. Since the late 1990s, the term's use has levelled off in relation to fiddle music; over the past decade the term Gaelic has come to be more frequently appropriated in categorizing and promoting the fiddle music. **[Hennessy 2008; Lavengood 2008].**

Celtic Music Interpretive Centre (CMIC). Located in Judique and opened in 2006, this was the outcome of a project by a dedicated group of volunteers, supported by the Municipality of Inverness, which sought to establish a gathering place and performance and information centre for Cape Breton music and culture. Initially located in the local community centre, keen interest and engagement from the outset made it apparent that larger, purpose-designed facilities were needed, this leading to the present 465 m² (5,000 ft²) building. The CMIC is a not-for-profit society and a one-of-a-kind facility in Canada. The centre's mandate is to collect, preserve and promote the traditional Celtic music of Cape Breton through education, research and performance. The CMIC offers an in-depth look into the history, culture and music of Cape Breton Island and received designation from the Nova Scotia Legislature in 2013 as "The Official Celtic Music Centre of Nova Scotia." The Centre offers year-round ceilidhs of live traditional music, educational workshops in fiddle, piano and dance and Scottish-Gaelic language immersion classes; the week-long Buddy MacMaster School of Fiddling is held there each October during Celtic Colours. The CMIC has a growing collection of archival materials and a resource library, a recording studio, an interactive exhibit room (The Tom Rankin Exhibit Room), a full-service restaurant and bar, a gift shop and an on-line store offering locally made products. CMIC runs research projects and has an evolving, online database of artist profiles as well as The Donald Angus Beaton project, which is documenting the life and music of the Mabou fiddler; it has also been responsible for several compilation CDs of Cape Breton fiddle music (the *Failte* series). Managed by a volunteer board, which includes a number of local musicians, its executive director between June 2006 and February 2013 was fiddler, Kinnon Beaton; its current (2015) executive director is Cheryl Smith and music director is Allan Dewar (since 2009). In 2015, the CMIC, along with Celtic Colours, launched the Féis Movement, Féis Cheap Breatuinn, as an initiative to support the transmission of the fiddle music and its performance environment for current and future generations.

Celtic Records. A record label started by Bernie MacIsaac in the early 1930s and operated from his Celtic Music Store on Main Street in Antigonish. There he was selling spring-wound phonographs but had no recordings of local artists to offer consumers, becoming inspired to become the first local record company to produce Cape Breton fiddle recordings. MacIsaac brokered a deal with the independent Compo company in Montréal, who recorded and pressed the recordings, and in 1935 he escorted the first local artists, fiddlers Dan J. Campbell, Angus Chisholm and Angus Allan

Gillis, with Mrs. W. J. (Bess Sidall) MacDonald on piano, to Montréal to record. This was a milestone in Cape Breton fiddle music, the first instance of a Cape Breton fiddler having recorded in Canada. In the course of that pioneer trip they recorded 20 selections for ten 78-rpm discs. One hundred copies of the first release were pressed and sold for 75 cents each from MacIsaac's Antigonish store and through his own distribution network, which involved him travelling around Nova Scotia, including to Cape Breton, selling discs to various outlets; later, in response to demand, 1,000 copies of each new release were ordered at a time. MacIsaac returned to Montréal on a second occasion with two Antigonish fiddlers, Hugh A. MacDonald and Wilfred Gillis. In 1960, Bernie MacIsaac sold the Celtic label and all the masters to George Taylor of Rodeo Records, who continued with the label until the late 1970s. In total, Celtic Records produced fifty-one 78s, one 45-rpm and 40 LPs of Cape Breton music. Artists included Winston Fitzgerald, Angus Chisholm, Bernie Ley and Joe MacDougall, the Five MacDonald Fiddlers, Dan R. MacDonald, "Little" Jack MacDonald, Dan Joe MacInnis, Joe MacIsaac, Joe MacLean, The MacLellan Trio, Jimmie MacLellan, Elmer Briand, Johnny Wilmot, Dan J. Campbell, Angus Chisholm, Angus Allan Gillis, Bill Lamey and Paddy LeBlanc.

Celtic Serenade. A broadcast of Gaelic, traditional and folk music from Cape Breton, Ireland and Scotland, from CJCB Radio, Sydney. Hosted for the first year by Sheldon MacInnes the show was passed over in 1975 to Donnie Campbell who, more than 40 years on, continues to host and produce it. The show is prepared and recorded by Campbell in his home studio and airs on Sundays from 6-9 p.m.; its also available online through the CJCB website. *See* **Campbell, Donnie; radio**.

Celtic Umbrella Ensemble, The. This was founded in 2011 to showcase the variety of instrumental and vocal music from the Maritimes, Ireland, Scotland and Scandinavia, which shapes sound and performance practice in contemporary Nova

Scotia. An occasional band with a fluid membership, to date it has included Gillian Boucher from Cape Breton (fiddle, step dance), Anna Ludlow from Antigonish (fiddle), Mary Beth Carty from Antigonish (accordion, guitar, percussion), Ward MacDonald from PEI (fiddle) and Cassie and Maggie MacDonald from Halifax (piano, fiddle, vocals, step dance); Seph Peters played guitar, banjo and mandolin. These artists represent a range of regional music traditions; their common interest is exploration of repertoire, arrangement and instrumentation in connected traditions. To date they have experimented with instrumental and vocal solos (in English, Gaelic and French), twin fiddles and piano, banjo and fiddle; a cappella harmonies; and tag-team-style step-dancing. The group has performed at festivals in the Maritimes and in Québec.

Centre 200. Cape Breton's largest sports and entertainment facility, it was conceived as a bicentennial project to celebrate the 200th anniversary of the founding of Sydney (1785). Constructed on the site of the old Sydney Forum in the downtown area, the venue opened in early 1987, with a concert by Bryan Adams. A versatile convention, exhibition, sports and entertainment facility, it has the capacity to accommodate up to 6,500 people. Aside from ice hockey, the centre hosts concerts, among them to date performances by Rita MacNeil, John Prine and The Rankin Family. Owned by the Cape Breton Regional Municipality, the centre is also seen as valuable to traditional music professionalism in its role as a venue used by Celtic Colours and the ECMAs.

Ceòlas. Annual one-week music and dance summer school held in the Gaidhealteachd area of South Uist, Scotland, it uniquely focuses on the connections between Scottish and Cape Breton traditions. The curriculum covers Gaelic language, piping (both *ceòl mor* and *ceòl beag*), instrumental dance music and dancing. A holistic teaching approach encourages students to engage in a range of art forms in order to fully understand the connectedness of language, music and dance.

It was founded in 1996 by piper Hamish Moore, who was convinced that Cape Breton musicians represented a link to traditions long forgotten in Scotland; since it's inception, the tutors have been a mix of Cape Breton and Scottish, with many fiddlers such as Joe Peter MacLean having a long-standing involvement in the project.

CFMA. The Canadian Folk Music Awards. *See* **awards**.

Chafe, Winnie and Pat. From Glace Bay, the Chafe's music lineage goes back several generations to the MacMullin settlers at Beaver Cove, near Boisdale, during the 1840s. Rod MacMullin (1912-1986), from Frenchvale, was a fiddle player; he married Christina MacDonald, from Judique, whose family tree included many well known Cape Breton musicians such as John Allan Cameron, Dan R. MacDonald and Buddy MacMaster. Theirs was a popular music house with many musicians visiting often; their daughters Winnifred "Winnie" (Chafe) is a noted exponent of the Cape Breton violin and daughter Ann (Boozan) is a champion piper.

Chafe, Winnie. (1936-). Fiddle, teacher. One of the first female fiddle players from Cape Breton to achieve prominence and often referred to as "Cape Breton's First Lady of Scottish Music" she has a distinct voice within the tradition, her sound and practice showing a combination of Cape Breton, post-Skinner Scottish and classical violin traditions. Born to parents Rod and Christina (MacDonald) MacMullin, as a young girl she heard Bill Lamey, Angus Chisholm, Joe Confiant and Johnny Wilmot, who visited her maternal grandfather's home. Her formal music education began with Prof. James MacDonald in North Sydney, and continued each Sunday for five years after the family moved to Glace Bay. Her music education was brought further by Sr. Louise Frances Reardon, a classical violinist and pianist; at 16, Winnie was performing as first violinist with the Cape Breton Orchestra; later in her career she was concert mistress with the Cape Breton Chamber Orchestra. Following her graduation from teacher's college she married Mike

Winnie Chafe at the 2015 Canadian Grand Masters National Fiddling Championships, where she received a "Lifetime Achievement Award." Courtesy of the Chafe family.

Chafe, a banker, travelling with him to live in Ottawa, Toronto, New York and Los Angeles, where he was variously posted. During this 10-year sojourn Winnie developed her music career, being lead violinist in the Ventura County Symphony Orchestra, California, and appearing on national television in the U.S. Settling back in Glace Bay, she taught grade school as well as teaching music and performing. Involved in many contests, she was the first woman to win the International Old Time Fiddle Contest in Pembroke, ON, in 1964; she later judged at the Canadian Grand Masters Fiddling Championship and at the Maritime Old Time Fiddling Contest. From 1972 to 1974 she worked on CBC-TV's *Ceilidh* program, arranging music for the fiddle ensemble. Her commercial recordings include *Highland Melodies of Cape Breton* (1979), *Cape Breton Scottish Memories (1979)*, *The Bonnie Lass of Headlake* (n.d.), *Echoes* (2002) and *Legacy (1996)*. Most tracks feature her daughter, Pat, on piano; she also released a compilation CD, *The Collective Works of Winnie Chafe*.

Winnie's albums show an individual approach to Cape Breton and Scottish music, a sound she developed from fusing classical training and technique with traditional repertoire, marked in her penchant for slow airs. Throughout her career

as a music teacher she believed in introducing classical violin techniques, posture and training methods into Cape Breton and Scottish music instruction, and she developed a specific methodology to facilitate this. She taught for many years at the Adult Vocational Training Centre in Sydney and for the Cape Breton/Regional School Board from 2004-2011, as well as in Port Hawkesbury; from 1999-2000 she was associate professor of Celtic Studies at CBU. Between 1977 and 1986 she produced a weekly series of summer concerts at the Savoy Theatre in Glace Bay; titled *Ceilidh*, each concert was built around the theme of a specific music gathering, such as a wedding or kitchen party; the series won several awards over its run, including Nova Scotia Event of the Year. Her student performance groups included the Cape Breton Strathspey and Reel Fiddle Society (a group of fiddlers, aged 9-62 years), who in 1975 were invited to perform in Edinburgh Castle for the inauguration of a chair and Centre of Canadian Studies at Edinburgh University. An ambassador for Cape Breton music, she has been invited to perform at prestigious events in Scotland and England, as well in Canada; a selection of her recordings were among the gifts from Canada to Pope John Paul II to mark the canonization of St. Marguerite Bourgeoys in 1982. Among her formal accolades for her contribution to music are: doctorates from St. FX (1986) and UCCB (1995), the "Cultural Life Award–Outstanding Professional Artist" (from the Cultural Federations of NS, 1993), and "Business Woman of the Year," from the Professional Women's Club of Canada. Indeed, such has been her repute that the Canadian Navy recognized her, in 1993, as official sponsor of the Maritime Coastal Defence Vessel HMCS *Glace Bay*. In 2015, Winnie Chafe became the first woman to be presented with the "Lifetime Achievement Award" at the Grand Masters National Fiddling Championships. [**MacGillivray 1981**].

Chafe, Patricia (Pat). (1960-). Piano, composer. Born in Brooklyn, NY, to Canadian parents Michael and Winnie Chafe, she was raised in Glace Bay, where she continues to live. Her mother is a renowned violinist, her father played accordion, her grandfather was a fiddler, and her aunt was a world-champion piper. Pat's formal music training and experiences were in western art music—lessons and grade exams—until the age of 17, competing in festivals and recitals associated with the Royal Conservatory curriculum and playing organ for church choirs such as St. Anne's Male Choir (1982-2002). Inspired by her mother's musicality and encouraged by a progressive piano teacher to find her own voice in music, Pat had begun to accompany fiddle players from the age of 13. A good ear, and aural and improvisatory skills supplemented her music literacy, rendering her a versatile accompanist who was in demand by singers and fiddlers in a range of styles – Scottish, old-time, Irish, country and western and contemporary. She was the house piano player for 5 years for the Dartmouth Old Time Fiddle Championship contest during the 1970s, playing with such fiddlers as Lee Cremo, Jerry Holland, Larry Parks and Arthur Muise. She was also her mother's regular accompanist from her early teenage years, and they performed Pat's first song composition together on CBC-TV's show *90 Minutes Live* when Pat was 13; her subsequent body of song has been in classical, traditional and urban folksong styles. Her classical commissions include the theme for the opening ceremonies of the Jeux Canada Games, works for theatre and for the Cape Breton Orchestra. Her traditional music compositions have been recorded by Cape Breton players such as Carl MacKenzie, John Allan Cameron and Winnie Chafe. Best known of these, "Stella's Trip to Kamloops" has been recorded by the San Francisco Scottish Fiddlers and The Boys of the Lough. While some of her tunes have been in collections published by Jerry Holland and Paul Cranford, in 2009 she also published her own volume of 209 fiddle tunes *Bits and Pieces, Volume I*. A psychologist of some 15 years experience, she moved to full-time music in 2005, since when she has been more visible, playing live and studio accompaniment for a range of fiddlers and singers, and teaching piano privately and at the Gaelic College. She is a regular performer in the Sydney area, at the Louisbourg Playhouse and at Celtic Colours, for example.

— ≈ —

Bits and Pieces: A Collection of Original Music by Pat Chafe. Marches, Strathspeys, Reels, Jigs, Waltzes, Slow Airs and More with Special Selections by Doug and Margaret MacPhee. A tune-book published in 2009 by August Musicworks, Glace Bay, this has 142 pages of tunes with a preface by Joey Beaton; acknowledgements; dedication to the compiler's parents, Winnie and Mike Chafe; a contents page with tunes arranged by tune-type, key and alphabetically; and an author's note. The collection has 236 tunes, 202 of them by Pat Chafe, including "Stella's Trip to Kamloops," a march popularized by Jerry Holland. Twenty-eight of the tunes are compositions by New Waterford piano player Doug MacPhee, 6 are by his mother, Margaret MacPhee, also a piano player. There are 56 reels overall, 52 jigs, 37 strathspeys, 32 marches, 17 waltzes, 21 clogs/hornpipes, 17 slow airs and 2 two-step polkas. Many of the tunes offer variations, through the use of first- and second-time endings, and four of the waltzes offer an accompanying harmony part. Chords are indicated for each tune, not as a blueprint but "as guides and choices for the player."

— ≈ —

Chapman, Stan. (1946-). Fiddle, teacher, composer. New Glasgow, NS. A respected contributor to the Cape Breton fiddle tradition, particularly through his role as a teacher, he had grown up in an environment listening music being played by his father and uncle and on recordings and the radio, mainly CJFX. He studied classical violin and progressed through the Toronto Royal Conservatory violin and theory exams; he received an elementary music education diploma from Nova Scotia Teachers' College in 1973 and taught music in the Nova Scotia school system for 32 years. In the early 1970s he began to teach a few students at home in New Glasgow and was soon persuaded by Margaret Dunn to set up a Cape Breton fiddle class in Antigonish. In the aftermath of the *VCBF* documentary it soon became evident that there was a demand for such teaching and soon he was giving classes in Mabou and in Creignish as well. Performance groups emerging from these classes, among them such as Highland Classics and The Special Seven, were in demand, evidence that the Cape Breton fiddle tradition was in safe hands for the future. Students from his classes included Natalie MacMaster, Ashley MacIsaac and Wendy MacIsaac, who have gone on to carve out international careers as Cape Breton fiddlers. Chapman's teaching was the focus of a PhD dissertation in the 1980s: "Traditional and Non-Traditional Teaching and Learning Practices in Folk Music: An Ethnographic Field Study of Cape Breton Fiddling" (Virginia Hope Garrison, 1985, University of Wisconsin-Madison). He has directed the CBFA in many performances and has given fiddle workshops in the U.S., Canada and New Zealand. He has taught at the Gaelic College, St. Ann's, for more than 20 years and is currently a part-time lecturer in Culture and Heritage at CBU, where he teaches performance courses in Cape Breton fiddle. He has composed about half-a-dozen tunes, two of which appear in *The Cape Breton Fiddlers' Collection*, and is featured on the Rounder album *Traditional Fiddle Music of Cape Breton: MacKinnon's Brook* (2008) and on three recordings by singer Hector MacIssac, including *The Legend of the Black Donnellys* (2009).

Chen, Tyson. (1981-). Piano. Ottawa, ON, and Mabou, Cape Breton. Born to a Chinese-Jamaican father (Patrick) and American mother (Beverley), he grew up in Ottawa taking classical and popular piano lessons, later diversifying to other styles including ragtime and rock. He moved to Mabou in 2008 to take up an engineering job and immersed himself in the Cape Breton fiddle-music scene as a piano accompanist; he was influenced and encouraged by many local musicians such as Kevin LeVesconte, Melody and Derrick Cameron, Anita MacDonald, Marianne Jewell, Pius MacIsaac, Willie Kennedy and Stanley MacNeil. By

the summer of 2010 he was performing regularly at the Glenora Distillery and the Red Shoe Pub, Mabou; he began playing for square dances with various fiddlers. He also maintains a profile as a classical musician and has been involved in local musicals including *John Archie & Nellie* and *The Weddin Dance*, for which he was musical director. He now has a full-time music career, which includes teaching alongside performing.

CHER Radio. Although the signal could only be heard in industrial Cape Breton (Sydney area), CHER radio made a concerted effort to carry traditional music on the airwaves. CHER-FM (MAX FM 98.3), Maritime Broadcasting System Ltd., began broadcasting in 1965 when Robert J. McGuigan received a licence. His business partner, David Neima, held a passion for all things Celtic, and through the 1970s put an emphasis on Cape Breton music and language, before regional and national broadcasters became interested in it. Rankin MacSween, president of New Dawn Enterprises (a Sydney community economic development agency) was also highly involved in starting this, wanting to promote local music and ownership out of concern of foreign media ownership dominating the island. In one of his first jobs as an on-air contributor, Ron MacInnis (of *The Vanishing Cape Breton Fiddler* fame) worked on the morning show and on remotes where he interviewed many of the key tradition bearers. A popular program, *Failte is Furan*, hosted by John Campbell and Linden MacIntyre became one of the focal points of traditional music in industrial Cape Breton. CHER has changed ownership and switched formats a number of times in the last several years, but remains an important part of the island's radio heritage. *See* **radio.**

Chéticamp Connection, The. A trio of Joe Cormier (fiddle), Ethel Cormier (piano) and Edmond Boudreau (guitar, mandolin), this group played only occasionally because its leader, Ethel, was Toronto-based while the others were resident in Boston. It recorded two albums: *The Chéticamp Connection* (1983) and *The Chéticamp Connec-*

tion, *Phase II / Homage a Chéticamp* (1985), the latter release of which coincided with celebrations for Chéticamp's 200th anniversary.

Chiasson, Hilda. (1962-). Piano, step dance. Grand Étang and Belle Côte, Cape Breton. Born in Toronto, ON, to parents Julie Hélène and Daniel Chiasson, the family moved to Cape Breton when she was one year old. Music was on both sides of the family; her mother was a step dancer and her father sang and played mandolin and harmonica. On her mother's side her grandfather played, repaired and made fiddles; her paternal grandfather's house was a popular party house in Chéticamp for many years; he was a fiddle player and an Acadian singer and storyteller; the folk collector Helen Creighton made regular visits to record him during the 1940s and 1950s. One of her uncles, Albert Chiasson, sang professionally and was one of the first in the Chéticamp area to record an album (a 45-rpm album that included two of his own compositions); he also regularly performed at dances, playing guitar, often with Sandy MacIntyre in Toronto. Another relative, Didace LeBlanc, played fiddle for dances and was well known in Cape Breton music circles, not least for his hospitality. However, it was her aunt, Yvette Bourgeois, a piano player who accompanied many fiddlers, including Arthur Muise, who was her greatest influence starting out. Largely self-taught, Hilda was inspired by the musicians she encountered at sessions and parties at her grandfather's house, in particular the Beatons of Mabou, John Morris Rankin, and Maybelle Chisholm MacQueen. From the late 1970s she was mentored by Jerry Holland and, along with Dave MacIsaac on guitar, the trio developed a very slick, prescribed and innovative approach to arranging Cape Breton fiddle tunes that proved inspirational for a whole generation of younger players and which was first introduced on Holland's *Master Cape Breton Fiddler* album (1982). Her distinctive rhythmic and harmonic stylings have made her a popular piano accompanist and she has contributed to more than 50 albums. She has played and recorded with many Cape Breton fiddlers as well as musicians from Scotland, Ireland and North America. Starting in the late 1990s Hilda toured and recorded for 16 years with J. P. Cormier; today she performs on a part-time basis, mostly at dances and with a variety of established and emerging fiddle players. She has composed a small number of tunes, one of which – "The Holland Wedding Reel" – has been published and recorded on several occasions. She is also a step dancer, and may have been the first to step dance and play the piano simultaneously. [**MacGillivray 1988**].

Chiasson, Joel. (1973-). Piano, step dance, fiddle, teacher. Chéticamp and Sydney. Regarded as an outstanding piano accompanist and stepdancer, he identifies himself as an Acadian who plays Cape Breton music. Growing up in Chéticamp he did not have immediate access to live Cape Breton fiddle music although he had heard and liked it through radio and TV broadcasts. Thus, though he was taught classical piano for a decade, his ambition was to accompany fiddle players. Inspired by Hilda Chiasson, Maybelle Chisholm MacQueen, John Morris Rankin and Betty Lou Beaton he taught himself accompaniment by watching the 1980s TV show, *Up Home Tonight*, recording and replaying sections repeatedly to learn the piano parts. He also learned by listening to fiddle players on cassette and working out accompaniments himself. As a young teenager, inspired by the dancing of Lucienne LeFort from Chéticamp at a local variety show, he sought basic dance instruction from James Cormier. Equally impulsively he decided to take up the fiddle around 1990 upon seeing Natalie MacMaster perform at the Saint-Joseph-du-Moine concert. He taught himself, listening carefully to players such as Buddy MacMaster, Natalie MacMaster, John Morris Rankin and Stephanie Wills. Chéticamp's music scene at the time centred around two local taverns, the Doryman and Le Gabriel, neither of which – under Nova Scotia liquor laws – Chiasson could enter until he turned 19. Reaching this age and getting his driver's license opened up a new world, one where he began to meet and perform with all ages of musicians. Though he trained as a teacher and works at Étoile de l'Acadie (the

French-language school in Sydney), he spent years touring with Ashley MacIsaac and the Kitchen Devils (1995-1997) and with Natalie MacMaster (1998-2000) as a piano player and dancer. He has taught workshops in the U.S. and Canada and has provided piano accompaniment on some thirty recordings.

Chisholm family of Margaree Forks. A prominent musical family whose talents were passed down through several generations and included some of the most influential and idiosyncratic players of fiddle and piano. The major names in modern times are Angus and Archie Neil, two of the nine children born to Archibald ("Archie the Teacher") and Isabel (MacLennan) Chisholm. The family was raised in Margaree Forks, surrounded by music; Archibald, although not a player himself, was an avid follower of fiddle music, particularly fond of the playing of Donald Beaton (Domhnull Iain an Taillear) while Isabel sang Gaelic songs and *puirt-a-beul*; on the MacLennan side a number of uncles and grand-uncles were fiddle players, among them Angus MacLennan and Danny MacLennan. Angus, Archie Neil and their brothers were given their first instruction on the fiddle by Johnny "Steven" White, from Margaree, who taught them to play "The Cock of the North." Angus Allan Gillis also guided them, while Jimmy MacInnis, of Big Pond, who spent a year living with the Chisholm family, introduced them to note-reading and to higher position work, which he had learned while living in Maine. The Chisholms are also noted for having been being particularly admiring of and influenced by the bagpipe tradition.

Chisholm, Archie Neil. (1907-1997). Fiddle, storyteller, broadcaster. A brother to Angus he has also become a legend within Cape Breton fiddle lore on his own merit for his involvement, in various ways, with the tradition; indeed the fact that he was a solid dance fiddler is often overlooked in light of his other achievements. Although he suffered from polio at a young age, which confined him to crutches, a cane and, finally, a wheelchair, he was determined to be independent; he studied

teaching, working in various schools around the Province and graduated from the Nova Scotia Teacher's College in Truro in 1936; his BA and BEd from St. FX (1967) earned him a *Time* magazine article for being the eldest member of his graduating class. Involved in politics, he ran as a Progressive Conservative candidate for Inverness County in the provincial elections of 1956 and 1966, and was appointed to a Canadian Consultative Commission for Multiculturalism. He was a founding member of the Committee for Cape Breton (later the CBFA) in 1972 and he was master of ceremonies at the first Glendale Festival of Scottish Fiddling in 1973; he assumed this role at many other events including the Broad Cove Scottish Concert (which he did for almost 40 years) and the weekly Fiddlers Concerts at the Normaway Inn. In 1979 he hosted *Archie Neil's Cape Breton* on CBI and CBC, a series of half-hour radio programs first broadcast in the Maritimes, then aired nationally in the early 1980s. In 1992 he worked with Mary Anne Ducharme in documenting his unique personal life story which was published in *Archie Neil: A Triumph of a Life!* (Breton Books). Regarded by many as "a true gentleman of Cape Breton" and a tireless advocate of many local causes and charities, he is one of the region's most highly decorated individuals, having been honoured with more than a dozen awards from island community groups. He and his wife, Margaret (Delaney), received a joint award of merit from the Nova Scotia Highland Village Society in 1991 for their contribution to the music and culture of Cape Breton. In 1996 he received an honorary doctorate from CBU and is immortalized in a life-size wood carving by Joe MacKinnon at the Normaway Inn. Archie Neil's grand-daughter, Chrissy Crowley, is a well-known contemporary fiddler who performs with the band Còig. [**Caplan 1986; Ducharme 1992; MacGillivray 1988**].

Chisholm, Angus. (1908-1979). Fiddle. Margaree Forks, Inverness County, and Cambridge, MA. His first public performance was a fiddle duet with his brother, Archie Neil, at a local dance at Peter Coady's; this was followed by playing at wood frolics, kitchen rackets, house dances and school house dances in the Margaree area. He befriended many of the fiddlers on the scene, such as Malcolm Beaton, Dan J. Campbell, "Big" Ronald MacLellan and Donald Angus Beaton; he was particularly inspired by the playing of Mary MacDonald and by the bowing style of Angus Allan Gillis. Having trained as a school teacher, he spent 6 years working in various communities; in the 1930s he moved to Boston, later returning to Cape Breton and taking up employment in the steel plant. During the 1950s he was a construction worker in Newfoundland, and later spent some time in Elliot Lake, ON, and Toronto. From the 1960s he made Cambridge, MA, his home and played an active part in the Cape Breton community there. Angus Chisholm was among the first Cape Breton fiddlers to record commercially for Decca in the U.S. and for the Celtic label in Montréal with Dan J. Campbell and Angus Allan Gillis. The 78s cut at this time (1935) were also the first Cape Breton fiddle recordings to be made in Canada. Chisholm's full catalogue was reissued as LPs on the Shanachie and Celtic labels in the 1970s. Due to tensions between himself and the record companies he ceased making commercial albums; much of his music that is now available was captured informally on home recordings made at house parties in Cape Breton and Boston, and often at his own instigation in response to requests for his music.

Angus Chisholm. Courtesy of Paul MacDonald.

repute. Angus Chisholm is often hailed as one of the greatest fiddlers – some would argue *the* greatest – in Cape Breton history. At his funeral in East Margaree, in 1979, the presiding priest summed up this regard: "What Caruso was to the singing world Angus Chisholm was to the Scottish music world – one of the best in his line."

Chisholm was indeed a catalyst in that he was one of those who made a distinction between music for dancing and music for listening to, so affirming Cape Breton fiddle music as an art form in its own right, rather than a support for the dance only. His preferred performance contexts emphasised that: he favoured a listening audience—something that was not common until that time. Indeed, his focus on this was so intense that he frequently performed unaccompanied, without the piano that had become requisite, something that further set him apart from his contemporaries. Increased access within Cape Breton to printed collections from the 1940s onward enabled him to expand his repertoire and deviate from the limited tune-type choices previously available to Cape Breton fiddlers. As a virtuoso player, he enjoyed the technical challenges presented by hornpipes and clogs, which until then had not been part of the core repertoire, and showpieces such as Scott Skinner's arrangement of "Tullochgorm" and "The East Neuk of Fife." In tuning and intonation he strived toward precision over the more varied and colourful interpretations found in the playing of earlier fiddlers. He was selective in his choice of embellishments and sharp and deliberate in his execution of these. By omitting many of the drones, double stops and left-hand ornaments used by other fiddlers, he created a cleaner, more transparent melodic line which was emphasized further by clearly articulated, controlled bowing patterns. The repertoire and style cultivated by Angus Chisholm, and the new listening context in which they were presented, were new to Cape Breton audiences; he attracted a huge following at concerts and house parties and was featured often on TV shows hosted by John Allan Cameron, Tommy Makem and Don Messer. He introduced a new dimension to the Cape Breton fiddle tradition in terms of practice and style, and set a new standard which continues to inform the tradition today. [**MacGillivray 1981**].

Chisholm siblings. The next generation of Chisholms, Cameron, Maybelle and Margaret were born to parents Willie D. and Annie Mae (Cameron) Chisholm. As well as having a strong musical pedigree on the Chisholm side of the family there was music also on the Cameron side. Their great-grandfather Charlie MacKinnon, from St. Rose, was considered a good fiddler in his day; his daughter (their grandmother) Margaret Cameron also played.

Chisholm McQueen, Maybelle. Piano. Margaree Forks. Steeped in music at home and having played her first dance with her uncles Angus and Archie Neil at the age of 10, Maybelle studied classical music with the Sisters of St. Martha for many years. She has recorded with many Cape Breton fiddlers, including her uncle Angus, Johnny Wilmot and, more recently, Howie MacDonald. She continues to play at dances and sessions, and often accompanies Ashley MacIsaac in concert, including at Carnegie Hall in 2015. Maybelle released her album *Pure Celtic Hearts* in 2001. She has been a major stylist in Cape Breton piano accompaniment, particularly recognized for her innovative rhythmic techniques and occasional flamboyancy. Maybelle's contribution to the Cape Breton tradition was celebrated in a special tribute concert at the 2014 Celtic Colours Festival. [**MacGillivray 1988**].

Chisholm, Cameron. (1945-). Fiddle. Mararee Forks. Although he started off playing piano he soon switched to fiddle, and received his earliest instruction from his grandmother Margaret Cameron and from Johnny Stephen White. At home, his father would jig tunes to him, his mother – a fiddle player herself – helped him to read music and his sister Maybelle, who played the piano, also taught him tunes. He heard a lot of fiddle music on the radio, particularly from CJFX. His uncle Angus was a significant influence as was the piper, Sandy Boyd, who stayed with the family for some time. From the age of 8 Cameron

was performing in public, at first solo, then with Maybelle accompanying him on piano. He moved to Toronto in the early 1960s, where he worked as a banker and then as a teacher. There he played at many Cape Breton events at the Slovak Hall and at the French Club. He also played at dances in Boston, Detroit, Windsor, Montréal, Sudbury and Hamilton, and was part of the fiddle group who performed on the weekly *Ceilidh* TV show out of Halifax in the early 1970s; he was also among the Cape Breton fiddlers profiled in the *Scotia Sun* in 1973. He moved back to the Margaree area of Cape Breton, where he still lives. Although he has not recorded or played often in public he has met and encouraged many young players who have visited him, and he is cited by many as a significant influence on their style. [**MacGillivray 1981**].

MacDonald, Margaret (Chisholm). (1947-). Fiddle. Margaree Forks and Toronto. Although she started off on the bagpipes she began playing the fiddle as a teenager, taught initially by her mother and influenced by members of her extended family, and by piper, Sandy Boyd, who often stayed with them. Other influences were Buddy MacMaster, Joe MacLean and Donald Angus Beaton. She married her husband, Peter, at the age of 17 and started a family and, for a number of years, had little time or opportunity to play. From the mid-1970s she gradually returned to performing on an occasional basis, preferring the presentational concert setting above playing for dances. She was among the performers at the first fiddle festival in Glendale and is featured on the 1979 Glendale album playing a tribute to Angus Chisholm, her uncle. In Toronto she is involved in the Cape Breton community and plays in duets with her husband on mandolin at various events; they return to Cape Breton most summers where she occasionally performs. [**MacGillivray 1981**].

chromatic. This refers to a 12-note scale built on a series of consecutive notes, each of which is a semitone apart. The term is also used (less accurately) to describe a tune which, although not in a chromatic scale, may involve semitone movement necessitating a lot of accidentals. Tunes of this nature are rare in the Cape Breton repertoire, with the exception of a small number composed, typically, by non-fiddle players, e.g., by accordionist, Stewart MacNeil. Such tunes do not translate easily to the fiddle within the parameters of the Cape Breton style, and thus have not generally become part of the wider repertoire.

Church, The. Religion was one of the main factors influencing settlement patterns of the pioneers who came to Cape Breton. Catholics gravitated toward Inverness County and parts of Victoria County, while Presbyterians dominated along the North Shore (Victoria County). Fiddle and pipe music was popular among the Catholic population while Gaelic song was favoured by the Presbyterians. In the Highlands of Scotland, particularly during the 19th century, the clergy were notorious for their campaigns against music, and are reported as destroying pipes and fiddles. This was a feature of the Cape Breton situation too until almost the turn of the 20th century, with certain clergymen holding to the archaic superstition that fiddles and pipes were instruments of the devil. The most notorious example was the Reverend Kenneth J. MacDonald, parish priest of Mabou from 1865 to 1894, who is reported as collecting all the instruments in his parish and destroying them; other priests are believed to have acted similarly and many fiddles were discarded under this regime (although local lore suggests that since many homes had multiple fiddles the best one was kept safely hidden). Lee Cremo has suggested a positive consequence of all this activity, in that the indigenous Mi'kmaq often came into possession of the instruments that the Scottish Catholics had to abandon. Activities surrounding the music such as the dance were also frowned on by the church, and the associations between music and dancing and liquor further incensed certain clergymen.

easing off. By the 20th century, however, a greater tolerance of music and its related practices was apparent among the Catholic clergy in particular. Perhaps this reflects an appreciation on their part of the financial potential in social activities associated with music. Certainly, in the early part of the century, the clergy were strong in their support of events such as the parish picnic, where funds were channelled back into the parish, financing the building of new churches, for example. Individual priests such as Fr. Dan MacDonald worked with parishioners in the Iona area in the organizing of local picnics. Parish halls were offered as venues for square dances, garden parties, picnics, and later concerts were held on church grounds. Key supporters for such events included Fr. Mike MacAdam, Fr. John Hugh MacEachern, Fr. John Angus Rankin and Fr. Colonel MacLeod. While not specifically related to fiddle music, the teachings and philosophy of Fr. Moses Coady and Fr. Jimmy Tompkins, promoting adult education, self-help and co-operative organization, have been important in Cape Breton cultural life. These gave rise to the philosophy identified as the Antigonish Movement and introduced new thinking and practices in society, which would prove invaluable tools for the organizers of the CBFA. Many clergy members indeed became enthusiastically involved in efforts to revitalize the fiddle tradition in the wake of the provocative 1971 *Vanishing Cape Breton Fiddler* documentary. Priests such as Fr. Colonel MacLeod in Creignish encouraged the start-up of fiddle classes; others such as Fr. John Allan Gillis in Mabou, volunteered to buy instruments for local children who wished to partake in the newly established fiddle classes in the area. Those for whom he provided instruments assembled at his funeral, in 1973, and played "Dark Island" as a tribute to him; since that time, fiddle music has come to be accepted as part of wedding and funeral services.

musical priests. Many priests became actively involved in the music themselves; among them Fr. Francis Cameron, Fr. Angus Morris and Fr. Colonel MacLeod are well-respected fiddle players; Fr. John Angus Rankin was well known as a piano player and Fr. Eugene Morris is widely admired as a step dancer. Such individuals have also played an important role at other levels: Fr. Eugene Morris, for instance, was involved in the teaching of step-dancing for a number of years and encouraged a number of his students, such as Betty Matheson and Margaret Gillis, to set up their own classes; Fr. John Angus Rankin was at the forefront of the Glendale Fiddler's Festival in its formative years, not least when he directed the massed fiddles finales; Fr. Francis Cameron, during his time as parish priest in Mabou in the early 1980s, opened the doors of the Glebe house to local fiddlers, so that it became a popular venue for ceilidhs; Fr. J. J. MacDonald in the Sydney Mines area encouraged similar social activities. Bishop Faber MacDonald (1932-2012), a fiddle player from Little Pond, Cape Breton, was the founder of the Prince Edward Island Fiddlers Society, in 1976, an organization modelled on the success of the CBFA; Fr. Allan J. MacMillan, currently directs the Gaelic choir, *Coisir an Eilein*; Fr. Hugh A. MacDonald (d. 2010) was a constant supporter of the music community, and contributed various writings, including poems, in praise of Cape Breton musicians; in industrial Cape Breton, Fr. Ora McManus supported the fiddle music through various initiatives, including some at Cape Breton Univiersty. [**Gibson and Beaton 1977; Le Blanc 1986; McDavid 2008**].

CIGO radio. *See* **Hawk, The.**

CIMA. *See* **Canadian Independent Music Association.**

CIRPA. *See* **Canadian Independent Record Production Association.**

CJCB. Radio and TV station based out of Sydney. It was founded as a radio station in the late 1920s by local entrepreneur, Nate Nathanson; he was selling battery operated "radio boxes" out of his music and book store and felt compelled to provide something for people to listen to, since reception of other stations coming from elsewhere in the province was limited and of poor quality. The business expanded into TV in the 1950s.

   CJCB Radio. A Sydney-based radio station, an affiliate of CRBC and then of the CBC, which went on air for the first time on February 14, 1929, as the only commercial station on the island. From the 1930s, CJCB recorded and

Cast of Cottar's Saturday Night *on CJCB Radio, 1935. 87-481-17011. Beaton Institute, Cape Breton University.*

broadcast Scottish-style fiddling usually for 15 minutes every weekday evening and on Saturday nights. The first popular program featuring fiddle music was a weekly program aired over the CBC network, *Cottar's Saturday Night*. Piano player Lila Abraham Hashem, who had moved to Sydney from Inverness, started her own radio show in 1936, sponsored by Brook's Grocery Store, using "The Road to the Isles" as her theme tune. Robbie Robertson was the announcer and she provided 15 minutes of piano solos, much of it in response to written requests. In the early 1940s, Bill Lamey hosted a weekly 15-minute program which he used to promote a regular dance he was organizing in the Sydney area. Lamey, along with a group called the Butt-Ender Boys, also featured on another CJCB show sponsored by Eastern Bakery, for whom he worked. Winston Fitzgerald and his Radio Entertainers, Estwood Davidson and Beattie Wallace performed live on the MacDonald Tobacco Company-sponsored show for 10 years. Through the 1950s Dan Joe MacInnis was also involved in this show and used it to promote his upcoming dances. Piano player and accordionist Elizabeth Northen Finnell hosted a show during the 1960s, which regularly featured Johnny Wilmot on fiddle. CJCB was noted for presenting a variety of popular musical genres, and has switched formats on occasion as audience tastes have evolved. The station has continued to support Cape Breton music and has presented the *Celtic Serenade* show since 1973. Initially a half-hour program hosted in its first year by Sheldon MacInnes, it was taken over by Donnie Campbell in October, 1975. He continues to host it in its current three-hour format. (*with* **WB**) See *Cottar's Saturday Night*; *Celtic Serenade*; **radio**.

CJCB-TV. The first TV station to broadcast in Nova Scotia, this was set up in 1954 as an extension of an existing commercial radio business, with the remit of reasonable regional coverage, aimed for by building broadcast towers in Inverness and Antigonish Counties. It's core programming was provided by the CBC, but from the outset, it devoted several hours per week to local, live, in-studio entertainment. The station joined CBC's national microwave network in 1958, linking it to all stations between Cape Breton and British Columbia; colour in local productions was introduced in 1975. A change of ownership in 1971 moved CJCB into the CTV network, when the CBC established a second station, CBIT-TV, in Sydney. Now part of the CTV Atlantic regional system in the Canadian Maritimes, CJCB-TV's studios are in Sydney and it carries the same programming as its sister station, CJCH-TV in Halifax, only a small percentage of which is of fiddle performances. Of its coverage of fiddle music, *The Cape Breton Barn Dance* was significant in that it was the first TV show to focus on Cape Breton fiddlers. This was a weekly show produced in Sydney and broadcast between 1962 and 1969. Co-sponsored by the Goodyear Company and Robin Hood Flour, it employed Winston Fitzgerald and Estwood Davidson as regular performers and introduced various guest performers such as fiddlers Carl MacKenzie and Buddy MacMaster. It was hosted by Robert Allison "Al" Foster (1915-2003); another signifincat show he hosted on CJCB-TV was *The Cape Breton Ceilidh*. *See* **television**.

CJFX Radio. One of the pioneer radio stations in Canada, CJFX first aired on March 23, 1943, from Antigonish, Nova Scotia. St. Francis Xavier University was the original licence holder, and the station, founded by Catholic priests, teachers and graduates of the university was aligned closely to the mission of the co-operative movement as it was being advanced by Fr. Moses Coady and Fr. Jimmy Tompkins; as such, CJFX was perceived as being of and for the people. The station was privately owned and run by a board of directors. It could be heard all over eastern mainland Nova Scotia, western Cape Breton, eastern PEI and in parts of Newfoundland. From its inception it was committed to featuring Scottish fiddle music even when it was not the popular or profitable thing to do. The availability of recordings from the era meant that music was readily accessible and abundantly used for broadcast purposes. Local music was seen to be an integral part of the broadcast offerings, weaving its way in and out of various programs and presentations. In fact, J. Clyde Nunn, the first managing director of CJFX, himself hosted the popular *Fun at Five* program, a mildly satirical presentation that drew some of its humour from joking about various aspects of daily life. Nunn's on-air persona, "The Old Man," was portrayed as a curmudgeon who was not always a fan of fiddle music. He and his sidekick, Percy Baker, would poke gentle fun at the culture and characters of the region.

The first fiddle music broadcast on CJFX came both from commercial releases – much of it coming from Bernie MacIsaac's Celtic label, which was based in Antigonish – and, certainly until the 1960s, from live performances. In the early days, fiddlers such as Sandy MacLean, Angus Allan Gillis and Angus Chisholm would play via telephone from Inverness to the station in Antigonish; later the CJFX premises, at 85 Kirk Street, provided a large room with a studio-quality piano. Cape Breton musicians, including those who lived away and returned annually on vacation, were frequently recorded there. Ray "Mac" MacDonald joined CJFX as an announcer and programmer in 1967 and, along with Gus MacKinnon, recorded a substantial body of material for broadcast at concerts and other events. Gradually, an extensive library of Cape Breton material, both commercial and original, was amassed as well as a substantial body of recordings from Ireland and Scotland. Fiddle music could be heard at any time of the day on CJFX including key slots such as before the evening news. There were two particularly prominent shows: *Scottish Strings* hosted by Gus MacKinnon, from the 1960s until MacKinnon's duties as station manager and current affairs talk show host took the majority of his time, and *Ceilidh*, which was a daily show, hosted by Ray "Mac" up until his retirement, in 1999; this show continues on a weekly basis in 2015, hosted by Barry MacKinnon. The impact that CJFX radio had in Cape Breton, particularly in Inverness County and central Cape Breton, was significant. The station played an important role in keeping a spotlight on the music, promoting both live and recorded material, advertising fiddle-music events such as concerts, dances, etc., and contributing to the dissemination of style and repertoire. Radio was, for many years, the most important media serving the fiddle community; star players emerged and set new standards in terms of style; new tunes were heard and shared through this medium and, as recently as the 1990s, it was playing a significant role in the transmission process as young players recorded the shows and learned new tunes and techniques from this source. Significantly, long before Canadian content was introduced or the ECMA awards established, CJFX was promoting the music of Cape Breton fiddlers; indeed, for a number of years during the 1960s, Ray "Mac" was the only radio host in North America playing this music. Interestingly, when a move was perceived away from this level of support, the fiddle-music community was mobilized into taking action. In 1981, for example, a group – the Committee of Concern for Improved Scottish Music Programming on CJFX – led by Donna Davis and Joey Beaton was formed to investigate moves at the station to reduce Cape Breton Scottish content. On March 25, 2013, CJFX changed its branding to 98.9 The Nish, and changed its format to popular hits of the '60s, '70s, '80s and '90s; shows, including "Ceilidh," now broadcast Sunday evenings, are available at www.989xfm.ca. (*With* **WB**) *See* **radio**.

CKJM. La Coopérative Radio-Chéticamp/ Cooperative Radio Chéticamp Ltée (CKJM) was developed in the early 1990s and made its permanent broadcasting debut in October 1995. The objectives of the station include operating an FM, French-speaking community radio station with an educational mandate, involving the direct participation of the residents of the Chéticamp, Saint-Joseph-du-Moine and Margaree areas; offering learning initiatives related to engineering and radio hosting through active participation in the preparation and broadcasting of radio shows; promoting regional cultural development and artistic expression with the presentation of folk and historical shows and Acadian plays; encouraging the development of new music appreciation with a variety of quality musical programming; organizing public-service educational shows such as round-table discussions, debates, etc.; and offering an informative news service in order to enlighten the community and favour social and economic regional development. The station operates out of *Le Studio Marcel Doucet*, opened in August 2000 and named after the Cape Breton fiddler who died in 1992. By the turn of the 21st century, this station was the only one in Cape Breton broadcasting a show that was substantially in Gaelic, *Aiseiridh nan Gàidheal* (The Awakening of the Gaels), produced by Geoff May and Rebecca-Lynne MacDonald-May, although the focus is largely on Gaelic language and song rather than on fiddle music. Another show, *Cape Breton Fiddle Tunes*, is presented by David Gillis. (*With* WB) *See* **radio**.

clappers. Used to provide idiophonic accompaniment to fiddle music with a sound reminiscent of castanets. Clappers is the Cape Breton form of (and term for) "bones," an instrument which has only ever been associated there with a small number of players. Hughie Young from North Sydney played and recorded on the clappers with The Inverness Serenaders in the U.S. in the 1930s; clappers were also featured on a couple of Angus

Chisholm's early recordings. Another known performer was John A. "Wild Archie" MacLennan (b. 1906 in Port Malcolm), who lived in Halifax after 1956, where he played at the Cape Breton Club, accompanying fiddlers such as Sandy MacLean, Jack MacQuarrie, Gordon MacQuarrie, Tena Campbell, Harry Bagnell and Neillie Gillis. Another player was Johnny Muise, from Inverness, who spent much of his life in Boston and featured on several recordings. Originally, clappers were two animal rib bones, although two pieces of hardwood were most often used in Cape Breton; generally, the clappers created a loud volume that did not suit the typical performance environments for Cape Breton fiddle playing. While the length and curvature of each of the pieces depends on the personal preferences of the performer, the bones are typically between four and eight inches long and are of similar size. The technique involves holding one bone firmly, with the thumb against the bone and the index finger up over the thumb; the middle finger is on the front edge of the bone, holding it firmly in place so that it does not move. The second bone is gripped by another finger and permitted to hang loosely; the sound is created by shaking the wrist so that this second bone "claps" against the stationary one. Different timbres can be created by moving the fingers along the bone while playing. Some players play two sets of bones simultaneously, one in each hand. Because body language is a key part of performance, and since gesture is required to produce the sound, the clappers have been considered something of a novelty in Cape Breton music. [**Caplan 2006**].

clog. A tune type related to the hornpipe, it dates to the mid-19th century. It is in 4/4 time and is played at a relatively slow tempo. Its structure is marked by dotted rhythms and often involves much triplet movement. There is a strong accent on the first and third beats of the bar, and a particular feature is the use of 3 accented quarter notes at the end of each part, creating a "pom-pom-pom" effect. Clogs appeared first in the Cape Breton repertoire in the late 1920s via the tune-book *Ryan's Mammoth Collection*, but did not become widely played until the 1940s. There is

some ambiguity in the use of the terms "clog" and "hornpipe" in Cape Breton (indeed the clog here seems to be closer to what the Irish understand as a hornpipe). This ambiguity is compounded by the fact that in printed collections the labels are, at times, interchanged, with many tunes being identified as simply "hornpipe or clog," thus leaving it open to the interpretation of the player. Generally speaking, the clog's more virtuosic style and consistently dotted rhythm make it a distinct entity, while the hornpipe in Cape Breton – as in much of North America – has even passage-work, and thus is easily interpreted as a reel. No specific dance has been associated with the clog in Cape Breton, although the tune type was originally (and indeed continues to be) associated with a dance type of the same name in places such as Lancashire, England. The clog was popularized by fiddlers Angus Chisholm and Winston Fitzgerald; others known to favour it include fiddlers Carl MacKenzie and Dwayne Côté, and piano player Doug MacPhee. Dan R. MacDonald was quite prolific in his output of newly composed clogs, but other fiddler-composers have composed only a few of this type of tune or have not engaged with the idiom at all. Though players like piano player Mac Morin and fiddle and guitar player J. P. Cormier favour clogs, interest in them generally appears to be on the wane and among the younger generation very few are playing them to any great extent. [**Graham 2006**].

CMRRA. See **Canadian Musical Reproduction Rights Agency Ltd.**

Coast, The. The 89.7. Coastal Community Radio Co-operative Limited (The Coast 89.7 in CBRM) was incorporated on June 12, 2003. Founded by current general manager Bill MacNeil, the concept was to develop a community-owned radio station dedicated to promoting local artists and culture to an interested group of individuals. In 2005, in conjunction with the ECMAs being held in Cape Breton, The Coast 89.7 began operating as a licenced special event station, limited to 50 watts and a temporary tower. This meant new licences for different events had to be secured for each broadcast. During the first year the station moved between Glace Bay and Sydney as it provided special-events broadcasts for various community groups and events. On December 3, 2007, The Coast 89.7, having had its permanent full-time FM licence approved earlier that year by the CRTC, began broadcasting. The Coast 89.7 (CKOA-FM) plays a minimum of 80% Canadian musical selections per week, with emphasis on local and regional musical acts. Cape Breton traditional fiddle music is featured in the daily music mix and also spotlighted in two programs. They are *Cape Breton Fiddle Tunes*, with David Gillis, which also airs on CKJM Chéticamp, and the *Cape Breton Kitchen Party*, hosted by Glace Bay's Charlie Clements. The station streams live at www.coastalradio.ca and is also available on the TuneIn app and throughout Atlantic Canada on the Bell Fibre-Op TV Channel 773. In 2011 the station won the ECMA Radio Station of the Year Award (small market) and was nominated for the Nova Scotia Music Award for Radio Station of the Year. (*With* **WB**) *See* **radio.**

Còig. (meaning "five" in Scottish Gaelic). A concert-format band originally with fiddlers Chrissy Crowley (Margaree), Rachel Davis (Baddeck) and Colin Grant (Sydney), piano player Jason Roach (Chéticamp) and guitar, mandolin, whistle and banjo player Darren McMullen (Hardwoodlands, NS). They were formed in 2010 when, as five solo acts, they were scheduled to participate in Celtic Colours and were invited to play together as a promotion for the event. The positive experience led to them continuing to perform occasionally as The Còig Ensemble, a band with fast tempo, slick presentation and high-powered drive; the repertoire is eclectic in its juxtaposition of old and new tunes from Cape Breton, Scotland and Ireland and the arrangements are generic in terms of contemporary "trad" bands representing any point of the Scotland/Ireland-North American axis; however, the piano stylings, maintain a strong distinctive Cape Breton element to the sound. The band's first album, *Five*, was released in 2014 and the band won a Canadian Folk Music Award in 2015; Colin Grant left the band in February of that year.

Colaisde na Gàidhlig / The Gaelic College. Located at St. Ann's in the centre of Cape Breton in one of the earliest Scottish settlements, it runs programs for students of all nationalities, ages and levels who wish to expand their knowledge of the Gaelic language, music and culture. It was established as a school for this purpose by a Presbyterian minister, Rev. A. W. R. MacKenzie, in 1938. As the Gaelic College of Arts and Crafts, it applied itself to the revival of and training in the production of Cape Breton Gaelic crafts (in particular, tartan fabrics), and most courses were taught in Gaelic, although the Canadian government did not formally recognize the language. By the 1950s the demand for "St. Ann's tartans" had grown to the extent that the school merited substantial government funding; by 1997 it could form a partnership with CBU to further promote Cape Breton Gaelic language and culture, set-

Còig

Colaisde na Gaidhlig / The Gaelic College, St. Ann's.

ting up the online Gaelic credit courses *Beul an Tobair* and a Gaelic Heritage Centre. Today, it is the only such institution in North America, now running programs in Gaelic language and song, fiddle, pipes, dance, piano and weaving. Its new pipe group, Nuallan, reflects the traditional dance style of piping played in Cape Breton and points to a renewed focus on local, vernacular traditions and away from the competitive piping scene. The college runs daily demonstrations, a daily lunch-time ceilidh, a weekly instructors ceilidh, and a new Cape Breton Island-wide festival called KitchenFest! / Féis a'Chidsin!; a series of online instructional videos is due for release in 2015. An Talla Mór / The Great Hall of the Clans seats 350 people for concerts and other events. A live-in institution, it's facilities include dormitories, classrooms, meeting rooms, cafeteria and halls; these facilities, coupled with its central location on Cape Breton, have rendered it an ideal centre of operations and late-night club venue for Celtic Colours and for the year-round CBFA rehearsals and annual concert. The Gaelic College is a charitable foundation and raises more than 80% of its revenue while receiving the remainder primarily from the Province of Nova Scotia. Its governance structure consists of representatives from their foundation as well as those appointed by the government of Nova Scotia. The current CEO of the college is a former premier of Nova Scotia, the Honourable Rodney J. MacDonald, ECNS. The underlying philosophy of the College was contemporary Scottish rather than Cape Breton in the early years, with an emphasis on pipe bands, kilts and highland dance. In recent years the focus has been very deliberately shifted to local traditions and practices, a celebration of Cape Breton and of its Gaelic heritage. In 2013, the Gaelic College was recognized by Queen Elizabeth II and given the opportunity to use the "Royal" prefix as part of its name. The college acknowledged this but, after much consideration, decided against using it. [**Lamb, 1992**].

Cole's 1,000 Fiddle Tunes; Ryan's Mammoth Collection. Compiled by William Bradbury Ryan (b. 1831) who, in 1882, with his mentor Elias Howe, published it as *William Bradbury Ryan's Mammoth Collection* (copyright 1883), it was later issued as *Ryan's Mammoth Collection*. In one volume, this is considered one of most important repositories of 19th-century North American music, with 1050 tunes for fiddle or any treble instrument. Tunes are compactly presented in 150 pages, some have named composers, and the music is basically from Scotland and Ireland, but with much material from England, Germany and America. In the 1890s the collection was listed in the Sears Roebuck catalogue – a measure of its popularity and potential availability. In 1940, the M. M. Cole Company published *1,000 Fiddle Tunes*, estimated by Alan Jabbour to be almost identical to *Ryan's Mammoth Collection*, although a (slightly) abridged version. Now better known as *Cole's 1000 Fiddle Tunes* or *Cole's Collection*, this became something of a "bible" for fiddlers who read music, and its versions of tunes have, over several generations, become standards in the U.S. The book was published again in 1995 (edited by Patrick Sky), this time reverting to the *Ryan's Mammoth Collection* title, with full historical information surrounding the collection. In all its forms, *Cole's* or *Ryan's* is a remarkable snapshot of the repertoire of 19th-century America and has been an invaluable source of tunes for countless fiddlers and other musicians, not least in Cape Breton. *See* **tune books.**

collecting. (i) The amassing and assembling of existing work, and (ii) the practice of collecting music, song and dance through notating and/or recording, either for posterity or as a resource for contemporary performers. This developed out of an awareness of folklore, which emerged as a discipline in the 19th century and was a key element in the maintenance and development of traditional music in all of Europe, notably in Scotland and Ireland. Collecting was not introduced into Cape Breton cultural life until the 1930s, at first focusing on Gaelic song and storytelling; that this was comparatively late is not too surprising, for neither the Scottish penchant for collecting material to fuel the music-publishing business nor the Irish intellectual pursuit of collecting as a hedge against potential cultural extinction – certainly in the case of the fiddle music – were relevant. The first formalized, strategic collection of the fiddle music did not happen until the 1940s; while preservation – from both "old country" (Scottish) and "new world" (Cape Breton) perspectives – was the impetus behind the collection of Gaelic song and story, the ideologies driving collection of dance music were somewhat different. Fiddle-music collection was associated with identity and heritage issues, with the primary objective being to generate material for dissemination and promotion, a subsequent outcome being the assembling of subject matter for critical discourse. As such, collecting in the context of Cape Breton fiddle music was never considered a pursuit in itself, but rather was linked to publishing (in print or audio/audio visual formats) and academic research, or was aligned to the wider agendas of archives or institutions. Collectors of fiddle music range from professional scholars and researchers to amateur fiddle enthusiasts, and include Cape Bretoners and non-Cape Bretoners. This collection was not done in ideological isolation, however, for the work of collectors and researchers in other disciplines including Gaelic language, song and story, English language folk song, piping, step and square dance and other ethnographic, anthropological, folklore and historical subject areas often intersects with the fiddle-music tradition; these bodies of work have provided important contributions to the Cape Breton fiddle-music narrative. The collection of music in Cape Breton can be summarized as follows: (1) Early collecting, (2) Academic research, (3) Archives and institutions, (4) Amateur collecting, (5) Collecting for publishing and dissemination.

1. Early collecting. The earliest collectors active in Cape Breton focused on the Gaelic song and story traditions and the motivation behind much of this work was preservation of what was perceived to be a tradition in decline. Originally these collectors visited from Scotland and the U.S., although, from the 1960s onward, local

and locally based scholars, many of them associated with the Celtic Studies Department at St. FX, Antigonish, became involved. Gaelic traditions in the region have continued to attract scholars, due in part to the role of St. FX and other institutions and organizations, such as the Beaton Institute and the Highland Village Museum, and indeed have experienced something of an upsurge in activity in recent times as part of a wider movement promoting the Gaelic language. While much of the work in the area continues to focus on song and story, there are some natural intersections with the fiddle-music tradition. A small number of early collectors (interestingly, American and female) who visited Cape Breton with the purpose of collecting folk material did include fiddle music as part of their work. Typically what they recorded eventually appeared to some extent in commercially released format, such as film or LP.

song collectors. The first efforts in the field of collection of Gaelic song and storytelling traditions were conducted by academics and scholars in folklore and musicology from the U.S. and Britain. In 1937, English-born Gaelic-speaker John Lorne Campbell (1906-1996) of Canna, Scotland, and his American wife, Margaret Fay Shaw, made the first organized recording expedition to Cape Breton (following up on a trip in 1932 to assess the state of Gaelic there); they sought to collect songs from the descendants of settlers from Barra and South Uist who were living near Boisdale and Iona. The linking of Scotland and Nova Scotia was a significant facet of Campbell's approach to Gaelic studies; he also made some recordings of the history and traditions of the Mi'kmaq while in Nova Scotia. Material collected by him in Cape Breton in 1937, and again in 1953, appears alongside material generated from fieldtrips to Benbecula, South Uist, Eriskay, Vatersay and Barra in *Hebridean Folksongs Volume II* (1977) and *Volume III* (1981), which he published with Francis Collison (Oxford: Clarendon Press) and is the focus of *Songs Remembered in Exile: Traditional Gaelic Songs Recorded in Nova Scotia in 1937 and 1953* (1989), which also gives contextual detail from his field work experience. In

1941, and again in 1942-1943, with the support of a Rockefeller Foundation Fellowship, Charles W. Dunn, a Scot based at Harvard University, home of the first Celtic Studies Department in North America, visited Cape Breton in search of Gaelic material. In 1953 he published *Highland Settler: A Portrait of the Scottish Gael in Nova Scotia* while he was associate professor of English at the University of Toronto; this described Scottish Settlers who came to Cape Breton. His collection, which is housed at Harvard University's Boylston Hall, includes 161 Gaelic songs and stories from Nova Scotia, including Cape Breton-American folksongs. Another ethnic-music collector and recordist, ethnographer, ethnomusicologist, teacher and writer, Sidney Roberston Cowell (1903-1995), whose work primarily focused on American folk song, visited Cape Breton in 1953 and carried out fieldwork there, material from which is housed as part of the Sidney Robertson Cowell Collection at the Library of Congress, Washington, DC, and from which was produced the LP (with detailed liner notes) *Songs from Cape Breton Island*. She also published "The Connection Between the Precenting of Psalms on Cape Breton Island and in Colonial New England Churches" (*Journal of the International Folk Music Council, 14*; 1962). Contrary to the advice of her mentor, Charles Seeger, who encouraged her to record everything, Cowell chose to concentrate her work in Cape Breton on the North Shore area, including the Gaelic Mod held at St. Ann's in 1953. Hector Campbell, a reciter of Gaelic folk tales, was the focus of the next tranche of collecting and publishing by Rev.Malcolm MacDonnell of Hillsdale; Kenneth Jackson of Harvard and the University of Edinburgh (1946), Sr. Margaret MacDonnell of St. FX. and Dr. Gordon MacLennan of University College, Dublin. and Ottawa recorded Campbell again toward the end of the 1960s. Results of Sr. Margaret MacDonell's recordings appear in *Luirgean Eachainn Nill/Folktales from Cape Breton*, published in 1981 with John Shaw. Campbell also informed the work of MacEdward Leach, an American scholar of medieval literature and folklore, known for his work on the Ulster cycle

(*Deirdre na nUisenach* / Deirdre of the Sorrows). Leach, who was professor at the University of Pennsylvania, was married to a Nova Scotian, and he spent his summers of 1949-1951 there carrying out fieldwork as part of a collaboration with the Library of Congress. The material he collected is deposited at the American Folklife Centre at the Library of Congress.

In 2004, Memorial University of Newfoundland and Labrador launched a website on *MacEdward Leach and the Songs of Atlantic Canada*. Further Gaelic material was collected and published by researcher Kathleen MacKinnon from Tiree in Scotland in 1964. A graduate of St. FX, she visited Cape Breton in the early 1960s to collect stories and songs for her 1964 Master's thesis ("A Short Study of the History and Traditions of the Highland Scot in Nova Scotia"); a report on her collecting activities in Cape Breton is lodged at the Beaton Institute. Ralph Rinzler, an American who became interested in Cape Breton song through his association with Sidney Robertson Cowell, had copies of her tapes in his personal collection that is now housed at the Smithsonian Institution; he showcased Cape Breton singers at Harvard University in 1955 and at the Newport Folk Festival, Rhode Island, in 1965. He visited Cape Breton in the 1960s and collected songs, compiling an LP for the Folkways label. The 1950s marks the beginning of activity in collecting and research by Nova Scotians themselves. Lilias Toward, a lawyer from Baddeck, known for her publication *Mabel Bell: Alexander's Silent Partner* (Breton Books, 1988), collected Gaelic and Acadian songs in the 1950s in Middle River and Whycocomagh; her tapes are housed at the Canadian Museum of History, in Ottawa. Helen Creighton's *Gaelic Songs of Nova Scotia* (1964), with Calum I. N. MacLeod, was significant since it contained, for the first time, music notation and song variants. She had first visited Cape Breton in August 1932 with Doreen Senior, her mandate to collect folk music from around the Maritimes, which she did in association with the Library of Congress, U.S., and the National Museum of Canada. Creighton's collection of Nova Scotia material on 307 audio discs, 15 audio cassettes, 4 audio cartridges, 4 cylinder recordings, 4 videocassettes and 3 film reels is held by the Nova Scotia Archives, while the Canadian Museum of History (formerly The National Museum) and the Library of Congress hold copies of selected audio recordings. Her LP *Folk Music from Nova Scotia* contains only one Gaelic song from Cape Breton and no instrumental music from the region. One of Creighton's collaborators, her Gaelic advisor Major C. I. N. MacLeod, was professor of Celtic Studies at St. FX, founder of the Celtic Studies Department there and, in the 1950s, advisor to the Department of Education. A Gaelic speaker from Kintail, Scotland, and a champion bard at the National Mod, he transcribed and translated material for Creighton and also directed her toward particular areas and singers. During his years in Nova Scotia he himself recorded Gaelic material and published some of it in *Sgialachdan a Albainn Nuaidh;* his recordings are held by the University of Glasgow. American-born John Shaw, who lived in Nova Scotia between 1964 and the 1980s, recorded extensively for St. FX and his work forms the basis of the Cape Breton Gaelic Folklore Collection, founded by Sr. Margaret MacDonnell, a Gaelic scholar and author of *The Emigrant Experience* (1982). In 2005, funded by the Department of Canadian Heritage, his field recordings were digitized and made available on the website *Struth nan Gaidheal* / Gael Stream. His fieldwork also resulted in two landmark publications, *Sgeul gu Latha (Tales Until Dawn),* based on the contribution of Joe Neil MacNeil, and *Brigh an Òrain (A Story in Every Song),* on that of Lauchie MacLellan. Prof. Kenneth Nilsen, who joined St. FX's Celtic Studies Department in the 1980s, had already recorded Nova Scotians living in Boston, during the 1970s. Working often with videotape (the first to do so extensively), he conducted more than a hundred hours of interviews with Nova Scotia Gaelic speakers. His fieldwork material, much of which informed his teaching, also appeared in local newspaper articles (in such as *The Casket*) during the 1980s and 1990s and in a number of academic articles. Other important

collecting work in the Gaelic communities was carried out between the 1970s and the 1990s by Rosemary and Brian McCormack, who were based in the Iona region and whose output included several commercial recordings, such as *A Tribute to the North Shore Gaelic Singers*. Seumas (Jim) Watson, former Gaelic editor of *Am Bràighe* and now manager of Gaelic Interpretation with the Highland Village Museum, recorded in Cape Breton from the early 1980s, and has published much of this material in *Sealladh gu Taobh / Oral Tradition and Reminiscence by Cape Breton Gaels* and in *Am Bràighe*. Since no systematic collecting of Gaelic folksong in Scotland itself began until 1946, Cape Breton emerges as a pioneer territory in this. Commercial recordings of Gaelic song (ranging from field recordings to modern representations of the tradition) have been available since the mid-1950s; publications featuring and focusing on Gaelic song include Creighton and MacLeod's *Gaelic Songs in Nova Scotia* (1964), Donald A. Fergusson's *Beyond the Hebrides (Including the Cape Breton Collection)* (1977) and John Lorne Campbell's *Songs Remembered in Exile: Traditional Gaelic Songs from Nova Scotia* (1990). There are public archival holdings of Gaelic song material in Cape Breton, as well as in the U.S., U.K. and Ireland, and private collections of song material in Canada and the U.S., as well as locally. On-line resources include *Gaelstream* (St. FX) and the Beaton Institute's *Diversity in Unity* project. Teaching in the song style and repertoire is increasingly available through workshops, summer schools and participatory events such as milling frolics, typically hosted as part of a wider program of events. Academic scholarship in the area has been conducted recently by such as Heather Sparling, Stephanie Conn and Brett Woods. [**Conn 2011**].

fiddle-music collecting. The first formal collection of Cape Breton fiddle music dates from 1941, when American ethnomusicologist, Laura Boulton, visited the island as part of a research project funded by the National Film Board of Canada and recorded fiddler Sandy MacLean from Foot Cape. Diane Hamilton, the American collector, visited Cape Breton in the mid-1950s and collected material from Gaelic singers primarily, although some instrumental selections were also included, notably from fiddler Mike MacDougall. Also in the 1950s, dance researcher Frank Rhodes collected in Cape Breton; his findings were subsequently published as part of the Flett writings on dance. [Conn 2011]. *See* **Boulton, Laura; Hamilton, Diane; Rhodes, Frank; song.**

2. Academic research. Since the 1970s, substantial amounts of material related to the fiddle tradition in Cape Breton have been collected by both researchers affiliated with an academic institution and independent scholars. The first category refers generally to the trained musicologists and folklorists, many of them (but not all) from outside of Cape Breton who have come to engage with Cape Breton music from a variety of circumstances; their collection is distinct in that the direction taken in each instance is the research question that was created to inform their individual Masters or Doctoral theses or for papers for conferences and/or publication; their collecting process is typically tailored to generate data relevant to this. The engagement with each of these individuals with the Cape Breton community has varied, as has the impact of their work on the local community; typically, their data is housed in the institutions supporting their research although copies may be available in Cape Breton and, more recently, online. A number of independent scholars from Cape Breton itself have also made significant contributions to the body of material available in published and private form. While outside scholars can bring an objective, or etic, viewpoint, for the Cape Breton scholars a significant strength is their "insider," or emic, perspective. Among the independent scholars (some of whom have been affiliated with particular institutions at points in their careers) whose work relates to the fiddle music tradition are: Allister MacGillivray, who, in the 1980s, published two volumes, *The Cape Breton Fiddler* and *A Cape Breton Ceilidh*; Paul MacDonald, whose extensive research includes areas such as home recordings, accompaniments and the

Irish influence; and Sheldon MacInnes, who was written extensively about fiddlers such as Dan Joe MacInnis and Buddy MacMaster, as well as on the dance tradition. Other scholars (historians, linguists, etc.) whose work has revealed data and perspectives valuable to the Cape Breton fiddle conversation include Ken Donovan (French influence), Barry Shears (piping), Richard MacKinnon (piano, song), Dave Mahalik (Celtic Colours) and notably Paul Cranford (style, repertoire). *See* **research.**

3. Archives and institutions. The Beaton Institute, the Celtic Music Interpretive Centre, the Highland Village Museum, CBU and St. F.X. have instigated collection and research projects, yielding both historical and contemporary material, which has been accessible on-site, through recordings, print publication and on-line. *See* **Archives; Beaton Institute; Cape Breton University; Celtic Music Interpetive Centre; Highland Village Museum; St. FX.**

4. Amateur collecting has played a significant role in the amassing and assembling of a substantial amount of Cape Breton fiddle music, both in written and in audio (and, to a lesser extent, audiovisual) formats. Such collectors can be classified as follows: (i) those who set out to collect or record fresh material, and (ii) those who amass it from retail and/or other sources.

(i) The practice of making home recordings of house sessions became popular among fiddle-music enthusiasts once domestic recording devices became widely and cheaply accessible; recordists progressed from large reel-to-reel, to cassette, DAT, minidisk and digital formats; they also used super-8 film, video and digital video. A recognized home-recording culture peaked during the 1950s and 1960s and played a key role in documenting the fiddle tradition in that era; this replaced, to a large degree, fiddlers' dependence on the recording industry. While these were amateur collectors, documenting what were often (but not always) spontaneous musical affairs, some substantial and significant collections have been generated as a result, such as those made by Doug MacMaster, Herbie MacLeod and Johnny

Muise in Boston. Some of these collections of house recordings – from both Cape Breton and the Cape Breton diaspora – have made their way into larger archives (e.g., at Boston College) and some material thus recorded has also been made commercially available.

(ii) A number of fiddle and piano players in Cape Breton were known for having substantial collections of tune books. Most appear to have been generous in sharing these in the wider fiddle community, and some of them were indeed quite careless about seeking returns, so that there was a scattering of such books throughout the island. Others maintained their collections intact, however, and among these was Joe MacLean, whose 104 books were donated to the Highland Village in Iona following his death; Winston Fitzgerald's 50 or so books from Scottish, Irish, American and Canadian traditions are now in the Beaton Institute. Collections such as these, and other collections of tune books and recordings amassed by musicians such as Malcolm Beaton, Johnny "MacVarish" MacDonald, John A. Campbell, Bill Lamey, Dan Joe MacInnis, Doug MacPhee, Francis MacDonald, Dave MacIsaac, Kyle MacNeil, Dwayne Côté and non-musician aficionados such as the late Danny Fraser, of Westmount, and David Gillis, of Margaree, contribute to an understanding of the 20th-century Cape Breton repertoire. So too do hand-written and self-assembled tune collections help build up the picture of the effort that went into acquiring new material prior to the advent of photocopiers and scanners. Others built substantial private collections of recordings either of those commercially available or of domestic home recordings. Dave MacIsaac has one of the most impressive of such collections; Donnie Campbell, for instance, shares much of private collection through his weekly radio show. *See* **note reading.**

5. Collecting for publication and dissemination. Collecting where the end product is made commercially available includes published tune collections and writings about Cape Breton fiddle music, audio and video recordings (and accompanying liner notes), radio, TV and Internet materi-

als. [**Conn 2011; Lavengood 2003; MacDonald 2000**] *See* **recordings;** *Cape Breton Fiddler, The; Cape Breton's Magazine;* **tune books.**

Colosimo, Mario. (1954-). Piano, teacher. Glace Bay. From a background in classical and popular musics, he was drawn into Cape Breton music in the early 2000s through the weekly sessions at Rollie's (a popular live-music venue, now closed), in North Sydney, where he became a regular player. He had taken piano lessons from the age of six and was exposed to a wide range of music at home; his mother sang, and his uncles were part of a country and western band during the 1950s. Also playing guitar, fiddle, mandolin and bouzouki, he is part of a trio with Lisa MacArthur (fiddle) and Paul MacDonald (guitar), and has been featured on recordings with Paul Cranford (2010), Allie Bennett (2013), Lawrence Martell (2013) and Stan Chapman, and with his student groups from CBU. Colosimo's music-notation skills have contributed significantly to Cranford's tune collections, such as *More Tunes from the Lighthouse* (2010), *The Celtic Colours Collection* (2011), *The Cape Breton Scottish Collection* (2013) and *The Cape Breton Highland Collection* (2015).

Columbia Records. Founded in Washington in 1888, Columbia is the oldest brand name in the recording industry. Its first 78-rpm discs were issued at the turn of the 20th century and included many "ethnic" music recordings, which were designated "F" (for foreign) as part of a strategy to provide musics for immigrant markets. Columbia Records of Canada was established in Toronto in 1904, with its discs pressed and distributed by Sarton Records there from 1939 to 1954; from then until 1979 it was reconfigured as CBS Records Canada. Columbia produced the first known recordings of Cape Breton fiddlers – released in a Scottish series of the "F" category. The players were fiddlers "Big" Dan Hughie MacEachern and Charlie MacKinnon, who were resident in the northeastern U.S. at the time. They were recorded as members of the ensembles The Columbia Scotch Band and The Caledonia Scotch Band. Antigonish fiddler Colin

J. Boyd had three 78s on the Columbia label at this time as well, but these were grouped with the Irish series. John Allan Cameron later released two LPs on the label, *Lord of the Dance* (1973) and *Weddings, Wakes and Other Things* (1976). *See* **recording industry**.

Columbia Scotch Band. A 1920s Boston-based ensemble which recorded with the Columbia label under this name and also as the Caledonia Scotch Band. *See* **Caledonia Scotch Band.**

Committee for Cape Breton. *See* **Cape Breton Fiddlers' Association**.

Competition. In music and dance, this takes two forms: (i) innate human competitiveness and (ii) organized competition for prizes or honours. Both apply in Cape Breton music. Innate, or unspoken competition continues to exist, as in any healthy, ongoing tradition. It is seen, not only in young players, but was part of the music's 20th-century development; fiddlers, for example, would try to outshine one another by producing a new tune at the first summer concert after a long winter spent perusing the printed collections. Inevitably, in such a small community, there will always be a degree of competition to secure a particular gig or a recording contract; hierarchies in fiddling are further determined by criteria such as the number and status of performance engagements, community recognition through tributes and testimonials, album sales, funding success, level of media coverage and, latterly, recognition though various award ceremonies. This same human urge fed into the competition ethos which peaked in the early-to-middle decades of the 20th century and were more significant in the past than in the present. Between the 1920s and 1980s, Cape Bretoners took part in a substantial number of fiddle and step-dance contests held in Cape Breton itself and as far away as Boston; many of them won prizes, and trophies have been named after renowned Cape Breton fiddlers. Contests were regarded as a viable performance context to be enjoyed by the fiddlers and the wider community, but they have not played a strategic part in, or become the driver of, the Cape Breton fiddlers' sound or practice; fiddlers played the same tunes as they would in any other performance situation, and in their own personal style as it was at any given time.

competition and standards. In other fiddle traditions in Canada and elsewhere, until the advent of modern-day, inexpensive album production and professional and semi-professional performance opportunities, competition played a central role in establishing "standards." On the down side, it can be seen to dictate repertoire and influence performance practices and styles, as performers tailor their playing to meet the conventions or expectations of judges; this tends to set "competition players" yet further apart from "at home" fiddlers. In the early decades of the 20th century, fiddle contests were fashionable and seductive for the better players, but addressed an all-around technical mastery rather than regional style, and were advertised as old-time or old-style where such terms were used to encapsulate all of the old-country styles (Scottish, Irish, French) that were still being maintained in the new-world environment. However, with the distinction between styles becoming more illuminated as the century progressed, and as the criteria for competitions narrowed, it became evident that in order to pursue the competition route the Cape Breton fiddlers would be required to compromise their style. For the majority of them, by unspoken consensus, this was out of the question. And despite enthusiastic indulgence in competition by at-home and diaspora Cape Breton fiddlers over a half-century, it is not acknowledged as having been a force in determining core elements of the fiddle style. Perhaps this is because, as the century progressed, Cape Breton fiddlers who followed the contest route as part of their performance profile tended to be either based off-island or were non-Scottish in their heritage (e.g., Lee Cremo, Tara Lynne Touesnard, Elmer Briand, Marcel Doucet, Joe Cormier); for such musicians, playing Cape Breton music was a personal choice. In any case, since the 1980s, contests have had no significant place in the music lives of the majority of Cape Breton fiddle players, despite their being challenged and derided occasionally in the media for this choice by representatives of other contest-focused fiddle styles. The 1970s revival of fiddle music effectively filtered out residual contest activity among Cape Breton fiddlers, whereas in other cultures, such as in Ireland, organized competition introduced in the 1950s has, in fact, contributed to the re-energizing of what was at that time a flagging tradition. In Cape Breton – perhaps because the fiddle community was so small, or perhaps because *The Vanishing Cape Breton Fiddler* documentary had challenged the tradition as a whole, causing that community to consolidate in retaliation – the focus turned to transmission, participation and, ultimately, professionalism. By the 1980s, it was clear that little interest remained in the ethos of competition as such.

overview of contests involving Cape Breton fiddlers. The competition attitude is not without some sense of irony or even paradox, considering that in the history of the art of fiddle playing, Cape Bretoners have made quite a mark and have enjoyed notable success in contests, many of these in Cape Breton itself. The first known competition involving a Cape Breton fiddler was held in Glendale, Inverness County, ca. 1891, when Malcolm H. Gillis was awarded first prize. Contests in fiddle playing, step dancing, piping and milling were part of the picnics held in the early decades of the 20th century in communities like Judique and Inverness. Much of the interest in contests which occupied the early-to-mid-20th century stemmed from a series of contests initiated by Henry Ford in Minnesota and replicated across North America. In 1926 The Intercolonial Club of Boston, an organization made up largely of Maritime expatriates, held a local contest and its success prompted the promotion of an open competition for fiddlers from the U.S. and Canada, the majority of them from New England, Québec and the Maritime Provinces. The impetus was to halt the popularity of jazz by promoting old-time music; the entry criteria specified that participants must be at least 50 years of age. Regional heats were held in various locations with the winners

convening in Boston for the final, which would be held over a week. In the end, there were several contests held in Boston as a result, the first two only a week apart as the winner at any given time could be challenged to defend his victory. Within Cape Breton, a number of regional contests were held in order to select the players to send forward to compete in Boston. In April, 1926, Dougald MacIntyre of Cape Mabou took first place at the Strand Theatre in Sydney, going forward as South Cape Breton's representative to the Boston finals where, adjudicated by J. Scott Skinner, he was placed second and was awarded a silver trophy; "Big" Dan Hughie MacEachern from Glenora was the winner. Malcolm H. Gillis, who had won first place in Glendale, was also placed second in one of the contests held in Boston that year, while Mick MacInnis (1870-1946) from Terra Nova came first among the competing 100 fiddlers and was presented with a trophy inscribed: "Michael MacInnis, Best Old Fashioned Fiddler, 1926, Intercolonial Club, Boston." MacInnis continued to excel on the competition circuit winning various awards in New Glasgow (e.g., Eastern Nova Scotia Fiddle Champion, 1926), Charlottetown, PEI, and again in Boston in 1929. Other Cape Breton fiddlers who participated in contests during this decade included Dan J. Campbell, who was placed first in a contest staged at Labour Temple Hall, Inverness, in 1926, judged by Sandy MacLean, Angus Chisholm (who was to win in Boston in 1927) and "Big" Dan Hughie MacEachern, who would take second place in 1929. Ronald Kennedy (1870-1958), "Red" John MacKinnon and James P. Campbell (1863-1942) were also successful contest players at this time. "Baby" Joe MacLellan, of Princeville, under the tutelage of his father, "Big" Ronald MacLellan, entered the contest scene in the 1920s as a young teenager and won prizes in Sydney, North Sydney and at the Judique Highland Games. In 1932, Tena Campbell took first place in a contest in Glace Bay sponsored by the fire department, and later won the Maritime Fiddle Championship. In 1933, Angus Allan Gillis won the St. Finian's Cup at Alexandria, Ontario. In the same year, Lila Hashem won a piano competition staged in Sydney as part of the city's 150th anniversary, where she performed a strathspey and two reels before judges Fr. Stanley MacDonald and Bernie MacIntosh. In the late 1940s, Bill Lamey won a contest held at the Gaelic College, sponsored by the Cape Breton Island Gaelic Foundation and adjudicated by Prof. Jimmy MacDonald from North Sydney. The last known fiddle contest held in the Iona area saw John Francis Campbell receive first place among competitors which included Hector MacLean, Kitchener MacDonald and Gordon MacQuarrie. The Glenora picnics continued to hold contests where John Alex "The Big Fiddler" MacDonald won many medals as did Ronald Kennedy of Broad Cove Chapel, and the Mod, first held in the 1930s, later included fiddle competitions.

decline. Contests began to wane in popularity on Cape Breton Island itself after the mid-1900s, although Cape Breton fiddlers continued to participate in contests held off-island. Mary MacDonald, for example, competed in Boston and Detroit, where she won a number of medals. Dan Joe MacInnis was awarded the Old Time Fiddle's Championship Trophy in a 1942 contest. In the 1960s, CJCB-TV, Sydney, developed the idea of a popularity contest as an alternative to the platform. Noted players such as Theresa MacLellan, Paddy LeBlanc, Joe MacLean and Winston Fitzgerald participated, with Dan Joe MacInnis emerging the winner. Fiddlers began to compete in contests outside of the established circuit, with Wilfred Gillis participating in the Canadian Fiddling Championships and Winnie Chafe entering the International Fiddlers Contest in Pembroke in 1964, and emerging as the first woman ever to win this. But by the 1970s contests had disappeared from the Cape Breton scene; this was the period when local fiddlers turned their attention to refuting the media suggestion that the Cape Breton fiddle tradition was in danger of vanishing. Off-island, some fiddlers continued to pursue success in the contest circuit; one of them, Joe Cormier, for example, winning several contests in Waltham, MA, (in 1971 he won first prize; in 1972 he placed third and won the prize for Federa-

tion Fiddler). At the Dartmouth Old Time Fiddle Championship contest in Nova Scotia, fiddlers such as Lee Cremo, Jerry Holland, Larry Parks and Arthur Muise participated while Donald MacLellan, who had previously won the Championship of Eastern Nova Scotia Cup, won the Mod Ontario Trophy in 1976 and 1977. In the late 1970s and early 1980s an attempt was made to revive fiddle contests in Cape Breton itself; in 1979 and 1980, Bill Lamey and Winnie Chafe were invited to judge contests in Port Hawkesbury as part of the Festival of the Strait; Hugh Angus Jobes won the Buddy MacMaster trophy for jig playing in 1980; the Angus Chisholm Memorial trophy was won by Karen Beaton. However, the level of local support for these was small and it was clear that the contest held little attraction within the local Cape Breton fiddle community. Fiddlers did continue to compete in contests elsewhere; many continued to participate in contests held at the Canadian-American Club in Boston. Don Campbell won several contests in Ontario and was a semi-finalist in the North American Old Time Fiddle Championships held in Shelburne, Ontario. Tara Lynn Touesnard won the Maritime Fiddle Championship on several occasions (where there has been an award named in her honour, following her death in 1994) and had been invited to compete in the Canadian Grand Masters Fiddling Championship in Ottawa. Troy MacGillivray and Cassie MacDonald are other Cape Breton-style fiddlers who have been involved in this contest since the 1990s. Mi'kmaw fiddler Lee Cremo, from Eskasoni, is undoubtedly the single most successful Cape Bretoner to engage in the contest scene, across both Canada and the U.S., and was the recipient of more than 85 awards and a number of prestigious titles. The absence of the better-known names among young fiddlers—many of whom are professional musicians—indicates that the more invisible, organic sense of competition in a commercial world is currently the favoured medium of achieving personal gratification outside of community appreciation. **[Doherty 1996; Hornby 1979; MacInnes 1997].**

Fiddle and Box

reel

Paul S. Cranford
contemporary Cape Breton

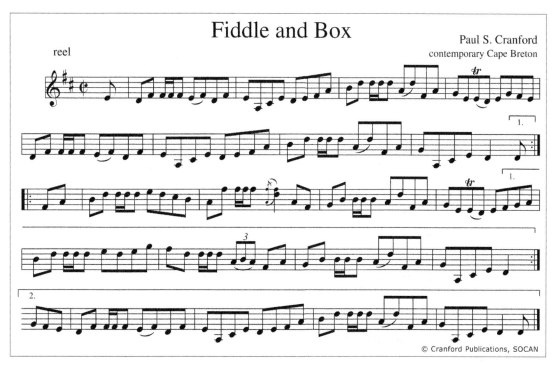

Composed by Paul Cranford for the wedding of Liz Doherty and Jim Woods, 2007.

composing. The practice of "making" new tunes is a vibrant one in the Cape Breton fiddle tradition as is evidenced by the substantial numbers of compositions appearing in published collections (in Cape Breton and, occasionally, elsewhere), on recordings and in private collections. The first documented tune composition from Cape Breton appears to be "The Charlottetown (Cape Breton) Caledonia Club," a 2/4 march by Archie A. Beaton of Mabou in David Glen's *Collection of Highland Bagpipe Music*, Book 7, published in Edinburgh, Scotland ca. 1905; this was followed by a 6/8 pipe march by Malcolm H. Gillis "The New Year", which appeared in Book 11 of the series, published in 1908. The publication of Gordon MacQuarrie's 1940 collection, *The Cape Breton Collection of Scottish Melodies for the Violin,* had 101 compositions by MacQuarrie himself, with the remainder by 13 others, including Dan R. MacDonald, Ronald MacLellan, Sandy MacLean, Dan Hughie MacEachern, piper Alex MacDonald and J. D. Kennedy; this suggests that the practice of composing new material was well established at that point. While several decades lapsed before there were any further publications of tunes, it is known that Dan R. MacDonald was busy composing by the 1940s. Dan Hughie MacEachern was the only other fiddler known to be composing any quantities of tunes at the time; however, others did dabble in it to some degree, including Angus Chisholm, Winston Fitzgerald and Johnny Wilmot. For whatever their reasons, they chose not to formally publish their newly composed materials and it was not until the 1970s that substantial evidence emerged relating to the extent of such composition. This in turn prompted a significant wave of tune making, which still carries on today. The prevalence of tune composition within the Cape Breton tradition may be a direct outcome of the restrictions imposed on the creative process by the notion of "correctness"; to be "correct" a tune must follow a specified melodic pattern and so, rather than engaging creatively with existing tunes by way of variation (as is the practice in Irish music), fiddlers instead channel their creativity into the construction of new material. A common practice was to add variations to existing tunes in the form of extra parts or turns. Also, once square sets became popular in the early 20th century, more jigs were needed and, as well as borrowing from such as the Irish tradition, many new tunes of this type were locally composed.

the composers. Best known of the early Cape Breton fiddler composers are Dan R. MacDonald and Dan Hughie MacEachern, the former with ca. 450 tunes published out of some 2,000 original compositions in his lifetime; more recently, Jerry Holland had a total published output of ca. 275 tunes. Over all periods, however, Kinnon Beaton is the most widely published of all the Cape Breton fiddler composers (with ca. 700 tunes in print), while John MacDougall, who allegedly has composed around 45,000 tunes, is considered the most prolific. Many others have published collections of their own tunes, among them John Campbell, Brenda Stubbert, Dougie MacDonald, Paul Cranford, Andrea Beaton, Otis Tomas, Francis MacDonald, Joey Beaton, Pat Chafe, Glenn Graham, Ray Ellis and Troy MacGillivray. Through the nine volumes published to date as part of the *Cape Breton Musical Traditions Series,* Toronto-born publisher Paul Cranford has made a vital contribution to the tune-composition element of the Cape Breton tradition by foregrounding the work of a wide range of composers, ensuring that the tunes are correctly associated with their sources for posterity. His 2007 publication, *The Cape Breton Fiddlers Collection,* for example, contains 267 pieces, the majority of them from 96 Cape Breton composers; it is testimony to the continued enthusiasm for this practice. Today, the majority of fiddlers compose a few tunes and include these in their personal repertoires, often recording them and (less frequently) publishing them in hard copy. Piano players (such as Doug MacPhee, Barbara MacDonald Magone, Ryan MacNeil, Stewart MacNeil, Pat Chafe and Gordon MacLean) and pipers have also contributed to the body of newly composed Cape Breton tunes played by fiddlers. Indeed, they too will often adapt and perform the new compositions of the fiddle players.

the process. No consistent methodology appears to exist in relation to tune composing within the Cape Breton fiddle tradition. Most fiddlers refer to it as something that happens quite casually – a tune might simply pop into their head at any point in time. Others admit that the creative streak may vary, and while some tunes "just appear," others will take more time to shape. Occasionally in published collections we see notes to the effect that a tune was composed over an extended period of time – sometimes years. An unusual instance is that of John MacDougall who is said to have composed substantial numbers of tunes within short time frames; he believed that these tunes had been "given" to him by the dead. Andrea Beaton carries a notebook and jots down ideas and melodic fragments several times over the course of a day; these she may later develop into a tune or a number of tunes. Dan R. Mac-Donald was known to have jotted down ideas as and when they came to him; "Heather Hill," for example, was composed while he was working in the woods in Scotland and written while sitting on a tree stump. Many engage in the composing process while they have the fiddle in their hands, and some fiddlers have composed tunes while trying out other instruments, such as mandolin or banjo. In some instances, fiddlers have collaborated on specific tunes and, in recent years, such collaborative opportunities have been formalized and extended to non-Cape Breton partners through project opportunities such as at Celtic Colours.

naming and registering tunes. The prevalence of written sources for much of the Cape Breton-composed repertoire suggests the importance of appreciating and acknowledging sources. The Cape Breton fiddler of the past certainly appears to have had a deep appreciation of and respect for tune sources; this, no doubt, is linked into issues of identity and integrity. And so, for locally composed tunes in the Cape Breton repertoire, the practice of correctly identifying composers and tunes has continued, supported today by the availability of a substantial body of published information against which to check material. Furthermore, the recording business, which demands precise identification and acknowledgement of sources, necessitates the practice. In more recent times, since virtually all tune composers wish to formally register and copyright their material, the legal imperative demands that composers continue with this practice. Yet self-composed tunes were not always afforded this type of esteem, least of all by the composers themselves. Dan R. MacDonald was known to have freely shared his compositions (although he always ensured his name was included in the hand-written copy) and was simply happy to have them played; indeed he was apparently surprised to receive his first royalties for performances of his tunes by the Cape Breton Symphony Fiddlers.

tune names. The names given to tunes composed in Cape Breton reflect the life and society of the fiddlers. As is the practice elsewhere, tunes are often named after an individual – a friend, a family member, another fiddler, a step dancer or piano player – and indeed it is considered quite a privilege to have a tune composed in one's honour. Events are also recognized in many tune titles; among such are weddings, anniversaries and deaths. Also, when travelling fiddlers would spend extended periods of time with a family, as was common up to and during the 20th century, they would often write a tune as a mark of gratitude to their hosts, in much the same manner as Turlough O'Carolan and other 17th- and 18th-century harpist-composers had done in Ireland. A survey of the names of tunes can reveal changes in the player's life or fortunes. For instance, Dan R. MacDonald's composition titles trace the course of his life, including his overseas travels during the Second World War; indeed, the increase in performance travel by all players, and their interaction with other musicians outside Cape Breton, can be traced through compositions of the 1990s onward. Such contemporary tunes may have more humorous titles that can generate or colour stage patter, something which was not needed for older players, who tended to speak little, if at all, during performances.

style. Within the broad range of tunes that make up the Cape Breton, locally composed repertoire, a number of stylistic features are included. There is often a marked difference between older tunes and more recent compositions, for instance. Older pieces are often modal in character, use a narrow range and may be built on gapped scales; the use of the double tonic is also a feature of many older tunes. Newer compositions sometimes display an increased harmonic awareness and a predominance of major keys rather than modes. Donald Angus Beaton's tunes, for instance, are generally narrow in range, rarely employ the lower G-string and never move out of first position, thus aligning to the older style of his playing. Tunes involving the entire first-position range of the fiddle, and more, were introduced in local compositions such as in the tunes of Dan R. MacDonald and Dan Hughie MacEachern. This represented a marked departure from the limited range typical of older tunes, largely dictated as they were by piping and vocal sources and ranges. Individual composers, however, have their own unique styles, and many of these are instantly recognizable by any musician familiar with the tradition. The majority of tunes conform to the AABB binary structure although, occasionally, extended and multiple-part tunes are to be found. Of the locally composed Cape Breton tunes to date, the most common forms are reel, strathspey and jig, followed by march, slow strathspey and air. Small numbers of other tune-types are also found in newer collections, the most recent type being "slip-tunes" in 3/2. Perhaps understandably, the more radical of the newer compositions tend to be played only by the composer rather than being picked up and assimilated into the wider Cape Breton repertoire.

interpreting the tunes. Individual tune composers express different views in relation to how their music might best be interpreted by other players. Typically, when published, only occasional directions are given in relation to individual tunes, perhaps a tempo or general style direction or some bowing suggestions. Kinnon Beaton, however, in his 2010 collection states in the introduction that while those playing the tunes are free to add their own expression, the melody notes should not be interfered with. From the opposite perspective, Dougie MacDonald and Pat Chafe both suggest that those interpreting the tunes do what they feel necessary to make them their own. **[Graham 2006; MacDonald 2009; McGann 2003].** *See* **tune books.**

Comunn Féis Mhàbu. Mabou-based organization whose purpose is to facilitate the progressive development of Gaelic language and culture with many of the programs it offers focusing on the transmission of cultural skills in intergenerational social settings. Although based in Mabou, CFM programs draw participants from the surrounding area, and in some instances, from all over Cape Breton and beyond. This is an organization without a building. CFM feels that this offers freedom to present their programs and events in the settings that best suit their needs. For more than 20 years, Comunn Féis Mhàbu has offered a wide range of workshops, programs and events to both youth and adults. These include weekend cultural workshops, music- and song-mentoring programs for youths based around the house-session context, with performance opportunities at local venues, Gaelic song circles, after-school programs, Gaelic immersion programs and family square-dance lessons. CFM has also partnered with Celtic Colours to host the "Mentors and Musical Minds" concert at Strathspey Place in Mabou, showcasing young players from its own program with high profile local artists and international guests.

concert. This kind of event, presentational in nature and involving formal stage performance before a live audience, has been popular in Cape Breton since the 1950s. The outdoor summer concert, hosted by individual local communities throughout the summer months, was popular throughout the second half of the 20th century, with the number of such events peaking in the late 1980s-early 1990s; typically, these highlighted local talent, with fiddle players, piano players and step dancers often dominating the program. While a small number of such events have continued, various other types of concert have been developed; today, concerts happen year-round, and many are held in a range of indoor venue types; concerts vary from the variety model of the outdoor concert to single, headline-act events. Concerts thus take three forms: (i) outdoor summer concert, (ii) indoor concert and (iii) pub concert/matinee.

(i) Outdoor summer concert. By the mid-20th century, the era of the parish picnic with its diverse program of participatory events and activities had begun to wane as the "Scottish concert" – where the emphasis was more on cultural entertainment – began to become more popular; the first of these was held at Broad Cove in 1957. Over the years, various local communities organized their own concerts and, by the 1980s, the summer calendar was crammed with these events. The concerts were held outdoors, in a field equipped with staging, sound, lights and basic catering and other facilities. Typically organized by a volunteer committee over several months, an even larger contingent of volunteers becomes

Ben Eoin Fiddle and Folk Festival. Courstey of Dan MacDonald.

involved in the implementation of the event itself, so that these are truly community occasions. Concert-goers come equipped with chairs, refreshments and suitable clothing, prepared for what was usually a marathon session, lasting for several hours; typically the concert would start in the early afternoon and continue until late evening. In some cases the concert would be followed by a dance in the local community hall; a tradition of late-night house parties also developed in association with particular concerts. While each concert has it own distinct identity, the program is generally populated primarily with fiddle and piano players (perhaps with additional guitar and/or percussion accompaniment), each performing a 10-15 minute set; this is supplemented with pipers, singers and perhaps a band; dancers feature quite frequently. Since the 1970s it became common to end such concerts with a finale featuring a massed fiddle group. An emcee – often someone who has held that position for many years – will make all the announcements and introduce the various acts; musicians themselves, especially fiddlers, generally choose not to speak on-stage; this is something that has changed since the 1990s and increased awareness of the fiddlers on-stage presentation skills.

Following the landmark 1970s Glendale concerts, programs were dominated by local fiddle players such as Buddy MacMaster, Theresa MacLellan, Jerry Holland, Howie MacDonald, Brenda Stubbert and Kinnon Beaton, gradually introducing the younger generation of players such as Natalie MacMaster, Ashley MacIsaac and Wendy MacIsaac. For that generation of players, the summer outdoor "Scottish" concert was often the stepping stone for them to begin life as a public performer; prior to that, the house party or square dance fulfilled that role; since the late 1990s, Celtic Colours serves that purpose for more recent emerging artists. Many of the acts who have gone on to international acclaim honed their craft through the experience of performing at the outdoor concerts, among these the Rankins, the Barra MacNeils, Natalie MacMaster and Ashley MacIsaac. Concerts were also an important plat-

form for celebrating musicians "from away," Cape Breton's first and subsequent generations who lived in places such as Detroit, Toronto, Boston and who often made their annual visit home to coincide with the local concert. The labelling of these concerts as Scottish (as was common during the 1950s and 1960s) is a significant indicator of the sense of identity felt by the Cape Breton music community and their acknowledgement of and pride in their Scottish roots. But from the 1970s onward, as a stronger sense of a Cape Breton "self" became embedded – partly in response to the perceived threat exposed by *The Vanishing Cape Breton Fiddler* documentary – the Scottish tag was pushed back, passing through a transition stage where concerts were referred to as "Cape Breton Scottish"; ultimately the concerts came to be celebrated as "Cape Breton," reflecting a new-found confidence in the region's own voice. Fiddle concerts following the same model became a feature of some of the non-Scottish communities such as that at St. Joseph-du-Moine, which was hosted by the Acadian community. Today, the outdoor concerts of this type are at Broad Cove (July), Highland Village (August) and St. Ann's (August).

concert formula. While the program content of the concerts has followed the same basic formula from the late 1970s on, some, particularly those outside of Inverness County, began to feature outside acts such as Runrig, Na h-Òganaich, the Battlefield Band and Ossian, all from Scotland, alongside local musicians. The mid-1980s and early 1990s were, arguably, the heyday of the outdoor fiddle concerts. Since then a number of these have ceased to exist (e.g., Saint-Joseph-du-Moine and Ben Eoin); others have evolved in different directions, expanding into community festivals where the fiddle concert (possibly indoors now rather than outdoors) is alongside a plethora of other events in a more varied program. Various factors have contributed to the demise in popularity of the outdoor concert. At a fundamental level, there is the issue of the organization of such an event, with many of those involved for many years no longer able to commit to the workload and with perhaps fewer interested young folk in the communities to take up the mantle. But, if the number of concerts of this nature has decreased, the number of fiddle-music events has increased to cater for the growing cultural tourism sector. Perhaps the typical tourist did not understand, appreciate or need the marathon concert setting, with fiddler after fiddler being showcased? Perhaps this was too intense an introduction to the local culture? Smaller snapshots of the tradition, preferably with an element of participation, seem to be more palatable. And, of course, the Cape Breton scene has been transformed since 1997 by Celtic Colours, which has brought a new and different context, dynamic and level of expectation to events across the island and has no doubt impacted on the outdoor concert circuit. That said, some concerts such as Broad Cove, Highland Village and the CBFA concert at the Gaelic College continue to deliver what has become, and *is*, a uniquely Cape Breton experience – an outdoor concert setting where fiddler after fiddler dominates the stage. And while even these stalwarts have modernized and moved toward having a headline act (which may or may not be a fiddler) – in some instances made possible by corporate sponsorship – the general program ethos and experience remains the same.

(ii) **Indoor concert.** Smaller concerts, easily accommodated in parish, community or fire halls became popular, outside of the summer months originally, and then gradually, as year-round fixtures on the Cape Breton scene. Such concerts may be organized by volunteer community groups as a fundraiser or, in more recent times, by commercial promoters and venues. They may be stand-alone events or be held in association with other activities such as summer schools and community festivals, or may mark specific calendar events such as St. Patrick's Day. Concerts have become a popular way of remembering past artists, and tribute concerts have been held to honour, for instance, the memories of John Allan Cameron, Jerry Holland, Estwood Davidson and Mike MacDougall. Typically these are 2-3-hour affairs and follow the variety concert model with

an emcee. Popular concerts include the weekly three-fiddler concert held at The Barn at the Normaway Inn in Margaree. Another particular type, the pastoral airs concert, was introduced by the Big Pond Summer Festival Committee in 1989; this theme continues today, held in St. Mary's Church and focusing primarily on air playing and song; other communities such as Iona, Marion Bridge, Glencoe and Mabou have taken up this type of event also. Only in recent years have single-headline-act concerts, possibly with a supporting act, been found, inspired by an awareness of contemporary practices since the Celtic boom of the 1990s; events such as the Granville Green concert series in Port Hawkesbury have successfully adopted this model.

(iii) **Pub concert.** Often referred to as a matinee, even when it happens late in the afternoon or early evening, this concert or gig sits somewhere between the formal concert and the public, commercial ceilidh. Typically, a fiddler and accompanist (piano, perhaps with guitar and/or percussion) are seated on a small stage and amplification is in place. Often there is a small floor area in front of the stage to allow for step dancing or a square set. The performance typically lasts a few hours; the fiddler is "spelled off" (i.e., given a break) by other fiddlers who show up, usually locals or perhaps some visitors known to the musicians. Little or nothing is spoken from the stage (unless there is a singer involved who likes to engage with the audience). Dancers take to the floor spontaneously or with encouragement from the audience or the musicians on stage. While the emergence of the pub as a significant venue in the context of Cape Breton music performance is a recent phenomenon – compared with say, Ireland, where it has been part of the culture since the 1950s – the pub matinee became an institution first in the Acadian village of Chéticamp, where such have taken place on Saturday afternoons, year-round, at the Doryman Tavern since the early 1970s; Le Gabriel, another tavern in the village, has also a long association with programming events of this nature, often again on Saturday afternoons. The Sydney area has seen a number of venues explore this type of event over the years (The Old Sydney Pub, The Bonnie Prince, The County Line, Daniel's, Governors, Ziggy's, The Crown and Moose, The Old Triangle, etc.); the Red Shoe Pub in Mabou hosts a music program with daily performances from May until October, as does the Glenora Distillery; most recently, the Frolic and Folk Pub and Grill opened at the Iona Heights Inn in Iona also offers a fiddle music events program. Intimate pub venues redolent of Irish pubs are different from the larger spaces, with dance floors also popular for fiddle-music events on the island (such as the various Royal Canadian Legions, Knights of Columbus halls and Elks Clubs where Saturday afternoon music/dance events may happen). Across the island other pub-type concerts or gigs focus on the contemporary folk singer, perhaps with a fiddler playing backup; sets of fiddle tunes may be included in this setting, one of the few instances in which fiddle may be accompanied by guitar without the presence of a piano. [Doherty 1996; Graham 2006; MacInnes 1997]. *See* **matinee.**

Confiant, Joe. (1900-1985). Fiddle. George's River and Glace Bay. Born in Little Bras d'Or, to parents Frank and Martha (Fortune) Confiant, Joe was among the first Cape Breton fiddlers to be well-versed in both Irish and Scottish music. His father was born on the French island of Saint Pierre, off the coast of Newfoundland. His uncle, Henry Fortune, was a noted Irish style fiddler and a note reader. Highly influenced by him and the various other Irish players along the Gannon Road, Confiant also took an interest in the Scottish musicians moving to the Northside, befriending harmonica player Alex Basker, from Mull River, who had moved there by the 1920s. Alex was a Gaelic speaker and played a different repertoire, coming from the Mabou district. Together they created a vibrant hybrid, a sound and repertoire unique to this long-time duo. Joe and Alex played dances and parties all over the Northside (being particularly popular in Frenchvale where Basker's wife was from) and performed often on radio. Joe Confiant's own home, located in Centerville, halfway between North Sydney and Sydney Mines, became a legendary household for sessions, attracting many musicians from the rural districts. Thus "old Joe," as he was known, became a very influential player. In addition to his large repertoire of Irish and Scotch tunes he included Acadian tunes, rare polkas, and old American fiddle tunes such as the "Arkansas Traveller" and "The British Grenadiers March." Joe also had a distinctive method of padding both feet as he played, similar to the Québécois style. His late sons Joe, William and Raymond also played the fiddle, the later two taking an iterest in the Bluegrass style. Today, tunes from Joe's eclectic repertoire can be heard performed by such as Larry Parks and Paul Cranford. Confiant himself, with John Willie Morrison on piano, can be heard on the album *Off to Georges River–Traditional Irish, Scottish and Cape Breton Fiddle Music* (2002), a recording which demonstrates his unique approach to bowing with cuts happening in both directions; it also displays his very solid, deliberate timing, which generates great lift and dynamics in his music. Rare recordings of his duo with Alex Basker exhibit even more dynamism, Basker punctuating with chords and double stops while maintaining a steady swing, allowing Confiant to play freely with his bowing and variations.

Conseil des Arts de Chéticamp (CAC). Founded in 1999, it was formed from local organizations such as The Swing du Suête Dance Company, the Échos des Montagnes Youth Choir and Théâtre Sans Détour in order to render arts and culture efforts more effective in the community; since then it has become a regional arts-promotion body recognized by the province of Nova Scotia's Department of Tourism, Culture and Heritage. Its primary focus is the preservation and promotion of Acadian culture in Chéticamp and it is in this context that it programs fiddle music as part of its mandate.

contests. *See* **competition.**

Copley. A record label established by Justus O'Byrne in Boston in the late 1940s to fill the gap in the market created when the major American labels ceased issuing Irish recordings. His Irish-born mother, Ellen O'Byrne and his Dutch father, Justus De Witt, had opened a store in New York in 1900 where they sold music instruments and cylinder recordings; Ellen convinced Columbia to begin recording Irish artists and this eventually led to the creation of its "F" (foreign) series. Following his mother's death, in 1926, Justus moved to Roxbury, MA, where he established a music shop, travel agency and record company, selling and distributing Irish, Scottish and Canadian music on disc. They then began recording all three genres, with an emphasis on Irish and Irish-American content. Titles such as *The Cape Breton Breakdown* are found in the listings, but in later catalogues Canadian musicians were listed as Scottish artists; Cape Breton fiddler, Dan R. MacDonald, for example, who recorded at least three 78s with Copley, was advertised as "Dan R. MacDonald, well known Scottish fiddler." Johnny Wilmot is also believed to have recorded with this label in duet with Joe Derrane, accordionist, although no discs exist to verify this. Typically with Copley, recording took place in New York at the Decca or RCA studios, and only a small amount actually took place in Boston. Copley ceased producing its own records at the beginning of the 1970s, and in 1986 ceased selling records and instruments. *See* **recording industry**.

copyright. This indicates the intellectual property right that a composer or creator has over his/her own compositions. When a work is performed by another artist or broadcast publically, a royalty must be paid to the original composer of the work. The Copyright Office is responsible for registering copyrights in Canada, and is part of the Copyright and Industrial Design Branch of the Canadian Intellectual Property Office (CIPO), a specialist operating agency of Industry Canada. All music, including traditional music, is subject to copyright. Generally, copyright lasts for the life of the composer or author, the remainder of the calendar year in which the author dies, and for 50 years following the end of that calendar year. In the case of a work where the identity of the author is unknown (as in older traditional tunes and

songs, for example), copyright for the work shall exist for whichever is the earlier: the remainder of the calendar year of the first publication of the work plus 50 years, or the remainder of the calendar year of the making of the work plus 75 years. When the period of copyright expires all music becomes "public domain." The *Canadian Copyright Act* recognizes three main rights: (a) The right to produce or copy a work (e.g., sheet music); (b) The right to reproduce a work, including mechanical rights (e.g., tape and digital audio reproductions) and synchronization rights (e.g., music in films, videos and multimedia productions); (c) Performing rights, which are the rights to perform a work in public (e.g., a live concert, a recording or any other type of public performance) and the right to communicate to the public by telecommunication (e.g., a broadcast). Different agencies deal with each of these, and most composers exercise their rights collectively through collective societies or organizations. SOCAN (the Society of Composers, Authors and Music Publishers of Canada) is the Canadian copyright collective that administers and protects the performance rights of its members. Today the majority of Cape Breton fiddlers active as professional or semi-professional artists are registered members of SOCAN and receive royalties as appropriate.

Cormier, J. P. (John Paul). (1969-). Fiddle, guitar, song, composer. London, ON, and Westville, NS. Born to parents Paul and Hazel Cormier, J. P. grew up listening to a range of music styles, with his early inspirations ranging from Winston Fitzgerald and Estwood Davidson to Chet Atkins. He moved to Cape Breton in 1994 and pursued a varied professional career in music; the diversity of his talents and interests have allowed him to present himself as a Cape Breton fiddler, guitarist and a singer-songwriter, a bluegrass musician and a country/mainstream artist as the occasion and opportunity demands; he is also a producer/recording engineer and has his own studio, where he and other artists have recorded. As a guitarist playing Scottish, Irish and Cape Breton dance tunes, he has recently recorded a duo album with

Irish/U.K. guitarist, Tim Edey, a collaboration that was borne out of the Celtic Colours annual "Guitar Summit." As a fiddler, he has recorded with his uncle, renowned Cape Breton fiddler, Joe Cormier on *Velvet Arm Golden Hand* (2002). Among his singer-songwriter successes are "Another Morning" and "Afghanistan." Self-taught, and relying on aural rather than music literacy skills, he plays an array of instruments including mandolin, banjo, bass, dobro, piano, ukulele and percussion. He has recorded almost 20 solo albums (some themed specifically, e.g., fiddle, banjo, mandolin and voice), and appears on more than 300 recordings with other artists, some 50 albums of which he has also produced. He has won more than 30 awards, including 12 ECMAs, 5 MNS awards and a Canadian Folk Music Award; his album, *Another Morning*, was nominated for a Juno in 1998. In 2005 the Bravo! network aired *J.P. Cormier–The Man and His Music*, a one-hour documentary examining his life and music; he was also featured on Bravo's program *Men Of Music*.

Cormier, Joseph "Joe." (1927-). Fiddle. Chéticamp, Cape Breton, and Waltham, MA. Of Acadian heritage, Joe Cormier is the son of Job and Adele (Deveau) Cormier; his father was a left-handed fiddler and an accordion player whose four brothers (one of the them the classically trained Prof. Marcellin Cormier) all played the violin. Among Joe's six siblings was Paul (d. 1977), the father of J. P. Cormier. A step dancer from a very young age, Joe started fiddle at age 8 or 9, picking out tunes by ear on a homemade instrument; by the age of 14 he was playing concerts and dances around the county. In 1948 he moved to Sydney to work; there, he performed regularly with Winston Fitzgerald at the Ashby Legion, the Venetian Gardens, the Midway Hall in Glenville and at other venues in Inverness County. During those years he was taught sight-reading by his uncle, Prof. Marcellin, and became interested in the published collections, particularly *The Athole* and *Middelton's*. In 1962 he moved to the Boston area and played weekly at the French Club with

Loudger LeFort and Joe Boudreau, also competing in and winning prizes at early-1970s fiddle contests. He played regularly on radio, mostly on the CJFX show *The Chéticamp Hour,* often in duet with John Campbell. In 1974 he became the first Cape Breton fiddle player to record for Rounder Records (*Scottish Violin Music from Cape Breton Island,* Rounder 7001); this effectively re-energized the Cape Breton commercial recording industry, which had fallen dormant after its initial 1930s and 1940s burst on account of fiddlers becoming disillusioned with its perceived lack of integrity. Cormier later recorded *The Dances Down Home* (1976), *Old Time Wedding Reels* (1992), *Chéticamp* (1998) and *Informal Sessions* (1998). His Rounder recordings are also notable for the extent of contextual information in their liner notes—the first time this level of information was provided about a Cape Breton performer. He has been involved in music collaborations such as *The North Atlantic Strings*, recording with Doug MacPhee, Edmond Boudreau, Gerry and Bobby Robichaud and recorded as part of *The Chéticamp Connection* with Ethel Cormier and Edmond Boudreau (1983, 1986); in 2002 he recorded *Velvet Arm, Golden Hand* with his nephew J. P. Cormier. His album titles and liner notes reveal something of the identity issues with which he is concerned, and while the 1970s work foregrounds a Scottish and Cape Breton identity, by the 1980s the emphasis has become much more Acadian-centred. In *The Chéticamp Connection,* for example, he writes: "the music is Celtic, the heart Acadian," while his *Chéticamp* CD is proclaimed as "Acadian violin music," although his same style and repertoire are maintained. In 1984 Cormier was honoured with an American Heritage Fellowship Award for his contribution to the preservation of Celtic music in the U.S., the first Cape Bretoner to receive such an accreditation. [**Cormier 2001; MacGillivray 1981**].

correctness. An aesthetic value regarded as critical in the Cape Breton fiddle tradition in the past, but, in recent decades, gradually diminishing in importance. The term indicates the degree of authenticity and integrity of the music elements of a given performance: a semantic template against which qualitative comparison—and hence judgments—can be made. It does not merely mean accuracy, precision and exactitude of a melodic line, but rather refers to choices made in shaping or interpreting it within the parameters of what is by consensus accepted and known as Cape Breton style. Correctness applies to (i) the melodic outline or "setting" of a tune and (ii) the individual style or "flavour" added to this.

(i) *melodic outline.* With regard to the outline or setting, it is not that one particular version or "setting" of a tune is regarded as correct within the tradition; rather, multiple settings are permitted, as long as they adhere to understood conventions and as such are deemed authentic. Neither does "correctness" prioritize literate sources over aural learning, although it is easier to substantiate when measured in relation to a printed source. And correctness is not just expected of music-literate players alone, but equally of ear players.

(ii) *flavour.* As for the stylistic aesthetics employed in the interpretation of a setting, there is a clear understanding within the community of practitioners as to what might be deemed appropriate or "correct"; this may be subtle, and unspoken, but it is enculturated by osmosis during the learning process.

Cape Breton vs. Irish fiddle approach. The value of correctness is one which distinguishes the Cape Breton fiddler from the Irish fiddler. With the latter, the practice of spontaneously varying the tune is core to the creative process, and is considered organic in that it applies to the melodic and rhythmic outline as well as to the additional elements of style; indeed, each time an Irish player performs a tune, the expectation is that it be slightly varied so that the performance is never fixed or static (an exception is found in competition playing, where a player will often rehearse and perfect a fixed setting of a tune). In this light it is little wonder then that Johnny Wilmot's impression of Irish fiddler Michael Coleman was as follows: "I listened to that Michael Coleman. I slowed that fellow down many's the time [on a re-

cording] and I played him too, to see if I could play his tunes ... every time I put him on he'd be doing something else" (Caplan 2006); his observation is analytically substantiated in Jesse Smith's 2008 transcription and analysis of all of Coleman's recorded performances. To this end, it is common in Ireland for each tune to be played at least three times in any given performance in order to permit the player to engage with this creative element. But in Cape Breton, since the tune is a much more fixed entity, it is normal for the tune to be played twice, and sometimes once (although in the past it appears that three or more repeats of a tune was common). In new Cape Breton tunes, composers differ on how others might interpret their music. Some (e.g., Dan R. MacDonald, Dan Hughie MacEachern, Kinnon Beaton and John Morris Rankin) feel that it should be treated "correctly" as would any other tune; others (e.g., Jerry Holland and Dougie MacDonald) encourage players to engage creatively with the melodic lines, perhaps coloured by both of their experiences as touring players and by their familiarity with Irish tunes and playing practices. To this end, MacDonald, in his published tune collection (1992), states: "if there are tunes you'd like to change to suit your ear, please feel free to do so." [**Caplan 2006; Doherty 1996; Dunlay 2000; Smith 2008**].

Cosy Cottars, The. A group formed in 1942 by fiddler Jimmie MacLellan (1910-1988), who was born in Inverness County and settled in Sudbury, Ontario; the title is borrowed from the weekly radio show with which MacLellan was associated in the 1930s. The Cosy Cottars also had local Sudbury musicians A. Rasi (accordion, saxophone), Len Nedard (guitar) and Grant Morrison (drums), as well as a then-recent emigrant from England, Bill Chandler on piano. While MacLellan's roots were in the Cape Breton Scottish tradition, his experiences away from home and performing for audiences across Nova Scotia and Ontario encouraged him to diversify his style and repertoire, so that The Cosy Cottars presented an eclectic mix of music including "The Sunnyside Waltz," "The Scandinavian Schottische," "Salty Cold

Breakdown," "Cincinnati Two Step," "Dalhousie Polka" and "The Road to Inverness Strathspey." Their three album titles on the Banff label – *Barn Dance Music–Presenting Jimmie MacLellan and the Cosy Cottars, Jimmy MacLellan and the Cosy Cottars Play Old Time Favorites, Saturday Night Hoedown with Jimmie MacLellan and the Cosy Cottars* – reflect this cross-genre approach. The band, which played on a part-time basis with the members maintaining full-time jobs elsewhere, was popular on radio programs on CKSO and CHND and on television. See **Cottar's Saturday Night; MacLellan, Jimmie.**

Côtés of Grand Greve, Richmond County. This family of pipers, fiddlers and singers has a heritage that is in part French (Côté), Irish (Kavanaghs and Barrons) and Scottish (Currie, of South Uist). This amalgam of cultures, an association with other music genres – including classical music, pipe bands – and a solid grounding in musical literacy, has shaped their musical stylings, and some members of the Côté family are particularly noted for the individuality of their approach to Cape Breton fiddle music.

Côté, Gordon. (1938-2003). Fiddle, bagpipes. One of a large family born to Donald (Dan) and Elizabeth (Barron) Côté, he grew up listening to fiddlers from the St. Peter's area such as Joe MacDonald, Johnny Stone, Don Martell and "Old" Dan Curry (a first cousin to his father); his maternal grandfather, Dan Barron, was also a fiddler who learned from the Cashes of Irish Cove. From a young age Gordon played guitar, sang and occasionally accompanied one of his older brothers' fiddle-playing. The battery-operated radio was an important source of music entertainment, and through shows on CJFX and CJCB he became acquainted with the music of Dan J. Campbell and Winston Fitzgerald. He was 14 when he first tried out the fiddle himself, and was given rudimentary music-reading instruction by "Old" Charlie MacKinnon of French Cove. In the Royal Canadian Army, from 1955 to 1958, he broadened his music skills, training as a piper with the Black Watch Regiment, developing his music literacy

skills and learning an extensive repertoire of tunes; many of these were from *The William Ross Collection*, arranged by Pipe Major Duncan Rankin. After 1958 he worked in Toronto until he came back to the fiddle in the 1970s following the Fiddlers' Festival in Glendale. He played frequently with guitarist Estwood Davidson and at many house parties with fiddlers such as Jerry Holland, Joe MacNeil and Ciffie Carter. In the 1980s, he was a member of The Cape Breton Symphony Fiddlers and has one album, *Partners To Places*. [**MacGillivray 1981**].

Côté, Dwayne. (1969-). Fiddle, guitar, piano, composer. A flamboyant and virtuoso fiddle player, his mother, Gladys Catherine (Stone), was a piper, step dancer and teacher who was particularly active during the 1970s and 1980s; his father, Gordon Côté, was a piper and fiddler. Encouraged at home (where his music-listening experience included such diverse artists as violinists Isaac Stern, Jascha Heifetz and Pinchas Zukerman, Irish fiddler Sean Maguire, classical pianist Glenn Gould and rock band AC/DC), he was further inspired by fiddlers Jerry Holland, Buddy MacMaster, Winston Fitzgerald, Angus Chisholm and Elmer Briand. He observed classical players on TV, picking up their techniques by imitation, and although he began playing by ear, he went on to develop music literacy skills and classical influences while on a scholarship to the Royal Conservatoire in Toronto. His repertoire is typically Cape Breton in tune types, but with a tendency to include more challenging melodies that permit demonstration of his technical versatility. He has composed more than 200 pieces and has a number of albums, the first (*Introduction*, 1991) released when he was in his early 20s; *The Journey Home* (2000) followed several months performing in Dubai. Doug MacPhee was Côté's regular accompanist for years, but collaboration with Newfoundland jazz guitarist Duane Andrews has permitted him to move away from the classic Cape Breton fiddle-piano combination into other arrangements, which resulted in two albums – *Dwayne Côté and Duane Andrews* (2010) and *The Empress* (2012), the first of which won awards from MusicNL, MNS and an ECMA; they also won the "instrumental album" category of the Independent Music Awards judged by Tom Waits, Seal and Ozzy Osbourne. In 2014, he released another album with his brother, Roger Stone, entitled *Unama'ki Wkwisk (Cape Breton Sons)*. While his musical openness has, at times, set him apart as something of a maverick, he has, nonetheless, ably represented Cape Breton at key events with fiddle players Natalie MacMaster, Wendy MacIsaac and Lucy MacNeil as part of the New Generation ensemble who performed for Pope John Paul II in Halifax in 1984, and as part of the Cape Breton contingent of players who showcased at *Éigse na Laoi*, University College, Cork, Ireland, in 1993; he has also toured in Scotland and Australia.

Cottar's Saturday Night. A radio program of Scottish entertainment produced by CJCB Sydney and broadcast across Canada on CBC, the first show to do so. Between 1935 and 1937 it ran with two 26-week seasons under musical director M. J. Ballah, a North Sydney baritone singer with Lebanese roots. The show was symbolically – and perhaps powerfully – named after a classic Robert Burns poem, which was in its time (ca. 1785) an influential affirmation of Scottish culture and the speech and lives of the Scottish people. The show's format followed a weekly visit to a fictional Scottish family, the Aikens, during which listeners were introduced to the setting (which varied from time to time as the family "visited" a neighbour's home, for example); the cast were Mae Cameron, Moses Ballah, Mrs. Hazel Matherson, Mr. and Mrs. Blendon Davies and Bernie MacIntosh; Tena Campbell and Jimmie MacLellan were the resident fiddlers. The entertainment consisted of a mix of conversations, stories, songs in English and Gaelic, fiddle tunes and comedy sketches, including the "Letter from Boston" purported to be sent from a displaced member of the family, a sister, Sarah. A key element of the show was the requests or greetings read out each week to listeners from all over Canada celebrating birthdays, anniversaries and other special occasions. From the scripts

of the show it can be seen that the producers were inundated with requests to the extent that they had to change the criteria: birthday requests could no longer be acknowledged for those aged upward of 90 years, but only for those of 100 years or more! *See* **Ballah, Moses; radio.**

Cottars, The. A band which has two sets of brother-sister siblings: Ciarán and Fiona MacGillivray from Mira (whose father is singer-songwriter and music historian Allister MacGillivray, and whose mother, Beverly, managed the band) and Roseanne and Jimmy MacKenzie from Baddeck. Formed in 2000 when the members were between 11 and 13 years of age, The Cottars were modelled on the local Barra MacNeils in presenting a mix of contemporary and traditional Cape Breton, Scottish and Irish tunes and English-language and Gaelic songs. Their instrumentation is fiddle, piano, guitar, bouzouki, tin whistle, harp and bodhrán, and each member step dances. They received the Tic Butler Memorial Award in 2001, enabling them to record *Made in Cape Breton* (2002); two other albums followed: *On Fire* (2004) and *Forerunner* (2006). While all still in school they achieved and managed a high profile career, touring variously with John McDermott, Natalie MacMaster and The Chieftains. They were the focus of a CBC-TV special, *Meet the Cottars* (2002), which was aired on PBS in the U.S.; they also won ECMA awards in 2003 and 2004 and a nomination for a Gemini award. In 2006, when the group disbanded, the MacKenzies pursued other music ventures, one of these being The MacKenzie Project; The Cottars later re-formed with the MacGillivrays and two new members, Bruce Timmins from Big Bras d'Or (guitar) and Claire Pettit, a New Yorker with Cape Breton connections (fiddle, viola, vocals and stepdance), and released an album, *Feast,* in 2010. *See* **MacGillivray family; MacKenzie siblings.**

Cranford Publications. Set up in 1979 by Paul Cranford, its mission has been to provide resources for musicians on Cape Breton and in the Canadian and global traditional-music communities. The company's first venture was the re-issuing of old Scottish collections which had been used by Cape Breton musicians in the early 20th century but which were no longer easily accessible. These were *The Skye Collection* from 1887 (reissued by Cranford in 1979), *The Simon Fraser Collection* from 1874 (in 1982) with a companion CD, and *The Alexander Walker Collection* from 1866 (in 1991). In 1988 Cranford also initiated a tune-book series, *The Cape Breton Musical Heritage Series*, in order to feature the compositions and settings of individual modern-day fiddlers, music from key Scottish Collections, music from the bagpipe repertoire and from the Irish-Cape Breton connection; a *Celtic Colours Collection* was published in 2011 in conjunction with that festival. A full catalogue of Cranford's Cape Breton, Scottish and Irish materials is online at cranfordpub.com, which also offers extensive information on Cape Breton music and musicians, tunes indexes and ABC notation files. It carries also an on-line catalogue of fiddle music from Cape Breton, Ireland and Scotland, as well as links to educational sites and other fiddlers, luthiers, and festivals. *See* **Cape Breton Musical Heritage Series**.

Cranford, Paul. (1953-). Fiddler, composer, publisher. Toronto and North Shore, Cape Breton. Cranford is best known as the founder of Cranford Publications, with which he has been responsible for collecting, recording, transcribing and disseminating much valuable Cape Breton, Scottish and Irish music. He grew up in Toronto, ON, the son of John and Margery (Stewart) Cranford; during his school years he experienced a wide variety of music, learned music theory and played tuba. His interest in Cape Breton music followed a visit in 1975, when he secured a job as lighthouse keeper on St. Paul's Island between Cape Breton and Newfoundland. A month-on- month-off schedule allowed him to spend four weeks at a time travelling around Cape Breton, playing with and learning from many great fiddlers, and the next month, in isolation at the lighthouse, practicing and notating the music he had collected. Talking to older players prompted him to seek out old printed collections, and being aware of their

Larry Parks, Paul Cranford and Sarah Beck at the CBFA Concert, 2013. Photo by Victor Maurice Faubert.

general unavailability, to set about re-publishing these as well as the new compositions of local fiddlers; this led to his establishing Cranford Publications, in 1979. An enthusiastic fiddle player and composer, he performs casually and formally with such as Sarah Beck, Mario Colosimo, Brenda Stubbert, Doug MacPhee, Otis Tomas, Larry Parks, Paul MacDonald and David Papazian, various of who work under the group name Rocky Shore. In 2010, he released a double CD of his own music, *More Tunes from the Lighthouse,* with more than a hundred previously unrecorded melodies, a follow-up to his first book and CD, *The Lighthouse Collection,* in 1996. Keenly interested in Irish music, he was inspired by the playing of Northside fiddler Johnny Wilmot, and was one of those responsible for introducing the concept of "session" (non-stage, ensemble) playing to Cape Breton and for instituting the island's only such occasion of music, which is held weekly. His Irish connections were further recognized by his selection as artist in residence for the 2009 Celtic Colours, which focused that year on Ireland; many of his tunes (such as "Union Street Session" and "The Lion") have become popular in Ireland, recorded by artists such as Sharon Shannon, Laoise Kelly and the Bumblebees. Cranford's final lighthouse posting was on Machias Seal Island, a bird sanctuary in the Bay of Fundy; since 2009, he is involved with music publication, composition and performance full time. [**Feintuch 2010**].

Lighthouse Collection of Newly Composed Fiddle Tunes–Original Melodies in the Cape Breton, Irish, and Scottish Tradition. Complied by Paul Cranford, this 1996 tune book is Vol. 3 of The Cape Breton Musical Heritage Series: 20th-Century compositions. It has 294 tunes in its 112 pages, divided into broad tune-type categories: (i) marches, strathspeys, reels and hornpipes, (ii) jigs, (iii) waltzes and slow airs. Within each category, tunes are numbered and arranged by key. There are 153 reels, 76 jigs and 27 strathspeys. The book includes a number of scordatura tunes, 3/2 pieces referred to as "slip-reels," single jigs and slides not commonly found in Cape Breton, tunes with 3 or 4 parts, tunes that modulate internally, and tunes which may be interpreted as any number of tune-types (e.g., clog, hornpipe or reel). Most of the tunes – such as "Union Street Session" – are composed by Cranford himself, one each are done in collaboration with Gordon MacLean ("Isabel") and Brenda Stubbert ("Surprise Shift"); another tune is arranged by Jerry Holland ("Fin Fever"). Other composers featured are Gordon MacLean, Tommy Basker, Paul MacDonald, Cameron Chisholm, Otis Tomas, Margaret MacPhee, Johnny Wilmot, Chris Langan, Kevin Roach, Eddie Poirier and Hector MacKenzie. The book has three associated CDs: the first is titled *The Lighthouse* (1996), with 18 tracks containing 57 tunes from the book performed by Paul Cranford and friends; the two other CDs are a double pack, *More Tunes from the Lighthouse* (2010) with 113 tunes from the book. The collection itself is introduced by Paul MacDonald, and lists the tunes according to tune type and key, with information on composers, structure and, in some instances, tonality. Additional information is given where composer's tunes may be found, and on alternative melodic variation or harmonies, as well as an alphabetical index. Cover and internal photos are by Wayne Barrett and Krista Amey.

Creative Nova Scotia Leadership Council, The (CNSLC). Created from the former Nova Scotia Arts and Culture Partnership Council in 2011, this is a link-up between the cultural sector and the government of Nova Scotia designed to foster better understanding and decision-making. The council has 16 members, who represent the diversity among the arts and culture industry in Nova Scotia. Thirteen of these are volunteers from the arts and culture sector, and two are representatives from the Department of Communities, Culture and Heritage; a member of Arts Nova Scotia also sits on the council in a non-voting role. Sector members include artists, writers, filmmakers, musicians, performers and other professionals actively involved in cultural industries. They are selected through a public call for interest, which is followed by open nominations and an approval process. Joella Foulds, then artistic director and co-founder of Celtic Colours, was a member of CNSLC from 2003 to 2011; Gaelic singer, Mary Jane Lamond, from Glendale, Inverness County, joined in 2012. The CNSLC has a variety of functions. It provides advice to government on cultural matters in the province, specifically to the Minister of Communities, Culture and Heritage; it also directly encourages community spirit through creative endeavors and arts/culture activities; it educates the public on the recreational, educational, social and economic importance of culture and the uniqueness of Nova Scotians' diverse cultural identities and invests in cultural development activity. Research is also carried out into the creative economy and culture sector, which feeds into the formulation of cultural policy. CNSLC is thus central to Nova Scotia's cultural strategy in relation to the government's ambitions for arts and culture. Since 2005, each October, the council hosts the Creative Nova Scotia Awards Gala, which makes two awards, one to recognize established artists, the other for community arts and culture organizations. CNSLC is associated with the Portia White Prize, which offers opportunities to Nova Soctian musicians. *See* **awards**.

Cremo, Lee Harvey. (1938-1999). Fiddle. Eskasoni, Victoria County. Of Mi'kmaw heritage, he was born to Simon Cremo (1900-1964) and Annie Denny in Barra Head, before the family moved to settle in Eskasoni when he was four years old. Fiddle music had long been in the family, and Lee's great-grandfather, Michael, played an instrument that was believed to have been made by one of the earliest Scottish settlers. This was passed on to Lee's father, Simon, who began playing at the age of five under the direction of the parish priest in Johnstown, Fr. Saulnier. Simon Cremo travelled around Cape Breton and Nova Scotia selling baskets and playing tunes for a small fee, and would be asked to play for dances in areas where there were no fiddlers available. During the summer months Lee often travelled with his father, accompanying him on guitar, and for many years was his father's regular accompanist at square dances. He took up the fiddle out of curiosity, unknown to his family, and for years he would practice at a friend's house, getting occasional tips from other fiddlers such as Neil Francis MacLellan of Benacadie and listening to the playing of Winston Fitzgerald and Dan Hughie MacEachern on the radio and, from time to time, when he could afford it, at dances; it was not until he was 18 that his father realized he played the fiddle. Lee then went on to have phenomenal success in fiddle competitions, winning more than 80 trophies all over North America. He won The Maritime Old Time Fiddling Contest at Dartmouth, NS, 6 times, and a major Western Canada contest 10 years in a row. He was Canadian champion at the Alberta Tar Sands Competition and was ranked 5th in the North American Fiddling Championship of 1974. At the Grand Master Fiddling Championships in Nashville he won the award for "Best Bow Arm in the World"; his success in this documented in the 1986 film *Arm of Gold* (Edwin Communications). Frequently asked if he considered himself a "Cape Breton fiddler," a "Scottish fiddler" or a "Mi'kmaw fiddler" his reply invariably was "a good fiddler!" His position and attitude were unique in his time, for he approached the music from outside of the tradition, with a Mi'kmaq rather than a Scottish identity; Cremo celebrated the freedom that this afforded him, rather than let it restrict him. He approached the repertoire and style with a flexibility that allowed him to shape it in accordance with other music sounds and experiences that challenged and excited him. With his natural showmanship he offered a fresh approach to fiddle music, one that was simultaneously familiar and unfamiliar (in part Scottish, Cape Breton, old-time and down east) across a range of traditions; indeed that element made his music all the more attractive in a contest setting. His repertoire, like his style, was eclectic and included older tunes, contest favourites and his own compositions such as "The Constitution Breakdown." A broken left arm interrupted his music career, but he eventually returned to fiddle playing, although forced to adopt a different posture, with the fiddle held on its side and against his chest. A flamboyant showman, Lee played often with accompanists Joe Vincent on piano and "Wild" Archie MacLennan on bones; his band, Eastern Variation, which included Gabrile Syliboy on bass, Wilfred Paul on lead guitar, Joseph MacMullen on piano, Peter Stevens on drums and James Poulette on rhythm guitar, featured on a number of his commercial recordings. Cremo made his first LP, *Champion Fiddler,* in 1968, and played on six others in the 1970s. Contractual issues prohibited him from recording for 10 years, but he resumed in 1995 with *The Champion Returns,* which was voted "Best First Nations Recording" at the 1996 ECMAs. He also featured on the Rounder Records *Bras d'Or House* CD, and on several Smithsonian-Folkways collections of Native American music. A significant ambassador for the Cape Breton Mi'kmaw community, Cremo has been accorded many honours: he was invited to perform at the 1999 launch of the Aboriginal People's Television Network and the Porcupine Awards for Folk Music offer the "Lee Cremo Award for Native Artists." With the exception of seven years in Maine working in lumber camps, Cremo spent his life in Eskasoni and, despite his profile as a successful musician, held down a long-term job as a school bus driver. **[Caplan 2006; MacGillivray 1981; Smith 1994].**

crossover. Also known as "fusion" or "blending," this refers to the intersections of Cape Breton fiddle music with other music genres and/or art forms with the intention of creating a new piece of music or a general sound that is simultaneously new, while incorporating recognizable elements of both its constituents. One of the earliest examples of Cape Breton meeting classical music in this way was the composition of "The Cape Breton Concerto," performed in Sydney and in New York in 1982. Composed by Daniel Goode (b. 1936), an American composer, clarinettist and director of the Electronic Music Studio of Livingstons College-Rutgers in New Jersey, it was scored for 6 Cape Breton violins (performed by Kinnon Beaton, Donny LeBlanc, Dave MacIsaac, Theresa MacLellan, John Morris Rankin and Brenda Stubbert), piano (Joey Beaton) and a symphonic band. In 2006, American ethnomusicologist and gamelan leader Barbara Benary composed "Jigalullaby" involving Gaelic song with violin and gamelan orchestra; the Gamelan orchestra, Gamelan Son of Lion, had been founded by Benary, Daniel Goode and Philip Corner in 1976. Cape Breton/classical music initiatives continued through the 1980s in the work of Scott Macmillan (e.g., "Songs of the Cape" [1985], a suite in four movements featuring The Octet, a classical string quartet and Celtic rhythm section, including Macmillan, Dave MacIsaac, Louis Benoit and Andrew Russell). Macmillan has subsequently composed other works in this crossover vein, including "Celtic Mass for the Sea" (1991) and "Aiseag" (2014), his most recent piece which was a U.K. New Music Biennial commission. David Greenberg, a specialist in Baroque violin music, has made several recordings with the ensemble Puirt-a-Baroque, presenting traditional Cape Breton fiddle tunes in arrangements inspired by the art-music/traditional-music crossover that existed in Scotland in the 18th century. Many Cape Breton fiddlers and bands have appeared with Symphony Nova Scotia through various initiatives such as the "Maritime Fusion Concerts"; these include Ashley MacIsaac, The Barra MacNeils, Natalie MacMaster, J. P. Cormier, Mary Jane Lamond and The Cottars. Some of these per-

formances have been recorded and subsequently released on CD, most recently featuring SNS and the Barra MacNeils (2011). A collaboration involving Cape Breton fiddle music and ballet was an element of a dance production in Des Moines, Iowa, which involved the music of John Campbell. Sandy MacIntyre was one of the feature artists in the Mirvish production *Needfire–A Celtic Musical* (1998-2000) at the Royal Alexandra Theatre and the Princess of Wales Theatre in Toronto. The Barrra MacNeils' *Cathedral* project in 2010 emerged from the idea of presenting Cape Breton music alongside other genres; the *String Crossings* project curated by Kimberley Fraser in 2013 explored common ground between Cape Breton, American and Scandinavian fiddle traditions; Natalie MacMaster collaborated on the album *Yo-Yo Ma & Friends: Songs Of Joy And Peace* (Sony Classical), which won a Grammy in 2010. Popular and rock music has also met Cape Breton fiddle music in various contexts since the 1990s. Bands such as Cullin and Kilt contributed to this type of fusion; however, Ashley MacIsaac's work in the 1990s (starting with his *Hi! How are you Today* album) set a new standard in this regard and introduced an entirely new audience to Cape Breton fiddle music; MacIsaac continues to work with such as Philip Glass, the influential contemporary composer and performer. **[Graham 2006]** *See* **Greenberg, David; MacIsaac, Ashley; Macmillan, Scott.**

Crowley Chrissy. (1990-). Fiddle, composer. Margaree and Sydney. A member of the Cape Breton band Coìg, she is a granddaughter of Archie Neil Chisholm of the renowned Margaree Forks family of musicians. Playing from a young age she has made showcase and collaboration performances nationally and internationally. Her repertoire is an eclectic mix of tunes, arrangements and stylistic traits influenced by the many artists she has encountered in various North American and European traditions. At the age of 17, through Offshore Gael Music, an independent label run by Lisa Butchard that helps emerging young Celtic musicians to make their first album, she released her self-titled debut (2007), for which she won a

LIZ DOHERTY

"Top 20 Under 20" Award from the CFMA. *The Departure* followed in 2010 and was nominated for an ECMA. *Last Night's Fun* was relased in 2013 and this won Crowley a Canadian Folk Music Award for Instrumental Solo Artist (2013).

crushed-bowstroke. A term first introduced in the *DunGreen Collection* (1996), it refers to a bowed ornament used to add texture to long (quarter) notes; it is executed by approaching the note with a sharp bowed accent then immediately relaxing this, almost slowing to a stop. At the point of accent, further emphasis may be added by using vibrato or a "warble." The crushed-bowstroke is epitomized in the playing of Winston Fitzgerald and Jerry Holland; these fiddlers often chose this type of ornamentation to highlight a long note, thus creating a sense of space within the melodic line where other fiddlers might apply a cut. [**Dunlay and Greenberg 1996**]. *See* **bowing style; warble.**

CTV. A television network developed in the late 1950s as part of a consortium to establish an alternative to CBC-TV programming, this Canadian English-language broadcaster, which is Canada's largest privately owned network, was launched in 1961. Fiddle-music programming on CTV began with a 17-week run of *The John Allan Cameron Show* in 1975, following his leaving the CBC *Ceilidh* Show in 1973. One of three programs in a music series called *Trilogy,* Cameron's was a variety half-hour devoted to the Scottish and Irish music traditions of the Maritimes. Operated by the CTV network is CTV Atlantic, a conglomerate of 4 TV stations in the Canadian Maritimes (CJCH-DT, Halifax; CJCB-TV, Sydney; CKCW-DT Moncton, New Brunswick and Charlottetown, Prince Edward Island; and CKLT-DT, Saint John, New Brunswick) and formerly ATV (Atlantic Television System). In the 1980s, this carried one of the most significant programs involving Cape Breton fiddle music, *Up Home Tonight.* Each week, CTV Atlantic dominates the ratings with some 27 hours of local programming, including news and local information; it augments this community engagement with various supports and funding

initiatives; among these is the *Christmas Daddies Telethon*, produced by volunteers from the staff of CTV in its 3 centres on the first Sunday in December each year. Established in 1964, the telethon is a pledge-based variety show broadcast live, with the funds generated being donated to various local children's charities. Cape Breton fiddlers are among those who contribute to the success of this event each year. *See* **John Allan Cameron Show; television;** *Up Home Tonight.*

Cullin. Band formed in 1999 to replace a previous band titled MacKeel and complete its contracted tour schedule in the U.S. Managed by Wayne O'Connor (who had managed MacKeel and Ashley MacIsaac), the members were Matt MacIsaac (bagpipes and whistles), Mairi Rankin (fiddle), Arthur O'Brien (vocals), Stuart Cameron (guitar), Stefan Morin (drums) and Dave Hoare (bass); later members included Seth Fraser and Pat Gillis (guitar) and Dave Carmichael (vocals). The band's only album was produced by Gordie Sampson (1999-2000) and reflected their eclectic sound, which ran from straight, acoustic traditional sets, folk songs and pipe solos to more pop and rock/reggae styles. The band toured mainly the northeastern U.S. and was short-lived.

Cultural Federations of Nova Scotia, The. The umbrella organization which oversees the infrastructure for eight individual non-profit federations, one of which is Dance Nova Scotia.

Currie, Alex. (1910-1997). Bagpipes. Sydney Mines and Frenchvale, Cape Breton County. Starting at the age of 10 he learned to play the bagpipes almost entirely from within his extended family; his father, Peter, was a piper as were his two grandmothers and two older brothers. From his father he learned to make chanters and from his mother and grandmother he learned his repertoire of tunes entirely by ear. He learned to read music when he joined the army, enlisting with the Cape Breton Highlanders and later transferring to the PEI Highlanders during the Second World War. Currie had a repertoire that consisted mostly of jigs, strathspeys and, mainly, reels. He had a unique fingering style and played always with the right hand above the left hand on the chanter (the opposite to the norm). He also played in a seated position. Currie's music, most notably his style and settings of tunes, was collected by local piper and music historian, Barry Shears, who understood it to reflect the older community piping tradition that had been prevalent in Cape Breton until replaced by pipe bands and competition culture. He was later "discovered" by Scottish piper, Hamish Moore in the 1990s who, in a manner similar to Alasdair Fraser in relation to the fiddle tradition, used his music to flag the authenticity of Cape Breton music in contemporary Scotland. Through his connections with Moore, Currie came to meet other Scottish pipers such as Fred Morrison; he performed at the *Dance to the Piper* concert at Celtic Colours, where his nephew John MacLean blew the pipes while he did the chanter work. He was interviewed by Ron Caplan for *Cape Breton's Magazine* a couple of days before he died. [**Caplan 2006; MacGillivray 1998**].

cut. A bowed ornament that is a prominent feature of the Cape Breton fiddle style, particularly in strathspeys and reels; it is used to add rhythmic interest to the melodic line, in a way that is believed to be a reflection of piping style. The ornament can be traced to Scotland, where it is referred to today as the "birl" and previousl as, the "gathering" (in the Skene MS, 1717). In Cape Breton, cuts or "cuttings" (sometimes called the "shake") remain a prominent characteristic of the fiddle style, although the extent of its use has been diminishing from the mid-20th century onward. Cuts are executed with very short bow strokes and involve applied forearm pressure along with a quick movement of the wrist or bow-hand fingers to shake the bow through the notes. Each individual bowed note of the cut is clearly articulated and the bow is kept in contact with the strings throughout. Most often involving a down-up-down bow motion it is, however, regarded as the mark of dexterity for a fiddler to be equally adept at bowing cuts in the opposite direction (i.e., up-down-up); Ashley MacIsaac, for instance,

favours the latter in his cuts. In the Cape Breton style, cuts are often followed by another stroke of the same note, resulting in four successive identical pitches. Sometimes two or more cuts are played consecutively (e.g., double cuts), adding heightened rhythmic interest to the tune. In Cape Breton the cut has three forms:

(**i**) A sequence of three notes of the same pitch created by breaking up a single quarter-note into smaller units of 2 sixteenth notes and an eighth note.

(**ii**) An extension of the regular three-note cut into a four-note sequence, where the quarter note is divided into 4 sixteenth notes. This type is most often found in strathspey playing and was a particular feature of the older Mabou Coal Mines style of playing.

(**iii**) A 3-note cut or treble achieved by extending a pattern of 2 notes on different pitches by cutting the first note in two; this creates a 3-note pattern, the first two of which are on the same pitch and the third on a different pitch. It was first termed a "strathspey treble" in the *DunGreen Collection* (1996), where it is described as the technique employed in "cutting up" a strathspey, something that was characteristic of an old Inverness County style. The bowing used on this type of cut again uses three distinct strokes, although it tends to start on the up-bow, and so is the opposite of the regular cut. When a "strathspey treble" does start with a down-bow, it involves slurring into or out of the embellishment and may involve other bowing patterns or techniques such as the loop. By the 20th century, in Scotland this type of ornament was already considered by players such as Scott Skinner as old-fashioned and was nicknamed "the doodle," thereafter coming to be more regularly replaced by the "Scots snap." In Cape Breton, and in other fiddle traditions such as Donegal, Ireland, this type of cut (there termed a treble) remains common. A recent variation, inspired by certain Irish styles, is a three-note cut where the middle note is on another pitch, usually a step above. [**Doherty 1996; Dunlay and Greenberg 1996; Graham 2006**].

D

Dàimh. Based in Lochaber in the Scottish Highlands, this group has an international line-up, featuring Cape Breton bagpipes and whistle player Angus MacKenzie from Mabou; members in 2015 are Gabe MacVarish from California on fiddle, Scotland's Ross Martin on guitar, Murdo Cameron on pipes, accordion and guitar, and Griogair Labhruidh on vocals and uilleann pipes. Self-styled a "Gaelic super-group," they play Scottish and Cape Breton music with a contemporary thrust. They have several albums to date on their own label Goat Island Music (*Tuneship*, 2013) and on Greentrax (*Moidart to Mabou*, 2000; *Pirates of Puirt*, 2003; *Crossing Point*, 2007; *Diversions*, 2010; *Tuneship*, 2013). Typically, other Scottish musicians join the band in festival performances for a big-band production; for a number of years the bands' members also ran The School of Dàimh each October on the Isle of Eigg off Western Scotland.

Dàl Riada. A Gaelic rock band active in 1992-1993 with a focus on songs, mostly covers of Runrig material, and occasionally joined by fiddlers Ashley MacIsaac or Jackie Dunn. The group was formed by Goiridh Dòmhnullach (vocals) from Glendale and Rob Morin (guitar, vocals) from Troy while they were students at St. FX. They were joined by Doug "Shifty" Hill (bass), Ivan Murray (drums), Derrick Martin (electric guitar) and Scott Long (pipes and whistle); Allan MacKenzie (pipes) joined them occasionally, and later members included Dave Morin (guitar, bass), Johnny MacDonald (piano, keyboards) and Sandy MacDonald (guitar, bass). Dàl Riada played several gigs organized by An Comunn Ceilteach St. FX, as well as concerts and festivals around Cape Breton over two summers, and played a role in popularizing Gaelic language, in particular, among younger age groups.

dance. Within Cape Breton there are two main strands of traditional dance, broadly regarded as (1) solo or step dance and (2) social or group dance. There is some degree of crossover between the two forms as, for example, step dancing is incorporated into particular figures within some social dances. Other discrete, but connected, dance forms in Cape Breton's cultural practices are Acadian dance, Highland dance, Irish competition-style step dance and Scottish country dance. *See* **under terms.**

1. solo step dance. A vernacular percussive dance form that involves close-to-the-floor foot patterns performed within a limited space and marked by emphasis on rhythm and a relaxed upper body stance. It is similar in style to Irish *seán-nos*, Northumberland clog dance, Appalachian buck dancing, and French and Acadian dance from Québec and elsewhere in the Maritimes, yet is uniquely identifiable. The term "Cape Breton step dance," which is used to describe this dance form today, is relatively new, appearing for the first time in the 1980s when Cape Breton dancers were first invited to perform and teach off-island. Prior to this, dance was simply part of the wider cultural tradition, associated with fiddle music which itself had evolved from being considered Scottish to being known as Cape Breton Scottish and, finally, Cape Breton; the need to define or label the associated dance (even as such changes occurred in relation to the fiddle music) simply never arose. Step dance's origins are believed to be Scottish, from the Highlands and Western Isles, although there has been considerable debate over the years in Cape Breton regarding a possible Irish connection. Today's step dance has evolved from specific choreographed dances into a more extempore practice that responds directly to the music. Once formal teaching of step dance resumed in Cape Breton in the 1970s, the dancing again became semi-structured with preordained routines becoming the norm among younger dancers. Step dancing was originally associated with both the bagpipes and the fiddle, but by the early 20th century it became associated primarily with the latter, and today it continues to be bound up with the fiddle music, affecting it in matters of repertoire, style and performance practice. While in the past it was common to have dancers who specialized exclusively in this art,form, today it is more typical to have dancers who are also instrumentalists.

history. Historian Ken Donovan has uncovered evidence of French dancing masters active in Louisbourg as early as the mid-18th century; MacDougall's *History of Inverness* (1922) refers to dance schools estblished in Inverness Country from the early 19th century. Other early references include a description by C. H. Farnham in 1886 describing social gatherings at Ingonish and East Lake Ainslie where the music was provided by bagpipes. Collecting carried out in 1957 by British scholar Frank Rhodes indicates specific solo dances, each of which had a fixed sequence of steps and was associated with a particular tune. Involving both percussive and softer "travelling" and "setting" steps, these dances were kept inside particular families such as the Beatons of South West Margaree, the Kennedys of Broad Cove and the MacMillans of Creignish and were not widely known. Much of the early dancing in Cape Breton was passed on by recognized dance masters; Scottish dance masters were among the earliest settlers to Cape Breton, so it was in the spirit of continuing their profession that dance schools were set up in Cape Breton; most such teachers were obliged to supplement their incomes in other ways in the new environment. The majority of the dance masters were male and operated in a peripatetic fashion, travelling around Cape Breton and offering tuition for short periods of time. In the early years of the 20th century, however, step-dance schools disappeared as a more extemporaneous form of step dance came to replace the older, choreographed solo dances in demonstrations and competitions. The introduction of square sets also contributed to making step dancing redundant as part of social dancing.

competitions were popular from the early years of the 20th century, some of them quite informal in nature, ranging from friendly duels to specific challenges among the dance masters. One of the latter was known as Smaladh na Coinnle/ The Smooring of the Candle, where a lighted candle was placed on the floor and the dancer was required to flick the top of the wick with the feet while dancing, without extinguishing the flame. Other challenges included taking turns to dance as many complete steps as possible on a short block of wood or to step dance on tables on which rested glasses full of whiskey without spilling a drop. As with the fiddle, there were contests at events such as picnics, and Cape Breton dancers also competed in off-island contests in Boston, Detroit and New York. Early dance competitions featured the older "set" or fixed-choreography dances such as "The Flowers of Edinburgh"; more extemporaneous performance later became the norm as the tradition changed.

teaching. In the late 1930s the Gaelic College started teaching various Highland dances and Scottish Country Dances from choreographies published by the Royal Scottish Country Dance Society and from collections made by Mrs. Mary Isdale MacNab of Vancouver. It was not until the post-*Vanishing Cape Breton Fiddler* revival of fiddle music in the early 1970s that the idea of step dance classes was revived. Margie Dunn, Minnie MacMaster and Geraldine MacIsaac were the first to start teaching step dance in this more formal, revival context; others soon followed, across Cape Breton itself, and in Antigonish on the mainland: Harvey Beaton, Alexander MacDonnell, Willie Fraser, Mary Janet MacDonald, Jean MacNeil, Mary Jessie MacDonald, Clare (MacDonald) Currie and Fr. Eugene Morris were among those who took up teaching dance. For these first teachers the class situation presented many challenges, for none of them had been formally taught themselves or had been given any guidance as to how they might pass on their knowledge. They devised individual systems by trial and error, for the first time naming steps or specific patterns of steps – such as shuffle, hop step, back step – learning to break steps down in order to explain them and using techniques such as holding hands to better transfer the beat. In 1979, these step-dance teachers came together for the first time to share their knowledge and experience at an event organized by Fr. Eugene Morris in Whycocomagh. Other teachers soon emerged from this example, including Betty Matheson, Patsy Graham, Sr. Dolina Beaton, Margaret Gillis, Lucy MacNeil, the Warner sisters and the Pellerin brothers. From the 1980s onward, off-island teaching opportunities developed, with invitations to teach Cape Breton step dance (as it was then being branded) at workshops in the U.S. and in Scotland itself.

costumes. Specific costumes have never been part of the step-dance performance tradition in Cape Breton. But from the 1970s on it became common for dancers to incorporate some degree of distinctive tartans (either common clan tartans or the Cape Breton tartan designed in 1957) into their attire; this was a vest (waistcoat) for males, a skirt for females, or a sash which could be worn by either. No bespoke footwear is involved although individual dancers show a preference for particular types of shoes, either hard-soled or soft-soled, depending on their dance style. Cape Breton lore has many stories of people walking to and from dances barefoot in order to save their shoes for dancing. In the 1970s a trend for "clickers" (metal plates) on the heels and toes of the shoes became common, and Fr. Angus Alex MacDonnell introduced a "staccato tap" (a loosely-fitted plate). These additions were seen to enhance the performance by permitting observers who were situated further away from the dancer to hear the detail of the footwork; they were also deemed useful for demonstrating particular rhythms in class settings. The move to such metal taps did coincide with the adoption of amplification of the music, which necessitated a corresponding volume adjustment by the dancers, but the practice was no doubt influenced too by the regular appearance on TV of dancers from traditions outside Cape Breton, on shows such as *Don Messer's Jubilee;* all of these used such audible supports. These practices clashed with another school of thought which was very firmly of the opinion that Cape Breton step dance should be "seen and not heard." A turning point in the trend came in 1983 when Mary Janet MacDonald stopped using clickers,

having been advised by Fr. John Angus Rankin to discard them ahead of teaching in Barra, Scotland, where she would be in an influential position.

the style. Cape Breton step dance as it exists today is danced primarily to strathspeys and reels; jigs are danced to in group or square-dance formations and only very rarely involve anything other than a few core, basic steps. A strathspey will always segue into a reel; however, reels may be danced in isolation. While these dances are solo, The Scotch Four, and the less common Eight-handed Reel, involve groups of four and eight individuals, respectively, who step dance as when solo but incorporate "travelling" steps in choreographed formations to create an overall sense of common purpose; of these, only the Scotch Four is found today. Step-dance displays are common on concert platforms or during square dances or ceilidhs, these often involving a number of dancers who will each take a turn to perform, as such sharing their steps; such displays happen more spontaneously in other contexts, with the dancer sufficiently moved by the music to perform, or encouraged to do so by the audience or the fiddler. In a concert setting, if more than one dancer is involved, a line will be formed and the dancers will take turns moving forward and showing their steps, then go back into the line; in the line formation they may collectively perform some basic steps or dance together, each dancer performing their own steps. Choreographed routines became a popular part of presentational dance from the 1970s onward, where two (and, in later years, more) dancers worked out carefully coordinated dances. Among those known for this type of dance routine were the Warner Sisters, and brothers, John and Bill Pellerin; the Rankin Family, the Barra MacNeils and Beòlach have all incorporated this type of routine into their shows. Step dancing may or may not also feature in some of the group or square social dances, most commonly in figure three of "The Mabou Set," which is danced to a reel; this has been popular practice since the 1970s.

technique. The Cape Breton step-dance style is described as being "close to the floor" in that no high leg movements are involved, and very little floor-space is required. Words such as "neat" and "graceful" are used to describe dancers, as are phrases such as being "light on his/her feet." The body is held straight but relaxed with the body weight distributed evenly; the point of balance is between the balls of the left and right feet. Facing forward, with the eyes fixed straight ahead, the arms are held in a relaxed position at the sides; some movement of the arms (swinging forward or backward) may be a feature of certain dancers' performances. Hip and – more so – knee movements generate the action of the legs, ankles are relaxed, the feet are held with a natural "turnout" and the balls of the feet and heels are used for making contact with the floor. Elevation is a matter of individual preference, although

Kelly Warner MacLennan and Melody (Warner) Cameron. Photo by Mats Melin.

most dancers opt for minimal balance on the toes. The feet are kept close together, with the "working" foot (alternating right and left) held close to the supporting foot; the working foot does not generally extend further than the toe of the supporting foot. Movement is primarily on the spot facing forward; some sidesteps and turning steps also feature, and most step-dance demonstrations conclude with a back-step. The best dancers have individual styles and unique characteristics; what distinguishes them may have to do with their steps or their body posture; the timing, however, is what is most important. Strathspeys and reels involve a series of individual patterns which are combined into individual steps and presented starting first on the right foot and then on the left foot in a balanced, symmetrical format. The basic steps involve toe and heel movements, brushing movements (heel to toe) and stamps (stomps),

marking out the beats of the particular tune-type. Dances generally start with a version of the basic step, and this may be returned to at various points in the routine, particularly if the performance is extemporaneous rather than choreographed. The style of steps has, of course, changed over time. Post-revival (and as a result of the demand for formal tuition), the number and patterns of steps expanded and became more diverse, occasionally taking on influences from other styles such as Irish, jazz, tap and popular dance. Common patterns informing contemporary step dancing in Cape Breton include over-ankle movements (where the ankle is twisted outward), winding and considerable syncopation. Steps are generally longer today; in the past steps were of 2 or 4 bars duration, but today, many last for a full 8-bar part of a tune. Some debate surrounds the issue of gender in relation to steps and whether specific male and female steps exist or have existed. The numbers of steps a dancer may have at their disposal can vary from 40 to 200, although quantity in this respect is not necessarily an indication of quality. In the past, whereas the step dance was extemporaneous, dancers introduced their steps spontaneously in response to the fiddle music within the musical moment. However, since the learning environment has moved from home to classroom, this has changed, and more fixed routines are now the norm; such dancers will often ask for specific numbers of tunes (mostly strathspeys) to be played. No fixed start time is involved in a Cape Breton step-dance performance (dancers can start at any point in the tune); in the past some dancers were known for having flamboyant markers at both the start and end of their performances. (*With* **MM**)

the music-dance connection. As Cape Breton step dance moved away from having fixed dances associated with specific tunes (e.g., "The Flowers of Edinburgh") toward a more extemporaneous style, one of the hallmarks of a good dancer came to be the ability to respond spontaneously to the music in the rhythm of their steps. Pipes and fiddles were both danced to in Cape Breton, either separately or, on occasion, together; the fiddle became the predominant instrument from the mid-20th century; however, as Cape Breton- or traditional-style piping has been re-introduced in recent times it is common to see the bagpipe (and indeed other pipe variants) and step dance partnered once again. Particular fiddlers were and are known for being good step-dance players, and dancers often requested specific tunes, such as "King George IV," "Calum Crubach" or "The Bird's Nest." Timing is the most important characteristic for both the dancer and the musician. While more fixed routines have become the norm for step dancers since the 1970s, the music-dance connection is still important and certain players continue to be favoured by the dance community. Indeed, many of the dance classes have from the outset included live fiddle music where the economics can allow it; Howie MacDonald played for years for Betty Matheson's classes, while Kyle MacNeil was the fiddler at Jean MacNeil's classes. The requirements of the step dance have continued to somewhat direct the fiddle music in terms of repertoire (the type and order of tunes played) and style (tempo, lift or drive), even where the music happens without the dance; it is only since ca. 2000 that this hold of the dance over the music in non-dance contexts has weakened.

the dancers. Allister MacGillivray's *A Cape Breton Ceilidh* (1988) offers the first insight into the dance tradition with regard to numbers of known step dancers (604) and their gender (more than 40% are female). This data reveals that up until the second half of the 20th century the better-known dancers were male, but once formal classes were re-established in the 1970s revival period, females began to balance and eventually outnumber males. An early trend too

was for dancing to be contained within certain families, often across several generations. While many fiddlers (and other instrumentalists) were often noted dancers, there was a community of dancers known specifically for such skill – particularly evident from the middle part of the 20th century onward. Since the 1970s many musicians are also dancers, and today most well-known dancers are also teachers of dance. A number of academic studies and publications have focused on the dance tradition and its primary exponents (e.g., MacGillivray, Le Blanc, MacInnes, Rhodes, Voyer); a comprehensive study of the Cape Breton step-dance tradition and its transmission, by Mats Melin, is scheduled for publication in 2015. For the purpose of this *Companion*, biographies of dancers who are involved in other aspects of the fiddle-music tradition only are included.

the Scottish question. The Scottish origins of Cape Breton step dance have been questioned by various authorities (e.g., MacInnes 1993, 1996); while an Irish connection has been suggested by some, sufficient evidence has been established to corroborate a Scottish ancestry. Much of the confusion surrounding the issue emerged from the Gaelic College which, in the 1960s and 1970s, prioritized Highland dance (and to a lesser degree, Scottish Country Dance) and dismissed any association with the locally practiced step-dancing tradition. The debate re-emerged in the 1990s when, along with the fiddle music, Cape Breton step dance was showcased in Scotland for the first time. Since then, the form and style has been adopted by many in Scotland; a robust schedule of workshops initially with Cape Breton step dancers (Mary Janet MacDonald and Harvey Beaton) led to a number of Scots embracing the style; classes continue to be offered, but now often the teachers are Scottish. Among those who have so embraced the form are such as the dance group Dannsa, which has Cape Breton step dance at its core; Scots such as Maggie Moore and Pat Ballantyne have contributed to research on the subject; Mats Melin from Sweden, who spent many years active in the dance community in Scotland, has also played a pivotal role in developing the current position of Cape Breton step dance there, besides contributing to the narrative in Cape Breton through his ongoing research and publications. [Doherty 1996; Graham 2006; Le Blanc 1986, 1997; MacInnes 1993, 1996; MacGillivray 1988; Melin 2012, 2015; Rhodes 1985, 1996; Voyer 1986].

2. square dancing. A popular element of Cape Breton culture and a mainstay of the fiddle tradition, this form of social dancing has its roots in European dance forms such as the quadrille and was introduced primarily by Cape Breton immigrants based in Boston at the turn of the 20th century. In Cape Breton, the square dance underwent many transformations; while many local variants existed at one point, square dances have now become standardized into a small number of forms (e.g., "The Mabou Set," "The Sydney Set"); these involve a number of figures (usually three), danced to jigs and reels, the number of which varies depending on the set involved. On the east side of the island, walking through the figures is common, but step dancing as part of the square set is prominent on the western side. By the end of the 20th century the square-dance experience in Cape Breton had crystallized into a particularly unique one; held usually in community or parish halls and with music provided by a single fiddler and piano player (amplified), a single form of the square set would be danced over and over for the entire night with only short breaks to allow for a change of partners between dances. For anyone accustomed to contemporary Irish set or *céilí* dancing, Scottish country dancing or contra dancing, where the focus is on variety of dances, this seems somewhat peculiar. As Cape Breton music and dance has been increasingly considered as a cultural commodity, with an emphasis on participation, from the 1990s onward the impact of this has been significant in relation to the square-dance tradition. Square dances and dancing have, in effect, fallen victim to the success of the cultural tourism campaign as, encouraged to participate by the apparent simplicity and inclusive ethos of the square dance, visitors have, in many instances, over the summer months taken

Scotch Four with Melody Cameron, Harvey Beaton, Gerard Beaton and Dawn Beaton, with Glenn Graham on fiddle. Photo by Victor Maurice Faubert.

over the local dance scene; they have at times outnumbered the locals, many of whom have begun to retreat for the summer season; this has caused something of a crisis in the dance scene and affected the fiddlers, for whom the square dance was both an opportunity to develop skill, stamina, repertoire and reputation, and to showcase their playing in the optimum environment of responding to able dancers. A movement is currently underway to re-energize the square-dance tradition; part of this is focussing on the size of the sets and re-introducing some of the many variants from different communities; in addition, during 2015 special dance events were held to recognize some of the legendary Cape Breton square dances (West Mabou and Glencoe) and to attract, once again, large informed crowds of participants to the dance floor.

contexts and venues. Dancing was an important part of social activities in early Cape Breton communities at weddings, in particular, which were held in winter. At this time, dancing was most commonly done to pipe music, particularly in communities where fiddle players were in short supply. At weddings the dancing began with "Ruileadh nan Càraid" ("The Married Couple's Reel"), a 4-handed reel for the bride, groom, best man and bridesmaid, followed by a second iteration of this danced by their relations; after this everyone danced. Another dance, "The Bedding

LIZ DOHERTY

of the Bride," a 4-handed reel, was danced later in the proceedings. Wedding celebrations could last for a week and, where the home of the host was too small, a stage might be erected outdoors to accommodate the dancing. Other occasions for dancing were the summer picnics, frolics and socials. Schoolhouses were next used to house dances; there the fiddler or piper would be seated on a chair and the small wooden building lit by a single lantern; these events were used as fundraisers for the teacher's salary and for the upkeep of the building. Proper dancehalls first appeared in the early 1900s, typically church or community halls, although by the 1940s some commercially built venues had started to appear in larger towns and in the Sydney area. In the 1950s, the picnics gave way to community festivals and concerts, which usually included a square dance to round off the day's activities; this practice continues today with the last remaining outdoor concerts. From the 1970s onward, union, association and community halls became the typical dance venues, and some of these – such as that at Glencoe Mills – have become legendary. During the summer months the number of square dances taking place around the island peaks, although there has been a noticeable drop in the numbers (and quality) of these since the turn of the 2000s. For the remainder of the year dances happen only occasionally, and by 2014 only one regular dance was held year-round, on Saturday nights in West Mabou (weather permitting). *See* **dance halls; picnic; social; wedding.**

the dance experience. The Cape Breton square-dance experience is something quite unique and is important, not only culturally, but also in generating a sense of community. The experience involves the location, the camaraderie, the atmosphere and the socializing, as well as the central elements of the music and the dance itself. In Glencoe, for instance, the venue is in a particularly remote and isolated location, several miles along a dirt track through deep forest; it is something of a surprise experience to eventually happen upon hundreds of cars, bright lights and crowds gathered around open trunks catching

up and having a drink; from the small hall whose windows and doors are flung open comes the distinctive amplified sound of the Cape Breton fiddle with piano accompaniment and the pulsating rhythm of pounding feet from dancers aged between 9 and 90. A small cover charge is paid to gain entry to the hall; once inside the 3-figure Mabou Set (2 jig figures and a reel) is in full flight; sets may vary from 4 couples to indeterminate numbers; typically the climax comes in the third figure, where all of the dancers assemble in a line of couples facing the fiddler; then, the top couple turns in toward each other and breaks through that line, before leading into a section of the dance where individual step dancing is featured, one of the highlights of this reel-time figure. After a few minutes' break the fiddler will start into a set of jigs, the signal that another set is about to begin, and gradually couples take to the floor and join in; there is no strict starting point. For anyone experienced in other dance traditions the Cape Breton approach may seem unorthodox in terms of the flexible approach to starting a set and the fluidity with which couples can choose to join in with no apparent regulations in place regarding optimum numbers (acceptable in some but not all dance halls), and the practice of dancing the same set all night. However, while the perception

The Chéticamp Set: hooked rug by Sylvia Roach, ca. 2007. Courtesy of Barbara Le Blanc.

may be that the square dance is very flexible and casual, in reality it is governed by a strict set of criteria and rules of etiquette that, although not articulated, are understood by its aficionados. The current concern in square-dance circles is due largely to these internally known "givens" remaining unarticulated even as the demographic of the practitioners has changed. [Doherty 1996; Graham 2006; Le Blanc 1986, 1997; MacInnes 1997; MacGillivray 1988; Melin 2012, 2015; Rhodes 1996; Voyer 1986].

3. Other forms of dance. While Cape Breton step and squaredance are most commonly related to the Cape Breton fiddle tradition, a number of other dance forms are practiced, to various extents, on the island that also intersect with the fiddle music. These include other Scottish dance forms (Highland dance and Scottish country dance), Irish and Acadian dance forms and a new, hybrid form, referred to as Celtic step dance. *See* **under terms.**

Acadian dance. In the Acadian communities, until the mid-20th century, the Roman Catholic Church dictated the framework in which dance occurred at such events as weddings, picnics and special feast days like la Chandeleur, la Mi-carême, Christmas and New Year. Outside of these contexts, however, the Church often opposed dancing, only relaxing its position in the later part of the 20th century. At local community picnics, the first of which was held in Saint Joseph-du-Moine in 1881, dancing was one of the main attractions. Two platforms were built to accommodate up to four square sets each; the fiddler had his own special elevated and protected corner, and he would play from one o'clock in the afternoon until midnight for 2 days in a row. Old French song dances or *rondes* also existed in Chéticamp. Dance ethnologist Simonne Voyer collected the following 3 group figure dances in 1957: Le Reel à Quatre (French Four), Le Reel à Huit (French Eight), both based on cotillion and quadrille structures, and a progressive longways dance, La Patate Longue. Locally these were referred to as *les vieilles danses* or "the old dances." According to residents who were interviewed in the 1980s,

by the 1940s these old dances were replaced by the square sets which had been steadily growing in popularity in some areas of North America since the early 20th century. Music teacher, Médéric LeFort began teaching these square dances in 1977 at the Chéticamp school, Notre Dame de l'Annonciation (NDA). He taught 6 figures; in Chéticamp, square dancing has always featured the same first figure, danced to jigs, with figures two and three danced to reels, chosen from the remaining five figures. Interestingly enough, the prompting or calling for these dances in Acadian communities has always been in English. Contrary to the Scottish communities, where the use of a caller disappeared in the second half of the 20th century, Chéticamp still uses a caller, who gives the dancers their prompts. Collectors refer to a particular style of the Chéticamp sets which is graceful in character, particularly in the passing of partners in the grand chain. Step dancing through the sets is also common. Dance in some Acadian communities has been well documented (Voyer, Le Blanc and Sadowsky) and various teaching resources have been developed (Le Blanc). [Caplan 1989; Le Blanc 1986, 1997, 2000; Le Blanc and Sadowsky 1986; Ross and Deveau 1992; Voyer 1986].

4. Dance research and resources. The dance tradition, in all of its permutations, has been well studied by academics and researchers. Early references to dance practices in the media date to, for example, 1929 and the *Toronto Star;* in the 1950s collectors Simonne Voyer and Frank Rhodes documented Acadian and Scottish dance respectively. Acadian dance was later the subject of research by Barbara Le Blanc, independently and with Laura Sadowsky; Sheldon MacInnes, based at CBU, contributed to the body of work on dance research, as did independent researcher, Allister MacGillivray with his publication *A Cape Breton Ceilidh* (1988). In the 1980s, MacInnes initiated contact with Dance Nova Scotia (DANS), which resulted in various teacher-training schemes and teaching resources being developed, among them *No Less, No More, Just Four on the Floor*, approved for use in the public school system as part of physi-

Square dance in West Mabou, 2015. Photo by Margie Beaton.

cal education programme. Two Scandinavians have carried out dance research, Jørn Borggreen (Denmark) on the square dance (2002) and Mats Melin (who completed his PhD research on the step-dance tradition at the University of Limerick in 2012 and subsequently published his findings in 2015.) Various teaching DVDs have been published by such as Mary Janet MacDonald, Jean MacNeil and Sabra MacGillivray. [**Borggreen 2002; Doherty 1996; Graham 2006; Le Blanc 1997; MacGillivray 1988; MacInnes 1993, 1996; Melin 2012; Rhodes 1985, 1996; Voyer 1986**].

dance halls. Dance halls have played a significant role in the Cape Breton fiddle tradition since they were first built in the early years of the 20th century. British dance scholar, Frank Rhodes, dates the first dance hall to Inverness County in 1900, although it was 1930 before they were the norm. Dance halls were often associated with the local church, and as such had a wider community function for all types of events. Only occasionally were dedicated dance halls established as independent, commercial ventures. Today, most dance halls continue to be church or community enterprises; other appropriate spaces such as firehalls, union or association halls (e.g., Elks, Rotary, Lion's Clubs, Legions) are also used to host dances around the island. Le Blanc and Sadowsky describe the early halls as being fairly basic in nature: pre-electrification, lighting was supplied by a lantern and, in the absence of a stage, the fiddler was positioned on a chair. Teams of 2 fiddles often played in order

to add volume since no other accompaniment (or amplification) was available. Gradually the halls evolved; stages became commonplace and as, first, pump organs and, later, pianos became established as the prevalent accompaniment instrument, halls began to invest in these; later, in-house PA systems became available. By the 1980s piano players began to supply their own electric instruments, eventually removing the need for halls to have acoustic upright pianos, although a small number of halls continue to have these. While some early halls had their dance venue on the second floor, this is no longer the case. Most of the popular dance halls in Cape Breton have a capacity in the region of 200 (strictly regulated by the fire marshall and licensed premises regulations); most have a canteen, and if the dances are designated "adult," they are permitted to serve alcohol; tables with seating around the perimeter of the dance floor are required as part of the licensing laws, but the dance halls where no alcohol is involved (as in Glencoe Mills and West Mabou) simply have benches placed around the walls for seating. A well-sprung hardwood floor is the optimum requirement for a good dance hall, as well as good acoustics so that the fiddle music can permeate all areas of the space. Values related to the quality of any dance concern the physical properties of the hall in this regard, as well as the obvious matters of the choice and form of the fiddler, the size and make-up of the crowd, and the general social ambience. Typically, dances are organized and hosted by community groups in a volunteer capacity, with funds generated being re-invested in the local community.

regional halls. Popular dance halls across Cape Breton in the past have been in communities such as Baddeck, Big Pond, Broad Cove (school), Brook Side/Section, Brook's Haven (Prime Brook), Brook Village, Bucklaw (Rainbow Hall), Caledonia, Centreville, Chéticamp, Christmas Island, Creignish (rec. centre), D'Escousse, Dundee (Rousseau's Barn), East Bay, East Margaree, Edgewater, English Island, Eskasoni, Glencoe, Glendale, Glenview, Glenville (Midway), Grand Mira, Grand River, Harbourview (Neili

Angus D. MacDonald's), Hayes River (school), Île Madame, Inverness (CMBA), Iona, Johnstown, Judique (hall), Inverness (Mabou, MacKinnon's Harbour, Marble Mountain, Margaree/Margaree Valley, Margaree Forks, Northeast Margaree (The Barn at the Normaway Inn), Port Hood Labour Temple Hall), Kenloch (Malcolm MacQuarrie's), Little Narrows (school), (old hall; arena), Princeville, Scotchtown, Scotsville, Southwest Margaree, Strathlorne, Troy (school), Valley Mills, Washabuck, West Bay Road, West Lake Ainslie, West Mabou, Westmount, Whycocomagh (Jack MacIntyre's, Legion, Smitty's Hall). In the industrial area around Sydney, popular halls during the heyday of square dances in the 1940s and 1950s were at Carpenter's Hall, The Cabin, Cedars Hall, the L.O.C., Mira Ferry, Nelga Beach, the Ritz, Spain's Hall and the Venetian Gardens. Off-island, among the displaced Cape Breton community, popular dance halls for Cape Breton events were located in Boston (such as the Orange Hall, the Rose Croix), in Detroit-Windsor, Halifax (Farrell Hall, Dartmouth, and St. Lawrence Parish halls), Toronto (St. Mary's, Liberty, Army and Navy, Legion) and in Antigonish. Until the West Mabou dances introduced a practice of varying the fiddler from week to week in order to attract different audiences and to give younger, emerging players an opportunity to gain experience in playing for dances, the common practice was for fiddlers to hold long-term residencies at particular dance halls. Buddy MacMaster, who played at the Glencoe Mills dances, was the last fiddler to hold such a residency from the 1970s through to the 1990s. Today the main dance venues are Brook Village Hall (Mondays), Scotsville (Tuesdays), the Barn at the Normaway Inn (Wednesdays, following the concert), Glencoe Mills (Thursday), South West Margaree Hall (Fridays), and West Mabou Hall (Saturdays); thus, a dance is held on most nights during the summer season. Various other halls and venues around the island are used on an occasional basis to host square dances (CMIC, Westmount). The only academic study specifically of the dance hall and its importance in Cape Breton to date is by Emily Addison, in an undergraduate paper at Trent University. [**Addison 2001**].

Dance Nova Scotia (DANS). The umbrella service organization for all forms of dance in Nova Scotia, this registered, charitable organization is governed by a board of directors elected from the dance community. Founded in 1974, it is funded by the province. DANS works with existing dance schools and organizations to promote and encourage all forms of dance and acts as a resource and professional development centre for the dance community. Although Cape Breton's Highland dancers are often affiliated with DANS, to date very few Cape Breton step dancers are involved. Yet, DANS has been a partner in developing specific Cape Breton dance resource packs for public schools in collaboration with dancers, dance teachers and researchers in a project initiated by CBU's Continuing Education Department. Notable in this regard is the 1992 publication, by Barbara Le Blanc with Mary Janet MacDonald, Betty Matheson, Dianne Milligan and Dolena Roach: *No Less, No More, Just Four on the Floor: A Guide to Teaching Traditional Cape Breton Square Sets for Public Schools.*

dance players. As distinct from "listening," "listening-to" or "presentational" players (i.e., those who perform in contexts without dance as the primary response), dance players have a repertoire and a style that is dictated wholly by the requirements of the dance, whether the solo step dance or the social square dance. Historically in Cape Breton, fiddle music was primarily functional for the dance, and so, by definition, all players were effectively dance players. As the 20th century progressed, a clear distinction began to emerge among these players and those whose music was increasingly for listening purposes only, where the focus was more on technique and virtuosity demonstrated across a much more diverse repertoire than concerned the dance players. The latter continued to focus on generating the volume and drive required to stimulate the dancers and a repertoire that was mainly confined to strathspeys, reels and jigs. While many players today cultivate both styles, most admit a preference (or ability) for one over the other; indeed, today the majority prefer performing in listening or presentational contexts.

dance-fiddling. This is the simultaneous performance of fiddle music and step dance by a single performer. Hugely popular during the 1980s and 1990s, but less-commonly showcased today, it had been a fashion in the 19th century, and was already evident in Scotland, in Ireland and in Irish-America, where noted players such as James Scott Skinner and Michael Coleman were known for it. Robbie MacIntosh, who emigrated from Scotland and settled in Earltown, Colchester County, in 1822, was one the first exponents of the practice in Nova Scotia; Ronald Joseph MacLellan (d. 1970) and Mikey A. J. MacDonald could also play and step dance at the same time. The practice of step dancing while playing the fiddle is a form of percussive self-accompaniment; a coordination skill requiring considerable ability and practice. A feature of contest fiddling across Canada, it was Jerry Holland who re-popularized the practice in Cape Breton. As a young boy playing Cape Breton music in Boston he made it part of his performance routine from the beginning; by the 1980s, among the early groups emerging from the formal classes which had recently been established, it was almost *de rigeur*. It became part of the act of high-profile players such as Natalie MacMaster and Ashley MacIsaac during the 1990s. Since then, while it still happens occasionally, the trend seems to have cooled off. Before it did, however, a number of piano players such as Tracey (Dares) MacNeil, Hilda Chiasson and Mac Morin took it dramatically further, demonstrating that they too were multi-talented and capable of dancing while they provided accompaniment on piano.

Dares, Tracey. *See* **MacNeil, Tracey.**

Davidson, Estwood. (1913-2005). Guitar. New Brunswick, Halifax and St. Peter's, Cape Breton. Growing up in New Brunswick he moved to Halifax, as a teenager, where he stayed with his sister who ran a business there. He started out playing guitar with Peter Briand from L'Ardoise, who played in the down-east style of Don Messer until Winston Fitzgerald sought him out; this was the beginning of a lifelong collaboration between these two musicians. Following their first performance together, in Dartmouth, Davidson, who admitted to being challenged by Fitzgerald's style, never having heard Cape Breton music prior to this, immediately enrolled for a music-theory course at the Halifax Conservatory of Music. With both Davidson and Fitzgerald enlisted during the war, it was not until 1946 that their paths crossed again in Sydney. They approached Charlie MacDougall, who gave them a Saturday night radio slot and advised them to engage a piano player; thus, Beattie Wallace joined them for the show that was sponsored by the MacDonald Tobacco Company, and which gained them a large following and invitations to play in venues such as the Navy League, Carpenters Hall and Venetian Gardens in Sydney, and later in Inverness County, the Magdalen Islands (Îles de la Madeleine) and Newfoundland and Labrador. Winston "Scotty" Fitzgerald and The Radio Entertainers (or, in the extended line-up employed for round and square dances, The Winston Fitzgerald Orchestra) had a long and varied career that saw them play all over Cape Breton and across Canada, featured in long-running radio and TV shows, and releasing several recordings. Davidson contributed to the slick, uniform sound of the ensemble through his careful charting of chords so that the guitar and piano complemented each other; the considered arrangements between the fiddle and the accompanying instruments set a new standard in Cape Breton and influenced the tradition for generations to come. Like the others in the group, despite the fact that they often played up to 6 nights a week, he held a steady daytime job. He also had issues with the music business, not least being unimpressed with the tendency for the fiddler to get all the acknowledgment, while the accompanists were often overlooked. The Estwood Davidson Memorial Concert was established in Richmond County to honour his memory with proceeds going towards a bursary for local youths; the tenth and final such concert was held in 2015. **[Caplan 1990].** *See* **guitar; Fitzgerald, Winston.**

Davis, Rachel. (1989-). Fiddle, step dance, composer. Baddeck. Her music experiences to date are typical of the early 21st-century Cape Breton fiddle tradition. Her parents, Lenard and Pauline (Long) Davis, both play music and her maternal grandfather, Clarence Long, taught her to play the fiddle; she recalls practising under his watchful eye in his barber's shop. In addition to this home environment, post-revival, external fiddle classes gave Rachel tuition opportunities with a range of teachers such as Karen Beaton, Kyle MacNeil and Stan Chapman, some privately and some at the summer courses offered at the Gaelic College at St. Ann's. Natalie MacMaster, John Morris Rankin and Howie MacDonald were others she listened to a lot during her formative years as a player. Performance opportunities offered by tourism were more significant for her than the then-declining informal house parties. She played for the weekly summertime Baddeck Gathering ceilidhs, developing her concert-performance skills in small and intimate environments. She also grew up with Celtic Colours as a regular element in her music calendar, experiencing performances and playing opportunities that have created for her and her contemporaries an international frame of reference. In 2007 she received the Tic Butler Award and, in 2009, the Frank "Big Sampie" Sampson Award, which enabled her to record a self-titled debut album; a second album, *Turns,* followed in 2013. Nominated for a Canadian Folk Music Award as Young Performer of the Year, Davis is one of a group of young players who live in Cape Breton and play music full time; her portfolio career includes performances at local events, international festivals and residencies such as at Dollywood in the U.S., and occasional fiddle teaching. She performs often with singer-songwriter Buddy MacDonald, has guested with The Cottars, is a member of the CBFA and is a founding member of the band Coig.

Decca Record Company. A record label established in Britain, its American branch was set up in New York in 1934 by Jack Kapp, who had previously worked for the Brunswick label. Though dealing mostly with popular music, Decca had an "ethnic" stream from the late 1930s to the early 1950s, part of which was a Scottish-music series of 33 discs and an Irish-music series with ca. 300 releases. Cape Breton fiddlers appeared in the Scottish series, some of them recorded in Boston: Alcide Aucoin, Colin Boyd, Dan J. Campbell, Angus Chisholm, Alick Gillis, Angus Allan Gillis and Hugh A. MacDonald. Not all of the recordings released by Decca were original; some duplication occurred between discs and a number of those released had appeared earlier on the Celtic label. *See* **recording industry.**

decoration. *See* **embellishment; ornaments.**

Detroit. The U.S. city of Detroit, MI, was a popular destination for many Cape Bretoners seeking work in the automobile industry; many of those who worked there lived across the border in the Canadian city of Windsor. There were two main periods of immigration to this urban area: post-Second World War from the mid-1940s to ca. 1953, and 1960-1965, when the automobile industry was expanding. Cape Bretoners followed a chain migration pattern with individuals encouraged to relocate by previous Cape Breton settlers, usually family or friends from their local community in Cape Breton. As in other pockets of settlement, Cape Bretoners in the Detroit-Windsor area tended to be drawn together by their shared cultural identity: organizing activities around their church, families and friends, maintaining the fiddle-music and step-dance traditions and passing these on to subsequent generations. In much of this, they were replicating, to a large degree, the approach of their earlier generations who had immigrated to Cape Breton from Scotland. Unlike the earlier experience, however, Cape Bretoners living in Detroit-Windsor maintained frequent contact with Cape Breton, such as inviting fiddlers to travel to play at dances or a concerts, and through regular vacations at home, typically during the summer months. In 1936, the Nova Scotia Club of Detroit was formed with Frank MacRae from Margaree as its first president. This held dances, picnics and benefit concerts with Leo MacDonald from Glengarry, Ontario, and "Little" Jack MacDonald from Judique as the regular fiddlers, accompanied by Ann MacNeil from Sydney on piano. Other fiddlers who often performed included Johnnie Archie MacDonald, Allan MacDonald (Foot Cape), and Bernie Mac-Neil (Big Pond). In the late 1940s, Frank Gillis from Inverness took over as president and ran events involving Cape Breton fiddlers who were based in the area, such as Dan R. MacDonald, Hughie MacDonald, Allan MacDonald, "Little" Bernie MacDonald, Leo MacDonald, "Little" Jack MacDonald and Ambrose Beaton, Johnnie Archie MacDonald, Bernie Mac Neil and Bob MacNeil. Regular piano accompanists were Marion (Mac-Donald) MacDougall, Ann MacNeil, Dorothy MacDonald and Joan (MacDonald) Boes. During the 1950s and through the 1960s, the club itself was inactive but the wider Cape Breton community in the region continued to congregate for social events including music sessions, concerts and dances; in this period, Johnnie Archie Mac-Donald of Judique, John Willie MacKinnon of Harborview and Bernie MacNeil of Big Pond were key players; invitations were issued to Cape Breton fiddlers back home to travel to perform at what they were advertising as "Down East dances" and which saw Buddy MacMaster, Sandy MacIntyre, Kinnon Beaton, John Campbell, Cameron Chisholm, Donald Campbell and Willie Kennedy travelling to take part over the years. Popular piano players during this era were Barbara (Mac-Donald) Magone, Kay (Campbell) White, Jessie Ann (Cameron) Beaton, Joan (Mac Donald) Boes and "Red" Mary (MacDonald) Beaton. Typically, the Saturday night dances were followed by a Sunday afternoon house party or ceilidh. At one of these events in the 1950s, John Archie MacDonald was inspired to assemble the group, The Five Mac-Donald Fiddlers, from musicians called MacDonald in the Windsor-Detroit area (who were for the most part unrelated); this group, the first massed fiddle band from Cape Breton, went on to record several albums. The Nova Scotia Club was revived again in 1972 through the efforts of Hughie Ferguson from Inverness, Andrew MacLellan from Glenview, Margaret Parker from Detroit, Hughie Jr. MacDougall from Judique, Bob Mac Neil from Detroit and Bob Willis from Saskatchewan. Again, they ran Cape Breton dances, benefit concerts, summer picnics and Christmas parties, and promoted Cape Breton musicians from the local area as well as continuing the tradition of inviting players from back home. The Nova Scotia Club of Detroit continues to hold dances 2 or 3 times a year. Current local musicians associated with it are fiddlers Morgan MacQuarrie, Jimmy MacNeil and Kenneth MacLeod, and piano accompanists Jessie Ann (Cameron) Beaton, Tom MacNeil and Marion MacLeod; the Rankin siblings Sara, Alistair (fiddles) and Cameron (piano) – students of Kenneth MacLeod – also frequently perform at Cape Breton events. [**MacInnes 1977, 1997**].

Deveau, Gerry. (1934-). Spoons, step dance. Chéticamp. Joseph Gerard ("Gerry") Deveau has been involved in the Cape Breton fiddle-music scene in a variety of capacities over the years, as a prompter for dances, the producer of the Saturday afternoon matinees at the Doryman Tavern for a decade and, perhaps most notably, as a spoons player. Something of a novelty act in Cape Breton, largely due to his highly energetic performances and the rarity of the spoons in the tradition, he recorded with Ashley MacIsaac on his award-winning *Hi, How are You Today?* album in 1995, and later toured Canada and the U.S. with him. A step dancer, he also sang and played guitar for over thirty years with his country and western band the Chéticamp Islanders, which included fiddlers such as Ephram Bourgeois and Arthur Muise at various points. [**Feintuch, 2010**].

Deveaux, Robert. (1977-). Fiddle, piano. Saint-Joseph-du-Moine and Louisbourg, Cape Breton. The son of Roy and Regina Deveaux, he grew up in an Acadian community where he was exposed to Cape Breton fiddle music as a teenager through recordings and in live situations such as kitchen parties at the home of Cameron Chisholm in nearby Margaree. He took lessons on fiddle with John MacDougall and Peter Poirier and on piano with Nettie LeBlanc. Among his greatest music influences were local players Johnny Aucoin and Arthur Muise as well as Cameron Chisholm and Jerry Holland. He also spent considerable time playing with Mary Jessie MacDonald when she returned to Cape Breton upon retirement from her job in Boston. As with all of the fiddle players who live in Cape Breton year round he plays for many tourism-related events during the summer season. He has recorded on *Pure Celtic Hearts,* Volume 2 (2004) and on compilations from the local Acadian community including *Le Théatre des Moineaux* (1995) and *Région de Chéticamp, Toujours Chantante, Compilation de 17 artistes de la région de Chéticamp* (2013), illuminating the complex identity typical of Cape Breton fiddlers from an Acadian background; further underlining this he has studied conversational Gaelic at St. FX. Deveaux has also carried out research into the French repertoire, stylings and practices of Chéticamp fiddler, Joseph Larade, one of his greatest influences.

Dewar, Allan. (1970-). Piano, fiddle. Antigonish, NS. Born to parents Roy and Marion Dewar he was raised in Halifax and Antigonish and exposed to Cape Breton music from a young age; his mother is a noted piano player and his maternal grandparents, Jean and Willie Fraser, often hosted parties and gatherings of musicians who were performing in or passing through Antigonish. Jean herself was a piano player who accompanied many fiddlers at dances in the Antigonish area. From a young age Allan performed at concerts for the Cape Club of Halifax; during the Highland Games in Antigonish he played guitar alongside his mother on piano and sister Joan on fiddle. Between 1992 and 2006 he toured professionally, playing piano with various Cape Breton fiddlers and singers including Ashley MacIsaac, Mary Jane Lamond, Glenfire, Natalie MacMaster and Jerry Holland. He continues to record and perform locally with players including Troy MacGillivray and Shelly Campbell. Since 2009, Dewar has been music director of the Celtic Music Interpretive Centre in Judique, where he is involved in producing concerts, recordings and organizing the annual Buddy MacMaster School of Fiddling.

diaspora. (i) Scottish diaspora. Cape Breton represents Gaelic Scotland's last diasporic region to exemplify a living culture which, while now shaped and re-formed according to its new world conditions, still maintains strong and proud roots in Scotland. (ii) Cape Breton diaspora. Cape Bretoners have for many years left their island for various reasons, generally in search of work. The potato famine of 1845-1851 saw people leaving the island for better prospects early in its colonial history, and the inclement winters and religious community were factors in the re-emigration of a Presbyterian population from St. Ann's to Waipu, New Zealand, in 1851. In the early 20th century, Boston was a popular destination, and the Detroit and Windsor region had two influxes of Cape Bretoners, first in the late 1940s and again between 1960 and 1965; Toronto was another primary destination in the 1950s while Halifax has been popular since at least the 1940s. Other areas which attracted Cape Bretoners periodically included Sudbury, Ontario; "out west," to places such as Alberta, became the primary option from the 1990s, and today the biggest draw continues to be that region. Finding employment was the primary reason Cape Bretoners had for leaving the island, and both males and females felt the need to emigrate. The pattern of migration has typically been a chain one, where emigrants, once settled, encouraged other Cape Bretoners – typically family members or others from their local communities – to join them if the prospects were encouraging. Cape Bretoners are known for their community tenacity; thus, in a pattern not unlike that of their forefathers who emigrated from Scotland, clusters of Cape Bretoners can be traced in many of the points of relocation. As they congregated together in these displaced communities, often a vibrant sense of culture and identity was cultivated. Religion (generally Roman Catholic), stories, songs, dance and music (both recorded and live) were practised, in some instances, more robustly than at home. Boston, for example, during the 1940s and 1950s was a hotbed of Cape Breton fiddle music, as was Detroit. Some of the key developments in Cape Breton music – including the first recordings, the proliferation of domestic recordings during the 1960s, the development of the piano style and the introduction of the new social dance form of the quadrille – came largely from displaced Cape Breton communities in the U.S. Expatriate communities regularly hosted dances and ceilidhs and frequently enabled Cape Breton musicians still based at home to travel to perform at these events. It was only in the 1990s that the tradition of Cape Breton communities bedding down in larger urban environments began to change; while large numbers of Cape Bretoners continued to emigrate, perhaps the relative ease with which they could return to Cape Breton on a regular basis (and communicate via the Internet and phone) meant that they did not need to create new communities, but could continue to tap into the community back home more regularly. Perhaps, too, it was as Cape Breton fiddle players became more at ease in assimilating with other traditions that they were content to do this rather than remain separate, promoting their own music only. Whatever the reasons, today there are no new large expatriate Cape Breton communities promoting a living strand of the culture, despite emigration levels remaining high. Furthermore, previous hotbeds of Cape Breton activity (Boston, Halifax, Toronto, Detroit-Windsor), while still in evidence, are arguably less active today, a generation or more down the line. [**Burrill 1992; Graham 2006; MacInnes 1977**]. *See* **Boston; Detroit; Halifax; Toronto.**

diatonic. Refers to a scale or interval involving only the notes proper to the prevailing key (i.e., the white notes on the piano) without the use of chromatic alteration (i.e., the use of accidentals or the black notes). While it may have different meanings in different contexts, it often refers to both major, minor and modal heptatonic scales. *See* **chromatic.**

dirt. A term used by Cape Breton fiddlers over the last few decades to refer to a fundamental aspect of the fiddle style. "Dirt" refers to the combined effect of such as bowed and fingered embellishments, drones and elements such as tone, intonation, accent and articulation; some might argue that this constitutes the older, Gaelic element of the music. While much of the interpretation of tunes is bound by conventions of "correctness," it is in the application of those elements contributing to the dirt that personal freedom may be exercised and where the individual discrepancies that energize Cape Breton style are in evidence. The dirt contributes to the "flavour" that an individual fiddler brings to the iteration of a given tune; the application of this distinguishes between individual Cape Breton fiddlers, and thus marks personal styles. *See* **flavour.**

Dòmhnullach, Goiridh (Jeff MacDonald). *See* **MacDonald family of Kingsville.**

Donovan, Ken. Ingonish and Sydney. Historian who worked for Parks Canada at Louisbourg from 1976 to 2011 and currently teaches history part-time at CBU. A self-proclaimed "Cape Breton nationalist, determined to write, publish and promote Cape Breton history," he has edited and co-authored 7 books, among them *The Island: New Perspectives on Cape Breton History, 1713-1900* (1990) and *Cape Breton at 200: Historical Essays in Honour of the Island's Bicentennial, 1785-1985* (1985); he has published more than 60 peer-reviewed papers and delivered more than 90 articles at national and international conferences and symposia on aspects of Cape Breton history, including pre-contact and settlement, slavery, astronomy, gardening, Ingonish, Cape Breton's cultural awakening and music, particularly as it related to the Louisbourg experience. He is past president of the Old Sydney Society, a non-profit organization that operates 4 museums in the Sydney area; he serves on the board of directors of the Jost House Museum and the Sydney Architectural Conservation Society. He is also historical editor of the *Nashwaak Review*, published by St. Thomas University.

Dorchak, Gregory. (1981-). Researcher, fiddle. Detroit. His 2006 Masters project at the University of Syracuse, NY – "Fiddling with Tradition: The Question of authenticity within Cape Breton Fiddle Music" – analyzes the social nature of culture, and change therein, by examining how Cape Breton musicians make decisions while performing. Although based in Boston, fieldwork done over two summers in Mabou led to his observation that the Cape Breton music community facilitates innovation and practical judgment in ways that other communities could benefit from; this has also been presented in papers at NAFCo (St. John's, Newfoundland, in 2008, and Aberdeen, Scotland, in 2011), the American Folklore Society (2007, Québec) and at the National Communication Association conferences (Chicago, 2009, and San Francisco, 2010); he has also published a paper on Jerry Holland and Winston Fitzgerald. While his academic work has moved largely in another direction, family ties in Sydney and his interests as a fiddle player keep him connected to Cape Breton.

Doryman Tavern, The. Opened in Chéticamp as The Surfside Tavern in 1966, since the 1970s this venue has become synonymous with the informal concert-style presentation event, the Cape Breton fiddle matinee. One of the first of its kind to be held in a licensed premises, this continues year-round on Saturdays, 2pm-6pm. Most of the island's fiddlers have performed at the Doryman. Starting in 1977, the resident house fiddler was local, Donny LeBlanc, accompanied by André LeBlanc on piano and Gélas Larade on guitar; Chester Delaney is the current resident fiddler. The guest musicians were programmed for many years by Gerry Deveau.

double stop. A fiddle technique which produces two simultaneous notes, it is achieved by bowing across two "stopped" (i.e., fingered) adjacent strings and is used to emphasize primary and secondary melody notes or in conjunction with particular ornaments such as cuts. How and when they are applied in tunes is a matter of choice for the individual fiddler. In the past, the frequency with which these were employed by some players within a given tune led to them being perceived almost as a drone, albeit broken up by single bowing patterns. Furthermore, the effect created was often dissonant; as the melodic line became thinner and more transparent the use of double stops became less frequent (often restricted to the end of phroases), more consonant and more often in strathspeys than reels. Another practice found in Cape Breton fiddle playing is "doubling," i.e., sounding an open string while, simultaneously, fingering the same pitch on the adjacent string. While this is occasionally referred to as "unison double stop" the term is not technically accurate, since only one of the pair of notes is actually stopped. [**Doherty 1996; Dunlay and Greenberg 1996**]. *See* **doubling**; **drone**.

double tonic. A term used to refer to tunes in which 2 primary-chord options, a tone apart, present as the main harmonic choices; in other words, 2 tonics exist. These two tonics may involve degrees one and two of the scale or degrees one and seven. The upper chord may be major or minor while the lower chord is always major. [**Dunlay and Greenberg 1996**].

double up-bow. A bowing pattern whereby two consecutive up-bows are used, not in a slurred pattern but, on the contrary, sounding quite separate. The bow may be briefly stopped or lifted between notes in order to articulate this separation. Typically, the first up-bow usually ends one idea and the second up-bow begins another, for example, where the second note acts as a pick-up note for the following phrase. [**Doherty 1996; Graham 2006; Dunlay and Greenberg 1996**] *See* **bowing style**.

doubling. Here a single pitch is doubled by sounding it simultaneously on an open string and on the adjacent string by employing the fourth finger. Typically found at the end of phrases, it contributes to the creation of a fuller sound, and may generate interesting tonal properties if (as is often the case) the two pitches are slightly unequal in tuning. The unison is often emphasized further by the addition of a single, first-finger grace note sounded concurrently on the open string; less frequently, a double grace note is used. While this practice was associated with particular types of tunes in different parts of Scotland (e.g., in the playing of airs in the Northeast), in Cape Breton it is employed across all tune types, although it is much less common today than it was among the players of the early 20th century. Although sometimes referred to as a "unison double stop," this term is not technically correct since it involves an open string (i.e., not stopped or fingered) along with a stopped string and, as such, only one stop is involved. **[Doherty 1996; Dunlay and Greenberg 1996; Graham 2006].** *See* **double stop; fourth finger; unison.**

Doucet, Marcel. (1949-1992). Fiddle, piano, actor. Chéticamp, Inverness County. Born to Alex W. and Annie (Larade) Doucet he had a core repertoire of Cape Breton, Scottish and Irish tunes. He was also Yukon fiddle champion and is known for composing the march "Space Available," which has become part of the Cape Breton fiddle canon. His life in music, however, was shaped by his improvisational abilities which gave him the opportunity to play back-up for singers and melody players alike. He performed in Canada, the U.S. and Europe with John Denver, The Band, Cornelia Boucher and Billy MacLeod, Matt Minglewood, Sam Moon, Sylvia LeLievre and Bruno Bourgois. He appeared in several music productions, including *The Rise and Follies of Cape Breton Island* and *The Cape Breton Summertime Revue*, and was also employed as a fiddle player at the Fortress of Louisbourg.

Doucette, Joe. (1958-). Fiddle, piano, guitar, mandolin. Neil's Harbour and Ingonish Beach. He grew up listening to tapes of local players such as Mike MacDougall and played with members of the MacDougall family over many years. His 1999 album, *Fiddlin' Around Down North*, was produced by Jerry Holland, who also played on it; Brenda Stubbert (piano) and Paul MacDonald (guitar) also feature. It includes several of Doucette's own compositions. A member of the CBFA, he has performed on local TV and radio shows including CBC's *Island Echoes* and *Talent Cape Breton*.

drive. Related to aspects of performance such as "lift," "lilt" and "swing" this is a term used in Cape Breton to refer to the energy generated within a given performance; this is created through particular choices made in relation to timing, metre, pulse, accent and articulation. Having "good drive" in their playing is something that most Cape Breton fiddlers aspire to and, along with good timing, is considered an essential component in successful dance playing. "Drive 'er!" (meaning "drive it" [the tune]) is a common call of encouragement to Cape Breton fiddlers; a comment such as "he/she was drivin'er last night" is a compliment on a good performance. **[Doherty 1996; Dunlay and Greenberg 1996; Graham 2006].** *See* **timing; tempo.**

drone. The drone, as it relates to fiddle playing, is created by sounding an adjacent string or stopped note alongside the melody line over an extended series of notes. Believed to mimic the drone of the Highland bagpipe, the effect is sometimes referred to as "blending" by Cape Breton fiddlers. Open strings were often used to create a drone behind a melody being fingered on an adjacent string; drones created by stopping a string on a particular note were also used. Drones were a prominent feature of the Mabou Coal Mines style of fiddling, a noted exponent of which was Mary MacDonald. While technically a drone involves a long continuous note being held, in Cape Breton another approach was to repeat a single note over and over in conjunction with a melody line, using a single bowing pattern; this created a drone effect through repetition. In some instances Cape Breton fiddlers preferred the practice of intermittent droning, whereby a tune would be peppered with short bursts of drones or these drone effects other than a single, long, continuous drone. Today, particularly in reel playing, drones are rarely used; often, they feature only in their intermittent form in conjunction with the bowed ornament, the "cut." [Doherty 1996; Dunlay and Greenberg 1996; Graham 2006]. *See* **double stop.**

Ducharme, Mary Anne. (1943-). Editor, teacher, playwright. Plattsburg, New York and Nevada Valley, Inverness, Cape Breton. Editor for a time of Inverness County's *Partici-paper*, a regional magazine published five times yearly that often covered music. In 1992 she produced the biography *Archie Neil: A Triumph of a Life!* (Breton Books), of Archie Neil Chisholm, the Margaree Forks fiddler, radio presenter, emcee and advocate of Cape Breton music, one of the legendary Chisholm family.

Dudley Street. *See* **Boston.**

Dunlay, Kate E. (1957-). Ethnomusicologist, researcher, writer, lecturer, fiddler, step dancer. Wayland, MA, and Halifax. A noted authority on Cape Breton fiddle music, she was among the first to explore it in an academic context. She is best known for *Traditional Celtic Fiddle Music of Cape Breton* (1986), a publication known in Cape Breton as "the little blue book," and *Traditional Celtic Violin Music of Cape Breton, The DunGreen Collection* (1996), which was co-authored with her husband, Baroque violinist and Cape Breton fiddler, David Greenberg; both of these are considered core literature on their subject. Dunlay's work on Cape Breton has ranged from detailed technical analyses of individual players' styles to more general socio-historical narratives; she has presented and published material in a variety of contexts (encyclopedias, album liner notes, magazines); she was also consultant and writer for the Cape Breton fiddle music and dance exhibit at the CMIC in Judique. Despite growing up in the Boston area, which had a strong Cape Breton community, her first encounter with its music tradition was not until the early 1980s when she met fiddler Carl MacKenzie, pianist Doug MacPhee,

and step dancer Betty Matheson while attending the Ashokan music camp in New York state. She then began to visit Cape Breton fiddlers living near Boston – including John Campbell, Joe Cormier, Bill Lamey and Ludger LeFort – before embarking on visits to the island where she studied step dance with Minnie MacMaster and fiddle with Buddy MacMaster. Observation and analysis of the latter's stylistic nuances led her to further investigation of the Cape Breton tradition through a Masters program in folklore/ethnomusicology at Indiana University in 1986. She has been teaching university courses on Cape Breton music since 1989. In 2003, she began teaching online courses on this subject for CBU and, since 2005, has taught modules on Irish music and the music of Atlantic Canada at Saint Mary's University, Halifax. She has composed a number of tunes, one of which is the reel "Keeper of Delight."

— ∼ —

Traditional Celtic music of Cape Breton Island. Kate Dunlay with David Reich. 1986. Harrisville: Fiddlecase Books. A tune book with substantial text included, it is the first of its kind on Cape Breton fiddle music; it contains 86 tunes, many of which are in previously unpublished settings. Each tune is accompanied by brief notes, recorded and printed sources and details of the player from whom it was transcribed. There is a brief introduction to the place of fiddling in Cape Breton life and a discussion of techniques such as bowing and left-hand embellishments; many new terms are introduced as the authors attempt to describe, often for the first time, such techniques as they are used by Cape Breton fiddlers.

— ∼ —

Traditional Celtic Violin Music of Cape Breton: The DunGreen Collection. 139 Transcriptions complete with historical and musicological annotations and descriptions of the performance practice by Kate Dunlay and David Greenberg. A tune collection and style guide and described by the authors "a field guide" to the Cape Breton fiddle tradition, this 1996 publication gives a socio-historical overview of the tradition, analysis of the style and performance practices, and transcriptions of recordings of core repertoire from major stylists. Its 68 pages have tunes arranged into categories by type and key, and also indexed alphabetically, a preface, intro-duction and historical background as well as commentary on modality, performance practice and technique, and an overview of research methodology; a discography, videography and bibliography of tune collec-tions with Cape Breton compositions is also provided, as is information on sources, and alternate tune titles. The bulk of the collec-tion is music "transcribed from the playing of some outstanding exponents of the tradi-tional style of Highland Scottish fiddling as cultivated in Cape Breton, Nova Scotia," spe-cifically Dave MacIsaac, Mary MacDonald, John Campbell, Fr. Angus Morris, Donald MacLellan, Theresa MacLellan, Carl MacK-enzie, Kinnon Beaton and Donald Angus Beaton, Jerry Holland, Johnny Wilmot, Alex Gillis, Donald Campbell, Buddy MacMaster, Joe MacLean, Dan J. Campbell, Angus Allan Gillis, Colin Boyd, Ashley MacIsaac, Paddy LeBlanc, Angus Chisholm, Alex Gillis and Alcide Aucoin, Hector MacKenzie, Winston Fitzgerald; some non-Cape Bretoners – Stan Myers and Ivan Laam – are also included. The transcriptions are descriptive of a single player's performance of a given tune; in many instances variations are also supplied and more than one fiddler's setting of a tune included. The name of each source is given and extensive notes offer additional analysis, commentary and information regarding alternative printed and recorded manifesta-tions of each tune, as well as alternative names by which the tune is known. All details of the performance are included in the transcription of one round of the tune using identified and described symbols. Of the 139 tunes, 68 are reels, 49 Strathspeys, 22 Jigs, 1

each of waltz and march/air; some of them are "high bass" tunes.

— ∼ —

Dunn family of Antigonish County. From Lower South River, Antigonish Co., NS, mother and daughter, Margie and Jackie, are part of the MacEachern family of Queensville; Margie is the niece of fiddler/composer Dan Hughie, whose music she has made available through publication; her father, John Willie, was a dance fiddler, and an uncle, Alex Joe, also played fiddle and recorded in the U.S.

Dunn, Margie. (1939-). Step dance, fiddle, teacher, publisher. Raised in Queensville, Cape Breton, the daughter of John Willie and Sarah Catherine (MacMaster) MacEachern, she started to play at a young age with her father, and much later in life joined Stan Chapman's adult fiddle class in Antigonish. A member of the CBFA – with which she performed on many occasions – she became better known as a step dancer having made her first public appearance at the age of 4 in Creignish, where people threw money on the floor for her! She continued to play fiddle and piano and taught step dancing, both privately and in groups, for 10 years in Antigonish; she performed in Scotland and, along with her students, on John Allan Cameron's CBC-TV show; she also orga-nized the Ceilidh Beag (Youth Concert) as part of the Antigonish Highland Games for a decade. She taught her daughter, Jackie, to step dance, started her off on the fiddle, and often accompanied her on piano during her first years performing as a fiddler. She manages the music of her late uncle, Dan Hughie MacEachern, and is responsible for the publication of the *MacEachern Collection Vol. 2* (1993). [**MacGillivray 1988**].

Dunn MacIsaac, Jackie. (1969-). Fiddle, piano, step dance, teacher, composer. Music was on both sides of the family, from Margaree and Dunvegan on her father's side and from the MacEacherns on her mother, Margie's, side. From a young age Jackie accompanied her mother, who was teaching step dance and performing at festivals and events in the Antigonish area, where they lived, and in Cape Breton; often she would join her mother on stage at the end of her routine, and in this way she gradually began performing her own solos. Again with her mother as her guide, she began trying tunes on the fiddle before she started as Stan Chapman's first student after he moved to the area, going on to perform solo on fiddle and, later, having taken classical piano lessons for a number of years, she began accompanying fiddlers as well. She was a member of the performing group, The Next Generation, organized by Chapman in 1986, and subsequent groups Highland Classics and The Special Seven; these groups involved mostly young players who were being taught by Chapman at the time, including Natalie MacMaster, Wendy MacIsaac and John Pellerin. Influences outside her family and by tuition came from Buddy MacMaster, Kinnon Beaton, Betty Lou Beaton, John Morris Rankin, Maybelle Chisholm MacQueen and Dave MacIsaac, whose guitar playing and chord progressions influence her piano work. A performer and teacher, Dunn MacIsaac has played with many of the recognized Cape Breton fiddlers over her career at such national and international events as the Washington, DC, Irish Folk Festival, Le Festival d'Été de Québec, Ceòlas (South Uist), Sabhal Mòr Ostaig (Skye), the Canadian-American Club (Boston and Toronto) and the Windsor Cape Breton Club, the Expo '86 World Fair in Vancouver and Celtic Colours. A music graduate of St. FX, her 1991 undergraduate thesis, "Tha Blas na Gaidhlig air a h-Uile Fidheir: The Sound of Gaelic is in the Fiddler's Music" (1991), contributed to the discussion surrounding the Gaelic language in Cape Breton and its connection to Cape Breton fiddling. She recorded the solo *Dunn to a T* album in 1995, and is on several other recordings: playing fiddle on Wendy MacIsaac's *Timeline* (2003) and step dancing on her *That's What You Get* (1998), playing piano with Glenn Graham on *Let 'er Rip* (1996), Buddy MacMaster's *The Judique Flyer* (2000), Brenda Stubbert's *In Jig Time* (1995), Kinnon Beaton's *Eoghan Dubh* (2003) and Andrea Beaton's *Cuts* (2004). She is featured on compilations—such as the Smithsonian Folkways *The Heart of Cape Breton* (2002)—and performs on various documentaries and commercial videos about Cape Breton music: *Cape Breton Island: The Video,* (Volume I and Volume II). In 2003, she and her mother released a double CD of Dan Hughie MacEachern's playing compiled from old reel-to-reel recordings, *The Land of My Love–The Music of Dan Hughie MacEachern*. Jackie continues to live in Antigonish County, where she works as a schoolteacher. **[Zinck 1999]**

dynamics. The effect of increasing or decreasing volume within a piece of music, creating a sense of light and shade. Historically, this is not a part of the Cape Breton fiddle style, which is governed more by rhythmic propulsion as necessitated by its primary function as dance music. However, as the divide between dance and listening contexts for the music became more distinct from the mid-20th century onward, increasing use of dynamics can be heard in Cape Breton playing, typically in more recent times, and associated with arrangements used by larger bands. Dynamics do feature at a micro level in Cape Breton fiddling, however, where, changes in bow pressure and accent within individual notes may result in a degree of dynamic colouring, for instanc, in the technique known as the "bow-push accent." **[Dunlay and Greenberg 1996; Graham 2006]**.

E

ear players. Term used in reference to players who learn their music aurally (i.e., without using written notation). It makes the distinction between these and players who use notated music as part of the learning process. Properly the term might be "ear learners" since in Cape Breton all fiddle players perform without reference to a musical score, irrespective of the source or method used in the learning process.

the process. Developing a good or accurate ear is not only necessary, it is almost instinctive among traditional musicians, and is often taken for granted by them. A well-developed ear allows players to commit the basics of a tune to memory following a few hearings, with attention to all the nuances and details picked up on subsequent listenings. In the past, Cape Breton fiddlers would hear a tune played at a social gathering and hurry home to replicate it; fiddlers also picked up tunes from various mouth-music sources, through *puirt-a-beul* or jigging. With the advent of recording (particularly personal, portable devices with play-back) the process of learning by ear changed significantly; rather than the learning having, of necessity, to happen in the moment, it could be delayed; equally, the source could be replayed multiple times creating, in effect, an extended learning opportunity. Rather than having to absorb a new tune in its entirely in a single hearing, particularly challenging phrases could be played over; the process of de- and re-constructing a tune in this manner came to be adopted in formal class settings which developed in the 1970s. While ear players, in theory, may have had limited repertoires in comparison with those musically literate players who were able to access the printed tune collections they did, indirectly, acquire a variety of tunes, picked up by ear as such tunes became part of the music canon. Today, while the majority of younger players have music-reading skills, there remain some key exponents of the tradition who are exclusively ear players.

style. Ear players were not exempt from playing "correctly" (i.e., within the accepted bounds of integrity); to be considered "very correct for an ear player" was high praise indeed. Critically, however, style can only be learned by ear; even for "note players" the written source supplies the tune outline; all the nuances of style – the "flavour" – can only be learned through an aural process. **[Doherty 1996; Garrison 1985; Graham 2006].** *See* **note players.**

East Coast Kitchen Party. East Coast Kitchen Party is an independent media organization reporting on Atlantic Canada's arts, entertainment and lifestyle news. It operates via a main web portal launched during the ECMAs in Charlottetown, PEI, in April 2011, a 24/7 radio station, East Coast Kitchen Party Radio (2012) and an extensive social media network on Facebook, Twitter and YouTube. The website was created by Michael Trenholm, a long-time journalist in Atlantic Canada who now resides in Ottawa, Canada. The website is owned and operated by Atlantic Multimedia Incorporated. Linda Rankin of Mabou, NS, is a senior associate for the company and regular contributor to East Coast Kitchen Party. *See* **radio.**

East Coast Music Association (ECMA). A non-profit association dedicated to the music of Atlantic Canada, established in 1991, it is a regional collaboration of ca. 1,000 members involved in various sectors of the music industry. Membership includes musicians, artists, agents, managers, record companies, studios, media, related corporations and retailers. Membership benefits include showcase opportunities, professional sessions, and online profiles. ECMA seeks to foster, develop, promote and celebrate East Coast Music and its artists locally, regionally, nationally and internationally, focused on the annual East Coast Music Week and The East Coast Music Awards; it also runs educational sessions and workshops throughout the year, trade missions and an International Export Program. Partnership with other industry organizations such as MNS assists in delivering its aims. Many contemporary Cape

Breton fiddlers who play professionally or semi-professionally, are members of the ECMA; many of them have won ECMA awards across a range of categories, something considered a mark of prestige; young emerging talent has also benefitted through participation in showcase events, for example, with the ECMA thus supporting professional development in relation to the Cape Breton fiddle tradition. *See* **East Coast Music Awards.**

East Coast Music Awards (ECMAs). These honour Atlantic Canadians in an annual ceremony that is one of the most important for Cape Breton artists with regard to prestige and professional development. Launched in 1989 as The Maritime Music Awards by Halifax music-industry promoter Rob Cohn, the tribute became known as the ECMAs following the creation of the East Coast Music Association in 1991, when it expanded to take in all the Atlantic provinces (New Brunswick, Nova Scotia, Newfoundland and Labrador and Prince Edward Island). The ECMAs are hosted by a different city in a different province of the region each year, and are presented at a ceremony which is part of a five-day event. It includes an international industry conference and festival that showcases high-status East Coast artists and music as well as the creative work of outreach schools and community programs. The presentation ceremony is broadcast as a two-hour, national show on CBC-TV. The city of Sydney, Cape Breton, hosted the ECMAs in 1995, 2000, 2005 and 2010, using the 2000 event to celebrate the influence of the Rankin family of musicians, and to commemorate the life of John Morris Rankin, who had died earlier that year; this event itself received a media Gemini Award for Best Music, Variety Program or Series. In response to the scale of that event, which pushed the organizational and infrastructure capacities of Sydney to the limit, by the time of the 2005 ECMAs, Sydney had developed its facilities to include the new, multi-million-dollar Membertou Trade and Convention Centre and the Sydney Marine Terminal. These hosted a greater number of sessions, boosted by an international program and a successful partnering with CBU. The awards themselves have expanded accordingly—from the original five categories (Album; Female Artiste; Male Artiste; Song; and Video [each "of the year"]) to 28 categories, for the music industry as a whole, 3 of which are in the category of traditional music. Various Cape Breton fiddlers and others have been nominated and have won awards across a range of the categories over the years, some recipients on multiple occasions. *See* **awards.**

Eaton's Catalogue, The. A mail-order catalogue published by chain store and mail-order consumer-goods retail outlet Eaton's from 1884 to 1976, one of the first such to be distributed by a Canadian retail store. Initially a 32-page booklet handed out at the Industrial Exhibition (now the Canadian National Exhibition), within 12 years the catalogue was generating more than 200,000 mail orders per annum; new subscribers, particularly in rural areas, were solicited by the offer of gifts for supplying contact information on non-subscribers. Initially only in English, the catalogue was published in French in 1910. The products on offer included everything from household goods to farm tools and pre-fabricated buildings. Apart from its social value in remote, rural Canada, in Cape Breton the Eaton's catalogue was an important resource for accessing instruments (including fiddles and pianos), strings, music collections, tutor books and books for dance callers.

ECMA. *See* **East Coast Music Association Awards.**

Ellis, Raymond. (1941-). Fiddle, composer. Little Narrows and Whycocomagh. Born to parents John and Mary (Northern) Ellis, he taught himself to play on a borrowed fiddle by listening to recordings and to the playing of his maternal grandfather, Charlie Northern, and his uncle Cosmos; he was also encouraged by his cousin John Gillis, of MacKinnon's Harbour. He played for school house dances from the age of 11 and although music was never his full-time occupation, he played, taught and recorded, mostly around Nova Scotia and occasionally in Boston and Toronto, where he lived for a year. A composer of tunes as well, more than 64 of his own compositions were published in the book *Cape Breton Fiddle Tunes–A Collection of Original Compositions by Raymond Ellis* in 2010, and four others are in the 2007 *Cape Breton Fiddlers Collection*; his tunes have also been recorded by Natalie MacMaster, J. P. Cormier, Brenda Stubbert, Kinnon Beaton and by Bert Murray from Scotland. He released two commercial albums, *Dedicated to Mom and Dad* (1994), with Hilda Chiasson on piano, and *More like Me!* (1999).

— ≈ —

Cape Breton Fiddle Tunes–A Collection of Original Compositions by Raymond Ellis. Published in 2008, this 32-page book has more than 60 tunes composed between 1987 and 2008 by Ray Ellis and one by Murray Gallant. A date or place is noted for the composition of the tunes, each of which references the type in its title; all have two turns save "Wendell Ellis's March," which has four. The pieces are loosely grouped according to key rather than type and are listed in an alphabetical index. There are 26 reels, 21 a jigs, 12 strathspeys, 4 marches, one hornpipe and one waltz.

— ≈ —

embellishment. The practice of adding decoration to a basic tune in order to enhance the melodic line and add individual expression or "flavour." Within Cape Breton, embellishing a tune is often referred to as "ornamentation," and is a central part of fiddle practice; it involves a range of bowed and fingered patterns that are a key part of the fiddlers' music vocabulary. Fingered ornaments are sometimes referred to as "left-hand embellishments." *See* **ornament.**

emigration. *See* **diaspora.**

events. The Cape Breton calendar for fiddle music and related events is populated year round, with a marked increase in amount and variety of activity (and audience engagement and profile) during the summer season, which is currently perceived as lasting from Canada Day (July 1) until mid-October (the conclusion of Celtic Colours); there are other peaks, such as around Christmas, Easter and other holidays; since 2014 Kitchenfest! / Féis a' Chidsin!, an initiatve of the Gaelic College, has brought the start of the season forward into June. The type and frequency of events has changed over the course of the 20th century; in the past, picnics, contests, frolics, garden parties, weddings and socials formed a core part of the social scene; while most of the these are no longer found, instead are ceilidhs, concerts, matinees, square dances and festivals. *See* under **terms.**

exhibition tunes. A loose term for technically-challenging, "showpiece" tunes that satisfied the demand for complexity and thus became more popular in the post-1940s "listening" contexts for fiddle music. The conscious incorporation of these into the repertoire challenged the technical ability of the Cape Breton fiddler and encouraged developments in this area; indeed, from this era increasing evidence exists of players seeking tuition from violin teachers or subscribing to distance music theory and technique programs. Such showpiece tunes might be of a type not common (certain hornpipes or clogs, for instance); in an unusual key or tuning; involve some particularly unusual or demanding technique or multiple parts or variations, each requiring increased technical dexterity. Tunes such as "The Banks Hornpipe" and "The East Neuk of Fife" became the mark of the technically accomplished fiddler; indeed, certain fiddlers became known for their rendition of particular tunes of this type: Angus Chisholm for "Listen to the Mocking Bird," Dwayne Côté and Kyle MacNeil both for "Tullochgorm," Shawn MacDonald for "The Hangman's Reel." While most fiddlers today can approach such exhibition pieces confidently, these tunes remain a minority in the repertoire. A number of fiddlers, such as Carl MacKenzie and Dwayne Côté, have a preference for including technically challenging tunes as part of their standard repertoire rather than reserving displays of technical dexterity for one or two discrete showpieces. *See* **repertoire.**

exhibits. Visual representations of Cape Breton fiddlers, other than photographs, are relatively scarce. The Finlay Walker Memorial Collection, the work of local artist, Ellison Robertson, includes pastel images of rural Gaels (including some fiddlers) and was acquired by CBU in the 1990s; it is permanently displayed there at the Centre for Cape Breton Studies. A photographic exhibit of Cape Breton fiddlers, curated by Allister MacGillivray with Sheldon MacInnes in collaboration with the Beaton Institute has been on display at the Sydney Marine Terminal since 2006. The Gaelic College houses an exhibit depicting the history of the Cape Breton fiddle in the Hall of the Clans and, in Inverness County, Judique's CMIC has an interactive exhibit in the Tom Rankin Exhibit Room. Online, the Highland Village Museum has developed a virtual exhibit, *Ceilidh air Cheap Breatunn / Cape Breton Ceilidh*, as part of Canada's virtual museum project. Internationally, the story of Cape Breton fiddle music informed an exhibit as part of the Balnain House project in Scotland (1993-2000) and was included in *The Fiddlecase Exhibition* as part of the North Atlantic Fiddle Convention in Derry/Donegal, Ireland, in 2012. Individual artists, in recent years, have also depicted Cape Breton fiddlers in occasional pieces such as paintings (e.g., Peter Rankin) and wood-carvings (e.g., William D. Roach). *See* **Balnain House Museum project; Celtic Music Interpretive Centre.**

F

FACTOR. Foundation Assisting Canadian Talent On Recordings. A private, non-profit organization formed in 1982 by CIRPA and CMPA in partnership with three Canadian broadcasting companies: CHUM, Moffat Communications and Rogers Radio Broadcasting. It aims to sustain and grow the independent Canadian music industry and does this through the administration and disbursement of significant funds contributed by private radio broadcasters and the Department of Canadian Heritage Canada Music Fund. Support is available to recording artists, songwriters, labels, publishers, managers and event programmers and industry bodies; they can fund recordings, demos, showcase events, marketing and promotion of recordings and offer some tour support – both national and international. FACTOR has added concerns since 2012 when Canada's entry to the negotiations opened through the Trans-Pacific Partnership that raised the possibility of losing the CanCon quota requirements. It would appear that while some Cape Breton artists have benefited from FACTOR support, the traditional music community has had, as yet, limited engagement with the various support programs run by this organization. *See* **CanCon.**

fairy lore. As in many other connected cultures, the intersection between music and the fairy world informs part of the Cape Breton historical and contemporary narrative in relation to the fiddle music and piping traditions, used typically to explain extraordinary musical gifts or as a source of repertoire. Indeed, some research supports the theory that fairy folk crossed the Atlantic along with the emigrants in certain instances; certainly numerous stories pertaining to the fairies having made the crossing continued to be handed down in the oral tradition. Latterly, it has been suggested that a significant alteration that occurs in the fairy lore of Cape Breton is its Christianization, in other words, that the supernatural manifests itself as spirits of good or evil. Examples of fairies appearing in Cape Breton relate to fiddler Donald Campbell (d. 1878) of St. Peter's who allegedly received his music knowledge, and a bow, from the fairies. "Big" Ronald MacLellan, as recounted by his daughter, piano player Marie MacLellan, also acquired a fairy bow and with it a legendary flair for fiddle music. [**MacDonald 2009; MacGillivray 1981; MacNeil and Shaw 1987**]. *See* **otherworld.**

families. Historically, much of the Cape Breton fiddle tradition was passed down within families, generating well-known dynasties of players, whose involvement and impact typically passed through several generations. Such families dealt with in the *Companion* are: Aucoin family of Sydney Mines, Beaton family of Mabou, Campbell family of Glenora Falls, Chisholm family of Margaree Forks, Gillis family of Scotsville, Graham family of Judique, MacDonald family of Ironville, MacDonald family of Kinsgville, MacDonald family of Margaree, MacDonald family of New Waterford, MacDonald family of Queensville, MacInnis family of Big Pond, MacLean family of Washabuck, MacLellan family of Riverside, MacMaster family of Judique, MacNeil family of Sydney Mines, Muise family of Boston, Rankin family of Mabou, Stubbert family of Point Aconi. Smaller family groupings such as a single parent and child or a group of siblings have also been presented together in this volume: Beaton sisters, Benoits of Halifax, Cameron brothers, Cameron family of Boisdale, Cameron family of Belle Côte, Chafe (Winnie and Pat) family, Cotés of Grand Greve, Dunn family of Antigonish, Foulds family, Fraser brothers, MacDonald family of Detroit, MacDonald siblings of Foot Cape, New Waterford and Detroit, MacDonald sisters of Halifax, MacDonald sisters of New Waterford, MacGillivray family of Antigonish, MacGillivray family of Mira, MacIsaac siblings of Creignish, MacKenzie brothers of Mabou, MacKenzie siblings, Morris brothers of Colindale and the Touesnard sisters. [**Graham 2006**].

Family Herald, The. See *Canadian Family Herald.*

fat-flat stroke. An even, one-dimensional bow stroke used most often in reels to distinguish certain clusters of notes from the rest of the melodic line in terms of their pulse. By applying a solid, equal and almost (but not quite) staccato treatment to these notes they are easily differentiated within the flow of the melody. This technique is only heard in the playing of a few older Cape Breton fiddlers – most noticeably that of Donald MacLellan – although it has been adopted more widely by contemporary players, who use it occasionally as a feature. The terms was coined by David Greenberg and first used in the *DunGreen Collection* (1996). [**Dunlay and Greenberg 1996**]. *See* **bowing style.**

Father John Angus Rankin Cultural Centre, The. Located in the former Glendale glebe house, it is named after the priest who ran the local parish for 32 years, and who played a key role in the preservation of the area's culture and music. Opened in 1997, the centre is managed by a not-for-profit co-operative whose mission is to generate activity based on local talent, resources and culture, to preserve the glebe house for its historical value to the cultural community and to promote local identity. The centre includes a CAP site (Community Access Program – an initiative of the Government of Canada that aims to provide Canadians with affordable public access to the Internet and the skills they need to use it effectively), weaving facilities and a gift shop; regular kitchen ceilidhs are hosted during the summer season. An in-house archive – Taigh-Tasgaidh Braigh na h-Aibhneadh – holds local documents, maps and photographs of historical and cultural significance to the area. *See* **Rankin, Fr. John Angus.**

Feintuch, Burt. (1949-). Folklorist, fiddle. Professor of Folklore and English and Director at the Centre for the Humanities, University of New Hampshire, he is a former editor of *The Journal of American Folklore* (1990-1995) and a member of the National Recording Preservation Board at the Library of Congress. Originally from Philadelphia, PA, his first encounter with Cape Breton music was as a fiddle student at the Ceilidh Trail School of Celtic Fiddle Music in Inverness (1997). Curious about the music, the place and the sense of connectedness between culture and local life he embarked on several fieldwork and interviews trips, these yielding a substantial body of published material including *In the Blood: Cape Breton Conversations on Culture* (2010), with photographs by Gary Samson, and for which he received an Independent Publishers Book Award. Other projects have included recordings with extensive accompanying liner notes for Smithsonian Folkways and Rounder: *Cape Breton Fiddle and Piano Music: The Beaton Family of Mabou* (2004), *The Heart of Cape Breton: Fiddle Music Recorded Live along the Ceilidh Trail* (2002), *Buddy MacMaster: Cape Breton Tradition* (2003, co-produced with Mark Wilson). Other published material has considered issues affecting the Cape Breton tradition, such as revival, out-migration and cultural integrity and sustainability. While his work in academia is diverse including, for instance, studies of the music and culture of New Orleans, Cape Breton remains at the centre of his interests.

Féis Cheap Breatuinn / Féis Cape Breton. Based on a popular Scottish initiative, the *féis* movement was introduced to Cape Breton in 2015 to bring new energy to the fiddle-music tradition, with a specific focus on youth participation and involvement. While the Cape Breton fiddle tradition has, since the 1990s, become a significant player on the international stage, there have been escalating concerns about the numbers of young people having access to and engaging with the local tradition; while international interest in learning to play Cape Breton fiddle music and step dance has peaked, at home the opportunities to experience certain elements of the culture have, paradoxically, diminished – a consequence of consistent out-migration of younger Cape Breton players, changes to the established performance environments such as fewer square dances, a rapidly diminishing cohort of older players as well as an unfortunate number of untimely deaths within the fiddle music community of players in the 40-60-year age group – that group, as identified back in the 1970s, already a particularly limited one in terms of numbers playing. The CMIC and Celtic Colours have taken the lead on this initiative with a view to connecting the many stakeholders across the island to ensure that the music and culture will remain a vibrant and living tradition for future generations. Piano player and step dancer Mac Morin was appointed to coordinate the new movement.

Ferguson, John. (1953-2012). Fiddle, guitar, bouzouki, mandolin, bass, bodhrán, singer, composer. Caribou Marsh, Sydney and Halifax. Born to parents Neil John and Lorraine (Dares) Ferguson, he became interested in folk music as a teenager and was a founding member of Halifax folk bands Miller's Jug and Kiltarlity in the 1970s. He went on to play with the band McGinty for 35 years, and recorded with them and in duos with singers Buddy MacDonald and Roger Stone. He toured extensively on the folk circuit in Canada and the U.S. as well as in Ireland, Luxembourg, Iceland and the Dominican Republic. Ferguson was among the first to introduce the bouzouki to Cape Breton music circles. He composed a number of tunes (e.g., "The Four North" [strathspey] and "Robert Hannigan's" [reel]), and a collection of his compositions is currently being complied by his widow.

Festival Volunteer Drive'er Association (FDVA). A not-for-profit society of ca. 40 people, it was formed in 2004 by the drivers who volunteered to transport artists around the island to their various gig commitments during Celtic Colours; the scattered geography of the island demanded such intense contact between performers and drivers that the latter came to be acknowledged as a key part of the welcome and hospitality which artists and other visitors experienced. The drivers are variously retired from other jobs, take their own vacation time to coincide with Celtic Colours, or are Cape Bretoners who live away but return home

annually for the festival. The term "drive'er" is connected to the common call of encouragement often made to Cape Breton fiddlers while playing to "keep it going" or "keep it up." Now part also of the wider fiddle-music scene in Cape Breton the mission of the association is to (a) promote, represent and support participation in Cape Breton arts, music, cultural heritage and hospitality; (b) promote and extend international and domestic awareness, appreciation and celebration of Cape Breton music and musicians, Celtic Colours and others for culture, heritage and hospitality of Cape Breton Island; (c) encourage, assist and/or enable participation of Celtic and Cape Breton music, arts and culture through the dispensing of occasional gifts, grants, accommodations and scholarships. The FVDA is funded by merchandise sales at Celtic Colours, which enables it to offer the Frank "Big Sampie" Sampson Award annually to young artist toward studio recording time. The FVDA also established the John Allan Cameron Bursary as a support for students attending courses at the Gaelic College, St. Ann's. *See* **awards; Celtic Colours International Festival; Frank "Big Sampie" Sampson Award.**

festivals. (a) Local festivals. The Cape Breton calendar, particularly during the summer season from late June until the end of August has numerous community festivals, many of which include a cultural dimension, usually a dance, ceilidh or concert. There are also a number of arts festivals – such as Bras d'Or Festival of the Arts – held annually which generally feature Cape Breton fiddle and dance, as do various ethnic festivals such as Mi-Carême and Festival de l'Escaoutte in Chéticamp, and the Multicultural Festival in Sydney. Dedicated Cape Breton fiddle and/or dance festivals are the annual Cape Breton Fiddlers' Festival (each August at the Gaelic College), and the Chestico Days Stepdance Festival. The concept of a specific fiddle festival was born in the 1970s with the Cape Breton Fiddle Festivals held in Glendale; these spanned a decade and were a core element of a wider revival. More typical at that time was the one-day outdoor concert (such

Dan R. MacDonald. Courtesy of Topic Records.

as at Broad Cove, Iona and Big Pond); these often grew out of earlier social gatherings such as picnics. Since 1997, Celtic Colours has extended the tourist season until mid-October, engaging the whole community in imaginative ways and raising the profile of Cape Breton and expanding accessibility to Cape Breton music; the formula and program of Celtic Colours was aligned more to international models than to anything previously existing in Cape Breton. Held in June since 2014, Kitchenfest/Fèis a' Chidsin! extends the tourist season in the other direction and is also based on a decentralized model; over a week this celebrates local music, food, stories and hospitality. Cape Breton fiddle music and dance is also featured at the various Gaelic festivals that have developed in recent years in Cape Breton, such as Féis an Eilein in Christmas Island.

(b) **International festivals.** Cape Breton fiddlers have, increasingly since the 1990s, developed busy touring schedules appearing at various folk, traditional and Celtic festivals internationally. While Cape Breton musicians occasionally were featured at established events such as the Mariposa and Newport Folk Festivals in the 1960s, the first significant and robust programming of Cape Breton music at such events was at The National Folk Festival in Wolf Trap, Washington, DC, organized by Mike Denny. Since then other festivals have focused on Cape Breton as a regular part of their program (e.g., Shetland Folk Festival, Tønder Festival, Denmark; Celtic Fests in Cuba and in Barbados) or as a special feature; examples

of the latter include the Éigse na Laoi Festival (Cork, Ireland, 1993) and Celtic Connections (Glasgow, 2009). [**Ivakhiv 2005; Mahalik 2014; Lavengood 2008**].

fiddle. (a) Generic term for any form of bowed stringed instrument. It includes the standard violin as well as such variants as the Chinese Erhu and the Scandinavian Hardangar.

(b) Specific bowed instrument typically made from a single block of wood, hollowed out and covered with a soundboard with originally 3 (later and typically 4) but up to 5 strings. From the 1500s, fiddles in Islamic areas were held upright resting against the player's knees or on the floor (like a double bass) and with the bow held palm-up; in other areas it was held approximately horizontally, lying across the player's chest, supported by a strap, or vertically supported by the chest or shoulder and with the peg box pointing to the ground. The Nyckelharpa, a keyed fiddle still popular in Scandinavia, is part of this fiddle family. Kit fiddles (easily transportable since they could be kept in a pocket, hence generating the nickname "pocket violin") were popular among French dancing masters in the 16th-19th centuries; this existed in four forms – the rebec, mandora, viola and violin.

(c) The term used in many folk-music traditions to denote the standard violin; there is a perception in some levels of society that a "fiddle" player is a lesser or untrained player as opposed to a "violinist"; this view, however, is ill-informed. The instrument is the same in both musical contexts although folk or traditional players may adopt different conventions in terms of instrument hold, bridge curvature, string type and action. In Cape Breton, the term "violin" was used widely until late in the 20th century and its players were violinists; since the 1970s, the terms fiddle and fiddlers have come to replace this in general usage (except in a few instance where older, legendary-status players are being referred to). *See* **violin.**

Fidheal Mhor a' Ceilidh / The Big Fiddle, Sydney, Cape Breton.

Fiddlesticks Music Publishing. Currently run by Roberta Head, this company administrates the licensing of Jerry Holland's original compositions, all of which are registered with SOCAN.

Fiddletree, The. A project involving instrument making, tune composition and performance led by Otis Tomas. *See* **Tomas, Otis.**

Fidheal Mhor A' Ceilidh. *See* **Big Fiddle, The.**

firehalls. Nova Scotia's fire departments range from large, paid, professional services in the urban regions, to totally volunteer services in small towns and villages. In Cape Breton, many of these have a dedicated building which in the past, and in some instances still, has served also as a community hall for local social events, including square dances.

First Nations. *See* **Mi'kmaq.**

Fitzgerald School of Irish Dancing, The. In 1973, the Irish Benevolent Society, under president, Mike Fitzgerald, invited Laura Masters, the North American Dance Champion, from the Butler Academy in Toronto, to Cape Breton to introduce and teach Irish dancing to children and members of the Irish Benevolent Society. Prior to this workshop, little was known about Irish dancing in Cape Breton; Highland dances such as The Irish Washerwoman were mistakenly assumed to be Irish. Fitzgerald's daughter Renie was captivated by the dancing taught at these initial

workshops and took further instruction, gaining a TMRF certification from An Comisiúin le Rincí Gaelacha, the governing body of Irish step dancing. She established the Fitzgerald School of Irish Dancing, based in in Sydney, but with classes held over the years in Glace Bay, St. Peter's and Antigonish. More than 1,600 dancers, mostly female, have been involved in the school, learning a number of solo dances as well as specific group, *céilí* or "figure" dances. As is typical in this dance genre, the Fitzgerald school has its own costume, with a white dress, embroidered with shamrocks, harps and a pot of gold; more advanced dancers can wear personal, "solo" dresses of any colour and design. Though not a priority for the Fitzgerald School, competition is the focus for this style of Irish dancing, and its dancers have been successful in competition (the *féis)* in Montréal and Ottawa. But because of the relative remoteness of the school from the wider competition circuit, its dancers have been more involved with community performances and have developed their own choreographed exhibition pieces. The Fitzgerald school has now a profile at Cape Breton festivals and community events, and has performed at the G-7 summit in Halifax, for Irish President, Mary McAleese's state visit to Cape Breton, on various television shows and at the Miramichi Irish Festival in New Brunswick. In 2005, supported by the Department of Communities, Culture and Heritage Cultural Division, the school visited Ireland, where they gave a number of performances and participated in workshops in Co. Donegal; dancers from the school have also guested with international and touring musicians (e.g., Bumblebees) and dance shows (*The Magic of Ireland*).

Fitzgerald, Mike. (1923-). Community organizer and dance caller. Tilton, Newfoundland, and Sydney. Advocate of the Irish community and Irish culture in Cape Breton, he has Irish roots in counties Kilkenny and Tipperary, Ireland. Born to parents John Fitzgerald and Mary Murray, there was music in the family – fiddlers, melodeon players, singers and dancers in the Irish-Newfoundland style. At the age of 18, Mike came to Cape Breton where he married Flora MacDonald with whom he had 8 children. He first called the sets at a dance at the old Lyceum in George Street, where fiddler, Tena Campbell, was playing, the regular caller being absent. From then he became a regular caller at Sydney-area dances and was a member of Joe MacIsaac's Dance Band in this capacity; he later formed his own dance band – The Eastern Aires – in which he played drums and was the prompter. He hosted a weekly half-hour radio show on CJCB, promoting this band's performances. A stalwart of the Irish community in Cape Breton, he joined the Ancient Order of Hibernians (AOH) in 1950 and for a time was its Canadian national organizer. In 1966 the AOH was succeeded in Cape Breton by the Irish Benevolent Society, of which Fitzgerald became president and a member of its executive. He became involved in running the Irish Club on Townsend Street, which opened in 1971, winding up his band performance in order to dedicate time to this. He was president of the local chapter of The Multicultural Society (a Government of Canada initiative to bring ethnic groups together), 1992-1994 and 1996-1998, and he also served on the board of the Multicultural Association of Nova Scotia; for the 25th anniversary of the latter, in November 2000, he was presented with a gold diamond pin by Lt. Governor Myra Freeman. Fitzgerald's family followed him in Irish cultural promotion activities: his daughter Maureen (Renie) is director of the Sydney-based Fitzgerald School of Irish Dance and his granddaughter Lyndsey has toured internationally as lead dancer with *The Magic of Ireland* dance show.

Fitzgerald, Winston "Scotty." (1914-1988). Fiddle. White Point, Victoria County. Of French and Irish parentage, he grew up surrounded by music. His father, George Fitzgerald, and mother, Mary Paquet, both sang; George and his brother, Jim, played fiddle. Another fiddler, Archie Gwynn from Sugarloaf, would stay with the family for a few weeks every winter, creating an extended opportunity for house parties. Inspired in this way, Winston began to play the fiddle at the age of 8; at 12 he made his first public appearance,

Winston Fitzgerald with Mary Jessie MacDonald. Courtesy of Paul MacDonald.

playing at a picnic to raise funds for a teacher's salary. Other young boys starting out to play at the same time included Mike and Angus MacKinnon from Smelt Brook, and Hector, Donald and Jack MacDougall from Sugarloaf. They were able to get together occasionally and share tunes, some of which were sent to them by Angus Chisholm, who had taught for a time in Sugarloaf. During 1933-1934, Winston spent a winter travelling through the Annapolis Valley with a black-face minstrel show, The Maritime Merrimakers, in which he played fiddle between sketches, accompanied by Max Cross on guitar, gaining professional experience and improving his sight reading. In the 1930s he returned to Cape Breton each summer, fishing the northern waters with his family, and playing music with his brother Bob on guitar and with Arthur Severance, a piper and guitar player from Forchu. Winston worked during the winters at the shipyards in Halifax; there he played for dances with Jack Vickery on piano as The Cape Breton Serenaders and, later, with Joe Morgan (guitar), Joe Nightengale (vocals, bones), Fred Broan (banjo) and Al Slaunwhite as The Ramblers. They played live 15-minute radio shows for free in order to advertise their dances. His reputation led to the invitation to perform with Hank Snow (who coined the nickname "Scotty"), both with the band Hank Snow and his Ranch Boys and on Snow's morning radio show on CHNS, where he played a tune and backed the host's singing. Winston toured Nova Scotia and New Brunswick with the band, doing concert, stage and movie theatre work (where they would play between shows), this experience providing him with further insights into the professional musician's life and challenging him to stretch his style and expand his repertoire. Back in Halifax, the growing Cape Breton community there provided many opportunities for performing, and he built up a dance circuit. From 1940 to 1946 he was with the Royal Canadian Army; then he moved back to Cape Breton where he married and settled in Sydney, working variously as a chef, a carpenter and with an aluminium company until his retirement.

bands. Fitzgerald's leisure time was spent in music, notably with his band – Winston "Scotty" Fitzgerald and his Radio Entertainers – which he formed with Estwood Davidson (guitar) and Beattie Wallace (piano) in 1947; occasionally he played with other piano accompanists such as Catherine Ann Lamey. Regulars on radio, the trio built up a dance circuit from Ingonish to Antigonish and played also in Sydney in venues such as The Venetian Gardens, The Navy League, The Ashby legion and Carpenters Hall. During the 1950s, as Winston Fitzgerald became increasingly popular, his regular performance group The Radio Entertainers expanded to become The Winston Fitzgerald Orchestra. Joining the core group of Fitzgerald on fiddle, Beattie Wallace on piano and Estwood Davidson on guitar, the orchestra members included, variously, Eddie Pastoni, Tupper MacAskill, Wes and Howie Pretty, Chippie MacDonald, Johnny Green, Murray Maxwell, Prof. Jim MacDonald, Jimmy Ruth, Sonny and Jimmy Slade and Murph Stag; Mike MacNeil and Dan Joe MacCormack were prompters. The band played a mixture of modern, round dance and traditional music at what were known as "round and square dances." The Venetian Gardens in Sydney was one of their regular performance arenas, and

they also travelled to Halifax, Toronto, Windsor and Detroit. In later years Fitzgerald also played with The Cape Breton Symphony, with which he toured Ireland, Scotland and Shetland.

recordings. He recorded a number of 78s with the Celtic label and became the first Canadian fiddler to record an LP: *Canada's Outstanding Scottish Fiddler–Winston Scotty Fitzgerald and his Radio Entertainers* (1953). Other recordings include *Canada's Outstanding Scottish Fiddler, Winston Scotty Fitzgerald* (Celtic), *Winston Scotty Fitzgerald and His Radio Entertainers* (Celtic), *It's New–Winston Scotty Fitzgerald* (Celtic), *The Inimitable Winston "Scotty" Fitzgerald* (Celtic); *A Selection of New Jigs, Reels, Strathspeys, Hornpipes and Waltzes* (Banff), *House Parties and 78s* (CBM) and *Classic Cuts* (Breton Books); posthumously, some of his earlier Celtic label material was re-released as *Traditionally Yours* (1997); Fitzgerald also appears on compilations such as *The Fiddlers of Cape Breton* and *16 Great Barn Dance Tunes.* He was also the first to attempt to maintain ownership of his own music by setting up the Mac label (with Lloyd Taylor from CJCB), on which he released a small number of recordings.

professionalism. With an extensive catalogue of recordings, much radio play, frequent TV appearances such as on the Cliff MacKay, Don Messer and John Allan Cameron shows and an intensive dance circuit that took in Sydney to Toronto, Detroit and Boston, Fitzgerald was, in fact, one of the first Cape Breton fiddlers to achieve "star" or "living legend" status. This he did while keeping up a day job throughout his life. He approached his music as a business and was quick to respond to changes in the market (e.g., by moving into the round-dance niche), and to redress copyright issues (by setting up his own record label). He was aware of what his audiences expected from him, in response to which he and his band dressed professionally and were configured in appropriate line-ups. He used live radio to draw in his potential audiences, but also had the ability to respond to the expectations of any crowd: for a number of years in the French Club he played only round dances, yet he had enough polkas in his repertoire to satisfy a crowd in Antigonish.

impact. As an artist he set new standards within the Cape Breton fiddle tradition and played a significant role shaping the sound and practice into what they are today. Inspired by classical violinists such as Jascha Heifetz and Itzhak Perlman, he constantly challenged his own technical limits on the instrument. He developed his music theory through a correspondence course with the U.S. School of Music, and he listened to the music of dance bands like Glenn Miller and Tommy Dorsey in order to better understand timing. In repertoire he was responsible for introducing both new tunes and tune types, and in particular he explored the creation of medleys of tunes. Many of his arrangements have come to be considered classics in Cape Breton in the same way that those of Michael Coleman were revered among subsequent generations of Irish fiddlers. Fitzgerald was one of a number of fiddlers of the time to extend the range of keys which the Cape Breton fiddler might employ, and was especially fond of keys such as E flat, B flat and F. When he acquired a new tune book he would first go through it and identify the best tunes in these keys to learn. He placed great emphasis on the value of a tune "setting," and often worked at a tune over extended periods of time in order to satisfy himself in relation to this. Like his contemporary, Angus Chisholm, Fitzgerald was interested in extracting a cleaner, more transparent sound from the older Cape Breton texture by developing a more definite approach to intonation, embellishment and bowing. Unlike Chisholm, his explorations included the accompaniment, as well as such as harmony and arrangement. Above all, however, he was a dance player, and all of his developments regarding style were within this context. While his tempo was deliberately faster than that of other fiddlers, his timing – and thus his drive – was pitched just right. Within the dance context he maintained a presence as an intense performer; even as he was creating the optimum experience for the dancers he was fully involved in the music as art. The impact of Winston "Scotty" Fitzgerald

on Cape Breton fiddle music of the late 20th century was immense, and he played a significant role in moving it away from an 18th-century Scottish sound toward something more distinctly Cape Breton. Within that evolving Cape Breton voice, many elements of the older sound and practice were, demonstrably, retained, to the extent that Scottish fiddler, Hector MacAndrew, upon meeting Fitzgerald, declared him to be "near(er) the truth." **[MacGillivray 1981; Caplan 1993, 2006; Cranford 1997; Fitzgerald and Cameron 1978].**

personal collection. Fitzgerald's personal archive of some 50 items of printed music was donated to the Beaton Institute by the fiddler himself. It offers an insight into the interest of the Cape Breton fiddler in printed music collections and practices in relation to this; it also highlights the diversity of Fitzgerald's repertoire. The collection consists of some of the significant Scottish fiddle books including the Skye, the Athole, various Gow collections, Captain Simon Fraser's, various of Scots Skinner's, the Middleton, various Mozart Allan collections, various of Kerr's, and Harding's. Bagpipe music is included with such as the *J. Wilson Collection*, P. M. James Robertson's collections and *The Glen Collection*. A substantial number of Irish and Irish American books are also included, such as Jerry O'Brien's collections and tutors, Ed Reavey's collection, Breathnach's *Ceòl Rince na hÉireann*, Walton's *Irish Dance Music*, the Joyce collection and *Allen's Irish Fiddler*. In addition, it includes several volumes of songs, waltzes and classics and tune books from other fiddle traditions such as by New Brunswick's Don Messer and Shetlander, Tom Anderson. The archive includes the U.S. School of Music *Home Study Course for the Violin* (New York), lessons 1-96, a music-education program which Fitzgerald was known to have pursued. Local Cape Breton collections include the 1940 MacQuarrie Collection, MacEachern's Collection, Volume 1 (1975), and the reprinted Skye and Fraser collections. There are also a number of handwritten tune compilations, including a 28-page set of tunes composed by Dan R. MacDonald, sets of handwritten tunes copied from various collections, and looseleaf sheet music which Fitzgerald himself had presumably assembled for his own use, as was the practice of the time. Multiple copies (up to 3) of some publications are included; others are only partially maintained and some are missing pages or front covers.

— ≈ —

Winston Fitzgerald: A Collection of Fiddle Tunes. Melodies Arranged from Performances by the Legendary Cape Breton fiddler. As vol. 4 of the *Cape Breton Musical Heritage Series: 20th Century Performers,* this 1997 book is a posthumous collection of 230 tunes from the repertoire of one of Cape Breton's most prominent fiddlers. It is presented under a series of tune type categories: hornpipes and clogs; pipe tunes; strathspeys and reels; jigs; polkas; and airs, melodies and waltzes. Within these categories tunes are individually numbered and arranged by key, with additional notes provided for specific tunes to highlight particular sources, further information, or offering melodic variations that Fitzgerald may have used. As is typical of Fitzgerald's repertoire, reels are the most prominent tune type (27%), with hornpipes and clogs being the next largest category (22%), followed by strathspeys (19%) and jigs (18%). It is worth noting that this was the only published fiddle-music collection from Cape Breton at the time to include a dedicated pipe-tunes category and a polka category, which contains some of the tunes that he popularized – "The Antigonish polkas #1 and #2." The tunes come from various sources, from 18th-, 19th- and 20th-century Scotland, from America, Canada, England, mainland Nova Scotia and from Cape Breton; all are presented in Fitzgerald's settings. While some pieces are referred to as "traditional," 53 composers in total are identified. Of these, James Scott Skinner's contribution is the greatest – 32 tunes in total. Five of Fitzgerald's own compositions are included. The collection also includes an introduction by the editor about Fitzgerald and his immense

contribution to the Cape Breton tradition, a section describing techniques that Fitzgerald used in his playing, an index of tunes by key and tune-type, an index of composers and an index of Fitzgerald's repertoire as it appears in other Cranford publications. Within the main key and tune-type index, alternative titles for certain tunes are given, and what are classified specifically as "pipe tunes" also appear under the relevant dance tune-type category. Quotations from Fitzgerald himself (from *Cape Breton's Magazine* interviews) intersperse the various tune categories along with 13 photographs internally and 2 cover photos.

— ≈ —

Five MacDonald Fiddlers, The. A group formed among the expatriate, Cape Breton community in Detroit, MI, during the 1950s following informal, regular Sunday-afternoon music sessions that were a big part of the Detroit scene. Twin fiddles had already been a popular combination in Cape Breton and, occasionally, multiple-fiddle ensembles had been formed in the stateside Cape Breton community, such as The Columbia Scotch Band

The Five MacDonald Fiddlers, 1953. 77-1393-1527. L-r: Allan, Bernie, Hugh, John A. and Dan R. MacDonald. Beaton Institute, CBU.

and The Inverness Serenaders. The Five Mac-Donald Fiddlers, however, represented the largest grouping of Cape Breton fiddles to date, thus creating both a sight and a sound that was unique at the time. Accompanied by Joan MacDonald (later known as Joan Boes) from Foot Cape on piano, the players were Johnny Archie MacDonald from Little Judique Ponds, Hugh A. MacDonald from Mabou, Bernie MacDonald from Whycocomagh, Allan MacDonald from Foot Cape and Dan R. MacDonald from Judique. Of these, Allan and Joan were brother and sister and Hugh was their first cousin; none of the others were related. The band changed as its members moved on: after Dan R. left, the band was re-named as The Five MacDonalds; Bob MacNeil played and recorded with them from that point, while Leo MacDonald from Glengarry, ON, also performed with them occasionally. At the suggestion of Johnny Archie, who was a key figure in maintaining and promoting Cape Breton music in the Detroit area, Celtic Records of Antigonish recorded the group. Subsequently they released 3 LPs on the Celtic label, one of which was re-issued by Rodeo: *The Five MacDonald Fiddlers, The Five MacDonalds,* and *Scottish Reels, Jigs and Strathspeys by the Five MacDonald Fiddlers*. They also featured on a number of anthology recordings: *24 Cape Breton Fiddle Medleys, The Fiddlers of Cape Breton* and *This is Sydney*, all of which include selections previously released. The band was hugely popular in the Detroit area where they played concerts, benefits and weddings, and entertained at private parties; in 1953 they played in Cape Breton's other diasporic community in Boston, for a benefit concert at the Inter-colonial Hall organized by Bill Lamey. Some of their recordings have been re-released in CD format as *The Five MacDonald Fiddlers with Joan MacDonald Boes*.

flavour. The term used locally in Cape Breton to refer to aspects of style as it relates to the fiddle sound. In other traditions, such as the Irish, the Gaelic term *blas* is sometimes used to refer to this; however, this equivalent is not generally used in Cape Breton. Within Cape Breton fiddle practice,

as in Baroque music, the melodic outline of a tune, once arranged into a specific "setting," becomes a fixed entity while the nuances of style are more flexible, varying from player to player and, with an individual, from one performance to the next. These flexible elements or variables – ornaments, accent, articulation – contribute to the "flavour," which is thus where individual expression and discrepancy shines through, where each fiddler puts his or her own stamp on the tune. The flavour or style enhances the basic tune, or melodic outline, which in Cape Breton practice is quite rigidly interpreted according to local conventions regarding "correctness." The flavour too, although it implies freedom and flexibility, is bound by the conventions regarding correctness, although these have changed, and continue to change, over time. Winston Fitzgerald, who was known for his unique style within the Cape Breton tradition, considered the significance of adding flavour to a tune in the following way: "You learn a tune out of a book, but if you don't put anything in it ... you might just as well wash your feet with your socks on." [**Caplan 2006; Doherty 1996; Dunlay 2000**]. *See* **correctness; ornament.**

flying spicatto. This is a four-note bowing pattern which involves the first down-bow being followed by three successive up-bows, played in a deliberate, detached fashion. A feature particularly of the Mabou Coal Mines style, and associated with the playing of Donald Angus Beaton, the effect of this bowing pattern is one of almost bouncing the bow. Mainly evident in the playing of strathspeys, less commonly in reels, the flying spicatto pattern is rarely used today by Cape Breton fiddlers. [**Doherty 1996; Dunlay and Greenberg 1996**]. *See* **bowing style.**

foot-tapping. Gesture in the form of foot-tapping thus keeping time with the music, is an omnipresent part of the Cape Breton fiddle-music practice and an integral element of performance; each individual player demonstrates his/her own style to a certain extent in this regard. To eliminate foot-tapping from a performance would, firstly, be a challenge for the player and, secondly, compromise the overall aesthetic. In the past, however, in recording situations, fiddlers often tried to at least reduce the noise of the feet and indeed were encouraged by recording engineers to eliminate it. Since the 1990s, however, foot-tapping has been prevalent in recordings; increasingly it is common for separately recorded "foot tracks" to be included in the recording process. Fiddler Howie MacDonald is known for his ability to engineer natural-sounding foot tracks and has brought this to bear on his own recordings as well as having been utilized by others for this purpose. Most Cape Breton fiddlers employ both feet when they perform from a seated position. Typically one foot (the primary foot) will mark the strong beats of the bar (e.g., beats 1, 2, 3 and 4 in a strathspey, and beats 1 and 3 in a march or reel). The other foot (secondary foot) will either remain in a sedentary position or may be used to further emphasize these accentual points and/or to mark the off-beats in a manner similar to the Québécois "French tap." The movement with the primary foot may involve the whole foot (in a flat-foot motion) or the heel, and, much more rarely, the ball of the foot; the secondary foot will typically involve tapping the ball of the foot; also common is a rocking motion between the heel and the ball of the foot. Many personal interpretations of this basic patterning can be found among fiddlers. Equally, the force and impact of the foot movements, governed in part by the height of the feet off the ground, may vary from one player to the next. The physiology of the player, interestingly, seems to have little impact on the sound and dynamism of the feet in this context. Players generally demonstrate a preference for one foot over the other or a particular stylistic pattern of foot-tapping, although it is not uncommon for this to shift within a given performance. Increasingly, choices are made in terms of footwear to accommodate this aspect of a player's performance; some players prefer hard-sole shoes to achieve clarity of foot-tapping while others in recent times have started to perform barefoot. Even when performing in a standing position time is still kept with the fiddler's foot, although

usually adjustments are made that result in a less-pronounced visual and less-audible outcome; in some instances, however, the opposite is true.

Forrester School of Celtic Dance, The. Established in Sydney in 1965 by Eileen (Pottie) Forrester (Fellow, BATD; Member, SDTA; Scottish Official Board of Highland Dancing Adjudicator's panel), who continues to co-direct it with her daughter, Shannon Forrester; the school has several branches throughout the Sydney area. A recognized Scottish Highland Dance school, it in fact offers teaching in a variety of dance styles, including Highland, Celtic step dance, Scottish national, specially choreographed and novelty dances; exam and competition-oriented training is offered; there is also a strong non-competitive program which revolves around the performance dance troupes in both Scottish Highland dance and Celtic step ("Reel Precision") and a junior dance company, "Highland Thistle." The school's dancers perform in approximately 50 shows a year; they have travelled to take part in various competitions and events internationally. Since 1992, Pipe Major Michael Campbell, of Sydney, has been the musical director for the dance company; other musicians who regularly perform with it include fiddle player, Shawn MacDonald. *See* **dance.**

Fortune, Henry. (1866-1935). Fiddle. Sydney Mines. Henry James Fortune was an Irish-style fiddler, one of the last fiddlers to solely represent that style in Cape Breton. A music teacher, he was known for his strict attitude towards preserving the local Irish fiddle style as it was practiced in the Northside area. For this reason, it was widely assumed that Henry was of Irish descent. However, the Fortunes were originally Acadian, with the surname Fortin. Henry's great-grandfather, Frances Fortune (Fortin), a fiddler, was among the Acadians returning to Little Bras d'Or at the end of the 18th century; many of these Anglicized their names. A number of the Fortunes married into the Irish community in the district, creating a large extended family connected with such as the Cahills from Co. Wexford and the Burkes. Fiddle playing passed through the generations; Henry's uncle Billy Fortune (1824-1901), a left-handed player, had been considered among the finest Irish-style players during his time on the Northside. Henry himself was known for his highly ornamented long-bowing technique. His nephew, Joe Confiant, was highly influenced by the Irish style; he in turn influenced his nephew, Johnny Wilmot, thus carrying on a rare strain of Irish music on Cape Breton's Northside, in the face of powerful Scottish influence.

Foulds family. Sydney and Boularderie. Joella Foulds and her sons Jamie and Mattie (Matthew) have been involved in the Cape Breton fiddle, music scene in various capacities over the years and have made an immense contribution. Joella, in her role as co-founder and current executive director of Celtic Colours, has been responsible for delivering on the cultural tourism potential of the fiddle-music tradition, raising the profile and presence of Cape Breton fiddle music internationally, creating an award-winning cultural event and, indirectly, shaping the conditions for the learning and practice of Cape Breton fiddle music for current and future generations of players.

Foulds, Joella. (1945-). Executive director of Celtic Colours. Born in Manitoba, she moved to Cape Breton in 1978 where she has worked variously as a musician (including as a singer with Rita MacNeil's band), a CBC journalist and broadcaster, a social worker, artist manager and event coordinator. In her capacity as president of Rave Entertainment she managed the band Realworld that featured her sons Jamie and Matt along with singer-songwriter Gordie Sampson. Along with Max MacDonald she founded Celtic Colours in 1997, inspired by the success of Celtic Connections in Glasgow. The festival, which is held over 9 days each October, has won numerous awards at the national and regional level, including the National Cultural Tourism Award in 2011. In 2012, Joella was honoured with the Order of Canada for her work in the Arts and Culture sector and she received an honorary doctor of letters (D. Litt) from CBU in 2011. From 2002 to 2009, she was a member of the Nova Scotia Arts and Culture Partnership Council, becoming chair for 2009-2011. She received the Industry Builder Award from the ECMA in 2000 and was inducted into the Cape Breton Business Hall of Fame in 2006. In 2014, she was one of 12 Nova Scotians appointed by the Premier to the One Nova Scotia Coalition, a volunteer group mandated to develop a new economic plan for the province. [**Feintuch 2010**].

Foulds, Jamie. (1969-). Lead singer, songwriter and multi-instrumentalist with the pop-rock band Realworld from 1986 to 1995, Jamie owns and runs Soundpark Studios based in the Sydney area. He is a recording engineer and record producer and has received the ECMA Studio Engineer of the Year award 8 times. He has recorded albums for such as The Barra MacNeils, J. P. Cormier and for Celtic Colours.

Foulds, Matthew. (1972-). Drummer and percussionist Mattie, besides being involved with various pop and rock bands, has performed and recorded with many Cape Breton fiddlers. He was a founder member of Beòlach, with whom he has recorded. Since 2001 he has lived in Scotland, where he has recorded and toured with artists such as Karine Polwart, Phil Cunningham and Aidan O'Rourke. He owns and runs Mobile with a Home recording studio in the Scottish Borders and has recorded and produced many award-winning albums.

fourth finger. The practice of using the fourth finger in preference to an open string was common among many old-style Cape Breton fiddlers where it avoided string crossing and allowed for the open string to be sounded against the stopped note as a unison, or doubling, thus creating a fuller sound. Later players, such as Winston Fitzgerald, also made considerable use of the fourth finger; however, he was influenced by the practice as it related to classical violin technique, whereby the fourth finger was used instead of an open string, in order to allow a consistent tone to be maintained and offering the option of applying vibrato to that note. [**Doherty 1996; Dunlay and Greenberg 1996; Graham 2006**]. *See* **doubling.**

Frank "Big Sampie" Sampson Award, The. An award set up in 2005 and named, since 2007, in memory of Frank Sampson, an inaugural member of the Celtic Colours Festival Volunteer Drive'ers Association. Jointly sponsored by the FVDA and Lakewind Sound Studios, it grants a young up-and-coming Cape Breton musician six days recording-studio time; recipients are acknowledged during the Celtic Colours festival. To date, these have been: Adrianne Chapman-Gorey and Mike Gorey (song, 2014), Joanne MacIntyre (Gaelic song, 2013); Maxim Cormier (guitar, 2012); Anita MacDonald (fiddle, 2011); Kenneth MacKenzie (fiddle/pipes, 2010); Rachel Davies (fiddle, 2009); Dawn and Margie Beaton (fiddles, 2008); Jason Roach (piano, 2007); Colin Grant (fiddle, 2006), all of whom released CDs with support from the initiative. *See* **Festival Volunteer Drive'er Association.**

Fraser brothers: Isaac. (1989-), piano, and **Robbie** (1986-), fiddle. Strathlorne, Inverness County. Born to Laurne and Joanne Fraser, the brothers were encouraged in music from a young age. The family tree includes connections with fiddlers Dan Hughie MacEachern and Sandy MacLean; both parents were enthusiastic music supporters and listened to Ray "Mac's" *Ceilidh* on CJFX radio almost every night. They were also regular square dancers, and Laurne played fiddle at home; he gave Robbie his first instruction at the age of five. Isaac began playing piano at the age of nine, having been given a few basic chords, but took lessons with Marianne Jewel in Scotsville, and was strongly influenced by Mac Morin, who inspired him to practice intensively. Robert took some lessons on fiddle from John Donald Cameron and John MacDougall, but perceives himself as being mainly self-taught, learning primarily by ear and with his interest in music being nurtured in the home environment. He is interested in good timing and what he calls the "pure, traditional old style." He cites Buddy MacMaster and Willie

Kennedy as his main influences; indeed, from his earliest years, he was recognized for adopting elements of these players' bowing styles. Robbie is featured on the Bravo channel documentary *And they Danced* (2005), and since 2005 has toured occasionally with Ashley MacIsaac, Glenn Graham and Rosie MacKenzie in the U.S. and in Canada. He performs mostly with his brother, however, something they have been doing since their first public performance, in Port Hood in 1998. Together they have recorded three albums: *Hear this, Here it is* (2004), *Right at Home* (2006) and *Everything Old is New Again* (2009). While the brothers have both pursued full-time professions in other areas and currently live off-island, they relish any opportunity to perform on visits home to Cape Breton.

Fraser, Alasdair. (1955-). One of the most influential Scottish fiddle players of the 20th-21st centuries. From Clackmannan, Scotland, he has lived in California since 1981, but has maintained deep ties and involvement with his native Scotland ever since. He is the founder and director of four fiddle schools: The Valley of the Moon Scottish Fiddle School (California, founded 1984), Alasdair Fraser Fiddle Week (Isle of Skye, Scotland, founded 1987), Sierra Fiddle Camp (California, founded 2006) and Crisol de Cuerda/Crucible of Strings (Spain, founded 2008). Initially influenced by the variety of fiddling styles he was exposed to growing up in Scotland – from Farquar MacRae and Angus Grant in the Highlands to Hector MacAndrew in the Northeast – Fraser discovered Cape Breton music in 1981 (through a chance meeting with Buddy MacMaster) and became a passionate advocate for reintroducing its fiddle music and dance to Scottish audiences. In the liner notes to his Cape Breton-influenced album *The Driven Bow* (1988) he states:

> the fiddle and dance traditions on Cape Breton Island in the Canadian Maritimes provide us with a window which sheds light on the way 18th and 19th century dance fiddlers, such as Neil Gow (1727-1807), used to play in the

Highlands of Scotland.... Let's hope that some of the great fiddle and dance tradition that has been absent from Scotland for so many years can be restored.

Fraser's belief, which initially met with considerable skepticism, led to an awareness of, and gradually an understanding and appreciation of, Cape Breton music in contemporary Scotland; many new networks and partnerships have developed as a result of his passionate insistence on giving attention to Cape Breton and its music. Fraser initiated the first Cape Breton fiddle workshops to take place in Scotland, bringing Buddy MacMaster and Harvey Beaton to his summer school at Sabhal Mór Ostaig on the Isle of Skye in 1992. Through his appreciation of Scotland's "golden age" fiddler-composers and his shared passion for tying the music to the dance and playing for dances, Fraser was keen to reintroduce the cello as the accompanying instrument of choice and today performs and records with American cellist, Natalie Haas. The duo has performed a number of times at Celtic Colours.

Fraser, The Captain Simon Fraser Collection. The Airs and Melodies Peculiar to the Highlands of Scotland and the Isles, edited by Captain Simon Fraser and chiefly acquired during the interesting period from 1715 to 1745 though the authentic sources narrated in the accompanying prospectus. Tune collection published in 1816 by The Highland Society of Scotland; a revised edition was printed by William MacKay and Angus Fraser in 1874. Simon Fraser was a Scots fiddler and composer who was born at Ardachie, near Fort Augustus in 1773; he moved then to Errogie in Stratherrick and later again to Knockie. "The Knockie" collection, as it came to be known, was successor to a 1795 publication *Thirty Highland Airs, Strathspeys etc. With a Bass for the Violoncello or Harpsichord, Consisting Chiefly of Tunes Entirely New With a Few Old Tunes Never Before Published.* The 1816 collection surpassed this in scale, and remains regarded as a classic collection of dance tunes and Gaelic airs arranged for fiddle and piano. Fraser continued to add to this

collection until his death in 1852, and his son had planned to publish this material as a "Volume 2," but died before this was accomplished; the originals are housed in Edinburgh University Library.

In 1982, Paul Cranford republished Fraser's main collection, a book that went on to become one of the most valued of the Scottish collections in Cape Breton, with more than 50 of its tunes now circulating in the region. This edition is a reproduction of the 1874 edition (made from a copy held in Joe MacLean's private collection) plus a few additions from the 1816 original from a copy owned by Winston Fitzgerald. The book has 128 pages, spiral bound on heavy cartridge, with an introduction by Cranford, the preface to the 1874 edition, the original "Letter" and "Prospectus" by Simon Fraser, a full alphabetical index of tunes in Gaelic and English, and melody and bass lines of 221 tunes with tune type or performance direction included; an appendix carries notes to the individual tunes, a list of Highland melodies already incorporated with Scottish song, and an English index. The tunes in this collection include the airs of traditional Gaelic songs which Fraser had heard from the singing of his father, grandfather and their acquaintances, and strathspeys, reels and jigs, some of them newly composed. A double cassette tape was originally issued to accompany the publication of this edition in Cape Breton (now remastered as a CD). This features 18 musicians playing the Fraser tunes: Donald MacLellan, Ronald MacLellan, Alex Francis MacKay, Loretto Beaudry, John Neil MacLean, Sonny Slade, Paul Cranford, Jerry Holland, Pat Cormier, Doug MacPhee, Mary Gillis, John Shaw, Sandy MacDonald, Dave MacIsaac, Carl MacKenzie, George MacInnis, Gordon Côté and Joe MacInnis.

Fraser, Kimberley. (1982-). Fiddle, piano, step dance, teacher. Sydney Mines. Music was not a big part of her home environment, although her grandparents' generation on both sides had fiddlers and step dancers; her grandfather, Bill Livingstone, was a noted fiddler and her great-grandfather on her father's side, Donald Anthony

MacNeil, was a fiddler and step dancer. Her sister took step dance lessons with Jean MacNeil, and Kimberley joined her at the age of four. In 1989 she started fiddle lessons (playing left-handed) with Kyle MacNeil, later taking classical violin lessons in North Sydney with Dan MacDonald, son of Prof. Jimmy MacDonald. Around then she started taking piano lessons at the Gaelic College with Ryan MacNeil and fiddle with Sandy MacIntyre during its summer programs. She heard local musicians such as Brenda Stubbert, the Barra MacNeils and occasionally Dougie MacPhee, Howie MacDonald, Carl MacKenzie and Dwayne Côté at local concerts, and encountered Inverness players such as Ashley MacIsaac through TV shows like *Up Home Tonight*. Her first participation in a ceilidh was at the Hillview Avenue home of Tic and Emily Butler in Sydney when Irish folk singer Tommy Makem was visiting. She went on to perform regularly at The Dockside Ceilidh held at the North Sydney Ferry Terminal, she joined the CBFA, and became an instructor at the Gaelic College during the summer months; she also took part in the 1998-2000 production *Spirit of the Island*. This was a particularly important step in honing her professional skills as it was before an audience of mostly tourists; it also got her thinking about releasing a CD, which she did in 2000 (*Heart Behind the Bow*). In 2002 she received the Tic Butler Award and her album *Falling on New Ground* (2006) earned her an ECMA (2008). This album featured Danish fiddle and guitar duo Harold Haugaard and Morten Alfred Høirup, whom Fraser had met first at Celtic Colours and again while working on a young musicians' collaborative project at the Tønder Festival in Denmark. Her engagement with other musics also led her to tour Sweden as piano player with Irish-American group, Cherish the Ladies. She studied Gaelic at CBU and jazz at St. FX and Berklee College of Music, Boston; at Berklee, she began to combine her enhanced theoretical and technical knowledge with Cape Breton fiddle-music performance and her growing interest in players and styles from the early 20th century. Fraser's focus now is on re-presenting Cape Breton music using new techniques and accompaniments. Being artist in residence at Celtic Colours in 2013 allowed her to work with Haugaard and the Nordic Fiddlers Bloc, and with Americans Darol Anger, and Natalie and Brittany Haas; with these she explored new ideas in arrangement and accompaniment, and setting—as presented in the "String Crossings" showcase—a new standard for collaborations built around Cape Breton fiddle music. Currently based in Sydney Mines where she teaches fiddle, piano and step dance, and runs an online fiddle and piano teaching service, Fraser has also contributed to fresh awareness of performance-related injuries affecting fiddle players, an area only recently receiving attention among traditional music communities in the Celtic world. [**Feintuch 2010**].

frolic. *Froilig* in Gaelic. A now extinct communal activity where people in a locality came together to make light of a task such as chopping wood. Once the work was completed a supper was provided and the end of the task celebrated in an evening of music and dancing. The term frolic was added to many activities: "chopping frolic," "spinning frolic," etc. For one of these – the "tucking" or "milling" frolic – the task itself was associated with music, specifically Gaelic songs, which had a regular pulse and a communal chorus. By the second half of the 20th century, frolics had fallen out of fashion along with communal, work-sharing practices, but the term has been maintained in relation to certain gatherings focusing on Gaelic song and where a traditional milling frolic is simulated. Typically held in a local community or parish hall, the work element of the frolic in these instances is staged, and even though it is participatory, no real task is actually being done. Thus, the milling frolic – the purpose of which was traditionally to mill or soften (mill, soften or "full") cloth that had been steeped in urine – in today's context will simply involve a bolt of dry cloth, or cloth dampened by water for effect. Eight to 12 people will sit along both sides of a long table and the cloth will be "fulled" as a repertoire of appropriate Gaelic songs is shared. Thus the frolic revolves around the body actions of the original task. Milling frolics are staged today in communities such as Johnstown, Christmas Island, and as part of the activities programmed by the Highland Village.

funeral music. Piping rather than fiddle playing was associated with funerals in Cape Breton in the past, and it was common practice for a piper to lead the procession accompanying the casket to the graveside playing an air or lament. Fiddle playing had no role in this ritual; however, starting in Inverness County in the 1970s, fiddle music began to feature in the funeral ceremony, sharing this role with, or occasionally replacing, the pipes or, more typically, the organ. It's inclusion or non-inclusion was entirely at the discretion of the clergy member officiating; while rigid protocols were maintained in some areas (e.g., as late as 1979 Winston Fitzgerald was forbidden to play at the funeral of his long-time piano accompanist, Beattie Wallace, in Sydney), in other parishes priests actively encouraged inclusion of fiddle music at funeral ceremonies and indeed, often participated themselves. When Dan R. MacDonald was buried in Mabou, in 1976, more than 75 fiddlers directed by Fr. John Angus Rankin performed a number of selections including many of MacDonald's own compositions. Fifty fiddlers played at the funeral of Angus Allan Gillis in 1978; another massed fiddle group performed at the funeral of Angus Chisholm the following year. Such performances continue to feature at funerals of the Cape Breton fiddle-music community. Alternatively, individual fiddlers and pianists provide music on request, one of these being Buddy MacMaster, who played at the majority of funerals around Judique for many years. The above relates to the practice within the Roman Catholic Church; fiddle music has never been included in religious ceremonies among the Presbyterian and other faiths.

LIZ DOHERTY

G

Gaelic. A member of the Celtic language family native to Scotland, Gaelic (Scottish Gaelic: A' Ghàidhlig) is a member of the Goidelic branch of the Celtic languages. Scottish Gaelic, like Modern Irish and Manx, developed out of Middle Irish, and thus is ultimately descended from Old Irish. As a result of voluntary immigration and forced evictions from the Highlands and Islands of Scotland commencing in the 1770s and lasting until into the mid-1800s, by the late 19th century it was estimated by churchmen that 250,000 people spoke Gaelic in Canada. They could be found in many different regions, including Nova Scotia, Prince Edward Island, the Codroy Valley of Newfoundland, New Brunswick, the Eastern Townships of Québec, Glengarry County in Ontario, Bruce County in Ontario, Vancouver, and Winnipeg. Gaelic scholar Jonathan Dembling has stated that in this period "Gaelic was truly a *Canadian* language," adding that it was the "largest non-official language at the time of Confederation (1867)," that is, only behind English and French in the number of speakers. Due in large part to the introduction of an Anglo-centric education system since this period, Gaelic language has sharply declined across Canada. Mockery, ridicule and in some instances corporeal punishment in the public schools resulted in the internalization of shame specific to speaking Gaelic. This resulted in effectively ending the inter-generational transmission of the language. Language attitudes impacted local economies and a majority of Gaelic-speaking parents were led to believe that prospects for their offspring depended on fluency in the English language, causing a sudden and drastic decline in the Gaelic speech community in the 20th century. Notwithstanding the educational and economic environments in which Gaels found themselves in 19th- and 20th-century Canada, in the 21st century, Nova Scotia remains the only Canadian jurisdiction where Gaelic language and cultural expression have persisted,

A Milling Frolic in Iona. Photograph from The MacInnes Collection.

having been passed down from generation to generation from the time of the earliest Gaelic speaking settlements. In 1773, the first group of Gaels from the Highlands and Islands of Scotland arrived in Pictou Harbour, NS, on the ship *Hector*. The Gaelic settlement period spanned almost 80 years (1773-1850). During this period, it is estimated that 50,000 Gaels settled on the northeastern Nova Scotia mainland and Cape Breton Island. Gaels settled along family and religious lines in eastern Colchester, Pictou, Antigonish, Northern Guysborough, Inverness, Richmond, Victoria and Cape Breton counties. Over generations, Gaels in Nova Scotia contributed to the province's diversity and cultural attractiveness, particularly through language, story, song, music and dance. Since the settlement period, it is estimated that over two dozen Gaelic dialects were introduced into Nova Scotia, thousands of fiddle and pipe tunes were composed, regional step-dance styles, thrived, thousands of songs—some brought over from Scotland and others composed locally—were shared, more than 300 placenames and thousands of personal nicknames were introduced; between 1791 and 1902 there were a dozen different Gaelic publications initiated. Local efforts at language preservation and development occurring throughout 20th-century Nova Scotia were inhibited due to lack of official recognition, exclusion, ineffective planning and allocation of resources, resulting in further loss of Gaelic language and its cultural expression. In 1920, a petition signed by

5,468 individuals from more than 230 communities throughout eastern Nova Scotia was sent to the Nova Scotia legislature requesting that Gaelic be included in the Nova Scotia public schools' curriculum. In 1921, the Nova Scotia Legislature approved Gaelic as an optional subject in Nova Scotia's public schools. In 1939, the Nova Scotia Assembly called for the enactment of measures to ensure the teaching of Gaelic in Nova Scotia schools and passed a resolution calling for the appointment of a Gaelic teacher at the Normal School, Truro. In the 1950s a Gaelic advisor position to the provincial Department of Education was created; later, in 1957 a Department of Celtic Studies at St. FX University in Antigonish was established; courses in Gaelic instruction were offered to full-time students. In 1969, the Gaelic Society of Cape Breton was formed giving wider support to Gaelic retention across rural Cape Breton Island in particular. Native Gaelic speakers from Scotland were invited to migrate to Cape Breton resulting in significant developments in Gaelic instruction in the Inverness County public school program and at CBU. In the 1960s, 70s and 80s, Gaelic learners and enthusiasts from the U.S. migrated to Cape Breton Island and the northeastern Nova Scotia mainland. Some persevered through immersion in the Gaelic speaking communities to learn Gaelic. These later assumed leadership roles in teaching Gaelic and advocating for Gaelic language and cultural identity in Nova Scotia. Throughout the 1980s and 1990s further development ensued with Gaelic instruction at the Highland Village and the Gaelic College and events such as Féis an Eilein (Christmas Island Festival) being developed. In 1987, an international conference with focus on the "Politics of Gaelic Cultural Maintenance" was held at CBU, the result of which was to actively organize grassroot advocates island-wide to form the Gaelic Council of Nova Scotia (Comhairle na Gàidhlig). Established in 1991, Comhairle na Gàidhlig, a non-profit society, dedicated its efforts to the maintenance and promotion of the Gaelic language and culture. In 1995, Gaelic was once again introduced into the province's *Education Act* with

the proviso that it would be built into the curriculum of a given school as a heritage-language/local-history study, provided there was demand from the student population and the teaching resources were available. In 1997, Comhairle na Gàidhlig's *Gaelic in Nova Scotia: Opportunities* report was submitted to the Department of Education. Out of 8 recommendations, one, the creation of a curriculum for public schools, was adopted. Various initiatives and reports (e.g., *Gaelic Nova Scotia: An Economic, Cultural, and Social Impact Study* [2002], *Developing and Preserving Gaelic in Nova Scotia* [2008], *Minority Language Renewal: Gaelic in Nova Scotia and Lessons from Abroad* [2008]) reflected community advocacy efforts and resulted in steps being taken by the government to recognize the language's decline and engage local speakers in reversing this trend. Recommendations from these reports include focusing on community development, strengthening education, legislating road signs and publications, and building ties between the Gaelic community and other Nova Scotia "heritage language" communities (Mi'kmaq and Acadian). Increased ties were called for between Nova Scotia and the Highland Council, Scotland, and a first such agreement, a memorandum of understanding, was signed in 2002. Significantly, in December 2006, Iomairtean na Gàidhlig (Office of Gaelic Affairs) was established. A provincial government division whose vision is that Nova Scotians reclaim their Gaelic language and identity as a basis for cultural, community, spiritual and economic renewal, Gaelic Affairs creates awareness, works with partners and provides tools and opportunities to learn, share and experience Gaelic language and culture. Today, Gaelic Affairs supports and manages the following government and community-based social-learning initiatives: language and cultural awareness, learning opportunities for government employees, language-learning sessions and cultural-awareness workshops for community groups, adult and youth language and cultural mentorship programs and the advancement of Gaelic-language and cultural programming with organizational and institutional partners in the

Gaelic Community. The Department of Education supports Gaelic Language and Studies courses, funding programming in 13 schools across the province with over 1,000 students enrolled; 3 universities offer post-secondary courses specific to Gaelic language, culture, heritage and history. Apart from institutional learning and study opportunities in the province, there are three Gaelic-related institutions offering a range of programs that work to promote local Gaelic language and culture and four major festivals offer Gaelic-language and cultural learning opportunities and stage performances. (*with* LMK)

language-music connection. Scholars have made a case for a close connection existing between the fiddle style and the accentual patterns of the Gaelic language (e.g., John Gibson, Jackie Dunn). Indeed, one of the greatest compliments for the Cape Breton fiddler (particularly in the past) was to acknowledge that he/she "had the Gaelic" in their music. However, when interrogated further it appears that this expression is one that was perpetuated through habit and that it refers, in fact, to the stylings of older players, who may or may not have spoken the language. Certainly it might be conceded that, through the aural transmission process, vestiges of a spoken, language influence on the music may have passed down through subsequent generations who do not speak that language; however, the language-music connection presented to date has never been fully substantiated; while the romanticized notion that it presents is appealing to some, from a music-analysis perspective, outside of specific *puirt-a-beul* connections, there is not yet been a wholly compelling case. The demise of the Gaelic language did have an impact on the fiddle tradition in specific instances—Gaelic sources of tunes, for example *puirt-a-beul*, have largely become redundant; however, language decline did not necessarily impinge upon the music style. While change affecting the music style may have coincided with linguistic changes in the community, these were not necessarily the result of such changes, but rather socio-musical changes instigated in response to multiple changing conditions. Alarmist commentary such as that suggesting that the future of Cape Breton fiddle music was dependent on the survival of the language sparked considerable debate and concern during the 1990s.

"Gaelic" fiddle music. The use of the term Gaelic as a label for the Cape Breton fiddle style can be dated to as recently as the 1970s. John Gibson, a Cape Breton-based Scottish scholar, writing in the *Scotia Sun,* described individual fiddlers as having a Gaelic style, marking what appears to be the first time such a label was applied in a fiddle-related context. "Gaelic" fiddle music had previously been referenced in the *Captain Simon Fraser Collection* from Scotland but had never assumed widespread usage. The "Gaelic" descriptor was rigorously applied by Gibson and by Gaelic scholar, John Shaw, throughout the 1970s. Over the next decade it came to be appropriated by the piping community as a means of distinguishing the competition-style piping tradition from the older vernacular styles and practices being rediscovered and re-presented in Cape Breton; however, among the fiddle music community, it was the label "Cape Breton fiddler" that emerged as the preferred the marker of identity, evolving from the previously popular "Cape Breton Scottish" label. It was not until the 2000s that the label Gaelic came into widespread use in relation to Cape Breton fiddle music. The success of many Cape Breton artists during the Celtic boom of the 1990s helped crystallize Cape Breton's position as a bona fide member of the Celtic world and the foregrounding of Gaelic song and *puirt-a-beul* by a number of these artists (such as The Rankins, The Barra MacNeils, Ashley MacIsaac and Mary Jane Lamond) helped shine a light on what was still, at that time, a language facing extinction. Since then there has been an increasing alignment of the fiddle music and the Gaelic language, something that has escalated over the past decade in a mutually beneficial arrangement. For the fiddle community, as it is faced with maintaining a distinctive identity on an increasingly homogeneous Celtic platform (both sonically and in terms of presentation), the appropriation

of a Gaelic identity adds a dimension of *gravitas* and historical significance that helps position it as somewhat unique. While the Gaelic element for the contemporary Cape Breton fiddler, to date, extends mostly to band names and CD titles it is encouraging to note that a significant number, specifically in the under-40 age group, have begun some practical engagement with the Gaelic language, or intend to. However, for now, the music and the language continue to exist as two elements of Cape Breton culture, connected certainly but not as interdependent as this recent branding suggests. [**Dembling 1997, 1998, 2005; Dunn 1991; Feintuch 2010; Gibson 1973; Kennedy 2002; Newton 2011**].

Gaelic College of Celtic Arts and Crafts, The. *See* **Colaisde na Gàidhlig**.

gapped scale. A scale involving less than the normal 7 notes, thus featuring gaps or intervals, at least one of which is greater than a whole tone. The use of gapped scales is quite common in Cape Breton fiddle music, found particularly in older music, often in pipe tunes. Among those used frequently are the hexatonic (6-note) and pentatonic (5-note) scales. [**Dunlay and Greenberg 1996**].

garden party. A parish-picnic-style event, but held over an evening rather than a number of days, this was a community-organized fundraiser that included music, dance and sporting events. Held during the summer months, garden parties were popular in communities such as Margaree and Mabou, where they were typically held in the church grounds or close to the schoolhouse, where a stage would be erected for the occasion. Garden parties began to decline in popularity in the middle decades of the 20th century.

Garrison, Virginia Hope. (1938-1993). A music teacher, education consultant, writer and researcher born in Indianapolis, Indiana. She worked in music education in the mid-western U.S. from the 1960s and taught at the University of Wisconsin-Madison from 1975 to 1978. From 1979 she was mostly based in Nova Scotia (although she taught at the University of Toronto in 1986-1987) where she worked as a music teacher and choir director; she was also a member of the province of Nova Scotia's task force on high-school music curriculum. Her PhD thesis combined her interests in folk music and music education: "Traditional and non-traditional teaching and learning practices in folk music: an ethnographic field study of Cape Breton fiddling" (1985, University of Wisconsin-Madison). [**Historica Canada 2015**].

Gillis family of Scotsville. John Richard (John R.) and Jessie Mae Gillis in Scotsville have a family of four children, three of whom are well-known musicians or are otherwise heavily involved in the music scene. John R. (1943-2012) and his brother Wallace (1946-2010) both played fiddle while their sister, Sandra, is a piano player and the family home was known for music. **Dale Gillis** (1969-) is a fiddle player and step dancer and was responsible for organizing the Scotsville square dances which take place on Tuesday nights during the summer season. **Kyle Gillis** (1971-), now living in Barrachois, Cape Breton, also plays fiddle and performs at concerts and occasionally at dances with his wife, Dawn (MacDonald), on piano. A composer too, one of his pieces, "Mrs. Campbell's Birthday," is included in *The Cape Breton Fiddlers Collection* and was also published in the regional newspaper, *The Victoria Standard*.

Gillis, Patrick. (1974-). Guitar, mandolin, banjo. A left-handed player, he taught himself guitar when young, and was influenced in music by players such as Dave MacIsaac and John Allan Cameron. He has worked as a full-time guitar accompanist at different times performing with many of Cape Breton's musicians including Natalie MacMaster, Ashley MacIsaac and Glenn Graham; he toured the U.S. with the group Cullin and was a prominent performer in Howie MacDonald's production, *Celtic Brew*. With the group Beòlach he made two recordings: *Beòlach* (2002) and *Variations* (2004). He has also recorded with Dougie MacDonald, Andrea Beaton, Kinnon Beaton, Mairi Rankin, Mary Jane Lamond, Mac Morin, Colin Grant, Chrissy Crowley, Ashley

MacIsaac and Ryan J. MacNeil, and plays regularly with Wendy MacIsaac, Kenneth MacKenzie, Glenn Graham and Rodney MacDonald. His forte is picking out tunes and he has featured often in the "Guitar Summit" showcase at Celtic Colours.

Gillis family of South-West Margaree. Malcolm H. and Margaret (MacFarlane) Gillis had a family of 17 children, many of whom were noted musicians: Alick, Ambrose, Bernie, Dougall, Jack, Jimmy, John Joe and Minnie on fiddle, Malcolm on bagpipes. They all received some instruction from their father, and many tunes, techniques and practices—in particular high-bass tunings—were passed down through the family. Malcolm H. was also a proficient step dancer who learned from John Gillis, son of the dancing master, Allan Gillis, and passed on much of what he learned to his family.

Gillis, Malcolm H. (1856-1929). Poet, fiddle, step dance, singer. One of Cape Breton's great talents, he was known as "The Bard of Margaree" for his poetry in Gaelic and English; his writing has been published and is featured in the CBC documentary, *The Celtic Peoples in Canada.* He played a range of instruments as well as fiddle—bagpipes, accordion, piano and uilleann pipes—and was also a singer. He was one of those invited to perform at the first Mabou Picnic in 1897, and was also successful in the 1926 Boston fiddle contest that was adjudicated by James Scott Skinner. [**MacGillivray 1981**].

Gillis, Alick. (1900-1974). Fiddle and step dance. Boston, MA. The son of Malcolm H. and Margaret Gillis, Alick left South-West Margaree for Glace Bay and then, with his brother Jack, moved to Massachusetts in 1922 in search of work, settling first in New Bedford and later in Boston. He continued his music education with a classical violinist there and played often in the burgeoning Cape Breton music scene, centre of which was the Cape Breton Club that had Saturday night dances and Sunday afternoon ceilidhs. Known as "The Dean" of the Scottish music scene in Boston, Gillis formed a band, The Inverness Serenaders, in the 1930s, styled after the Irish dance bands that were popular in Boston at the time; the band configuration was a relatively new departure in Cape Breton fiddle music, the only precedents being the Caledonia Scotch Band and the Columbia Scotch band, both Boston-based. Gillis recorded with The Inverness Serenaders for Decca, including some solo tracks, and his reputation was further expanded by WHDH radio, on which he broadcast a fiddle-music show each Saturday; this could be picked up in parts of Cape Breton. Gillis visited Cape Breton during the summer months, where he teamed up with Angus Allan Gillis to play at concerts and ceilidhs in the Margaree area. [**MacGillivray 1981**].

Gillis, Angus Allan. (1897-1978). Fiddle. Upper Margaree, Inverness County. The son of Alexander Gillis and Catherine Gillis, he spent most of his life on the family farm. His father had played fiddle until he lost a finger, but his cousin, James D. Gillis, encouraged Angus Allan to play and introduced him to the rudiments of note reading. Of his 8 siblings, his brothers Hughie, Jim (James A.) and Jack also played fiddle, and he found another musical peer in Sandy MacLean from Foot Cape once he started attending school at Broad Cove Banks. Angus Allan and Sandy often provided the music for dancing at school; they practised together at Sandy's house and later were joined by Lila MacIsaac, who accompanied them on the organ. Angus Allan was influenced by local-area players such as Donald Beaton from Mabou, Malcolm Gillis from Margaree, "Little" Jack MacDonald, Johnny "MacVarish" MacDonald from Broad Cove, and Ranald MacDougall

Angus Allan Gillis. Courtesy of Bill Aucoin.

from Margaree, who was a regular visitor to the Gillis home. Gillis developed a reputation for his tune settings and style, particularly for his bowing and cuts which, with his timing and drive, earned him a reputation as a dance player. At the time when he was in his twenties, dances were popular and many halls held these regularly. Gillis built up a circuit which included Glenville, Brook Village, Kenloch, Inverness, and South West Margaree, and played with fiddlers Dan J. Campbell, Angus Chisholm, Jimmy Gillis, Ambrose Gillis, Buddy MacMaster and pipers Malcolm Gillis and Allan "Black Angus" MacFarlane, often playing 6 nights a week. In 1926 and 1927 he was based in Boston, where he played for dances at the Winslow Hall near Dudley Street; he also played for dances and on WHDH radio with The Inverness Serenaders on visits to Boston in the 1930s. In 1933, representing the Scottish Catholic Society of Cape Breton, he travelled with piper, Malcolm Gillis, and a Sydney-based, Scottish priest, to Alexandria, Ontario, where he was placed first in a competition for his performance of "Johnny Cope," winning The St. Finnian's Centenary Cup. In 1935, with Angus Chisholm and Dan J. Campbell, and Bess Siddall MacDonald on piano, he recorded three 78s for the Celtic label. Among these pioneer discs, released in 1936, was an additional duet with Dan J. Campbell of "The Old-Time Wedding Reels," which has come to be regarded as a Cape Breton classic. Gillis is synonymous with the old-style Cape Breton fiddle tradition, but his contribution can be considered progressive in terms of his recordings and his membership of one of the first bands to feature Cape Breton fiddlers; in repertoire, he has been credited with popularising the hornpipe (previously associated with "set" dances) as a discrete tune type. His fiddle duos— with Dan J. Campbell, Sandy MacLean, Angus Chisholm, Bill Lamey, Donald Angus Beaton and Joe MacLean—added to his repute. [**MacGillivray 1981**].

Gillis, James D. Fiddle and bagpipes. Margaree, Inverness County. A teacher, Gaelic scholar and a writer who travelled extensively around the world. His reputation merited his inclusion in J. J. MacInnis's 1943-44 overview of Cape Breton music, *Scottish Music in Cape Breton, Nova Scotia: Violin Players I Have Met.*

Gillis, Malcolm H. *See* **Gillis family of South-West Margaree.**

Gillis, Wilfred. (1923-2002). Fiddle, composer. Arisaig, Antigonish County. Born to parents Lauchlin and Mary Ann (MacDonald) Gillis, fiddle was prominent in his family; his father was a note reader, as was his grandfather, Stephen Gillis, who was formally trained and who conducted a string quartet providing music in church. Outside of his family Wilfred was inspired by New Brunswick's Don Messer, whom he heard regularly on radio. He also trained for a time with Profs. Jimmy MacDonald and Pat Cormier, who helped his music-literacy skills. In 1953-1954, when he was already well established as a musician, he studied further at the Halifax Conservatory, redressing what he felt were poor habits he had developed. He was a regular performer on CJFX in the 1940s, recorded 78s with Colin MacInnis on piano and a solo LP, *Arisaig Airs,* in the 1960s. Moving to Ottawa in 1966 he joined the music scene there and took part in competitions such as the Canadian Fiddling Championships, winning various awards and later being asked to sit on judging panels. Gillis was one of the early members of the Cape Breton Symphony set up in 1974 for CTV's *John Allan Cameron Show,* and recorded and toured internationally with them. His style was more representative of mainland Nova Scotia and more eclectic than was typical of Cape Breton players. He had a particular interest, passed down throughout his family, in slow air playing, and was also a composer of tunes such as "Welcome to the Trossacks," "The Highland Centenary" and "The Goldenrod Jig," which were played widely in Cape Breton. In 1997, he was elected an honorary member of the Antigonish Highland Society in recognition of his contribution to the music heritage of Nova Scotia. [**MacGillivray 1981**].

Glencoe; Glencoe Mills Hall. Arguably the most famous of the dance halls in Cape Breton, this status is partly so due to its remote location and legendary family dances where Buddy MacMaster was the resident fiddler for 35 years. An important part of the Glencoe experience, for many, happens in the parking lot, where people, hot and exhausted from dancing congregate to take a break and socialize, before venturing back in for another set. Constructed originally as a schoolhouse ca. 1905, the hall is linked to the local St. Joseph Catholic Church. Weekly square dances are on Thursdays from 10 p.m. to 1 a.m. in July and August; occasional dances are held throughout the year. [**Addison 2001**].

Glendale Fiddlers' Festival. A festival devoted exclusively to Cape Breton Scottish fiddle music, the Cape Breton Fiddle Festival was first held in the summer of 1973 on the grounds of St. Mary's RC Church in Glendale. For a number of years Scottish concerts had been held on the site, initiated by the parish priest, Fr. John Angus Rankin. However, the Glendale '73 event was a unique and historic occasion in the history of the Cape Breton fiddle in that it was the outcome of a campaign which had been sparked in response to the 1971 CBC-TV documentary *The Vanishing Cape Breton Fiddler*. The festival was organized by a group of volunteer enthusiasts whose ambition was to redress the situation highlighted by the documentary—that the Cape Breton fiddle tradition, on account of not being handed down to younger players, could be in danger of becoming extinct. Organizers Frank MacInnis and Fr. Eugene Morris spent a summer meeting with and encouraging existing players to take part in a festival, and initially succeeded in staging an impressive fiddle concert. It had, as its finale, 102 fiddlers playing together, accompanied by Joey Beaton on piano and directed by Fr. John Angus Rankin; this was the first ever massed fiddle performance of that scale in Cape Breton. Since it included a group of young players who had recently begun taking instruction from John MacDougall, it sent a strong message that "the Cape Breton fiddler" was alive and well—and indeed, was taking note of criticism. The Glendale

Glendale '77 album cover, 1977. Beaton Institute, Cape Breton University.

festival was recorded, and selections later released on LP. Subsequent festivals were held in 1975, 1977, 1979 and 1981; then the event, by this time under the organization of the newly named CBFA, relocated to St. Ann's; other festivals continued to be held in Glendale up until the 1990s. Following a few years' hiatus, the concert, in conjunction with a local community festival, has recently been revived. [**MacInnis 2007; Thompson 2003, 2006**]

Glenora Inn and Distillery. Located in Inverness County this is a popular venue in which to experience the public ceilidh, hosted by a local fiddler and piano player every evening during the summer season. It is unique in that its distillery, set up in the 1980s, produces North America's only single-malt whiskey (since 1990), Glen Breton Rare, and in 2014 launched a new whiskey, Fiddler's Choice.

golden age of Scottish fiddling. *See* **Scotland**.

Gosse, Jeffrey. (1984-). Fiddle. Toronto. Born in Toronto, he has strong Maritimes connections with his grandmother being from Judique, Cape Breton; his father is from Corner Brook, Newfoundland and Labrador. Having encountered fiddle music at the age of 6 at a family event in Cape Breton he began taking lessons with Sandy

MacIntyre in Toronto, returning to Cape Breton each summer to attend courses at the Gaelic College. Along with MacIntyre he performed in the Celtic musical production, *Needfire*, in Toronto in 1998, and also featured alongside his mentor at a special tribute show during Celtic Colours in 2009. He is featured on the video *Carrying on the Traditions: Cape Breton Scottish Fiddling Today* (*Fiddler* Magazine, 1996) alongside such fiddlers as Buddy MacMaster, Theresa MacLellan, Jerry Holland and Brenda Stubbert.

Gow, Niel. (1727-1807). Fiddle, composer. Inver, Perthshire, Scotland. A famous Highland Scottish fiddler and dance master, he was patronized by a number of Dukes of Atholl and considered by his contemporaries to be the finest musician of his day. A key figure in the so-called golden age of Scottish fiddling, he broke new ground as a professional musician and is credited with composing some 87 dance tunes and airs, a number of which may have been wrongly attributed to him. These were published in 7 collections with a further 3 appearing posthumously. One of his sons, Nathaniel (1763-1831), was a noted player and composer and other members of his family also composed and published fiddle music. Gow is acclaimed for his use of the "up-driven bow," a specific bowing technique utilized in strathspey playing; this pattern is one which has been maintained in the Cape Breton fiddle style and was particularly noted by Scottish fiddlers such as Alasdair Fraser to support the theory that Cape Breton fiddle music represented an old, unchanged Scottish sound. [**Alburger 1983; Hunter 1979; Purser 1992**].

grace-notes. Grace-notes, provided by the left hand (for the typical, right-handed player), are added to the basic melody line as a form of finger ornament. They exist in two broad forms, as (a) "single" and (b) "double," although extensions of these forms are also found and various interpretations are possible according to the manner in which they are articulated. For example, a grace-note may be executed in a clean, definite fashion

where it is realized as a subsidiary note, one that does not impinge on the rhythmic value of the main melody note. Alternatively, a grace-note may be given more prominence and executed in a deliberate and measured fashion; in this instance it acquires some of the value of the melody note and results in a lack of distinction between the melody note and the ornament. This more relaxed approach to sounding the grace-notes was favoured by early Cape Breton fiddlers, and those later emulating an older sound (such as John Morris Rankin). While grace-notes continue to be a feature of the Cape Breton fiddle style, since the 1940s the extent to which they are employed has gradually decreased, particularly in reels.

(a) *single grace-note.* This is a short, decorative note that precedes the main melody note. It is used to break up 2 notes of the same pitch, and can be used in relation to any note within a tune, but most commonly on the main accented notes. As regards the pitch configurations used in such grace-notes, old style/new style distinctions are evident for, whereas in the past, grace-notes (both single and double) generally involved pitches immediately above or below the main melody note, increased intervals—often a third—have gradually become popular, thus opening up and adding a sense of space to the melodic line. Another approach involves the grace-note repeating the pitch of the melody note directly preceding it. In most instances the grace-note is found on the same string as the melody note being graced; often the grace-note is pitched above the main melody note, but it may occur below it, particularly where the grace-note involves an open string (referred to as an "open-string grace-note" the term "hammer-on" is also occasionally used, although technically this only refers to such an ornament where it assumes main melody note [and hence beat] status). Particularly common in Cape Breton is the use of a first-finger grace-note above the open string while the pitch of the open string is being doubled by the fourth finger on the string below. Winston Fitzgerald was particularly noted for his use of this technique. In music notation the grace-note is joined to the main melody note by a slur, and in practice it is most often executed in this manner, joined to the main melody note in a single bow-stroke. A few players such as Dougie MacDonald and Ashley MacIsaac have experimented with changing bow direction between the grace-note and the main melody note, adding additional rhythmic interest.

(b) *double grace-note.* A sequence of 2 decorative notes, the first of which is the same pitch as the main melody note and the second, generally a pitch (or 2 pitches) higher; occasionally this may be lower. Typically, the 2 notes of the double grace-note are clearly articulated; however, where an interval of more than one scale degree is involved between the pitches (e.g., using a first and third finger motion to decorate a first finger melody note) the second pitch may not be distinct, and so will be more percussive in effect. The speed at which the double grace note is executed may create some ambiguity regarding its position after or before the main melody note. Most prevalent is the practice of sounding the double grace note before the main melody note, on the beat (so that it basically reduces the value of the main melody note). David Greenberg refers to this technique as a "one-cycle trill." **[Doherty 1996; Dunlay and Greenberg 1996; Graham 2006]**

(c) *extended grace-note figures.* Occasional extended forms of the grace-note feature in the playing of certain fiddlers. A 3-note example used by Jerry Holland and Mary MacDonald among others is perhaps best considered a form of roll, specifically a short roll. A figure involving 2 consecutive iterations of a double grace-note is also found in the playing of certain fiddlers, amounting to what is effectively, a trill. A popular technique in Cape Breton fiddling is the "warble" (a term first used in the *DunGreen Collection,* 1996) that involves the double grace-note being realized as an indistinct mordent. **[Dunlay and Greenberg 1996; Graham 2006]** *See* **ornament; roll; slide; warble.**

Graham family of Judique. The Graham family tree connects with many of the greats of the Cape Breton fiddle tradition. Danny Graham is an accomplished Gaelic singer and also plays fiddle; he was one of the fiddlers who participated in the finale of the first Glendale Fiddlers' Festival. His father Alex Graham was a step dancer as was Alex's grandfather, Stephen, and the Grahams are related to such fiddlers as Buddy MacMaster, Natalie MacMaster, Alex Francis MacKay and Dan R. MacDonald. Mary (Beaton) Graham, a piano player, is of the renowned Beaton family of Mabou; her parents were Donald Angus and Elizabeth, her siblings include fiddler, Kinnon Beaton and pianist Joey Beaton, while nieces and nephews include Andrea Beaton and Rodney MacDonald. Danny and Mary's children all took up the fiddle, some of them taught by Kinnon Beaton as part of a group of cousins. **Eileen** (1976-) and **Amy** (1979-) both step dance and as children performed at many of the outdoor concerts. Amy is a noted singer songwriter who has recorded alongside her brother Glenn on two of his albums.

Graham, Glenn. (1974-). Fiddle, composer, teacher, academic. Judique and Halifax. Born to parents Danny and Mary (Beaton) Graham, Glenn's roots in music are extensive. Growing up surrounded by music and aware of the Gaelic language he took up the fiddle at the age of ten, when along with a group of cousins, he was taught by his uncle, Kinnon Beaton. Although he abandoned lessons for a few years his interest returned in his later teenage years; at that time he took some lessons from local fiddler, Neil Beaton. Largely self-taught, he learned tunes mostly from recordings and from tune books; he was particularly drawn to the older sound and style of the Mabou Coal Mines and inspired by the playing of such as Donald Angus and Kinnon Beaton, John Morris Rankin, Alex Francis MacKay, Buddy MacMaster and Howie MacDonald. He began regularly playing for concerts, dances and ceilidhs as a teenager and in 1996 recorded his first solo album *Let 'er Rip*; a year later he teamed up with Rodney MacDonald and released the twin fiddle album *Traditionally Rockin'*, which was a double nominee for Instrumental and Roots/Traditional Artist of the year at the 1998 East Coast Music Awards. As "Rodney and Glenn" they were in high demand at special events, festivals and dances. In 1999, Glenn began actively pursuing a solo career and released Step Outside in 2000, which featured his sister Amy (singer-songwriter and step dancer) and also showcased his own song-writing and singing; Amy is also featured on *Drive: A Traditional Cape Breton Fiddle Recording* which followed in 2004; in 2007 *Decade: A Compilation* was released, an 18-track retrospective of his previous recordings with some previously unreleased material. During this time he also recorded with the Beaton family for the Smithsonian Folkways label.

He has toured internationally and has taught at such institutions as the Gaelic College, Ceòlas (South Uist, Scotland), Musicamp Alberta (Red Deer, AB), and Celtic Arts Foundation Winter School (Seabeck, WA). His music has been featured on international TV shows for *Dawson's Creek* and *Party of Five*, multiple CDs and CD compilations, TV specials and independent films and DVD productions. As an academic, Cape Breton fiddle music was the subject of Graham's Master's thesis (Saint Mary's University, Halifax, 2004) and informed his book *The Cape Breton Fiddle: Making and Maintaining Tradition* (CBU Press, 2006); he has also published a collection of his own compositions *The Glenn Graham Collection of Cape Breton Violin Music* (2010). Graham is nearing completion of a PhD in political science at Dalhousie University, NS; his project is a historical political economic study of Cape Breton Island and is tentatively titled "Regionalism on the 'Celtic' Fringe: How a Peripheral Community Resists, Negotiates, and Accommodates Political And Economic Integration." Notably the pertinence of the region's culture and its language and musical revitalizations figure into the analysis.

— ∼ —

The Glenn Graham Collection of Cape Breton Violin Music (2010). Self-published, this is a collection of over 200 original compositions by Graham, some in collaboration with family members Danny and Mary Graham, Kinnon Beaton, Andrea Beaton and Rodney MacDonald. It features slow airs, marches, clogs, hornpipes, strathspeys, reels, jigs and waltzes and includes an introduction written by Glenn.

— ∼ —

gramophone. *See* **recordings.**

Grant, Colin. (1984-). Fiddle. Toronto, Ontario and Sydney, Cape Breton. Born in Toronto and raised by Nova Scotian parents, Carolyn and John Grant, both musicians, his father being a noted piper. He began taking violin lessons, initially following the Suzuki method, at the Royal Conservatory of Music at age 4; at the age of 12 he started taking instruction from Cape Breton fiddler, Sandy MacIntyre in Etobicoke, ON, while continuing his classical studies. He first attended the summer courses offered at the Gaelic College in 1996, where he was taught by Stan Chapman, Sandy MacIntyre and Sheila Cameron. In 1998 the family relocated to Sydney and Colin took lessons on fiddle and guitar with Allie Bennett until he left for university in 2003. Besides being inspired by the Cape Breton "stars" of the time, such as Buddy MacMaster, Jerry Holland, Howie MacDonald, The Rankins, The Barra MacNeils, Natalie MacMaster and Ashley MacIsaac—many of whom he had encountered in Toronto—Grant was exposed to the music of other Celtic artists, and cites The Chieftains, The Tannahill Weavers and Shaun Davey as influences. This eclecticism has continued to shape his musical tastes, and more recent favourites include Shooglenifty, Croft No. 5, Treacherous Orchestra, Millish and The Olllam. A full-time professional musician based in Cape Breton, Grant has, of necessity, developed a portfolio career in order to sustain this, drawing on his varied experiences, training and influences. At home he performs occasionally at dances and ceilidhs, acts as a live sideman and studio musician for various acts such as Crowdis Bridge (bluegrass), Tom Fun Orchestra (rock), Jason MacDonald (singer/songwriter) and Dave Sampson (singer/songwriter). He has also toured, mostly on the international festival circuit, with two Cape Breton bands, Sprag Session and, until 2015, Còig, of which he was a founding member. His recordings include *Colin Grant* (2006), *The Toy* EP (2008), *Fun For The Whole Family* (2010), *Sprag Session* (2012), *Còig* (2014); he also featured on the *An Drochaid* documentary soundtrack (Watercolour Music, 2014). His music has featured on recordings by Troy MacGillivray (*Eleven*, 2005) and Andrea Beaton (*Branches*, 2009), and his tunes published in *The Cape Breton Fiddlers' Collection* and *The Celtic Colours Collection*. Grant is an example of a Cape Breton artist who has engaged fully with the business side of the industry, emerging as both artist and entrepreneur and who balances an international profile with local, community activities. A member of the board of directors of CBMIC, which administers showcase and export funding opportunities to Cape Breton-based musicians, he is also president of the Centre Communautaire Étoile de l'Acadie in Sydney, which programs various arts events including one in association with Celtic Colours every year.

Greenberg, David. (1965-). Baroque violin, fiddle. Maryland, Washington, DC, and Halifax, NS. Born to parents Jeanette and Leon Greenberg, both musicians and interested in international folk dance, his introduction to music was via the Suzuki method, through which he took instruction from the age of four. Interested in a range of fiddle styles, he first encountered Cape Breton music in the mid-1980s at a session in Bloomington, Indiana, where he was attending university, studying Baroque violin. Kate Dunlay, who was the performer, shared tapes of various fiddlers with him and he became interested in the style of Mary MacDonald and Donald MacLellan and, later, Theresa Morrison. During his first visit to Cape Breton around that time, he met and befriended Cape Breton piano players Doug and Margaret MacPhee and gave his first performance at the Saint-Joseph-du-Moine concert. A full-time, professional musician, he was a member of Tafelmusik in Toronto, 1988-1998. He has

lived in Halifax since 2000, where he directs the baroque group, Tempest; he tours internationally with Chris Norman (flute, pipes, song), French baroque group, Les Musciens de Saint-Julien and U.K. baroque group Red Priest. He founded the unique baroque/Cape Breton outfit, Puirt a Baroque, recording three albums with them: *Return of the Wanderer* (Marquis Classics, 1998), which was nominated for a Juno award, *Kinloch's Fantasy: A Curious Collection of Scottish Sonatas and Reels* (Marquis Classics, 1997) and *Bach Meets Cape Breton* (Marquis Classics, 1996), which won an ECMA for Best Classical Recording. He is featured on various traditional music and cross-over recordings with artists such as Concerto Caledonia (Scottish/various), Ferintosh (Scottish/Cape Breton) and Suzie LeBlanc (Acadian); on compilation CDs including *Celtic Colours International Festival* (vol. VII, 2003) and on EMI Music Canada's *Pure Moods Volume 2* (1999); he has also appeared with Ian McKinnon and Symphony Nova Scotia performing *MacKinnon's Brook Suite* (Ground Swell Records, 2001). In 2000 he released *Tunes Until Dawn* with Doug MacPhee. Along with his wife, fiddle player and academic, Kate Dunlay, he published the influential *Traditional Celtic Violin Music of Cape Breton: The DunGreen Collection* in 1996, and has authored a number of other articles pertaining to Cape Breton music as it intersects with early music. He has composed several tunes in the Cape Breton idiom including "Allan 'Big Alex' MacDonald" (strathspey), "Francis Xavier MacDonald" (jig) and "Buddy's Detour" (jig), which have been recorded by him and other fiddlers including Jerry Holland, Buddy MacMaster and The Rankins. *See* **Dunlay, Kate.**

groove. A term that, like "drive," "lift," "lilt" and "swing," refers to the underlying metrical impulses in a given performance. The term is not in widespread use among the Cape Breton fiddle community, although it has emerged in relation to the playing and performance practices of some contemporary fiddlers such as Ashley MacIsaac and Colin Grant, typically in fusion contexts. The term was foregrounded by Jeffrey Hennessy in his

2008 PhD dissertation: "Fiddle Grooves: Identity, Representation, and the Sound of Cape Breton Fiddle Music in Popular Culture."

GroundSwell Music. Halifax-based record label and management company with a focus on East Coast Canadian artists. Started in 1992 by musician Ian McKinnon as the artist-management and record company for his group, Rawlin's Cross, it expanded in subsequent years and forged a partnership with Warner Music Canada in 1994; Warner continues to work as GroundSwell Music's distributor in Canada. GroundSwell acts as artist management for The Stanfields, The Town Heroes, Carleton Stone and Rawlins Cross. The company has produced other music projects, including the Celtic Symphonic project *MacKinnon's Brook Suite* (McKinnon with Scott Macmillan and Symphony Nova Scotia). It has also built business relationships within the industry, including international live-performance bookings with The Agency Group and Paquin Entertainment.

group. In recent Cape Breton parlance this is the common term used to identify a selection or "set" of tunes presented in performance; previously referred to as "medley." As in other traditions, the practice of building sets of tunes coincides with the advent of the commercial recording industry; prior to this, tunes tended to be played individually. Indeed, some players such as Lee Cremo continued the practice of playing individual tunes for much of their recording careers, and contemporary players will often feature an occasional exhibition-piece or show in isolation. The number of tunes in a group in the Cape Breton tradition varies; at square dances such a group may have 10 or more tunes, and on recordings, sets may still feature 6 or more tunes. This practice of generating long groups of tunes became common from the 1970s onward; earlier players such as Winston Fitzgerald, tended to favour sets of 2 and occasionally 3 tunes at a maximum. Certain players were and are noted for having a particular talent for selecting appropriate tunes in creating a group and some specific tune combinations have become standards within the tradition.

rationale. The norm is for the group of tunes to be constructed around a single tonal area and players refer to such a group as being "on" a particular key, for instance "on" A major. This practice distinguishes Cape Breton performance practice from others, such as the Irish, where the tendency is to create momentum in a given set of tunes through the use of modulation. Cape Breton fiddlers began experimenting with such modulation within tune groups only since the 1970s, the first such developments happening with the Cape Breton Symphony; more traditionally, however, momentum is generated by an acceleration in tempo as different tune-types are introduced (such as the change from march to strathspey to reel) or through some tonal changes or colours, for example moving from major to minor to modal in relation to a single tonal area. In Cape Breton today there is a distinction between tune-groups for dancing to, and tune-groups for listening to. While the structures used in the dance contexts are easily transferred into a listening or presentational context, the opposite is not possible as, increasingly, players are experimenting with the construction of groups that are not restricted by the demands of dance. For instance, when playing at a square dance, the norm is that the tune group is decided upon spontaneously; fiddlers may certainly have tunes that they like to run together, but other factors related to the dynamics of the dance will also contribute to the tune choices made. In other situations, such as house parties, a similar spontaneity may also impact on the form, even though there may be no element of dance involved. For concert performances or in a recording studio, the tune-group is more likely to be pre-arranged. Similarly, in ensemble performances—such as at the massed concert finales by the CBFA or with any of the increasing number of bands within the Cape Breton tradition—predetermining of the tune group is essential.

groups for dancing to. The strathspey-reel combination is the basis for much of the medley construction in both solo step-dance and listening contexts. Typically the dance strathspey will segue into the reel; the strathspey is characterised by a sensation of growing anticipation, with the beat accelerating during the final turn before making a smooth transition into the reel. Larger groups are constructed around this strathspey-reel core; such a group might include an air, a march, a slow strathspey, or any combination of these, before progressing into the dance strathspey-reel pairing, at which point a dancer may take to the floor. In the solo step-dance tradition this is by far the most common tune-type combination. For social group dancing in square sets, the groups feature a single tune-type only; this will be either jigs or reels. Groups of waltzes (often instrumental versions of song-airs or newly composed pieces) are only occasionally found in a dance context, although during and post-Second World War the fashion for round and square dances called for more inclusion of such as these.

groups for listening to. In terms of music for listening to two scenarios exist, one being a live situation, the other, involving recording; the latter is generally affected by conditions determined by the very process of recording and the medium being used which affects the length of time allowed per cut or track, ultimately affecting the size of the tune-group. In live contexts, certainly since the 1970s, the trend was for increasingly longer tune-groups. However, in the first decade of the 2000s there is evidence of younger players moving back toward shorter tune-groups. This may be due to these younger players having only limited opportunities to perform at square dances (and thus being less accustomed to building the longer sets required for the dance); equally it could be motivated by their growing engagement with international audiences (both at events abroad and at Celtic Colours and other tourist-dominated local events) who may not be accustomed to long (and uni-tonal) sequences. The strathspey-reel combination, central to the dance tradition, does however form the basis for much of the "listening" tune-group (as performed at a concert, house party, session or on a recording); strathspeys are only rarely played without being followed by a

reel. Other tune-types used for dancing (reels, jigs and waltzes) are also regularly found in listening contexts, but generally there will be no change in performance style. As opportunities for Cape Breton fiddlers to perform away from the dance increased throughout the late 20th and into the 21st century, there has been a parallel growth of interest in players experimenting with the construction of tune groups. Ashley MacIsaac, Howie MacDonald, Glenn Graham and Brenda Stubbert, for instance, have recorded tune combinations that use the tune-types typical of the Cape Breton repertoire, but in unexpected order, such as jigs into reels. Sets of polkas, clogs and airs make up other tune-groups, although these are much less common. Since the 1990s the combination of vocals intertwined with a tune or group of tunes has become popular, seen with such as Krysta MacKinnon, Wendy MacIsaac, J. P. Cormier, Natalie MacMaster, Glenn and Amy Graham, Cynthia MacLeod, Melody and Derrick Cameron, Andrea Beaton as well as, of course, The Rankins, The Barra MacNeils and Ashley MacIsaac. *See* **structure of Cape Breton music.**

guitar. This instrument may have arrived from Europe with French settlers, but it is not until the early 20th century that there is evidence that it featured in the music of the Scottish settlers. Factory-manufactured guitars were available after 1884 from such as Eaton's and Simpson Sears catalogues (which were a source of other instruments in Cape Breton at the time). Hawaiian steel guitars were, in fact, popular mail-order catalogue items; this was the first instrument played by Marie MacLellan, for instance, and recordings exist of Sandy MacLean being accompanied in this way by Hilda Murphy. A date for the guitar's entry can be surmised from observing recordings; the first of these of Cape Breton fiddle music in 1928 actually had banjo providing rhythmic accompaniment alongside the piano (in the Caledonia and Columbia Scotch Bands); however, the next group to record, the Inverness Serenaders, included a guitar. The first Cape Breton recordings released in Canada (in the 1930s) featured piano as the accompanying instrument, but soon recording artists began to experiment with other forms, including guitar. However, it was the 1940s – and no doubt in part due to the shared musical experiences of fiddlers and jazz players in the Sydney area of Cape Breton – when the instrument became a regular addition to the fiddle and piano combination. Guitar accompaniment to fiddle music, generally alongside of the piano rather than as an alternative to it, has continued to the present day; since the 1960s, the instrument has also been utilized as a melody instrument, usually in a solo capacity; this too continues to be developed. Almost without exception the guitar players in Cape Breton have been, and continue to be, male. Some fiddlers are also guitarists, among them Jerry Holland (who accompanied Bill Lamey and Angus Chisholm for years), Dave MacIsaac, John Allan Cameron, J. P. Cormier, Kyle MacNeil, John Morris Rankin and Allie Bennett. Other prominent guitar players are Paul MacDonald, Patrick Gillis, Sandy MacDonald, Brian Doyle, Matt MacIsaac, Maxim Cormier, Gélase Larade and Edmond Boudreau.

accompaniment instrument. Among the first recording artists playing guitar along with the fiddle-piano duo was Mickey MacIntyre, who recorded 78s with Angus Chisholm; J. D. MacKenzie recorded with Dan R. MacDonald on the only 78 to feature fiddle and guitar without piano. His style of playing involved laying the instrument across his lap and playing it with a slide. Bill MacDonald on guitar regularly teamed up with Margaret MacPhee to accompany Johnny Wilmot and is featured on his 78s. Estwood Davidson is perhaps the most influential of the guitarists to emerge from this era. Having teamed up with Winston Fitzgerald on fiddle and Beattie Wallace on piano, he felt compelled to expand his music theory knowledge in order to better understand the challenges presented by Fitzgerald's repertoire and thoughts on appropriate accompaniment. The carefully worked out arrangements between guitar and piano, which included extending the chord patterns beyond basic triads to include 6ths, 7ths and 9ths and being able to play in less com-

On guitar, Allie Bennett, John Allan Cameron and Dave MacIsaac in Big Pond. Photograph from The MacInnes Collection.

mon keys, established the music of this ensemble as a new standard. In the 1970s, Halifax-born Dave MacIsaac (who is also a Cape Breton fiddle player) brought guitar accompaniment to a new level, modelling his style on the piano, particularly on the techniques developed by Mary Jessie MacDonald, using melodic fragments, walking bass lines and chord substitutions. MacIsaac was part of the fiddle-piano-guitar ensemble that set a new standard for accompaniment and arrangement in the early 1980s, recording as part of Jerry Holland's *Master Cape Breton Fiddler* LP. In the 1990s, Gordie Sampson from Big Pond, from an intense family background of Cape Breton music but with eclectic musical interests, also brought in fresh techniques and sounds, including the use of open tunings such as DADGAD, as did J. P. Cormier with new right-hand techniques and alternative tunings. But though these players dominated the recording scene in Cape Breton, they always appeared in conjunction with a piano player, or in larger configurations with drum and bass. In fact, the guitar on its own has only rarely been used to accompany the fiddle. In 1951 American folklorist Diane Hamilton recorded fiddler Mike MacDougall accompanied on guitar, by Tim Donovan; he played 12-string guitar and had quite a distinctive individual style. Following MacDougall's death a tape of his music was released which again featured him performing with guitar accompaniment. MacDougall, of course, had been influenced to a considerable extent by his experience in performing with Irish-style folk bands such as Ryan's Fancy where guitar played a prominent accompaniment role. Sonny Slade in Sydney and Peter Poirier in Chéticamp also occasionally accompanied fiddlers with no piano present. By the first decade of the 2000s guitar and fiddle was becoming more common. Jerry Holland's posthumous CD release, *Helping Hands* (2009), features Irish guitarist John Doyle, Ashley MacIsaac and Dave MacIsaac recorded with fiddle and guitar, and Melody and Derrick Cameron regularly perform as a fiddle-guitar duo. The folk-song and fiddle scenes do have quite a fluid relationship within Cape Breton, and singer-guitarists (such as Buddy MacDonald who regularly partners with fiddle players) have created a regular platform where fiddle and guitar team up without piano accompaniment. Furthermore, two publications of Cape Breton fiddle repertoire explicitly refer to guitar: *Scottish and Cape Breton Fiddle Music in New Hampshire for Violin, Mandolin and Guitar* (Jason C. Little, 1984) and *Cape Breton Traditional Style Fiddle Sets with Guitar Tablature* (Sandy MacIntyre and Leigh Cline, 2011).

melody instrument. John Allan Cameron, already a fiddle player, in the 1950s was the first to attempt to play fiddle tunes on the guitar (12-string), developing his own style that involved only down-strokes executed using a thumb pick. Cameron, who in the late 1960s, was the first Cape Bretoner to achieve mass popular appeal as a folk singer, regularly accompanied fiddlers such as Dan R. MacDonald, Bill Lamey and Angus Chisholm and often performed as part of the Cape Breton Symphony Fiddlers throughout the 1970s. The guitar as a solo instrument has continued to be developed since that time, both in Cape Breton and across the Celtic world. Dave MacIsaac's CD *Celtic Guitar* was the first guitar solo CD to be released locally (1988), followed by *Nimble Fingers* (1995); MacIsaac has also recorded with Scott Macmillan on *Guitar Souls* (1993). Celtic Colours hosts an annual "Guitar Summit" as part of its program, showcasing the instrument in both a solo and accompaniment capacity. This event, which has featured players such as MacIsaac, Macmillan, Gordie Sampson, J. P. Cormier, Brian Doyle, Patrick Gillis and Maxim Cormier, has led to interesting collaborations, such as that between J. P. Cormier and Irish guitarist Tim Edey. [**MacDonald 2000**].

H

Halifax. The capital city of Nova Scotia, Halifax has long been a vibrant cultural centre, featuring an active Cape Breton music scene due to the relocation there for decades of many Cape Bretoners affected by economic circumstances. A number of high-profile Cape Breton musicians, second-generation Cape Bretoners, have also been born in the Halifax area, among them fiddler/guitarist Dave MacIsaac. As in other urban centres such as Boston and Detroit, where clusters of Cape Bretoners settled, Cape Breton expatriates did not take long to establish a rich musical community in Halifax. House ceilidhs continued in their new locale, just as they were practiced in Cape Breton. Entering the 1940s fiddlers and enthusiasts would visit the home of fiddler Alec Dan MacIsaac in Drummond Court; other popular gathering places were the homes of Donald Meagher and Johnnie Beaton on Barrington Street. House sessions in the 1960s, typically held after square dances, were found at the residences of Roddie MacDonald, Johnnie Beaton and Sonny Murray. Fiddlers such as Buddy MacMaster, Joe MacLean, Carl MacKenzie and Winston Fitzgerald would gather to play and, at Roddie MacDonald's home, for example, enjoy access to his impressive collection of recordings, often coming away having found a "new" tune for their repertoires. Since at least the 1940s, "Scotch" and Cape Breton-themed dances, most often organized by the Halifax Cape Breton Club, have been a fixture in the metro area. Dances were held at the Sisters of Service Hall in in the 1940s and 1950s, featuring the music of Charlie MacKinnon. Dances also occurred at Seagull Hall in Halifax's downtown as well as Carpenter's Hall on Gottingen Street, with Elmer Briand often being the featured fiddler. St. Theresa's Church Basement Hall often featured the music of Buddy MacMaster and Carl MacKenzie. Other venues popular in the 1960s included the Labour Temple and the Horseshoe Club. Around 1973 or 1974,

the Cape Breton Club relocated its dances from St. Theresa's to Farrell Hall in Dartmouth, where the dances continued for several years. Performing were fiddlers such as Buddy MacMaster, Carl MacKenzie, John Campbell, John Morris Rankin, Howie MacDonald and, later, younger fiddlers such as Wendy MacIsaac, Rodney MacDonald and Glenn Graham. The dances then moved to St. Lawrence Hall, in Fairview, Halifax, and most recently to the Lion's Hall, Connolly Street, where they are still held once a month, on the last Saturday, for eight months of the year.

pub scene. The pub scene in Halifax has also played host to Cape Breton traditional music. Fiddler Jarvis Benoit and his multi-instrumentalist son Louis, played at Alexander's Pub in the early 1980s. Local folk bands such as McGinty emerged in the city in response to demand from the many pubs and in the 1990s, Cape Breton pipers Paul MacNeil and Jamie MacInnis, both members of the Halifax Police Pipe Band, began to explore the older Cape Breton dance piping-style in The Open Door Gang. In 1986 John Morris Rankin and Dave MacIsaac began performing regularly at the Thirsty Duck tavern for a few years for large crowds of young Cape Bretoners and music enthusiasts; in the 1990s into the 2000s, Cape Breton fiddle music followers filled Your Father's Moustache Pub and Eatery in huge numbers—all of these indictors of the success of the Celtic boom. Other players on the scene at that time included Rodney MacDonald, Glenn Graham, Andrea Beaton, Wendy MacIsaac and bands such as Beòlach and Slàinte Mhath . A levelling off in the popularity of Celtic music saw performances in such venues declining, although since 2010 there have been efforts to revitalize the presence of fiddle music in the central part of the city in venues such as the Rockbottom Brew pub; there Cape Breton fiddlers are now often included on their Friday and Saturday night multi-act billings. When The Olde Triangle opened in Halifax, Dave MacIsaac and Louis Benoit were hired, and continue to play there every Monday night. In the late 1990s the Cape Breton Store and Tearoom was a popular, albeit short-lived alternative to the pub. Beginning in the early 2000s, Glenn Graham and Wendy MacIsaac played regularly on Sunday afternoons at the Celtic Corner Public House in Dartmouth; they would occasionally be accompanied by Dave MacIsaac, Harvey Beaton and others. Also around the same time, Ceilidh's Pub in Dartmouth began featuring Cape Breton music with Marc Boudreau as its house fiddler. He is often accompanied by various pianists, and most often includes Dave MacIsaac as his accompanist on guitar. Durty Nelly's Pub, in the Argyle Street pub district, has featured fiddle music with such musicians as Anna Ludlow, Cassie and Maggie MacDonald, Renee Doucet and Seph Peters. Casino Nova Scotia, in partnership with Music Nova Scotia, hosts regular music events spotlighting Nova Scotia musicians, at times featuring Cape Breton traditional acts. Cape Breton fiddlers have also diversified into Pop and Rock bands in the city, such as the Worry Birds, which features Cape Breton fiddler Bhreagh MacDonald.

concerts and festivals. Cape Breton fiddlers, both resident in Cape Breton and Halifax, have also been invited to perform in various fiddle and Celtic-themed concerts and performances. In the 1970s the Cape Breton Club sponsored Scottish concerts at Queen Elizabeth High School. Also around that time, a number of prominent fiddlers visited Halifax regularly to take part in the CBC-TV show *Ceilidh.* In 1972 and 1973 Sheldon MacInnes from Big Pond produced a series of concerts there to showcase Cape Breton performers, among them Paddy LeBlanc, Mike MacDougall and members of the Rankin Family. In the 1990s and early 2000s Charlie MacIsaac staged well-attended Cape Breton-themed concerts, bringing in popular fiddlers from Cape Breton as the featured acts. The concerts were held at such venues as Exhibition Park and the Halifax Forum multipurpose room. Cape Breton music has also been included in festivals and events such as Halifax-Re-jigged Festival, Halifax Celtic Festival and Fiddles of the World. Cape Breton fiddlers in Halifax have also capitalized on the vibrant cultural-industries scene by having their music placed on theme-based promotional music compilations (e.g., for Alexander Keith's beer, various tourism promotion advertisements and occasional theatre appearances). Some fiddlers such as Wendy MacIsaac, Glenn Graham, Dave MacIsaac and Leanne Aucoin have regularly taught lessons in the city and step-dance classes have also been taught by such as John Robert Gillis. In the university sector, Cape Breton music has also had a presence with courses being delivered by Kate Dunlay at Saint Mary's University; the Master of Arts in Atlantic Canada Studies program has also attracted scholars researching aspects of the Cape Breton music tradition. (*With* **GG and SMI**) [**Glenn Graham 2006; MacInnes 1997**].

Hall, Mike. (1982-). Fiddle, piano, button accordion, teacher. Saint John, NB, and Alberta. Of French descent, he grew up in a music environment, as his father, Sean Hall and his uncles Jack, Victor and Ivan all played the accordion, and there were many step dancers in the family. An avid musician, by the age of 14 Mike had recorded a CD (*Steppin 'er Out,* 1996), on which he played accordion, guitar and bass; after this he became captivated by Cape Breton fiddle music, which altered his music focus. He was inspired by the playing of Howie MacDonald, Jerry Holland, Natalie MacMaster, Cameron Chisholm and Arthur Muise, and learned a great deal from piano player Maybelle Chisholm McQueen, who lived near him in the 1990s. After several years listening to the music and frequently visiting Cape Breton he moved there in the early 2000s, settling in Judique; he began playing at concerts, dances and ceilidhs and was particularly popular around Chéticamp. In 2009 he recorded a second album, *A Legacy–Not to be Forgotten,* with Joel Chiasson on piano and featuring an old house-party cut of Alex "Lewis" MacDonald, an Inverness County fiddler (d. 2008) who lived in Saint John and who had been an important influence in Mike's younger years; this was done at the home of Alex and Minnie MacMaster in Troy. A second CD, *Dance Halls,* was released in 2012. A full-time player for a number of years, Hall taught fiddle locally, at fiddle camps and via Skype in addition to playing gigs and, occasionally, touring. He moved for a short time to Newfoundland but currently lives and works in Alberta, returning to Cape Breton periodically.

Hamilton, Diane. (1924-1991). The pseudonym of Diane Guggenheim (1924-1991), an American mining heiress, folksong collector and patron and founder of Tradition Records, which she ran with Irish ballad singer, Paddy Clancy. Having become acquainted with Clancy and his brothers in New York she travelled to Ireland in the 1950s where, with Liam Clancy, she visited and recorded a number of noted singers such as Sarah Makem; it was on that trip that Sarah's son Tommy and Liam first met and they went on to form some of the most successful commercial folksong collaborations, the Clancy Brothers and Tommy Makem and later, Makem and Clancy. While her main focus as a collector was Irish song, and later instrumental music, Hamilton made one field trip to Cape Breton in the early 1950s where she recorded a number of Gaelic singers and players, mostly around the Ingonish area. Material from this was released on the album *Nova Scotia–Music from Cape Breton* in 1955. The Irish Traditional Music Archive in Dublin houses a number of field tapes from the Cape Breton expedition as part of the Hamilton collection. [**Clancy 2002**].

harmonica. The harmonica, or mouth organ, is a free-reed instrument designed in Germany in the 1820s. Matthias Hohner of Trossingen, who began production in 1857, is the most significant name associated with it to the present day, although harmonicas are now made elsewhere as well, notably in China. Harmonicas are made in different keys and may be diatonic or chromatic. The instrument, affordable and accessible, was popular in Cape Breton. While it was sometimes used for dances in the absence of a fiddle player in communities such as Frenchvale, it was generally regarded as a toy, although many musicians started out playing this instrument, including Winston Fitzgerald. Women often played it, including Gertie Boutilier Turnball (mother of

Beattie Wallace) and Mary (Beaton) MacDonald (mother of Joan MacDonald Boes), who played the harmonica alongside her sister Sarah Catherine (Sarah MacArthur) on fiddle. Later, Joe Burke recorded on the instrument in duet with fiddler Johnny Wilmot for the 1978 Topic LP *The Music of Cape Breton, Volume 1: Gaelic Tradition in Cape Breton*. Alex Basker was the best known early exponent. His son, Tommy Basker, recorded *The Tin Sandwich* in 1994; this recording, demonstrating his own with brand of "Irish music with a Cape Breton swing," remains the only dedicated harmonica recording from the region.

Hashem, Lila (Abraham). (d. 2006). Piano. Inverness and Sydney. The daughter of Mustafa and Mary Ann (MacDonald) Abraham, her father was Lebanese while her mother was one of a well-known family of fiddlers from Foot Cape, whose father, Neil R. MacDonald, played fiddle, while his siblings, Joan (piano) and Allan (fiddle), played with the Five MacDonald Fiddlers in Detroit. While growing up, Lila heard much fiddle music and singing at the house when musicians such as Sandy MacLean (fiddle) and Lila MacIsaac (piano) would visit. Starting with piano lessons from Jessie Maggie MacLellan of Inverness, Lila later took some classical training from the local nuns. She was largely self-taught, however, learning by listening to Lila MacIsaac's chording style and learning melodies from a book by Scott Skinner. Her first public performance was at a July 1 picnic where she accompanied Angus Allan Gillis and Dougald Burke and later, on the pump organ, Angus Chisholm. Having moved to Sydney, in 1935 she won a piano competition there after which she began to team up with Robbie Robertson for a regular radio show; during that 15-minute slot she played piano solos in response to requests, most often "The Road to the Isles," which became her signature tune. She was soon established on the dance scene as a regular accompanist for fiddlers in the Sydney area such as Bill Lamey and Joe MacLean, playing in many of the popular dance halls such as Carpenter's Hall and Nelga Beach for many years. Other fiddlers she accompanied on a more occasional basis around the island included Charlie MacLellan of Dunvegan, Philip Chiasson of Chéticamp, Angus Chisholm, Johnny "Washabuck" MacLean, "Little" Jack MacDonald, Donald MacLellan, Winston Fitzgerald, Paddy LeBlanc, Sandy MacLean, Joe MacLean and Theresa (MacLean) Morrison. She played regularly in Valley Mills with Sandy MacInnis, and joined his group The Sydney Scottish Violins as accompanist, eventually becoming the leader, at which point it came to be known as Lila's Scottish Fiddlers. Like the vast majority of musicians in Cape Breton, she did not play full time, and had two businesses in Sydney, a beauty salon and a bowling alley. She featured on some fourteen 78s with various fiddlers and on a 1956 LP with Joe MacLean. [**MacGillivray 1988**].

Hawk, The. 101.5 (CIGO FM). Radio station located in Port Hawkesbury, Cape Breton. Established in October 1975, CIGO is a full-service adult contemporary station with a focus on servicing the community through public service, news, sports and weather information. CIGO began as 1410 AM and converted to 101.5 FM on April 3, 2000. While it can be picked up from New Glasgow to Sydney its primary target audience is Inverness and Richmond counties in Cape Breton, and Antigonish and Guysborough Counties on the Nova Scotian mainland (the "Quad Counties"). It's most significant contribution to the Cape Breton fiddle tradition has been the *Highland Fling* program, first broadcast in 1975 and hosted in 2015 by Bob MacEachern on Sundays at 6 p.m. *See* **Highland Fling; MacEachern, Bob; radio.**

Hayes, Ian. (1984-). Guitar, research. Halifax. He grew up in Shubenacadie and Whycocomagh and developed an interest in Cape Breton during the 1990s when he was inspired to take up the fiddle and guitar by recordings of The Rankins, The Barra MacNeils, Natalie MacMaster and Ashley MacIsaac who were popular, nationally, at that time. With Chéticamp piano player Jason Roach he played Cape Breton music as an accompanist

and as a session musician with such as Chrissy Crowley and Kenneth MacKenzie. While studying for a Master's degree in jazz guitar performance in Louisville, Kentucky, he became involved in the Irish session scene there and developed an interest in exploring music from an academic perspective. Cape Breton fiddle music is central to his research work; he has published on Cape Breton fiddle in relation to intellectual property rights; he has been conducting festival fieldwork on amplification practices, and has recently completed his doctoral studies in ethnomusicology at Memorial University, Newfoundland; his thesis title is "It's a Balancing Act. That's the Secret to Making this Music Fit in Today: Negotiating Professional and Vernacular Boundaries in the Cape Breton Fiddling Tradition" (2015).

Head, Gillian. (1988-). Fiddle, step dance. River Ryan. She took fiddle lessons first with Stephanie Wills, then with Jerry Holland, who became her principal inspiration; influenced too by Ashley MacIsaac, she used his recordings to practise her step dancing to. Her parents, Dan and Roberta Head, were drawn into Cape Breton music through Gillian's interest; Roberta became co-director of The Ceilidh Trail School of Celtic Music (2007-2010) and also managed Jerry Holland's career for a number of years. Gillian plays with Jason Roach on piano, hosts sessions and delivers illustrated talks on Cape Breton music on Sydney-bound cruise ships for tourists. Her debut CD, *Spirit*, was released in 2014.

Henderson, James Murdoch. (1902-1970). Scottish fiddler, composer and music critic. Aberdeenshire, Scotland. A player who admired violinists James Scott Skinner, George T. Taylor, and James F. Dickie he was regarded as an authority on strathspey and reel playing. In 1935 he published *The Flowers of Scottish Melody*, with 130 tunes, including 40 original contributions; this was reprinted by The Buchan Heritage Society in 1986. He edited and published *The Scottish Music Maker* in 1957, a book that preserved a number of Skinner's melodies that may otherwise have been lost. Henderson's Cape Breton connection is significant in that Dan R. MacDonald met him while stationed in Scotland with the Canadian army during the Second World War; Dan R. acquired many books from him and, passing on his contact details to other fiddlers upon his return, started a new era in tune sourcing (via postal contact with Henderson) in Cape Breton. [**Alburger 1983**] *See* **tune books.**

Hennessey, Jeffrey. (1971-). Musicologist, piano. Wolfville, NS. He became interested in Cape Breton music as a teenager when playing on tourism promotions, and was drawn to the piano accompaniment associated with Cape Breton fiddle. In this he heard parallels with the rock, blues, and country piano stylings with which he was familiar as a player. His PhD dissertation, "Fiddle Grooves: Identity Representation and the Sound of Cape Breton Fiddle Music in Popular Culture" (University of Toronto, 2008), explored this further, examining Cape Breton fiddle music with regard to identity and representation in regional musics and their relationships to rhythm, metre and musical time. He lectures in music at Acadia University, Wolfville, NS, where he is (2015) acting aean of Arts.

Herdman, Jessica. (1982-). Classical violin, fiddle, researcher. She grew up in Ajax, Ontario, but spent her childhood summers in her mother's home region of Cape Breton. She experienced Cape Breton fiddle music and dance on a regular basis and, from the age of 13, inspired by the contemporary successes of Natalie MacMaster and Ashley MacIsaac, she began taking fiddle lessons with Sandy MacIntyre in Toronto and at the Gaelic College. A violin performance graduate, her Master's dissertation was entitled "The Cape Breton Fiddling Narrative: Innovation, Preservation, Dancing" (University of British Columbia, 2008); she has further presented and published on this topic since. Currently (2015) a PhD student at the University of California, Berkeley, her research now concerns music, social identity and conflict in early modern France, but she occasion-

ally writes on Cape Breton-related issues, with the focus on globalization, identity and marketing, and continues to perform Cape Breton fiddle music.

high bass. The commonly used Cape Breton term for *scordatura*, from the Italian word meaning "mis-tune." Scordatura is the practice of re-tuning the strings of the fiddle from the standard G,DAE'. The most common alteration used in Cape Breton involves tuning the bottom two strings up a tone each to sound A,EAE'. In Cape Breton this is referred to as "high bass," "high bass and counter" or "high bass and tenor." Other tunings such as A,DAE' are not as common, although the tuning F,DAE' was believed to have been a favourite of fiddler Ranald Kennedy, learned from Donald "The Tailor" Beaton. While the use of scordatura is sometimes perceived as an easy way to approach tunes that have difficult cross-fingering passages, the main reason behind its popularity in Cape Breton is linked to the enhanced acoustical properties such tuning produces; these are added volume and octave layering; some also link it to the drone sound produced by the bagpipes. For volume, the resonant qualities created through sympathetic ringing strings (e.g., for a tune "on" A at least 2 strings will ring sympathetically with every note made when the fiddle is tuned A,EAE') and the increased potential for using open-string drones made scordatura a popular option among Cape Breton fiddlers playing for dancers, particularly before amplification was widely available. High-bass tuning also facilitated the playing of a single tune in two octaves; thus, when two fiddlers played together one could play the tune in the lower register and the other in the upper register, using the same fingering. Certain fiddlers were noted for their ability to play high-bass tunes and indeed for the substantial number of high-bass tunes in their repertiores. Mary MacDonald, for example, is reputed to have had 30-40 high bass-tunes at her disposal, while Dan Allan MacLellan (1870-1946) is said to have had hundreds. Today in Cape Breton, scordatura is used only by a small number of fiddlers, such as

strathspey
scordatura (AEAE)

Christy Campbell

traditional
arr: P.S.C

Dave MacIsaac, and is certainly never employed just for the purposes of adding volume. However, many fiddlers have at least one high-bass group of tunes in their repertoire that is performed generally as an exhibition feature or novelty; popular choices include "Christie Campbell." In the printed collections, high-bass tunes are featured to a limited extent. Directions for re-tuning are generally indicated at the beginning of the tune, to the left of the clef sign. Once the instrument is re-tuned, the melody line should be fingered as normal, although of course the notes generated will sound at the altered pitch. [**Cranford 2013; Dunlay and Greenberg 1996; Graham 2006; MacGillivray 1981**].

Highland Classics. A group of young fiddle players, most of them students of Stan Chapman, that formed in the late 1980s following a previous performance group, The Next Generation.

Highland Dance. *See* **Dance.**

Highland Fling. A radio show broadcast on The Hawk 105.5 (CIGO FM) on Sundays at 6 p.m. The history of *Highland Fling* is very closely connected to the resurgence of Cape Breton fiddle music. The program first aired in November 1975 with noted piano player, composer and cultural activist Joey Beaton, who was very much involved in the Cape

Breton fiddle music revival, hosting what was then a Saturday night half-hour show. It quickly gained in audience and popularity with its focus on fiddle, piano, bagpipes and Gaelic song, which resulted in the show being lengthened to one hour and moved to Sunday evenings. Subsequent hosts included Dan MacDonald and John MacDonald before Bob MacEachern took it over in January 1982. The station has accumulated an impressive library of commercial recordings of Cape Breton fiddle music as well as a number of home recordings from concerts, ceilidhs and house sessions, and has partnered with the CMIC in Judique and the Beaton Institute at CBU in making this material publically available. Often, guests will perform live. Since 2001 the show has been streamed live on the web. Several months of archival programs are always available on their web site. *See* **Hawk, the; MacEachern, Bob; radio.**

Highland Village Museum (Baile nan Gàidheal). Founded in 1959 as the Nova Scotia Highland Village Society and originally proposed by NS Premier Angus L. Macdonald, who held office in 1933-1940 and 1945-1954, Highland Village Museum has been part of the Nova Scotia Museum family since 2000, one of its 28 thematically diverse museums across the province. A living-history museum, it aims to tells the story of Gaelic settlement in Nova Scotia and to research, collect, preserve and promote the Gaelic language, culture and heritage, as it is found in Nova Scotia. It is set on 43 acres in Iona, with 11 historic buildings, an outdoor performance area and a genealogy centre; costumed interpreters recreate Scottish rural Gaelic life in the province; demonstrations and workshops in crafts, culture and language are held and Gaelic immersion programmes are offered; it also has virtual museum exhibits such as *Ceilidh air Cheap Breatunn / Cape Breton Ceilidh* (virtualmuseum.ca). Highland Village Day, held on the first Saturday of August each year, continues as one of the few outdoor "Scottish" concerts remaining in the Cape Breton calendar. The Highland Village Society continues to operate the site on behalf of the province; this is a non-profit Society led by a volunteer board of trustees elected by the membership. In June 2009, the Nova Scotia Highland Village Society's board of trustees formalized the sites' commitment to Gaelic with the adoption of a Gaelic policy, the first for any Gaelic-related institution or organization in Canada. Various teaching and immersion projects are ongoing such as Stòras a' Bhaile, a short Gaelic immersion folk-life school for advanced Gaelic learners, Cainnt mo Mhàthar, an online project of video-recorded Gaelic speakers from varying dialectal areas of Cape Breton, and An Drochaid Eadarainn (The Bridge Between Us), a virtual Gaelic folk life school. The Highland Village also has a publication mandate; following on from *Naidheachd a' Chlachain* (1994-2001/2), The Highland Village currently publishes *An Rubha: A Gaelic Folklife Magazine.* Since 1979 it presents an annual Award of Merit recognising individual and/or groups who have made an outstanding contribution to the Highland Village and/or to Gaelic culture in Nova Scotia; more recently it has established the Stòras na h-Òigridh / Treasures of Youth, a scholarship for young players in memory of local fiddle player, Michael Anthony MacLean (1911-2007). It annually features a number of expert lecturers for its Seòmbar na Grèineadh (Summer Room Series), invited to give talks at such as the Joe Neil MacNeil Memorial Lecture and the Alex Francis MacKay Scotch Music Presentation. The library has more than 1,600 books, including a substantial collection of Gaelic books; and the museum is engaged in ongoing collection of recorded Gaelic songs, oral history and stories, including the Nòs is Fonn archive. It also houses the MacLean Collection of Music Manuscripts, the personal collection of local fiddler, Joe MacLean. *See* **MacLean Collection.**

Highland Village Day. An outdoor Scottish concert first held on the site of the Highland Village Museum on August 4th, 1962 to mark its official opening, this concert continues on the first Saturday of each August. The first Highland Village Day involved competitions, and performances by fiddle players, Gaelic singers, step dancers and the Gaelic College Pipe Band; since then, while the competition element has disappeared, the programme continues to celebrate fiddle music, dance, piping and Gaelic song. Many of Cape Breton's high-profile artists have performed at this, including those with local family connections such as the Barra MacNeils, Slàinte Mhath and the Iona Gaelic Singers. In the past, part of the experience was the long traffic line-up waiting for the ferry to transport concert-goers across to Iona (and which led to much socializing), but since the Barra Strait Bridge was opened in 1993 this no longer happens; however, the location of the concert site, where the audience stretch up a steep hill, is unique and Highland Village Day continues to be one of Cape Breton's remaining few outdoor concerts of this type.

Holland, Jerry. (1955-2009). Fiddle, composer. Brockton, MA, and Belle Côte, Cape Breton. His father, Jerry, of Irish-French descent was from Acton, NB, and his mother from Saint Pamphile, Québec. Jerry Sr. was a fiddler, playing Irish, Scottish and down-east music, who, having settled in Boston in the 1930s, became interested and involved in the Cape Breton music scene there through his friendship with fiddlers such as Angus Gillis, Fred and Dan Landry, and Lambert Foley and his family, Bert, Aubey, Norman, Earl

Jerry Holland. Courtesy of Fiddlesticks Music Publishing.

and Winifred. Young Jerry thus grew up in a rich music environment with regular house parties in his own home and at Angus Gillis's in Rockland, MA. As a child he also had the opportunity to see and hear Winston Fitzgerald play and he attributed much of his early interest to this occasion. Jerry began playing fiddle, piano and guitar and step dancing at the age of 5 under the guidance of his father, and soon came to the attention of some of the leading figures of Cape Breton music in Boston. Bill Lamey invited him to play at the Rose Croix hall when he was just 6 years old, where he played a waltz and a reel and had to stand on a chair to be seen; by the age of 10 he was playing for sets at the dances organized by Lamey at the Orange Hall, and later he accompanied Angus Chisholm for a couple of years on guitar at Tom Slavin's Club on South Huntington Avenue. Holland's reputation as a child prodigy had been cemented by the age of 7 when he participated in the TV variety show *Boston: Community Auditions,* and later on the *Ted Mack Amateur Hour,* a national TV talent competition which he won with his simultaneous fiddle and step-dance routine. He later appeared on the popular *Don Messer's Jubilee* and he was a regular winner at both fiddle and step-dance contests held at the French Club in Waltham. With the waning of the Boston-Cape Breton scene by the 1970s, Jerry, who had played fiddle for John Allan Cameron at an Irish

restaurant there (The Harp and Bard), was invited to join The Cape Breton Symphony, a group of fiddlers that was to feature as part of *The John Allan Cameron Show* on TV Since that group included many famous players in its 20-year history, such as Winston Fitzgerald, John Donald Cameron and Buddy MacMaster, for the young fiddler with no Cape Breton family connections this was a significant opportunity and one which he always considered the key to his acceptance in Cape Breton, although that group in itself was never especially popular there. Holland's experience with the symphony also challenged him in many ways, most especially in his note-reading abilities and in discipline, and taught him much about harmony, arranging and the de- and re-construction of melodies, much of which informed his own music development. In the mid-1970s the Holland family moved to Cape Breton, where Jerry spent the rest of his life. Although technically an "outsider," his understanding of the music and his empathy with the tradition ensured his acceptance, to a large degree, as a Cape Breton fiddler, one of the first to achieve such recognition. Internationally, Jerry Holland is arguably one of the best known of Cape Breton's fiddlers. His impact on the tradition has been immense on many levels. As a composer he has contributed a significant body of tunes to the repertoire, many of which (e.g., "Brenda Stubbert's" and "Stan Chapman's") have become embedded as classics. Many of his tunes have been published in two collections (Cranford), while a number appear on various recordings by himself and other artists, both in Cape Breton and worldwide. He recorded 9 solo albums, including *Helping Hands* with Irish guitarist John Doyle, which was released posthumously in 2009, and *Jerry Holland and Friends* in 2010. Others include *Crystal Clear (2000),* on which he performs solo, inspired by Angus Chisholm, and *Parlor Music* (2005), with Doug MacPhee on piano. However, it was his 1982 release, *Master Cape Breton Fiddler,* which established him as a significant post-revival Cape Breton player and a massive influence on emerging fiddlers at the time such as Howie MacDonald, Dougie MacDonald and Allie Bennett. Perhaps the most significant aspect of this recording was the attention given to the role of accompaniment by Dave MacIsaac on guitar and Hilda Chiasson on piano; with them, Holland pioneered a new, more modern sound, one in which the harmonic lines and styles were carefully charted and co-ordinated, building further on what Winston Fitzgerald had been doing since the 1950s. Holland also appears on recordings by the Cape Breton Symphony Fiddlers and is one of the featured artists on *Music from Cape Breton Island*, the live recording from the Éigse na Laoi Festival of Cape Breton fiddling held in Cork, Ireland, in 1993.

sound. Jerry Holland has an individual sound: he cultivated a distinctive, sweet tone characterized by the regular use of vibrato as an ornamental device and much use of the upper reaches of the bow. He was particularly interested in the variation opportunities inherent in any given tune; while these were never realized in a spontaneous fashion, as would be typical of an Irish style, he often worked out variations for tunes that became his personal settings. This approach also coloured his thinking in terms of accompaniment, and he would chart variations in chordal patterns and/or rhythmic motifs for subsequent turns of a given tune. He generally avoided extended groups or medleys of tunes, something that had become popular during the 1970s, believing that 4-5 tunes per group was sufficient. While he was keen that his own compositions be suitable for dancing to, it was in listening contexts that he himself preferred to play. He did a great deal of his work with Hilda Chiasson and Dave MacIsaac, but also worked regularly with other accompanists such as Alan Dewar and Mary Jessie Gillis. A carpenter by trade, and an occasional fiddle maker and restorer, he was one of the first Cape Breton fiddlers to attempt, at various times, to pursue a music career as his main profession. He did a lot of work in the U.S. in particular, teaching at fiddle camps, which was a new type of opportunity for a Cape Breton fiddler from the 1980s onward. He had strong views on his experiences within the music industry due to his dealings with some of the major record labels and as such was one of the first Cape Breton fiddlers to properly deal with issues of ownership and copyright. He set up his own publishing company, Fiddlesticks Music, and blazed a trail for the younger musicians who, following his lead, became much more informed about such areas of the business. Jerry was the musical director for the Ceilidh Trail School of Celtic Music, Inverness, in 1996 and again in 2007-2009. *A Tribute to Jerry Holland* was held by Celtic Colours in 2009, following his death earlier that year. His son, Jerry "Junior" Holland (1985) is a drummer who has played and recorded with many Cape Breton fiddlers and is involved in the music industry. [**Caplan 1988; Feintuch 2010; MacGillivray 1981**].

— ≈ —

Jerry Holland's Collection of Fiddle Tunes. A Compilation of Traditional and Original Melodies from the repertoire of Jerry Holland; 282 Tunes. Originally published in 1988 by Paul Cranford as vol. 1 of the *Cape Breton Musical Heritage Series: Contemporary Performer* and now in its fifth edition (2004). Its 94 pages have 282 tunes from the repertoire of Jerry Holland, divided into: (a) marches, strathspeys and reels, clogs and hornpipes; (b) jigs; (c) waltzes and slow airs. Tunes are numbered individually and arranged by key. There are 133 reels, 83 jigs and 37 strathspeys; some of these may be interpreted as a number of tune-types (e.g., strathspey or reel, hornpipe or reel). Holland composed 139 of the tunes (7 of them in collaboration with other composers), including such popular pieces as "Brenda Stubbert's Reel" and "Stan Chapman's Jig." 41 other named composers' tunes are included, these representing: (i) Scotland from the 18th century onwards (John Bowie, Daniel Dow, Charles Duff, Simon Fraser, Neil Gow, William Gow, Robert Lowe, Joseph Lowe, John Lowe, Robert MacIntosh, Bert Murray, James Walker, William Marshall, William Morrisson, Robert Petrie, John Riddell, William

Shepherd, J. Scott Skinner), (ii) Ireland and Irish-America (Martin Mulhaire, Brendan Mulvihill, Máire O'Keeffe, James O'Beirne), (iii) America (Lew Alpaugh, George Wilson), (iv) Nova Scotia (Aubrey Chapman) and (vi) Cape Breton (Paul Stewart Cranford, Otis Tomas, Dave MacIsaac, Elmer Briand, Hilda Chiasson, Angus Chisholm, Pat Chafe, Alex MacEachern, Dan R. MacDonald, Dougie MacDonald, Paul M. MacDonald, Pipe Major Alex MacDonald, Mike MacDougall, Donald MacLean, John Morris Rankin, Harry Slaunwhite). The collection has a preface with detailed information on Holland's style and technique; there is an alphabetical tune index including alternative titles and a list of composers whose tunes are included. Some personal reflections on Holland's life in music are quoted from various sources, mostly his *Fathers and Sons* recording; additional notes offer further information and variation options. The cover image and other photos are by Carol Kennedy; rear cover photo is by Ronald Caplan. An accompanying cassette to the first edition was published and Holland's commercial recordings are referenced in later editions.

— ≈ —

Jerry Holland: A Totally New Compilation of Traditional and Original Melodies, complete with chords arranged by Jerry Holland. Volume 5 of the *Cape Breton Musical Heritage Series: Contemporary Performer,* this 128-page collection with 322 tunes from the repertoire of Jerry Holland was published in 2000 by Cranford. It is divided into three categories: (a) marches, reels, strathspeys, clogs and hornpipes; (b) jigs; (c) waltzes and slow airs. Tunes are numbered individually and arranged by key; there are 138 reels, 84 jigs and 44 strathspeys; two barn dances are among the other 56 pieces. The material includes pipe music and raised-bass tunes, and is both old and new, traditional and from known composers; there are also many examples from Ireland, Scotland,

England, Shetland, America, Canada and from other Cape Breton composers. 61 known composers in total are represented, with 121 compositions from Jerry Holland himself (5 of these composed in collaboration with Dougie MacDonald and 1 with Lew Alpaugh) and the others from named tunesmiths: Dan Hughie MacEachern (2), John MacDougall (2), Malcolm MacDonald (2), Dougie MacDonald (5), John MacLean (1), Ronald MacLellan (2), Elmer Briand (2), Billy McComiskey (3), Joan MacDonald Boes (2), William Morrison (2), Pat Shuldon Shaw (2), Mrs. Robertson of Ladykirk (1), Tom Marsh (10), Charlie Mulvihill (1), Howie MacDonald (3), Neil Gow (1), John Gow (1), Eddie Poirier (2), Kitchener MacDonald (1), Ed Reavey (3), Wilfred Gillis (2), John Mc-Coll (1), David Greenberg (7), D. MacLeod (1), G. S. MacLennan (1), James Walker (2), J. Scott Skinner (9), Duncan MacIntyre (3), Paul Stewart Cranford (3), William Marshall (9), Dan R. MacDonald (3), Dave MacIsaac (1), Mike MacDougall (2), Howdy Forrester (1), James Hill (2), Ward Allan MacDonald (1), Allie Bennett (1), Joey Beaton (1), John Morris Rankin (3), J. D. Kennedy (1), Scott Macmillan (1), Abraham MacIntosh (1), Tom Anderson (1), Paddy O'Brien (1), piper Alex MacDonald (1), Brenda Stubbert (1), Peter Hardie (1), Daniel Dow (1), Angus Fitchet (1), Doug MacPhee (1), James Stewart Robertson (1), Seamus Connolly (1), Sandy MacLean (1), Frank Livingston (1), Liz Carroll (1), Peter MacPhee (1), Phil Cunningham (1) and Robert Petrie (1). As a Cape Breton fiddle-tune collection this is not only the most diverse for sources, but it was the first to include chords. Each tune is presented with considerable information – type, chords, composer, era, publisher and the relevant Holland CD – as well as some melodic variations and harmonies. There is a preface by editor Paul Cranford and some instructional information on chord choices, embellishments and bowing, an interview with Jerry Holland (excerpts from

Fiddler Magazine, Vol. 6 No. 4) and a full alphabetical index, including alternative tune titles. The book is illustrated with photos by Carol Kennedy.

– ∾ –

home recordings. By the late 1940s consumer recording machines became more accessible and there emerged a group of amateur engineers and collectors from within the circle of Cape Breton fiddlers. These engineers were close friends of the music and hosted countless sessions in their homes or attended other house sessions specifically to record and document the music. Included among them were Johnny Archie MacDonald (Detroit), Doug MacMaster, John Muise, Herbie MacLeod and Joe Beaton (all Boston), Roddy "The Plumber" MacDonald in Halifax and Hughie "Shortie" MacDonald from Inverness. *See* **collectors; house session; recordings.**

hornpipe. A dance and its related tune originating in England, which appeared in print for the first, time in 1525 and is sometimes referred to as "single hornpipe." In its original configuration the hornpipe was in triple time (most commonly 3/2) and was generally regarded as representing a characteristically English rhythm. Hornpipes had particular Maritime connections since many ships' companies carried a resident fiddler so that music for dancing was readily available to stave off ennui on long voyages. The word "hornpipe" was quite loosely used, and any step dance tended to be referred to by this name, even if it was clearly related to another tune type. Around 1760 the hornpipe developed into the "double hornpipe" and was frequently performed by professional dancers between acts of plays. Two styles of hornpipe (one dotted, one more even rhythmed) are now prevalent; in Cape Breton these are clearly distinguished as clogs and hornpipes respectively. The hornpipe is in either common time (for slower hornpipes) or cut time (for faster hornpipes), and is characterised by even-rhythm passagework that coincides with the style of the reel, as does the accentual pattern, where beats 1 and 3 are emphasized. It was first introduced as an ac-

companiment to specific solo dances such as "The Flowers of Edinburgh" (believed to have been transported with the earliest settlers) and "The Sailor's Hornpipe." Once these dances became defunct in the early 20th century, the hornpipe as a tune type was redundant and has never since been associated with a specific dance within Cape Breton. The tune type, however, remained in the repertoire in a somewhat peripheral capacity; this has been attributed variously to its lack of association with the dance, to its non-Gaelic origin and to the technically challenging nature of many of the tunes that may have been considered unnecessary for some fiddlers in the past. While it had been associated with certain players such as Angus Allan Gillis, it was in the 1940s that the hornpipe rose in popularity in the hands of players such as Angus Chisholm and Winston Fitzgerald. These fiddlers made it legitimate for the even-rhythmed style of hornpipes to be found in combination with reels, a practice common across North America; the clog, however, was retained as a distinct tune type used in a listening context only. In Fitzgerald's published collection, some 50% of the tunes are hornpipes, an indication of the popularity of the tune type among certain players. In the early decades of the 21st century, however, the hornpipe appears to have become less popular; where it is played, it tends to be featured in isolation, as a distinct tune type and no longer as a reel substitute, perhaps reflecting an increased awareness of how these tunes are used in Ireland and Scotland. A small number of local tunes in this idiom have been created over the years. Dan R. MacDonald composed several tunes of this type. Conversely, the 1996 *DunGreen Collection*, which is considered an authoritative source of old-style repertoire, contains no hornpipes.

house party. A more informal event than the house ceilidh or session, the house party may be a spontaneous or a planned affair. While fiddle music is an important element of such an event, it is not necessarily the focus and there is no expectation of those in attendance to sit quietly to listen – although many may choose to do so. A small number of house parties have, informally, become part of the part of the Cape Breton events calendar; these are quite large annual productions and include the installation of a sound system for the musicians and the provision of temporary car parking and even camping facilities; invitations to such parties are highly sought-after. *See* **ceilidh; house session.**

house session. The ultimate music setting for some is a small select gathering of musicians and listeners where music is played and discussed. Quite distinct from the, at times, "staged" ceilidhs (house or public) and the informal house parties (although the terms are often interchanged), the session was a gathering where the focus was on exploring the music. Often such sessions were recorded on domestic reel-to-reel recorders, later on cassettes; these home recordings became a resource in the dissemination of the fiddle music, particularly significant since they captured the music of many players who were otherwise undocumented or who – having become disillusioned with the commercial music industry – did not wish to record commercially. For subsequent generations of fiddlers, home-recorded tapes became an impor-tant part of the learning process. Before formal music-teaching opportunities were developed in the 1970s, the session played an important role in the transmission of the music and its associated traditions; this is where emerging young players often experienced prominent fiddlers playing and absorbed much in the way of repertoire, style and performance practice. Attentiveness to the music was imperative. The late-20th century sessions became more fiddle- and piano-centred, with less of the diversity of activities of the early ceilidhs being in evidence. As well as being popular in Cape Breton, house sessions were a key event for displaced Cape Breton communities, for example in Boston and Detroit, during the mid-1900s, when they often took place on Sunday afternoons. It was common for such sessions to conclude with all the fiddlers present playing a few groups of tune together; as such these provided the context for the introduction of the formal ensemble. In Detroit during the 1950s, for example, the group The Five MacDonald Fiddlers emerged from the Sunday-afternoon sessions held at the home of John Archie MacDonald. *See* **home recordings; session.**

I

Iggy and Squiggy. Nicknames which appear in a tune composed by Jerry Holland as a tribute to two enthusiastic followers of Cape Breton music—Susan Beaton (1969-) and Patricia (Pat) Phee (1970-), both from Antigonish. In the late 1980s and early 1990s they travelled throughout Cape Breton following the fiddle-music scene; their exuberance and youth is seen as having acted as something of a catalyst in loosening what they perceived as rather staid reactions to the fiddle music. Musicians indeed viewed their advent positively, and their presence at a concert or ceilidh could be socially and musically transformative; while Cape Breton audiences were never particularly reserved but always keen to engage with the music through whoops and calls of support for the player, Iggy and Squiggy brought this to a new level. Marking this, Jerry Holland dubbed them with their frivolous pseudonym. Superficially, they described themselves as "poster girls" for the fiddle-music scene; they attended particular musician's performances in almost a groupie fashion. Their humour and attitude was, however, underpinned by a deep interest in and respect for the music, something that was understood and appreciated by musicians. There had already been music experience: Susan's father, Stuart Beaton, followed the music and was a fiddler himself; his father, Herman, had been a piper, and the Beaton home was known for house parties, many of them featuring Irish music played by Grady Poe and Kim Vincent and, on occasion, Jerry Holland. Susan later organized events and dances, in one period managing Jerry Holland's career. Pat had become interested in step dance after attending a square dance in Glendale, and performed at some of the major outdoor concerts and events. The duo's hilarity and gregariousness was surpassed only by their generosity in looking out for visiting students and others interested in the music: advising and guiding, and transporting music aficionados and musicians to all parts of Cape Breton and the Mainland. Although no longer particularly involved in Cape Breton music, their contribution serves as a reminder that musicians need audiences, and that good reception for music inspires players to excel, keeping music alive.

instruments. The main melody instruments used in Cape Breton music have been fiddle and Highland bagpipes, while piano and guitar are the main accompanying instruments. Of these, the fiddle (referred to commonly as the violin until the late 20th century and still occasionally so) is iconic, and is thus depicted widely, particularly

Iggie and Squiggie

Jerry Holland, 1955-2009.

LIZ DOHERTY

with regard to tourism, notably monumentalized in The Big Fiddle, which dominates the port area at Sydney Harbour. From the second half of the 20th century the fiddle, partnered with a very unique and robust style of piano accompaniment, became synonymous with the Cape Breton sound heard in dance halls, on concert stages, at ceilidhs and on recordings. Sometimes the fiddle-piano combination was supplemented by guitar and occasionally a percussion instrument, such as clappers (bones); only rarely is the fiddle heard without piano. However, while it may be perceived that the Cape Breton tradition has always centred on this instrument duo, this has only been the case since the revival period of the 1970s. Prior to that, the fiddle-piano combination had often been part of larger fiddle groups, or with other melody instruments such as harmonica and banjos, rhythm instruments such as knitting needles, snare drums and, on occasion (on a Bill Lamey recording), kettle drums, or drones performed on the Jew's harp; unaccompanied solo fiddle or, more typically, teams of two fiddles, were also common, particularly in the early decades of the century. Bagpipes were of great significance in earlier times, embodying Scottish roots, and these were also played in combination with fiddles. Significantly, and often overlooked, various other instruments such as mandolin, harmonica, accordion and flute contributed to Cape Breton music independently of the fiddle, albeit much less commonly. Clusters of certain instruments in particular places around the island emerged, for instance, accordions in the Iona area; a number of the early fiddle players were in fact proficient on a range of instruments. In the opening decades of the 21st century this diversity in instrumentation has resumed, perhaps because the fiddle no longer has to prove itself as being alive and relevant, in danger of disappearing. The fiddle dominates, of course, but the omnipresence of the fiddle-piano duo has given way to larger ensembles which, while maintaining these at their core, are added to with more lead and accompanying instruments. Much of the subsequent diversification in terms of soundscapes is related also to the acceleration in connection to and collaboration with other traditional musicians – those of Ireland, Scotland, Scandinavia and North America – due to increased regular participation by Cape Breton musicians in international festivals and events and through Celtic Colours. Cape Breton musicians are now more accustomed to hearing and seeing the different group/band formats which dominate many of these other traditions' practices, and are keen to explore those models, but in the context of their own style and repertoire. While "the band" concept has been a part of the Cape Breton tradition since the earliest recordings, and particularly so after the 1990s, this format has now become very common (outside of the square-dance tradition) among younger players. It is interesting to note, however, that in some of the contemporary band configurations, depending on choices made in relation to tune type, medleys and arrangements, the strongest defining Cape Breton feature is in fact often the piano, not the fiddle. *See* **under terms**.

Inter-Media. A record label and production company based in Halifax. Started in the mid-1970s by Dave Miller, it offered musicians low-cost recording by providing a mobile studio that could be brought to their homes. Inter-Media's package included the cost of production, pressing (with World Records, Ontario), artwork and delivery of records, and the artist could purchase the finished product at a price per unit. Winnie Chafe's *Cape Breton Scottish Memories* (1979) and *The Bonnie Lass of Headlake–Cape Breton Scottish Violin Favourites, and* The Sons of Skye's *Both Sides of the Water* (1981) and the *Festival of Scottish Fiddling* (1973) all appeared on the label. The advent of digital technology and the opening up of CD production meant that, gradually, musicians moved to using Inter-Media for the recording process only doing the production end themselves; fiddler Kinnon Beaton was the first to try this approach, followed by Carl MacKenzie and Doug MacPhee (piano). The company ceased business in the mid-1980s.

intonation. Refers to a fiddler's realization of pitch accuracy, i.e., whether or not a note is in tune, sharp or flat. It is one of the elements of style on which qualitative judgements regarding a player may be made, and attitudes to it in the Cape Breton fiddle style have changed over time as indeed they have in many other music traditions. With older and older-style fiddlers the intonation typically and deliberately varied, with a range of neutral notes (specifically the 3rd and 7th degrees of the scale and the note C, irrespective of its position within the scale) being frequently employed, adding colour and complexity to the melodic line; this ambiguity in intonation is often considered as being related to the tuning of the bagpipe chanter. In the 1940s, fiddlers Winston Fitzgerald and Angus Chisholm had to reconsider intonation with regard to recording and piano accompaniment, and conscious decisions were made to reduce tonal ambiguities in favour of aligning pitches with their equal tempered equivalences. The piano's increasingly busy and syncopated stylings called for the melodic line to become somewhat simplified, less dense and more transparent and true; thus any features which generated dissonances between the fiddle and piano (such as neutral notes) were eliminated. As new contexts for performance emerged, removing the music from its function as supporting the dance to establishing it as an art form in its own right (i.e., music to be listened to only), the fiddle-piano pairing stabilized, with the necessary adjustments being made to the fiddle style. New opportunities were presented to the fiddle-music community through these changes, including new performance contexts and new repertoire made possible. New techniques were developed, which encouraged them to move toward more standardized tunings as a baseline from which they might then engage with challenges such as different keys, higher-position work and such. This move has been most visible since the 1970s establishment of formal fiddle teaching structures, and today the intonation of the majority of Cape Breton fiddlers is generally truer in relation to standard violin practice in other genres. Indeed, many fiddlers from this time onward are very clear in their perception of what is "in tune" and what is "out of tune." Still, certain players continue to employ some flexibility in terms of intonation. [**Dunlay and Greenberg 1996, Graham 2006**]. *See* **key; tuning.**

Inverness County Centre for the Arts. A venue and exhibition space opened in 2003 to cater for the creation, presentation and performance of the arts in Inverness County. Developed and maintained by the Inverness County Council of the Arts (ICCA).

Inverness Oran (Oran Inbhir Nis), The. (Trans. "Song of Inverness"). A publication started by Rankin and Eleanor MacDonald, Lawrence and Jackie Ryan, and Fr. Bob Neville in 1976. Conceived as "a voice for the community," its original Gaelic title was changed to the English some years later. Over the years it has published numerous articles about music and culture including debates and editorials by Frank MacDonald. This weekly paper (published on Wednesdays) continues to serve as a key information source relating to music and associated events in the Inverness area. [**Feintuch 2010**].

Inverness Serenaders, The. A Cape Breton band formed in Boston in the 1930s, it was led by Alick Gillis from Margaree and featured Alcide Aucoin from Chéticamp and Charlie MacKinnon from Lake Ainslie, all on fiddles; Angus Chisholm also played with the group on occasion. They were joined variously by Betty Maillet or Malcolm Gillis on piano, Jim Aucoin on accordion, Paul Aucoin on guitar and banjo, and Hugh Young, who played clappers and danced. Loosely modelled on Irish dance bands popular in the U.S. at the time, the Inverness Serenaders became an icon of Cape Breton fiddle music in Boston during the 1930s. On Saturday nights the group performed live for 15 minutes on Boston's WHDH radio from the Hotel Touraine (a broadcast which could be picked up in Nova Scotia) before playing a dance in O'Connell Hall on Dudley Street. The band was recorded by Decca for 6 78-rpm releases between

1934 and 1937, in what were among the earliest recordings to feature Cape Breton fiddling. These tracks feature solos by Gillis and also Alcide Aucoin; another documents an informal recording session that includes greetings and conversation in Gaelic and English. *See* **bands.**

Irish Benevolent Society of Cape Breton, The (IBS). Organized in 1966 and chartered in 1970, this is a non-political, non-profit and non-denominational organization and a member of The Multicultural Association of Nova Scotia. Its primary purpose is to create awareness and an appreciation of the contribution Irish culture has made to Cape Breton, and to keep that alive. Included in the Society's pledged objectives is "the promotion and perpetuation of the traditions of Ireland," including Irish music. The Society was spearheaded by expatriate Newfoundlander Mike Fitzgerald, who has been its president and an executive member over many years. Key activities include the introduction of competitive Irish dance to Cape Breton and the facilitation of the Fitzgerald School of Irish Dance in 1974. Since 1965 the IBS has hosted a St. Patrick's Day concert and surrounding events that, in its early years, included the crowning of the "Queen of the Shamrocks," a beauty/talent/Irish-ness contest. The Society has also contributed to the research and documentation of the Irish in Cape Breton through various initiatives, including a one-hour documentary on the Irish directed by historian Ken Donovan (*The Irish of Cape Breton, 1713-1900*), and the hosting of an Irish Cultural Symposium at Louisbourg in August, 1995. The IBS has also provided a cultural centre for the Irish of Cape Breton at the Irish Club in Sydney since 1971; this was originally on Townsend Street and later moved to Dorchester Street.

Irish Music. A generic term which in the past indicated the older music of Ireland, including the more formal harp repertoire, today it implies, and is generally replaced by, "traditional Irish" music. It has a distinctive and well-documented repertoire and styles, and has a clear lineage with forms

Jim Woods, Matt MacIsaac, Liz Doherty, Andrea Beaton and Troy MacGillivray, Ireland, 2012. Photo by Lorcan Doherty Photography.

and practices dating to the middle ages. Irish music has been a contributing factor to the Cape Breton fiddle tradition in general and in certain communities, most especially in "the Northside" area (North Sydney, Sydney Mines, Point Aconi, Florence, George's River and Bras d'Or, with the Gannon Road stretching through it) where it has played a significant role in shaping style, repertoire and performance practice. Irish settlement is believed to have taken place in Louisbourg since 1713, although scholars such as Ken Donovan and Mike Kennedy suggest that there was, in fact, an earlier Irish presence. Caught between the imperial rivalries of France and Britain, hundreds of Irish came to Cape Breton during the 18th century because they shared a common religion with the French and distrust of the English. After the fall of Louisbourg in 1758, immigrants from southern Irish counties such as Wexford, who initially made for the fortress, relocated to such as St. Peter's, among them Lawrence Kavanagh, one of the most prosperous businessmen on the island. An influx of Irish settlers arrived from counties Wexford, Waterford and Kilkenny following the 1785 Wexford Rebellion; they centred mostly in the Irish Grant (Lingan, New Waterford) and also in Sydney Mines and St. Peters; other small isolated Irish communities were established in such as Boisdale, Port Hood, the North Shore, Irish Cove, Ingonish and the Margarees, and single Irish families settled in areas such as Mabou Coal

Mines and Washabuck, areas that were otherwise heavily populated by Scots. By 1815 there had been a considerable influx of Irish from Newfoundland, and Irish from the smaller communities across Cape Breton moved to join them, consolidating the Irish population in five major districts: the Northside, Lingan, Ingonish, the Margarees and St. Peter's. New genealogy research reveals that there was considerable intermarriage between the Irish and the Scots in Cape Breton, much of this with those of Barra descent. Irish settlers in Cape Breton, it seems, continued to return home for particular events, mainly since they had no priest in Cape Breton; this changed in 1816 when Fr. William Dollard, an Irish Gaelic-speaking priest arrived. The Irish communities were known as having a lively social scene and much music and dancing at such as weddings and wakes; in the Lingan area, parties allegedly lasted for up to a week; as such, they were harshly criticized by Bishop Plessis during his visit in 1815. Evidence of instruments such as accordions, uilleann pipes and harps being played in the Irish communities also challenges the assumption that fiddles and bagpipes were the only instruments available on the island until pump-organs and pianos were introduced in the early 20th century.

repertoire. English-language song in the Cape Breton repertoire is dominated by Irish ballads and songs, adapted by, and assimilated into the repertories of contemporary folk singers such as Buddy MacDonald, Darryl Keegan, Cyril MacPhee and Malcie MacPhee. Such Irish songs have a long provenance in Cape Breton, dating back to the 1800s. Not only were Irish songs popular, but it became common for new, local songs to be composed, albeit set to existing Irish song airs; this practice infiltrated some of the most profoundly Gaelic areas of the island, such as Christmas Island and Washabuck. The Newfoundland Irish – specifically, fishermen based in Bay St. Lawrence, White Point, Ingonish and Neil's Harbour – influenced local musicians in the community such as Mike MacDougall, as well as Winston Fitzgerald who, being of French and Irish parentage, was already particularly

Natalie MacMaster and Sharon Shannon performing at Celtic Colours, 2014. Photo by Corey Katz. Courtesy of Celtic Colours International Festival.

familiar with Irish songs, one of his signature pieces being "The Rose of Tralee." The North American ballad boom of the 1960s, among the chief exponents of which were Irish singers such as the Clancy brothers from Co. Tipperary and Tommy Makem from Co. Armagh, also had a huge impact in Cape Breton, not least on John Allan Cameron. Since the 1970s, local Maritime Irish folk and ballad bands became popular, such as Ryan's Fancy, Barley Bree (with Donegal fiddler P. V. O'Donnell), and Evans and Doherty; visits to Cape Breton by such as Makem and Clancy added to this popularity and, even today, bands such as The Irish Rovers continue to maintain an audience in Cape Breton. From the 1940s onward the great interest in printed collections among the Cape Breton fiddle community included inexpensive publications such as *Cole's 1000 Fiddle Tunes* (1882, 1940) and the Scottish, four-part *Kerr's Collection,* both of which contained many Irish tunes; influential Irish books were the O'Neill's collections published in Chicago (1903, 1907) and *Allan's Irish Fiddler.* Irish tunes had currency in Cape Breton on account of the fact that the "square sets" – which were brought to Cape Breton from Europe via the U.S. – involved figures danced to jigs. They became popular in the early decades of the 20th century, rendering the Irish repertoire an important resource for this type of tune that was less commonly found in Scottish music. Many hornpipes played in Cape Breton are also from Irish sources, although the style of playing them is markedly different. A great amount of Irish material on 78s, which was available in Boston and elsewhere in the U.S. from the beginning of the 20th century, found its way back to Cape Breton; Johnny Wilmot's mother, for instance, was an avid collector of such recordings, notably those by Sligo, Ireland, fiddler Michael Coleman which were significant in shaping Wilmot's style.

diaspora. Crossover between Cape Bretoners and the Irish was inevitable in Boston and other urban centres in the northeastern U.S. Both communities based much of their social activities around dances held in the Dudley Street area, and house parties were commonplace, typically involving musicians from both communities. Some intermarrying took place (e.g., Irish fiddle- and banjo-player Jimmy Kelly married Sally MacEachern of Sydney, and their home became a gathering place for both Cape Breton and Irish musicians). Eddie Irwin was a popular piano accompanist who regularly played for both Cape Breton and Irish fiddlers in Boston, as did his mother, Mary, who was born in Cape Breton (Irish Cove) to Irish descendants. The first known recording of Cape Breton fiddlers – by Charlie MacKinnon and "Big" Dan Hughie MacEachern – was in the context of the Irish-influenced dance band known as both The Caledonia Scotch Band and The Columbia Scotch Band, led by Irish-American piano player, Dan Sullivan, himself married to a Nova Scotian. Later Cape Breton ensembles such as The Inverness Serenaders were, no doubt, influenced by the popular Irish dance bands of the day in their configurations of musicians and music arrangements. In cities such as Boston, music partnerships were formed, such as Johnny Wilmot playing with Irish accordionist Joe Derrane. Dan R. MacDonald released two 78s on the Boston-Irish Copley label, and Johnny Wilmot is also believed to have recorded in duet with Joe Derrane for Copley, although nothing was ever released. Irish-style fiddlers from Toronto, The Yonge Street Fiddlers (Kim Vincent, David Papazian and Steve Jeffries), performed at

the Glendale Festival in 1979; Papazian later settled in Cape Breton, as did another Torontonian, Paul Cranford. Both of these men came to play an important role in spotlighting the Irish-music presence in Cape Breton and in establishing the Irish-style session (first at Rollie's, North Sydney) as a viable performance context, albeit adapted to suit Cape Breton ways; other sessions are now found in Sydney. Boston-born Jerry Holland (whose New Brunswick-born father was of Irish-French descent and played Irish and Scottish music on fiddle) was brought up in a Cape Breton community but where Irish music was very much present; he maintained an interest in Irish music throughout his life and has long been familiar to Irish musicians, many of whom play a number of his compositions.

exchanges. Cape Breton was little known in Ireland until 1991, not least because only a handful of recordings were available (on the U.K.-based Topic and the Ontario-based Brownrigg labels, and some on Rounder), mostly through only one outlet, Claddagh Records in Dublin. One group of Donegal fiddlers had previously been in Cape Breton, Meath, Ireland-based fiddle player Tony Smith had also visited with his family, and Kerry fiddler, Máire O'Keeffe, spent time there and occasionally played Cape Breton fiddle music on *The Long Note*, an RTÉ radio show she presented; a film crew with personnel from Ireland had also filmed Cape Breton players at home in the 1980s, making the documentary film *The Magic Fiddle*. Mike MacDougall played in Dublin and Meath during a trip in the 1960s and Winston Fitzgerald and John Allan Cameron visited Killarney, Co. Kerry, in the 1980s as part of the Pan-Celtic Festival; Jerry Holland made his first visit in 1991, when he played at Mother Redcaps in Dublin's Liberties area. Since that time, exchanges between Ireland and Cape Breton have become much more common, and in 1993, as part of the Éigse na Laoi Festival at University College, Cork, which celebrated the music and dance of Cape Breton Island, a group of 15 performers were invited to participate, with 30 or more players, dancers and supporters from Cape Breton and Boston coming to join in also. The event was recorded by Nimbus Records and subsequently released on CD. Many Cape Breton musicians have returned to Ireland to perform at various festivals and events in the interim, among them The Barra MacNeils, who were supported by the Irish state agency Music Network, to do a nation-wide tour in the mid-1990s and, in 2007, retuned as a headline act at the ESB *Beo* Festival at the National Concert Hall, Dublin. Tommy Basker, Paul Cranford, Paul Mac-Donald and Ryan MacNeil were among the first Cape Bretoners to attend Scoil Samhraidh Willie Clancy at Milltown Malbay, Co. Clare (the major Irish-music summer school); by 2014, Leanne Aucoin was teaching step dance at the school; indeed, Scoil Samhraidh Willie Clancy partnered with the Gaelic College in 2004 to host a week of Irish music and dance workshops there. Cape Breton fiddlers have appeared at many of the major Irish music events such as those organized by Cairdeas na bhFidléirí in Co. Donegal (Boyd MacNeil) and at Fleadh Cheoil na hÉireann as well as at the 2012 North Atlantic Fiddle Convention held in Derry and Donegal. A number of these performances have been documented by RTÉ (the Irish national radio and TV service), on programs such as *The Pure Drop* (1993), and on TG4, the Irish-language TV station; in 2007, Manus Maguire (who along with his brother Seamus Maguire) has long been a supporter of Cape Breton music organized a tribute night for Cape Breton fiddler Jerry Holland, testimony to the impact that fiddler has had on the Irish tradition; This was broadcast by TG4 as *Oíche do Jerry Holland*. Irish connections have been furthered through the presence of Irish faculty and students at St. FX in Antigonish, who spent much of their time in Nova Scotia attending and participating in events around Cape Breton; among these are Clare concertina player and academic, Gearóid Ó hAllmhuráin and Irish-American concertina player Rory Ann Egan. Connections between Cape Breton and Irish-Americans accelerated during the 1980s, when events such as the Washington Irish Festival brought both communities of musicians together; Seamus Egan and Eileen Ivers were among those who had a significant impact on young players like Natalie MacMaster, who subsequently incorporated many of Ivers's variations and stylings into her playing; Egan's *A Week in January* (1990) is a collaborative effort with Cape Breton musicians, including Hilda Chiasson on piano and Dave MacIsaac on guitar. The dance tradition has also seen connections being fostered; notably at the 1993 Cork-Cape Breton event: a Cape Breton ceilidh was held, alternating Cape Breton and Irish square sets, with musicians from both areas taking turns to provide the music. In 1996 and 1997, Natalie MacMaster and Ashley MacIsaac toured with the Chieftains, as did The Cottars and Slàinte Mhath later. The Chieftains' album *Fire in the Kitchen* features many collaborations with Cape Bretoners, including The Rankins, The Barra MacNeils, Ashley MacIsaac and Natalie MacMaster. In 2009, Celtic Colours celebrated the Ireland-Cape Breton connection by introducing, as its first festival theme, *The Irish are Coming*, as a reciprocal event to Cork 1993; Celtic Colours continues to foster this connection with Ireland and the Irish-American community.

research. While a number of scholars have researched and written about the Irish in Cape Breton (Donovan 1999; Punch 2009), the music has received little scholarly attention in this context; the only published material to date is an essay by Paul MacDonald in *The Irish in Cape Breton* (1999); MacDonald is pursuing research on this topic. However, 2 PhD dissertations on Cape Breton music and dance have come from students at the University of Limerick. Swedish-born dancer Mats Melin's 2012 thesis deals with Cape Breton step dance; he teaches Cape Breton step dance at the University of Limerick, and a number of his students have spent Erasmus periods of study at CBU. Earlier, in 1996, Liz Doherty's PhD thesis was on the topic of Cape Breton fiddle music. Fintan Valley also did comparative research in Cape Breton for his study of traditional music and identity (*Tuned Out*, 2008).

musicians. One of the earliest Irish players identified to date in Cape Breton is John Burke, an uilleann piper; born in Ireland in 1821 he resided for a time in the Lingan area before moving on to the mainland. Among the few Cape Breton fiddlers to be considered as having an Irish style were Henry Fortune (1866-1935) and his uncle Billy (1824-1901), both from Bras d'Or in Cape Breton's Northside area; the Fortunes were of Acadian descent and married into Irish families. Connected to the Fortune family, Joe Confiant was known for his ability to straddle both Scottish and Irish styles and tunes, something for which his nephew, Johnny Wilmot, later became well known. Wilmot influenced many other Northside players such as Robert Stubbert and his daughter Brenda, and Larry Parks; he played often with Tommy Basker, a popular step dancer and Irish-music-style harmonica player. Other players known for their favouring of Irish tunes included such as Hughie Jackson, piano player John Willie Morrison, Jerry Holland, Dougie MacDonald, Natalie MacMaster, and the MacNeil family from Sydney Mines, who went on to form The Barra MacNeils and Slàinte Mhath. From the outset, the Barra MacNeils, while maintaining the fiddle-piano combination of Cape Breton as their core sound, have demonstrated an Irish influence from bands such as the Chieftains, the Bothy Band and Planxty, in their instrumentation and arrangements and, less frequently, in their choice of tunes. Earlier in the 20th century, the fiddle community known collectively as the Lingan fiddlers was considered to have a strong Irish influence on their music.

style. While Irish tunes and songs certainly contributed to the Cape Breton repertoire, it was very rarely that the style was adopted. A somewhat random instance is an early recording of Inverness fiddler, Dan J. Campbell, playing the hornpipe, "Flea as a Bird," which he models on the playing of James Morrison, a Sligo fiddle player who was based and recorded in the U.S. during the early years of the 20th century. Some players do incorporate Irish bowing patterns (usually slurs) in their playing, and some use ornaments such as the "roll" occasionally (for example Jerry Holland, Brenda Stubbert, Kyle MacNeil, Dougie MacDonald). The Irish influence has also been seen in the tendency, since the late 1980s, to move away from long groups of tunes based around a single tonal area to more frequent modulations. Occasionally a snatch of the Irish approach to spontaneous variation in tunes may be heard but, in line with the common Cape Breton ethos, such variations tend to be worked out in advance rather than being created in the musical moment; an interesting insight into the difference in approach regarding this element of the creative process is heard in Natalie MacMaster's recording of "The Dawn" on her *Four on the Floor* album (1989). While this attracted some attention in Cape Breton, at the time being flagged as moving away from the value of correctness and adhering to a set musical line, MacMaster had, in fact, replicated a spontaneous performance by New York fiddler, Eileen Ivers, widely circulated in a private recording named "The Turning Point"; what had been a spontaneous artistic expression by Ivers became a fixed model for MacMaster; yet this was still perceived as being beyond the bounds of what was deemed acceptable in terms of the local canon. [**Caplan 1989, 1991; Doherty 1994; Donovan 1999; MacDonald 1999; Vallely 2008**].

Irwin, Eddie. (1940-1997). Piano. Cambridge, MA. The son of Mary and Alexander Irwin his family roots are both Cape Breton and Irish. His father, whose parents were from Co. Tyrone, Ireland, was born in Cambridge, MA. His maternal great-grandfather, John Cash, immigrated to Cape Breton from Waterford, Ireland, in 1826. His mother, Mary, was born into the Cash family in Irish Cove, Cape Breton, and later moved to Boston with many of her family members; she was a piano player who played in both Irish and Cape Breton circles. Irwin learned to play piano in the Cape Breton style, taught by his mother who also introduced him to the music of Irish American, Dan Sullivan. He played often at dances and house sessions around Boston; besides performing as part of a regular duo with Bill Lamey he also accompanied fiddlers such as John Campbell, Angus Chisholm and Joe Cormier, with whom he recorded for Rounder.

Island Echoes (*Mac Talla an Eilean*). The first Gaelic-language program to be broadcast on CBC Radio. First aired for just fifteen minutes in May 1971, it was the outcome of a campaign to encourage CBC to broadcast a Gaelic program and to build on connections already made with BBC Scotland, which had been recording in Cape Breton for several years. Early hosts were Hugh MacKenzie (who died in 1971 after being on air for 6 months) and Norman MacLeod (who died after presenting only a single episode); Rosemary Hutchinson (McCormack) from the Outer Hebrides, and working at the Fortress of Louisbourg at the time, took over. She expanded the show from its original 15 minutes to a longer presentation; broadcast on Saturday mornings, it featured fiddle and song recordings, the host's own fieldwork materials and invited guests. The show was challenged in 1973 in what came to be known as "The *Island Echoes* language debate": Scottish-born Lister Sinclair, a senior executive at CBC had proposed that the show might be expanded to include one of Canada's official languages, a position that was further strengthened in light of the fact that Canada had recently introduced a multiculturalism policy (1971) and growing support was emerging for the notion that no single European culture should be valorized over any other. The issue made it all the way to the Canadian parliament in Ottawa; however, a lobbying campaign and international media attention led to the decision being reversed, with Liberal MP and Inverness County-native Allan J. MacEachen emerging from the controversy as the defender of the Gaelic language. For a while the show continued as it had been, although McCormack took a break from it at that time before returning in the 1980s. Several other personalities hosted the show in the interim, most notably Kay MacDonald (1921-2014), who made it bilingual (Gaelic and English) and steadily built an audience for over a decade in what is considered by some as the heyday of the show; other guest presenters included BBC Gaelic broadcaster John Alick MacPherson, scholar Norman MacDonald and Dr. Robert Morgan from CBU. In 1992, with McCormack once again the host, the program moved to a Saturday-evening primetime slot, but presented in English and with some feature interviews only in Gaelic; it was picked up by Radio Canada International in the 2000s and today it continues its popular, weekly, one-hour, Saturday-evening airings hosted by Wendy Bergfeldt. (*With* WB) *See* **radio.**

J

Jewell, Marianne. (1948-2014). Piano, fiddle, teacher. Milwaukee, WI and Mabou, Cape Breton. Born in the U.S. to Lee and Margaret (Johnson) Jewell, Marianne studied piano and violin growing up, becoming interested in Cape Breton music while a student at Evergreen State College, WA. This was the topic for her senior thesis as part of her degree in ethnomusicology and she spent several months in Cape Breton conducting research. She later moved to Mabou and became a sought-after piano and fiddle teacher. She also recorded with Cape Breton fiddlers such as Fr. Angus Morris and Rannie MacLellan on Rounder's *Traditional Fiddle Music of Cape Breton, Volume 1: Mabou Coal Mines* (2002) and is featured on Mary Jane Lamond's *Orain Ghàidhlig* (2001).

jig. A tune-type typically in 6/8 time. It likely originated in England in the 16th century and became popular in European art and folk music circles. During the 17th century the tune and associated dance made its way to Ireland and Scotland, where it was widely popularized. In Ireland, a letter from Sir Henry Sidney to Queen Elizabeth in 1569 refers to the jig being danced by the Anglo-Irish ladies of Galway; it was next mentioned in 1674 when the Archbishop of Dublin condemned the dancing of "giggs and countery dances" in taverns. Many of the jigs popular in Ireland today (known as either jig or double jig) are native in origin and date from the 18th and 19th centuries. In Cape Breton, while examples were likely to have existed in the earliest repertoires, the jig was only widely adopted toward the end of the 19th century in order to accommodate the new square sets which were introduced ca. 1890 from the north eastern U.S. where they had been imported from Europe; such dances were popular among the Irish in the dances halls in Boston and in this environment were encountered, adopted, and adapted by Cape Bretoners. Irish jigs were popular initially, although Cape Breton composers soon created their own. In this regard the jig has come full circle, with a number of Cape Breton examples such as "Stan Chapman's Jig" by Jerry Holland and "Peggy's Jig" by Mike MacDougall now popular among Irish players. Today, jigs are considered a staple of the Cape Breton fiddle repertoire, and they are the largest tune-type body after the reel and strathspey; indeed in a number of printed collections—such as those by Dan R. MacDonald, Kinnon Beaton, Dan Hughie MacEachern and Brenda Stubbert—jigs form the

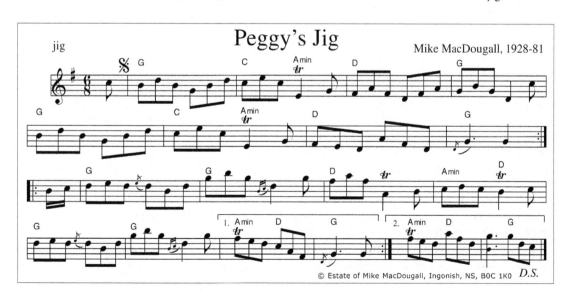

Peggy's Jig

Mike MacDougall, 1928-81

© Estate of Mike MacDougall, Ingonish, NS, B0C 1K0

largest tune-type category. But in younger players' collections they are not so prominent.

use. Jigs are used for square sets and in listening or presentational contexts. In the past, jig tunes accompanied specific solo dances, but since these dances disappeared over the course of the 20th century, the jig is no longer common in the context of solo step dancing; dancers such as Melody Cameron have begun to engage with it again in recent times and it has long been a favourite of Alexander MacDonnell. The two most common square dances – The Mabou Set and The Sydney Set – use several jigs played together in a medley; the former requires jigs for Figures 1 and 2, and the latter for its first figure only. Buddy MacMaster was particularly highly regarded as a jig player, and thus was in great demand for playing square dances. In listening contexts, the jig tends to be presented in a number of ways: (a) in a medley made up exclusively of jigs as for the square sets, (b) occasionally alongside other 6/8 tunes such as a marches or quicksteps, or (c) very occasionally in combinations involving tunes of different metres (e.g., jig-reel, jig-strathspey).

style. The jig is a dance tune consisting primarily of 2 groups of 3 eighth notes per bar. In Cape Breton it is typically played anywhere between a moderate to a sprightly tempo. The Cape Breton fiddler has a distinctive approach to both choosing and playing jigs. In terms of choice, the preference is for a melody in which the regular run of eighth-notes is broken up by longer notes; thus the note content is not quite as dense as that favoured in some other traditions. This was particularly true of older jigs associated with Inverness County players and is a characteristic that is found in many recent Cape Breton compositions. Indeed, the style of jig favoured by the Cape Breton fiddler is almost a hybrid between the 6/8 double jig and the 12/8 "single" jig or slide (which has a more pervasive presence of the quarter-note to eighth-note rhythm). The first note of each 2-bar phrase is typically lengthened, and is often emphasized by some form of ornamentation such as a grace-note or vibrato. The groups of eighth-notes are played with a slight dotted-rhythm ap-

plied, creating a measured, yet bouncy, feel to the tunes and, ultimately, a distinctive Cape Breton swing.

jig family. Other forms of the jig are the slip-jig (9/8), single jig (6/8) and the slide (12/8). In Cape Breton these variants appear only rarely in the repertoire; this is because they have no function within the step or square dancing traditions (in that there is no specific dance in Cape Breton associated with them); single-jigs and slides may, occasionally, be interpreted as jigs; slip-jigs, however, are found only in listening contexts. Many contemporary fiddlers will have some of these jig variants in their repertoires; published examples are to be found in collections by Jerry Holland and Paul Cranford, while others such as Ashley MacIsaac, Mac Morin and Còig have recorded them. [**Vallely 2011; Graham 2006**].

jigging. A form of mouth music found in Cape Breton, particularly in the past, where dance music is performed vocally, mostly using nonsense syllables. This is the equivalent of what is termed "lilting" in the Irish tradition. Jigging is an extemporized form of music and is distinct from the form known as *puirt-a-beul*. Jigging was a common way in which tunes were taught and women, in particular, were often noted for passing on repertoire in this manner.

John Allan Cameron Show, The. A 17-week TV show started in 1975 on CTV following his leaving of the CBC *Ceilidh* Show in 1973. One of three programs in a music series called *Trilogy*, Cameron's was a half-hour variety show devoted to the Scottish and Irish music traditions of the Maritimes. It was through this show that The Cape Breton Symphony Fiddlers was assembled (originally as part of the pilot show), under the musical direction of Scotsman, Bobby Brown. The show moved to CBC for the 1979-1981 seasons. *See* **Cameron brothers; Cape Breton Symphony Fiddlers; CTV; CBC; television.**

Juno Awards. Presented annually to Canadian music artists and bands to acknowledge their artistic and technical achievements in all aspects of music, the Juno Awards are named in honour of Pierre Juneau, the first President of the Canadian Radio-Television and Telecommunications Commission and former President of the CBC. Following a less formal system started by *RPM Magazine* in 1964, the Junos were established in Toronto in 1970 as The Gold Leaf Awards. Re-named the following year, their base remained in the city until 1991; since then they have been hosted in various locations; the closest the awards have come to Cape Breton was Halifax, Nova Scotia in 1996. They are held in the March/April period as the culmination of a week-long celebration of Canadian music; the event has been televised nationally since 1975, and is now broadcast internationally. Juno Award winners are chosen by members of the Canadian Academy of Recording Arts and Sciences (CARAS) or by a panel of experts, depending on the award. Nominations are made by musicians or their representatives and winners receive trophies with a design commissioned from Ontario artist Shirley Elford. Cape Breton musicians who have been recognized with Juno awards include The Rankin Family, Ashley MacIsaac and Natalie MacMaster while others such as The Barra MacNeils and J.P. Cormier have received nominations. *See* **awards.**

K

Kennedy, Ronald. (1870-1958). Fiddle. Broad Cove Chapel. One of the earliest known left-handed fiddlers, he was admired as both a dance player and a listening player and was among the first to successfully straddle both performance contexts. He is remembered for his winning of fiddle contests held during the 1920s and for his use of various scordatura tunings. [**MacGillivray 1981**].

Kennedy, Willie. (1925-2014). Fiddle. Kenloch. Born to parents Danny Michael Kennedy and Euphemia MacAllen, he grew up surrounded by music. His father (d. 1954) was a fiddler who teamed up with Jack MacQuarrie, a neighbour, to play for local dances; his uncle, Joe Kennedy, contributed a number of compositions to MacQuarrie's 1940 *Cape Breton Collection of Scottish Melodies*. His mother's uncle was Ronald Kennedy, a fiddler in the early decades of the 20th century; his aunt, Mary C. Gillis of New Waterford, also played fiddle, as did his brothers Alex and Roddy. He began on a tin fiddle purchased from the Eaton's catalogue, going on to learn to play in earnest at the age of 10, picking up tunes he would hear at home and from other local fiddlers such as Malcolm Beaton, Charlie MacKinnon and Sandy MacLean. As a teenager, Angus Allan Gillis invited Willie to "second" with him (i.e., join him as second fiddle) and they spent a summer playing dances at Kenloch Hall; at other schoolhouse dances he teamed up with fiddlers such as John Alex MacLellan, Jack "Malcolm" Gillis or Morgan MacQuarrie. As the popularity of square dances and fiddle music waned in the mid-20th century, Kennedy abandoned the fiddle for a decade and a half. On moving to Mabou, he credits Fr. Francis Cameron with encouraging him back to music as, in the wake of the *Vanishing Cape Breton Fiddler* documentary, the priest promoted local fiddlers such as Kenneth Joseph MacDonald, Sandy Cameron and Gregory Campbell. It was

Willie Kennedy, Mabou. Courtesy of Mark Wilson.

the 1990s before Willie began performing again in public, often with Kenneth Joseph MacDonald; he is featured on Rounder's *Traditional Fiddle Music of Cape Breton: The Rover's Return, Volume 2* (2002), and released a solo album on the same label, *Willie Kennedy, Cape Breton Violin* (2002), accompanied by Gordon MacLean on piano. Kennedy's repertoire was mostly older, traditional, dance tunes; his style is distinctive and quite ornate in its left-hand embellishments, with long, fluid bow work; his transition from strathspey to reel is much more subtle and flowing than with many other fiddlers, who bridge this in a much sharper fashion. Kennedy has influenced a number of younger players such as Wendy MacIsaac, and, indeed, his first recorded track was with her on her 1996 album *That's What You Get*. [**Wilson 2002; MacGillivray 1981**].

Kerr Collections, The. During the latter part of the 19th century, James S. Kerr (1841-1893) of Glasgow published several collections of dance music, some of which became extremely popular not only throughout Scotland, but throughout the Scottish- and Irish-influenced music world. Not much is known about the compiler or the publishing house, save that the books were issued from 1875 on, most notable of which is *Kerr's Collection of Merry Melodies for the Violin,* in four volumes, with Scottish, Irish and North American music. In Cape Breton these books were affordable and accessible – more so than some of the other tune books – and as such came to be widely used by the fiddle community.

key. This is the scale in which a tune is played. In Cape Breton parlance, groups of tunes built around a single tonal area are referred to as being "on" or "in" a particular key. Within this, individual tunes may be within a particular scale or mode. The range of keys used by Cape Breton fiddlers has expanded over time. While there were always exceptions, many of the early fiddlers had a limited number of keys in which they performed; much of this likely links to the bagpipes as a source of repertoire, since the range of keys possible on that instrument was limited. However, players such as Hugh A. MacDonald, Mary MacDonald, Donald John "the Tailor" Beaton and Dan J. Campbell were among those known for their ability to play in more unusual keys. Others such as Sandy MacLean, "Big" Ranald MacLellan, and Johnny "MacVarish" MacDonald were noted for their skill in transposition, being able to play any single melody in a variety of keys. Certain keys such as B flat were regarded as particularly challenging and as such were rarely used, although some players such as Johnny "Ranald" Beaton and "Little" Simon Fraser, in the early 1900s, were particularly noted for being interested in these. While tune books have long been available in Cape Breton, their increased accessibility from the 1940s onward brought the option of exploring other keys to the attention of many of the fiddlers, and the popularizing of such keys as F, B flat and E flat, owed much to the playing of Winston Fitzgerald and Angus Chisholm; Fitzgerald marked tunes in these keys as priorities to learn in any new tune-book he acquired. Fiddler-composers such as Dan R. MacDonald and Dan Hughie MacEachern began to compose tunes in these keys, and

developments in piano accompaniment enabled further expansion of key choices as the piano players became increasingly familiar with music theory and the rudiments of harmony. Today, many Cape Breton fiddlers can play comfortably in a wide range of keys. Though standard practice still entails extended groups of tunes being created around a single tonal area, modulation between keys within a tune group has become a popular alternative over the past 20 years, most likely an influence from contemporary Scottish and Irish bands. [**Dunlay and Greenberg 1996; Graham 2006; Cranford 2013**].

kilt. (a) The distinctive traditional-Scottish and old-Irish form of pleated, wrap-around, lower-body dress for men. Heraldic-style tartan patterning has been used for these, particularly since the mid-1800s, by now rendering the garment an icon of Scottishness, and of clan identity within Scottishness. **(b) Kilt.** A Cape Breton-Newfoundland Celtic rock group formed in Halifax in 1997. Popular on the pub scene initially, and gradually working up to main-stage performances at festivals in Canada and the U.S., the band was modelled, to an extent, on the Newfoundland group, Great Big Sea. Its original members were Tony Ronalds (lead vocal/whistles/percussion), Brennan MacDonald (acoustic guitar/vocals), Brian Buckle (drums/percussion/vocals) and Bonnie Jean MacDonald, who was the band's Cape Breton fiddler; later members included Scott MacFarlane (bass/vocals) and Chris MacFarlane (drums/vocals). The band had two albums: *Kilt* (1997) and *Four in the Crib* (1999), both of which won ECMA nominations. Disbanded in 1999, Kilt re-formed for a short time in 2000.

KitchenFest! / Fèis a' Chidsin! A festival initiated by the Gaelic College in 2014, it is held over a week or more in late June, as such kick-starting the tourist season. Its focus is on presenting Cape Breton music, culture, food and hospitality through more than 100 events spread right across the island.

kitchen fiddlers. A term used within various traditions to refer to fiddle players who are competent, although not regarded as exceptional players. Within Cape Breton the term was sometimes used in the past to identify "ear" players whose playing was regarded as lacking somewhat in correctness, the Cape Breton fiddlers hallmark of quality and authenticity. Kitchen fiddlers had ample opportunity to participate in music life in Cape Breton, particularly at house parties or ceilidhs, as well as occasionally at more high-profile public events in order to "spell off" (i.e., relieve) the "master" fiddler. In the 1970s, as part of the move to marshal substantial numbers of Cape Breton fiddlers into a collective as a statement in response to the insinuation that the fiddle music was "vanishing," those initiating the massed fiddle groups for performance at the Glendale Festivals had no hesitation in incorporating the tier of kitchen fiddlers into their plan, since the focus was on generating critical mass rather than presenting an elite group of star performers. To this day, the CBFA exists as an opportunity for fiddlers of all levels of experience and ability to join forces in a performance context.

kitchen racket. Popular during the early 20th century in Cape Breton, and elsewhere in the Maritimes as well as in New England, as a semiformal, social event held in a family home and involving music, song, dance, stories, food and drink; a small admission fee of perhaps 25 cents might be charged. Kitchen rackets were less dependent on high-quality fiddlers in the way a dance necessarily was, and the term "kitchen fiddler" came into use to refer to fiddlers who could ably contribute to such social events but who perhaps were not in the same league as the "master" fiddlers. Although no longer a specific event, the term kitchen racket is still occasionally used today and understood as being synonymous with ceilidh and house party. *See* **ceilidh; house party; house session.**

knitting needles. An idiophone percussion form used during the early years of the 20th century in a number of traditions, including American old-

Kay (MacEachern) Livingstone plays knitting needles with her grand niece, Jackie Dunn MacIsaac on fiddle. Courtesy of Jackie Dunn MacIsaac.

time music. Knitting needles were tapped on the body of the fiddle as the fiddler played, to provide a rhythmic accompaniment. In Cape Breton the practice was rarely found. Dan Hughie MacEachern's sisters, however, were known to accompany his fiddle music by standing alongside him and striking the body of the fiddle with knitting needles in this way as he played. The technique was demonstrated by Kay (MacEachern) Livingstone to her grand-niece Jackie Dunn MacIsaac's fiddle playing at a concert tribute to Dan Hughie MacEachern during Celtic Colours in 2003.

L

Lakewind Sound Studios. A recording studio set up in 1996 in Point Aconi by musicians and producers Gordie Sampson and Fred Lavery. A multiple ECMA and MIANS Studio of the Year award winner, Lakewind personnel, including engineer Mike (Sheppy) Shepherd, have also won numerous individual and industry awards. Many Cape Breton fiddle albums have been recorded at Lakewind; it is also the partner studio for the Frank "Big Sampie" Sampson Awards which each year facilitate a young, emerging artist to make their debut recording.

Lamey, Bill. (1914-1991). Fiddle. River Denys, Inverness County, and Boston, MA. Born William H. to parents John H. and Margaret (MacLean) Lamey in Inverness County, his family ancestry was Irish on his father's side and Scottish on his mother's. In 1932, six years after the family moved to Sydney Mines, Bill started to play the fiddle, encouraged by his mother, who had a great love for the music, and inspired by fiddlers such as "Big" Ranald MacLellan, Gordon MacQuarrie and Mary "Hughie" MacDonald. He was interested in learning to read music and in accessing tunes through the published collections from the outset, a factor which led to him amassing one of the most substantial and significant personal libraries of fiddle-tune books; this included standards such as Gow, Marshall, MacKintosh, Fraser and Skinner, as well as some less common in Cape Breton, such as the Anderson collection. Lamey acquired many of these

Joe MacLean and Bill Lamey.
Courtesy of Mark Wilson.

tune books from Scotland and in fact it was he who first identified and connected with Grants Booksellers in Edinburgh, Scotland, a key contact for Cape Breton fiddlers and tune book collectors. Lamey developed a reputation for scouring the printed collections, identifying the best tunes and arranging these into settings and medleys. Many of his choices and arrangements have been passed on through subsequent generations of Cape Breton fiddle players, and are considered classics. Lamey was also known for his attention in following notation precisely and was one of the only Cape Breton fiddlers to attempt to replicate the bowings suggested in the printed sources. Moving to Sydney in 1936, he became well known through regular performance on CJCB and CJFX in the 1940s with a group called The Radio Entertainers which included pianist, Lila Hashem and Joe MacLean, on fiddle; the Lamey-MacLean fiddle duo became one of the most highly regarded in Cape Breton music history. With Lila Hashem on piano they maintained a schedule of dance playing during the 1930s and 1940s that included venues such as Nelga Beach and St. Theresa's Hall in Sydney, and halls in other communities such as Big Pond and Christmas Island. In 1938 he played at the first Gaelic Mod at St. Ann's, and in 1948 he won the Premier of Nova Scotia Cup in competition there. During the 1940s and early 1950s he recorded several 78s for the Celtic label, which at this time had opened a recording studio in Antigonish. In 1954, with his wife, Sarah Anne (Sally) MacEachern from Glendale, and family, Lamey moved to Jamaica Plain, Boston, MA, joining the Cape Breton diaspora community. A charter member already of the Cape Breton Island Gaelic Foundation that was formed at St. Ann's in 1938, he joined its Boston branch, where he served as its president for a decade and a half. He promoted Cape Breton music in the city for some 30 years, and organized weekly dances at the Rose Croix and Orange halls for 18 years. His weekly radio program on WVOM provided yet other performance opportunities for Boston-based, Cape Breton fiddlers, sponsoring frequent visits by others such as "Little" Jack MacDonald, Winston Fitzgerald, Donald and Theresa MacLellan, Angus Chisholm, Buddy MacMaster, John Allan Cameron, Joe MacLean, Donald Angus Beaton, Cameron Chisholm, Dan J. Campbell, John Campbell and Mary MacDonald. Many of Bill's performances were recorded at house sessions and, through dissemination of the tapes, he became hugely influential. A collection of his 78 recordings was released by Shanachie in 1979 as *Bill Lamey: Classic Recordings of Scottish Fiddling*, and in 2000 Rounder released a collection of his home recordings: *Full Circle–From Cape Breton to Boston and Back: Classic House Sessions of Traditional Cape Breton Music, 1956-1977*. These provide a valuable sound bite of the Boston-Cape Breton scene and of the Cape Breton-Irish connections that were an integral part of the narrative in the city throughout the 20th century. Popular Cape Breton accompanists are also heard on these albums, such as Lila Hashem, Mary Jessie MacDonald, Eddie Irwin, Doug MacPhee, Margaret MacDonald, Sally Kelly and Mary MacLean Gillis. On them too are Irish musicians Jimmie Kelly on banjo and Jimmie Corrigan on drums. Much can be learnt from Lamey's style and repertoire, for on the recordings is his distinctive snappy bowing technique, his rhythmic strathspeys and reels, and haunting slow airs. Bill Lamey holds the honour of being the first Cape Breton fiddler to formally perform in Scotland, appearing at the Mod in Inverness in 1963. He returned in 1977, but did not play at that time due to the chronic muscle and tendon problems that caused him to retire from public performance the following year. Upon retiring in 1983 from his day job at the Massachusetts Bay Transit Authority, he returned to live in Kingsville, Cape Breton. [**MacDonald and Lamey 2000; MacGillivray 1981**].

Lamey, Doug. (1983-). Fiddle. Boston, MA, and Glendale, Cape Breton. The grandson of renowned Cape Breton fiddler Bill Lamey and Gaelic speaker Sarah Anne (Sally MacEachern) Lamey, Doug grew up in Norton, MA, where he studied Cape Breton and Irish fiddle as well as classical violin at Wheaton College. His influences included such as John Campbell, Jerry Holland, Sandy MacIntyre, Buddy MacMaster (Cape Breton) Seamus Connolly and Tommy Peoples (Ireland), and Alasdair Fraser (Scotland); however, his greatest inspiration was always his grandfather, although he never had the opportunity to hear him play in person. An active figure on the Boston music scene he performed at venues such as Club Passim and the Canadian-American Club in Watertown, and at events such as the ICONS Festival and Boston College Music Festivals; he also recorded with the band Trí in 2009. In 2011 he and his family relocated to Cape Breton; that same year he recorded his first solo album, *A Step Back in Time*, which features his wife, Kaitlin (MacDonald) Lamey, on piano. Living in Glendale, he teaches fiddle and works seasonally at the CMIC in Judique as a performer and archive technician.

Lamond, Mary Jane. (1960-). Gaelic singer. Glendale. Although she spent only four years of her childhood in Cape Breton, otherwise growing up in Ontario and Montréal, Lamond spent her summers visiting her grandparents in Cape Breton and there became interested in the Gaelic language, particularly the songs; she later pursued this interest as a student on the Celtic Studies program at St. FX. Her first recording, *Bho Thir Nan Craobh*, included fiddle music by Ashley MacIsaac; however it was their collaboration on the track "Sleepy Maggie" for MacIsaac's 1995 album, *Hi, How Are You Today?* that brought them national recognition. Since then, Lamond has received many awards and honours for her own recordings, including ECMAs as well as a Juno Awards nomination. As an advocate for the preservation and promotion of the Gaelic language in Cape Breton she has played an important role as a member of the Gaelic Council of Nova Scotia and

Creative Nova Scotia Leadership Council. She has continued to engage directly with the fiddle music through collaborations with such players as Gillian Boucher and Mairi Rankin, and has had musical collaborations with Gaelic singers in both Scotland and Ireland. With fiddler Wendy MacIsaac she has recorded the album *Seinn*, which won a CFMA in 2013, among other accolades.

Lavengood, Kathleen Elizabeth. Researcher, violin. Oregon and Elkins, West Virginia. Although her formal studies focused on classical music, growing up she was interested in folk fiddle traditions and engaged at various points with Irish music, Bluegrass, Scottish and Cape Breton fiddle (participating in fiddle contests and performing at Highland games in the U.S.). While taking graduate studies in ethnomusicology, she was drawn to Cape Breton fiddle music and analyzed the Boulton recordings, which she published in 2004 as *A Journey Through Time and Tradition: Laura Boulton's Discovery of Cape Breton Fiddler Sandy MacLean.* In 2008 she produced a PhD dissertation "Transnational Communities Through Global Tourism: Expressing Celtic Culture Through Music Practice on Cape Breton Island, Nova Scotia," at Indiana University, Bloomington. She spent extended periods living in Cape Breton from 2003 until the completion of her research work, and while there was a regular at the Thursday night Rollie's sessions in North Sydney. She performed at Celtic Colours in 2005, at the Baddeck Gathering Ceilidhs over 2003-2004, and was guest concertmaster with the Cape Breton Chamber Orchestra the following year. *See* **Boulton, Laura; research.**

Le Gabriel Restaurant and Lounge. A Chéticamp venue, that along with its near neighbour, the Doryman tavern, has a long reputation for hosting Cape Breton fiddle matinee events, mostly on Saturday afternoons.

Leadbeater, Mildred. Piano. Glace Bay and Antigonish, NS. Her adoptive mother came from Gillis Point and her father was raised in Grand Narrows, where he had learned music from Rod MacKinnon of Cooper's Pond; it was he who bought Mildred a piano at the age of 9. She took classical lessons with the nuns, but having obtained a book of Scottish tunes she opted for that music. At 10 she met John Angus MacNeil, who taught her to chord to the fiddle music heard nightly in the family home. She first played with Johnny Wilmot in 1936—when she was 16 and he was 20—at a house party; she found Wilmot's Irish music quite difficult to chord to, but his style and approach ensured that she developed as a resourceful accompanist. She married Len Leadbeater and moved to Antigonish, where she hosted her own live, 30-minute, Saturday-night program for a few years on CJFX radio: *Piano Melodies by Mrs. Len Leadbeater;* generally a solo player on this, she took requests sent in by letter. Lloyd MacDonald played for her on a few occasions when at university there, as did Dan Joe MacInnis, Sandy MacInnis and many step dancers. Leadbeater recorded with Johnny Wilmot on CJCB with Robbie Robertson. She now lives in upper Canada. [**MacGillivray 1988**].

Le Blanc, Barbara. (1951-). Dance researcher, teacher. Cap-le-Moine, Low Point, River Bourgeois, New Waterford, and Terre Noire. Despite growing up learning Acadian French, the language of her parents and her home, most of Le Blanc's formal schooling was in English. A self-proclaimed "born-again Acadian," from the early 1980s a renewed interest in her Acadian culture and history led her to research work in Acadian group dances, some of it conducted in collaboration with Laura Sadowsky. She has published widely on the subject and has been involved in producing a number of resources for dance-education purposes. Her MA thesis, "To Dance or Not to Dance: The Case of Church and Group Social Control in Chéticamp" (Laval University, 1986), was completed in the same year she conducted the Inverness Dance Project for the Museum of Man, Ottawa. In 1992 she produced *No Less, No More, Just Four on the Floor: A Guide to Teaching Traditional Cape Breton Square Sets for Public Schools* in collaboration with Mary Janet MacDonald, Betty Matheson, Dianne Milligan and

Dolena Roach (DANS). In 2004 she published *All Join Hands: Guide to Teach Traditional Acadian Dance/ Tous Ensemble: Guide pour l'Enseignement des Danses Traditionnelles Acadiennes* in association with Dance Nova Scotia in Halifax (DANS). Another teaching resource, a guide to teaching 12 Acadian song dances, or *rondes*, is in production. Her current work relates to education and identity issues around drama and theatre as well as cultural institutions such as museums. Her PhD thesis from the History Department at Laval University, Québec, was titled "Ethnologie des Francophones en Amérique du Nord" (1994), and in 2004 she received a Doctor of Letters, *honoris causa*, from Acadia University. A past president of the Fédération Acadienne de la Nouvelle-*Écosse* (FANE), she remains remains involved in dance research and transmission. [**Caplan 1989**].

LeBlanc, Didace. Fiddle. Chéticamp. Although he did not play the fiddle until the age of 25, after he got married, he had heard a lot of music at home over the years. His brother gave him an instrument and he had a number of tapes from house parties featuring players such as Angus Chisholm, Donald Angus Beaton and Winston Fitzgerald. Gordon Côté helped him with the rudiments of note reading and, under the guidance of local music teacher, Medric LeFort, a group of players in the Chéticamp area would get together over the winter months and read tunes from books. Of his own family his children André, Lorna and Kathleen were all musically inclined and became noted musicians. The family home became a favourite spot for musicians and the LeBlanc hospitality was legendary; a key event for 17 years was the house party there that followed the annual Saint-Joseph-du-Moine concert and that attracted many of the island's top players.

LeBlanc, Donny. (1955-). Fiddle, guitar, mandolin, composer. Petit Étang, Cape Breton. Born to parents Joseph and Lucy (Aucoin) LeBlanc he grew up close to the Acadian village of Chéticamp listening to Cape Breton fiddle music played by his uncles Didace and Neil LeBlanc and by his cousin

(second) Arthur Muise. He had also come in contact with local fiddler "P'tit" Placide Odo and, as a child, often imitated him playing. Starting out on the mandolin from the age of 7 he was a teenager when he made the switch to the fiddle, learning tunes by ear initially from both radio and recordings, and later taking music reading lessons from local music teacher, Medric LeFort. His style developed shaped by the styles of those he admired, such as Arthur Muise, Winston Fitzgerald, the Chisholms of Margaree and Buddy MacMaster, some of who played at dances in Chéticamp at the time. He played his first solo at the Glendale concert in 1973; in 1975 he began playing occasionally at the Doryman Tavern in Chéticamp; by 1977 he was playing regular Saturday-afternoon shows there with his cousin André LeBlanc on piano and Gélase Larade on guitar. He has played in Boston, Toronto and New York, and was a member of the group of Cape Breton fiddlers assembled to perform Daniel Goode's "Cape Breton Concerto" along with John Morris Rankin, Howie MacDonald, Brenda Stubbert, Dave MacIsaac, Joey Beaton and Theresa MacLellan in the 1980s. His first album, *Traditional Cape Breton Music*, was released on LP in 1985, followed in 1993 with a CD, *Rosining up the Bow*, with Hilda Chaisson on piano and Paul MacDonald on guitar; more recently he released *Les Reels des Cap-Rougiens* (2002). [**MacGillivray 1981**].

LeBlanc, Placide Patrice (Paddy "Scotty"). (1923-1974). Fiddle. East Margaree, Inverness County. Of Acadian descent, he was born to parents Jim and Margaret (Poirier) LeBlanc. His father often played the fiddle at local dances, and from a young age Paddy took lessons on this instrument and in step dance. He studied music with Prof. James MacDonald of North Sydney, who taught him to read music, and he later learned Highland drumming during his 12 years with the Cape Breton Highland Regiment. A versatile musician, he performed weekly on CJCB-TV with singer Charlie MacKinnon and The Lumberjacks group; he played many dances and also appeared with Winston Fitzgerald on the

Ceilidh TV show. Following a recommendation from Dan R. MacDonald he was approached by George Taylor to record; under the name, "Scotty" LeBlanc he released two albums on the Celtic label – *The Fiddling French Canadian Scot* and *Fiddlin' Scotty LeBlanc* – in the 1950s. He played in Sudbury, Ontario, as well as in Ayr, Scotland, in 1973 (with the Cape Breton Gaelic Society and fiddler Dan Joe MacInnis), where his performances were broadcast by the BBC. He was known for his interest in the published collections as a source for new tunes, and was regarded as having good timing and loud volume. He particularly liked to play in duets with other fiddlers (such as with Wilfred Prosper) or in trios (with Dan Joe MacInnis and Mike MacLean or John Archie MacIsaac and Duncan MacQuarrie). A popular character, who often played tunes at the back of his barbershop in Sydney, he was honoured in compositions by Dan R. MacDonald and Donald Angus Beaton, who, respectively, wrote "The Barber of Spring Road" and "Memories of Paddy LeBlanc." [**MacGillivray 1981**].

left-hand embellishments: *See* **ornament.**

left-handed players. Within Cape Breton there have been a number of fiddle players who are known as "lefties" or left-handed players. These include Ronald Kennedy of Broad Cove, Fr. Colonel MacLeod, Billy Fortune and Archie Neil Chisholm. Among today's fiddlers Kinnon Beaton, Ashley MacIsaac and Kimberley Fraser are well-known players, all left-handed. Of these, Beaton and MacIsaac play with the fiddle strung as normal, while Fraser choses to reverse the order of the strings. A number of guitarists are also left-handed players.

Ley, Bernie. (1917-1974). Fiddle. Little Lorraine, Cape Breton County. Living in Sydney since his teenage years, he there befriended Joe MacDougall, who became his lifelong music partner in one of the most popular twin-fiddle acts in Cape Breton. They began their career playing on Sydney sidewalks, something both their fathers, also fiddle players, had done before them. In the 1950s

they joined Joe Murphy's Swing Band before forming their own duo, Fiddlers Two. They played the local circuit at venues such as Nelga Beach and the Imperial Hall, and later were invited to travel to communities in other parts of Cape Breton, such as Inverness, Lower River Inhabitants and Grand Anse. They were a regular feature on the 1957-1969 CBC-TV show *Don Messer's Jubilee* and, in the 1960s, on the CJCB-TV show, *Cape Breton Barndance*. Renowned for playing round and square dances in a typical down-east style, their repertoire included a number of Ley's own compositions, including "The Waltz Quadrille" and "Debbie's Jig" (which was published in Don Messer's collection). They made a number of commercial recordings, including two 45s (*The Four Jacks* and *On the Road to Boston*) and an LP, *Fiddlers Two* (1965), which featured Calvin Ledrew on guitar and Laurens Ledrew on piano. Ley and MacDougall feature on several anthology recordings on the Banff and Celtic labels (e.g., *16 Great Jigs and Reels* and *16 Country Waltzes*). Bernie's daughter, Florence (Flo), played piano with them from the age of 11 as they maintained a full schedule of public performances and private house functions; music has continued on down the generations with Ley's grandsons, Gordie Sampson (an internationally recognized singer-songwriter and occasional fiddler) and Keith Mullins (a singer-songwriter and drummer who has performed with fiddlers such as Jennifer Roland, Glenn Graham and Rodney MacDonald). Ley also contributed to the professionalizing of Cape Breton music, being one of the founder members of the local musician's union; his daughter, Debbie Mullins, continues to be involved with this today.

lilt. *See* **drive.**

Lingan fiddlers, The. In the Lingan area of eastern Cape Breton in the mid-20th century there was a vibrant fiddle music scene, one that is often not acknowledged in the Cape Breton narrative. Fiddlers there such as Tom Marsh and Vincent MacGillivray were among the local fiddlers involved in a lively house party scene; parties there often lasted for several days and homes such as that of the Marsh's were among the favourite performance venues for fiddlers such as Winston Fitzgerald.

listening fiddlers; listening-to fiddlers. The distinction between fiddlers whose music was for dancing to and fiddlers whose music was for listening to became increasingly evident after 1940; this was due to a significant expansion of the repertoire which came about as post-Second World War access to published collections from overseas was greatly increased; furthermore, there was an increase in opportunities (e.g., on radio and recordings) for players to perform in non-dance contexts, presenting the music as a stand-alone art form. The distinction between such players had, however, been in evidence prior to that, as noted in a number of biographies in MacGillivray's *The Cape Breton Fiddler* (1981). While dance players cultivated a style that was primarily concerned with generating "drive" for the dancers and a repertoire that was strathspey- reel- and jig-based, "listening" players focused more on tone, technique and with a wider array of tune-types, such as the air, hornpipe and clog, which they added to the core repertoire. Their preferred performance involved presentation of the music, where a listening audience would appreciate the nuance of their style and choices of material. Indeed, Cape Breton is often known for having "good listeners," audiences who understand and know intimately the music being played. Certain players became known as either dance or listening-to players but many were equally proficient in both contexts, although they generally expressed a personal preference for one or the other. Winston Fitzgerald, for example, preferred the dance setting, while his contemporary, Angus Chisholm, preferred a listening audience. Today, younger players often prefer such a listening context; this may in part be due to the fact that this is where they find most opportunity to play since, as the local square-dance circuit has diminished, players do not have the same opportunity to engage in dance playing to the extent that previous players had. In fact, the listening context has evolved further into a presentational one, where additional demands (such as working the stage, talking to the audience) have, since the late 1990s, been placed on the player in many contemporary performance environments. *See* **presentational style fiddlers.** [Doherty, 1996; Graham 2006].

Loop. *See* **bowing style.**

M

Mabou Coal Mines-style. A specific style and repertoire that is distinct within Cape Breton; associated originally with the Mabou Coal Mines area of Inverness County, specifically with descendants of Alexander Beaton who emigrated from Skye in 1809, and perpetuated ever since through members of the extended Beaton family. Prominent among them were Donald John "The Tailor," "Johnny Ranald," "Curly" Sandy and Danny Johnny Ranald Beaton; later, in the 20th century, the key players were Donald Angus Beaton and Mary (Beaton) MacDonald; elements of the style are found more recently in the playing of Kinnon and Andrea Beaton, Rodney MacDonald, Glenn Graham, John Morris Rankin and members of the Campbell family; others such as Baroque violinist and fiddler David Greenberg have modelled their playing on this style. The Mabou Coal Mines style is the singular localized style that has been persistently maintained to the present day; other local stylistic clusters became increasingly less defined over the course of the 20th century, ultimately disappearing as clearly articulated entities. That the Mabou Coal Mines style has been the only one of these to be maintained in a robust and cohesive manner is due to several circumstances: the extent of the Beaton family, specifically the number of individuals within it playing fiddles and thus practicing this style right up to the present day, plus the fact that many of these players emerged as "master" fiddlers, bringing further attention to the style. The Mabou Coal Mines style is widely considered as reflecting an "old" Cape Breton sound and, as such, is often described as old style. It is showcased in a number of recordings such as *The Beatons of Mabou* (Rounder, 1978) and on *Traditional Fiddle Music of Cape Breton: Mabou Coal Mines* as part of the North American Traditional Music Series (Rounder, 2002).

style. The Mabou Coal Mines style is often described as the musical expression of the Gaelic language, a claim which many scholars have endeavoured (perhaps not wholly convincingly) to fully substantiate; indeed the descriptor of fiddlers "having Gaelic in their music" is often related to exponents of the Mabou Coal Mines-style. Marches, strathspeys and reels are the dominant tune types; jigs are also found, many of them featuring a rhythmic pattern of a quarter note followed by an eighth note, which creates a very distinctive metrical pulse, further emphasized by slurring across the beat. The style is characterized by a dense musical line, full of left-hand embellishments; many of these are executed in a deliberate and measured fashion so that distinction between the main melody note and the applied ornament is blurred. Drones and double stops abound, creating many passing dissonances that add colour. High-bass tunings for the fiddle were also frequently employed adding to the potential for textural density through ringing sympathetic strings. Intonation generally included a myriad of tonal inflections, many of them influenced by the bagpipe-tuning spectrum (in terms of range and tonality), adding additional colour. The tunes themselves often used mixolydian and dorian modes and, frequently, gapped scales. Various bowed ornaments (e.g., double up-bows) contributed rhythmic interest and complexity to the basic single-stroke bowing pattern. In particular, the technique described as "flying spicatto" (a series of three up-bows articulated in a specific manner) was regarded as a particular thumbprint of the style, and Donald Angus Beaton was considered a master of this. [**Doherty 1996; Dunlay and Greenberg 1996; Graham 2006**] *See* **style, bowing styles, flying spicatto.**

Mac. The first independent record label established by a Cape Breton fiddle player, Winston Fitzgerald, along with Lloyd Taylor, an employee of CJCB, Sydney, in the 1950s. Short lived, it had a small output of three 78s; these and other unissued cuts were later sold to George Taylor of Rodeo Records who released them in 78 and, later, LP format.

MacArthur School of Dance. Based in Sydney since 1997, this dance school is under the directorship of Kelly MacArthur, a champion Highland dancer from Cape Breton, who has competed and performed all over the world. Teaching both Highland and Cape Breton step dance in both traditional and more contemporary forms, the school also has an active performance troupe, the CapeLand Dancers, which consists of top-level dancers from all over Cape Breton.

MacArthur, Lisa. (1977-). Fiddle. Codroy Valley, Newfoundland, Cape Breton, and Halifax, NS. She was introduced to the music of Cape Breton during the 1990s as acts such as the Rankin Family, The Barra MacNeils, Natalie MacMaster and Ashley MacIsaac were enjoying commercial success and attracting a wide and young fan base. Access to Cape Breton music was relatively easy at this time and she began accumulating recordings and magazines, viewing CBC-TV specials and attending concerts, finding an ally in her father, Neil, a fan of Cape Breton and Irish musics, who had a collection of recordings of fiddlers such as Carl MacKenzie, Natalie MacMaster, Buddy Mac-Master, Joe MacLean and Winston Fitzgerald. Deciding that she wanted to give the fiddle a try herself, her father borrowed an old Chinese fiddle from a neighbour and arranged for her to have lessons with Gordon Bennett in Stephenville, NL, who played Cape Breton music. He introduced her to the playing of Cameron Chisholm, Dwayne Côté, Brenda Stubbert, Jerry Holland, Stephanie Wills, Wendy MacIsaac and Jackie Dunn, and through him she met Maudie and Jeanie Hill and Vonnie (Hill) MacDonald, who were important as she began, from a young age, to further her studies of the fiddle music in Cape Breton. She enrolled at the Gaelic College for the entire summer of 1995, an experience out of which she was able to progress her fiddle playing with a variety of tutors, learn note reading, piano accompaniment and step dancing, and to discover and be inspired by a host of players from Cape Breton and Ireland. The following summer she attended both the Ceilidh Trail School and the Gaelic College, and

eventually moved to live in Cape Breton. Her debut CD, *Lisa MacArthur*, was released by Odyssey in 2003; she now plays occasionally in a trio with Paul MacDonald (guitar) and Mario Colossimo (piano).

MacCuaig, Viola. Piano, fiddle. Glengarry County, Ontario, and Dalhousie, Québec. Born to parents Norman B. and Mary Jane (MacMillan) MacRae, she was raised at Lochiel, ON, in an area which had been settled by Scottish emigrants during the late 18th century and in which the Scottish culture and traditions had been maintained. Her mother played piano and her father sang Gaelic songs, and from a young age she attended music classes, gradually emerging as an accompanist to local fiddlers who visited the family home. In 1940 she married Walter MacCuaig and moved to Dalhousie, Québec, where she teamed up with Cape Breton fiddler "Little" Jack MacDonald and became his regular piano accompanist for more than three decades. They played for many years at Bob's Hotel, Dalhousie Station, where Cape Breton musicians visited regularly. Following "Little" Jack's death she joined a local fiddle group, Lochiel Strings in 1982, initially as a piano player and later on fiddle. After her death in 1994, Québec flute player and scholar Jean Duval, composed a lament in her honour, "Farewell Viola," which was performed at her funeral. She was inducted posthumously into the Glengarry Celtic Hall of Fame in 2005 and later, as part of the Lochiel Fiddlers, in 2009.

MacCuspic, Charlie. (1931-2001). Fiddle. Baddeck, Victoria County. Born on Hunter's Mountain, his main music influences came from outside the family and indeed outside of the predominantly Presbyterian Baddeck area where there were few fiddlers. His father played some fiddle, but since the family were sabbatarian Charlie wasn't permitted to play music on the main recreation day, Sunday. He learned by ear, inspired by the music of Joe MacLean, Winston Fitzgerald, Buddy MacMaster and Carl MacKenzie, and became involved with the CBFA with whom he performed. He made a number of recordings, the earliest on cassette, the last, *The Baddeck Gathering*, on CD in 1993. He is also featured on a number of compilations, including *Traditional Fiddle Music of Cape Breton: Bras d'Or House* (Rounder, 2008). **[Wilson 2008]**.

MacDonald, "Little" Jack. (1887-1969). Fiddle, bagpipes, step dance. Judique, Detroit, Dalhousie, Québec and Glengarry County, Ontario. Born to Donald Rory and Flora MacDonald, his parents died when he was very young and he was raised in Judique by his maternal uncle Allan "Tal" Mac-Donnell and his wife, Annie MacMaster. Another uncle, Angus "Hughie" MacDonnell, who lived on River Denys Road, introduced him to music, being a piper and a step-dance teacher whose own four sons – Allan, Archie, Hughie, Alexander – all played fiddle. "Little" Jack and his brother, "Little" Roddy, were taught the fiddle in their home by "Big" Dan Beaton from Mabou. Jack started on a homemade half-sized fiddle, and by the time he was a teenager was proficient enough to join a travelling show, *Home Products and Medicine Man*, travelling to Montréal where he continued his music education and developed basic music notation skills. Following a period in New England he lived in Timmons, ON, before moving in 1923 to Detroit, where he became part of the Cape Breton music scene playing, typically, with a guitarist or with Ann MacNeil on piano, at the Nova Scotia Club of Detroit, the Maritime Club in Windsor and at the various Scottish Societies; he also broadcast regularly on WMBC radio. In the 1940s he moved to Dalhousie, Québec, where he formed a music partnership with piano player Viola MacCuaig. "Little" Jack MacDonald is regarded as a particularly expressive player, who was one of the first Cape Breton fiddlers to emphasize the value of the music as an art form that might be experienced through listening, rather than always being danced to. He had a great interest in the classical violinists Fritz Kreisler and Jascha Heifetz, and was keen to transfer some of the ethos surrounding their performances into his playing of Cape Breton fiddle music. He was particularly renowned for his playing of airs that had only a limited presence in the tradition until then, and certain tunes – such as "Our Highland Queen" – came to be associated with him. In these he found a perfect vehicle for displaying his command of the bow, his confident and sweet tone, and his use of ornamental devices such as vibrato and slides. In his dance music, he was noted for his ability to employ distinctive bowing patterns and embellishments such as the double cut, a thumbprint of his style. Although "Little" Jack did not have a huge impact on Cape Breton music at home during his lifetime (having only returned on a few visits during his 50-year absence), he was a significant figure within the displaced Cape Breton community in the Detroit-Windsor area, and he influenced younger players such as Bobby MacNeil of Dearborn, Michigan. In 1939, he recorded the first of five 78s for the Celtic label, and, in the 1950s, an LP, *The Bard of Scottish Fiddling*; he also is featured on various anthologies of Cape Breton music for the Celtic and Banff labels. **[MacGillivray 1981]**.

MacDonald family of Detroit, Michigan. One of several discrete family groupings of MacDonalds in the Detroit-Cape Breton community, father and daughter John Archie and Barbara (Magone) recorded together and individually.

MacDonald, John A. (Johnny Archie). (1893-1974). Fiddle. Little Judique Ponds, Inverness County, and Detroit, MI. Born in Superior, Wisconsin, to parents J. A. and Florence (Beaton) MacDonald, both from Little Judique, he moved to Little Judique Ponds at the age of seven, following the death of his mother. There was music on both sides of the family. His grandfather, Donald MacDonald was the only fiddler in Little Judique in his day, and played at all local weddings and dances; Donald had passed the music on to his own children, including Johnny Archie's father and uncle, Hugh, who later played frequently with Angus R. Beaton, the father of Donald Angus Beaton. Donald MacDonald's mother and her brother, John Archie Beaton, were also step dancers and singers in both Gaelic and English. In such an immersion it was perhaps inevitable that Johnny Archie would play; as a child he mimed playing the fiddle with two pieces of wood but it was not until he was 17 that he began in earnest, first working alone on the instrument his father had left behind as he headed to California and Alaska in search of work. Though there were no other fiddlers in the Judique area at the time, he heard music at social events such as the July 1 picnics held in Inverness, and he regularly heard fiddlers such as "Big" John Alex MacDonald and Alex Michael MacDonald, who were based in the Port Hood area. Johnny Archie's first public performance was for a local schoolhouse dance in Judique, when he "spelled off" Allan MacDonnell, who was providing the music, unaccompanied; after that he often played at formal and informal dances in the area. In 1921 he moved to Moncton, New Brunswick, then to Detroit in 1924. He had eight children with his first wife (Florence MacKillop, from Judique), who died in 1938, and a further five with Dorothy Hogan (from Medford, MA), whom he married in 1946. Detroit's reputation as a hub of Cape Breton music owes much to MacDonald's playing and promoting of the music and dance traditions, though his full-time profession was actually as a police officer. He organized regular dances to which he invited Cape Breton fiddlers such as Angus Chisholm, Cameron Chisholm, John Campbell, Donald Campbell, Winston Fitzgerald, Donald MacLellan and Buddy MacMaster to perform. He was involved in Scottish concerts there too, from the 1930s to the 1950s, which had fiddlers such as Mary (Beaton) MacDonald, Gordon MacQuarrie, Fr. Hugh Allan MacDonald and Bill Lamey. During the 1920s, "Little" Jack MacDonald stayed with Johnny Archie's family for a time and was a significant influence on his host's music. Sunday afternoon music sessions at the MacDonald family home were a regular occurrence, and were attended by musicians from the Cape Breton community. It was at one of these sessions that the idea for the group, The Five MacDonald Fiddlers, emerged, including, of course, Johnny Archie. It was he who effectively managed the band, liaising with the record company and

acting as musical director, a role he was able to fulfil even though an "ear" player. He had several solo recordings: three 78s on the Celtic label in 1946 (accompanied by Ann [MacDonald] MacNeil of Whitney Pier), and 3 LPs, starting in 1960, for Rodeo Records (accompanied on the first LP by Kathleen [MacMaster] Beaton of Halifax, and by his daughter, Barbara, on the last two).

Magone (MacDonald), Barbara. (1948-). Piano, composer. Detroit and California. She grew up in a home that was the mainstay of Cape Breton traditional music for a substantial transplanted community. Her father was John Archie MacDonald, fiddler and founding member of the Five MacDonald Fiddlers; her mother was Dorothy Hogan, who was of Cape Breton (mother) and Irish (father) parentage; she played piano but passed away when Barbara was 9 years old. Music sessions were a weekly feature of her childhood, and from the age of 5 Barbara was picking out tunes guided note by note by her father; Joan (MacDonald) Boes was her great mentor. Betty Lou (MacMaster) Beaton and her sister, Lorraine, also played roles in shaping Barbara's music, a female mentoring which reflected the gender alignment typical of the 1950s and 1960s, where men played fiddle and women accompanied them on piano. During summers spent in Cape Breton, Barbara accompanied fiddlers at dances and weddings, primarily Buddy MacMaster, Carl MacKenzie, John Campbell and Theresa MacLellan. From there she went on to work as a piano player not only with Cape Breton fiddlers, but with Irish, American and Scottish artists, including concertina player, Gearóid Ó hAllmhuráin, Irish-American fiddle player, Seamus Connolly and Scottish fiddle player Alasdair Fraser. She toured the west coast of Scotland in early 1990s with Alasdair Fraser and Buddy MacMaster as part of *The Driven Bow* tour and Fraser's campaign to champion Cape Breton music in Scotland. MacDonald was an accompanist on the *Masters of the Folk Violin* tours of the U.S. (1988-1990) sponsored by the Smithsonian Institution and the National Council for the Traditional Arts, alongside fiddlers Seamus Connolly, Joe Cormier,

Kenny Baker, Alison Krauss, Claude Williams and Michael Doucet; she was also involved in *The Well*, a theatre production in Dublin, Ireland, by John McColgan of *Riverdance* fame (2001). Based for many years in San Diego, California, she has taught piano at a number of music schools and camps including: Fiddle Tunes in Port Townsend, WA; Valley of the Moon Scottish Fiddling School in northern California; Ashokan Celtic Week in upstate New York and Gaelic Roots at Boston College. Her two solo recordings are *Scottish Piano Selections* (1966) and *The Fiddler's Friend* (1989), the second of which features some of her own compositions; she also accompanies her father, John Archie MacDonald, on his two LPs , the second in the early 1960s, titled *Tribute to the Detroit Scot*. Most recently Barbara has been performing with Dwayne Côté in the U.S. and recorded a CD with Ashley MacIsaac in 2012, *Beautiful Lake Ainslie*. [**MacGillivray 1988**]. *See* **Detroit**.

MacDonald siblings of Foot Cape, New Waterford and Detroit, Michigan. Born to parents Neil R. and Mary (Beaton) MacDonald, brother and sister **Allan MacDonald** (1920-2004) and **Joan MacDonald Boes** (1930-1998) were brought up in a Gaelic-speaking household where English became the order of the day only after the children began to attend school. They became known as fiddle and piano players, respectively; a cousin, Hughie MacDonald of West Mabou, who came to live with the family, also played fiddle. Neil R. was a fiddle player who could sight-read and was especially interested in the correct interpretation of tunes and in the process of building tune groups or medleys; Mary played organ, piano and harmonica, and was also a Gaelic singer and step dancer; before she was married, she and her sister, Sarah Catherine, played for dances and she also accompanied some of the legendary Mabou Coal Mines players such as Dan (*Domhnull Iain an Taillear*) Beaton. There were many noted musicians in the area who regularly visited the MacDonald home, including fiddlers Sandy MacLean, "Curly" Sandy Beaton and Malcolm Beaton, and pianist, Lila MacIsaac. When the family moved to New Waterford, in 1937, other musicians they heard often were Mary "Hughie" MacDonald, Lauchie Marr, "Black" Jack MacNeil and Duncan MacQuarrie. After the war, during which Allan was stationed in Halifax with the Canadian Navy, the family relocated to Detroit, where work was plentiful at General Motors. "Little" Jack MacDonald often visited and they would encounter players such as Jack MacDeagle and Bernie and Bobby MacNeil at dances and house parties. Allan and Joan became established as part of the thriving Cape Breton scene in Detroit and were members of the recording group The Five MacDonald Fiddlers, later the Five MacDonalds. Joan was introduced to the piano by her mother, but in Detroit she learned much from Ann MacNeil, "Little" Jack's accompanist, and from "Little" Jack himself, who had strong views on what was expected from an accompanist. Joan attended formal music lessons from a young age and at the Detroit Conservatory of Music as a teenager where, in addition to the classics, she studied popular, boogie and jazz styles. She composed her first tune at the age of 12; her best-known composition is the march, "The Sweetness of Mary," which was popularized by Jerry Holland. She released two recordings: *I Mourn for the Highlands* and *On Foot Cape Road* (as Joan MacDonald Boes), both of which demonstrate her skills as a melody player; as an accompanist she can be heard on recordings of The Five MacDonald Fiddlers; these LPs have been re-released in CD format as *The Five MacDonald Fiddlers with Joan MacDonald Boes*. *See* **Detroit; Five MacDonald Fiddlers**.

MacDonald family of Invernesss and South-West Margaree. Francis "Rory Sis" and Corrine (MacPherson) MacDonald, a husband-and-wife fiddle and piano duo, and their family, including son Roddy, a multi-instrumentalist based in Halifax, and Francis Jr., a film-maker and photographer. Francis Snr. and Roddy together published a collection of music in 2007, *Margaree Melodies, A Book of Original Fiddle Tunes*.

MacDonald, (Joseph) Francis. (1932-2014). Fiddle, pipes, composer, teacher. Born in Inverness and known as Francis "Rory Sis," his parents Rory "Sis" MacDonald and Sara Anne MacLellan, although not players themselves, encouraged music in the home; gramophone recordings were played regularly and his mother often sang. His father's cousin, John Alex MacDonald of Port Hood, played violin, and Malcolm Beaton of Strathlorne was a regular visitor and taught Francis his first fiddle tune, "Hector the Hero," as a teenager. He played by ear initially, until local fiddler Malcolm Burke taught him sight reading; he played first on a fiddle borrowed from a neighbour, listening and learning from players such as Donald Angus MacPherson of Dunvegan, Lauchie Walker (who often substituted for Malcolm Beaton at the dances) and John Willie Campbell from Glencoe, all players who had their own styles, repertoires and settings of tunes. In April 1953, MacDonald joined the army as a piper and following an intensive music-theory course joined the Black Watch Regiment piping unit at Camp Georgetown, ON. He toured and recorded with them, performing on the *Ed Sullivan Show* in the U.S., playing for John F. Kennedy and the British Royal family, and meeting Elvis Presley. He played the fiddle only occasionally through these years, but when he moved to a regular corps in Sydney he connected with the fiddle-playing community again and frequently teamed up with Raymond Ellis, Mac Campbell and Dan Joe MacInnis. He also joined Dan Joe MacInnis and Sandy MacInnis in teaching fiddle at CBU through the Continuing Education Department during the early 1970s. His piping was military in style, and some crossover is evident with his fiddle playing, in particular on marches, where he includes piping-influenced drones and ornaments. His last public performance as a piper was a 1976 telecast of the *Ryan's Fancy Show*; on that same show he played fiddle in a trio with Cameron Chisholm and Angus Allan Gillis. His music literacy led to him becoming an avid collector of tune books and, as was the practice at the time, he would copy out and share particular tunes with other fiddlers. A composer himself of both songs and tunes, throughout his life he played fiddle to the piano accompaniment of Corrine MacPherson, who he married in 1954. The family had moved from Dartmouth, NS, to South-West Margaree in 1973; in the late 1980s, Francis and Corrine moved back to Inverness town, where they had both been born. In 1993, MacDonald released an instructional video for beginner fiddle players, the first of its kind in Cape Breton. [**MacGillivray 1981, 1988**].

MacDonald, Roddy. (1956-). Fiddle, small pipes. He took up the violin as a teenager, learning tunes from his father, Francis, from listening to 78-rpm recordings of Angus Chisholm, Angus Allan Gillis and Bill Lamey, and from perusing the fiddle and pipes tune books which he had access to at home. Composing since 1974, he has made some 250 tunes, some of which appear in the 2007 *Margaree Melodies* collection. In Halifax since the late 1970s, he has performed with bands such as McGinty, Kiltarlity and The Farriers, playing fiddle, guitar, bouzouki and small pipes, and is featured on the 1995 CBC fiddle-music documentary *Heart of the Gael*.

— ∾ —

Margaree Melodies. A Collection of Cape Breton Violin Music Consisting of Original, Traditional and Favourite Tunes Selected and Arranged by J. Francis MacDonald and Rod MacDonald. A 2006, 30-page tune collection with 102 tunes listed in three sections according to type and arranged alphabetically by title; additional information on a small number of tunes is included, with some photographs. There are 36 jigs, 29 reels, 14 strathspeys, 8 marches, 6 slow airs, 6 hornpipes, 2 clogs and 1 waltz. The tunes are loosely arranged according to key, and the scale or mode is indicated in each instance. 57 of the tunes are compositions by piper and fiddler Francis MacDonald, 20 are by his son (fiddler and multi-instrumentalist Roddy MacDonald), and 4 are by his wife, piano player Corrine MacDonald. Of the other newly composed tunes, 4 are by Hugh Murray, 2 by John Ferguson, and one each by Rev. Hugh A. MacDonald, Paul Cranford,

A. Martin MacPherson, Angus MacPherson, Ray Ellis and Neil A. Beaton. The remainder are traditional melodies, some of which are in arrangements by MacDonald. The collection includes the march "Grahame MacDonald of Clan Donald," composed by Francis MacDonald in honour of his cousin who was responsible for promoting Scottish culture for many years in Australia; this tune, arranged by Pipe Major James McConnell, is the signature tune of the Noosa Queensland Pipe Band.

— ≈ —

MacDonald family of Ironville. Fiddle player, Lloyd MacDonald and his wife, Winnie, a piano player, had 12 children, many of whom have gone on to pursue careers in music within the Cape Breton, Irish and classical traditions. The family formed a band, Scumalash, in the early 1980s; together they recorded an album in 1992 and toured internationally, performing at festivals, folk clubs and theatres all over Europe, Canada and the U.S., including the Edinburgh Fringe Festival, Festival Inter-Celtique Lorient, Douarnenez Folk Festival, the Inverness Dance Festival and the Goderich Celtic Roots Festival.

MacDonald, Lloyd. (1931-2013). Fiddle. Born on the Gannon Road to parents James R. MacDonald, Beechmount, and Belle (Gouthro) MacDonald, Frenchvale (both in Cape Breton County), he was only a few months old when his father died in the Florence coal mine. When his mother then became ill he was taken to live with his aunt Elizabeth (Lizzie) MacDonald and her husband, John (Jack) MacDonald, in Ironville; later they moved back to North Sydney and lived next door to Lloyd's mother and his older siblings Hector and Sylvia. His father, James, had played violin, as did his brothers Murdoch and Hector; their ancestors were from Barra, Scotland, but it was not until the late 1800s, generations later, that there was evidence of music in the family, when Lloyd's great-grandfather James married into the MacKinnon family of MacKinnon's Harbour and Cooper's Pond, a very well-known musical family. Lloyd's step-parents both encouraged him in

music; Lizzie was recognized as a great lilter of fiddle tunes, while Jack was a Gaelic speaker and historian. Lloyd studied violin with Prof. James MacDonald, developing into a proficient musician. By the late 1930s he was winning contests at the Gaelic College in fiddle and highland dancing; by the 1950s he was involved in a weekly radio show on CJCB, with Mildred Leadbeater on piano, and he also took part in music productions in Antigonish when he attended St. FX. He worked in the automobile sector, as a Nissan dealer – hence his nickname "Tokyo Lloyd." His business success was honoured by the Cape Breton Business Hall of Fame in 2006 and by CBU with an honorary doctor of laws in 2012. Although for a number of years he concentrated on his business he encouraged his young family to play sending them to lessons with Mary Gillis and Prof. Jimmy MacDonald; when his son, Shawn, took up the fiddle Lloyd himself was once again inspired to play. As well as performances with the family band, Scumalash, he gave instruction at Cape Breton fiddle workshops worldwide and was invited to judge Scottish fiddling competitions in Canada, the U.S. and in Scotland. At the age of 80, he released a solo album titled *Aires in Bloom*, in 2011, one of the very few Cape Breton recordings to focus primarily on airs and slower pieces, demonstrating his ability in marrying his classical training with the Cape Breton fiddle style. He was also the first Cape Breton fiddler to explore the music of the Shetland Islands, having encountered Aly Bain and Boys of the Lough in Mabou in the 1980s; he and Shawn later studied with Tom Anderson at Stirling University, Scotland in 1983 and subsequently introducing many Shetland and modern Scottish tunes into the Cape Breton repertoire. In his later years he and his wife visited Ireland often, playing at various events such as Fiddle Fair in Baltimore, Co. Cork.

MacDonald, Winnie. (1934-). Born to Archie and Ethel MacDonald from the North End of Sydney, her grandfather, Angus "Scumalash" MacDonald, from Gillis Lake, East Bay, was a well-known figure in the Sydney area; he was a founding member of the Scottish Catholic Society and was involved in presenting Gaelic plays there. Her father, Archie, played harmonica and guitar and sang folk songs. Her mother, who had been raised by John and Ethel Coakely from Florence, sang in blackface minstrel shows in Sydney and played tenor banjo. Along with her sisters, Winnie received piano training from the Sisters of Notre Dame at Holy Angels in Sydney's North End. She became a school teacher and, having married Lloyd MacDonald, encouraged all of their children to pursue music lessons. When Lloyd returned to the fiddle she began working on piano accompaniment and had ample opportunity to play as the children became proficient and the family band, Scumalash, emerged. She continued to maintain an active interest in classical music, specifically working as a fund-raiser with the Nova Scotia Youth Orchestra in Halifax to create opportunities for young Cape Breton musicians. She returned to university in the 1960s to study folklore and history and, along with Joe L. MacDonald, completed research on the Gaelic bards of Boisdale and Ironville and their narrative songs; she had also been involved in church music in the local parish and, at 84, has recently taken up the cello.

MacDonald, Paul. (1959-). Guitar, recording engineer, researcher. Born in North Sydney, Paul (the third-eldest son, after Jim and Chris) was ill as a child and was cared for by various family members, which led to him, inadvertently, being exposed to a range of musics, from the lilting of his father's aunt Lizzie to the playing of Mike MacDougall and Tim Donovan, who he heard in Ingonish while staying with his father's brother, Fr. Hector MacDonald; Hector himself was a guitar player and singer of Irish ballads; another uncle on his mother's side was Sid Martell, the yodeler and singer who recorded for the Celtic label. Paul took guitar lessons with Prof. Jimmy MacDonald, who encouraged him to develop his natural improvisation skills; he learned to read by playing trumpet in a marching band in North Sydney; along with his older brothers, he had an interest in contemporary rock music. When his father returned to playing the fiddle, Paul, with a 12-string guitar, began accompanying him to various fiddlers' gatherings, although his interest in that scene was short lived and he turned to the electric guitar. At the age of 21 he was introduced to jazz music (incidentally at the Glendale fiddle festival) and shortly after enrolled on the jazz program at St. FX. In 1984 he moved to Boston, then to Halifax, ending up in Montréal in 1986; although still focused on avant-garde jazz he had increasingly become interested in Celtic guitar stylists, and in Montréal encountered his first Irish music session with such players as David "Papper" Papazian, Kim Vincent, the Laport brothers and the Marchands. He immediately recognized in Irish music a potential freedom where his creative improvisatory skills might develop. Having visited Scotland and England with the family band, Paul found himself based back in Cape Breton in 1987 where he met Tommy Basker, who he credits as his "professor" of Irish music; Basker encouraged him away from contemporary commercial releases and introduced him to 78s and home recordings, and MacDonald became fascinated with the piano accompaniment of Dan Sullivan and guitarist Whitney Andrews. By 1989 he was back living in Cape Breton, hungry now to learn about his local music tradition and drawn, in particular, to those he considered improvisers, such as Johnny Wilmot, Alex Currie and Tommy Basker. Befriending Paul Cranford, the two spent months travelling around the island meeting musicians; MacDonald also began to study piano; he was most interested in an Irish style based on the playing of Dan Sullivan and Charlie Lennon, although in Cape Breton his piano hero was unequivocally Mary Jessie MacDonald. In the 1990s, he travelled to Ireland on several occasions with various other Cape Bretoners and met and played with Irish musicians such as Sean Maguire, Sharon Shannon and Máire O'Keeffe; since 2010, he has made many return visits. He also spent time in Boston and became involved in the Irish scene there, recording and touring with such as Joe Derrane, Frank Ferrel and Brendan Mulvihill. His interests also extended to other traditions including U.S. old-time and Danish folk music.

guitar. Irish guitar player, Arty McGlynn introduced him to drop D tuning in the late 1980s and MacDonald has maintained this ever since. However, his preference is for more closed chords, bar chords, and substitution chords rather than the open fingering style most Cape Breton and Irish guitarists use. His influence came mostly from piano players and he focuses on melodic embellishments and bass lines. He has recorded with Irish and U.S. musicians and, in Cape Breton, has played with Otis Tomas's Fiddletree ensemble, the POE Trio, Scumalash, Rocky Shore and in duos with his brother Dan on fiddle and with John MacLean on bagpipes; a recent ensemble is with Lisa MacArthur on fiddle and Mario Colosimo on piano.

recording. Interested in recording engineering from a young age, it was the 1980s when MacDonald became interested in recording fiddle players; his first project was with Paul Cranford, recording 22 Cape Breton musicians for the release, *A Tribute to Dan R. MacDonald.* Using the same 14-bit PCM machine he also began his first digitization projects, editing some of Cape Breton's classic home recordings. A conversation with Carl MacKenzie about the quality of new versus old recordings led him to reimagine aspects of the recording practice; his recording of Jerry Holland from a farm house on the North Shore (released as *A Session with Jerry Holland*) met with much local acclaim for its natural acoustic properties. He further studied this area of sound production in Ireland with Harry Bradshaw, a leader in the field, returning to Cape Breton where he began recording fiddlers using a portable DAT player and exploring multiple spaces to identify the best possible acoustics. He worked with a number of players, and established a method and a sound that was unique. In 1995 MacDonald started to work for Rounder Records alongside Dr. Toby Mountain, a highly regarded engineer and audio research expert; they worked with the Sonic Solutions desktop system, mastering CDs on computer. Inspired by the work of jazz sound engineer Pierre Sprey in Washington, DC – particularly the high resolution and realism ach – ieved through using pressure zone mics (PZM)—MacDonald sought him out and together they worked on sev-

eral recordings from 2000 to 2004 for Mapleshade Records. MacDonald has used this PZM microphone ever since, and has recorded many Cape Breton fiddlers such as Jerry Holland, Natalie MacMaster, Brenda Stubbert and Mike Hall, as well as others for the online project, Cape Breton live. Remastering old recordings has been another passion; early examples of his work in this area include *Mike MacDougall's Tape for Fr. Hector* and other recordings for *Cape Breton's Magazine*; later having developed his technique in this area he worked on several projects for Rounder Records (e.g., Bill Lamey's *Full Circle* CD) and others such as *Here Comes John Allan Cameron*; he is currently working on Winston Fitzgerald material which he had convinced Holburne Records to house at the Beaton Institute. His digitization portfolio includes home-recording collections by such as Doug MacMaster, Herbie MacLeod, Neil MacDougall; he also worked on Gaelic collections by such as Ralph Rinzler and John Shaw and was involved in the preliminary work for the Gaelstream website at St. FX.

scholar. Although not a Gaelic speaker – and misunderstood at times by the Gaelic community for his reluctance to personally embrace the language – MacDonald is unique in his position as a scholar who has extensive experience and familiarity with the various Gaelic song collections in Nova Scotia; his explorations and observations are unique in that he has approached the songs and singers, not as a linguist, but as a musician; he is interested in their sonic stamp – the discrepancy between each singers' interpretation of the melodic line; this he perceives as being a significant marker of the individual performer, and equally as valid as their Gaelic. In terms of fiddle music, MacDonald has published several magazine articles and liner notes on individual players (e.g., Bill Lamey, John Allan Cameron, Wilfred Prosper) and on wider topics such as the history of the piano.

MacDonald, Shawn. (1969-). Fiddle, violin, viola. Sydney. He started to play the fiddle under the tutelage of his father while taking classical violin lessons from Prof. James MacDonald in North Sydney, and also later in Halifax. He continued his bi-musical journey on fiddle/violin, being involved with the Nova Scotia Youth Orchestra from the age of 12 and progressing to study music at Acadia University while regularly performing with the family band, Scumalash. His versatility as a musician has enabled him to pursue a wide range of activities in Cape Breton that include teaching and studio work, where he is in demand for his improvisatory skills. He performs with a number of bands including the Pub Boys and Privateers and is concert master with the Cape Breton Orchestra. He is featured on several recordings, including the *Celtic Colours Compilation CD* (2004), Lloyd MacDonald's *Aires in Bloom* (2011) and on many Cape Breton country and pop albums. He recorded the underscore for the CBC-TV movie *Pit Pony* (1997) and is featured on the Channel 4 documentary, *The Magic Fiddle* (1991).

MacDonald, Martin. (1977-). Orchestra Conductor, cello, fiddle. Toronto, ON. Bi-musicality was encouraged from a young age as he attended lessons in classical music (cello and piano) locally, in Antigonish and in Halifax, while simultaneously being tutored in fiddle music by his father and Prof. James MacDonald. He was exposed to a variety of fiddle styles through his father's diverse music interests that included contemporary Scottish bands such as Boys of the Lough and Silly Wizard. A full-time, professional musician he is one of a small number of classically trained musicians from the island thus occupied, and possibly the first cellist; furthermore, he is the first and, to date, the only orchestra conductor to emerge from Cape Breton and is currently associate conductor of Symphony Nova Scotia (2013-2015); prior appointments included resident conductor of Symphony Nova Scotia (2008-2011) and associate conductor of National Academy Orchestra of Canada (2006-2008); he is also a guest conductor with several orchestras across Canada. As part of his work with Symphony Nova Scotia, he has conducted collaborative performances with the orchestra and Cape Breton musicians such as The Barra MacNeils, Natalie MacMaster, Ashley Ma-

cIsaac and J. P. Cormier, and was conductor for *The Barra MacNeils and Symphony Nova Scotia: Live in Concert* CD (2011) that won an ECMA. As a performer he is featured on recordings with Scumalash and on his father's CD, *Aires in Bloom* (2011), playing cello.

MacDonald, Dan. (1976-). Fiddle, bodhrán, drums. Toronto, ON. He followed his father and older brother, Shawn, in taking up the fiddle, taking lessons in classical music from a young age and being exposed to the traditional playing of a range of Cape Breton, Scottish and Irish players, including Kyle MacNeil, Jerry Holland, Johnny Cunningham, Aly Bain, Kim Vincent, Frankie Gavin and Michael Coleman; his first public performances were as part of the family band, Scumalash. A graduate of the Jazz Studies program at St. FX, he moved to Toronto in 2003 where he has pursued a full-time career in music. He toured Europe and North America with Irish dance show, *The Magic of Ireland*, for which he acted as musical director for a year; he is also involved in a dance show, *Brogue*, and is a member of a trio, North Atlantic Drift. He offers classes in Cape Breton and Irish fiddle in Guelph, Ontario, and appears on various recordings, including *Scumalash* (1990), *Magic of Ireland* (2008), *Skerries Traditional Music Weekend* CD (2010; 2011), *North Atlantic Drift* (2011), *Aires in Bloom* (2011), *Riverside Celtic College compilation CD* (2013), *Celtic Colours Compilation CD* (2013). MacDonald is featured also in the 2010 CMT movie *Reel Love* and on the 2012 TV show, *Copper*.

MacDonald family of Kingsville. A branch of the extended family of musicians, singers and Gaelic speakers from Queensville, Inverness County, known as the "Dougald" MacDonalds. Alex "Dougald" MacDonald married Kathleen (MacEachen) MacDonald; they settled in Kingsville, where the local community of Bràigh na h-Aibhneadh (Kingsville and Glendale) had a rich tradition of fiddle music, Gaelic language and storytelling, and was also the location for events such as the renowned fiddle festivals in the 1970s. There was music on both sides of the family. Alex played mouth organ and step danced and the "Dougald" MacDonalds included many uncles, aunts and cousins who were musicians or dancers. Kathleen's father, John Alex MacEachen, was a fiddle player who played often at local dances; his father, Angus D., had also been a fiddler. Kathleen herself chorded on the piano, step danced and sang. They had four children, all of whom have carried on various elements of the tradition, maintaining close musical ties with members of the wider "Dougald" MacDonald family such as their cousins, fiddle players Howie, Dougie and Brian. The eldest, Lynne (MacDonald) MacNeil, (1966) is a step dancer and singer and plays piano. Her daughters, Molly and Hannah, are also step dancers.

MacDonald, Jeff / Dòmhnullach, Goiridh. (1967-). Gaelic singer, composer, storyteller, educator. A passionate advocate for the Gaelic language and traditions, the young Jeff's interest in Gaelic song was sparked about the age of 9; he went on to win a gold medal at Mòd Ontario in 1989, then sang in the Gaelic rock group Dàl Riada with his own brothers and the Morin brothers of Troy in the 1990s. He has contributed to documentary broadcasts on Gaelic language and culture in Canada and Scotland, performed at Éigse na Laoi in Cork, Ireland, in 1993, and at Ceòlas in Scotland in 2002; he is also a frequent performer at concerts and other events in Cape Breton, most recently singing alongside his son, Pàdruig. He has researched Gaelic locally, publishing *Dualchas a' Bhràigh – Gaelic Traditions of Glendale and Kingsville*, which includes the names and sloinneadhs of many local singers, storytellers, dancers and musicians of the older generations, and he completed his Masters thesis in Folklore for Memorial University, Newfoundland in 2014. He was curator of www.capebretonceilidh.com, a Cape Breton, Gaelic-culture website which was given a provincial award in 2005, and has worked with the Gaelic-language organizations Comunn Gàidhlig is Eachdraidh a' Bhràigh, Comhairle na Gàidhlig, Highland Village and Taigh an t-Sagairt / The Fr. John Angus Rankin Cultural Centre in Glendale. He is currently employment as Oifigear

na Gàidhlig / Gaelic Field Officer for Gaelic Affairs, a branch of the Nova Scotia Department of Communities, Culture, and Heritage. He has taught extensively in Nova Scotia's Gaelic communities and works often with youth. As a singer he has recorded with such as Ashley MacIsaac, Natalie MacMaster, Douglas Lamey, Féis an Eilein singers, Mary Jane Lamond, and is featured on some of the Celtic Colours' compilation CDs. His son, Pàdruig, one of Cape Breton's new generation of native Gaelic speakers, is presently learning the fiddle, and performs Irish step dancing.

MacDonald, Sandy. (1963-). Guitar. A popular player at dances, festivals and parties throughout Cape Breton he has performed and recorded with many Cape Breton fiddlers, including his cousins, Howie and Dougie MacDonald, Mac Morin, Kinnon Beaton, Andrea Beaton, Douglas Lamey, Natalie MacMaster and Dawn and Margie Beaton.

MacDonald, Johnny. (1964-). Piano, step dance. From a young age he has accompanied many fiddlers at concerts and dances, among them his cousins Howie, Brian, and Dougie MacDonald. His wife, Claire, of Acadian descent, is a step dancer and teaches this locally; his daughters Breah and Regyn are also continuing the tradition playing various instruments, dancing and learning Gaelic. *See* **MacDonald family of Queensville.**

MacDonald family of New Waterford. With roots in Inverness County and strong musical associations with the Mabou Coal Mines style, Mary (Beaton) MacDonald, one of the first female fiddlers to rise to prominence in Cape Breton, is recognized as a significant contributor to the fiddle tradition; her daughter, Mary Jessie, also played an important role in relation to the piano style, with much of her input shaping the development of the Cape Breton accompaniment sound. Another daughter, **Claire MacDonald** (Currie), was also a noted step dancer. [**MacGillivray 1988**]

MacDonald, Mary (Beaton). (1897-1983). Fiddle. MacKinnon's Brook and New Waterford. Born to parents Alexander R. and Margaret

Mary "Hughie" MacDonald. Courtesy of Paul MacDonald.

(MacIsaac) Beaton, "Little" Mary, Mary "Hughie" or "Mairi Alasdair Raonuill," as she was variously known, was a direct descendant of one of the pioneer settlers of Mabou Coal Mines, Alexander Beaton (Alasdair an Taillear) who arrived in 1809 from Glen Spean in Scotland. Her family had many generations of fiddlers: her grand-uncle, John Beaton, played fiddle as did her uncles Johnny Ranald, Angus Ranald, "Young" Donald Beaton and Alexander R. Beaton Jr., and her cousins Danny, Jessie, Ronald Dan, Johnny "Johnny Ranald," Janet, Ronald and Donald Angus Beaton. It has been said that her greatest influence growing up was fiddler and step-dance master, Alexander J. Beaton, an immigrant from Glen Spean, who taught Mary, her sister Jessie and their mother. However, Old Allan Gillis from Foot Cape (whose name appears in relation to several highly regarded players such as Sandy MacLean and Angus Allan Gillis) also taught her note reading and bowing techniques. MacDonald's repertoire, settings and style, coupled with her family lineage, positioned her as an ideal representative of the older Cape Breton fiddle tradition, particularly in the 1970s as the revival of the fiddle music became paramount. Her playing came to be synonymous with what is known as the Mabou Coal Mines style and scholars and linguists, keen to support a language-music paradigm, suggested that "she played as she spoke" or "there was Gaelic

in her fiddle" – in other words, that her playing was imbued by the Gaelic language in terms of nuances, rhythmic patterns and inflections. As a step dancer she had similarly valued uniqueness, having in her repertoire a number of old steps taught to her by Alexander J. Beaton; indeed, the dance greatly informed her playing style.

Mary MacDonald also gained distinction as one of the few female fiddlers of the time, playing at concerts and picnics in Inverness County, and was held in high regard by many fiddlers, including Angus Chisholm, Winston Fitzgerald and by those classically trained violinists in Cape Breton who had close connections with the fiddle-music community. Having married Hugh MacDonald of Glencoe Mills she settled in New Waterford and became a prominent figure on the music scene in that area, playing with Margaret MacPhee on piano; in later years she often performed with her daughter Mary Jessie, on piano. At the encouragement of "Red" Gordon MacQuarrie and Mary Jessie, she travelled to perform in Boston and Detroit; her first visit to Boston was in 1951 when a reception was held for her at the Cape Breton Club. She occasionally participated in fiddle contests off-island, winning several awards. Her playing can be heard on the 1978 Topic LP, *The Music of Cape Breton: Cape Breton Fiddle Music* (Vol. 2), as well as on several home recordings. **[MacGillivray 1981].**

style. MacDonald's music was marked by a strong sense of timing and drive; in particular, her style was marked by the use of complex bowing patterns superimposed on the underlying single-stroke bowing style. She created a dense texture using a lot of right-hand bowed ornaments (cuts and double cuts); left-hand ornaments such as single and double grace notes, drones, double stops, unisons and warbles also featured; her intonation was influenced by the bagpipes; and some of her slower pieces are imbued with a very distinctive melancholy feel. MacDonalds lineage, geographic location and inherited style positioned her – particularly during those years where the Cape Breton fiddle tradition was considered to be in danger of disappearing – as something of an icon for the Mabou Coal Mines style and the old sounds of Cape Breton. However, recent research and home recordings reveal that MacDonald never considered herself musically conservative. Certainly she shows herself to have been musically versatile, adapting her style to playing in an equally compelling manner, with traditional style piano players such as Margaret MacPhee on the one hand, and the progressive Mary Jessie MacDonald, her daughter, on the other. Her defined and polished interpretation of the older tunes, settings and stylings is also what attracted players such as Angus Chisholm and Winston Fitzgerald to her music.

MacDonald, Mary Jessie. (1929-2007). Piano. New Waterford, Boston and River Ryan. Mary Jessie's family home was the venue for many music gatherings where, drawn by her mother's reputation as a player and dancer, many of the top fiddlers visited often. Her mother taught her to step dance; when she was 8 years old she began to play the pump organ, and in the ceilidhs at home had the opportunity to accompany some of the finest fiddlers of the time. In 1952 she moved to Boston, where she experienced a range of music genres including jazz, and she introduced many of the new sounds and techniques into the basic chording style she had developed at home, thus developing a distinctive, compelling style that was to have an impact on the developing Cape Breton piano tradition. She replaced the basic vamping pattern previously employed by Cape Breton piano players with a richer, more complex chording marked by a busy left hand using regular octave motion, and interpolated with a syncopated right-hand movement based on broken chord patterns. This became the basis for the Cape Breton piano style from the late 1950s onward and affected fiddle style – which gradually became less dense in texture, likely to compensate for the growing complexity of the accompaniment. Mary Jessie was held in high regard as a piano player in the Boston-Cape Breton community and performed at key venues such as the Greenville Café on Dudley Street, the Orange Hall in Brookline and the Canadian American Club in Waltham, ac-

companying fiddlers Angus Chisholm, Winston Fitzgerald, Bill Lamey, Alex and Malcolm Gillis, Catherine and Rannie Graham, Alcide Aucoin, Murdoch MacPhail and John Campbell. Touring fiddlers from the Scottish and Irish traditions also sought her out, and so she performed with such esteemed figures as Sean Maguire, Hector MacAndrew, Ron Gonnella and Alasdair Fraser. She was also among the first of the Cape Breton piano players to be invited to teach her style, and was on the staff of the Festival of American Fiddle Tunes, Port Townsend, WA, for many years. In 1988 she was honoured for her contribution to American folk music by the Smithsonian Institute, Washington, DC, where she performed with fiddler John Campbell for the Smithsonian Folklife Festival. She returned to live in Cape Breton in 2001 after 50 years as an émigré, and was honoured at Celtic Colours the following year in a tribute concert titled *Fiddlers Choice*. She recorded commercially with many fiddlers including Winston Fitzgerald, Joe MacLean, Donald Angus Beaton, Bill Lamey, Dave MacIsaac and Natalie MacMaster. She is also featured on the 1978 Topic LP *The Music of Cape Breton: Cape Breton Fiddle Music* (Vol. 2), where she accompanies the fiddle playing of her mother; her music is also to be heard on many home recordings made in Boston and Cape Breton from the 1950s onward. [**MacGillivray 1988**].

MacDonald family of Queensville. The "Dougald" MacDonalds of Queensville are descendants of Gilleasbuig Bàn MacEachern, who arrived in Cape Breton from Arisaig, Scotland, in the early 1800s and settled in Bràigh na h-Aibhneadh, the area today known as Kingsville and Glendale in Inverness County; his family was known to include many fiddlers and pipers and music continued to be passed through the generations, right up to the present day. It is through this family line that such 20th- and 21st-century Cape Breton musicians as brothers Dan Hughie and John Willie MacEachern of Queensville, Alex Francis MacKay of Kingsville, "Big" Ranald MacLellan and his children Donald, Theresa, Marie and "Baby" Joe MacLellan, Jackie Dunn MacIsaac,

Glenn Graham and Howie, Brian and Dougie MacDonald are connected. "Big" Dan Hughie MacEachern, one of the first Cape Breton fiddlers to record, was a great-grandson of Gilleasbuig Bàn; his father, Dòmhnagan a' Bharain (Dan the Barrens) MacEachern, was a fiddler, and others of his siblings also played, including brothers John Angus and John R.; his sister Ceiteag Bhàn was a step dancer and another sister, Kate Jess, a button, accordion player and Gaelic singer. Kate Jess married Dougald MacDonald from Creignish Rear; it was from this family connection that the "Dougald" name has continued down the line. They had a family of five: Kathleen (guitar), Francis (fiddle), Anna (fiddle), Alex (mouth organ and step dance) and Donnie (fiddle). Raised in Queensville, their music has been handed down through successive generations of "Dougald" MacDonalds and an extensive network of musical cousins now exists: Kathleen's son Brian MacDonald is a noted fiddler and composer of tunes; of Francis' sons, Dougie MacDonald was a noted fiddler and composer of tunes and Randy is a piano accompanist, while daughters Cathy and Maureen are step dancers; Anna's family, again MacDonalds and raised in Westmount, includes Michael (piano), Judy, Evelyn (step dance), Marilyn (piano and song), Howie (fiddle, piano) and Cheryl (step dance); Alex's family includes Gaelic singer Jeff MacDonald, guitar player Sandy MacDonald and piano player, Johnny MacDonald. Events such as the Glendale Fiddle Festivals in the 1970s and the Glendale concerts through the 1980s, which generally coincided with the annual haymaking season, would see the wider family congregate around the old homestead and provided the occasion for much music-making involving the family and the wider community. *See* **MacDonald family of Kingsville; MacDonald family of Westmount; MacDonald, Brian; MacDonald, Dougie; MacEachern, "Big" Dan Hughie.**

MacDonald family of Westmount. Of the six children of Howard (Sr.) and Ann MacDonald, many of them are noted fiddlers, piano players, step dancers and singers: Michael (piano), Evelyn (step dance), Marilyn (piano and song), Howie (fiddle, piano) and Cheryl (step dance). Music has been passed down from both sides of the family and the MacDonald family tree connects them with many other Cape Breton players. Ann (Anna "Dougald") (1931-2006) – herself a highly regarded fiddle player who encouraged her children to play and performed with them often – was the daughter of Kate Jess MacEachern; she was a button accordion player and Gaelic singer, and the sister of "Big" Dan Hughie MacEachern, who was one of the first Cape Breton fiddlers to record. Anna's siblings were also musical with Donnie and Francis being fiddle players, Alex, a step dancer and Kathleen a guitar player. Music was passed down through their families leading to an extensive network of musical cousins. Howard Sr. was a step dancer and his brother Wilfred a fiddle player; family connections on his side include nephews Harvey Beaton (step dance, piano) and Brian MacDonald (fiddle). *See* **MacDonald family of Queensville.**

MacDonald, Howie. (1965-). Fiddle, piano, composer, comic. When Howie started to play at the age of 7 or 8, besides his own family members, there were very few of his peers playing fiddle music. One young player he met and played with, the pair often switching between fiddle and piano, was John Morris Rankin from Mabou; one of their first performances together was at the Glendale Fiddle Festival in the 1970s. Howie later went on to record and tour for 10 years with the Rankin Family. Their shows featured much of the music partnership between himself and John Morris and the duo was a popular one at local events in Cape Breton when scheduling permitted. Howie has released 11 albums and a DVD; among his albums he has included live performances, a slow air recording (*Just Relax*, 1998) and duos with Ashley MacIsaac (*Cape Breton Fiddle Music Not Calm,* 2001) and Dave MacIsaac (*Auld School,* 2010). Some of his albums also bring in his comic and mimicry skills, and include ambient noises and scripted conversations that reflect the real conditions of a live Cape Breton square dance or ceilidh in much the same way as the old home re-

Howie MacDonald. Photo by Murd Smith.
Courtesy of Celtic Colours International Festival.

cordings had done (e.g., *WhY2Keilidh*, 1999); his CD *The Dance Last Night* from 1997 is the first live square-dance recording from Cape Breton. He is also featured on many compilation albums and has recorded with other Cape Breton fiddlers such as Natalie MacMaster, J. P. Cormier as well as on most of the Rankins' catalogue. He has composed many tunes including the "The Westburne Reel," popularized by Leahy, and his arrangement of "Skye Boat Song" (from *The Ceilidh Trail,* 1993) was used in the movie *White Squall*; he has also received many ECMAs nominations and won an award in 1991 for his *Live and Lively* album. Since his dual role as comedic actor/musician in the *Cape Breton Summertime Revue* in 1997 MacDonald has become increasingly recognized for his talents as a mimic. He developed his own comedy and musical-revue-type show, *Howie's Celtic Brew*, which toured the Maritimes in 2000-2001; much of the material from this was later incorporated into a show, *Canadian Loonie*, which ran in 2002 in Ontario. No longer involved in the music business on a full-time basis, Mac-Donald has pursued further study and a career in the health-care services; he does continue to perform on an occasional basis; often members of his family—including his daughters Kristen and Jillian (both step dancers)—are involved in such performances.

MacDonald Sisters, Halifax, NS. Cassie (1991-), fiddle, and **Maggie** (1993-), piano, guitar, accordion. Both are Highland and step dancers. Born to parents John and Anita MacDonald, they are paternal grand-daughters of Hugh A. MacDonald, Antigonish's "polka king," and his wife, Winnie. Cassie and Maggie started with Suzuki method on the violin and Cassie stayed with this instrument, inspired by her cousin Kendra MacGillivray, with whom she took classes at the Gaelic College from the age of 9. Maggie switched to piano and attended classes with Kolten MacDonell at the Ceilidh Trail School of Music, various workshops at the Gaelic College and classes with Kimberley Holmes, a down-east-style fiddler and piano accompanist. While Cape Breton music and musicians has been their focus, their influences have been eclectic and include the Leahy Family and Gordon Stobbe; Maggie indeed describes her style as a "hybrid" of the Cape Breton and down-east styles. Cassie has also competed as part of the Grand Masters Fiddle contest. The sisters play a circuit of concert-type gigs around the Maritimes and at festivals in the U.S.; they have two CDs *Fresh Heirs* (2011), which has an accompanying tune book (*Tunes*), and *Sterling Road* (2014).

MacDonald Sisters, New Waterford. Dawn (1977-), step dance, piano, and **Helen** (1980-), step dance, fiddle. They grew up listening to fiddle music on records, radio and TV, encouraged largely by their mother and her family, who were from the Iona area. Inspired by the step dancing they saw on the TV show *Up Home Tonight* they persuaded their mother to send them to classes, where they were taught by Kay Handrahan. Dawn was encouraged by Brenda Stubbert to try chording on the piano and later got regular tutelage from Marilyn MacDonald; she practised by playing along with cassettes of fiddlers such as Buddy MacMaster, Natalie MacMaster and Howie Mac-Donald, and by accompanying Helen, who had started playing fiddle. Through the Cape Breton Gaelic Society in Sydney, the sisters, along with other young players, were given opportunities to play onstage and to meet established musicians such as Marie MacLellan and Doug MacPhee, who greatly encouraged them. They have performed choreographed dance routines with the Barra MacNeils, Natalie MacMaster and Howie MacDonald, live and on recordings; Helen has performed with the Scottish dance group, Dannsa and teaches step dance. The sisters are now living in Barrachois, Cape Breton (Dawn), and Victoria Mines (Helen), and continue to perform together in Cape Breton; their partners Kyle Gillis (Dawn) and Scott MacKenzie (Helen) often join the duo on fiddle and guitar, respectively.

MacDonald, Allan. *See* **MacDonald family of Foot Cape and Detroit.**

MacDonald, Anita. (1991-). Fiddle, step dance, singer. Little Narrows, Cape Breton. She received the Frank "Big Sampie" Sampson Award from the Festival Volunteer Drive'ers Association to record her debut album, *Stepping Stone*, in 2011. A Gaelic singer also she currently works for Féis an Eilein in Christmas Island. With a BA in History and Gaelic from CBU, she is often sought after to conduct workshops in music, dance and song and has toured throughout New England with Cape Breton trio, The Goin's On.

MacDonald, Brian. (1964-). Fiddle. Brian is the second youngest of ten children of Kathleen "Dougald" MacDonald of Queensville and Lawrence MacDonald of Troy. On his mother's side there are many musicians, dancers and singers in the family tree, among them cousins, Howie MacDonald and Dougie MacDonald; Kathleen herself played guitar often at dances with her brother, Francis, on fiddle. Brian was one of the active younger players on the Cape Breton scene during the revival years of the late 1970s and into the 1980s; he then moved away to live in Québec then to British Columbia to work as a teacher of the deaf. He returned home to Nova Scotia and settled in St. Andrews, Antigonish County, where he formed a group, the Antigonish County Fiddlers. He has continued to perform at events in Cape Breton and has been a guest at such as Celtic Colours and a regular fiddler instructor at the Gaelic College. Married to Jennifer Fiorini

from Ontario, their five children, Anna, Olivia, Brienne, Abigail and Mark are all immersed in various aspects of the music tradition as fiddlers, pipers, drummers, guitarists, dancers and singers. *See* **MacDonald family of Queensville.**

MacDonald, Buddy. (1951-). Guitar, vocals, singer-songwriter. North Shore and Boularderie. Growing up he heard much fiddle music and Gaelic song, as his father, Thomas Angus (Tommy "Peggy") MacDonald, was a member of the North Shore Gaelic singers, and fiddlers such as Mike MacDougall were regular visitors to the home. Buddy's style is folk and contemporary folk, and he has composed a number of songs, including the popular "Getting Dark Again." His professional career has involved residencies in such as hotels, restaurants, pubs and clubs throughout Cape Breton, concert appearances and, increasingly, international tours; he is the regular host of the late-night Festival Club at Celtic Colours. Buddy has several recordings, both solo and in collaboration with others including John Ferguson, Donnie Campbell, Dave Gunning and John Allan Cameron. They include: *Buddy and Donnie ... at the Gaelic College* (1990); *Getting Dark Again* with John Ferguson (1995); *We Remember You Well* (2000); *Song Book ... Getting Dark Again ... Buddy Mac Donald* (2007); *Live at the Pub* (2005); *Six Strings and Me "live"* (2009); *Myself ... My Shadow and Me* (2012) and *Feel the Air* (2015). Buddy MacDonald has been a major player in developing the common ground between the fiddle and the folksong traditions in Cape Breton; during the early 1990s he teamed up with fiddlers such as Natalie MacMaster, later with Jennifer Roland and, most recently, with Rachel Davis, generating performances where the fiddle played mostly backup to the vocals; tune groups would always be included though, representing one of the few occasions on which fiddle is heard with guitar accompaniment only, without piano.

MacDonald, Cassie and Maggie. *See* **MacDonald Sisters of Halifax.**

MacDonald, Dan. (1953-). Event organizer, promoter, writer, media broadcaster, entrepreneur. Creignish and Sydney. His background includes several significant families of fiddlers, the MacDonalds of Creignish and the MacEacherns of Queensville on his father's side, and the MacDonalds of Kingsville on his mother's; this leads to a web of musical relations across Cape Breton and beyond – indeed, he claims to be the first in five generations not to play the fiddle. His father was in charge of booking music for the local dances and parish concert in Creignish for several years during the 1960s and, as a teenager, Dan was responsible for booking rock bands for the local dances at the youth club. Upon moving to Sydney in 1980 he coordinated, stage managed and acted as emcee for a series of Celtic music concerts hosted by the university. During the 1980s and 1990s he worked with the ATG, which spearheaded many initiatives and events in the promotion of Cape Breton music, including the Ben Eoin Fiddle and Folk Festival, which ran for 12 years. As a founding member, he served in various roles (including president) until the society's demise in 2000. In the late 1990s he worked with Sydney's Rave Entertainment, acting as a booking agent for artists such as John Allan Cameron and J. P. Cormier. His primary business interests are linked to music: Creignish Hills Entertainment (which deals with event management and PR), The Poster Guy (a poster distribution service) and Masked Man Enterprises, which released the album *Tamerack'er Down* with Brenda Stubbert in 1984. As a broadcaster in the 1970s and 1980s he hosted Celtic and East Coast music shows on three different stations – CIGO in Port Hawkesbury (where he took over from Joey Beaton in hosting *Highland Fling* in 1978), CKEC, New Glasgow, in the late 1970s, and CHER in Sydney in the early 1980s. He has written for a number of publications over the years, contributing columns and articles to such as *The Scotia Sun, Celtic Tides, Celtic Life* and *The Cape Bretoner*. Since 2000 he has contributed a regular column on fiddle music and entertainment to *The Cape Breton Post*. He has also written poems, some of which have appeared as songs on a recording by Marilyn MacDonald-MacKinnon. A regular square-dance follower, he

has also been a volunteer for Celtic Colours since its inception, he has acted as a stage manager, site manager, emcee and trainer, coordinating stage and site volunteers; he has also volunteered at the Stan Rogers Festival in Canso, and at the East Coast Music Week. MacDonald's and his wife Vonnie's promotion of Cape Breton fiddle music has been acknowledged over the years by several organizations, including the CBFA (1979), the Canso Causeway Anniversary Celebrations (1980, 2005), MNS (2000), the ECMA (2005, 2010) and Celtic Colours (2006, 2012).

MacDonald, Dan. *See* **MacDonald family of Ironville**.

MacDonald, Dan R. (1911-1976). Fiddle, composer. Judique and Mabou, Inverness County. Born in Rear South Judique to parents John R. (Johnny "the Carpenter") and Jessie (O'Handley) MacDonald, his mother died when Dan R. was four, resulting in his moving around the homes of family members. His father was a fiddler who played by ear and performed for dances; he was Dan R.'s earliest example when, in 1921, he began playing on his grandfather Allan O'Hanley's fiddle. He listened also to local fiddlers such as Angus A. and Allan MacDougall, Alexander MacDonnell and Kitchener MacDonald of Whycocomagh. He met and played with Sandy MacLean from Foot Cape and became a devoted fan of "Big" Ronald MacLellan. Around 1930 John Willie MacEachern in Glendale introduced him to the rudiments of music notation, which helped him expand his repertoire. He played for dances locally and in the late 1930s, at the invitation of Bill Lamey, made his debut on radio from Sydney. In 1939 he released his first commercial recording, and in 1941, during the Second World War, while stationed with the Canadian Army in Britain, he composed a number of tunes, performed for the BBC and befriended composer and collector J. Murdoch Henderson of Aberdeen, Scotland, who introduced him to the many published collections of Scottish music. Through his association with Henderson, Dan R. acquired many of these collections, often in obscure locations, and sent them home. He also established contact between Henderson and Cape Breton fiddlers, effectively opening the door for a music export business that impacted greatly on the direction Cape Breton fiddle music was to take over the next 20 or more years. Returning to Canada after military service, he settled first in Boston; there he recorded at least 4 sides for the Copley label. He moved on to Hamilton, Ontario, for a short time and then to Windsor, Ontario, where he spent 12 years. There he was part of the Cape Breton music scene in the Windsor-Detroit area. An original member of the Five MacDonald Fiddlers there, he recorded two LPs with them. Having already recorded a number of 78s dating from 1930, he released 4 LPs on the Celtic and Rodeo labels, one each with piano players Lila Hashem, Marie MacLellan, Kathleen Beaton and Colin MacInnis; he is also featured on the compilation, *The Fiddlers of Cape Breton*. He returned to Cape Breton in 1967, where he lived in Sydney for a while before moving to Mabou, where he lived with his sister Katie Ann (mother of John Allan and John Donald Cameron). A colourful character, he spent much of his time travelling around the island and staying for extended periods with various friends and relatives. He was a regular performer at festivals and house parties and featured on CBC-TV's *Ceilidh* for one season in the early 1970s; in 1971 he was a prominent player in *The Vanishing Cape Breton Fiddler* documentary.

composition. Dan R. MacDonald is regarded as one of the most prolific Cape Breton fiddle composers. It is estimated that he had "made" something in the region of 2,000 tunes over a 45-year period, this at a time when composing tunes was not common. A number of these pieces have become established in the tradition as standards (to the extent that some were in fact published as "traditional" on other fiddlers' recordings) and now feature in the repertoire of virtually every Cape Breton fiddler. The Cape Breton Symphony Fiddlers, in particular, recorded many of Dan R.'s tunes, including "The Trip to Windsor" and "The Glencoe March." His music was named after people he knew or experiences he had had, and he often composed tunes to thank individuals or families who had hosted him on his travels around Cape Breton. His music is more representative of an evolving Cape Breton voice than the old Highland Scottish sound; his melodies are more expansive than is typical of the older repertoire, yet they never challenged any of the conventions of the day and thus were easily embraced by other players and assimilated into the repertoire with ease. He was generous about sharing his music, often presenting other fiddlers with handwritten copies of his latest creation. While he did, as a matter of practice, attach his name to all his handwritten scores, he was little concerned with issues of copyright; indeed, it was his nephew John Donald Cameron who registered his tunes to ensure that he was appropriately compensated. He was, however, quite particular regarding how his tunes be played and encouraged correctness in the interpretation of the melodic line. His first composition, "The Red Shoes," appeared in Gordon MacQuarrie's 1940 collection. Two books of his compositions, *The Heather Hill Collection* and *The Trip to Windsor Collection*, were published posthumously in 1985 and 1994 respectively; subsequent editions of the 1985 collection have been published. A cassette collection of his compositions—*Tribute to Dan R. MacDonald*—performed by 22 Cape Breton musicians, was released by Cranford Publications in 1989, the first Cape Breton recording devoted to the compositions of an individual. [Caplan 2006; MacGillivray 1981; McGann 2003].

— ∼ —

The Heather Hill Collection: Fiddle Music of Dan R. MacDonald. Hornpipes, Clogs, Jigs, Marches, Strathspeys, Reels. Compiled and edited by John Donald Cameron in 2000, this is a new edition of a 1985 collection, now with 84 pages and 230 original compositions by Dan R. MacDonald. These are indexed alphabetically and are grouped in categories according to type: there are 44 clogs and hornpipes, 73 jigs, and 8, 28 and 77 respectively of march-strathspey-reels; tunes are not arranged in any other particular order. The collection includes some of the popular Dan R. tunes such as the strathspey "The Lime Hill" and the reel "Heather Hill." Occasional composition dates, locations and/or dedications are indicated; there are 2 photographs and a biography of Dan R. by Daniel Graham. Performance directions included beside some of the tunes were taken from the notes of J. Murdoch Henderson, who had a significant influence on Dan. R. A cassette tape, *A Tribute to Dan R. MacDonald: 22 Musicians play Tunes from the Heather Hill Collection,* has 74 of these tunes that were previously unrecorded, performed solo by Kinnon Beaton, Elmer Briand, Dwayne Côté, Gordon Côté, Paul Cranford, Raymond Ellis, Wilfred Gillis, David Greenberg, Jerry Holland, Lloyd MacDonald, Shawn MacDonald, Dan Joe MacInnis, Alec Francis MacKay, Carl MacKenzie, Hector MacKenzie, John Neil MacLean, Buddy MacMaster, Natalie MacMaster, Kyle MacNeil, Lucy MacNeil, Wilfred Prosper and Courtney MacPherson (highland pipes).

— ≈ —

Trip to Windsor Collection: The Music of Dan R. MacDonald, Volume 2. Compiled and edited in 1994 by John Donald Cameron, fiddler and nephew of Dan R. MacDonald, this 76-page collection has 236 tunes which are arranged by key inside categories of "march-strathspey-reels," "jigs" and "clogs and hornpipes." Cameron's introduction states that the impetus behind the work is to ensure that the legacy of Dan R. lives on through his tunes being remembered and accredited to him. He also refers to tunes presented as being "exactly as written by the composer," but points out that the slurs and grace notes included should be used at the discretion of the individual player, as Dan R. would have recommended. A small number of tunes have additional performance directions included (e.g., "pointedly, with great force" is suggested for the strathspey

"Carron Bridge.") Included are 94 jigs, 88 reels, 24 Strathspeys, 23 hornpipes, 3 clogs and 3 marches; among them are the popular tunes "Trip to Windsor," "Glencoe March" and "The River Bend." Occasional composition dates, locations and/or dedications are indicated. Performance directions included beside some of the tunes, were taken from the notes of J. Murdoch Henderson, who had a significant influence on Dan. R.

— ≈ —

MacDonald, Dougie. (1968-2009). Fiddle, composer. Queensville, Inverness County. One of five children born to parents Francis H. and Mary A. MacDonald, Douglas Ian (Dougie) had an extended family of fiddlers that included cousins Howie and Brian MacDonald, from Westmount. His father played fiddle and was a member of the CBFA; there were often music gatherings at the house and Dougie heard other musicians in the community at a young age; these included Dan Hughie MacEachern and Dan R. MacDonald, who he regarded as his mentors. He started to play the fiddle at five, guided initially by his father; later he attended classes held by Stan Chapman with a group of some 30 children including Jackie Dunn and John Pellerin. Chapman taught him to read music and he used this skill to learn tunes from the CBFA newsletter. A key resource at the time were the recordings made at house parties or ceilidhs circulating among the music community; Dougie, like many of the other emerging players of that time, learned much from these, as they introduced him to different players, styles and to new tunes. Radio too played a role, and MacDonald, again like many of his peers, would systematically record fiddle music played on CJFX. He was one of those smitten by Jerry Holland's 1982 recording, *Master Cape Breton Fiddler,* and the impact of that on his developing style was marked. His music taste was quite diverse overall, and he listened to fiddle musics from a range of genres including Irish, country and bluegrass. This eclecticism came to shape his own sound and style, as well as his ca. 150 composed tunes, most of which are reels and many of which have been recorded both by himself and by other musicians in Cape Breton, the U.S. and Ireland, including Jerry Holland, Sharon Shannon, Howie MacDonald, The Barra MacNeils, Solas, Rodney Miller, Otis Tomas, Liz Doherty and Máire O'Keeffe.

A collection of 27 of his tunes was published in 1993, some of which were composed in collaboration with Jerry Holland, Howie MacDonald and Kinnon Beaton. Many of his tunes are created around a specific chord progression or modulation, and indeed many of them were created on guitar rather than fiddle. Some are based upon a particular technique, such as a shuffle bow pattern learned from country fiddling (e.g., in "The Parker Twins"). Variations to the melodic line are often written into the tune, rather than being highlighted as options. But MacDonald adopted quite a relaxed approach when it came to others interpreting his tunes, and encouraged players to make changes to accommodate their personal tastes. This flexibility (perhaps influenced by his understanding of Irish fiddle styles) informs his own playing, resulting in him taking a more relaxed approach to correctness, as it is understood within the Cape Breton fiddle tradition, than was common at the time. His style, described by some as "intense," is quite distinctive on a number of levels: the use of vibrato to embellish certain long notes (in his case the third-finger notes especially) was a regular feature; this, along with the use of a 3-note, consecutive upward pattern – executed in a single bow-stroke and almost emulating a slide – points to the influence of Jerry Holland. Elements of certain Irish fiddle styles may be detected in a type of roll he uses often, his choice of the fourth finger rather than the third in realizing grace notes and in the inclusion of an upper note in the middle of a cut; he also moves away from the more evenly articulated bow strokes of the Cape Breton style toward the more dramatic "pressure-and-release" patterns used in some Irish fiddle styles – such as that of Donegal, for instance. He uses the fourth finger in unison with the adjacent open string quite often, upward slides are used regularly, and pizzicato is occasionally employed. His style is further marked by the use of abrupt, heavily accented stops at endings and also at points within the melody. He occasionally moves into higher positions (even when lower-position options are available) at the ends of phrases.

While he experimented for a time with modulations within a group of tunes, again influenced by traditions outside of Cape Breton, he reverted to the local practice of building extended medleys around a single tonal area. MacDonald's awareness of his somewhat unique place within the Cape Breton fiddle tradition is referenced in the strapline of his first commercially released album, *Cape Breton Times–Music of Uncompromising Quality with the Traditional yet Contemporary Swing*. Later recordings were *Staying in Tune*, *Fiddle Tunes* and *A Miner*. One of the artists who participated in the 1993 Cape Breton Festival in Cork, Ireland, he is featured on the Nimbus recording of that event and on other compilations, including those by Celtic Colours and The Ceilidh Trail School. Although he performed often, and typically in presentational rather than in dance contexts, MacDonald did not make music his full-time profession, but worked variously as a woodlot operator and a miner at several sites across Canada, including the Northwest Territories. He died tragically in a car accident in December 2009, having just played at the Doryman Tavern in Chéticamp. *See* **MacDonald family of Queensville.**

— ∼ —

Cape Breton Fiddler Dougie MacDonald: Fiddle Tunes. Including Jigs, Reels, Strathspeys. Published in 1993 by Mabou Communications, Inverness County; 25 of its 27 tunes are composed by Dougie MacDonald himself; the other two ("Chums" and "Ciaran Tourish") were in collaboration with Jerry Holland. There are 18 reels, 3 jigs, 4 strathspeys, 1 slow strathspey and 1 march. Brief notes give information on the titles, all of which are dedicated to friends or in honour of local events. The collection has a foreword by MacDonald, acknowledgements and pencil sketches by Jimmy and Peter Rankin. Unusually for a copyrighted collection, within his introductory comments MacDonald invites readers to contribute to the creative process in using the book: "if there are any tunes you'd like to change to suit your ear, please feel free to do so."

— ≈ —

MacDonald, Francis. *See* **MacDonald family of Inverness and South-West Margaree.**

MacDonald, Howie. *See* **MacDonald family of Westmount.**

MacDonald, Hugh A. (1889-1976). Fiddle. Lanark, Antigonish County. Born to parents Angus and Mary (MacInnis) MacDonald, his family background was musical, with his father being a note reader, his mother a violinist and pianist, and all of his five siblings, Jim, John Duncan, Mary, Janie and Kate, playing violin; of these, his brother Jim was also a composer and an occasional violin maker, one of whose instruments Hugh A. played on his first recording. Known as Hughie "Eleven" (after the land-lot number given to his ancestors when they settled in Lanark), and later, Hughie "the Fiddler" and "The Polka King," Hugh A. began playing fiddle at the age of 9, learning mainly by ear and influenced by his immediate family as well as by two uncles, Dan MacInnis and John MacDonald, and by his neighbour, Dan "The Ridge" MacDonald, who had Mabou connections. He was soon in demand at local gatherings such as barn raisings and frolics, and later was invited to perform at concerts, picnics and dances including at the Town Hall in Port Hawkesbury where he played for many years. During the 1930s he was a member of the Antigonish Orchestra playing for dances; he also teamed up with his cousin, John William MacDougall from Westville, on fiddle to play dances in Pictou County. In 1935, along with Colin J. Boyd, he became one of the pioneer recording artists of Scottish violin music in Canada, featured on two 78s on the Celtic label with Bess Sidall MacDonald on piano and Jim Dale on bass. Hugh A. was a regular performer at the Highland Ball organized by the Antigonish Highland Society, he played for step dancers at the Antigonish Highland Games, he broadcast on CJFX radio accompanied by his wife, Winifred, on piano, and in the 1950s won two competitions in Antigonish. As a mainland fiddler he remained somewhat distinct from the Cape Breton players (although he played there often and was influenced by Dan R. MacDonald, John Campbell and Winston Fitzgerald), particularly in his repertoire. Besides strathspeys, jigs and reels, his typical tune choices included waltzes, foxtrots and, in particular, polkas, which were popular in the Antigonish area and of which he was considered a master. An ear player until an advanced age, he was nevertheless drawn to challenging tunes and to keys such as F and B flat, as were many of the top fiddlers of the time. Posthumously, he received a Stompin' Tom Award at the ECMAs (2001), was inducted into the Clan Donald Hall of Fame (2002) and to the Nova Scotia Country Music Hall of Fame (2003). The music continues to be carried on through the family with grandchildren Troy (fiddle and piano), Kendra (fiddle) and Sabra (step dance and Highland dance) MacGillivray being an internationally recognized family of musicians, as are his other grandchildren, sisters Cassie and Maggie MacDonald from Halifax. [**MacGillivray 1981**].

MacDonald, James. (1907-1985). Violinist, teacher. "Professor Jimmy" taught music in North Sydney from around 1933. He was a descendant of Alexander (Alasdair Ailein Mhór) MacDonald, known locally as Bàrd na Ceapaich (The Keppoch Bard), who was born in Glenuig, Moidart, Scotland, in 1820; he settled first at Cape Breton's Mabou Ridge, where his family became known as "the Ridge" MacDonalds; eventually they settled at Lower South River, near Antigonish, a Gaelic-speaking district at that time. In the 1940s, members of this family (whose tradition of poetry can be traced back to the 16th century) were recorded by Patrick Nicholson, the president of St. FX University, and a collector and publisher of Gaelic stories, representing some of the earliest field recordings of Gaelic material made in Nova Scotia. Jimmy's father, "Dancing Dan" MacDonald, was a well-known character who worked as an engineer for the railway and his mother, Janet, the daughter of Roland Stevenson, a well-known Halifax band leader of the late 19th century. MacDonald received his training at the Halifax Conservatory. Although he had numerous opportunities to travel, teach and perform, Jimmy remained home and married Mary Regis Long, the daughter of James Long, a fiddler from the Northside. From his home, Professor Jimmy taught piano, saxophone and guitar as well as violin; over several decades his impact was immense. His earliest students included Pat Cormier (later referred to as "Professor") and Lloyd MacDonald; through the 1950s and '60s many of the recording fiddlers sought tuition from him, among them Paddy LeBlanc, Joe MacIsaac, Winnie Chafe, Winston Fitzgerald and Angus Chisholm, sometimes to help them with specific techniques such as playing in higher positions; during the late 1960s guitar became popular and demand for classes with him on this instrument increased. It was common for him to teach several members of a single family, and in the 1970s these include the MacDonalds of Ironville and the MacNeils of Sydney Mines. A versatile musician, MacDonald played in various bands, pit orchestras and often played saxophone in Winston's Fitzgerald's ensemble. In addition to his widespread fame for his musicianship, Jimmy was also a well-known track and field winner at highland games throughout the province. Professor Jimmy continued teaching right up until the early 1980s. Since then his sons, James and Dan, have continued teaching music in the area. *See* **professors.**

MacDonald, John Alex. (1877-1958). Fiddle. West Mabou and Port Hood, Inverness County. Known as "the big fiddler" he was a contest-winning and influential player, one of the first in Cape Breton to generate a personal following as a dance player at venues in Mabou, Glencoe and Port Hood. **[MacGillivray 1981],**

MacDonald, John A. (Johnny Archie). *See* **MacDonald family of Detroit, Michigan.**

MacDonald, John L. (1926-2007). Fiddle. Foot Cape, Inverness County, and Toronto. Born to parents John Angus and Katie Ann MacDonald, he was one of a large family of 10 boys and 4 girls who were reared on a family farm where Gaelic was the first language; his father could whistle or "jig" tunes, and his mother and an older brother knew many Gaelic songs. Brothers Lawrence and Jonas played the fiddle, and there were often house parties when fiddlers such as Malcolm Beaton from Strathlorne and Sandy MacLean from Foot Cape visited the home. Beaton gave John L. his first fiddle, bought him a bow from the Eaton's catalogue, and taught him his first tune ("Put Me in the Big Box"). Other players John L. encountered when he was starting out were Danny Campbell, who played many of the dances in Kenloch, John Archie MacIsaac from Sight Point and, on occasion, Willie Kennedy. John L. also heard music on the family's gramophone: 78s of fiddlers such as Dan J. Campbell, Angus Allan Gillis, Angus Chisholm and the Inverness Serenaders. Following the death of both his parents in 1947, he moved to New Glasgow, then Truro and, in 1949, to Brantford, Ontario, and Toronto by 1950. There he picked up the fiddle again, playing at occasional dances organized by Angus MacKinnon. In the 1960s, John L. teamed up with Bill MacDonald, a fiddler from Middle River, and started a regular series of Saturday night dances at Liberty Hall, with Kay Jamieson on piano and a few other musicians to build out the band, particularly for the round dances. John L. then took up with Sandy MacIntyre, playing some sets together at the dance. These Cape Breton square dances in Toronto had a strong following for more than a decade; many visiting musicians played at them, and those who were based in the Toronto area often got a chance to play a set. John L. MacDonald's style and sound remained close to that which he had been surrounded with in Inverness County of the 1930s, despite having lived in Toronto for more than 50 years. His music appears on the CD, *Formerly of Foot Cape Road* (Rounder, 2005) with pianist Doug MacPhee, and on *Traditional Fiddle Music of Cape Breton: MacKinnon's Brook, Volume 4* (Rounder, 2008). *See* **Toronto.**

MacDonald, Johnny "MacVarish." (1852-1934). Fiddle. Broad Cove Marsh, Inverness County. An itinerant fiddle player and one of the first to amass a collection of printed tune books, he was known for his unique repertoire, including novelty pieces, and exhibitionist, trick fiddling techniques, such as playing with his left hand inverted on the neck of the fiddle or running the bow hair under the strings to create a drone effect; as such he and preferred playing where he was listened to rather than danced to. [**MacGillivray 1981**],

MacDonald, Fr. Kenneth Joseph. (1821-1910). South River, Antigonish County, and Mabou, Inverness County. Born to parents Alexander and Catherine (MacLellan) MacDonald, he was ordained a priest in 1856 and was posted to various parishes in Cape Breton and the Nova Scotian mainland before becoming the first pastor of Port Hood and Mabou in 1865, where he remained until his retirement in 1894; Port Hood was dropped from his jurisdiction in 1868, and West Lake Ainslie was added in 1871. During his tenure at Mabou he built the glebe house there and made preparations for a new church to be built. A strict disciplinarian, he was an earnest worker in the cause of temperance, vehemently opposed to social events such as dances and picnics, which he saw as opportunities for alcohol consumption; thus the fiddle music that was an attractive part of such events was regarded by him as central to the problem. Stories about his attitude to Cape Breton fiddlers and their music cite him as physically destroying instruments, and Jodi McDavid's essay "The Fiddle Burning Priest of Mabou" (2008) refers to him going from door to door demanding fiddles and then burning them. Equally popular, however, are stories about local fiddlers outwitting the priest; Johnny "Ranald" Beaton, for instance, according to the CBF (1981), handed over the poorest of his fiddles to be destroyed while secretly keeping a better one. Described in a newspaper article, "A Tribute to the Late Danny Beaton (1894-1950)," as "an implacable warrior who kept the faith in the people, the devil in hell, and the violins in their cases." Fr. MacDonald was

responsible for the Cape Breton version of what also took place in other countries, notably in Scotland and in Ireland (until as late as the 1930s). In all cases, as in Cape Breton, music traditions and local musics were damaged and devalued by such activity. [**MacGillivray 1981; McDavid 2008**],

MacDonald, Lloyd. *See* **MacDonald family of Ironville**.

MacDonald, Margaret (Chisholm). *See* **Chisholm family of Margaree Forks**.

MacDonald, Martha. (1960-). Researcher. Dartmouth, NS, and Goose Bay, NL. Now the associate director at the Labrador Institute of Memorial University, she grew up listening to Cape Breton music through her father, Robert (Bob) MacDonald, a Cape Breton piano player originally from Florence, Cape Breton, and through family visits to his parents there. As an undergraduate student at Mount Allison University, New Brunswick, MacDonald originally researched the tradition of bards in Cape Breton. Interested particularly in the Gaelic language and the social context of the ceilidh, she researched this for her MA at Memorial University, Newfoundland, which led to her 1986 dissertation, "Group Identity in Social Gatherings: Tradition and Community on the Iona Peninsula, Cape Breton." She is now studying narratives of Inuktitut language loss in Nunatsiavut for her PhD.

MacDonald, Martin. *See* **MacDonald family of Ironville**.

MacDonald, Mary. *See* **MacDonald family of New Waterford**.

MacDonald, Mary Jessie. *See* **MacDonald family of New Waterford**.

MacDonald, Paul. *See* **MacDonald family of Ironville**.

MacDonald, Ray "Mac." (1934-). Radio host. Sydney Mines and Antigonish. His career in radio started at the age of 19 at CJCB in Sydney, NS; he went on to work in virtually every aspect of radio production in Sydney and Bathurst, New Brunswick, before he moved to CJFX in Antigonish in 1965, starting as news editor, and later becoming the "Morning Man," a role he held for 10 years. After that he was exclusively involved in music programs until his retirement in 1999. His on-air skill, experience and genuine affinity for the music brought a new level of professionalism to the presentation of Cape Breton fiddle music on the radio, and he became one of the most celebrated and influential hosts in this regard. He began with a show called *Scottish Strings* that ran from 6-7 p.m. on weeknights; this was replaced by *Ceilidh* in the 1980s, a show which continues to be presented in 2015, with Barry MacKinnon as host. The popularity and influence of these shows was immense, giving a platform to Cape Breton fiddlers at a time of significant change (post-*The Vanishing Cape Breton Fiddler*); involving a mix of live performances and recordings, Ray "Mac" would also interview musicians, contextualize the music for his listeners, ensure that younger emerging performers were included, and kept audiences informed about upcoming events and activities; he was also admired for representing fiddlers from all across the island, and not exclusively those from Inverness County. His contribution to the Cape Breton fiddle tradition has been celebrated in various ways; he was presented with the Clan Donald Canada Achievement Award in 2004 and was given an Award of Merit from the Highland Village in 2000; in 2015 he was recognized by a special concert in his honour at Celtic Colours. [**Caplan 1993; Bergfeldt-Munro 2015**]. *See* **CJFX; radio.**

MacDonald, Robert. (1981-). Bagpipe, whistle, banjo and fiddle. Utah. He was originally introduced to Cape Breton music through a local friend and fellow piper, Larry Erdmann, who held regular ceilidhs with music and dancing at his home in Springville, UT, and who had visited Cape Breton to study piping with Barry Shears and Hamish Moore. MacDonald similarly became interested in the dance-style piping of Cape Breton, finding it "lively and liberating," having previously only experienced the pipe-band and competition piping traditions. He first visited Cape Breton in 2007 on a fieldwork trip to research the fiddle music; this yielded his 2009 Master's dissertation "Music from the Dead: The Tune-Making of John MacDougall" (Utah State University). He continues to perform Cape Breton music in a local band and at ceilidhs.

MacDonald, Roddy. *See* **MacDonald family of Inverness and South-West Margaree.**

MacDonald, Rodney. (1972-). Fiddle, step dancer, composer, teacher. Mabou. Born to Alex Angus and Elizabeth Ann (Beaton) MacDonald, he is connected to the Beaton family of Mabou on his mother's side, a grandson of Donald Angus and Elizabeth Beaton. His parents were both keen dancers and he was taught from a young age by Mary Janet MacDonald; he learned also from watching such as his uncle Donald Roddy MacDonald, Harvey Beaton, Willie Fraser and the Pellerin brothers, developing himself as a highly individual step dancer and, like other members of his extended family, with certain dance steps unique to the Mabou Coal Mines area. From the age of 8 he was involved in The Mabou Square Set, a group directed by Maureen MacKenzie from Mabou; he performed as part of this at concerts and events across the island. He got his first fiddle at the age of 9 and recalls spending hours moving the bow pretending to play along with tunes on *The Beatons of Mabou* LP. At 12, along with Glenn Graham and other cousins, he began to receive instruction from his uncle Kinnon Beaton. Their first public appearance was 9 months later (1985) at the Mabou Ceilidh Concert. Another uncle, piano player Joey Beaton, provided encouragement and guidance in bringing out old tunes and settings and unpicking the intricacies of the Mabou Coal Mines style for which Rodney's grandfather, Donald Angus Beaton, was renowned. Rodney's grandmother, Elizabeth Beaton, often provided piano accompaniment for him as he practised, and in 1988 it was she who accompanied him as he played for his first square set at a wedding. Buddy MacMaster, a keen dance-player, helped Rodney too in this regard, often according him the honour of playing for a set at the weekly dances in Glencoe Mills. He kept up his interest in dance when he left for college to study a Bachelor of Science in Physical Education at St. FX, teaching some 100 students at classes in Antigonish; during the summers he also taught step dance and fiddle in Mabou, Port Hood, Judique, Inverness, Whycocomagh and at the Gaelic College Following a short time as a teacher, in the late 1990s he entered politics, becoming a Member of the Legislative Assembly for the riding of Inverness (1999-2009) and held various ministerial portfolios from 1999-2009, including minister of tourism, culture, and heritage, minister of health promotion, minister of immigration, minister of sport and recreation, and minister of intergovernmental affairs. He succeeded Dr. John Hamm as premier of Nova Scotia (2006-2009). This did not afford him much time to pursue music, but he did manage occasional playing and teaching across Canada, in Boston and Detroit, and in Scotland. Today, however, he is much more active musically, with a second album in progress (the first was *Dancers' Delight* in 1995). Rodney is also featured on the Smithsonian CD *Cape Breton Fiddle and Piano Music: The Beaton Family of Mabou* (2004) and on other compilations, including *Cape Breton Lullabies*. He regularly teams up with Glenn Graham (with whom he released *Traditionally Rockin'* in 1997) for double-fiddle performances, accompanied on piano by Joel Chiasson, Allan Dewar, Jackie Dunn, Howie MacDonald or Mac Morin, but he also favours guitar accompaniment and performs with Patrick Gillis, Sandy MacDonald, or Colin MacDonald. Currently the CEO of the Gaelic College, he has overseen some significant developments there, including new policy directions in relation to step dance and piping and in nomenclature, some of which have attracted significant public debate. He also hosts weekly music performances during the summer season in his restaurant, Fiddler's, at the Ceilidh Cottages and Campground in West Mabou. **[Feintuch 2010]** *See* **Beaton family of Mabou.**

MacDonald, Shawn. *See* **MacDonald Family of Ironville.**

MacDonald, Winnie. *See* **MacDonald Family of Ironville.**

MacDougall, Ian. (1981-). Fiddle. Foot Cape, Inverness. Born to parents John Donald and Catherine (MacIsaac) MacDougall, it was his grandfather Angie D. MacIsaac, a fiddle player himself, who played often in the home and kindled Ian's interest in music. His cousin, local fiddler John MacDougall, gave him his first instrument and all his formal instruction. Ian also listened to a lot to dance tapes of Buddy MacMaster, Kinnon Beaton, Howie MacDonald and John Morris Rankin as well as to older records. He also sought out music in older print collections, thus generating a repertoire and style that were firmly old school. MacDougall sees himself as a dance player and has a reputation for having a lively style; he has played for dances organized by Cape Breton clubs in Toronto, Windsor and in the U.S. His playing can be heard on two recordings produced in supportive environments: *From Foot Cape* was recorded live in 2003 at a house party in Mabou, with Mac Morin on piano and Pat Gillis and Pius MacIsaac alternating on guitar; *Before You Arrive* was recorded in 2005 in the West Mabou dance hall, with Mac Morin on piano, playing in the empty hall before the dance. He has taught at the Ceòlas music school in South Uist and at the Gaelic College during several of their summer sessions.

MacDougall, John. (1925-2008). Fiddle, composer, teacher. Egypt, Inverness County. Born to parents George and Margaret (MacLellan) MacDougall his background in music can be traced back to his great-grandfather, Neil Jameison, a piper who lived in Piper's Glen, Inverness County, and who had a family of nine, all of whom could play the pipes. On the MacLellan side of the family his great-uncle and next-door neighbour, Donald MacLellan, was a good ear player. He got started on the fiddle by Dave Kennedy of Kenloch, who was married to his Aunt Annie; as a teenager he played a lot of parties and at dances in the schoolhouse. For about a year he regularly teamed up with Angus Allan Gillis to play at a dance at North Lake every week. While he learned a lot from watching the older players in relation to bowing and cuts in particular, by the age of 20 he was keen to learn to read music. Upon seeing an ad in the *Family Herald*, he signed up for a distance course with the Conservatory of Music, Vancouver. Later, Alex Glabais, a barber in Inverness, gave him a whole set of lesson books from the School of Music in New York. Following the broadcast of *The Vanishing Cape Breton Fiddler* (1971), Fr. Colonel MacLeod approached John about teaching fiddle to a group of students. The classes – the first formally organized instruction of fiddle music in Cape Breton – started in February 1972 and by July the students made their first public appearance, performing at the annual Scottish concert in Broad Cove. Following this, Fr. John Allan Gillis, parish priest at St. Mary's Parish, Mabou, offered to buy instruments for any local children interested in taking lessons and John started classes there in August 1972 with 15 students. He also began teaching adult classes in Mabou (from September 1972) and in Creignish (October 1972), with 12 students in each. Over the years he taught in Inverness, Broad Cove, Mabou, Judique, Creignish, Glendale, Scotsville, Margaree Forks and at the Gaelic College. Among his students was his young cousin, Ian MacDougall, who has recorded a number of Cape Breton fiddle albums. He operated a violin and piano repair shop out of his home and performed frequently at the Glenora Inn and Distillery with various piano accompanists including Penny Kennedy, Gregory Campbell and Isaac Fraser. His fiddle playing, by his own definition, was rugged and full of "scrapes and snarls"; he also held the fiddle in the old-fashioned manner, low on the chest.

MacDougall is particularly known for his eccentric claim that some 45,000 tunes have been channelled through him from dead Cape Breton fiddlers, those who, when they passed away, were musically illiterate and thus unable to impart many of their tunes to younger generations. Since 1975 these "lost tunes" would invade him in a veritable onslaught (up to 65 tunes at a time)

requiring him to write them down as they would come to him, fully formed. Consequently he generated paper copies of this substantial repertoire (by far the most prolific output from a single Cape Breton source), transcribed in staff notation and locked for safety in a chest in his home. MacDougall has described the tunes as being in an older Cape Breton style, many of them within the limited range of the Highland bagpipe or in high bass. Anxiously protective of his "compositions" he was notoriously reluctant to share hard copies of any of the tunes (although he would perform them) and largely resisted publication (although one tune, "John Charlie's Lament," appears in *Jerry Holland's Second Collection*, Jerry having learned it by ear from his father). MacDougall's music was the topic of an Master's dissertation, "Music from the Dead: The Tune-Making of John MacDougall," by Robert MacDonald (Utah State University, 2009); this examines the connection between MacDougall's tune "composing" and the supernatural as an extension and a Christianized revision of a traditional Scottish motif that connects music-making with fairy lore. [**MacGillivray 1981, MacDonald 2009**].

MacDougall, Mike. (1928-1981). Fiddle. Ingonish Beach, Victoria County. Born to parents Dan Rory and Mary Anne (Whitty) MacDougall in northern Cape Breton, he was reared in an environment long associated with music. Both his father and his grandfather, Rory MacDougall, played pipes and fiddle, while his mother sang. Mike and his brothers became interested in music at a young age, and by the time he was eight he was trying out the fiddle. Never formally taught, he was guided, however, by his father, who would listen to him practise and intervene if necessary. He also heard other musicians in the area, including "Little" Charlie Williams and Murray Hawley of Ingonish Ferry, Joey Doyle of Ingonish Center and Simon Morris of North Ingonish. As a teenager, Mike was already playing at dances and concerts in Cape North, Dingwall and Ingonish often with his brother, Tim. Through his involvement with Nova Scotia-based Irish bands such as

Ryan's Fancy and Barley Bree, Mike became the first known Cape Breton fiddler to visit Ireland, where he performed at some of the popular venues of the day such as The Embankment in Tallaght, Co. Dublin, and on various radio shows in the mid-1970s. He met Irish fiddler Sean Maguire and was responsible for introducing his music to Cape Breton players back at home, some of whom (such as Doug MacPhee) became avid followers. Although a fisherman by trade and never pursuing music as a full-time occupation, MacDougall played an important role in the wider Cape Breton tradition, particularly during the 1960s when fiddle music was being undermined and replaced by other forms of music and popular entertainment. At a time when fewer younger players were active on the scene, he was a source of inspiration to many, including Dave MacIsaac. He was regarded as bringing a special energy to his performances and having the ability to ignite and energize an audience. With a distinctive bow hold, which involved his arms being tucked in close to his body at the elbow, his style was lively and driving and, in its embellishments and intonation, evocative of the bagpipes. He played most often with guitar accompaniment provided by players such as Tim Donovan, Buddy MacDonald, Kevin Donovan, Donnie Campbell and Ralph Williams; this may not necessarily have been a matter of choice since there were few piano players in his area at the time; however, he also was involved with folk bands such as Ryan's Fancy, where guitar was the main accompanying instrument and this, no doubt, contributed to his ease in playing with this instrument. Mike started to compose in 1965 and many of his tunes – such as "Memories of Fr. Angus MacDonnell" and "Fr. Eugene's Welcome to Cape North" – have become standards in the Cape Breton repertoire; some, such as "Peggy's Jig," have also been popularized in the Irish tradition. He recorded with Ryan's Fancy and also appears on various anthology albums. While he had not made any solo recordings at the time of his death he had, however, made many tapes of his playing over the years in response to requests by friends for his music; one such, with an hour

Mike MacDougall. Courtesy of Topic Records.

of his playing, accompanied by Tim Donovan on guitar, was made in the months before his death for Fr. Hector MacDonald, and later released by *Cape Breton's Magazine* as *Mike MacDougall's Tape for Fr. Hector* (1985). He was also recorded by folk-music collector Diane Hamilton in the 1950s, the tapes from which are housed at the ITMA in Dublin, Ireland, as part of The Hamilton Collection; tracks from these appear on a 1995 album released by Hamilton (*Nova Scotia Folk Music from Cape Breton*). A Mike MacDougall Memorial Music Festival was established in his memory at Ingonish, and an annual scholarship in his name is awarded to a local student toward furthering their studies in music. [**Caplan 2006; MacGillivray 1981**].

MacEachern, "Big" Dan Hughie. Fiddle. Glenora, Kingsville, Inverness County, and Boston, MA. A great-grandson of Gilleasbuig Bàn MacEachern, who arrived in Cape Breton from Arisaig, Scotland in the early 1800s and settled in Bràigh na h-Aibhneadh, the Kingsville and Glendale areas of Inverness County; the family line included many fiddlers and pipers down through the generations. "Big" Dan Hughie was introduced to music from a young age; his father, Dòmhnagan a' Bharain (Dan "the Barrens") MacEachern, was a fiddler, known to be a good strathspey player; his siblings were musical – two brothers, John Angus and John R., both played fiddle; a sister, Ceiteag Bhàn, was a step dancer and another sister, Kate Jess, played accordion and sang in Gaelic. Moving to Boston,

MacEachern took part in one of the first major fiddle contests held there in 1926 and, judged by Scotland's James Scott Skinner, took first prize. Along with another Cape Breton fiddler, Charlie MacKinnon from Lake Ainslie, he collaborated with the Irish-American piano player and dance band leader, Dan Sullivan, in the group known as both the Columbia Scotch Band and the Caledonia Scotch Band. The first Cape Breton fiddlers known to have recorded commercially, they released three 78s on the Columbia label. MacEachern is related to subsequent generations of Cape Breton fiddlers, among them Howie MacDonald, whose grandmother (on his mother's side) was his sister Kate Jess. *See* **MacDonald family of Queensville; MacDonald family of Westmount.**

MacEachern, Bob. (1961-). Broadcaster. Judique and Port Hastings, Cape Breton. He began his broadcasting career with CIGO as an announcer on the graveyard shift and worked through management positions until, along with his wife, Brenda, he bought the station in 1993; it forms part of his portfolio of business interests. In 2000, CIGO was the first Nova Scotia station to make the transition from AM to FM and is now known as 101.5 The Hawk. He has hosted the weekly show *Highland Fling* on that station since the early 1980s. MacEachern is active with community organizations including the Strait Area Chamber of Commerce, Board of Governors of NSCC, Festival Antigonish and the Port Hastings Historical Society. In 2013, he received the Radio Television Digital News Directors' Lifetime Achievement Award and, in 2014, the Jack Hartery Lifetime Achievement Award in recognition of his commitment to business and community in the Strait Region. [Feintuch 2010]. *See* **Hawk, The; radio.**

MacEachern, Dan Hughie. (1914-1996). Fiddle, composer. Queensville, Inverness County. Born to parents Duncan and Mary (MacMillan) MacEachern, he grew up in a household where his brothers John Willie and Alex both played fiddle and where his sisters Kay and Marcela would provide unique rhythmic accompaniment by tap-ping the fiddle with knitting needles as the tunes were being played. The home was a gathering place for musicians, and fiddlers such as Gordon MacQuarrie, "Big" Ronald MacLellan and Dan R. MacDonald would frequently call, as did a cousin, Peter MacFarlane, who introduced Dan Hughie to music notation. Dan Hughie performed first in public for a wedding and went on to play dances at the schoolhouse in Sugar Camp and in Creignish, where he would typically team up with his brother, John Willie, playing in octaves. Dan Hughie's repertoire was extensive, and much of it was acquired from printed collections. Inspired to make his own tunes by the compositions of such as Gow and Skinner, he became one of the first Cape Breton fiddlers to produce a significant body of self-composed music. He particularly liked slow airs and marches, idioms in which he regularly composed. Some of his tunes that have now become standards are regarded as being quite distinctive and complex; the descriptor "twisty" is frequently used within the local fiddle music community to describe them. In 1975 the first volume of *MacEachern's Collection* was published—the first collection of Cape Breton tunes to appear in print since the 1940 MacQuarrie collection and the first collection to focus on the work of a single fiddle-composer from the region; a second volume

Dan Hughie MacEachern. Courtesy of Topic Records.

was published in 1993. MacEachern's contribution to the Cape Breton tradition was celebrated in a Tribute Ceilidh held in Sydney in 1980, and again in 2003 during Celtic Colours in a show titled "Trip to Mabou Ridge: Dan Hughie's Legacy." He did not record commercially, although an album of his playing was mastered from home recordings and released posthumously in 2003 by his niece and grand-niece, Margie and Jackie Dunn, as *The Land of My Love*, after one of his own tunes. [**MacGillivray 1981**].

— ❧ —

MacEachern's Collection, Cape Breton Scottish Music for the Violin. A 1975 tune collection by Dan Hughie MacEachern. The only previous publication of tunes from Cape Breton had been Gordon MacQuarrie's 1940 work (reprinted in 1975), which contained tunes by 14 Cape Breton composers; this volume represents the first collection from a single composer. Its 44 pages have 108 tunes in total – 39 jigs, 17 strathspeys, 31 reels, 10 marches, 4 slow strathspeys, 3 pastoral airs and 4 hornpipes – all transcribed by hand by Hector MacKenzie. Among the tunes are some of Dan Hughie's most famous compositions: "Bell Piano Strathspey," "Bell Piano Reel," "Fraser's Jig," "My Friend Buddy Jig," "Alex MacEachern's Strathspey," "John Allan's Jig," "Champion Jig," "Red Mill Reel," "Snow Plough Reel," "Alex Francis MacKay's New Fiddle Reel," "Margaret Chisholm's Jig" and "Canso Crossing Hornpipe."

— ❧ —

MacEachern's Collection: The Music of Dan Hughie MacEachern. Volume 2. Researched and published by Dan Hughie's niece, Margaret (MacEachern) Dunn in 1993, with music notation by Stan Chapman and Scott Macmillan. This collection has 170 tunes, all but three of them composed by Dan Hughie. There are 20 pastoral airs, 23 marches, 35 strathspeys, 42 reels, 45 jigs and 5 "miscellaneous" tunes, among which are a hornpipe and a clog; there are also compositions by others, including Alex Joe MacEachern ("Alex Joe's Jig"), Dave MacIsaac ("Dan Hughie's Kidney Stone," a reel) and Jackie Dunn ("Dan Hughie MacEachern's Reel"); the tune types are for the most part indicated in the titles. An alphabetic index lists the tunes within tune-type categories, a MacEachern family tree and profile by Margaret Dunn locate the composer in his milieu, and information is given on tune titles. The collection includes popular Dan Hughie compositions such as "Kennedy Street March," "Trip to Mabou Ridge March," "Juanita's Jig," "Marie MacInnis's Jig" and "The Deepdale Jig."

— ❧ —

McGillivray family of Antigonish. A trio of siblings from mainland Nova Scotia who have made a significant and varied contribution to the Cape Breton music tradition of the past twenty years. Kendra, Troy and Sabra are the grandchildren of Hugh A. MacDonald, "the Polka King" of Lanark, Antigonish County; another family connection, also on their mother's side, is Mike Denny, who was director of the National Folk Festival at Wolf Trap, Washington, DC, for many years and a regular visitor to their home, bringing with him many home recordings and introducing them to various Irish and Irish-American musicians. Their parents are Anthony (Tony) Jerome and Janice Anne (MacDonald) MacGillivray (1951-2005); their mother step danced, played fiddle and piano and accompanied her children at all of their early performances.

MacGillivray, Kendra. (1972-). Fiddle, piano, music teacher. Antigonish and Charlottetown, PEI. She started taking formal lessons with Stan Chapman at the age of 9, part of a group that included Natalie MacMaster, Ashley MacIsaac, Jackie Dunn, Neil Beaton, John Pellerin, Wendy MacIsaac and Stephanie Wills; as a teenager she took instruction in classical violin from Bob Murray. Living in Antigonish, listening to commercial recordings and home tapes was a big part of the learning process; Howie MacDonald's first album was a particular favourite, and Kendra would learn each of the tunes and play along to the recording.

Local house parties, such as those at Stuart and Mary Beaton's, where Jerry Holland would often visit, were also important; she would learn a new tune each time to play for Holland. During the summer months the MacGillivray family would attend many of the outdoor concerts in Cape Breton, where they would get to hear players such as Buddy MacMaster, Dave MacIsaac, Theresa MacLellan, Kinnon Beaton, The Barra MacNeils and The Rankin Family. Kendra began playing in public from around the age of 10, accompanied by her mother or her brother on piano. She released her first album in 1990 (*Antigonish's Own*), followed by *Clear the Track* (1996), *Over the Waves* (2000) and *Love o' the Isles* (2008), all issued on her own label, Kenroy Music Productions. For 25 years she has been teaching group and private lessons under the banner of the Kendra MacGillivray School of Celtic Music, first in Antigonish, later in Halifax and most recently in Charlottetown, PEI. She also teaches at Holland College School of Performing Arts in PEI (a performing arts school that is partnered with Berklee College of Music, Boston) and she has taught at the Ceilidh Trail School of Celtic Music.

MacGillivray, Sabra. (1976-). A champion highland dancer, a step dancer and bodhrán player who has performed and taught across Canada, the U.S., Australia, Scotland and Ireland. She is founder, director and choreographer of the Celtic Touch Dancers, a group of award-winning highland and step dancers.

MacGillivray, Troy. (1980-). Fiddle, piano, composer, step dancer, teacher. Antigonish. Encouraged by his mother and his two sisters, from the age of 8 he sat in in on fiddle classes being taught by Kendra. He began taking classical piano lessons (following the Toronto Conservatory of Music curriculum), with Sr. Rodriguez Steele, who appreciated Cape Breton music as she had grown up in Boisdale; she would let him practice chording to fiddle tunes at the end of each class. Growing up, his focus was on Cape Breton fiddle and piano music (with John Morris Rankin, Howie MacDonald and Hilda Chiasson being his main inspiration), but his influences also included local Pictou County musicians, Western Canadian players (such as Andy de Jarlis), and Irish players, Máire O'Keeffe and Brendan Mulvihill, who he heard on home recordings made in Cape Breton in the early 1990s. A graduate of St. FX, majoring in music, and with an Applied Music Technology Diploma for recording engineering, MacGillivray was 22 when he made his first solo public appearance playing fiddle at The Red Shoe Pub in Mabou; previously he had been a regular on the Cape Breton circuit playing piano with fiddlers such as Kendra MacGillivray, Rodney MacDonald, Glenn Graham and Jackie Dunn. He has played, and continues to play, dances and, as is typical of most contemporary players, appears with various musicians – most often with Allan Dewar or Brent Chiasson from PEI – when he is playing fiddle. As a piano accompanist, he performs often with Andrea Beaton on fiddle, although their roles typically interchange. Along with Shane Cook, a Canadian and U.S. National Fiddle champion, who spent time studying Cape Breton fiddle music, Troy released *When Here Meets There* in 2008, which positions Cape Breton, Irish and old-time fiddling together. While working on this project in Ontario he became interested in the contest scene and has participated in the Canadian Grand Masters Fiddling Competition. He has also been involved in that as a judge (2008, 2011) and currently he sits on the board of directors of the association. He has performed at major U.S. festivals and fiddle camps, and often plays in New England and the Boston area; in Europe, he has played at the Tønder Festival in Denmark, Celtic Connections, Glasgow, and at Ceòlas in South Uist. In 2008 he played on the Irish Spring Tour of Germany with Irish flute player, Nuala Kennedy, and in 2013 he performed at Fleadh Cheoil na hÉireann in Derry, following on from his performance there with Shane Cook at NAFCo in 2012. 50 or so of his compositions are published, and he has several albums (including *Music for Highland Dance*, 2011), these earning him awards from both ECMA (2008, 2009) and MNS (2008). In style, MacGillivray is a unique voice, not only for his fiddle playing, but also his piano accompaniment, in which can be heard his classical and jazz training and the influence from other traditions which affect his chord choices, voicings and voice leadings, and his approach to modulations. Troy MacGillivray has performed and taught Cape Breton music across Canada, in the U.S., Europe, Asia and Australia, and his versatility has led to much collaborative work. For his contribution to culture he was awarded a Diamond Jubilee medal in 2012.

— ≈ —

Troy MacGillivray, Fiddle Tunes. This 2008 collection is unique for being an online, PDF-format publication only. It has 17 of MacGillivray's tunes (one made in collaboration with Gabrielle MacLellan), biographical information on the composer and on his grandfather (fiddler Hugh Angus MacDonald, for who the jig "Hughie No. 11" was composed), a brief introduction to the author's home area of Lanark, Nova Scotia, and occasional references to recordings where particular tunes may be found; artist images, CD artwork and maps are also included. The flexible format is intended to facilitate both distribution and ongoing updating and additions.

— ≈ —

MacGillivray family of Mira. Although none of them are fiddle players, the MacGillivray family have contributed to the Cape Breton fiddle tradition in many ways across two generations. Allister MacGillivray is a noted songwriter and scholar, whose publications *The Cape Breton Fiddler* (CBU Press, 1981, re-issued by Sea-Cape Music, 1997) and *A Cape Breton Ceilidh* (Sea-Cape Music, 1988) continue to be a significant resource. His wife, **Beverly**, is a singer, manager and supporter of the arts in Cape Breton, and their two children, **Ciarán** (1987-) and **Fiona** (1989-) formed the band The Cottars while still at school, going on to record and tour internationally with artists such as John McDermott and The Chieftains. *See* **Cottars, The.**

   MacGillivray, Allister. (1948-). Songwriter, guitar, folklorist, author. Born in Glace Bay, Cape Breton, MacGillivray began singing at a young age

with the Immaculate Boys' Choir in Bridgeport, NS, and as a member of a touring variety show, Joe Gaul's Parade of Stars. He toured with such artists as John Allan Cameron (1969-1972), Ryan's Fancy (1973-1979) and Tommy Makem and Liam Clancy (1979-1980). His focus shifted to songwriting and he has composed many songs in the folk idiom – among them "Song for the Mira," which has been recorded across the world over 135 times and translated into multiple languages. His material has been used widely by Cape Breton artists such as John Allan Cameron, The Barra MacNeils and The Cottars, as well as by many high-profile international artists, groups and choirs. Beside his surveys of Cape Breton fiddlers, dancers, pianists and pipers, MacGillivray's other publications include folios of traditional and contemporary material: *Song for the Mira* (New Dawn Enterprises, 1979), *The Cape Breton Song Collection* (Sea-Cape Music, 1985) and *The Nova Scotia Song Collection* (Sea-Cape Music, 1989). As a record producer, he has worked with fiddler Buddy MacMaster and the Men of the Deeps, and produced two albums for The Cottars that won ECMAs. A graduate of St. FX, he was awarded an honorary doctorate from CBU in 1997. He was invested into the Order of Canada in 2013; as part of the ceremony one of his compositions, "Away from the Roll of the Sea," was performed in The Peace Tower on Parliament Hill by Ottawa carillonneur, Andrea McCrady.

MacInnes, Sheldon. *See* **MacInnis family of Big Pond.**

MacInnis family of Big Pond. Fiddler Dan Joe MacInnis and his wife Christie raised a family of 11 in Big Pond. The house was a regular visiting spot for many Cape Breton fiddlers, and in this rich musical environment most of the children learned to step dance and a number became noted musicians – Jamie on bagpipes and George on piano; Sheldon is a piper, dancer, researcher and advocate for Cape Breton music. The music connection has continued on through marriage; Trese, a step dancer, lives in Windsor, Ontario, with her husband, fiddle player Jimmie MacNeil of Dearborn, Michigan; Marie lives in Big Pond, married to singer-guitarist Malcie MacPhee; their son Calum is also a singer-guitarist; Patricia lives in Sydney with her husband, Kenny Hutchins, a well-regarded guitarist and fiddler who plays jazz and rock as well as Cape Breton fiddle music.

MacInnis, Dan Joe. (1922-1991). Fiddle. Born to parents Dan Peter and Mary (Campbell) Ma-cInnis (Mary "Danny Peter"), and a descendant of Scottish settlers who had emigrated from South Uist to Woodbine, Cape Breton, in 1842, he was brought up in Alexander Street, Sydney, listening to Gaelic being spoken and sung. Dan Joe was introduced to the fiddle by "Old" Peter Campbell of Woodbine, who would call at the MacInnis family home selling buttermilk and vegetables. He started to play at around 8 years of age on a fiddle he discovered in the attic, and made his first public appearance accompanied by Steve Googoo on guitar at the Membertou Reserve; later he developed a dance circuit in the Sydney area. Bill Lamey – another regular visitor to the house – was a major influence on his playing (to the extent that Dan Joe would position a picture of Lamey in front of him when he practiced). Lamey encouraged him to sight read, and Dan Joe, like a number of other fiddlers during the 1950s, became obsessed with the Scottish collections and established sources in Scotland, who would mail old tune-books to him. He purchased a substantial number of these (including the Gow, MacGlashan, Simon Fraser and Athole collections) and dispersed them among the local fiddle-playing community across Cape Breton Island. He also borrowed books from other fiddlers and, as was the practice of the day, would copy tunes from these by hand. He was always interested in discussing and analyzing the interpretative possibilities emerging form the printed sources and, as such, might be regarded as what later commentators have referred to as a "scholarly" fiddler. He had a knack for being able to identify good tunes from the collections, and so could assemble impressive medleys. Local fiddler-composers such as Dan R. MacDonald and Dan Hughie MacEachern would often send him copies of their latest compositions, confident that through his interpretation the tunes would enter the common repertoire "correctly." He thus had

Dan Joe MacInnis from Big Pond. Courtesy of the MacInnes collection.

an impressive repertoire that reflected the older Scottish tradition as well as the contemporary Cape Breton one. While he was inclined toward performing in listening environments (and was particularly drawn to non-dance tune types such as airs and marches), it was, nonetheless, the dance circuit that occupied much of his life as a semi-professional performer, with occasional competition participation and victory.

Over a five-year period in the late 1950s and early 1960s, Dan Joe performed each Saturday night on CJCB radio's *MacDonald Tobacco Show* and announced details of his upcoming dances in Big Pond, Sydney, Grand Mira, Eskasoni and Bucklaw. Through his regular radio broadcasts he acquired many fans for his music outside of Cape Breton, especially in Newfoundland, which he discovered when he visited there in 1965; he visited Scotland once, in 1973, as part of a group from the Cape Breton Gaelic Society. He made his first recordings in the 1950s – 78s on the Celtic label; in the 1960s he recorded 3 LPs with Celtic and Banff-Rodeo (*The Cape Breton Fiddle of Dan Joe MacInnis, The Scottish Canadian Fiddle of Dan Joe MacInnis*, with Doug MacPhee on piano, and *Scottish Canadian Fiddle Music*, with Loretta Beaudry on piano). He was also featured on a number of Cape Breton fiddle-music anthologies, including *Celtic Music of Cape Breton–Volume 1* with his son, George MacInnis, on piano (1984). Along with Jack MacNeil, Dan Joe was a founder of the first Big Pond Concert in 1964 and his popularity among the fiddle community across the island drew many of them to the annual event. The MacInnis home in Big Pond was a frequent venue for ceilidhs and house sessions; while these were typically instigated by Dan Joe, they were made possible, to a large extent, through the hospitality offered by Christie and the sense of fun and joy she created around the music for visitors and family alike. [**MacGillivray 1981; MacInnes 2007**].

MacInnes, Sheldon. East Bay, Cape Breton. Piper, step dancer, researcher and writer. The eldest of the MacInnis family, Sheldon grew up with music and dance part of the fabric of everyday life; many of the island's best-known performers were regular visitors to the home in Big Pond. As a young adult, Sheldon was heavily involved in the production of the popular Big Pond Summer Concert (1969-1992). As a musician and vocalist he toured and recorded with folk group, Sons of Skye (1974-1984); a CD of the group's 1981 LP recording *Both Sides of the Water* was released in 2014. Following university (St. FX and Merrill Palmer Institute, Wayne State University, Michigan, where he produced a Master's dissertation on the Cape Breton diaspora community in Windsor), MacInnes taught in the public education system in Halifax and became involved in presenting and producing Cape Breton music performances (1971-1975). At CBU from 1976 until 2008, he was active in teaching, research, publishing, producing and administrating programs and courses in Celtic music, Gaelic language, and traditional dance. Segments of his fieldwork

remain at the CBU archives. In the 1980s and the 1990s, independent TV and radio broadcasts, as well as CBC, MITV, CTV and BBC, included his work in documentaries and special programs. His professional work in Celtic music at the university and in the community helped to pave the way for CBU's Centre for Cape Breton Studies and CBU's unique program in ethnomusicology. In addition to a series of short articles, Sheldon has published two books, *A Journey in Celtic Music–Cape Breton Style* (1997) and *Buddy MacMaster–The Judique Fiddler* (2007). In his retirement, he continues to write with a view to further publications.

MacInnis, Frank. (1943-). Port Hawkesbury and Creignish, Inverness County. Although not a musician, he is related to many Cape Breton fiddlers such as Buddy MacMaster and the MacLellans of Riverside and was raised in a music environment. His paternal grandmother, who played the bagpipes, had seven brothers who were fiddlers and, on his mother's side, various members of the MacMaster family played fiddles and accordions. He was always involved in local events such as concerts and dances, which led to him taking a pivotal role in establishing the first fiddle festivals in Glendale in the 1970s as well as the Committee for Cape Breton (later the CBFA). Such events and activities were central to the revival of the local fiddle tradition and had been sparked by the implications inherent in the 1971 CBC-TV documentary, *The Vanishing Cape Breton Fiddler*. MacInnis co-hosted a radio program, *Scottish Strings*, for a period of 7 years on CJFX. A stalwart supporter of and authority on Cape Breton music, he remains involved in a limited capacity with the CBFA and continues to be an avid square-dance attendee.

MacInnis, Joseph J. (J. J.). (1887-1944). Sydney. Born to Joseph and Mary (MacDonald) MacInnis of East Bay. His mother died when he was 12 and he went to live with his maternal grandfather, John MacDonald, at Blackett's Lake; there he was exposed to the Gaelic language and to an extensive collection of books on Scottish history. He moved to Sydney and married Margaret MacNeil of Pipers' Cove. Their home on Campbell Street became a popular house for fiddlers to gather, MacInnis being a fiddler himself and owner of a collection of almost 40 published tune books that he readily shared. A member of the Scottish Catholic Society he was involved in the promotion of Scottish culture in Cape Breton. His articles in the Cape Breton editions of the *Canadian-American Gael, Eilean Cheap Breatann,* were titled "Scottish Music in Cape Breton, Nova Scotia: Violin Players I have met" (Vol. 1, 1943-1944) and "Scottish Violin Music in Cape Breton, Nova Scotia: Violin Players I have met" (Vol. 2, 1948), and represented some of the earliest biographies of Cape Breton fiddlers in print. Fiddlers featured were Vincent A. MacLellan, Ronald MacLellan, Malcolm H. Gillis, Sandy MacLean, William (Bill) Lamey, Angus Chisholm, Duncan J. MacIntyre, Angus Allan Gillis, Malcolm Beaton, Dan R. MacDonald, Daniel (Dan J.) Campbell (Vol. 1) and James D. Gillis, Charles MacLellan, John (Johnny "MacVarish") MacDonald, Dougald MacIntyre and Tena Campbell (Vol. 2).

MacInnis, Mary Elizabeth (MacMaster). *See* **MacMaster family of Judique.**

MacInnis, Mick. (1870-1946). Fiddle. Terra Nova, Glengarry, Cape Breton. Born to parents Rory and Mary (MacPherson) MacInnis; among his seven siblings, brothers Jonathan (1863-1946), Martin (1865-1928) and Jim (1879-1954) all played fiddle and spoke Gaelic. Self-taught and an ear player, he won a contest in North Sydney in 1926 and subsequently won the finals held in Boston; he won various other contests throughout his career. *See* **competition.**

MacInnis, Ron. (1944-). Sydney, Halifax and Woodside, NS. Although he left Cape Breton with his family as a teenager he returned after graduating from university and worked for CHER radio, often on remote broadcasts of Scottish concerts, a job which he credits with sowing the seeds of his interest in and love of Cape Breton fiddle music and culture. Later working for the CBC in Halifax he put forward a proposal for a documentary called *The Vanishing Cape Breton Fiddler,* which he worked on originally for radio and then for television. When this was broadcast in the early 1970s, it provoked a response from a small number of fiddle-music enthusiasts, who mobilized the wider fiddle community, ultimately creating a revival movement; events such as the Glendale Fiddlers' Festival, the establishment of the CBFA, various recordings, documentaries, academic research and publications all emerged as a consequence of this movement; furthermore, long-term changes in relation to the transmission of the music (through the setting up, for the first time, of formal teaching programs) also resulted, as did a shift in the sense of ownership of the music and a move from it being referred to as Scottish or Scotch to being celebrated as Cape Breton. MacInnis made efforts during the 1980s to document the response to the *VCBF* in a live show that was staged in Halifax. In 2001 and 2002 his work was further profiled in a number of TV documentaries (*Gzowski and Co., The Fate of the Fiddle* and *The Wakeup Call*). Invited to sit on the board of Celtic Colours in its early years, that festival also acknowledged his role in the Cape Breton fiddle story in shows in 2002 (*The Thriving Cape Breton Fiddler*) and in 2008 (*Salute to the Cape Breton Fiddler*). A freelance writer, newspaper columnist and an occasional fiddle player, MacInnis is currently working on a documentary entitled *The Return of the "Vanishing" Cape Breton Fiddler* intended for broadcast in 2015. *See* **Vanishing Cape Breton Fiddler, The.**

MacIntyre, Dougald. *See* **MacPhee family of New Waterford.**

MacIntyre, Sandy. (1935-). Fiddle, composer, teacher. Inverness, Cape Breton, and Toronto. One of 14 children born to parents Ronald and Cassie MacIntyre, both fiddle players and Gaelic speakers, Hugh Alexander ("Sandy") grew up in a rich music environment. Among his family members who played music (fiddles and pipes), step danced or sang were his grandfather John Angus MacIsaac, his brothers John R. and

Francis, and several uncles and aunts. He started playing the pump organ at age 8 or 9, chording for family members and visiting fiddlers; he took up the guitar in high school and also played drums with the Inverness pipe band. He began playing the fiddle as a teenager but it was not until he was in Toronto, at the age of 19, that he began to pursue this – and music literacy – in earnest. Linking up with other exiled Cape Bretoners to bring musicians to Toronto for Cape Breton-style dances and to keep the music alive, he played a large part in creating a vibrant Cape Breton music scene in the city. During the 1970s, just as the fiddle tradition was being revitalized back home in Cape Breton, MacIntyre was making appearances at such events as the Mariposa Folk Festival (1971, 1972). He managed and performed at Toronto's Scottish Talent Club for about eight years and later ran the sessions held at the Bow and Arrow pub. Along with Winnie Chafe, Buddy MacMaster, John Campbell, Cameron Chisholm and Doug MacPhee he was a member of the group of Cape Breton musicians featured weekly on the CBC-TV show, *Ceilidh,* recorded in Halifax in the early 1970s; he was also a member of the Cape Breton Symphony Fiddlers for many years. His albums include *Let's Have a Ceilidh with Sandy MacIntyre, Cape Breton–My Land in Music, Island Treasure* Vol. 1, *Cape Breton Fiddle Music: Steeped In Tradition, Steeped and Served: The Sandy MacIntyre Collection* (2-CD Compilation) and he has published a book, *Cape Breton Traditional Style Fiddle Sets with Guitar Tablature* (Sandy MacIntyre and Leigh Cline, 2011), which includes some of his own tune compositions, a number of which have become part of the Cape Breton canon. MacIntyre has also become one of the most established teachers of Cape Breton music, both in Toronto and, each summer, in Cape Breton, where he taught for more than 25 years at the Gaelic College. Since 1991 he also taught and performed at various events in Scotland and at U.S. fiddle camps and festivals such as the American Festival of Fiddle Tunes (Port Townsend, WA) and the Rocky Mountain Fiddle Camp (Colorado). In 2009, Celtic Colours paid tribute to him in a

show in Inverness where he was joined by former students Jeffrey Gosse, Colin Grant, Kimberley Fraser and Dawn and Margie Beaton. A number of fiddlers have composed tunes in Sandy's honour: "Sandy MacIntyre's Trip to Boston" (composed by John Campbell), "Sandy MacIntyre's" (composed by Brenda Stubbert), "Sandy MacIntyre's March" (composed by Donald Angus Beaton). [**MacGillivray 1981**].

– ≈ –

Cape Breton Traditional Style Fiddle Sets with Guitar Tablature. A tune book published by Cape Breton fiddler Sandy MacIntyre and Toronto guitarist, Leigh Cline, in 2011, part of the Mel Bay series. It is unusual in that it foregrounds the guitar, which is rarely heard within Cape Breton without the piano; off-island, however, Cape Breton musicians have often been accompanied by guitar in the absence of pianos and, indeed, piano players. The book's 120 pages have a brief introduction to fiddle ornaments, photographs of the authors, and the tunes themselves arranged in sets (jigs, reels, strathspey-reels, march-strathspey-reels, air-hornpipes, air-waltz-strathspey-reel); this is a unique approach which is clearly aimed at making Cape Breton music accessible to an "outside" audience. Among the 78 traditional and contemporary tunes, 16 are by MacIntyre himself.

– ≈ –

MacIsaac siblings of Creignish. Brother and sister Ashley and Lisa MacIsaac are both full-time professional musicians, who have, separately from each other, taken their roots in Cape Breton fiddle music and step dance into many new contexts and soundscapes. Born to parents Angus and Carmelita MacIsaac they grew up surrounded by music. Angus is himself a fiddle player who played often at home and performed with the CBFA, and various members of the extended family, including cousins Wendy MacIsaac and Natalie MacMaster, who lived nearby, and who were also involved in music. In the post-*VCBF* revival activity of the 1970s-early 1980s, the MacIsaacs and their peers were afforded many opportunities to pursue their musical interests through classes and performances. While their professional paths have not often intersected, the siblings did collaborate on an album released in 2009, *New Family Tradition*.

MacIsaac, Ashley. (1975-). Fiddle, piano, step dance, vocals. MacIsaac has made a significant contribution to the music, not only as an outstanding exponent of the traditional sound and style but also in terms of demonstrating its potential in relation to crossover with other genres, introducing it to new audiences and raising its profile on the international stage. A 3-time Juno Award winner he broke through to the mainstream with his double-platinum album *Hi, How Are You Today?* (1995) and the single "Sleepy Maggie" (featuring Gaelic vocals by Mary Jane Lamond), which achieved international radio play. Through the 1990s and early 2000s he maintained a high-profile career, one of a small number of Cape Breton musicians who, due to the attentions of the wider Canadian music industry, came to prominence at the time as part of a wider Celtic music revival. Following a distinctly different path from his Cape Breton peers, MacIsaac collaborated with such artists as Paul Simon, David Byrne and composer Philip Glass, while developing his own approach, which saw him experiment with marrying Cape Breton fiddle tunes and performance practices to rock, punk, pop and other genres. He toured with acts from The Chieftains to The White Stripes, The Smashing Pumpkins and Sting, guested with Symphony Nova Scotia, collaborated with members of Celtic rock band Spirit of the West and performed at the opening ceremonies for the Winter Olympics in Vancouver (2010). Sometimes highly controversial, he is indeed regarded by some as the *enfant terrible* of the Cape Breton fiddle tradition. He frequently invited a strong media focus, appearing on such shows as *Late Night with Conan O'Brien* (1997), where his performance led to an indecent-exposure scandal; he was the featured artist on *Star Portraits* (Bravo!) and on the CBC-

Ashley MacIsaac with Maybelle Chisholm MacQueen on piano. Photo by Corey Katz. Courtesy of Celtic Colours International Festival.

TV documentary *Me, Myself and the Devil: The Life and Times of Ashley MacIsaac* (2005). He signed with A&M Records, Decca, Loggerhead and Linus at different times, although throughout his career to date he has been involved with various other labels as well as having independently released some material.

Encouraged in music and dance at home and attending lessons with Stan Chapman (fiddle) and Harvey Beaton (step dance), MacIsaac released his first album *Close to the Floor*, in 1992 at the age of 17; this was followed with *A Cape Breton Christmas* in 1993, making MacIsaac one of the first Cape Breton fiddler to tap into in the specialist Christmas-music market. Since then he has released several albums. Many of these demonstrate his innovative and experimental tendencies (e.g., *Hi, How Are You Today?* [1995], *Helter's Celtic* [1999], *Crossover* [2011]); *Pride,* released in 2005, is in fact a non-fiddle album but rather a collection of pop songs that saw him venture into completely new territory. Other albums are much more rooted in the Cape Breton tradition (e.g., *Fine, Thank You Very Much* [1996]) while some are collaborations with Cape Breton musicians such as Howie MacDonald (*Cape Breton Fiddle Music, Not Calm*, 2001), Dave MacIsaac (*Fiddle Music 101*, 2000) and piano player, Barbara Magone (*Beautiful Lake Ainslie*, 2012). His catalogue includes a "best-of" album (2008) and a "live" album from the Savoy Theatre, with Maybelle Chisholm MacQueen on piano; in recent years this duo has played often at events in Cape Breton and in 2015 they performed at Carnegie Hall, sharing the bill with such as Philip Glass.

MacIsaac toured with the production *TapEire* in 2006-2007, a stage show based on the life of tap dancer James Devine, the "fastest dancer in the world" according to *Guinness World Records* and is featured on the associated CD release (Linus). Some of his video releases gained much airplay on such as MuchMusic and his music is featured on the soundtrack of several films and documentaries; he appears in an acting role in films such as *The Hanging Garden* (1997), *New Waterford Girl* (1999) and *Marion Bridge* (2002). In his autobiography *Fiddling with Disaster* (2003) he talks candidly about his career and the personal issues he faced including substance abuse and his sexuality. MacIsaac's music (specifically his 1995 album, *Hi, How Are You Today?*) was the subject of an MA dissertation at McGill University: "Devil on the Fiddle: The Musical and Social Ramifications of Genre Transformation in Cape Breton Music" (MacDonald 2006). His colourful narrative has continued with stories of bankruptcy, auctioning off a percentage of his future earnings on eBay, announcing (and later retracting) his intentions to pursue a political career, and his position on gay rights. Although he maintained a somewhat lower profile for a number of years MacIsaac has in 2015 publically declared his renewed ambition to achieve global fame. A left-handed fiddler, a piano player and a step dancer, he remains unique in his ability to perform Cape Breton fiddle tunes that can completely engage a discerning local audience and energize a hall full of dancers while, equally comfortably, break all of these conventions in presenting this music to new audiences in new contexts. [Caplan 2006; Historica Canada 2015; MacDonald 2006; MacIsaac and Condron 2003]

MacIsaac, Lisa. Fiddle, vocals. Besides playing Cape Breton fiddle tunes, Lisa gained experience as a back-up player for songs through her role in productions such as the *Cape Breton Summertime Revue* and *Dream a Little Dream* with former Mamas and Papas member, Denny Doherty; she also performed in this capacity with Bruce Guthro, a Cape Breton singer-songwriter and lead singer with Scottish band, Runrig. Since the late 1990s she and Brenley MacEachern have comprised the group Madison Violet (originally Madviolet), having originally met in Toronto and becoming involved in the band Zöebliss. A busy international touring outfit, Madison Violet have released 3 albums independently in Canada (*Mad Violet,* 2002; *Worry the Jury,* 2004; *Caravan,* 2006) and then signed a record deal with True North Records for their next album, *No Fool For Trying* (2009). Following a Live CD, *Live Crossroads März* (2010), *The Good in Goodbye* was released in 2012 followed by *The Year of the Horse* in 2014. Their music – involving close vocal harmonies and fiddle backup – has been described as acoustic folk and pop country, and the duo has been has been recognized with various awards from such as the ECMA, CFMAs and the Independent Music Awards. [Caplan 2006].

MacIsaac, Dave. (1955-). Guitar, fiddle, bass, mandonlin, tenor banjo and mandola. Halifax, NS. Born to parents Alex Dan MacIsaac and Frances MacDonald his family roots on his father's side were in Inverness County. Originally from St. Rose, his father was a fiddle player who played for Cape Breton dances in Halifax in the 1950s; fiddlers visiting or based for a time in Halifax would often visit the family home and recordings of Cape Breton fiddle music were regularly played. He started playing guitar at the age of 9, accompanying his father at house parties and playing in rock groups at school. While he had been trying out the fiddle from the age of 6 it was not until he was a teenager, and inspired by hearing Angus Chisholm play, that he returned to it, often playing in a twin-fiddle combination with his father. He developed an extensive repertoire much of it comprising old traditional tunes that were not part of the popular canon. Encouraged by Chisholm to learn to read music, he became an avid note reader and collected a substantial library of printed collections and private manuscripts; he also amassed one of the largest collections of home tape recordings, much of which he received from Roddy MacDonald in Halifax. Besides having an extensive and unusual repertoire of tunes he is also known as a source of information on tune names and settings, and is frequently consulted by other fiddlers on such matters. MacIsaac's versatility as a guitarist has enabled him to pursue a full-time professional career in the music industry, playing in a variety of styles and contexts and with such artists as John Allan Cameron, Rita MacNeil and Natalie MacMaster. He has been featured on a significant proportion of all Cape Breton fiddle recordings since the 1980s and, alongside pianist Hilda Chiasson, contributed to the highly coordinated and polished arrangements that were first presented on Jerry Holland's *Master Cape Breton Fiddler* album (1982). Following in the footsteps of John Allan Cameron in adapting Cape Breton and Scottish fiddle tunes to the guitar, MacIsaac was the first to release an album in this vein; *Celtic Guitar* appeared in 1988, followed by *Nimble Fingers* in 1995. The fluidity with which he can traverse and combine musical styles is evident in much of the material he presents on guitar; this crossover approach is further explored in partnership with fellow guitarist Scott Macmillan through frequent performance and their duo recording *Guitar Souls* (1993). As a fiddle player, MacIsaac's style demonstrates many of the characteristics of an older Cape Breton sound in terms of tone, intonation, left-hand embellishments and bowing patterns. While he is featured on compilation albums, his first solo fiddle album was not released until 1999, titled *From the Archives*. In 2001 he recorded with Ashley MacIsaac for their joint album *Fiddle Music 101*. An ECMA winner, MacIsaac continues to perform regularly in the Halifax area, and often in Cape Breton, at events such as Celtic Colours and some of the summertime concerts. [**Fleming 1997; MacGillivray 1981**].

MacIsaac, Jackie (Dunn). *See* **Dunn family of Antigonish.**

MacIsaac, Joe. (b. 1928). Fiddle. East Bay, Cape Breton County. Considered something of a child prodigy, he was playing fiddle by the age of seven under his mother's tutelage and was perform-

ing on local radio by the time he was eleven. He studied with Prof. James MacDonald and formed his own dance band, playing throughout Cape Breton and on the CBC-TV's *Don Messer's Jubilee*. A composer of tunes, he can be heard on a number of compilations, including *The Sound of Cape Breton*, *The Fiddlers of Cape Breton*, *Fifty Fiddle Favourites* and *16 Great Barn Dance Tunes*.

MacIsaac, Lisa. *See* **MacIsaac siblings.**

MacIsaac, Matt. (1980-). Highland pipes, tin whistle, flute, guitar, banjo, percussion, composer, teacher. Sydney and Toronto. He is the great-grandson of Pipe Major, John A. "Black Jack" MacDonald; three uncles on his mother's side play pipes, as do three cousins, all of whom influenced his music. He attended piping courses at the Gaelic College and at the College of Piping in Summerside, PEI, with tutors from Canada and Scotland: Scott MacAulay, Dr. Angus and Iain MacDonald, and the MacKenzie brothers – Kenny, Allan and Ian. Progressing through the competition scene from the age of 10, he has won every major piping championship in Atlantic Canada. MacIsaac is typical of the contemporary pipers whose musical training and practice encompasses both the highly regulated competition style and scene and the more individual, vernacular Cape Breton piping style. A full-time musician, he tours and records with Natalie MacMaster, performing also with his wife, the singer Kate Quinn, Mac Morin,

Joe MacIsaac's Dance Band. Courtesy of Mike Fitzgerald.

Nate Douglas, Eric Breton, Shane Hendrickson and Mairi Rankin; he also teaches. In 2012 he performed as part of the Nova Scotia Kitchen party at Fleadh Cheoil na hÉireann in Derry, Northern Ireland, along with Troy MacGillivray and Andrea Beaton. He has recorded *Cool-in: Cuillin* with the Nova Scotia band, Cullin, in 2000, and his solo album *The Piping Album–Matt MacIsaac* was released in 2005.

MacIsaac, Pius. (1959-). Guitar, mandolin, singer. Inverness and Mabou. He taught himself to play at home, inspired by musicians such as John Morris Rankin, going on to become a regular performer on the local scene, where his contribution to the community through his music is noted. He has had the opportunity to play guitar with many of the great Cape Breton musicians, including Natalie MacMaster, Kinnon Beaton and Buddy MacMaster, and has composed a number of songs and tunes. He has two albums: *Music from the Heart* (2003) and *The Greatest Gift* (2005).

MacIsaac, Wendy. (1971-). Fiddle, piano, step dance, teacher, composer. Creignish, Cape Breton, and Halifax, NS. Born to parents Donald and Geraldine (Campbell) MacIsaac, she heard much fiddle music on radio and on tapes during her childhood, both at home and at her grandparents' in Glencoe Mills. Her father played guitar and fiddle and her mother step danced. She also heard local fiddlers Archie A. MacNeil, Norman MacIsaac and Fr. Colonel MacLeod, the parish priest. With her cousin Ashley MacIsaac, she took classes with Stan Chapman in the early 1980s and later took a summer course with Kyle MacNeil at the Gaelic College; other influences included John Morris Rankin, Arthur Muise, Angus Chisholm and Willie Kennedy. Since moving to Halifax she has pursued a full-time music career, which has seen her perform with Ashley MacIsaac, the Rankin Sisters, *The Summertime Revue*, The Unusual Suspects, and *Lilith Fair*, an all-female music tour led by Sarah McLachlan. Wendy's collaboration with Gaelic singer, Mary Jane Lamond, led to the release of *Seinn* in 2012, for which they have won many accolades, including

a MNS award for Traditional/Roots Recording of the Year (2013), a Canadian Folk Music Award for Traditional Album of the Year (2013) and an ECMA for Group Recording of the Year (2012). *Seinn* was also named one of the top 10 folk albums of the year by NPR's *Folk Alley* in 2012. Though a musician who favours the old traditional style and repertoire, MacIsaac has a versatility and technical ability that allows her to shine in other roles, notably ensemble arrangements and vocal accompaniments. She is a founder member and manager of the band Beòlach, with whom she has two albums (*Beòlach*, 2002; *Variations*, 2004). She also has four solo albums: *The Reel Thing* (1994), *That's What You Get* (1996), *Timeline* (2003) and *Off the Floor* (2014).

MacKay, Alex Francis. (1922-2012). Fiddle. Kingsville, Inverness County. Born to Angus and Mary MacKay, the family roots are in the Kintail area of the Scottish Highlands, from where they immigrated to Cape Breton, settling first in St. Peter's, Richmond County, and in later generations the Glendale area. For Alex Francis there was music on both sides of the family: his father played the fiddle, as did his grandfather John MacKay, his paternal uncles Peter and John Willie, and maternal uncle John MacDonald. Both parents spoke Gaelic, and although English was the language of school, Alex Francis and his nine older siblings grew up in a Gaelic-speaking home environment. The family fiddle hung on the dining room wall and his father and older brothers Peter and Dannie would often play a few tunes in the evenings. Alex Francis also heard the fiddle-music recordings of Angus Allan Gillis, Dan J. Campbell and Angus Chisholm on the gramophone, as well as players such as Gordon MacQuarrie and Ronald MacLellan on CJFX and CJCB radio. He took up the fiddle at 14, guided initially by his brother, Dannie, who taught him some tunes by ear. Later he learned to read music from Jimmy Gillis, a piano tuner from Margaree and eventually collected a couple of dozen published tune books, many of them from Dan R. MacDonald. The MacKay home was a gathering place for musicians, and fiddlers Gordon MacQuarrie, "Big"

Ranald MacLellan and "Little" Jack MacDonald attended house parties there; Dan R. MacDonald spent a winter living with the family during the 1930s, as did the piper Sandy Boyd. One of Alex Francis's earliest public performances was in 1941 when he played with Peter MacPhee and Angus Chisholm for the opening of the National Park in Ingonish. He went on to play schoolhouse dances in the Kingsville, Princeville and Glendale areas and, during the 1950s and 1960s, performed at picnics in Broad Cove, Judique, Port Hawkesbury, Glendale, Big Pond and Margaree, and later in the Scottish concerts that began to replace them. From 1955-1957 he lived in Windsor, ON, where he played at Cape Breton house parties and at community dances organized by John Willie MacKinnon (from Port Hood) at the Cape Breton Club; J. D. MacKenzie from Ottawa Brook, Victoria County, was his regular accompanist on guitar. Although he featured on the Topic anthology albums of the 1970s and on *Music From the Simon Fraser Collection* (Cranford 1982), most of his commercial recordings date from his later years as fiddle-music enthusiasts and scholars came to recognize the distinctiveness and value of his musical voice; he was seen as representing a fast-disappearing link to the older, Gaelic way of life, language and style of fiddle playing. *A Lifelong Home* was released in in 1997 and *Gaelic in the Bow* in 2005, both on the Rounder label. **[MacGillivray 1981; Wilson 2005].**

MacKenzie Baillie, Pipe Major Kenneth. (1859-1924). Bagpipe, fiddle. Pictou and Colchester County, NS. Raised in the Gaelic-speaking home of his uncle in Colchester County where he learned to play the violin, he enlisted in the Royal Marine Artillery in 1879; his military career included campaigns in Egypt, the Sudan and Africa. During this time he began to learn the bagpipes as a pastime; later, when posted to Glasgow, Scotland, he was able to develop his piping abilities. In Inverness, he came under the influence of former Inverness Gold Medalist, Pipe Major Sandy MacLennan, and later married his only daughter, Catherine, also a piper. Together,

Alex Francis MacKay. Courtesy of Mark Wilson.

in 1901 they moved back to Nova Scotia, settling in Loganville, Pictou County. He joined the 78th Regiment Pictou Highlanders and music became his life's work, teaching and performing. Involved in recruiting in Canada and the U.S. during the First World War, he instructed several pipers who had enlisted. These included Rod Nicholson from Cape Breton. He is believed to have had a direct influence on the fiddle tradition of Cape Breton; each year he taught with the militia and many of the pipers were also fiddlers, among them Angus "the Ridge" MacDonald of Lower South River, Kenny Matherson of River Denys, Rory MacDougall of Ingonish, James D. Gillis of Inverness and several MacIntyres from Glace Bay. His influence might explain the existence of late-19th-century published Scottish pipe tunes in the repertoires of fiddlers who were exclusively ear players in early-20th-century Cape Breton. *See* **bagpipe.**

MacKenzie brothers of Mabou. Angus, Calum and **Kenneth MacKenzie** are the sons of Ronald Joseph MacKenzie from South Uist and Rita Maureen (Rankin) MacKenzie (d. 2000), a descendant of the original Mabou pioneer settlers. Both parents spoke and sang Gaelic and were active in promoting the language and culture in the Mabou area. The brothers were brought up speaking Gaelic; they had the opportunity to hear fiddle players such as Fr. Angus Morris, Joe Peter

MacLean, Willie Fraser and John MacDougall, and were encouraged to perform themselves. Being granted the Frank "Big Sampie" Sampson Award enabled Angus and Kenneth to record the album *Piob is Fidheal* in 2010. Along with their other brother Calum on piano and fiddle they perform occasionally as a trio, showcasing various combinations of piano, fiddle and pipes.

MacKenzie, Angus. (1977-). Bagpipes, whistle, composer, teacher. Portree, Isle of Skye, Scotland. His first formal tuition in music was on piano, from a peripatetic music teacher, Ed Rogers of Heatherton. His interest moved to bagpipes (inspired by Dr. Angus MacDonald of Glenuig, particularly his album *A'Sireadh Spòrs),* but he also listened to fiddle (which he heard at home and locally) and to Scottish bands such as Ossian, Wolfstone and The Battlefield Band. He went on to win piping competitions in North America both as a solo piper and as pipe major of St. Ann's Gaelic College Pipe Band. Pursuing his interest in Cape Breton's older style of dance piping, which has been receiving renewed recognition since the 1980s, he moved to Scotland to study Gaelic at Sabhal Mòr Ostaig and took up teaching whistle and pipes in Skye and Lochalsh. There, he joined the band Dàimh, playing bagpipes in a high-energy, contemporary format which brought Scottish and Cape Breton musics together. He also plays with the band Seudan and has performed and recorded with Gaelic singers Kathleen MacInnes, Anne Martin, Rachel Walker and Margaret Stewart.

MacKenzie, Kenneth. (1983-). Fiddle, bagpipes, small pipes. Mabou Coal Mines. He took fiddle classes with Stan Chapman in Mabou and Antigonish and performed along with other young players such as Dawn Beaton, Mairi Rankin, Bonnie Jean MacDonald and Tammy MacDonald in the group The Young Mabou Fiddlers. He took summer courses at the Gaelic college, learning both pipes and fiddle and spent a year at Sabhal Mòr Ostaig, in Skye, studying Gaelic. Inspired by older players Willie Fraser, Kenneth Joseph MacDonald, Buddy MacMaster, Theresa MacLellan, Alex Francis MacKay, Angus Chisholm and Donald Angus Beaton, he also cites John Morris

Rankin as influencing his fiddle playing. He has toured with The Beaton Sisters, playing at Celtic Connections and Festival Interceltique in Brittany. He is a member of Nuallan, the piping group formed at the Gaelic College which specializes in Cape Breton's older dance-style of piping. Kenneth has been featured on many recordings from Cape Breton and from Scotland both as a fiddler and as a piper, for example with Chrissy Crowley and Dawn and Margie Beaton. He has served as president of the board of directors of the Celtic Music Interpretive Centre in Judique and is also involved in organizing the program of music at the Red Shoe Pub in Mabou during the summer season. Kenneth's wife, Jenny MacKenzie, is a Highland dancer and step dancer from Cape Breton who has performed professionally for several years with various performing arts groups including the Macquarrie dancers and DRUM!, as well as with the MacKenzie brothers.

MacKenzie, Calum. Fiddle, piano. He started learning to play at an early age and was tutored by some of the island's foremost teachers. While in high school, he was a member of the group Celtic Crew; he taught fiddle and piano at Ceòlas in Scotland in 2004 and, during an extended stay there, performed with many prominent musicians such as piper, Iain MacDonald, and Dàimh.

MacKenzie family of Washabuck. John Stephen and his wife, Mary Anne (Deveaux) MacKenzie, had four boys and two girls who were musically inclined, among them fiddlers Carl, Hector, Simon and Charlie. Music has continued through the extended family with daughters Jean, the mother of the Barra MacNeils band members, and Charlotte and her husband, Vince MacLean, have well-known fiddlers, piano players and step dancers among their children. The MacKenzie family was featured on the CBC *Canadian Express* show in 1979 as guests of Ryan's Fancy; four generations of the family were involved, including 8 fiddlers and 20 step dancers. *See* **MacLean family of Washabuck; MacNeil family of Sydney Mines.**

MacKenzie, Hector. (1933-) Growing up in the small community of Washabuck, their home was a popular one for house parties that were well attended by local musicians; there were also frequent dances in the area. The first fiddle came into the home from a neighbour, Johnny Brown, and Charlie was the first of the siblings to learn to play, guided by a local player, Philip MacKinnon, and inspired by the playing of Michael Anthony MacLean from nearby Iona. Hector next followed in his brother's footsteps; he had a well-developed ear and was able to pick up tunes quickly; Charlie also taught him the rudiments of note reading and he developed an interest in the published tune collections, both Scottish (such as William Marshall) and Cape Breton (such as Dan Hughie MacEachern). He took up the guitar and would accompany players such as Archie MacKenzie and John Y. Gillis at dances and house parties, being the only guitar player in the area. He made his first radio appearance in 1947 on CJFX and continued to play locally until 1953, when he moved to British Columbia. Returning to Washabuck in the late 1950s he became involved in the local music community, playing at events in the Iona Highland Village and at the local Legion as well as becoming the emcee at various concerts and events. He has composed a small number of tunes and an LP of his music was released though the Iona Highland Village. [MacGillivray, 1981].

MacKenzie, Carl. (1938-). Fiddle, composer. Sydney Forks. The youngest of 12 children, Carl started to play fiddle at the age of 9. Besides his immediate family, most of whom were musical, he was inspired by his uncle, Neil Deveaux, a popular fiddler in the Washabuck area, and by Dan Hughie MacEachern, who visited them often. A major influence on his music was Winston Fitzgerald who he heard on radio and at dances; in particular he emulated Fitzgerald's grip of the bow, using thumb and index finger only. For a while he accompanied John Y. Gillis on guitar, but by his teenage years he himself was playing fiddle at dances at the Legion in Iona with his sister, Jean, accompanying him on piano. Based in Halifax in the 1960s (where he went first as an engineering student), he played often with Fr. Angus Morris, Fr. Francis Cameron and Dan Cormier, and was a regular

performer at the Cape Breton Club, the Labour Temple and the Horseshoe Club. House sessions were also popular after the dances, often at the home of Sonny Murray. MacKenzie then moved to Port Hawkesbury and began playing dances all over Cape Breton. In the 1970s he was a member of the fiddle group on the CBC-TV *Ceilidh* show and appeared on several of the CBC *Canadian Express* shows; he was also a frequent performer at the outdoor Scottish concerts. Along with his wife and family he moved to Sydney Forks, and while pursuing his career in engineering he managed to maintain a busy playing schedule. He taught fiddle for a time at CBU and was the fiddle player for weekly step-dance classes. He recorded 10 albums, among them *Welcome to your Feet Again* (1977), *Tullochgorm* (1979), *Fiddle Medleys* (1996), *It's a Corker! (2003)* and *Highland Classic* (2007). He taught and performed at many of the most prestigious festivals and fiddle camps in the U.S., including Valley of the Moon in California, the American National Folk Festival in North Carolina and Lowell, MA, and the Fiddle Tunes Festival in Port Townsend, WA. He also toured Scotland and Ireland, where he was part of the contingent at the 1993 Cape Breton Festival in Cork. An avid collector of published collections, he is a fan of James Scott Skinner and was one of the first Cape Bretoners to record Skinner's multiple variations on "Tullochgorm"; he has also composed several tunes.

MacKenzie siblings. Sister and brother **Roseanne** and **Jimmy** MacKenzie from Baddeck were origi-

Carl MacKenzie. Courtesy of Mark Wilson.

nal members of the band The Cottars, Roseanne (Rosie) playing fiddle, step dancing and singing while Jimmy played guitar and bodhrán. Leaving that band in 2006 Rosie toured with singer, John McDermott. Later, the siblings were involved in The MacKenzie Project, a collaboration with Irish musicians including Donogh Hennessy (guitar), Damien Mullane (accordion) and Pauline Scanlon (voice) from Ireland, and Howie MacDonald (fiddle), Brian Talbot (percussion) and Dave MacIsaac (guitar, dobro) from Nova Scotia.

MacKenzie, Angus. *See* **MacKenzie Brothers of Mabou.**

MacKenzie, Calum. *See* **MacKenzie Brothers of Mabou.**

MacKenzie, Carl. *See* **MacKenzie family of Washabuck.**

MacKenzie, Hector. *See* **MacKenzie family of Washabuck.**

MacKenzie, Hugh F. (1895-1971). Radio host, fiddle, bagpipes. Christmas Island and Sydney. A prominent advocate of the Gaelic language, who taught Gaelic classes, wrote Gaelic poetry and was a leading member of the Gaelic Society of Cape Breton. He was the original host of the radio show *Island Echoes* (*Mac Talla An Eilean*), a weekly presentation on the CBC network from CBI in Sydney, first broadcast in 1971. A chronicle of the life of this 20th century bard, including songs and stories (featuring Rod C. MacNeil of Barra Glenn) was released in 2012: *Mar a b'àbhaist 's a' Ghleann/ As it was in the Glen* (Síol Cultural Enterprises).

MacKenzie, Kenneth. *See* **MacKenzie Brothers of Mabou.**

MacKenzie, Maynard. (1929-2015). Fiddle. Middle River. The son of John D. "Jack" and Georgie C. (MacRae) MacKenzie, he was encouraged by his family to take up the fiddle at the age of 8, making progress with the help of a music-notation tutor he purchased through the Eaton's catalogue. Local players who influenced him starting off were Willie Danny MacDonald and Willie Probert; other fiddlers he had the opportunity to hear included Dan Hughie MacEachern and

the MacLean family from Washabuck. A regular performer with the CBFA, with whom he visited Scotland, and a composer of tunes (a number of which are published in *The Cape Breton Fiddlers Collection*, 2007), his playing is featured on the Rounder album *Traditional Fiddle Music of Cape Breton: Bras d'Or House* (2008). [**Wilson and MacLean 2008**].

MacKenzie, Roseanne. *See* **MacKenzie siblings.**

MacKinnon, Angus "Gus." (1924-1998). Radio host. Antigonish and Maryvale, NS. His career with CJFX, starting in 1961, saw him become, over a 30-year period, assistant general manager of the radio station and program director. As host of the show, *Scottish Strings* from 1968 to 1981, he took the initiative to supplement the limited supply of recorded discs with live recordings of Cape Breton fiddlers, which he made himself at various concerts. As such, the music he played on the show represented the contemporary players of the day. His recordings, along with Bernie MacIssac's 78s on the Celtic label, became the backbone of CJFX's music library and from which came its playlist; his was one of the shows that was regularly taped by Cape Breton fiddlers listening at home as a source of repeated listening and learning tunes. MacKinnon is also credited with having "discovered" John Allan Cameron. *See* **CJFX; radio.**

MacKinnon, Barry. (1962-). Radio host, producer and events organizer. Sydney and Antigonish. Currently host and producer of the CJFX radio show *The Ceilidh*, which is broadcast weekly on Sunday evenings; the show is also live-streamed and is available as a podcast. MacKinnon had previously been involved in the fiddle-music community as Brenda Stubbert's manager for a time; he produced her CD *In Jig Time* in 1996. He later produced *Why2Keilidh* by Howie MacDonald (1999) as well as the two compilation CDs, *Bridges of Cape Breton County* (1999, Celestial Entertainment, and 2002, Celtic Music) and *More Bridges to Cross* (2001), which featured various Cape Breton fiddlers. During the 1990s he programmed much of the music for The County Line bar in Sydney, a popular music venue at that time; he was also the producer for the Ben Eoin Fiddle and Folk Festival in the 1980s. *See* **CJFX; radio.**

MacKinnon, Charlie. (b. 1901). Fiddle. St. Rose, Inverness County, Boston, MA and Halifax, NS. A prominent player in the Cape Breton community of Boston during the 1920s and 1930s, he was a member of The Columbia/Caledonia Scotch Bands and, later, of The Inverness Serenaders. These the first ensembles featuring Cape Breton fiddlers to record. He moved back to Nova Scotia, settling in Halifax, where he continued to play often with fiddler Alex Dan MacIsaac who was also from St. Rose.

MacKinnon, Ned. (1876-1926). Fiddle. Cooper's Pond, Victoria County. Descended from one of the pioneer settlers of the Christmas Island area, he is documented as being one of the first skilled note readers and one of the first to gather a collection of printed tune books, including some by James Scott Skinner, which came to inform much of his repertoire. An itinerant musician who spent many years in the U.S., he relied largely on his music to make a living, possibly the first Cape Breton fiddler to do so. **[MacGillivray 1981].**

MacLean Collection, The. An archive of music books and ephemera that was assembled by renowned fiddler, Joe MacLean; after his death in 1999, the material was donated to the Nova Scotia Highland Village, Iona; an index of the material contained within the collection was compiled by Doug MacPhee. It includes 104 published books of Scottish and Cape Breton fiddle music dated between 1793 and 1996, all of which were either purchased by or were given to MacLean. Other items in the collection are correspondence between he and others regarding purchase of books and copies of new fiddle tunes for him to try; newsletters of the CBFA of 1974-1996; handwritten music composed by MacLean himself, and by Dan R. MacDonald, Dan H. MacEachern, Arthur Scott Robertson and others; scrapbooks of music scores – favourite MacLean tunes and other tunes he liked, including some of Dan R. MacDonald's;

copies of tune groupings collected for playing together in sets. While parts of the collection are public domain, some under copyright. Overall, it provides an insight into the life of the Cape Breton fiddler of the mid-20th century, an era where a number of fiddlers became fascinated with printed collections. There is evidence here of the practice of sharing and copying of tunes among the fiddle community, many of these carefully written out by hand before the advent of photocopiers. There is also correspondence between Joe MacLean and J. Murdoch Henderson, and receipts such as one for the purchase of the Gow Collection No. 2 from John Grant Booksellers. The book collection indicates the shaping of the modern Cape Breton repertoire within the 20th century. It includes publications of Scottish, Cape Breton, Irish and old-time musics, some piping collections, some other non-fiddle collections (e.g., accordion and concertina). A complete index of the books in this collection is available online. *See* **MacLean family of Washabuck.**

MacLean family of Washabuck. A family of fiddlers, some of them among the most well-known on Cape Breton Island, and whose music has been passed down through generations. The family's roots are in the Isle of Barra in Scotland, from where their ancestors emigrated in 1817, settling in MacKay's Point, Washabuck. Vincent and Theresa (MacNeil) MacLean had a family of twelve; Theresa was a Gaelic singer and Vincent a fiddle player and dancer who encouraged all of his sons and daughters to play. Music was also part of the wider community and other prominent families in the area included Dan MacKinnon and his children of Washabuck, and Hector MacLean and his family from Gillis Point, who were known as "The Lighthouse" boys and girls. The history of the MacLean family has been documented in *These Were My People: Washabuck, An Anecdotal History* by Vincent W. MacLean (CBU Press, 2014).

MacLean, Michael Anthony. (1911-2007). Fiddle. Michael Anthony spent all of his life in MacKay's Point, where he played fiddle for square dancing. He started playing at the age of 16, learning by ear, inspired by the many fiddlers from the

Washabuck peninsula who visited the MacLean home, including Dan MacKinnon, John Alex "the Fiddler" MacNeil, John Francis Campbell, Agnes Campbell, Red Rory MacLean and Jimmy MacInnis from Whycocomagh. Over the years he built up a large repertoire of tunes, initially playing unaccompanied, but later joined by John S. MacNeil or Jean MacKenzie on piano or Stephen and Joe I. MacLean ("the Lighthouse Boys") on the organ and banjo. A founding member of the CBFA, he can be heard on the CD, *Good Boy M. A.*, which has more than 30 tracks of his fiddling recorded between 1955 and 2003; many of these are home recordings, with pianist Gordon "Lighthouse" MacLean, made during the 1990s when Michael Anthony was in his eighties. Proceeds from the sale of this album have supported the recently established Stòras na h-Òigridh / Treasures of Youth Endowment Fund set up by Iona's Highland Village Society to support young people to continue their cultural studies based on the Gaelic traditions. [**MacGillivray 1981; MacLean 2014**].

MacLean, Joseph W. (Joe). (1916-1996). Fiddle. Washabuck and Sydney. He took up the fiddle at 12, learning initially by ear, picking up tunes at home from visiting players, including Hector MacKinnon and Fr. Sam Campbell, and from others who would jig them. By the mid-1930s he was playing at dances in communities at Middle River, Bucklaw and Baddeck, these typically held in schoolhouses, with no accompaniment to the fiddle. In 1939 he moved to Sydney, where he played with Donald MacLellan, Tena Campbell and Bill Lamey, and with the many musicians in nearby New Waterford such as Duncan MacQuarrie, Jack MacNeil, Mary MacDonald, Johnny Archie MacIsaac, Margaret MacPhee, Mabel Beaton and Mary Jessie MacDonald. He played dances at the popular venues – Nelga Beach and St. Theresa's – accompanied by pianists, including Lila Hashem, Beattie Wallace, Marie MacLellan and Janet Cameron. Though he excelled as a dance player, he was also noted for his duet playing with his sister Theresa (MacLean) Morrison and with Bill Lamey. A favourite of

Joe MacLean. Courtesy Topic Records, Ltd.

Cape Bretoners in Detroit, Toronto and Boston, he travelled often to play at dances there. In the 1950s and 1960s he made ten 78s on the Celtic and Rodeo labels, and three LPs. *Joe MacLean, Old Time Scottish Fiddle* included Lila Hashem on piano and Peter Dominic on drums. Admired for his dexterous playing of strathspeys he was also known for his extensive repertoire of tunes, much of which was gleaned from his library of Scottish, published collections. Inspired by Bill Lamey to learn to read music shortly after he moved to Sydney, MacLean became obsessed with printed sources, as did a number of other fiddlers at the time. Using contacts he made through Lamey and Dan R. MacDonald he acquired old and valuable books from J. Murdoch Henderson in Aberdeen and Grants Booksellers in Edinburgh. His library of more than a hundred of these is now at the Highland Village Museum, titled "The MacLean Collection." [**MacGillivray 1981; MacLean 2014**]. *See* **MacLean Collection.**

(MacLean), Theresa Morrison. (1919-). Fiddle. Washabuck and Sydney. She learned the rudiments of music notation at home, and, as well as fiddle, tried guitar and banjo. As a teenager, like her male peers, she played at local dances, picnics and concerts, and when she moved to Sydney in the late 1940s she was invited to play at local dances and concerts, despite the fact that it was rare to see female fiddlers in public. She also performed on radio, most frequently on a program organized by A. W. R. MacKenzie of the Gaelic College, and in the mid-1930s she performed often with her brother, Joe. In 1948 she married Peter Morrison, a Highland piper from Piper's Cove, and consequent child-rearing removed her from public performance. She did, however, continue her playing and there were many house parties at their family home in Sydney, for which she would constantly challenge herself to learn new tunes. She was a member of Lila Hashem's Scottish Strings ensemble for many years, and was fond of slow airs, particularly as played by James Scott Skinner and Hector MacAndrew; she developed a keen ear for unusual tunes and in later years began to compose herself. Equally at home playing for a dance or for listening to, her style is marked by solid timing and many of the left-hand embellishments and bowing patterns typical of old-style Cape Breton players. In 1999 the first recording of her music was released – *Laments and Merry Melodies from Cape Breton Island* (Rounder) with Gordon MacLean on piano – followed by *Lake Bras d'Or: Scottish Violin Music from Cape Breton Island* with Doug MacPhee on piano (Rounder, 2008). [**MacGillivray 1981; MacLean 2014; Wilson 1999**].

Theresa (MacLean) Morrison.
Courtesy of Mark Wilson.

MacLean, Vincent W. (Vince). (1944-) Michael Anthony's son Vincent married Charlotte MacKenzie, who comes from a long line of musicians and dancers from the Washabuck area; they settled at MacKay's Point, Washabuck, and raised their children Lauchie (1968-), Calum (1972-), Susan (1976-) and Jill (Franklin) (1977-) surrounded by music. Vince often step danced at home to recordings of fiddle music while Charlotte taught

Jill, Lauchie and Calum their first tunes on the fiddle. A retired Nova Scotia Community College teacher, MacLean is a noted local historian who has contributed much to Cape Breton culture and community initiatives. In 2014 he published a history of the Washabuck area with CBU Press.

MacLean, Susan. (1976-). While her siblings concentrated on the fiddle Susan took up the piano; her aunt Jean taught her the scale before she began taking lessons from Maureen MacDougall at the Highland Heights Inn in Iona and, late from Gary Watson and Sr. O'Reilly in Baddeck, and from Tracey Dares and Ryan MacNeil at the Gaelic College. Around that time, in the early 1990s, she and her sister Jill were members of a group, the Washabuck Connection, which played at many of the local concerts and community events. She continued to hone her accompanying skills by chording along to her grandfather, Michael Anthony, playing fiddle and, although she has no "regular" fiddle partner, she has performed and recorded with a number of players such as Anita MacDonald and also with singers such as Andrew McFayden. She has had compositions published in *The Cape Breton Fiddlers Collection* (2007) and in *The Victoria Standard* newspaper (2000, 2003). A member of the CBFA she teaches regularly at the Gaelic College and is featured on its on-line teaching resource which is in production. She has also been regularly involved in the Baddeck Gathering Ceilidhs organized by Nancy MacLean and is a founding member of the Stòras na h-Oigridh / Treasures of Youth Fund in association with the NS Highland Village Society at Iona.

MacLean, Gordon. Piano, pump organ, composer. Gillis Point, Washabuck. One of the "Lighthouse" MacLeans of Washabuck he grew up in a musical family; his uncles Hector, Mick John and aunt Veronica all played fiddle while his uncles Joe and Steve played banjo. Gordon plays pump organ and piano, and developed a very distinctive light accompaniment style. He has recorded on both instruments with a number of fiddle players, including on the Rounder album *Traditional Fiddle Music of Cape Breton: Bras d'Or House* (2008). He has also composed a number of tunes, some of which have become part of the standard repertoire in Cape Breton; his reel, "The Mortgage Burn," has been recorded also by artists from Scotland and Ireland. [**Wilson and MacLean, 2008**].

MacLean, Joe. *See* **MacLean family of Washabuck.**

MacLean, Joe Peter. (1945-2013). Fiddle and guitar. MacAdam's Lake and Boisdale. He was born to parents Charles and Kathleen (Katie) (Campbell) MacLean in one of the last Gaelic-speaking pockets of the region. Of South Uist ancestry, Joe Peter was raised in a Gaelic cultural environment, speaking the language and hearing Gaelic songs and stories as well as witnessing piping, fiddle music and dance. His father played fiddle and had a repertoire of old and unusual tunes, and Joe Peter's uncle, Danny Peter Campbell, was a Gaelic singer. Others who had influenced the music in the area included piper Johnny MacLean (who was born in South Uist) and fiddlers Dan MacIsaac, John and Dan MacIntyre, Dougall and John Campbell and Danny Campbell. Joe Peter also absorbed music from the radio after the family got electricity in 1960, in particular from *Scottish Strings* on CJFX, with such players as Winston Fitzgerald, Joe MacLean, Angus Chisholm and Donald Angus Beaton; he also listened to a lot of country and western music. He started off on guitar, then banjo and mandolin; his initial ambition was to be able to provide accompaniment to his father's fiddle playing. Taking up the fiddle himself at 18 he and his father played together accompanied by Hawaiian guitar. House parties and weddings, lasting for up to a week, provided opportunities for playing and musicians from the Northside area often were part of such events. MacLean

moved to Boisdale in 1980, where he played for round and square dances at the local hall as part of The Boisdale Trio with Paul Wuckitch on fiddle and Janet Cameron on piano. He became known to a new generation through his involvement with Celtic Colours, contributing much to each year's festival, particularly through his participation in the backstage sessions. For several years he was a regular tutor at Ceòlas in South Uist. MacLean had maintained a style and repertoire (particularly of jigs) that was not common in late-20th-century Cape Breton, one that was strongly linked to the piping tradition. His music can be heard on the albums *Back of Boisdale* (Rounder, 2005) and *Orain Ghàidhlig: Gaelic Songs of Cape Breton* (2001) by Mary Jane Lamond. [**Wilson 2005**].

MacLean, John Neil. (1930-2006). Fiddle. Gabarus Lake, Cape Breton County. Born to parents George W. and Effie (MacDonald) MacLean, John Neil grew up speaking Gaelic and listening to local Scottish song and music. Fiddle music was popular here, with such players as "Little" Angus MacDonald and Duncan L. MacIntyre of the French Road, Joe MacDonald and his son, John Joe, of Fiddler's Lake, "Old" Allan MacKinnon, Philip MacLean and Allison MacCormick of Forchu, and Donald John MacKinnon, who used to stage dances on wooden bridges in the area. John Neil was taught his first tunes at the age of 12 by a neighbour, Earl MacVicar; later he got the opportunity to play regularly with Alex Ferguson from Ferguson's Lake, who had moved to the area as the schoolmaster and boarded at the MacLean's home. Radio was a big influence, and on it John Neil first heard Tena Campbell play; he learned to read music too, and sourced tunes from the published collections. He played each week at dances in Gabarus, Forchu, Marion Bridge and Grand Mira, accompanied by either guitar or piano; with Phyllis MacLeod he is featured on Topic's 1978 LP, *Cape Breton Scottish Fiddle* and on *Music from the Simon Fraser Collection* (1982). He was a member of Lila Hashem's Scottish Strings ensemble in Sydney and of The Mira Fiddlers. [**MacGillivray 1981**].

MacLean, Johnny "Washabuck." (1925-1982). Fiddle and step dance. Lower Washabuck, Victoria County. Born to parents "Red" Rory and Ellen Ann MacLean, his father played fiddle and step danced, and relatives Joe, Michael Anthony MacLean and Theresa MacLean were fiddlers too. Johnny learned to step dance at a young age, emulating his father's style and acquiring steps that had been passed down from the MacKinnon family of Washabuck. Johnny began to play music at the age of nine on a tin fiddle given to him by a neighbour, Francis MacDonald, learning by ear, through listening to players such as Willie Danny "Betsy" MacDonald and Willie Probert from Middle River, and John Alex "The Fiddler" MacNeil of Gillis Point. By the age of 15 he was playing for dances at the schoolhouse in Washabuck and at the Masonic Hall in Baddeck. In 1942 he joined the army for a number of years and later settled in Sydney, where he worked at the steel plant. Through the capital's music scene he met Bill Lamey (who encouraged him to learn to read music) as well as fiddler John Willie Campbell and pianist Lawrence MacDougall, with whom he performed on CJCB radio. While based in Toronto in the 1960s he was regularly featured on the radio show *Opry North,* and in the 1970s he appeared on CBC-TV's *Ceilidh* from Halifax. His son John MacLean is an internationally known bagpiper. [**MacGillivray 1981**].

MacLean, Michael Anthony. *See* **MacLean family of Washabuck.**

MacLean, Sandy. (1893-1982). Fiddle and composer. Foot Cape, Inverness County. One of seven children, his family roots can be traced back to the Isle of Rum off Western Scotland, from where his great-grandfather Donald Bàn (1794-1874) and his family emigrated in 1826. Sandy's grandfather, John MacLean (1823-1911) played fiddle, as did his father and his uncle, Charles William MacLean; two of his brothers, Kenny and Murdoch, also played fiddle and most of the family spoke Gaelic as their first language. Sandy started off on the

bagpipes for a few years before taking up the fiddle in 1905, but after an illness in 1916 he concentrated on the fiddle; he sold perfumed lockets around Strathlorne and Broad Cove Banks to raise money to buy his first instrument by mail order. Allan Gillis, who had returned to Cape Breton from Minnesota, taught him for a few years, initially emphasising music notation and theory, then bowing; soon he was performing at local dances, with Malcolm Beaton and Angus Allan Gillis. In 1912, he moved to Boston, to western Canada in the 1920s and back to Boston. In 1929, he won a fiddle contest at the Intercolonial Hall there, receiving a prize of $20; out of the 21 contestants second prize went to another Cape Bretoner, "Big" Dan Hughie MacEachern. He returned to Cape Breton in 1930 where he played dances and house parties, and as a musician for the silent movies at the Temple Hall in Inverness. Considered to be one of the great Cape Breton fiddle players of the 20th century, MacLean was known for his settings of tunes and for being a "correct" player as well as for his unique style that included the use of the entire length of the bow for tone and volume. Technically ingenious, he often transposed tunes and was among those singled out for praise by J. J. MacInnis in the 1943-44 edition of *Eilean Cheap Breatann*, who referred to him as a "leading strathspey and reel player." The fiddlers who influenced his music included Donald A. Beaton, John A. MacDonald, Alex Young, Ned MacKinnon, Mary "Hughie" MacDonald, Alex "John Y." Beaton, Malcolm Beaton and, in particular, "Little" Jack MacDonald. He composed a number of tunes including "Sandy MacLean's Dream," "Lila MacIsaac's Favourite," "Palace Theatre Clog" and "The Dismissal Reel" that are included in Gordon MacQuarrie's 1940 collection. He refused to be recorded commercially, but did record for CJFX radio and for American anthropologist Laura Boulton. Along with Lila MacIsaac on piano he recorded 20 tunes in total for Boulton, half of these from *The Skye Collection;* the others, including some of his own compositions, were 2 airs, several hornpipes, 2 strathspeys and what he refers to as "a slow and fast Scottish dance." Some

LIZ DOHERTY

critics of the Boulton tapes, however, are of the view that these recordings do not represent MacLean at his best. [**MacGillivray 1981; Lavengood 2008**]. *See* **Boulton, Laura.**

MacLean, Susan. *See* **MacLean family of Washabuck.**

MacLean, Theresa Morrison. *See* **MacLean family of Washabuck.**

MacLean, Vince. *See* **MacLean family of Washabuck.**

MacLellan family of Riverside (Cleveland), Inverness County. Another significant family grouping in Cape Breton music. It includes "Big" Ronald and his children "Baby" Joe, Donald, Marie and Theresa, the latter three who recorded as The MacLellan Trio. [**Caplan 1996**].

MacLellan, "Big" Ronald. (1880-1935). Fiddle, composer. Born in Broad Cove to parents John and Peggy (MacEachern) MacLellan he began playing fiddle while living with his uncle, Archie MacEachern, in Glendale. According to Cape Breton lore "Big" Ronald was predestined to be a fiddler. His aunt discovered a bow-shaped arrow in a field near her house and interpreted this as "a fairy bow," which she took home and hid in a basket over the doorway, believing that this would one day enhance the abilities of some great fiddler who would know it was meant for him/her. Ronald found it, and strung it up with the white tail-hair of a horse, and from that point on he came to be regarded as an impressive fiddler. Initially an ear player, he was taught the rudiments of note reading by Vincent MacLellan. He was known for his settings of tunes, his use of high-bass tunings and for his interpretation of marches in particular. He was also regarded as a fine composer and a number of his tunes were published in Gordon MacQuarrie's 1940 publication *Cape Breton Collection of Scottish Melodies for the Violin*. He married Mary Ann (MacDonald) MacLellan, who played pump organ and, later, piano; like him, she was a fluent Gaelic speaker and was particularly known for her *puirt-a-beul* renditions. Fiddlers such as Dan R. MacDonald, Dan Hughie MacEachern and Gordon MacQuarrie were frequent visitors to the MacLellan home and inspired all of their children, as did other musicians in the local area such as Alexander MacDonald and Ernie Morrison, who played fiddle, and their sisters, Sadie MacDonald and Alice Morrison, who played organ. [**MacGillivray 1981**].

MacLellan, "Baby" Joe. (1915-1935). Fiddle. Nicknamed "Baby" due to his frail and youthful appearance, he was regarded as a child prodigy who, by the age of 12, was already playing for schoolhouse dances, house parties and kitchen rackets around the local area and as far away as Port Hawkesbury. He often played at picnics with his father on fiddle and his mother providing accompaniment on organ or piano. Under the guidance of his father he was introduced to the contest circuit and began accumulating prizes across the island, including a first at an old-time fiddling competition in Sydney's Capitol Theatre when he was 17. His achievement was noted in the local press and he was featured on CJCB radio, although no one at home heard his performance since they did not have a radio at that time. He died from TB at the age of nineteen. [**MacGillivray 1981**].

MacLellan, Donald. (1918-2003). Fiddle. Toronto. Donald began playing at the age of 11 when he was living for an extended period with his cousin, Jimmy "Ranald" MacDonald, in West Bay Road. Upon returning to Riverside (Cleveland) he paid more attention to the music being played at home, and to local fiddlers Alexander MacDonald and Ernie Morrison. By the age of 14 he was playing for dances in Port Hawkesbury, Point Tupper and at schoolhouses in Glendale and Princeville, generally with organ accompaniment. When he was 17 Gordon MacQuarrie taught him the rudiments of note reading and later he took further instruction from classical music teachers. He became interested in the printed collections as a source of tunes and amassed a substantial library of Scottish tune books, among them some unusual ones not commonly found in Cape Breton, such as those published by Elias Howe (*Ryan's Mammoth Collection*) and Peter Milne (*The Middleton Collection*). After a short period in Halifax he moved to Sydney where, along with Bill Lamey on fiddle and Lila Hashem on piano, and occasionally Joe MacLean, he featured on a weekly CJCB radio program sponsored by Eastern Bakeries. He joined the army in 1943 during the last years of the war, after which he returned to Sydney where he played Friday night dances at Carpenter's Hall. In 1947 he moved to Toronto, where he met other Cape Breton musicians such as Johnny Wilmot, Johnny MacLean and Sandy MacIntyre. There he became involved in the Cape Breton Club and Gaelic Society, performing not only for the Toronto branches but also for others across Ontario and the U.S. He played dances locally and in Ottawa, Sudbury, Windsor, Hamilton, Brantford, St. Catherine's, Detroit and Boston – anywhere there was a displaced Cape Breton community. He was a regular performer at the St. Andrew's concerts in Alexandria, ON, and at the Maxville Highland Games. He had previously succeeded in competition, winning the Eastern Nova Scotia Cup and, in 1976 and 1977, the Mod Ontario Trophy. He recorded in the 1950s on the Celtic label, six 78s and two LPs, with his son Ronald on piano, and *The Dusky Meadow* in 2003 with Doug MacPhee on piano; he also made 2 recordings with his sisters, Theresa and Marie as The MacLellan Trio. Donald MacLellan's style and repertoire are of the old Cape Breton style; he was known in particular for his strathspey playing. [**MacGillivray 1981**].

MacLellan, Marie. (1921-2006). Piano. Sydney. Interested in music from an early age, she started to play on the organ, guided by her mother who had schooled herself in music to accompany the fiddle music of her husband. Marie played organ at the local church in West Bay Road, where she learned to pick out melodies, encouraged by choir director and organist, Steve MacGillivray of Glace Bay. She took lessons from Miss Burton, who came from Margaree during the summers to teach organ and basic music-reading skills to youngsters in the area. She made her debut playing for dances as a guitar accompanist since the halls at that time were generally not equipped with organs or pianos. With the guitar tuned Hawaiian style and played with a bar, herself and her sister Theresa on fiddle became a popular fixture on the dance circuit in communities such as River Denys, Lower River, Kempt Road, Dundee and Grand Anse. In the mid-1940s Marie moved to Sydney for work, where she got herself a piano and began studying with Bernie MacIntosh. She also met with piano accompanists there, most of whom were female – Lila Hashem, Bessie MacKinnon, Margaret MacPhee. The Cape Breton fiddle-music scene was thriving at the time and Marie had the opportunity to accompany players such as Winston Fitzgerald (with whom she played on a local TV show), Joe MacLean and Angus Chisholm. In later years she played with Billy MacPhee, Raymond Ellis and Carl MacKenzie. However, she continued to play with her sister, most often at dances, notably in Big Pond each Saturday night for more than a decade; occasionally they were joined by their brother Donald, becoming The MacLellan Trio. Marie also recorded with various other fiddlers, including Buddy MacMaster on his *Judique Flyer* album (2000). She was the pianist chosen to accompany the first massed Cape Breton fiddle group at the Glendale Fiddlers Festival in 1973, and she was also a regular participant in annual events such as the Irish concert in Sydney and the Canada Day concert in Westmount as well as events organized by the Cape Breton Gaelic Society and at the Ashby Legion, the Elks Club and the Inter-Continental Lounge. Her style of piano playing simultaneously combines elements of the simple chording available on the old pump organ on which she trained, and the more progressive piano styles developed in the mid-20th century. While she liked to play the melody of the tune along with the fiddler, she was aware of individual fiddlers' differing views on this practice and worked with these. She was sensitive, too, to the variations in style among the fiddlers she accompanied, and tailored her sound to accommodate this. However, she had clear opinions on the significance of the piano within the Cape Breton tradition and the recognition it was afforded and, if asked, was quite happy to share these views. [**MacGillivray 1988**].

MacLellan, Theresa. Fiddle. One of the first female fiddlers in Cape Breton to develop a public profile, she generally performed and recorded with members of her family. Although she started on piano and guitar, her brother Donald encouraged her to take up the fiddle at the age of 8. Her music education – which included some basic sight-reading tuition from her brother and her mother – was furthered by Steve MacGillivray, director of the local church choir. Her first public performance was at age 9, for a picnic at West Bay Road in the company of Dan C. MacDonald, Kitchener MacDonald and Bernie MacDonald, at which she made an impact – as much for her age and gender as for her ability as a player. The fiddle and piano duo of Theresa and her sister Marie followed, becoming something of an institution in Cape Breton over the years, popular at concerts and particularly in demand for dances such as at Big Pond. An album, *A Trip to Mabou Ridge*, featuring Theresa and Marie MacLellan, with Blanche Sophocleus on guitar, came out in 1976; Theresa also recorded a solo 78 in Halifax with Rodeo Records and appears on compilation albums from *Cape Breton's Magazine* and on the Celtic and Topic labels. Her music career has primarily been centred in Cape Breton, where she worked as a school bus driver, but she has also travelled to perform, for example, to Montréal for the Olympic Games (1976) and to Halifax for the CBC-TV's *Ceilidh* show in the early 1970s, where she was part of the house fiddle band. A strong player with a vigorous bow-stroke and a distinctive touch, she is particularly regarded for her playing of marches and her ability to emulate the complex ornamentation of the bagpipes. [**MacGillivray 1981**]. *See* **MacLellan Trio.**

MacLellan family of South West Margaree. John Alex MacLellan (b. 1917) was born in Mount Pleasant to Hughie S. and Jessie Anne (Gillis) MacLellan and the family moved to the Margarees in 1928. He came from a long line of fiddlers on both sides of the family, including his father's granduncle and his maternal grandmother and uncles John Archie, Alex and Ranald Gillis. Encouraged

Theresa MacLellan. Courtesy of Mark Wilson.

by his relatives and by local fiddle player Malcolm H. Gillis, he took up the fiddle at the age of 12. His uncle Ranald showed him the rudiments of music notation, which made it possible for him to learn tunes from books borrowed from such as Fr. Rory MacNeil, who had an impressive library. He became particularly interested in airs, many of them sourced from these collections. He played often at weddings and at dances teaming up with players such as Angus Chisholm, Angus Allan Gillis and Sandy MacLean until an injured finger affected his playing; nevertheless he and his wife Johenna (MacDonnell), a piano player, passed music on to their children with two sons Rannie and Dougald taking up the fiddle and daughters Ann and Mary Jessie the piano. **Rannie MacLellan** (1951-) now lives in PEI where he performs often; a popular reel named in his honour was composed by Brenda Stubbert. [**MacGillivray 1981**].

MacLellan, "Baby" Joe. *See* **MacLellan family of Riverside (Cleveland).**

MacLellan, Dan Allan. (1870-1946). Fiddle. Glenville, Inverness County. Born to parents "Red" Allan and Catherine MacLellan, he was a descendant of one of the early pioneer settlers of the area, "Red" John MacLellan, who came from Morar in Scotland. In his day he was considered the master fiddler in the local area, although his two brothers, Malcolm (1876-1959) and Johnnie (1859-1951), were also good players; he was among those invited to perform at the first Mabou Picnic in 1897. An ear player, he excelled at dance playing and was particularly known for the number of tunes he could deliver in high-bass tuning; his style, particularly his tone, bowing and use of cuts, influenced later players such as Donald Angus Beaton and Dan J. Campbell. [**MacGillivray 1981**].

MacLellan, Donald. *See* **MacLellan family of Riverside (Cleveland).**

MacLellan, Jimmie. (1910 -1988). Fiddle and composer. St. Rose, Inverness County, and Sudbury, ON. He was inspired to take up the fiddle upon hearing Angus Chisholm play; largely self-taught, he also took a correspondence course in music theory. He played at some 500 dances in the local community and surrounding area before coming to prominence in the 1930s when, along with fiddle player Tena Campbell, he appeared regularly on the live, national radio show, *Cottar's Saturday Night*. He worked for a time in Truro, NS, where at a lumber camp he joined with other musicians from Scottish, French and Irish backgrounds and played for dances or hoedowns; later he had a Country band in Tatamagouche, Nova Scotia and also travelled to perform in PEI. He moved on to Timmons, ON, before settling, in 1942, in Sudbury. He had already developed an eclectic style and repertoire from his time on the mainland of Nova Scotia and he continued to adapt his playing style to suit the demands of the local dance audience, opting for a brisker tempo as popularized by Don Messer, and a more transparent melodic line with less embellishment and simpler bowing patterns than would be typical of a Cape Breton fiddler. His repertoire also continued to diversify, and though he maintained a core of Cape Breton and Irish tunes, his focus became increasingly on the popular Canadian fiddle tunes of the day. He formed Jimmie MacLellan and The Cosy Cottars, a band which became a popular fixture on the dance -usic scene and which, in the 1950s and 1960s, featured on a number of anthology recordings representing a cross-section of Canadian fiddle styles, including *Barn Dance Music, Saturday Night Hoedown, Country Hoedown: Coast To Coast In Canada, Fifty Fiddle Favourites, 16 Great Barn Dance Tunes*, and *16 Great Jigs And Reels*. He also appears on the Celtic label's compilation LP *The Fiddlers of Cape Breton*. In his later years MacLellan became interested in the authentic music of his native Cape Breton again and he composed many tunes in the style, often dedicating them to members of the Cape Breton community in Sudbury. A number of these were published in 1992 by his protege, Ontario fiddler Mike Farrell, as *Cape Breton Medleys: Scottish Violin Music by Jimmie MacLellan*.

— ≈ —

Cape Breton Medleys, Scottish Violin Music by Jimmie MacLellan. Published in 1992 and complied by Mike Farrell, Westport, Ontario, this celebrates the compositions of Cape Breton fiddler and long-time Sudbury resident, Jimmie MacLellan. Farrell was a friend and fellow fiddler who had been given MacLellan's music, including notebooks of his own compositions, by his daughters following his death. The collection has 59 tunes, among which are four reels by Farrell; the others, by MacLellan, are selected from the total of a hundred or so tunes he is understood to have composed, most of them in his later years. 26 of these are reels, 13 are jigs, 7 strathspeys, 5 hornpipes; there are two each of slow airs, waltzes and marches, and one each of slow strathspeys and clogs. In two sections, the first part is presented as "Scottish Dance Medleys" arranged so that tunes on adjacent pages may be played as medleys; the second part, with "Jigs, Reels and Hornpipes" does not link tunes. An introduction has information on the composer and the editor, and a commentary on the style of composition with brief information on some individual tunes. Many of the tunes are named for Cape Breton community members living in Sudbury, ON, such as Finlay Walker.

— ≈ —

MacLellan, Marie. *See* **MacLellan family of Riverside (Cleveland).**

MacLellan, Ronald. *See* **MacLellan family of Riverside (Cleveland).**

MacLellan, Theresa. *See* **MacLellan family of Riverside (Cleveland).**

MacLellan Trio, The. Siblings Donald, Theresa and Marie MacLellan of Riverside (Cleveland), Inverness County, performed and recorded under this name, with two fiddles (Donald and Theresa) and piano (Marie). Their first recording in this formation was a 78 rpm on which they were accompanied by Peter Dominic on drums. They followed this with two LPs on the Celtic label; later, tracks from these recordings were re-mastered and released on CD as *The MacLellan Trio*, part of the Breton Books *Classic Cape Breton Performances* series. While individually each of the MacLellans performed and recorded, and Theresa and Marie played a great deal together, as a trio they continued to perform on an occasional basis over the years including at the Broad Cove Scottish Concert in 1996 and at Celtic Colours 1999, where they were honoured in a special tribute concert. *See* **MacLellan family.**

MacLellan, Vincent A. (1856-1935). Fiddle, composer, poet. Broad Cove Intervale, Inverness County, and Grand Mira North, Cape Breton County. Born to parents Donald and Mary (MacIsaac) MacLellan into an artistic background; his father was known as a bard who had himself composed many songs; a brother, Frank, was a dancer and another brother, Angus, a fine fiddler. The community in Grand Mira North where the family settled had other fiddlers, such as the two Duncan MacDougalls, Steve and Dan MacEachern, and Jim and Archie Gillis, all from Victoria Bridge, and John Gillis, John R. MacDougall and several others on the French Road. Vincent became known as a step dancer and fiddle player and was often called to play for dancing, usually at weddings. In the 1880s a number of the brothers moved to California, although Vincent returned to Cape Breton in 1890, where he adopted something of an itinerant lifestyle, moving around the island, spending months at a time with different families and working at various occupations. He

often performed with his nephew W. J. MacDonald at St. Agnes Parish Hall in New Waterford. He was convinced of the value of note reading and was responsible for helping many Cape Bretoners, such as Gordon MacQuarrie, with the study of music theory. A versatile artist, he often judged fiddle contests, taught dance and a range of instruments including piano, fiddle, bagpipes and some brass; he directed choirs and orchestras and in the dramatic arts composed and directed plays. He composed the reel "My Brother's Letter," which was published in MacQuarrie's 1940 collection. A creative writer in both Gaelic and English, he published a book of songs, *Failte Cheap Breatuinn* (1892), which has been hailed as a landmark of Cape Breton's Gaelic tradition; as a musician, Vincent was highly praised by J. J. MacInnis in the 1943-1944 edition of *Eilean Cheap Breatann*. [**MacGillivray 1981**].

MacLeod, Allison Joseph "Bussie." (1935- 2009). Fiddle. Middle River. Growing up in Victoria County Bussie MacLeod heard local fiddlers such as Willie Danny MacDonald, A. A. Gillis, John Y. Gillis and fiddlers from Washabuck such as Joe MacLean. He lived in Toronto for some 13 years and, although he played at some parties while there, it was not until he returned to Cape Breton that he took up the fiddle in earnest. He teamed up often with fellow Baddeck resident Charlie MacCuspic and, later, Maynard MacKenzie. He was a regular performer with the CBFA, with whom he visited Scotland; his playing is featured on the Rounder album *Traditional Fiddle Music of Cape Breton: Bras d'Or House (2008)*. [**Wilson and MacLean 2008**].

MacLeod family of Dunvegan, NS, and Windsor, ON. Award-winning author Alistair MacLeod (1936-2014) is known for his Cape Breton-inspired short stories, including *The Lost Salt Gift of Blood* (1976) and *As Birds Bring Forth the Sun* (1986), and his novel, *No Great Mischief* (1999), which won him many awards, including the International IMPAC Dublin Literary Award (2001). MacLeod, his wife, Anita (MacLellan), and the family would leave Windsor each year to spend their summer in Cape Breton. Two of the MacLeod children, Marion and Kenneth, have become recognized musicians both in Cape Breton and among the Cape Breton community in Windsor-Detroit. Their musical influences represent the Cape Breton and displaced Cape Breton communities in which they grew up and include players such as Joan MacDonald Boes, the MacNeil family (Bob, Steve, Jim, Tom), Allan Neil R. MacDonald, Kaye White, Morgan MacQuarrie, Willie Kennedy, Greg Campbell, John MacDougall and John Morris Rankin. **Kenneth** (1975-) is a fiddle player and singer-songwriter and teaches fiddle and guitar in Windsor. His fiddle playing is featured on the Rounder recordings *Traditional Fiddle Music of Cape Breton: Bras d'Or House* (2008). **Marion** (1979-) plays piano and accordion. An ethnomusicologist at the University of Chicago, she maintains music ties with both Inverness County and Windsor-Detroit musicians and also frequently accompanies her brother Kenneth (fiddle). She is featured on the Rounder recordings accompanying Morgan MacQuarrie (*Kenloch Ceilidh*, 1997, and *Loch Ban*, 2001) as well as on *The Heart of Cape Breton: Fiddle Music Recorded Live Along the Ceilidh Trail* (Smithsonian Folkways, 2002). She also conducted the choir that performed Scott Macmillan's *Celtic Mass for the Sea* at Celtic Colours in 2007.

MacLeod, Herbie. (1913-2000). Arlington, MA. Based in Boston but with family roots in River Denys, Cape Breton, MacLeod was an avid supporter of Cape Breton music and was responsible for generating a substantial collection of reel-to-reel tapes that he recorded himself at house sessions often hosted after a dance. Using a mono 3M Wollensak recording machine, he recorded fiddlers such as Angus Chisholm, Winston Fitzgerald, Theresa MacLellan and Donald Angus Beaton and these tapes contributed to the practice of sharing tapes (in person and by post) among the Cape Breton fiddle community. In advance of a trip to Scotland, MacLeod made a recording of Bill Lamey at Lamey's own house; this he played for

Scottish fiddlers such as Hector MacAndrew, Bill Hardie and Ron Gonnella at an event at Queen's Hotel in Aberdeen. MacLeod also made the now classic recording of Bill Lamey and Eddie Irwin featured on the CD, *Full Circle–From Cape Breton to Boston and Back: Classic House Sessions of Traditional Cape Breton Music 1956-1977* (Rounder, 2000). *See* **home recordings.**

MacLeod, Katie. (1988-). Fiddle. Dunvegan, Inverness County. Her father, Rory, played and her granduncle was the renowned Fr. Colonel MacLeod, a left-handed fiddle player and an advocate of Cape Breton music who encouraged many young people to play; it was he who gave Katie the fiddle she still plays. Her formal music tuition began with lessons from Rodney MacDonald and Dougie MacDonald when she was 8, and she was also a regular attendee at the summer and March-break music sessions at the Gaelic College. In 2002 she began performing at the Glenora Distillery, often doing two shows a day, accompanied by Isaac Fraser on piano. In 2005 she performed at an ECMA showcase and appeared on *And they Danced* for Bravo! TV. In recent years she has worked for Destination Cape Breton, in Cape Breton and Halifax, promoting tourism, specifically Cape Breton music. She has also been involved with the recently opened Cabot Links Golf Club in Inverness, coordinating their program of local Cape Breton music.

MacLeod, Kenneth. *See* **MacLeod family of Dunvegan, NS, and Windsor, Ontario.**

MacLeod, Marion. *See* **MacLeod family of Dunvegan, NS, and Windsor, Ontario.**

MacMaster family of Judique. John Duncan and Sarah Agnes (MacDonald) MacMaster had a family of five girls (Kathleen [Beaton], Jeannie [Brennan], Genevieve [Whalen], Betty Lou [Beaton] and Lorraine [MacDonnell]) and three boys (Buddy, Alex and Jerry), many of who went on to become leading exponents of Cape Breton music. There was music on both sides of the family: John Duncan's family, whose ancestors arrived in Judique from Scotland in the early 1800s, had many musicians, including his mother who played fiddle. Sarah's people arrived from Moidart, Scotland, in 1798; her family tree connects many great Cape Breton fiddlers, among them Dan R. MacDonald, Alex Francis MacKay, Wilfred Gillis and Winnie Chafe. John Duncan played fiddle while Sarah often jigged tunes and contributed to making the MacMaster home a welcoming one for house parties. Music has continued through to the next generation; Buddy's daughter, Mary Elizabeth, is a piano player; Alex, who plays fiddle, is the father of Natalie MacMaster. All of the sisters played piano: Betty, married to Kinnon Beaton, of the Beaton family of Mabou, is a highly regarded piano player; her daughter Andrea is a fiddle player and composer while Allison is a step dancer. Genevieve is also known as a singer; her daughter Jennifer is also a singer, as is her daughter, Kate.

MacMaster, Hugh A. "Buddy." (1924-2014). Although he was born in Timmons, Ontario, the family moved back to Judique when Buddy was 4 years old. He was 11 when he started to play on his father's fiddle, trying out tunes from memory and later imitating what he heard on the recordings of Angus Chisholm, Angus Allan Gillis and Dan J. Campbell. He made his first public appearance at an amateur hour in Port Hood, accompanied by his sister, Kathleen, on piano; his first dance was in Troy where he played with Vincent MacMaster from Port Hastings at a school dance; twin fiddles was the norm at that time before amplification. Growing up, there were not many musicians in the Judique area although the MacMaster home, where there was a piano and the girls all played, attracted any local or passing fiddlers. Buddy worked with the railway for 45 years, retiring in 1988; during that time he maintained a busy secondary career as a fiddle player. He first played on radio in 1948 for a MacDonald's furniture store sponsored program in Antigonish; in 1949 he began playing for dances on a regular basis starting in Kenloch, then on Saturday nights at the Labour Temple Hall in Inverness and later in Glenville at the Midway Hall; by the 1950s he was in demand in Boston and Toronto, where he would often play

a weekend dance. From the 1970s through to the 1990s he was the resident fiddler at the dances at Glencoe Mills, the last fiddler to hold such a residency. Particularly since his retirement Buddy made several international trips to perform at such as Celtic Connections in Glasgow, Scotland, and Éisge na Laoi in Cork, Ireland; he also made many festival appearances across Canada and in the U.S. It was through him that Alasdair Fraser discovered Cape Breton fiddle music in the 1980s and Fraser invited him on several occasions, from 1992 onward, to teach at his annual fiddle school at Sabhal Mor Ostaig on the Isle of Skye, the first Cape Breton fiddler, to do so in Scotland. MacMaster also had a high profile on radio and on TV; he was a regular on shows such as *Ceilidh* and was a member of the Cape Breton Symphony Fiddlers.

music. Having learned to read music Buddy started up a correspondence with John Grant Booksellers in Scotland and acquired many of the printed tune collections; Dan R. MacDonald would also send him copies of newly composed tunes. He had an extensive repertoire as well as an impressive knowledge of the sources and the evolution of particular settings; in this regard he was the consummate scholarly fiddler. MacMaster has been hailed as one of Cape Breton's finest dance players and was highly regarded for his timing in particular – something he found somewhat ironic having been highly criticized as a young fiddler for playing too fast! Although he was encouraged to record for many years it was not until 1989 that he made his first album, *Judique on the Floor*. This was followed by *Glencoe Hall* (1991), *The Judique Flyer* (2000), *Cape Breton Tradition* (2003) and *Traditional Music from Cape Breton Island*, as a twin-fiddle album with his niece, Natalie MacMaster; he also recorded with the Cape Breton Symphony Fiddlers and is featured on numerous compilation albums and on the video, *Buddy MacMaster*, which includes two productions, *Master of the Cape Breton Fiddle* and *In Concert* (SeaBright Productions). His life in music was the subject of a publication by Sheldon MacInnes in 2007: *Buddy MacMaster: The Judique Fiddler* (Pottersfield Press).

Buddy and Natalie MacMaster with the Cape Breton Fiddlers' Association at Celtic Colours. Photo by Murd Smith. Courtesy of Celtic Colours International Festival.

recognition. MacMaster is one of the most decorated of the Cape Breton fiddlers to date. In 1995 St. Francis Xavier University awarded him an honorary doctorate; in 2006 he received an honorary doctorate from CBU. In 2000 the Governor General of Canada named him to the Order of Canada and in 2003 he was invested into the Order of Nova Scotia, the only Cape Breton fiddler to hold this honour. He is also the only Cape Breton fiddler recognized in the Scottish Traditional Music Hall of Fame (2006). That year he received the Dr. Helen Creighton Achievement Award at the ECMAs and, in 2014, a Lifetime Achievement Award from Folk Alliance International. **[Feintuch 2010; MacGillivray 1981; MacInnes 2007].**

(MacMaster), Elizabeth MacInnis. Piano, fiddle, step dance. Fiddler Buddy MacMaster's daughter and his frequent piano accompanist since she was 14 years old, she often played with him at the Glencoe Mills square dances and is featured on his recording, *The Judique Flyer*. She continues to perform occasionally with some contemporary Cape Breton fiddlers. *See* **MacMaster, Natalie.**

MacMaster, Doug. (1908-2005). Jamaica Plain, MA. A lifelong fan of Cape Breton fiddle music he, along with others such as Herbie MacLeod in the Boston area, contributed to an outstanding collection of Cape Breton fiddle music through home recordings. Like the others, he had no training as a recording engineer or as a folklorist/ethnographer; their involvement was fuelled by a genuine enthusiasm and love for the music. His own family roots were in the Creignish-Judique area of Cape Breton. MacMaster would record house sessions and ceilidhs hosted in his own home or at the homes of others such as that of "Toots" Gotovich also in Jamaica Plain. Typically, the ambient noise was also recorded, such as the conversation between tunes and comments by those present on the music, thus capturing the real experience. The tapes thus recorded, typically using reel-to-reel machines such as the Webcor, led to an informal but robust practice of sharing recordings among the fiddle communities in Boston, Detroit, Toronto and back in Cape Breton. Later, the musicians themselves acquired tape recorders and continued this practice of home recording and sharing of tapes. Selections of MacMaster's recordings of Bill Lamey are featured on the CD *Full Circle–From Cape Breton to Boston and Back: Classic House Sessions of Traditional Cape Breton Music 1956-1977* (Rounder 2000). His entire collection was digitized first by Paul Cranford (some of which was used for the *Cape Breton's Magazine* tape: *Winston Fitzgerald–House Parties and 78s*) and later by Paul MacDonald; much of it is now in circulation among the Cape Breton community. *See* **home recordings.**

MacMaster, Natalie. (1972-). Fiddle, piano, step dance, composer. Troy, Inverness County, and Lakefield, ON. One of three children born to Alex and Minnie (Beaton) MacMaster, Natalie comes from a strong music background on both sides of her family. Her father, Alex, himself a fiddler, is one of the MacMasters of Judique and his siblings include fiddle players Buddy MacMaster and piano player Betty Lou (Beaton). Her mother, Minnie, the daughter of well-known step dancer and jigger of tunes, Maggie Ann (Cameron) Beaton, is herself a noted step dancer and teacher. MacMaster started dancing (both step dance and Highland Dance) at a young age and took up the fiddle at the age of 9, making her debut performance at a square dance in Glencoe Mills within a year. Guided by her father and uncle she also took classes with Stan Chapman in Antigonish and, along with her fellow students such as Wendy MacIsaac, Jackie Dunn and Ashley MacIsaac, was part of performing groups, Highland Classics and the Special Seven, which were, in some ways, perceived as representing the success of the Cape Breton fiddle-music revival in force from the early

1970s. MacMaster recorded her first album, *Four on the Floor* (in cassette format) at the age of 16, followed in 1991 by *Road to the Isles*, which she co-produced with John Morris Rankin. She developed a busy playing circuit locally (while finishing school and completing her teacher training at the Nova Scotia Teachers' College in Truro); besides playing at many dances and concerts around Inverness and Richmond Counties she was featured in the *Cape Breton Summertime Revue* and played often with guitarist and singer Buddy MacDonald in various Sydney pubs, which brought her considerable exposure. Already recognized for her eclectic tastes, which saw her bring tunes and techniques from other musical traditions (from Irish to American Bluegrass to Flamenco) into her presentation of Cape Breton music and developing a unique hybrid style of step dance, MacMaster was perfectly positioned to benefit from the 1990s Celtic boom which saw an unprecedented level of industry attention focus on Cape Breton. she is widely considered one of the (if not *the*) foremost stars of contemporary Cape Breton fiddle music and has received many awards, among them two Junos, several ECMAs, Canadian Music Awards, Canadian Country Music Awards, as well as honorary degrees from St. Thomas University, the Atlantic School of Theology, Niagara University, NY, and Trent University. She received the Arts and Letters Award from the Canadian Association of New York and was invested into the Order of Canada in 2006. She has released 12 albums to date (many on the Rounder label), including one in duet with her uncle, Buddy MacMaster (2005) and, most recently, with her husband, Donnell Leahy of The Leahy Family (*One*, 2015). She is featured on several compilation albums, has released several videos and DVDs (including an instructional fiddle DVD); she also co-wrote the coffee-table book *Natalie MacMaster's Cape Breton Aire: The Story of a Musical Life and Place* with Pulitzer Prize-winning wordsmith Eileen McNamara and by photographer by Eric Roth (2010). MacMaster has collaborated with artists such as Alison Krauss, Sharon Shannon, The Chieftains, Luciano Pavarotti, Faith Hill, Paul Simon and Yo-Yo Ma, the latter on a Grammy-winning recording. Natalie continues her career as a full-time professional Cape Breton fiddle player; her stage shows now often include her husband and most of her 6 children playing fiddle and step dancing. *See* **MacMaster family of Judique.**

— ≈ —

Natalie MacMaster's Cape Breton Island Fiddle. Part of the "Mel Bay Presents" series, this 2001, 64-page, collection has 41 tunes transcribed by Stacy Philips from the playing on three of MacMaster's albums – *Fit as a Fiddle* (1993), *No Boundaries* (1996) and *A Compilation* (1998). The music is ordered by album and track listing and organized in medleys, with the layout designed to avoid page-turns and thus facilitate easier play through. Each tune is transcribed as played, chords are indicated and ornaments included; advice is given on interpreting the notation and "careful listening to the three albums" is recommended by the author. The book has 18 reels, 10 jigs, 7 hornpipes/clogs, 3 strathspeys, 2 marches and one air.

— ≈ —

Macmillan, Scott. (1955-). Guitar, keyboards, composer, conductor, teacher. Halifax. Born to parents Bob Macmillan and Jessie MacLeod, his early music interest was in blues and rock, expanding to include classical through his studies in composition and arranging at Toronto's Humber College. The diversity of his experience permits him to focus on discrete genres such as with his 12-piece jazz ensemble, Scott 'n the Rocks, or to engage in crossover and collaborative projects, which has led to him working with artists such as The Chieftains, Rita MacNeil and The Rankin Family. He has worked with the Nova Scotia Mass Choir and in 1995 became host conductor and principal arranger for Symphony Nova Scotia's *Maritimes Pops* series, through which he developed a number of orchestral arrangements of Cape Breton fiddle music and song. *Celtic Mass for the Sea* (jointly composed by Macmillan with Halifax librettist Jennyfer Brickenden) premiered

in 1991; in 2002 and 2015 it was performed at Carnegie Hall in New York. *MacKinnon's Brook Suite* was written for bagpipe player, Ian McKinnon and Symphony Nova Scotia and won an ECMA for Best Classical Recording in 2002. In 2012 Macmillan again won the ECMA classical award for *Within Sight of Shore,* the score to an award-winning documentary of the same name directed by his son, Ian, and which tells the story of his father's ship, the last Canadian warship, sunk in the Second World War. Other compositions in this vein include *Currents of Sable Island, Suite Africville* and *The Gallery Project. Suite Silver Dart* was commissioned by Celtic Colours, Centre Bras d'Or Association and the Silver Dart Centennial Association to commemorate the 100th anniversary of the first powered flight in Canada by Alexander Graham Bell and the Aerial Experiment Association; it was written for violin, harp, guitar, piano and string orchestra, and premiered at Celtic Colours in 2009. In 2014, a new piece, *Aiseag: The Ferryboat* was composed as a U.K. New Music Biennial Commission and performed at Sabhal Mòr Ostaig in Skye, in London, and at the Commonwealth Games in Glasgow. Macmillan has also been involved in recording projects; he has released albums with guitarists, Brian Doyle (*Live off the Floor,* 2010), Dave MacIsaac (*Guitar Souls,* 1993), *Songs of the Cape* with The Octet (1992) and he worked on Rita MacNeil recordings both as an instrumentalist and arranger. He was a member of Puirt a Baroque with David Greenberg and David Sandall, with whom he recorded *Bach Meets Cape Breton* (1995). In 1996, he established a series of recordings of house sessions with well-known Cape Breton musicians at his home in Hillsborough, Inverness County, that led to *The Minnie Sessions* Volumes, 1-3. Macmillan has taught guitar at Dalhousie University since 2008; in 2014 he was the recipient of Arts Nova Scotia's Portia White Prize.

— ≈ —

Scoobie Tunes, A Family Fiddle Frenzy. Cape Breton Style Fiddle tunes composed by Scott Macmillan. This 1996 book has 78 tunes categorized and arranged by key over 60 pages. It has 36 jigs, 30 reels, 5 hornpipes/clogs, 3 each of strathspeys and marches, and a single waltz. All are composed by guitarist, Scott Macmillan, with the exception of "The One On One Reel" and "The Crosswords Jig," both made in collaboration with Richard Burke in 1993. Chords are provided for all tunes and the overall key of each is noted. Commentary by Jennyfer Brickenden describes the people, places and events associated with the music, and the years of composition; cross-referencing links some pieces to the CD album *Scott Macmillan Presents Minnie Session, Vol. 1*. A foreword by Macmillan contextualizes the music, an alphabetic tunes index aids searching, and a discography and biography of the author place him in the Cape Breton music world.

— ∼ —

MacNeil family of Dearborn, Michigan. A family grouping in the expatriate Cape Breton community in the Detroit area and with on-going connections to the Big Pond community.

   MacNeil, Robert "Bob." (1936-2012). Fiddle. Born to parents Bernie and Ann (MacDonald) MacNeil, he was brought up in an atmosphere of Cape Breton fiddle music in a small but thriving Cape Breton community in the Detroit-Windsor area. His father, a fiddler, was originally from Glengarry (Rear Big Pond) and his mother was from the Whitney Pier area of Sydney; she was a piano player who often accompanied "Little" Jack MacDonald from Judique. Bob was classically trained on violin at the Detroit Institute of Music and Arts and played with the Detroit Scandinavian Symphony Orchestra. Many of the techniques he learned in this context came to inform his Cape Breton playing, particularly in his rendition of airs and in his use of higher positions; in this he was also influenced by the playing of "Little" Jack MacDonald. An active member of the Cape Breton community, he was one those responsible for regenerating the Nova Scotia Club in 1972, after a number of years of inactivity, and he was involved as a promoter and a performer at many of that organization's concerts and dances.

When he married (Barbara Fraser) he continued the family tradition of returning to Cape Breton for the family summer vacations and he, and in turn his sons Thomas (piano), Stephen (pipes) and Jim (fiddle), came to be considered an integral part of the Big Pond community's summer music events, particularly the pastoral airs concerts held at St. Mary's church in which they were regular participants.

   MacNeil, Jim. (1966-). Jim currently lives in Windsor, ON, with his wife Trese (MacInnis), daughter of Christie and Dan Joe MacInnis (Big Pond, Cape Breton) and his two daughters, Christie-Marie and Mae. His grandfather, Bernie was his first violin teacher and he played with his grandmother, Ann at an early age. His trips to Cape Breton started with travelling with his grandfather and participating at the annual Scottish concert in Big Pond for the first time at age 16. Jim is still actively playing the violin for Cape Breton functions and events in the Detroit-Windsor area, and vacations each July and August at his summer home in Rear Big Pond.

MacNeil family of Sydney Mines. The 6 children of Columba and Jean (MacKenzie) MacNeil have been professionally involved in music and are well known as the Barra MacNeils, managed initially by Columba; another band popular in the late 1990s, Slàinte Mhath , involved the 2 youngest family members. Jean, a piano player, step dancer and teacher, is one of the MacKenzies of Washabuck and the family spent a lot of time in that area with their musical relations. Other musicians, Monica (MacDougall) MacNeil (saxophone) and Lisa (Gallant) MacNeil (fiddle, step dance, bodhrán) are now married into the MacNeil family. *See* **Barra MacNeils.**

   MacNeil, Jean. (1940-). Piano, step dance, composer. Washabuck and Sydney Mines. Brought up in Washabuck, her family, the MacKenzies, was one of musicians. Her siblings included fiddle players Carl, Hector, Simon and Charlie; she was the first in the family to play the piano, teaching herself by ear. She soon had opportunities to chord for fiddlers including her brothers and other local fiddlers such as Joe MacLean, Michael Anthony

MacLean and Archie MacKenzie. She learned her first dance steps watching family members Joan and Charlie and later by Bernie Campbell; she was further inspired by seeing dancers such as Willie Fraser and Angus MacIsaac perform at picnics. Having moved to Sydney Mines she came in contact with players such as Robert and Lauchie Stubbert and Winston Fitzgerald. There, Fr. Eugene Morris encouraged her into teaching and she developed a wide circuit teaching step dance from Big Pond to North Sydney and Washabuck. She also taught in Sydney Mines and, for 15 years, at the Gaelic College; in 2002 she released an instructional step-dance DVD, *Spring in your Step*. She has also taught piano and shared the position of house accompanist at the Rollie's Wharf sessions (North Sydney) for a number of years; and she shares piano duty at the sessions held in the Blue Mist in Bras d'Or. Jean also taught each of her 6 children as they started off in music. She has also composed tunes such as "Dan Hughie MacEachern's March" and "Storm Party." **[MacGillivray 1988].** *See* **MacKenzie family of Washabuck.**

MacNeil, Sheumas. (1961-). Piano, pipe organ, fiddle, guitar, vocals. Caribou Marsh. He started playing music under the guidance of his mother, Jean MacNeil, before taking lessons on fiddle with Prof. James MacDonald of North Sydney and on piano with James Taylor of Sydney Mines. Besides his mother, he cites Doug MacPhee and Mary Jessie MacDonald as being among his major influences at this time. From the age of 10 he was performing along with his brothers Kyle and Stewart at concerts and ceilidhs around Sydney Mines and in Iona where his mother's family lived. This was the genesis of the Barra MacNeils, which expanded over the years to include sister, Lucy, and later, younger siblings Ryan and Boyd. Over the years Sheumas has spent periods of time acting as manager and agent for the band while also its piano player; his style and approach have been a significant contributor to the band's distinctive sound. His piano accompaniment is innovative in chord choices, textures (in particular his use of pedal notes and suspensions) and rhythms, and he has influenced younger

players, most notably Ryan MacNeil and Tracey (Dares) MacNeil. While studying for a music degree from Mount Allison University in New Brunswick, Sheumas majored in pipe-organ performance and, in 2010, this instrument provided the inspiration for a series of shows, *Cathedral*, which saw the Barra MacNeils showcase a range of material from Bach organ works to traditional and contemporary tunes and songs in cathedral settings; pipe organ featured again in the orchestrated arrangements performed and recorded in 2012 by the Barra MacNeils with Symphony Nova Scotia. Contributing bass harmony vocals to the band's arrangements Sheumas is also an occasional fiddle player, and the inspiration for Paul Cranford's reel, "The Twice a Year Fiddler." Sheumas is married to Monica (MacDougall), who plays Cape Breton fiddle tunes on saxophone and they perform together on occasion. *See* **MacNeil, Monica.**

MacNeil, Kyle. (1963-). Fiddle, guitar, mandolin, vocals. Sydney and Albert Bridge. Kyle started playing guitar at age 7 and soon after switched to violin, on which he was classically trained by Prof. James MacDonald and later at Mount Allison University. His tone and technical clarity owe much to his classical music experience; however, he is rooted in the traditional Cape Breton style and cites his mother, Jean MacNeil, uncles Carl and Hector MacKenzie, and local fiddlers Lauchie and Robert Stubbert as his greatest influences. He has also explored Irish fiddle-music techniques and is one of the few Cape Breton fiddlers to comfortably employ such as rolls in his playing. Kyle currently teaches Cape Breton fiddle music at CBU, and also offers private lessons in both the Cape Breton and the classical violin styles. **[MacGillivray 1981].**

MacNeil, Stewart. (1964-). Vocals, accordion, piano, tin whistle, flute, bouzouki, guitar, step dance, composer. Sydney Mines. Starting off on harmonica at the age of 6 Stewart evolved into a multi-instrumentalist, playing mainly accordion, tin whistle and flute, instruments that were more commonly heard on the Irish recordings he listened to than in Cape Breton. Alongside his siblings who played fiddle and piano, Stewart worked on weaving these less familiar sounds into Cape Breton tunes and arrangements, something that has distinguished the Barra MacNeils throughout their career. Stewart is also a singer who has composed many of the songs the Barras have recorded, such as "Nancy" and "Dance With Me Daily"; he has also composed a number of tunes, some of them characterized by a level of chromaticism not typical of Cape Breton fiddle tunes (e.g., "The Flower Basket" and "Toonik Time").

MacNeil, Lucy. (1968-). Vocals, fiddle, bodhrán, harp, step dance. North Sydney. The only girl in the MacNeil family, Lucy, like her brothers, was classically trained on the violin by Prof. James MacDonald and later by his son, Dan; like Sheumas, Kyle and Stewart, she too is a music graduate of Mount Allison University. Step dancing alongside her mother from a young age she also began playing fiddle tunes and joined the band originally set up by her brothers, The Barra MacNeils. Lead vocalist and step dancer she also plays bodhrán, harp, and joins Kyle and Boyd for fiddle groups. While the band has been her focus professionally, Lucy has taught often at the Gaelic College and is increasingly invited to perform with other artists as a soloist; among such performances were with Symphony Nova Scotia in a tribute to singer Rita MacNeil in 2014.

MacNeil, Ryan. (1976-). Piano, uilleann pipes, low whistle, step dance. Summerside, PEI. A founder member of the band Slàinte Mhath that enjoyed international success during the late 1990s and early 2000s, Ryan went on to join the Barra MacNeils with his older siblings, playing uilleann pipes, low whistles and step dancing with them until 2013. The uilleann pipes were not common in Cape Breton and it was mainly from listening to recordings, and later making trips to Ireland, that he mastered the instrument. His distinctive piano style, influenced by the playing of his brother Sheumas, his versatility and his familiarity with Irish music has led to him recording with Irish fiddlers such as Máire O'Keeffe, Seamus Grant and Liz Doherty.

MacNeil, Boyd. (1981-). Fiddle, mandolin, guitar, banjo, percussion, step dance. Sydney. The youngest of the MacNeil family, Boyd, along with his brother Ryan, was a founding member of the band Slàinte Mhath, which continued until 2005. He too joined the Barra MacNeils at that point, with all 6 siblings involved in the band until Ryan left in 2013. Classically trained, he brings a high level of technical ability to his fiddle playing and is steadily gaining a reputation as an excellent fiddle teacher of Cape Breton music. Boyd is married to Lisa (Gallant), who played fiddle, bodhrán and step danced with Slàinte Mhath ; she no longer works as a musician in a full-time capacity.

MacNeil, Bob. *See* **MacNeil family of Dearborn.**

MacNeil, Boyd. *See* **MacNeil family of Sydney Mines.**

MacNeil, Jean. *See* **MacNeil family of Sydney Mines.**

MacNeil, Jim. *See* **MacNeil family of Dearborn.**

MacNeil, Kyle. *See* **MacNeil family of Sydney Mines.**

MacNeil, Lucy. *See* **MacNeil family of Sydney Mines.**

MacNeil, Monica (MacDougall). (1968-). Saxophone. Antigonish and Caribou Marsh, Cape Breton County. Born to parents Cameron and Gladys MacDougall, who played music and square danced, she took piano lessons as a child and later learned to play saxophone in a school music program, continuing her instrumental studies at St. FX. She and her sister Maureen step danced at the Highland Village concerts as children, but it was not until she was in her twenties that she began to play Cape Breton music. Inspired by a range of musicians from Cape Breton, Ireland and Scotland, she explored traditional music repertoires and adapted tunes to the saxophone. During the 1990s she played at concerts and ceilidhs in Cape Breton and contributed to albums with Charlie MacCuspic, Buddy MacDonald and John Ferguson. While the sax has been used in the performance of other folk music traditions including Irish (marginally) and Québecois, it had not previously been associated with Cape

Breton, and was regarded as a novelty. MacNeil teaches music at Riverview High School (concert band, Celtic and rock classes) and performs occasionally at concerts with her husband, Sheumas MacNeil of the Barra MacNeils, on piano. *See* **MacNeil family of Sydney Mines.**

MacNeil, Ryan. *See* **MacNeil family of Sydney Mines.**

MacNeil, Sheumas. *See* **MacNeil family of Sydney Mines.**

MacNeil, Stewart. *See* **MacNeil family of Sydney Mines.**

MacNeil, Tracey E. (Dares). (1972-). Piano, step dance. Marion Bridge, Castlebay, and West Mabou, Cape Breton. Born to Jessie Marie and Dennis John Dares in Cape Breton County, where she was raised, her parents both enjoyed square dancing and enrolled Tracy in piano lessons as a child. Among her teachers was George MacInnis, who taught her to play fiddle tunes on the piano; during Saturday morning visits with an elderly neighbour, Percy Peters, she was encouraged to accompany his fiddle playing and thus developed her skills in chording to the tunes. Opportunities to work closely with Dave MacIsaac on guitar during the early 1990s allowed her to refine her technique in this regard and she also studied John Morris Rankin's accompaniment style. A teacher at the Gaelic College during the summer months, Tracey toured for a number of years with Natalie MacMaster and recorded with many Cape Breton fiddlers. She was a member of the band Celtic Trio with Jackie Dunn (fiddle) and Marilyn MacDonald (vocals), and with bagpipers Paul MacNeil and Jamie MacInnis she formed The Open Door Gang in the early 1990s. Her album, *Crooked Lake* (1994), was the first solo-piano recording from the post-revival generation and was a significant influence on younger players. She also released what is the only existing Cape Breton piano accompaniment tutor to date, *A' Chording to the Tunes,* in 1997. With a young family, Tracey became less visible during the early 2000s although she now performs more frequently around Cape

Breton. Along with her husband, Paul MacNeil, she developed Castle Bay Music, an online music store specializing in Atlantic Canada music which operated for a few years from 2000; the couple also released a bagpipe and piano CD of that name. She worked for a short time as director of music programming at the Gaelic College and is now based in the Mabou area where she is involved in learning and promoting the Gaelic language; her daughters are all continuing the tradition as musicians, dancers and Gaelic speakers.

MacPhee family of New Waterford. Mother and son, Margaret and Doug MacPhee, have family and music roots in Inverness County; they have contributed enormously to Cape Breton piano stylings, both in terms of accompaniment and in foregrounding the practice of piano as a melody instrument. Margaret's father, **Dougald MacIntyre** (1878-1934), from Cape Mabou, was a fiddler and step dancer whose own father, John Dan MacIntyre, was a player and his mother, Mary (MacIsaac), a step-dance teacher. He was one of many Inverness County residents to relocate to industrial Cape Breton during the early 1900s, contributing to the growth of fiddle music in areas such as New Waterford. While he was known for his duo playing with Joe Smith he was also a player in his own right, winning first in a local fiddle contest in 1926 and placing second at the finals in Boston where James Scott Skinner adjudicated. [**MacGillivray 1981**].

MacPhee, Margaret (MacIntyre). (1912-1997). Piano and step dance. The New Waterford family home was a gathering place for the many Inverness County musicians living there at the time, and weekend house parties were regular. Fiddlers such as Duncan MacQuarrie, Lauchie Meagher and Eddy Penney (a classically trained violinist originally from the mainland who would impress the local fiddlers with his renditions of Scott Skinner tunes played from the books) visited to play music with her father, and Margaret and her sister Florence took up step dance, absorbing what they experienced at home without formal lessons. Although there were few piano accompanists at the time, Margaret's cousin Mary Margaret (MacDonald) Mullins was the first one in the area to accompany fiddlers; Margaret followed her lead at 17 when her father bought her a piano. She herself became something of a pioneer of the Cape Breton piano, developing her own style, guided by the preferences of her father who particularly liked the piano to double the melody line of the fiddle. Other fiddle players who influenced her playing style were Duncan MacQuarrie, Mary MacDonald, Bill Lamey, Jack MacNeil, Mike MacDougall, Joe MacLean, Paddy LeBlanc and Johnny Wilmot. Partially blind since she was a teenager, Margaret developed an exceptional ear and sense of timing; these became her greatest strengths as an accompanist, which enabled her to bring the best out of a fiddler. She perfected her skills in intensive playing for the many musicians who visited the house and was in great demand to play at dances and for social occasions. She developed a partnership with Mary MacDonald during the years she lived in New Waterford, and she recorded several times with Johnny Wilmot: in 1951 for the O'Byrne de Witt company in Boston, and in 1963 for the Celtic label in Toronto. She was a frequent performer on radio too, highlights from which include playing with her father in 1932 and on the *Irish Hour* with Johnny Wilmot in Boston. She also composed a number of tunes, some of which have been published in collections including Pat Chafe's 2009 *Bits and Pieces*. Her contribution to Cape Breton music for more than 60 years was celebrated by the Cape Breton Gaelic Society in 1980 when 600 people attended a night in her honour. Her son Dougie became one of Cape Breton's best-known piano players, maintaining much of his mother's style and approach. [**MacGillivray 1988**].

MacPhee, Doug. Piano and composer. His mother began teaching him piano at 12, and he played publicly for the first time the following year, accompanying fiddler Johnny Wilmot at a square dance in Glace Bay. Wilmot tutored him in sight-reading, which led to him becoming an avid collector of notated fiddle tunes. J. Murdoch Henderson from Scotland was corresponding at the time with fiddlers such as Bill Lamey and Joe

MacLean, and it was common practice among the fiddle community for players to spend the winter months perusing the latest collections, emerging in the summer with new tunes with which to impress their peers. Dougie became particularly adept at finding "good" tunes and garnered a reputation for himself for this skill. With few employment opportunities in Cape Breton, like many others during the late 1950s he was forced to migrate to Toronto, where he lived off and on until 1968, with occasional periods back in Cape Breton and short stints in Boston and California. In both Boston and Toronto he was part of a Cape Breton music society that nurtured the displaced community, and in Toronto he developed a life-long friendship and music partnership with fiddler Donald MacLellan and indeed boarded with him for a year. Johnny Wilmot lived there for a time too, as did Johnny "Washabuck" MacLean; they also met "Little" Jack MacDonald, who was based in Detroit, on occasion, and characters such as Hughie "Shorty" MacDonald who were interested in the music; MacPhee was also friendly with Scottish violinist Ron Gonnella while there. In Boston, which had many Inverness County musicians, he played with fiddlers such as Angus Chisholm, Joe Cormier, Bill Lamey and John Campbell. At the Orange Hall, Alcide Aucoin and Henry MacPhee played with Eddie Irwin on piano for the round dances while Dougie played with them for the square sets. In 1968 he moved back to New Waterford and worked as sound archivist, music consultant, and conservator at the Beaton Institute at CBU. His albums include *Cape Breton Piano I-III* (1977, 1979, 1981), *The Reel of Tulloch* (1985), and *Cape Breton's Master of the Keyboard* (1989). Selections from these LPs were released on CD in 2002 as *Favourite Cape Breton Piano Solos*. He has also appeared on more than 40 recordings accompanying fiddlers; some of his memorable partnerships have been with Donald MacLellan, John Campbell, Carl MacKenzie, Johnny Wilmot, Dan Joe MacInnis and Dwayne Côté. His music is rooted in the old style and is he is inspired by both piano players such as his mother, Margaret MacPhee, and by Lila MacIsaac, and by fiddle players he had the opportunity to hear and to play with, including Mary MacDonald, Duncan Mac-Quarrie and Winston Fitzgerald. His approach to music is informed by his awareness of correctness as it pertains to the Cape Breton sound; he scrutinizes collections to find his preferred setting of a tune. As an accompanist, he likes to play the melody along with the fiddle, often in a different register, which was an older practice; in his solo performances he employs many of the same embellishments used by the fiddlers to add flavour to the melodic line. He has composed over 50 tunes (something he started in 1999), some of which are published in Pat Chafe's collection *Bits and Pieces* (2009). A core member of the music group on CBC-TV's *Ceilidh,* he has also toured Scotland (1975, 1977, 1979 and 1985), taught at the Ceòlas summer school, and has performed in Scandinavia and across North America. Also interested in Irish music, he met and performed with one of his heroes, Sean Maguire, at Celtic Colours in 2000. In recognition of his contribution to music he was awarded the Order of Canada in 2008. [**Caplan 1986; MacGillivray 1988**].

MacQuarrie, Gordon. (1897-1965). Fiddle, bagpipes, composer, poet. Born to parents Angus Forbes and Margaret (MacLean) MacQuarrie in Dunakin, Cape Breton, his mother died when he was an infant and he was raised by Neil Mac-Lennan in Melford, Inverness County. Literate in both Gaelic and English, he began playing music on both bagpipes and fiddle. He became interested in music theory and pursued this through a correspondence course and through instruction locally with fiddle-maker John Alex Gillis of Alba, Inverness County and with Vincent A. MacLellan. Known as "Red" Gordon on account of his hair, he was considered creative and eccentric, he lived an itinerant lifestyle, spending periods of time with different families around Cape Breton, such as with the MacKays of Glendale and at Rannie MacIsaac's in Creignish. He also performed on occasion beyond Cape Breton, for example, in 1939 with Mary "Hughie" MacDonald in Detroit. He was supposedly booked to participate in the pioneer recording sessions of Cape Breton fiddlers

in Montréal for the Celtic label in 1935, but was replaced by Angus Chisholm at the last minute. In 1940, along with Joseph Beaton of Medford, MA, he was responsible for the first publication of Cape Breton fiddle music—*Cape Breton Collection of Scottish Melodies for the Violin*—which had tunes by himself and other Cape Breton fiddlers and pipers. Among his own compositions the best known is perhaps "The Bonnie Lass of Headlake." Of his poetry, his tribute to "Big" Ronald MacLellan, composed following his death in 1935, is published in *The Cape Breton Fiddler*. A piper with the Cape Breton Highlanders, he served in Britain during the Second World War and while there obtained many of the published collections not previously accessible in Cape Breton. [**MacGillivray 1981**].

— ∼ —

Cape Breton Collection of Scottish Melodies for the Violin, The. Printed first in 1940 and later in 1975, this was compiled and arranged by Gordon F. MacQuarrie, fiddler, piper and composer, and published by Joseph Beaton at Medford, MA. It is the first published tune collection from the Cape Breton tradition. Its 152 pieces are presented in categories as: (i) Scotch reels and strathspeys, (ii) slow airs or marches, (iii) bagpipe marches, (iv) hornpipes and clogs, (v) jigs. There are 58 reels, 44 strathspeys, 20 jigs, 14 hornpipes, 1 clog, 9 marches, 3 airs, 1 slow strathspey and 2 other medleys. MacQuarrie's preface states that the aim of the work was to "form a comprehensive Collection of the National Music of Scotland, as composed and performed in New Scotland." He notes that this had been "considered for some time past, a long, felt want" and stresses the urgency for such an endeavour since any delay "might mean the loss of at least some, if not all the numbers.... Now is the time to gather together all that can be had of this kind of music which may be worth preserving, before it is lost beyond recall." He is also keen to stress that he is an amateur who "has not had the advantage of professional training in music" but believes that this important work "should be so done, than not done at all." The repertoire included in this collection consists entirely of previously unpublished melodies composed in Cape Breton, mostly in the Inverness County area. Of the tunes, 101 are by MacQuarrie himself, 11 by Dan R. MacDonald, 6 each by J. D. Kennedy, and Ronald MacLellan, 9 by Pipe Major A. MacDonald, 4 each by Sandy MacLean and Dan Hughie MacEachern, 3 by Dan Rory MacDonald, and 1 each by Vincent MacLellan, Allan MacFarlane, Ronald Beaton, Vincent MacGillivray, Peter MacPhee and Kitchener MacDonald; 1 each are also arranged by Dan Beaton and John MacKinnon. The tunes are ordered by key, with title, tune type and composer's name. Some Cape Breton favourites are included: "The Baddeck Gathering," "Red Shoes," "The Scotsville Reel" and "The Bonnie Lass of Headlake."

— ∾ —

MacQuarrie, Morgan. (1946-). Fiddle. Kenloch, Inverness County and Detroit. The son of Zina (Alexandrina MacDougall) MacQuarrie of Scotsville and Jack MacQuarrie of Loch Ban (later known as Kenloch), he inherited much music from his father's family: his grand-uncle, William MacQuarrie from Orangedale, was a violinist, another grand-uncle, Hector J. MacQuarrie, was a prizewinner in a pipe competition in 1891 and his aunt, Christie MacQuarrie Gowell, played the violin. His father played occasionally, teamed with Danny Michael Kennedy. Morgan and his sister Ann, a piano player, and brother Allan, experienced music at ceilidhs at their neighbour, Angus ("Sandy John") Kennedy's, and at dances in the Kenloch Hall and in Mabou, and heard it on *Scottish Strings* on CJFX radio from Antigonish. Morgan took up the fiddle at 12, going on to play at parties, school dances and concerts; since Ann had also begun playing piano, the two would practice together, and local fiddlers would drop in to join them. Since there were few of his own age playing Morgan began to play with Willie Kennedy who was some 20 years older. Later he

played with Cameron Chisholm and they roomed together in Windsor in 1965 after he spent some time in Toronto. Michigan state's large Cape Breton population at that time was dominated musically by John Archie MacDonald, of the Five MacDonald Fiddlers recording group, but MacQuarrie and Danny MacPhee found a niche and sponsored weekly dances at the Saxon Club Hall in Windsor. MacQuarrie settled in Detroit in 1970 and married Marie Cameron whose family roots were in Mabou. His playing has an old-style aesthetic featuring a lot of double stops and drones; he is a noted jig player, although his favourites are marches. He recorded three solo albums: *Kenloch Ceilidh* (1990), *Loch Ban* (2002) and *Over the Cabot Trail* (2007), all on the Rounder label. Indeed, MacQuarrie worked closely with Mark Wilson of Rounder Records on co-production of *The Traditional Fiddle Music of Cape Breton* volumes, part of the North American Traditions series. [**Wilson 2007; Wilson and Dunlay 2008**].

Mac Talla an Eilean. See *Island Echoes.*

Magone, Barbara MacDonald. *See* **MacDonald family of Detroit.**

Maillet, Elizabeth ("Liz" and "Betty"). (1907-1960). Piano. Digby, NS, and Boston, MA. Her mother was Margaret (MacNeil) Cameron from Scotch Hill in Margaree Harbour, Cape Breton. Elizabeth was born of a second marriage to Captain Maillet, in Digby, NS. Her mother's first husband, Archibald Cameron from West Lake Ainslie, had died of TB at the age of 36, leaving her a widow with three young daughters. Elizabeth grew up in Digby but spent her summers at Scotch Hill in Cape Breton. She played piano, having been taught by the French nuns, and was sought out by fiddle players such Angus Chisholm, Alick Gillis and Alcide Aucoin, accompanying them at many house parties. Later, when Gillis started the group The Inverness Serenaders, she joined them as their piano player; she is thus featured on some of the earliest recordings of Cape Breton fiddlers on the Decca label. This group was based in Boston and while there she also played often at the house parties of her niece Mary Eleanor ("Gacie")

Muise and her husband, John; they had a piano in the home and Gacie herself played; their daughter (Maillet's grand-niece) Janine (Muise) Randall is also a Cape Breton-style piano player. Maillet's style showed some evidence of her exposure to jazz music and included elements of syncopation.

march. Historically the march is a tune type used by the military in order to add diversion to an otherwise mundane and lengthy chore, to meter the progress and speed of that activity, and to enhance an air of comradeship, in much the same way that work songs were created to accompany domestic chores; it thus came to be part of military band performance. Associated with bagpipes in Scotland, the march, along with dance tunes, forms part of the *Ceòl beag* or "light music" repertoire. Marches may reflect their original functional role to accompany; they may be celebratory in nature to mark a victory or may be slow and funereal to reflect defeat. As a tune type, the march has a strong, regular rhythm and may be in any of a number of metres, but most commonly are in 4/4, 2/4 or 6/8. In Cape Breton, as in Scotland, bagpipe marches have been adapted for fiddle playing and

generally appear at the start of a medley of tunes or following a slow air. A 6/8 march will segue easily into a medley of jigs while duple time marches generally precede a strathspey-reel configuration. Only rarely is the march played in isolation. A good many marches have been composed specifically for fiddle, and some tunes—such as "Space Available" by Marcel Doucet and "The Glencoe March" by Dan R. MacDonald—are popular tunes, and often introduced into a fiddlers' repertoire at an early stage of the learning process. Most fiddlers have marches in their repertoires, and the tune type is relatively prominent in the published collections of fiddler-composers, representing up to 14% of the material in some instances (e.g., Dan Hughie MacEachern's collection, vol. 2). Certain players are noted for being exceptional march players, one of these being Theresa MacLellan, who is particularly regarded for her interpretation of pipe marches.

Marshall, William. (1748-1833). Scottish composer, regarded as one of the greats and referred to by Robert Burns as "the first composer of Strathspeys of the age." He is credited with having composed

march   Glencoe   Dan. R. MacDonald

© Cameron Music, Port Hawesbury, NS, SOCAN, CMRRA

LIZ DOHERTY

an estimated 257 tunes; a number of these such as "The Duke of Gordon's Birthday" have become part of the Cape Breton fiddle canon, likely entering the repertoire via his published collections, which were in circulation in Cape Breton mostly from the mid-20th century. [**Hunter 1979**].

master fiddlers. A term used to denote a small number of exceptional or "star" players within the Cape Breton fiddle tradition. It was used to distinguish between the small, elite group considered fiddling greats and the other capable, albeit less distinguished, fiddlers who made up the majority of the fiddle-playing populace. The term became particularly prevalent in the 1980s, following its appropriation by Jerry Holland for his 1982 album; today it is used typically to refer to iconic fiddlers of the past and is rarely used as a descriptor for contemporary players irrespective of their profile (Buddy MacMaster being a most recent exception).

Matheson, Betty. Step dance, teacher and a director of the CBFA. Glace Bay and Dominion. Born in Glace Bay, her parents were Ben and Kaye McIvor. Her father was a guitar player and singer and her mother took part in square dancing; many of her relatives could step dance and one of her uncles, Dan Charlie MacKinnon, was a prompter for local square sets. An only child, Betty spent the summers on the shores of the Bras d'Or in Malagawatch, Inverness County, her mother's home area. There she experienced square dances at Marble Mountain and was encouraged in her own dancing, having attended classes in tap, ballet and jazz. During the 1970s, while living in Boston, she witnessed both Irish and Cape Breton music and dance; when she moved back to Cape Breton and settled in Dominion, with Margaret Gillis of North Sydney she joined Fr. Eugene Morris's stepdance class. Encouraged by Sheldon MacInnes the two women began teaching together, offering classes at the Gaelic College and in Sydney. Such was the demand that step-dance teaching became almost a second job. Since 1975, Matheson has been a major driving force behind the CBFA, the office of which is located in her home. Significant projects she has been responsible for include the CBFA's 40th anniversary celebrations (2013) and its performance tour of Scotland (2008). She was a founding member of the board of Dance Nova Scotia and was involved in research projects on Cape Breton dance through this organization.

matinee. Informal presentation or concert-style event that takes place in a pub environment during an afternoon. In the present context, the matinee was first introduced in Chéticamp, at the Doryman Tavern, in the 1970s; since then it has become a popular type of event in a number of venues across the island. Typically there is a host fiddler and piano player who perform, on stage and amplified, for much of the afternoon; other musicians who show up may be invited to play a set and dancing, both step and square may happen. The audience is not expected to sit in silence as at a concert; people are free to chat and to move about the room; alcohol and food are always available. *See* **Concert.**

McCarthy, Brandi. (1987-). Fiddle, step dance. Fergus, ON, and Port Hawkesbury. Although neither of her parents played themselves, she heard Cape Breton fiddle music played by the Rankins, Natalie MacMaster and Ashley MacIsaac on recordings. She took step dance lessons locally and at the Gaelic College with various tutors such as Mary Janet MacDonald, Sabra MacGillivray, Betty Matheson, Jean MacNeil and Cheryl MacQuarrie and, at the age of 9, became interested in fiddle, attending various classes and workshops with John Donald Cameron, Dawn Beaton, Melissa Emmons, Andrea Beaton and Eddie Rogers. Membership of the CBFA played an important part in her music education, introducing her to the music of players from all over the island as well as affording her performance opportunities as a step dancer at Celtic Colours and in a number of TV productions such as *Rita MacNeil's Cape Breton* and *Steps with Sabra* on Bravo!, and as a fiddler and step dancer at the Celtic Music Interpretive Centre in Judique. She has taught both dance and fiddle at the Gaelic College and for the Port Hawkesbury Recreation Department; during 2009-2010 she spent a year in Ireland where she taught workshops at the University of Limerick and furthered her own studies in Irish dance.

McDonald, Chris. (1971-). Research, guitar. Burlington, ON, Vancouver, BC, Ottawa and Sydney, NS. Assistant professor in ethnomusicology at CBU, he comes from an academic background in popular music studies and has published on alternative rock, jazz and on the Canadian rock band, Rush. He became involved with Cape Breton music around 1998 initially as a performer in a Toronto-based Celtic music group led by Maureen Redden and including his partner, Heather Sparling, on flute. Sparling was working on Cape Breton's Gaelic-language and song traditions and this led to them moving there in 2005 when she was appointed to the faculty at CBU. There, McDonald began playing guitar with local musicians at the Thursday night session at Rollie's Wharf in North Sydney and at Cape Breton Gaelic Society events; gradually his own research interests shifted to the local culture. Currently his work – funded by the Social Science and Humanities Research Council of Canada – is on the history and style of Cape Breton piano accompaniment. He has also conducted research on local singer-songwriters, many of whom integrate aspects of Cape Breton traditional music into what they play.

McGann, Joseph Clifford ("Cliff"). (1970-). Guitar, song, academic, producer. Westford and Chelmsford, MA. Cliff's mother, Catherine Frances (MacDonald) McGann came from a musical family from Lanark, Antigonish County, Nova Scotia; his grandfather was a first cousin to Hugh A. MacDonald, "The Polka King." Known as "the number 11" MacDonalds, fiddle music was a mainstay on the family farm. McGann attended St. FX in the late 1980s and started to become interested in the Cape Breton artists who were gaining popularity nationally at the time, among them The Rankins and The Barra MacNeils. He also began learning more about the local musical traditions and met many of the last generation of Gaelic-speaking singers and fiddlers during that time; his maternal grandmother, who he visited often, was a Gaelic speaker from one of the last *gaidhealtachd* areas of mainland Nova Scotia. Inspired by Dave MacIsaac he began to explore fiddle accompaniment on guitar. McGann went on to enrol at the Folklore Department at Memorial University of Newfoundland and Labrador and wrote his MA thesis on the life and music of Cape Breton fiddler-composer Dan R. MacDonald: "Dan R. MacDonald: Individual Creativity in the Cape Breton Fiddle Tradition" (2003); he is presently working on a book version of this. He moved back to Boston in the mid-1990s and is an active musician on the Irish and Cape Breton scenes there.

McKinnon, Ian. (1961-). Highland bapipes, tin whistle, bodhrán, radio host, artist manager, label owner. Since 1992, the owner of GroundSwell Music, a record label and management company, he is a member of the Celtic rock group Rawlins Cross, with who he performs what has become their signature pieces, "MacPherson's Lament" and "Reel 'n Roll." Growing up in Halifax his interest in the music was fostered by his father, Alex McKinnon, and his grandmother, Mary Anne (Jamieson) McKinnon, a Cape Breton pianist. His graduate dissertation at Memorial University's Folklore Department dealt with the recording industry and commercialism: "Fiddling to Fortune: The Role of Commercial Recordings Made by Cape Breton Fiddlers in the Fiddle Music Tradition of Cape Breton Island," in 1989.

McMullen, Darren. (1975-). Guitar. Truro, NS. His parents Donna Mason and Chester McMullen were both musicians and his music education started at home playing first piano, then guitar. Rock and folk were his main interests until he was in his mid-twenties and living in Halifax; there he played with the band, Hair of the Dog (later the Gig Dogs), which featured fiddle player Martin St. Maurice with whom he released *Fingerboard Grooves* in 2001. From 2004 to 2008 he toured with J. P. Cormier across Canada, the U.S. and the U.K., playing guitar, bass, mandolin, tenor banjo, mandola, piano, cello and whistles; in 2010 he toured with the Rankins. He works with a range of bands representing Celtic, folk, rock and popular music genres, these including the Colin Grant Band, Pogey, Dave Gunning, David Francey, Matt Andersen, Bruce Guthro, Matt Minglewood, Gillian Boucher, Troy MacGillivray, Andrea Beaton, Rachel Davis, Anna Ludlow and Chrissy Crowley. He is also a member of contemporary Cape Breton band, Sprag Session and is a founder member of Còig. His solo recordings, *Decades* (2008) and *Shoes for Molly* (2011), have been recognized with ECMA and CFM nominations.

medals. Symbolic awards, typically with Royal authority and related to significant commemorations, these mark outstanding contributions to Canadian culture. Buddy MacMaster received the Canada Medal, issued on the 125th anniversary of the founding of Canada, in 1993. For significant cultural contributions, MacMaster, along with John Allan Cameron and Scott Macmillan were awarded The Golden Jubilee Medal in 2002; Troy MacGillivray and David Greenberg were among the recipients of the Diamond Jubilee Medal in 2012. *See* **awards**.

medley. *See* **group**.

Melin, Mats. (1965-). Dance research, step dance. Stockholm, Sweden, and Limerick, Ireland. A dancer, and a lecturer in that subject at the Irish World Academy of Music and Dance at the University of Limerick in Ireland, his interest in Scottish dance led to him to move from his native Sweden to Scotland in 1995, where he became involved in teaching, promoting and developing it for a period of 13 years. He worked with the Fèisean movement, the Scottish Traditions of Dance Trust and in local government-funded Traditional Dance Artist posts in four regions of Scotland. He has been involved in the Cape Breton step-dance tradition as a researcher and practitioner since 1992, having been introduced to it while attending Alasdair Fraser's summer school at Sabhal Mòr Ostaig on the Isle of Skye, where Harvey Beaton and Buddy MacMaster were instructors. By 1995 he was actively involved in promoting Cape Breton dance in Scotland. He was a founding member of the dance performance group, Dannsa, which has Cape Breton dance traditions at its core and was responsible for introducing Cape Breton step dancing into the curriculum of the Scottish music degree course at the Royal Conservatoire of Scotland (formerly RSAMD). In 2008, he moved to Ireland to work at the Irish World Academy. Besides teaching Scottish and Cape Breton step dance, he has worked as a choreographer on projects in Scotland (including Orkney), Ireland and North America, produced an instructional DVD and published several papers on aspects of these dance traditions. His 2012 PhD dissertation through the University of Limerick was "Exploring the Percussive Routes and Shared Commonalities in Cape Breton Step Dancing"; this was the basis of his 2015 publication on the subject: *One With the Music: Cape Breton Step Dance Tradition and Transmission* (CBU Press).

Membertou Trade and Convention Centre. A state-of-the art, multipurpose venue for the Mi'kmaw community of Membertou within the Cape Breton Regional Municipality; opened in 2004, it is a venue for large-scale music events such as Celtic Colours concerts and the ECMA awards show.

metre. A borrowing from poetry where it is used to describe rhythmic pulses, the term refers to the organization of music into regularly recurring measures or bars of stressed and unstressed beats. Metre is indicated in Western music notation by a "time signature" (sometimes called the metre signature) consisting of two numbers, one above the other, placed at the start of a piece of music immediately after the treble clef; the lower number indicates the type of beats per bar, and the upper the number of beats per bar. Since many of the tune types that make up the Cape Breton repertoire share identical time signatures, the key defining feature of individual tune types goes beyond mere time-signature, and involves metrical impulses—patterns of stressed and unstressed beats within a bar. Metre is further articulated in performance though externalized body gestures, specifically foot-tapping patterns. It is in the interpretation of metre that distinctions between a single tune played in different traditions are often most noticeable (e.g., a jig as played in Cape Breton versus Scotland or Ireland).

The Cape Breton player's style is based on patterns of alternating long and short notes and stressed and unstressed beats that create a baseline, metrical pulse. This is realized through the bowing, both the bowing patterns themselves and the articulation involved in realising these patterns. The bowing style primarily involves alternating down-bows and up-bows in a simple, single-stroke pattern; the down-bow generally coincides with the rhythmically strong beats in a bar (often, but not exclusively), those that are longer in duration. Irrespective of the duration, however, equal emphasis is given to the bow in both directions. The regularity that this creates is then energized by the application of various bowing techniques such as the bow-push accent (which creates dynamic within a single note), and the whip-bow technique (which relates to the connections between notes). *See* **bow-push accent; bowing style; whip-bow technique.**

Milling frolic. *See* **frolic.**

Mi'kmaq. A First Nations people, indigenous to Canada's Maritime Provinces and the Gaspé Peninsula of Québec; others today live in Newfoundland and the northeastern region of Maine. The nation has a population of about 40,000, more than 25% of whom speak Mi'kmaw. Mi'kmaw territories are divided into seven traditional "districts," each with its own independent government and boundaries. The independent governments had a district chief and a council made up of band chiefs, elders and other worthy community leaders. In addition to the district councils, there was a grand council comprised of district chiefs, which was the senior level of self-government.

In 1876 Canada passed *The Indian Act* requiring First Nations to establish representative, elected governments; after implementation of this, the grand council adopted a more spiritual function that it maintains today. In 2010 the governments of Canada and Nova Scotia signed an historic agreement with the Mi'kmaw Nation, establishing a process whereby the federal government must consult with the grand council before engaging in any activities or projects that affect the Mi'kmaq in Nova Scotia, the first such collaborative agreement in Canadian history.

Cape Breton has five Mi'kmaw communities: Eskasoni (population ca. 3,800), Membertou (near Sydney, 1,051), Wagmatcook (623), Waycobah (900) and Potlotek/Chapel Island (576). While the Mi'kmaq have their own language, beliefs and rituals, a rich oral tradition of folktales, and music traditions around song and drumming, interaction with other population groups has impacted on aspects of their culture. In Cape Breton, the aboriginal population interfaced with French, Irish and later Scottish settlers; as in other North American native cultures, from Peru to Alaska, the fiddle and its music was adopted by the native populace and, by the early 20th century, the fiddle was a popular instrument on all the reserves. There was no native Mi'kmaw fiddle music; rather those who took up the instrument (many of whom were itinerants, travelling great distances selling Mi'kmaw crafts) learned tunes and styles as they encountered them; as such their sources were eclectic, and learned aurally, which allowed them to put their own stamp on any music they learned. The discussion concerning the impact of language on fiddle music arises in relation to the Mi'kmaw players also; while it is often suggested that Mi'kmaw fiddlers bring a unique rhythm to Cape Breton fiddle music, influenced by the rhythm of the language (and while a popular game was to make up Mi'kmaw words for the first four bars of a tune that mimicked the rhythm of the phrase, not unlike *puirt-a-beul*), there has been no robust analysis conducted to date to substantiate this. A number of significant Mi'kmaw fiddle players from Cape Breton have been identified from the early 20th century; among them Lee Cremo (1938-1999) is the best known, having made a significant impact on the competitive circuit with over 80 wins to his credit; he made several recordings, played many high-profile gigs representing Cape Breton and composed a number of tunes. Square dances were popular, particularly in Eskasoni, and various local and visiting players provided the music for these. Roman Catholic priests stationed in the reserves or nearby played a role in supporting such events and in developing music-literacy skills among the Mi'kmaw players. To date, however, the Mi'kmaw contribution to the Cape Breton fiddle narrative has not been fully explored although some research has been carried out by Gordon Smith. *See* **individual entries**. [**Smith 1994**].

modes. Particularly associated with Gregorian chant (plainsong) and folk music, these are specific configurations of notes that generate a scale. Each mode contains five intervals of a tone and two of a semitone; they are easily identified if played on the white keys of the piano from a given starting note. It is the different placement of these intervals that creates each mode's individual character. While seven modes exist, each of which can be applied to any tonic note, the ones that feature most prominently within the Cape Breton fiddle tradition are the Ionian (C), Mixolydian (G) and Dorian (D) modes and, less commonly, the Aeolian (A) mode. The Ionian mode is essentially the major scale; the Mixolydian is the major scale with a flat 7th note; the minor modes are the Dorian (using a flat 3rd and 7th) and the Aeolian or natural minor (using a flat 3rd, 6th and 7th). The Mixolydian and Dorian modes are commonly used in bagpipe music; this may explain the popularity of these modes within the Cape Breton fiddle tradition. The Ionian, Mixolydian and Dorian modes share five of the seven pitches and only the 3rd and 7th degrees vary. It is therefore easy to move between modes within a single tune while maintaining the same tonic, simply by switching between the raised and lowered 3rd and 7th notes. [**Dunlay and Greenberg 1996; Graham 2006**].

Mombourquette, Allison. (1990-). Fiddle, step dance. L'Ardoise, Richmond County. She grew up listening to the fiddle music of her grandfather, who first taught her to play, and family friends such as Ciffie Carter and her neighbour and contemporary, Kayla Bona. Attending summer courses at the Gaelic College, becoming a member of the CBFA and participating in the music initiatives of Comunn Féis Mhàbu provided additional opportunities to develop her music interests and skills. She participated in the CBFA's youth exchange to Victoria, BC, in 2006, and a tour of Scotland and England in 2008; while studying French in Québec she also had the opportunity to perform with various artists including Natalie MacMaster, one of her fiddle heroes. Three of her compositions are included in the *Cape Breton Fiddlers Collection* (2007), and her debut CD, *Allie Mombourquette*, was released in 2014.

Moore family from Perthshire, Scotland. Hamish (1950-), **Maggie** (1954-), **Fin** (1979-), **Duncan** (1977-) and **Fiona** (1976-). Scottish lowland and small-pipes innovator, maker and player Hamish Moore discovered the playing of Cape Breton bagpiper Alex Currie in the 1980s and became interested in this as a style of playing as it was performed for step dance. He interpreted Currie's music as an opportunity for Scottish pipers to re-engage with an older, authentic style and through his own performances and recording did much to progress this in Scotland. His 1994 album *Dannsa' Air An Drochaid* (Stepping on the Bridge) is based on his Cape Breton experience. Moore went on to found the Ceòlas Summer School that has taken place in South Uist annually since 1996 and where the Gaelic commonalities in Cape Breton and Scottish fiddle music, piping, song, language and dance are celebrated. Maggie Moore developed an interest in the step-dance tradition and carried out research on this during several trips to Cape Breton and subsequently published some of her findings. Introduced to Cape Breton music through their parents – Fin, Duncan and Fiona have all spent time in Cape Breton where they have all performed at such as Celtic Colours, while Fin has taught at the Gaelic College.

Morin, Mac. (1975-). Piano and step dance. Troy, Cape Breton. Born to parents Ken and Mary Catherine (MacDonald) Morin, he grew up with music in the home. His father and brothers played fiddle and guitar and his mother played piano and was a step dancer and Scottish country dancer who had performed across Canada and in the U.K.; her own father, John R. (Roddie Eddie) MacDonald, was a dancer and fiddler. Having been taught a few steps initially by his mother, Mac was given formal instruction from a young age, in dance from the Warner sisters, and on piano with a local classical music teacher for a year. While as a teenager attending the Gaelic College for a language course, he met Tracey Dares and was encouraged to once again take up the piano. His first public appearance, accompanying Buddy MacMaster, led to him touring with Natalie MacMaster from 1999-2001 and from 2006 onward. He also toured with the Rankin Family and Howie MacDonald's *Celtic Brew*. He was a founder member of the band, Beòlach, in 1998, with whom he has toured Europe and North America and recorded two albums: *Beòlach* (2002) and *Variations* (2004). He has also performed and/or recorded with various other fiddle players including Jerry Holland, Ian MacDougall, Andrea Beaton, Rodney MacDonald, Glenn Graham, Howie MacDonald, Jackie Dunn, Wendy MacIsaac, Troy MacGillivray and Shelly Campbell; international artists with whom he has performed include Alison Krauss, The Chieftains and Yo-Yo Ma. He also teaches at home and internationally at such as Sabhal Mòr Ostaig and the University of Limerick. In 2015 he was appointed coordinator for Féis Cheap Breatuinn/ Féis Cape Breton, a new education, participation and networking initiative introduced by CMIC and Celtic Colours. An eponymous piano album released in 2003 reflects his individual style and his interest in and influences from other players such as John Morris Rankin, Tracy Dares MacNeil and, from Ireland, Mícheál Ó Súilleabháin. Also a step dancer involved from time to time

with the Scottish dance ensemble Dannsa, he has a neat style marked by gracious, clean and defined movements, and a repertoire of steps which combine old style and contemporary motifs. In 2014 Morin's contribution to Cape Breton music and dance was recognized in his role as artist in residence at Celtic Colours; his work in this capacity included collaborations with U.S. dancer Nic Gareiss.

Morris brothers from Colindale, Inverness. Two brothers, both Roman Catholic priests who have played many roles in the Cape Breton tradition including as artists and advocates for that tradition.

Morris, Father Eugene. (1935-). Step dance, teacher. He graduated from St. FX before continuing on to theological studies at St. Paul's Seminary, Ottawa. Following his ordination at St. Ninian's Cathedral (Antigonish) in 1965 he was allocated appointments in Antigonish, Glace Bay and Big Pond before spending a year in Swaziland, South Africa. Back in Nova Scotia he served in various areas including Port Hawkesbury, Creignish, New Waterford, Dingwall, Smelt Brook and St. Margaret's Village. He was Pastor at St. Theresa's Parish, Sydney for 9 years during which time he celebrated his silver anniversary in the priesthood (1990) with a mass and ceilidh. Since then he has been based in Bishop's Falls, Newfoundland. He participated in square sets all his life, but at the age of 30 he began to engage with the step-dance tradition, leading to impromptu house-party displays performed to his brother, Fr. Angus Morris's, fiddle playing. Following the broadcasting of *The Vanishing Cape Breton Fiddler* in 1971, Fr. Eugene set out on a mission to prove that Cape Breton fiddling was a vibrant art form. Along with school teacher and music enthusiast Frank MacInnis of Creignish, he spent the summer of 1972 travelling all over Cape Breton Island, meeting fiddlers and encouraging them to participate in a forthcoming fiddle festival. The Glendale fiddle festival of July 1973 – considered by Fr. Eugene to be part of his pastoral duties – thus culminated in a grand finale featuring more than a hundred fiddlers performing en masse. This event is considered as marking a turning point in the fortunes and practices of Cape Breton fiddle music. As part of the revival of music and dance during this era, modes of transmission were revised, and Fr. Eugene was among the first to promote formal step-dance classes in the Sydney area. While he taught these himself initially, he also encouraged others to do so, resulting in some of his students, Betty Matheson and Margaret Gillis, becoming key participants in the revival. An authority on Cape Breton step dance, Fr. Eugene has been the focus of various dance studies and publications and is featured in such as Allister MacGillivray's book, *A Cape Breton Ceilidh*. [**Melin 2015; MacGillivray 1988; Voyer, 1986**].

Morris, Fr. Angus. (1936-). Born Angus Roderick Morris to parents Patrick Morris and Florence (MacDonald) he was the fourth youngest in a family of nine. He first heard fiddle music on the radio and from local fiddlers of the day such as his father's cousins, Alex, Jim and John "Lewis" MacDonald, John Alex "the Big Fiddler" MacDonald, Donald Angus Beaton, Buddy MacMaster and Winston Fitzgerald. Although he started playing piano he took up the fiddle as a teenager. Excused from school for an extended period following the breaking of his arm and shoulder, taking up the fiddle seemed like a way to exercise the arm and stave off boredom. Jim "Lewis" MacDonald helped him tune up the family fiddle and gave him some basic instruction on note reading. He was soon among the fiddlers given the opportunity to "spell off" Buddy MacMaster at his dances in Neily MacDonald's Hall in Harbour View. Following high school, Angus spent 6 years working on the home farm and in the mines before beginning his studies for an arts degree at St. FX at the age of 22. He found ample opportunity to play there at gatherings with other students interested in Scottish music. In his last year at St. FX he entered the priesthood and spent 4 years in seminary training. Following his ordination he was appointed curate at St. Agnes parish in New Waterford (1966), and there became aware of the Mabou style through the playing of Mary MacDonald. From 1969 to 1976 he was stationed

as a missionary in Honduras; he did not bring a fiddle with him but bought one there and used the opportunity to listen a great deal to records and tapes. In *The Scotia Sun* (No. 14) there is a lovely tale of himself and an old Honduran man spending an afternoon sharing music on a fiddle with a bow made of alder and strung with the hair from a donkey's tail. Following his years there he moved back to Cape Breton, and to Sydney Mines (1976). There he became active on the music scene and saw Joe MacLean, John and Alex MacDougall and Billy MacPhee on a regular basis. He was later appointed parish priest in Eskasoni and has been serving as parish priest in Mabou for many years. An active player and a member of the CBFA he has also encouraged the inclusion of fiddle music into the liturgy. [**MacGillivray 1981**].

Morrison, Theresa (MacLean). *See* **MacLean family of Washabuck.**

mouth organ. *See* **harmonica.**

Muise family of Boston, MA. Ex-patriate Cape Bretoners John and Mary Eleanor (Edmonds) Muise were prominent figures in the Cape Breton music community in Boston in the mid-20th century; their commitment to the Cape Breton music tradition has been continued by their daughter Janine (Muise) Randall, piano player, teacher, researcher and founder of the Ceilidh Trail School of Celtic Music.

Muise, John. (1923-2005). Step dance, clappers. Born in Inverness to parents Peter and Annabelle (Walker) Muise, his mother was a step dancer, as were all the Walkers. As a step dancer John attended dances around Inverness, some of them held on the beach on a temporary wooden platform. He was influenced by the Inverness Serenaders' clappers player Hughie Young, most likely from the band's mid-1930s recordings; he started playing the bones or clappers while a young volunteer in the Canadian Army during the Second World War, while stationed in Scotland and France. After the war he moved to Boston where he ran dances, often for charitable causes, in various venues in Watertown and Brookline, and became very involved with the Canadian American Club and the Down East Bowling League, for which he served as president for a time. He also was a regular caller for square sets and played clappers along with many of the Cape Breton fiddlers who performed in the Boston area including John Campbell, Bill Lamey, Jerry Holland, Joe Cormier, Johnny Wilmot, Willie Kennedy, Buddy MacMaster, Carl MacKenzie, Raymond Ellis, Morgan MacQuarrie, Joe MacLean, Angus Chisholm, Alcide Aucoin, Theresa MacLellan and, in later years, Ashley MacIsaac. A flamboyant performer, he could play with up to three bones in each hand simultaneously with faultless timing. Muise and his wife, Mary Eleanor ("Gacie"), who he married in 1951, were central figures in the Boston-Cape Breton community's house-party era. She was a niece of Elizabeth Maillet who played piano with The Inverness Serenaders. Having a piano in the house, she taught herself to accompany fiddle music; she also played often at square dances in the Boston area. From the 1950s through to the 1990s the Muises, who in fact had a piano both upstairs and downstairs, hosted many house parties for Cape Breton fiddlers as well as Irish musicians, including Seamus Connolly, Larry Reynolds, Tommy Sheridan and Jimmy Kelly. Muise recorded music at these events and built up a collection of reel-to-reel tapes which his daughter, Janine, donated to the Burns Library at Boston College in 2011. Johnny Muise's playing can be heard on the Rounder CD *Traditional Fiddle Music of Cape Breton: MacKinnon's Brook* (2008) where he accompanies Joe Cormier on fiddle with Janine, on piano. *See* **home recordings.**

Randall, Janine (Muise). (1953-). Piano and Ceilidh Trail School of Celtic Music founder. Boston. Growing up in a home that was a popular venue for house parties she grew up listening to the playing of many Cape Breton and Irish musicians living in or visiting Boston, including Johnny Wilmot, Bill Lamey, Angus Chisholm, Alcide Aucoin, Angus Allan Gillis, Alick Gillis, Arthur Muise, Jerry Holland, Dave MacIsaac, Mary Jessie MacDonald and Jimmy Kelly. Janine learned to step dance by watching and learning

and took formal piano lessons, but it was only in her teenage years that she became seriously interested in accompanying fiddle tunes, inspired by Mary Jessie MacDonald, Eddie Irwin and later, by Hilda Chiasson and Tracey Dares. She performed often at Cape Breton square dances at the Canadian American Club with fiddlers John Campbell, Ludger LeFort and Joe Cormier; she also played regularly with Jerry Holland and today performs with Boston-based Irish fiddler Rose Clancy, PEI banjo player Ken Perlman, fiddler Frank Ferrel and with Cape Breton and PEI musicians who regularly visit the area. Although the Boston-Cape Breton scene is today greatly diminished, Randall continues to promote the music there, organizing events via the Canadian American Club of Massachusetts and other local venues. She has recorded with several fiddlers (such as Frank Ferrel, Joe Derrane, John McGann, Peter Barnes and Shane Cook) and is featured on *Traditional Fiddle Music from Cape Breton: MacKinnon's Brook,* part of Rounder's "North American Traditions" series (2008), accompanying Joe Cormier alongside her father on clappers. She has also recorded with Grammy-nominated classical violinist, Caroline Goulding (Telarc Records, 2009). Janine Randall's major contribution to Cape Breton music has been her founding of The Ceilidh Trail School of Celtic Music in Inverness, with which she was involved from 1995 to 2007. She continues to teach Cape Breton-style piano, and has presented papers on aspects of Cape Breton music at NAFCo in Aberdeen (2001), St. John's (2008) and Derry (2012).

Muise, Arthur. (1950-). Fiddle and step dance. Chéticamp. Born to parents Simon and Maggie (Camus) Muise he was brought up in a French-speaking family in the Acadian community of Chéticamp. Along with his brother, Lionel, and his sister, Corinne, Arthur started out step dancing at around the age of 5; when he was 8 he started to play the fiddle, initially under the tutelage of his father. His style developed, influenced by the playing most particularly of Angus and Cameron Chisholm, the latter who lived in nearby Margaree. Although he never recorded professionally, some home recordings of Muise were treasured items handed around among the fiddle community and these influenced many younger players. One of the fiddlers profiled in the *Scotia Sun* series (No. 27, 1973) – an indication of the esteem in which he was held – he performed often at the outdoor Scottish concerts, occasionally on CJFX and was a regular player at the Doryman Tavern with Donny LeBlanc. However, over the past twenty years, he has rarely been known to play in public. [**MacGillivray 1981**].

Muise, John. *See* **Muise family of Boston, MA.**

Multicultural Association of Nova Scotia, The (MANS). Founded in 1975 and mandated by the provincial government of Nova Scotia to represent the interests of multicultural organizations and communities in the province, this voluntary, non-profit organization addresses multicultural education, advocacy and information sharing. A member of the Cultural Federations of Nova Scotia, MANS was the catalyst that sparked Nova Scotia's *Multiculturalism Act,* the aims of which include the preservation of cultural traditions. It provides leadership to the hundred or more ethnocultural groups living in Nova Scotia and encourages people to work together on inclusive programs. Mike Fitzgerald, a promoter of the Irish community in Cape Breton, was among the first on the island to be involved in MANS, and served as its president from 1992-1994 and 1996-1998; Archie Neil Chisholm was also involved for a number of years.

Murphy, Joe and his Radio Swing Band. A popular dance band assembled in the 1950s with Cape Breton fiddlers Bernie Ley and Joe MacDougall, Helen MacAuley (piano), Miles MacDonald (bass) and Joe Murphy himself on drums. They released two LPS in the 1950s, *Barn Dance Music with Joe Murphy and his Band* and *Famous Canadian Fiddlers, Vol. II: Joe Murphy and his Band Play the Immortal Music of Jim McGill,* a tribute to the Toronto-based, Northern Irish old-time fiddler and composer (1902-1954) whose band, The Northern Ramblers, was popular at square dances, although

not in Cape Breton. Joe Murphy and his band also appear on various audio anthologies on the Banff, Rodeo and Celtic labels; marketed under such titles as *16 Great Jigs and Reels by Canada's Top Fiddlers;* these give an indication of the level of regard in which this group was held at the time across Canada.

Murphy, Peter. Antigonish. Photographer turned film-maker Peter Murphy owns Seabright, a production company that has released several DVDs of Cape Breton music and dance, some of his material broadcast nationally and internationally. His catalogue includes such as *Cape Breton Island, Volumes 1 and 2, The Best of Buddy MacMaster, Music in the Blood, The Pipes the Pipes are Calling* and the step-dance tutorial by Mary Janet MacDonald, *A Family Tradition.*

music industry. Since at least the 1950s, Cape Breton fiddle players have demonstrated an awareness of the business side of the music industry and have, although reluctantly in some instances, engaged with it over the years. Despite many fiddlers developing busy, multi-faceted careers that included live performances, radio and television work and the making and (often marketing and distributing) of recordings, music was never a full-time professional career for most of them. Rather, they maintained "steady" jobs and managed their music lives around this. This economic value of music can be seen from archived documents and artifacts. One early fiddler was noted for his professional fees being "more expensive" than his peers, suggesting that there existed a hierarchy in terms of popularity; fiddlers typically remember how much they were given for their first paid gig, and there is anecdotal evidence (documented by MacGillivray, 1988) that coins and notes were thrown on the floor for step dancers as they performed. From the late 1920s on, fiddle players were dealing with record companies (initially in the U.S.), showing that they were aware of the commercial potential of recorded music as well as its value in building live audiences; posters and advertising often point to outlets where the recordings were available. Musicians also became attuned to the marketing potential of live radio for promoting their various dances. Despite these tendencies, the main enticement for players continued to be primarily the music itself, and few seemed to get rich from it or consider professional playing a career option. Indeed, at the core of the Cape Breton fiddler's ethos, a clear sense of integrity remained intact and fiddlers appeared to be prepared to turn their back on financial and promotion opportunities if they felt their music was being compromised. This explains, perhaps, why during the 1960s more home recordings emerged than those released commercially; disillusioned with their experiences in dealing with certain record companies, Cape Breton fiddlers detached themselves from the industry. It was the 1970s before the concept of ownership of newly composed music was taken seriously in Cape Breton, when John Donald Cameron insisted on registering Dan R. MacDonald's music so that the composer could receive royalties for the performance of his tunes by the Cape Breton Symphony Fiddlers. CBC – which was broadcasting Cape Breton fiddlers during this time – was also a key player in bringing copyright issues to the attention of the performers. It was not until toward the end of the 20th century, however, that a significant cohort of full-time professional musicians emerged from the fiddle-music community. Initially these were the artists picked up by the major labels during the boom of the 1990s, such as the Rankin Family, the Barra MacNeils, Ashley MacIsaac and Natalie MacMaster, and most of these have maintained a full-time career in music. But other career artists emerged too, although the numbers are small; many have only managed to survive by moving to larger urban centers outside of Cape Breton and/ or by developing portfolio careers that also involve teaching and studio work. The majority of Cape Breton fiddlers, however, continue the tradition of being part-time or semi-professional musicians. Critically, nowadays they are generally aware of the range of supports and structures available to them and, for the most part, are inclined to engage with these. Very many fiddlers have recorded

at least one album (indeed, it is common in Cape Breton for fiddlers to have several albums to their credit), typically as an independent production, so have taken responsibility for the recording, mastering, reproduction, marketing and distribution of the product; to that end most will likely have registered any of their own compositions with SOCAN and may have established their own independent publishing companies in order to facilitate licensing. Besides a very few high-profile fiddlers/bands most artists act as their own managers, although some may occasionally use the services of booking agents, particularly internationally; some (but by no means all) have their own websites and most are affiliated with one or more industry bodies as members.

supports. Supports (both arts and industry) to the Cape Breton fiddler at local, provincial and national level are as follows: (a) government and government-affiliated agencies such as the Nova Scotia Department of Communities, Culture and Heritage, Canada Council for the Arts and Arts Nova Scotia; (b) membership bodies such as the East Coast Music Association, Music Nova Scotia, Cape Breton Professional Musicians Association; (c) industry and trade organizations such as Cape Breton Music Industry Cooperative; this also includes umbrella organizations such as the Cultural Federations of Nova Scotia and DANS; (d) copyright and licensing organizations such as: Canadian Music Reproduction Rights Agency, SOCAN, Musicians' Rights Organization Canada. Additional support may be available through Gaelic-language and tourism bodies. A small number of professional Cape Breton fiddlers are affiliated with organizations such as the American Federation of Musicians. *See* **profession; under terms.**

music literacy. The understanding of music notation, specifically the ability to read and write western staff notation or, indeed, any other form of notation where the symbols are established and understood by the community involved. *See* **note players; note reading; teaching.**

Music Nova Scotia (MNS). A non-profit organization established in 1989 to encourage the creation, development, growth and promotion of Nova Scotia's music industry; it provides education, information and resources for its membership, acts as an advocate for the industry to all levels of government and private enterprise, and supports its membership in the promotion of Nova Scotia music regionally, nationally and internationally. Members include Nova Scotian songwriters, musicians, agents, managers, promoters, distributors, photographers, associations, lawyers, accountants and other industry professionals. Services to members include education (workshops, seminars and consultations), funding opportunities, an Emerging Music Business Program, an Export Development Program and a Community Presenters Assistance Program; MNS also offers performing opportunities in Halifax and Sydney. As part of its remit, MNS researched and published *Music Sector Strategy 2007,* a rationale and proposed framework for provincial investment in music. The pinnacle of its activities is the **Nova Scotia Music and Industry Awards** ceremony, which is the culmination of Nova Scotia Music Week held in a different location around the province each November. These awards celebrate the province's music and industry professionals. MNS members make the nominations across a range of categories, and these are assessed by a committee of jurors; winners are then determined by vote by all members of MNS. Besides the Traditional/Roots Recording category they continue to dominate, Cape Breton fiddlers have, over the years, been nominated and won across a range of other categories including best classical album and best artist (male and female); the wider Cape Breton music industry has also won various awards.

music schools. Although the dominant form of music transmission has been informal and oral in nature, there is evidence that formal music teaching was available in Cape Breton from the early 1800s; while much of this was advertised in the urban centres around Sydney, "professors" were known in rural areas; itinerant fiddlers (often having returned to Cape Breton "from away") also fulfilled this role, teaching style, repertoire and music literacy skills. A more coordinated, formal approach was developed in the 1970s; as part of the response to *The Vanishing Cape Breton Fiddler* (CBC, 1971) the newly formed Committee for Cape Breton (later CBFA), supported by members of the clergy, initiated group classes for Cape Breton fiddle, and later step dance. Classes – led by a number of individuals coaxed to take on the role – sprung up around Inverness and Richmond counties and Antigonish. The Gaelic College (founded since 1938 but focusing initially on such as Highland dance and competitive piping) eventually followed suit, incorporating fiddle, piano and step dance into its extensive summer teaching programs; it has developed into the only institution of its kind in North America and continues to evolve its teaching practices and policies. A new online program of instructional videos (including fiddle with Andrea Beaton, piano with Susan MacLean, piping with Kenneth MacKenzie and step dance with Anna MacDonald) is scheduled for release by the college in 2015. The Ceilidh Trail School of Celtic Music was established considerably later (in 1996) with the wider mandate of Celtic music; Scottish and Irish fiddlers and guitarists made up the teaching staff along with high-profile Cape Breton players and, at various times, with Jerry Holland as the patron; this has been discontinued since 2010. Billed as The Buddy MacMaster School of Fiddling, the week-long fiddle program is offered annually at CMIC during Celtic Colours. Each of these schools typically attracts a local and a visiting clientele, with the visitors often outnumbering the locals. Year-round, however, teaching provision is still available island-wide; associated with individual teachers, the preference is for private, one-to-one classes; however, group tutelage still happens through programs, typically sponsored by community and language organizations (e.g., Mabou Music Mentorship Program); the most most recent teaching initiative is Fèis Cape Breton, launched in 2015 by CMIC and Celtic

Colours. Compared with other traditions only a few teaching resources in the form of printed instruction books or DVDs have been published; on-line initiatives include Skype lessons with individual teachers (e.g., the Kimberley Sessions with Kimberley Fraser). *See* **under terms.**

Musicians' Rights Organization Canada (MROC), The. A Canadian non-profit society for the collection and distribution of performer remuneration due from radio stations and other music users by Re:Sound (formerly known as the Neighbouring Rights Collective of Canada). MROC receives the funds from Re:Sound and distributes to musicians the performer's share of royalties stipulated under various tariffs and levies approved by the Copyright Board of Canada.

N

neutral notes. Certain degrees of the scale can be played either sharper or flatter than would be suggested by equal temperament (i.e., where equally spaced whole tones and semi-tones are used throughout the scale, as on the piano). The presence of these neutral notes – generally the 3rd or 7th degrees of the scale (and occasionally the 6th) – was common in Cape Breton, certainly prior to the introduction of fixed-pitch instruments, in particular the piano, in the early 20th century; the practice of choosing them over their more "in tune" equivalences was continued by many players for several decades after this. The presence of the neutral notes may be a legacy from the bagpipe, which was the only other widely available instrument in earlier years. While the resulting intonation where these neutral notes are employed is perceived by more contemporary players simply as being "out of tune," for many older players such as Mary MacDonald, Donald Angus Beaton, Willie Kennedy and Buddy MacMaster, the neutral notes were deliberately placed and the tonal ambiguity that resulted added to what is referred colloquially as "flavour" and "dirt" to the music. An extension of the practice involves the note C in particular; this note may appear in various guises, flatter or shaper than the scale or mode would suggest (but never quite a semi-tone in either direction), and this neutral status can be applied, irrespective of its position in the scale. [**Doherty 1996; Dunlay and Greenberg 1996**].

Newfoundland and Labrador. While this area has its own distinctive instrumental music and song traditions, much of it connected with the Irish and French traditions, Cape Breton fiddle music has also been an influence. This was affected by migration from Cape Breton to Newfoundland between 1820 and 1860, when Acadians from the Chéticamp area settled in the Port-au-Port peninsula. The Codroy Valley, in western New-foundland, was settled mainly by Scottish-Cape Bretoners from Inverness and Margaree around the same time. Descendants of both these groups continued the fiddle traditions. From the late 19th century, as a result of faster shipping, expanding fishery and the industrialization of Cape Breton, exchanges between Cape Breton and Newfoundland increased; radio in particular played a significant role in disseminating Cape Breton fiddle music as signals from CJFX and CFCY often had a better reach in the south and west of the island than did the local Newfoundland signals. Listening to such players as Winston Fitzgerald, Angus Chisholm and Dan Joe MacInnis could thus affect the style of many local players to greater or lesser extents, particularly when opportunities for playing not associated with dancing became more frequent. Even dedicated French-style players such as Emile Benoit adopted some stylings from Cape Breton players. Fiddler Ron Formanger took on board the style in a more robust manner, declaring that once he heard Cape Breton fiddlers on the radio he believed what he had been playing all along was wrong and allegedly never played a French tune again.

regional styles. According to some ethno-musicologists, the Newfoundland fiddle tradition (Labrador has its own tradition and stylistic variations within that) may be analyzed according to four predominant regional styles: (a) East Coast, (b) Codroy Valley, (c) Port-au-Port Peninsula, (d) Northern Peninsula; of course, today, as with most traditions, geographic styles are increasingly less relevant as technology enables access to diversity while paradoxically resulting in homogeneity; Newfoundland music scholar Evelyn Osborne refers to such as "media styles." The Northern Peninsula has been least affected by the Cape Breton tradition; the east coast, particularly around the area of St. John's has shown a degree of interaction between local and Cape Breton musicians; indeed this is where Rawlins Cross – a band featuring Cape Breton and Newfoundland musicians – was born. The Port-au-Port Peninsula in western Newfoundland is predominantly French, with a population descended both from French fishermen who settled there from the end of the 18th century and from Acadians, mainly from Cape Breton; by the 1900s, English and Scottish also settled there. The fiddle style, subsequently, has traces of Scottish, Irish and Canadian influences along with distinctive French traits including clogging (specific foot patterns to accompany the instrumental music). Fiddlers such as Ivan White (of Cape Breton ancestry), Ron and John Formanger, Howard Olivier (with Chéticamp connections) and Cornelius Rouzes all played a repertoire and style that was part Irish, Scottish and Cape Breton with some French and many local tunes; the Cape Breton tunes tended to be associated with listening contexts, while the older French material was used for dancing to. In the southwestern corner of Newfoundland, the Codroy Valley fiddle style is reminiscent of both the Cape Breton fiddle style and the Scottish fiddle style; it also displays characteristics of the Irish, Donegal fiddle style. This style has been shaped by its population group that included Acadian, Scottish, Cape Breton and Irish settlers. Here, the main tune types played are the strathspey, march and reel, combined in a single medley.

Scottish scholar Margaret Bennett states that many tunes in this region were brought over from Scotland in the mid-1800s, added to by Gaelic airs and waltzes that had been learned in Cape Breton or via the Sydney radio station. Popular tunes played in the Valley include "Calum Crúbach" and "Lord MacDonald's Reel" as well as many Irish jigs. Codroy Valley fiddle players also employ a number of bowing techniques similar to those of the Cape Breton style, and there is a strong sense of the downbeat pulse, lots of Scots snaps, cuts and double stops. Fiddle players with the Codroy Valley style include Walter J. and Jim MacIsaac, Joe AuCoin and David MacDonald. Danny Macdonald, one of the last of a generation of fiddle players from the Codroy Valley, started to learn fiddle at the age of 13 from playing with his father, John Archie Macdonald and other musicians at "house times" and square dances. Danny describes his own fiddle style as that of Cape Breton; he has modelled his playing on that of Cameron Chisholm, Jerry Holland, Buddy and Natalie MacMaster. Much of Danny's repertoire, like other fiddlers' in the area, consists of marches, reels and strathspeys but few waltzes or laments. As with most fiddlers in the Codroy Valley, he prefers to play with some form of accompaniment, preferably the guitar or piano vamping. Lisa MacArthur is a young fiddler from Newfoundland who has wholly embraced the Cape Breton style and practice. Recent research on fiddle playing in the western regions suggests that along with Canadian fiddle music and Cajun music, Cape Breton fiddle continues to be the main music listened to and emulated. In 1982 Gordon Bennett, a fiddler from the Codroy Valley, invited "Scottish music lovers" to assemble with the intent of forming a fiddle group and organization similar to the CBFA and its sister group in PEI. And, since its inception, Celtic Colours has provided an opportunity for regular performance opportunities for Newfoundland musicians in Cape Breton. **[Bennett, 1989; O'Connell 2007, 2009; Osborne 2007, 2013].**

newspapers and magazines. *See* **print media.**

Next Generation, The. A performing group organized by Stan Chapman in 1986, it included fiddle students from his own classes and those of other Cape Breton fiddle teachers. Members were Ashley MacIsaac, Natalie MacMaster, Kevin MacMaster, Wendy MacIsaac, Stephanie Wills, Kendra MacGillivray, Lucy MacNeil, Neil Beaton, Dougie MacDonald, Dwayne Côté, Shawn MacDonald, Catherine MacKinnon, John Pellerin, Joan Dewar and Jackie Dunn. The group featured at many local events including two showcases held at CBU and in St. Peter's, and re-enforced the message of the time that the Cape Breton fiddle tradition was very much alive and well in the hands of the younger generation. Following on from The Next Generation two later groups, involving different configurations of many of the same members, were formed – Highland Classics and The Special Seven.

Normaway Inn, The. A live-music venue and inn in the Margaree Valley which has had an association with music-related gatherings since the 1940s and where music is staged most nights during the tourist season from June to October. The Barn at the Normaway is known for its fiddle concerts and dances; on Wednesday nights it is the venue for the unique Three Fiddler Concert, where established names, emerging talents and impromptu guest performers perform in concert followed by a square dance.

North American Tradition Series. *See* **Rounder.**

note players. Those who use written sources to access repertoire or to inform learning. The term note players is in fact misleading and should properly be note "readers" or note "learners" since in Cape Breton no fiddlers employ written scores of any kind in performance (Winnie Chafe is a single exception). Indeed, many of the Cape Breton fiddlers who learned to read music did so at a point where they were already players; its function was primarily to increase their repertoire. Fiddlers, hearing a tune they liked at a dance or on the radio no longer had to capture it aurally in the moment; rather, once they had identified the tune name and located it in a printed collection it could be learned at a later date. Likewise, the books served as a system of mnemonics that could be consulted again and again, ensuring that a tune, once learned, would never be forgotten. Printed sources also offered a tangible yardstick against which levels of correctness could be measured and, as such, contributed much to this aspect of integrity within the performance practice. It is commonly accepted that in Cape Breton the fiddle tradition was primarily passed on aurally (by ear) until post-Second World War when new opportunities emerged for acquiring printed tune collections. While this era witnessed a significant increase in music literacy and the divergence of "ear" and "listening" players, nevertheless there is also enough evidence to suggest that music literacy did play a role in Cape Breton much earlier than this. *See* **ear players; note reading.**

note reading. Although the Cape Breton fiddle tradition has been essentially an oral tradition, literacy has existed concurrently since the time of the earliest settlers and has undoubtedly influenced the transmission of the music. In the 17th century, the Jesuits introduced music notation in order to teach vocal music; in the 18th, literate musicians lived in Louisbourg. One of the earliest trained Scottish fiddlers was Mabou Ridge pioneer Allan Cameron who immigrated in 1821; he trained in Edinburgh, and once established in Cape Breton he taught many, including Donald John "the Tailor" Beaton (1856-1919), to read and interpret written music. Beaton in turn passed this knowledge on to many others in his community; other early note-reading fiddlers were Johnny "MacVarish" MacDonald (1852-1934) from Broad Cove Marsh and Alexander Beaton (1835-1923) from Black River. Elsewhere on the island, sometime prior to 1860, The Sisters of Notre Dame taught music in the Arichat area. Later in that century, some of those nuns established the Holy Angels convent in Sydney and for the next hundred years that institution taught thousands of people the elements of musicianship. In Antigonish, the nuns at Mount St. Bernard gave rudimentary music training. Often it was young girls who benefitted from this; they in turn brought these music reading skills home and passed them on to the family members, usually male, learning to play fiddle. Less formally, many second- and third-generation traditional Cape Breton Scottish fiddlers left the

Francis "Rory Sis" MacDonald getting into the books. Francis MacDonald Photography.

island for employment opportunities; often on their travels they found the opportunity for music training and later passed on their knowledge. Examples include Vincent A. MacLellan (1856-1935) who, on his return from the U.S., taught a number of fiddlers to read, such as "Big" Ranald MacLellan (1880-1935); Allan Gillis of Deepdale spent nine years in the U.S. and on his return taught Sandy MacLean (1893-1984) the rudiments; Jim MacInnis, a Big Pond fiddler who had furthered his music education in the U.S. taught 14-year-old Angus Chisholm (1908-1979) to read music; Ned MacKinnon (1876-1926), upon returning from the U.S., taught a number of fiddlers near his home in the Christmas Island Parish; and early recording artist Alick Gillis furthered his own music training in the U.S. In addition, throughout 20th-century Cape Breton, there were a number of "professors" in classical music circles, including Prof. Cormier of Chéticamp, his son Pat Cormier of Sydney, and Prof. Jimmy MacDonald of North Sydney. All of those men were trained musicians whose students included many Cape Breton fiddle players. As well, after the First World War, trained pipers returned to Cape Breton bringing music literacy skills, books and new influences to both the fiddling and piping traditions. In the mid-20th century, some fiddlers sent off for tutor books through mail-order catalogues or in response to newspaper advertisements (e.g., in *The Casket*) or enrolled for music-theory distance-learning programs (e.g., Winston Fitzgerald). Understanding music notation became important to the Cape Breton fiddler when printed sources became accessible. Beginning in the 1940s, coinciding with connections with Scottish book suppliers (such as J. Murdoch Henderson, John Grant Booksellers and *The Oban Times*) made initially by Dan R. MacDonald, there was a marked interest in the numbers of fiddlers learning to read. Once acquired, this skill was passed on from one fiddler to the next, one outlining the notes of the staff for another. For the majority of Cape Breton fiddlers, knowledge of the notes on the staff was sufficient; no understanding of rhythms or accidentals was deemed necessary as their aural skills

provided this information. Many players in the 1940s made such efforts to master music-literacy skills to enable them to learn from the printed collections. Some of those known for their interest in amassing tune collections included Gordon MacQuarrie, who was possibly the first to own a copy of *The Skye Collection,* Ned MacKinnon (a known fan of Scott Skinner's tunes), Donald Angus Beaton, Bill Lamey, Dan J. Campbell, Angus Chisholm, Donald MacLellan, Alex Francis MacKay, Dan Joe MacInnis, Winston Fitzgerald and Joe MacLean. Later, Buddy MacMaster, John Campbell, Cameron Chisholm, Carl MacKenzie, Doug MacPhee, John Donald Cameron, Dave MacIsaac, Kyle MacNeil and Dwayne Côté continued the tradition of building personal collections of tune books; other, non-musicians such Danny Fraser from Westmount, who was in regular contact with Bert Murray in Scotland, also assembled impressive personal collections. While such individuals had eclectic collections of published books (including pipe music and Irish and American collections along with the Scottish ones) the core books supporting the tradition appear to have been *The Cape Breton Collection of Scottish Melodies for the Violin* (Gordon MacQuarrie), *The Scottish Violinist* (James Scott Skinner), *Cole's One Thousand Fiddle Tunes Collection* and the four volumes of *Kerr's Merry Melodies*, which were relatively cheap; something like *The Skye Collection* was regarded as "gold" since it went out of print in the 1920s; similarly the re-issue of the Athole Collection in 1961 helped fuel the revival in that decade. While local and provincial outlets supplying published music were limited in the early-to-mid-20th century (the Celtic Music Store in Antigonish being the key one) from the 1970s others appeared including Cameron Music Sales in Port Hawkesbury, McKnight's in Sydney, the CJFX store in Antigonish, Charlie's Country Music Store in Chéticamp, the Gaelic College and the Halifax Folklore Centre, with more recent additions including the Celtic Music Interpretive Centre in Judique. Various mail-order catalogues became important to further meet the demand (e.g., Shanachie and Green Linnet in the U.S.) and local organizations such as An Tullochgorm Society and a plethora of seasonal retail outlets also became involved in supplying locally published material. A dedicated music publishing business – Cranford Publications – was established in Cape Breton in 1979, its first issue being *The Skye Collection,* followed by re-issues of older printed collections. Paradoxically, however, even though the amount of printed material is now greater than ever, and accessibility to it is easier, the interest in published collections for repertoire building has diminished. Since the 1970s in group-learning situations, emerging fiddlers learned to read music as part of the basic music training and there is a much more casual attitude to this skill today; many of those who *can* read prefer, in fact, to learn tunes by ear. Furthermore, after the revival of the 1970s onward, access to new material has been more in aural form, done increasingly through new technologies and made accessible though changes in the transmission process, increased travel opportunities and collaborations. This has been a cause of lament for some older players concerned that the current generation is simply not "digging into the collections."

impact. From the 1920s onward, access to published collections impacted on the Cape Breton fiddle tradition in many ways. Certainly the increase in activity associated with these sources encouraged fiddlers to learn to read music, and ability in this markedly increased. Musicians shared tune collections, passing them on to other fiddlers once they had gone through them themselves. Often, tunes were copied out by hand, and fiddlers in this way created their own, personal collections. As for the Cape Breton repertoire, in the period after the 1940s it expanded rapidly, both in the number of tunes and in the types of tunes being played, as unlimited choices became available through literacy. Hungry for new material, fiddlers spent the winter months digging into the collections, emerging at the summer concerts and dances (or on a new recording) anxious to show off what they had unearthed; particular musicians became known for their ability to find the best material in a published collection;

indeed, it became almost a form of competition among musicians to come up with something new with which to impress their peers. A bonus was that if a new tune was heard on the radio it could now be identified, and if it was in print could be learnt more easily. Published collections further embedded the concept of "correctness" since they provided a reference point against which accuracy might be measured. Equally, alternative "settings" of tunes could be explored.

respect. For fiddlers of this mid-20th-century era, the obsession with tune books was underpinned by a great respect and reverence for them. In Cape Breton fiddlers' homes, the most recent or the most unusual tune books were given pride of place, perhaps displayed on the piano, if one were present. Fiddlers became fastidious about ensuring they could identify the source of any tunes learned, including tune name, book, edition and often, page number. Buddy MacMaster, at Celtic Connections in Glasgow in the late 1990s, delivered a powerful insight into this practice during a performance in which he spoke at length about the source of each tune he played (a practice which at the time was not common for Cape Breton fiddlers who tended to play more and speak less), offering a spellbound audience an informed and real account of the journey of tunes across an ocean and down through several generations. This event highlighted the significance of printed collections within the Cape Breton tradition; at a time when the tradition was referred to as Scotch or Scottish, the published collections provided a tangible link to the old country, adding substance and gravitas to what had been passed on orally for generations. For local Cape Breton composers, there has been the great advantage that literacy encourages the publishing of new tunes, ensuring wider dissemination of their material, and a greater awareness of the tune source. And, as composers protect themselves in copyright and register with relevant agencies such as SOCAN and CMMRA, there is also a financial benefit.

style. While published sources may have shaped the tradition in many ways, they have had little impact on performance style and practice. A divergence between ear and note players did emerge in the mid-20th century, but this mainly referred to the way in which material was accessed; ultimately the books provided new repertoire but did not indicate style in any way. Non-readers benefited indirectly from literacy as well, in that they were able to expand their repertoires learning by ear, second-hand, the new tunes being introduced from the written sources. For the majority of players the book was a source of new material and once it fulfilled that purpose, it was dispensed with as the learning process now focussed on performance.

Nova Scotia Country Music Hall of Fame. *See* **awards.**

Nova Scotia Department of Communities, Culture and Heritage (NSDCCH). Created in 2011, it promotes and celebrates Nova Scotia's diverse cultures and senses of heritage. The NSDCCH is responsible for bringing forward and implementing culture- and heritage-related legislation, one element of which was the 2012 *Status of the Artist Act*, through which Arts Nova Scotia was established as an independent body to oversee provincial government direct funding to artists. NSDCCH has an advisory board (the Creative Nova Scotia Leadership Council), and allocates finance (directly and indirectly) to funding programs for artists and arts organizations. These include Arts Nova Scotia Funding and Awards, Creative Nova Scotia Leadership Council Awards, Community Funding, Culture Funding, Heritage Funding and Youth Funding. Cape Breton music organizations benefitting from this to date include The Gaelic College Foundation, Celtic Colours, CMIC, Comunn Fèis an Eilein, The Strathspey Place Association, local Arts Councils in Inverness and Chéticamp and smaller, one-off projects such as those started by *Cape Breton's Magazine*.

Nova Scotia Music Week. *See* **Music Nova Scotia.**

Nuallan. A piping group formed by the Gaelic College in 2011 and significant in that it focused on the old-style community piping that had all but disappeared in Cape Breton by the end of the 20th century. The college had, for many years, supported an award-winning pipe band; however, the move to instate a contemporary band of this nature – with its focus on a vernacular style and repertoire informed by the dance and with performance practices that are aligned to contemporary traditional-music bands as opposed to competition – speak to some of the recent policy decisions made by the college executive. Nuallan has Paul K. MacNeil, Keith MacDonald, Kevin Dugas, Rankin MacInnis and Kenneth MacKenzie on pipes with Tracey MacNeil on piano, Pat Gillis guitar, and Kyle MacDonald on drums and percussion.

O

Odyssey Records. A Chicago-based label managed by Alf McConnell which has, since 1997, produced an annual compilation CD of artists performing at Celtic Colours. The project was instigated by McConnell as a support for the festival, a contribution that was recognized in 2009 when he was the inaugural recipient of The Order of Celtic Colours award. *See* **recording industry.**

Open Door Gang. A group popular in the early- to mid-1990s when they were regular performers on the festival circuit and released their album *Fosgail an Dorais.* Led by the twin bagpipes of Paul MacNeil of Barra Glen and Jamie MacInnis of Big Pond, the group also included Dave MacIsaac (guitar), John Ferguson (bouzouki) and Tracey Dares (piano and step dance). The formation of bagpipes, fiddle and piano had previously existed in Cape Breton in the 1950s and 1960s, but was never very common; more significantly, the band represented an old, vernacular style of piping (which was at that time beginning to get renewed attention in Cape Breton) as well as Gaelic song. Both MacNeil and MacInnis had trained as competition pipers and were involved in the Halifax Police Pipe Band, before being inspired by contact with Angus, Iain and Allan MacDonald of Glenuig, Scotland, to explore the older piping sound and practice associated with their own rural Cape Breton communities.

oral tradition. A term used in music to indicate a form which is practised and passed on without the necessity for text or other documentation as distinct from traditions that rely on notated sources. The tune, song or story is heard, absorbed, internalized and reiterated through a process of aural transmission (i.e., learning by ear as opposed to by note). At this point, the process begins again, already in multiple form, since the original deliverer may continue to transmit the tune, song or story, as, too, will the individual who has recently learned it and who, upon performance, will likely become the source for someone else to pick it up; and so the process continues. Developments in technology since the early 20th century have subverted the inherent simplicity of the oral tradition and the handing down of music from one generation to the next. The tape-recorder and other reproduction devices have become significant in the transmission process, reducing and often negating the need for personal contact and the immediacy of the musical moment. The oral experience may now be recreated ad infinitum, even when removed through time and physical space, making *delayed* oral transmission possible. In other words, rather than a tune being learned upon a single hearing, it can be played over and over, perhaps even slowed down, to allow it be learned. Notation is proven to be a critical support as a tool for collection, preservation, dissemination and transmission of materials as well as acting as a resource for expanding an existing repertoire; however, the choices made by the practitioners are what will ultimately dictate the oral-literacy balance within a given tradition. Ultimately, aspects of style will be passed on orally, irrespective of the method used in learning the tune.

in Cape Breton. The Cape Breton fiddle tradition is an oral one, albeit one which has long been supported by literate sources and practices. While the majority of players learned and passed on their music by ear, it is clear that music literacy was not uncommon, long before the 1940s, although this is the decade generally understood as marking the start of a blossoming of interest in written collections as a source of repertoire. From that time, fiddlers increasingly came to be described as being either "ear" or "note" players. From the 1970s, when group classes for teaching fiddle music began, notated sources took on another value as a means of coordinating the settings of tunes shared in this context and for simply managing large numbers of learners in a single class situation. Certainly from this period, music literacy skills became de rigeur for the majority of emerging Cape Breton fiddlers. Critically, however, notated scores have never been used in performance contexts (unlike in certain contemporary Scottish contexts, for instance); as such, the style and the performance practice has continued to be guided and shaped by the aural experience, specifically playing from memory. Within Cape Breton music literacy has effectively been used to reinforce and sustain the oral tradition. *See* **aural transmission; ear players; note players; note reading.** [**Doherty 1996**].

Order of Canada. Established in 1967, the Order of Canada is the highest civilian honour available in Canada's honours system and recognizes a lifetime of outstanding achievement, dedication to the community and service to the nation. Administered by the Governor-General-in-Council, it recognizes people in all sectors of Canadian society, representing a variety of contributions deemed to have enriched the lives of others. Approximately 6,000 people to date have been appointed. Among these have been Cape Breton musicians Buddy MacMaster (2000) and John Allan Cameron (2003), Doug MacPhee (2008) and Natalie MacMaster (2007). Others awarded it for contribution to Cape Breton culture are Joella Foulds of Celtic Colours, Ronald Caplan of Cape Breton's Magazine (2011) and singer/songwriter and authority on Cape Breton fiddle music, Allister MacGillivray (2013). *See* **awards.**

Order of Nova Scotia. The highest civilian honour of the Province of Nova Scotia, established in 2001 this honours any current or former long-time resident of Nova Scotia who has demonstrated a high level of individual excellence and achievement in any field and thus brought honour and prestige to themselves and to Nova Scotia. Buddy MacMaster, appointed in 2003, is the only Cape Breton fiddler to be recognized with this honour to date; singer Raylene Rankin of the Rankin Family was awarded this honour posthumously in 2013. *See* **awards.**

Organ. *See* **pump organ.**

ornament. A suite of bowed and fingered decorations that may be added to a basic tune in order to enhance the melodic line and add individual expression or flavour. Such ornaments are sometimes referred to as embellishments. Choices made in relation to the type of ornament used – where it is placed and how it is executed – help define each fiddler's individual sound. The ornaments themselves and the practice of applying them have changed over time; most notably, there has been a decrease in the extent to which ornaments are used within the fiddle style. While earlier players often displayed a style that was richly populated with a range of ornaments, from the 1950s, Winston Fitzgerald, in an effort to achieve a cleaner, more transparent texture in his fiddle playing, began to deliver a melodic line that included far fewer such ornaments. The rich, busy piano style that was developing around the same time also contributed to an increased emphasis on clarity from the fiddle player, resulting in less ornaments being employed. There has also been a change in the manner in which individual ornaments are executed. Whereas older players approached them in a relaxed and measured manner – to the extent that the ornament was often given as much space as the actual melody note – it became increasingly common to articulate them in a crisper, more definite manner, so that they become quite distinct within the melodic line.

ornaments and correctness. In the past, the application of ornaments was at the discretion of the individual fiddler and was an important element in defining personal style; ornaments were applied in a spontaneous manner and were part of the flavour added to the melodic line, which itself was bound by the conventions of correctness. Over time, however, this freedom exercised in relation to the application of ornaments has gradually diminished; increasingly since the mid-20th-century fiddlers have tended to approach the ornamenting of a tune in a more fixed way: at the same point in each turn of the tune and in each performance; however, the choice of ornament employed in each instance may vary. As such, current practice favours a clearly defined melodic line with a small number of diverse ornaments strategically and regularly placed, and crisply delivered; this approach still enables sufficient individual expression, or flavour, to be recognized. *See* **correctness; flavour.**

the ornaments. The ornaments used by Cape Breton fiddlers mostly have roots in early Scottish (and Baroque) practices, but there are also forms that imitate other instruments – in particular the bagpipes – and some come from other traditions such as the Irish. All forms used by fiddlers have also influenced players on other instruments such as piano. The two forms of ornaments are **(a) bowed ornaments** and **(b) finger ornaments**. In both types there is a suite of optional patterns that a fiddler may or may not choose to employ in the personal iteration of a given tune. While the pattern for each type of ornament is fixed, the application of it may vary from player to player who will bring to it other personal factors such as tone, intonation, bow pressure ,etc. Within Cape Breton, certain players are known for favouring specific ornaments or for being particularly capable in their execution of such. Much valuable work in identifying and labelling specific embellishments has been carried out by Kate Dunlay and David Greenberg in *The DunGreen Collection* (1996) which introduced, for the first time, terminology which has since been widely adopted within the fiddle community. [**Doherty 1996; Dunlay and Greenberg 1996; Graham 2006**]

(a) bowed ornaments. A range of specific bowed patterns used by Cape Breton fiddlers at their own discretion, or not at all. Bowed ornaments are often chosen over (or in addition to) finger ornaments since, by increasing the amount of bow-work, they add additional rhythmic interest to the melody. Within the Cape Breton tradition the most prevalent type of bowed ornament is the cut (which exists in several forms); other types are the crushed-bowstroke and the fat-flat stroke, while a specific bowed percussive ornament is indicated in some printed sources by an "X." *See* **under terms.**

(b) finger ornaments. Also referred to as "left-hand embellishments" these add additional notes to the melodic line; they may be executed in a relaxed manner, adding a lyrical dimension to the melodic line or, as is often the case in contemporary Cape Breton, in a more defined, rhythmic manner. The choice in this is entirely at the discretion of the individual player. The common types of finger ornaments used by the Cape Breton fiddler are: grace note, roll, slide, unison, vibrato, warble and wild note. *See* **under terms.**

otherworld. The Cape Breton fiddle music and dance traditions have some documented "otherworld" connections. Fiddler John MacDougall from Egypt, Inverness County, for example, often testified to a unique supernatural connection in that he claimed to be a conduit for the tunes of deceased Cape Breton musicians; "lost tunes" would possess him and he transcribed them for posterity; he accumulated some 45,000 tunes in this manner. In a perhaps not unconnected vein, esteemed dancer, Willie Fraser (1915-2015) acknowledged that he acquired many of his steps at the age of six in a series of dreams. [**MacDonald 2009; MacGillivray 1988; Melin 2012**]. *See* **fairylore.**

out-migration. *See* **diaspora.**

Outside Track, The. An international collaboration initiated in the early 2000s with members from Canada, Scotland and Ireland. Current members are Ailie Robertson from Scotland (harp), Fiona Black from Scotland (piano accordion) and Teresa Horgan from Ireland (flute and vocals); Cape Breton fiddler and step dancer Mairi Rankin has been with the band since 2009. Their multi-genre arrangements reflect their individual origins and experience with traditional and contemporary Cape Breton, Scottish and Irish tunes and songs. They have recorded a number of albums to date (most recently *Light up the Dark*, 2014) and have achieved honours such as Group of the Year at both the Live Ireland Music Awards, 2012 and the TIR Irish Music Awards.

P

Parks, Larry. Fiddle. North Sydney. Growing up on the Gannon Road his greatest music influence was fiddler Joe Confiant (1900-1985), who was known for playing both Scottish and Irish music. A left-handed player, Parks has adopted many tunes and stylistic nuances from Confiant's playing. An active member of the CBFA he has also played a key role over the years in the presentation of the Irish-style sessions held weekly on the Northside. His nephew, Mike Barron, is also a talented fiddle player.

pastoral air concert. A specialized concert where the program focuses on slow airs, an element of the Cape Breton repertoire that was not especially prioritized in the past. The pastoral airs concert was introduced in 1989 at St. Mary's Church in Big Pond and since then the model has been adopted by other communities across the island and held typically in a church venue; songs and instruments other than fiddle and piano may also be included in the programming.

peer recognition. Based on prestige, personality and skill – and in many ways the highest accolade among musicians – this principle underlies the selection of recipients of many of the awards associated with Cape Breton music. *See* **awards.**

PEI. *See* **Prince Edward Island.**

Pellerin, John. (1966-). Fiddle, step dance, mandolin. Antigonish. His father, Kenneth, was a fiddle player and a step dancer himself, and John began taking fiddle lessons at the age of 10 with Stan Chapman. His first public performance was at a student fiddlers' concert at the Antigonish Legion Hall, where he performed a solo with John Morris Rankin accompanying him on the piano. As he developed, his fiddle style was influenced by such as Buddy MacMaster, Arthur Muise, Donald Angus Beaton and Theresa MacLellan. He was also gaining a reputation at that time as a step dancer; the synchronized dance routines he performed with his brother, Bill (1964-), were particularly popular through the 1970s and 1980s and the duo, The Pellerin Brothers, was featured on TV shows such as *Up Home Tonight* and regularly at concerts across Cape Breton. Antigonish had its own Cape Breton music scene, generated in part by the substantial numbers of Cape Breton students taking courses at St. FX, and John had many opportunities to perform. He went on to play with Buddy MacMaster throughout the U.S., including at the Library of Congress; he also performed with piano player, Barbara Magone, in a production, *The Well*, at the Dublin Theatre Festival, Ireland, in 2001. He has recorded with Natalie MacMaster and Buddy MacMaster (step dancing and playing fiddle) and has composed a number of tunes. He continues to perform in summer concerts in Cape Breton, doing stepdance routines, with his brother Bill.

Performance rights. *See* **copyright.**

Peters, Pierce ("Percy"). (1911-1999). Fiddle. Sydney, NS. Born to parents Charles and Gertrude (O'Grady) Peters, he was encouraged to play from a young age by his father, uncles Austin and Pierce Peters, cousins Joe and Jimmy Peters and brothers Dick, John and Barney. One of his first experiences of Scottish violin music was hearing a J. Scott Skinner cylinder recording. He started to play at the age of 9, encouraged by his father, who bought him a fiddle at Menzie's Music Store in Sydney; he went on to play with his brother Dick as an unaccompanied, acoustic fiddle duo for local dances which were "called" by a prompter; the dances were typically the Plain Lancers, the Saratoga and the Caledonia. By the mid-1920s their circuit had widened to include Spain's Hall in Mira Ferry, halls in Gabarus, Belfry, Sydney River, Dominion and The Cabin, The Ritz and the LOC in Sydney. He was also a regular performer at the parish picnic held in East Bay. As the demand for dance bands grew he assembled The Percy Peters' Square Dance Orchestra and was one of the first to play Cape Breton music on CJCB radio; his wife, Helen, accompanied him on piano from time to time. He was a member of the CBFA and performed with them in 1980 at the Rollo Bay festival on Prince Edward Island. He recorded one album, *Party at Marion Bridge,* which featured Tracey Dares on piano on what was her first recording. [**MacGillivray 1981**].

piano. "To me the violin is a beautiful instrument but without the piano it's like a bell without a tongue." So declared Cape Breton piano player Marie MacLellan in MacGillivray's *A Cape Breton Ceilidh* (1988). The Cape Breton sound has, for most of the latter part of the 20th century, been defined by the combination of solo fiddle along with a very distinctive style of piano accompaniment. The style evolved from a simple block chordal harmonic support, or a doubling of the melodic line, to one that is marked by a highly syncopated right hand, a busy, stride-style left hand, much use of chord substitutions and occasional glissandi. This has had a significant impact on the fiddle style, for as the piano stylings became increasingly complex, the fiddle style responded by becoming cleaner and more defined in order to best accommodate it. As such, the elevation of the piano to the status of equal partner with the fiddle has arguably been the greatest contributing factor in creating a distinct Cape Breton sound in this century.

the instrument. Pianos were being imported to Nova Scotia as part of an early transatlantic trade long before they were produced in Canada. The first pianos made in Canada began to appear in the early 19th century when German immigrants developed a dry-kiln technique that enabled them to produce durable wooden frames that could withstand the Canadian climate. Canadian manufacturers became famous for the upright piano and, by the late 1800s, more than 260 such companies were active in Canada, some 30 of them across Nova Scotia. The Sisters of Notre Dame had introduced pianos to Cape Breton by the 1880s and had begun providing piano instruction in Sydney and Mabou, thus developing a potential market. Newspapers such as the *North Sydney Herald* carried adverts for pianos and organs from the 1870s, while the

Eaton's and Sears-Roebuck catalogues were also a popular source of pianos by mail order, once delivery was enabled by developments in the railway transport system; "Blind" Collie MacDonald sold pianos directly in Antigonish. Pianos appeared first in the homes of the better-off families, and Cape Breton lore has many stories about these instruments being transported around the community for various events, by horse and sleigh if it was during the winter months; where a piano was loaned to a community event such as a parish picnic a "guard" was tasked with protecting it through the night on the outdoor stage erected for such occasions. It was the 1940s before pianos were found in local halls. But by the mid-20th century pianos were common, and held pride of place in homes, often used to display printed tune collections as well as family photos; most parish and community halls where dances were regularly held had also invested in upright, acoustic pianos by this time, and a number of piano tuners were kept busy around the island. By the 1980s, however, electric pianos had taken over and today, even in private homes, the upright acoustic piano is less common. [**MacKinnon, 2009**].

evolution of the style. Early Scottish collections often included simple bass lines arranged for harpsichord or cello, and later piano, but the first actual directions for accompanying Cape Breton fiddle music emerged from pump-organ accompaniment, which was connected to church music or the simple vamping accompaniment used in Irish dance bands emerging from the northeastern U.S. Among the first piano players to appear on the Cape Breton scene was Margaret MacIntyre (later MacPhee) (1912-1997). Along with other female piano players – including Lila (MacIsaac) MacDonald (1900-1985), Lila (Abraham) Hashem, Jessie Maggie MacLellan – she developed the practice of playing out the melody on the right hand. Other piano players to emerge from the Inverness area around that time included Marie MacLellan, Elizabeth MacEachen (later Beaton), Janet Beaton and Danny MacEachen. The first Cape Breton fiddlers to record, Charlie MacKinnon and "Big" Dan Hughie MacEachern of the

Columbia and Caledonia Scotch Bands, were accompanied on piano by the Irish-American Dan Sullivan, in a formation and arrangement that was closely aligned to the popular Irish dance bands of the day in the Boston area. Sullivan had a distinctive style of accompaniment that included many techniques (including syncopation, extended chords and glissandos) associated with swing music, but in fact predating this; his influence on the subsequent development of a Cape Breton piano style is likely more significant than has been acknowledged to date. The next Cape Bretoners to record included the Inverness Serenaders in the U.S. (on Decca from 1934) and Dan J. Campbell, Angus Allan Gillis and Angus Chisholm in Montréal (on Celtic in 1935). The piano players involved were Betty Maillet (1907-1960), originally from Digby, Nova Scotia with family connections in Scotch Hill, Margaree, who accompanied the Inverness Serenaders and whose style emulated that of Dan Sullivan; Bess Siddall MacDonald, a British-born woman who married into an Antigonish family, accompanied the others and her style more reflected the older pump organ tradition which preceded the piano in Cape Breton. The stride style (properly known as "Harlem stride piano") was developed in the 1920s and 1930s in the U.S.; it involved the left hand playing a four-beat pulse (with a single, bass note, octave, 7th or 10th interval on the 1st and 3rd beats, and a chord on the 2nd and 4th beats) while the right hand played syncopated melody lines with harmonic and riff embellishments and fill patterns; other influences came from country music, blues and boogie-woogie. In the early 1950s, Mary Jessie MacDonald (1929-2007) from New Waterford took the lead on integrating elements from such popular styles with the basic chording that accompanied the fiddle tunes; inspired by a performance by the Gib Whitney Swing Band in Glace Bay and by other swing musicians she encountered later in Boston, she developed the idea of a walking bass line, adding a further level of complexity to the piano stylings. To this, Maybelle Chisholm MacQueen, from Margaree, added a distinctive, flamboyant touch through the addition of highly

Maybelle Chisholm MacQueen. Photo by Corey Katz. Courtesy of Celtic Colours International Festival.

syncopated chording and glissandi, this, in turn, influencing new generations of emerging players including Hilda Chiassson, Joel Chiasson and Jason Roach. The MacMaster sisters from Judique (Lorraine, Kay, Kathleen and Betty-Lou) also contributed to the evolving style; Betty-Lou (MacMaster) Beaton in particular was known for her "correct" chord choices. Joey Beaton from Mabou – whose primary influence had been his mother, Elizabeth Beaton – favoured an older, simpler style, yet incorporated some contemporary stylings into his own performances, resulting in his unique personal style. The players who were active in the revival period of the 1970s and 1990s added still further levels of complexity to the evolving Cape Breton piano style. To complement the (by then) well-established rhythmic patterns – such as the walking bass and right-hand syncopations – players turned their attention to the harmonic language, experimenting with new chord progressions and substitutions; some of this was influenced by Irish groups such as The Bothy Band (the harmonic language of Dónal Lunny, and Tríona and Mícheál Ó Domhnaill) and much of it came from popular and rock music. Also relevant was the fact that from the 1980s on, certain Cape Breton musicians (in particular the piano players) were in music-degree programs in jazz and classical music at St. FX and at Mount Allison University in New Brunswick. The significant innovators in this regard were John Morris

Rankin, Hilda Chiasson, Jerry Holland, Sheumas MacNeil and Tracey (Dares) MacNeil. These are the players who have influenced virtually all the subsequent piano players such as Ryan MacNeil, Troy MacGillivray, Mac Morin, Jason Roach and Joel Chiasson; they in turn have influenced a further generation.

the style. The Cape Breton piano style is characterized by its rhythms and harmonies. Rhythmically, it has a rolling octave movement, walking bass lines and chromaticism in the left-hand, with much right-hand syncopation; harmonically it has a wide palette of chords, inversions and substitutions, and uses stacked harmonies and pedal notes with occasional glissandi. Some of the rhythmic patterns prevalent in the piano style are closely aligned to the rhythms of the Cape Breton step dance tradition. As the step dancers have come to favour more syncopated steps, so too have the piano players—particularly in right-hand motifs—indicating that the dancer-piano player connection is still important. Even though piano players and fiddlers increasingly work together to plan out chords and arrangements, the style is nevertheless effectively an improvised one with which the player engages in the musical moment.

partnerships. Once pianos were introduced and had become established as the preferred accompanying instrument for Cape Breton fiddlers, musicians began to gravitate toward homes that had a piano for ceilidhs and house parties. The limited numbers of piano players (often female) were kept busy playing for a great many fiddlers. For the first recordings and live radio broadcasts of Cape Breton music, any piano player who was available was engaged, but the focus was entirely on the fiddler, and the accompanist was often not even acknowledged. By the second half of the 20th century, most Cape Breton homes had a piano and the numbers of accompanists had greatly increased. Established fiddle-piano duos became the norm with popular examples including Theresa and Marie MacLellan, Mary MacDonald and Margaret MacPhee; husband-and-wife duos were also common, as were brother-sister combinations. Winston Fitzgerald, in the 1940s, was

possibly the first player to employ a regular piano player, Beattie Wallace who, with Estwood Davidson on guitar, carefully worked out harmonic and rhythmic accompaniments, formalizing what had previously been an entirely spontaneous and improvised practice. This practice was cemented further in the early 1980s by Jerry Holland on his *Master Cape Breton Fiddler* LP; Holland had no doubt been inspired in this capacity by his tenure in the Cape Breton Symphony Fiddlers, where piano player Bobby Brown had charted out the music arrangements. From this point it became imperative for fiddlers to feel that their skill was matched (not simply supported) by the piano player, and that such duet performances were true partnerships. A key factor in this movement toward the fiddlers taking an active role in working out the accompaniment stemmed from the fact that, during the 1970s revival period, there was a trend for young musicians to be proficient as fiddlers, piano players and step dancers; by being able to interchange their roles in a performance, such fiddlers were better informed as to what they themselves needed from their accompanist. Among the duos emerging at this time were Natalie MacMaster and Tracey Dares, Kyle and Sheumas MacNeil, John Morris Rankin and Howie MacDonald, Kinnon and Betty-Lou Beaton and later, Hilda Chiasson and J. P. Cormier. This has led, finally, to a general increase in recognition of the piano-players' contributions to music performance style.

impact on the fiddle music. As this piano style evolved and became accepted, modifications in the fiddle sound were required in order to fully integrate the piano. Certainly other factors were also at play that encouraged Cape Breton fiddlers toward a more clean and polished sound, much of this coming from exposure to other musics on the radio (especially the playing of Don Messer) and the increase in opportunities for performance in presentational contexts (from recordings, to house sessions to concerts). Whatever the reasons, the developing role and style of the piano paralleled a marked change in intonation in the fiddle playing. The use of tonal inflections (a feature of the High-

Stella's Trip to Kamloops

Pat Chafe, SOCAN

march

© August Musicworks, Glace Bay NS, B1A 4P4

land bagpipes and the Gaelic language) were discarded in order to suit the equal-tempered piano. Likewise, the drones (also an echo of the bagpipe influence) were largely dropped, as they came to be perceived as clashing with the piano. As the piano players began to explore the range of the piano and experiment with syncopated rhythmic and melodic motifs in the right hand, the fiddling compensated for this increase in activity by opting for a thinner, more transparent texture, facilitated by reducing the quantity of embellishments used, and emphasizing those which remained. The expanding harmonic knowledge displayed by the piano players allowed (and encouraged) experimentation with tonal sequences. Likewise, the less-rhythmic tune-types – such as the slow air – were experimented with, something which was also made possible by the increased potential and capabilities of the piano players; indeed, the steady beat in Cape Breton slow air playing can be linked to the fact that accompaniment is generally always present in their performance. The rubato evident, for instance, in the recording of Winston Fitzgerald playing the air "Bovaglie's Plaid" unaccompanied indicates that there was more much more flexibility in metre on the rare occasions on which piano accompaniment was absent. In addition, many of the piano players who had received some formal instruction (e.g., from the nuns) were often responsible for sharing their knowledge of music literacy with the fiddle players.

piano as melody instrument. In Scotland, James Scott Skinner was quite vehement in his exhortation that piano players should not play the melody line of the tune on the right hand while accompanying a fiddle player. But in Cape Breton this was done from the outset, and came to be recognized as a characteristic of certain accompanists' styles. Generally, those players who favoured it introduced it sporadically within a group of tunes, interspersing it with sections of straight accompaniment; among these were Marie MacLellan, Elizabeth Beaton and Doug MacPhee. But even though the majority of older players expected to hear the melody as part of accompaniment, by the mid-20th century others expressed distaste for the practice; Theresa MacLellan, for instance, was known to complain to her sister Marie when she used it. Most fiddle players who learned after the 1970s appear to disapprove of the style, but don't mind occasional fragments of the melody line to be picked out

LIZ DOHERTY

Doug's Jig

Margaret MacPhee, 1912-97

© Doug MacPhee, New Waterford, NS, B1H 4H1

in the course of a medley or as an introduction that is part of the arrangement. Outside of the fiddle-piano partnership, solo piano performance of Cape Breton fiddle music has increased in popularity. In the mid-1930s, Lila Hashem hosted a weekly radio show on CJCB where she played piano solos in response to public requests. The first recording of this nature was by Alexander MacLean from Iona in 1962 (*Piano Stylings of the Cape Breton Scot*) on the Celtic label; others who followed, performing and/or releasing albums in this vein, include Lila Hashem, Eddie Irwin, Doug MacPhee, Barbara Magone, Joan MacDonald Boes, Elizabeth Beaton and, more recently, Troy MacGillivray, Tracy Dares MacNeil, Mac Morin, Jason Roach, Sheumas MacNeil and Ryan MacNeil. Piano players have also contributed to the repertoire through their own compositions; some of their tunes—such as Gordon MacLean's "The Mortgage Burn"—have become staples of the fiddlers' repertoire. Acknowledging this trend, Celtic Colours has long included a dedicated piano concert in its program allowing many of these artists a rare chance to take center stage.

recognition of piano players. While the fiddle-piano duo was at the core of the Cape Breton fiddle tradition for much of the 20th century, dominated it after the 1970s, and continues to largely hold that position to the present day, piano players were not always afforded the level of recognition that their role would suggest they be entitled to. On the earliest recordings, while players are generally mentioned by name, this is often in the form of an acknowledgement, in small print, on the back of the album sleeve and rarely with any images to identify them; meanwhile the fiddler was profiled on the front. This was standard practice until the 1970s. Piano players were, naturally, not happy with this, and a number of them did, on occasion, complain to the record labels, albeit to little effect. Two of the first to break the taboo were Barbara MacDonald and Marie MacLellan by being named on the front sleeves of LPs. Since the 1980s, piano players, in most instances, have come to be acknowledged as equal partners on recordings, and have mostly earned parity of esteem in live performance contexts also. Aside from duets, there are some 20 solo recordings of Cape Breton piano music today, the first of these, by Alexander MacLean, dating to the 1960s; Doug MacPhee is the most recorded solo piano player; Buddy MacMaster's 2000 release, *The Judique Flyer*, features each track using a different accompanist. Of the ca. 1,000 Cape Breton fiddle music recordings commercially released since 1928, only a couple feature no piano (Angus Chisholm was one fiddler who chose to play completely unaccompanied Jerry Holland on one of his recordings, *Parlour Music* [2005]); those who eschew the piano generally replace it with another instrument (guitar mainly, though cello has recently been used).

gender issues. The typical fiddle-piano duo in Cape Breton has a male fiddler and a female piano player; in Allister MacGillivrays' book *A Cape Breton Ceilidh* more than 70% of the piano players listed are female. This is in contrast to the data presented in the same author's earlier publication *The Cape Breton Fiddler* (1981), where fewer than 10% of the fiddlers profiled are female. As the 20th century progressed, however, and particularly since the revival period of the 1970s, the introduction of formal teaching streams broke down old barriers and habits, opening all aspects of the music tradition to both genders, altering the old male/female, fiddle/piano role patterns. Today, there is not only a high percentage of professional and semi-professional female fiddle players, but there are more male piano players, too.

research. As recognition of the role of the Cape Breton piano-accompaniment style has advanced, it has become the subject of research by a number of scholars including Chris McDonald, Richard MacKinnon and Paul MacDonald; various others such as Jeffrey Hennessy give it some attention too in wider studies of the Cape Breton tradition; Allister MacGillivray's 1988 publication, *A Cape Breton Ceilidh*, is one of the first contributions to scholarship in this field. As teaching opportunities for Cape Breton fiddlers developed since the 1980s, piano players have come to be valued in this regard also (albeit less so internationally). In terms of teaching resources, Tracy Dares's instructional video, *A' Chording to the Tunes: A Cape Breton Piano Accompaniment Lesson* (Crooked Lake Productions), published in 1997, remains the only one of its kind; however, the Gaelic College will launch an online instructional program in 2015 and several piano players already offer on-line teaching. [**Hennessy 2008; Kelly 1991; MacGillivray 1988; MacDonald 2014; MacKinnon 2009**].

picnic. Also known as the parish picnic, this was a popular, typically two-day outdoor event that was held in various communities during the summer months. Neighbouring parishes coordinated the scheduling of picnics to ensure that there were no overlaps and to encourage people to travel to similar events in nearby communities. While generally held over a weekend, in Iona, for example, the picnic was held on a Wednesday, which was the free afternoon for those who worked in the industrial area of Sydney. Sanctioned by the Church, the picnic was primarily a fundraising event for building or maintaining local church properties or schools or to pay a teacher's wages. Money was raised through various sporting activities at these events, as well as at games such as bingo, crown-and-anchor and from box socials and catering.

Music and dancing were a central part of the program, and a fee was charged to participate in a Scotch Four or a square set; typically the male partner would pay 5-10 cents per dance. A platform was erected to accommodate the fiddler and displays of solo step dancing. In the 1920s and 1930s, before communities had invested in organs or pianos, such an instrument was borrowed for the picnic, transported to the area and someone appointed to guard it through the night until it was returned. Picnics became an important part of the Cape Breton fiddlers' calendar of performances, and the most sought-after players spent the summer months travelling from one to the next. The first of them was held in Mabou in 1897 during the pastorate of Rev. Dr. J. F. MacMaster. The program included many of the well-known musicians of the time: Angus Archibald MacDonald from Mount Young (pipes/fiddle), Alex Archie MacDonald Jr. from Mabou Coal Mines, Malcolm H. Gillis from South West Margaree,

Johnny Ranald Beaton from Mabou Coal Mines, Angus Ranald Beaton from Mabou Coal Mines, John "Sandy" Beaton from Mabou Coal Mines, Donald John "The Tailor" Beaton from North East Mabou, John Alex "The Big Fiddler" MacDonald from West Mabou, John MacQuarrie from Black River, Donald Allan "Red John" MacLellan from Glenville, Johnny "MacVarish" MacDonald from Broad Cove Marsh, John Campbell (Aonghas Iain) from Glenora Falls, Archibald Beaton from Mabou Coal Mines (piper), Johnny MacIsaac from Blackston; it is believed that Dr. Kennedy and Domhnull Mòr Cameron both danced. Several popular picnics were held over the years, mostly but not exclusively in Inverness County, including at Mabou, South West Margaree, Inverness, Judique, Lower River Inhabitants, Broad Cove, Chéticamp, Iona and Big Pond. Picnics were phased out in the mid-20th century as the outdoor concert became more popular and the shift from participation to entertainment began, although they have more recently been reincarnated in the form of community festivals designed for fundraising.

pig-'n-whistle. A borrowing from a popular Canadian TV series broadcast from 1967 to 1977 and set in a fictional English pub. In Cape Breton, a pig-'n-whistle typically involved rock and roll and occasionally fiddle music; alcohol was always available, unlike at many of the other fiddle-music events at the time that were liquor-free. The pig-'n-whistle format quite possible provided the template for the pub matinee, which brought fiddle music into the pub setting. *See* **matinee**.

polka. A round dance and associated music that originated in mid-19th century Bohemia and spread throughout Europe and the Americas. The polka made its appearance in Cape Breton around the turn of the 20th century, associated with the new square sets being imported from the north-eastern U.S. The polka's function in this was short-lived, after which it was relegated to the periphery of the repertoire, appearing on an occasional basis and only in listening contexts. However, polkas were (and continue to be) popular on mainland Nova Scotia, in the Antigonish area in particular; fiddler Hugh A. MacDonald, for example, was known as "The Polka King," and his grandchildren Troy and Kendra MacGillivray continue to play some polkas in their repertoires. Other fiddlers with an interest in American and other Canadian fiddle traditions which maintain the polka also included this tune type such as Krysta MacKinnon, Joe Murphy, Tara Lynne Touesnard, Joe Cormier and Jennifer Roland; those more regarded as traditionalists rarely include polkas, if at all. While typically the polka is in 2/4 time and has a simple melodic and rhythmic structure, those from Antigonish are of the "double polka" variety, effectively using consistent 16th-note movement (as opposed to regular eighth-note movement typical of the simple polka) resulting in a busier melodic line. This type of polka is not unlike the type found in the Sligo-Roscommon-Leitrim region of Ireland (which is significantly different from the Sliabh Luachra polkas of south-west Ireland), and is also the type that would have been most commonly played by the Irish dance bands active in the north-eastern U.S. in the early 20th century. The melody of these polkas tends to be more through-composed in nature, with longer phrase structures that thus lead to less repetition than is found in other dance-tune types; polkas often include accidentals and may involve a modulation in terms of key for the second part of the tune. Winston Fitzgerald was responsible for popularizing a small number of polkas, among these "The Antigonish Polkas" nos. 1 and 2.

Port Hawkesbury Civic Centre. Open since 2004 this is a state-of-the-art facility serving residents, tourists, and the business community of Port Hawkesbury and the surrounding area. A "green building," it houses an arena, fitness centre, meeting and conference facilities, performance space, gallery and retail space, municipal offices, racquetball courts, and a walking track. The arena has 1,000 fixed seats with the capacity on the arena floor to host an additional 1,000 in theatre style; this space has come to be used annually for the opening concert of Celtic Colours.

positions. A term used to refer to the placement of the melody-playing hand on the neck of the fiddle. The hand's "home" position is with the fiddle neck resting between the thumb and first finger of the left hand; this is referred to as first position. The highest note possible to achieve on the fiddle in standard tuning using "first position" is B' (an octave and a 7th above middle C). To achieve higher notes the left hand must move further up the neck allowing the fingers to be placed higher up the fingerboard. The various options possible in realizing this are referred to as the "higher positions." In order to achieve higher position work

John MacDougall demonstrates his hold of the fiddle. Courtesy of Mark Wilson.

some classical violinists employ the support of a shoulder rest, something that is relatively uncommon within Cape Breton fiddle practice even today (although there are signs that this is beginning to change). In general, the typical physical approach of the Cape Breton fiddler, does not lend itself to the frequent use of higher positions; since the vast majority of traditional fiddle tunes are created to be played within the first position this has not been a major issue. However, some fiddlers such as Dougald MacIntyre, "Little" Jack MacDonald, Angus Chisholm and Dan Hughie MacEachern did challenge the normal practice in this regard and composers such as Dan R. Mac-Donald composed some tunes that require higher position work. Many Cape Breton fiddlers, for several generations, have received some classical violin training and have transferred the relevant skills to their fiddle playing. Today, tunes requiring the use of the higher positions, such as "The Contradiction Reel," the strathspey-reel, "Hughie Jim Paul" and the air "The Sweetness of Mary" (the latter two, incidentally, composed by a piano player, Joan MacDonald Boes) are all common within the fiddlers' repertoire.

posture. Unlike in classical music, the approach to posture (the position of the body when playing) is less standardized when it comes to traditional fiddle playing. In Cape Breton, the norm is to hold the fiddle in the typical classical manner, placed under the chin on the left side of the body, extending outward and supported between thumb and forefinger at the end of the neck piece; the bow is held in the right hand and is moved across the strings, between the bridge and the fingerboard. However, there are considerable discrepancies in the angle at which the fiddle is held as it extends from the body, the degree to which the chin and/or left shoulder grips and supports the instrument, and the position of the left hand, which may see the wrist arched outward or, conversely, inclining inward to any degree right up to, and including, resting against the neck of the fiddle. The angle of the wrist itself indeed affects the position of the fingers in relation to the strings. It should be noted that there are a number of left-handed players in Cape Breton; for them, these positions are reversed. More so in the past than today, variations in posture were evident in Cape Breton; some players rested the fiddle against the chest rather than under the chin and others held the instrument almost vertically. Such positions developed as habits borne out of playing in cramped environments where the fiddler had to protect himself and his instrument from being jostled by boisterous dancers; other players have had to re-think their posture in order to accommodate a physical injury. Today, although most performance contexts involve the fiddler playing in a seated position, increasingly in concerts, more and more players are opting to stand, where they can be better seen by the audience and can "work" the stage.

presentational style fiddlers. This is ethnomusicologist Thomas Turino's term adopted here to describe those fiddlers who since the 1990s, have acknowledged and engaged with the craft of stage presentation (e.g., standing up, moving, dancing, speaking) as part of their performances; in this context the fiddle playing is presented as a wider entertainment package, not simply for listening to. [**Turino 2008**]. *See* **listening fiddlers.**

Prince Edward Island (PEI). One of Canada's Maritimes Provinces, lying to the northwest of Cape Breton, it has its own fiddle tradition, which has been researched and documented primarily by Jim Hornby (1982) and Ken Perlman (1996, 2015). A hybrid of Scottish, Irish and Acadian styles and repertoires, "the Island" sound has distinctive nuances that distinguish it from other fiddle styles; the repertoire is eclectic and includes tunes from Scotland, Ireland, Cape Breton and mainland Nova Scotia, New Brunswick, Québec, Ontario, New England and the southern U.S., as well as many locally composed tunes. Fiddle music is both for dancing to and listening to, with the style of dance being solo step dance and social square dance, as in Cape Breton. Solo fiddle with pump-organ accompaniment was once predominant but in the last number of decades piano and/or guitar accompaniment have become the typical combination; massed fiddle groups and more diverse instrumental band formats have also become common. Perlman (1996) identifies 6 stylistic areas: Northeast, Central, and Southern Kings County; Queens County; and East and West Prince County; by and large, as one moves east on PEI (that is, toward Kings County), Scottish musical influence is more pronounced; as one moves west (toward Prince County), Acadian influence and tune choices come to the fore. Cape Breton and PEI have much shared history; in the 1800s, PEI, Cape Breton and parts of eastern and northeastern Nova Scotia were all part of a single *Gaidhealtacht* area and several PEI pioneers relocated to Cape Breton. Beginning in the 1930s, radio broadcasts featuring both live and recorded fiddle music from Cape Breton had an immediate

and broad-based impact on PEI repertoire and standards of performance practice, and in effect became a countervailing force to the local influence of Don Messer's music. This media-based trend was amplified by personal contact between PEI fiddlers and prominent Cape Breton players, notably Angus Chisholm and Winston Fitzgerald. Fitzgerald, in particular, not only conducted frequent concert tours on PEI but was often invited to judge local fiddle contests. Ultimately, the Cape Breton influence on PEI repertoire was so pronounced that old-timers in many parts of the island were soon lamenting that they rarely heard local favorites being played. Cape Breton influence on PEI playing styles, however, was at first confined primarily to northeast Kings County (closest in proximity to Cape Breton); in the rest of the island players tended to adapt the tunes to their own stylistic nuances, thus maintaining their own idiosyncratic sounds. This began to change in the 1990s; two important factors involved were the rise of a new generation of young fiddlers who had not been significantly exposed to older local players, and the Celtic boom of the 1990s, in particular the rise of such young Cape Breton fiddlers as Natalie MacMaster and Ashley MacIsaac.

Today, the Cape Breton stylistic influence has become so ingrained that it would take an extremely practiced ear to distinguish the playing of some young PEI fiddlers from their Cape Breton counterparts. The older island styles have continued to decline, and by 1997, a Rounder album, *The Prince Edward Island Style of Fiddling,* warned that the material included "may represent one of the last opportunities to hear these older Island styles." The post-*Vanishing Cape Breton Fiddler* revival of the 1970s also had an impact in PEI, where the visibility of fiddlers was also declining and fewer young people were engaging with the tradition. When Fr. Faber MacDonald from Little Pond, Cape Breton, was posted in Charlottetown he, along with Joe Pete Chiasson and others, established the Prince Edward Island Fiddlers' Association, modelled on the Cape Breton organization. Three branches of this were eventually formed across the island (Eastern Kings County, Queens County and Prince County); in 2009 a new branch was formed, the Southern Kings Fiddlers. Group classes aimed primarily at young people were created; festivals such as the Rollo Bay Fiddle Festival allowed opportunities for emerging players to perform and for inviting Cape Breton musicians to visit. Today, events such as the Festival of Small Halls and the PEI Fiddle Camp meet the demands of cultural tourism and music transmission in much the same way, although on a smaller scale, than they do in Cape Breton. Fiddlers such as Richard Wood, members of the Chiasson family and Eddy Arsenault (1921-2014) have generated international attention for themselves as fiddle players whose style, repertoire and presentation is closely aligned to contemporary Cape Breton examples; other music exports from the island – such as Barrachois in the 1990s and Vishten in more recent times – have foregrounded the Acadian connection particularly where it intersects with current Celtic music practices; thus a dualism in PEI's fiddle music is still very much in evidence today. Recordings featuring older Prince Edward Island playing styles are now available on www.bowingdownhome.ca, a new website co-sponsored by the University of Prince Edward Island and the Canadian Museum of History. **[Hornby 1982; Perlman 1996, 2015].**

print media. Cape Breton has a sizeable history of publishing both in the English language and in Gaelic. In Sydney, among the early newspapers published were the Gaelic and/or bilingual *Mac-Talla/The Echo* (1892-1904), *Am Mosgladh/The Awakening* (1922-1933), *An Solus Iuil/The Guiding Light* (1925-1927), *Fear na Ceilidh/The Visitor* (1928-1930) and *Teachdaire nan Gaidheal/The Messenger of the Gael* (1924-1934); later, English language papers carried features and provided contextual information on Cape Breton fiddle music. While these are no longer in print, many are available in public libraries, archives and online through various newspaper digitization projects (e.g., nsarchives.ca; librariesns.ca). Particularly since the 1970s, a variety of publishing

institutions have produced a substantial body of material that reflects the wider Cape Breton cultural revival brought on by an awareness of the many threats to the local economy and culture. In the wake of *The Vanishing Cape Breton Fiddler* documentary in particular, the local press played an important role in promoting and profiling subsequent fiddle-music events, all part of a revival movement. Among those were *The Cape Breton Highlander* (1969-1975), published by John Campbell and his family in Sydney, and *The Scotia Sun*, which carried a series of informative articles on individual fiddle players in the early 1970s written by John Gibson, Frank MacInnis and Joey Beaton. Community, local and regional print media became vital sources of information on music, song, dance and other cultural and artistic activities and networks, through advertising, event notices, previews, review, opinions, reporting and obituaries. All major fiddlers, singers and dancers have been profiled or promoted in these presses, typically in relation to their participation in community events and where they have roots in, or reside in, a particular region. Although pushed aside by the Internet today, in the past the presses have also been important in facilitating music-making directly by carrying advertising for instruments and for music books available otherwise only in urban centres or in the U.S. The only daily newspaper in Cape Breton for years was *The Cape Breton Post*, until the *Chronicle Herald* launched a Cape Breton edition in 2014. Others which carry substantial cultural content are the weekly *Inverness Oran*, *The Victoria Standard*, *The Reporter* and *The Casket*; other cultural "papers" are issued periodically by local and regional tourism bureaus,e.g., the *Participaper of Inverness County*, a quarterly cultural, magazine founded in 1979. Musicians and scholars of language and culture are regular contributors to these publications; some (e.g., *The Victoria Standard*) carry a regular tune column. Besides newspapers, magazines have also been an important source; key publications no longer in print include such as *Cape Breton's Magazine*, which presented many profiles of Cape Breton fiddlers and *Am Bràighe*, which contributed to many of the debates of the 1990s surrounding fiddle music in relation to stylistic change and to the links (or otherwise) between the fiddle music and the Gaelic language. International magazines such as *Fiddler Magazine, The Living Tradition, Irish Music Magazine* and *Celtic Life International* (formerly *Celtic Heritage Magazine* and *The Clansman*) have also focused on aspects of Cape Breton music over the years. Catalogues such as *the Canadian Family Herald, the Sears Roebuck Catalogue* and *Eaton's Catalogue*, once a vital source for accessing such as instruments and sheet music, are also defunct. Newsletters from individual organizations (CBFA, Cranford Publications) have been a particularly significant source of information and tune sharing through the 1970s-1990, and although they are less critical are still appreciated today.

prizes. Substantial financial awards given to support particular cultural or artistic activities. *See* **awards**.

profession. Cape Breton musicians have made their main income in a huge spectrum of professions; even those who maintained a busy dance circuit in the middle of the 20th century, often playing up to 6 nights a week, generally held down another job. Bill Lamey worked for Eastern Bakeries; Donald Angus Beaton worked for a time as a taxi driver and mail carrier; Buddy MacMaster worked all his professional life for the Canadian National Railway. Early occupations included blacksmithing; working in the mines (originally in Inverness County and later across the island in Cape Breton County) was the occupation of many others, while employment opportunities in the steel plant in Sydney also drew many away from rural Cape Breton to the industrial capital. Some fiddlers such as the Chisholms (Angus and Archie Neil) followed the teaching profession while Carl MacKenzie lectured in engineering; others such as Mike MacDougall and Winston Fitzgerald worked seasonally in fishing. A very few made their career as music "professors" or teachers. Women were typically homemakers or followed

careers as care workers or teachers. Those who went away often found work in domestic service; the men who left Cape Breton in search of work followed various employment paths and carried out their music activities on a part-time basis working in factories, forestry, mines or oil fields as work became available. While a number of individuals who chose an itinerant lifestyle did manage to survive by virtue of their musical prowess (often teaching music in return for room and board), it was not until the late 20th century that fiddle music became a viable prospect as a full-time occupation; even then, those that made that career choice often had other options to revert to during quiet times (Jerry Holland, for instance, worked periodically as a carpenter). In the 1990s, however, a small number of full-time fiddle and piano players began to emerge from the scene; for some they have sustained this career choice; others have chosen to balance it with another occupation. Today, only a small number of individuals resident on this island are full-time professional musicians and, of course, they spend considerable time off-island on tour; many other prominent players on the current scene retain another career, although such careers may now be in a related aspect of the arts or cultural tourism industries.

"Professors" (Prof.). The term applied to an individual engaged in the teaching profession to acknowledge formal qualifications and/or experience. Evidence of such professors exists in Cape Breton, related to both the fiddle and bagpipe traditions (qualified dance teachers were referred to as masters). This can be dated at least to 1820 with Allan Cameron, a professor with a degree from a college in Edinburgh, tutoring on the violin (MacGillivray 1981). Since the 1880s, advertisements began to appear in newspapers such as *The North Sydney Herald* for music tuition by such professors. In the early 1900s, Allan Gillis of Foot Cape was teaching fiddlers such as Sandy MacLean, while Jimmy MacInnis of Big Pond taught fiddlers such as Angus Chisholm to read music. The term professor, as it pertained to fiddle music continued until almost the end of the century; Prof. Jimmy MacDonald, for instance, taught in the North Sydney area until the 1980s; Prof. Pat Cormier was taught by Professor Jimmy; Prof. Marcellin Cormier taught in the Chéticamp area. **[MacGillivray 1981]**. *See* **MacDonald, James.**

prompter. *See* **caller.**

Prosper, Wilfred. (1927-2005). Fiddle, composer. Eskasoni, Cape Breton. A Mi'kmaq, born to parents Peter and Clara (Young) Prosper from Guysborough and Antigonish Landing, Nova Scotia, respectively, he had music in his family down through the generations. His maternal grandfather played the tin whistle, and his great-grandfather, William Nevins, played violin; his mother could jig tunes. In 1937 the family moved from Chapel Island to Barra Head and, later, to Whycocomagh. He was based in Halifax during the Second World War, and in 1947 when local indigenous peoples were obliged by the government to live on reserves, the Prosper family relocated to Eskasoni. As a teenager Wilfred had tried out a neighbour's fiddle, and while in Halifax he learned to play guitar. On his return, his parents bought him a fiddle through Simpson's catalogue and George MacKenzie from Pictou taught him rudimentary music theory. He was familiar with Don Messer's music on the radio and knew of fellow Mi'kmaw fiddler Simon Cremo, who travelled around the Indian communities selling baskets and playing French, Irish and Scottish tunes. Prosper improved his music reading with the nuns who ran the local choir, while priests stationed on the Reserve at various times (including Fr. Angus Cameron and Fr. Raymond MacDonald) encouraged him with loans of music books, as did Sydney music collector Danny Fraser and fiddler Dan Joe MacInnis. He and another local musician, Joe Googoo, began playing together, taking turns on fiddle and guitar and joined occasionally by other local musicians such as Frank Googoo and Frank Paul; Lee Cremo also played frequently with him. Radio was an important music source for Wilfred; on CFCY from PEI he heard Don Messer, and on CJFX heard fiddlers such as John Y. Gillis, Colin

Wilfred Prosper. Courtesy of Mark Wilson.

Boyd, Hugh A. MacDonald, Tena Campbell, Winston Fitzgerald, Bill Lamey, Joe Cormier and Angus Chisholm, most of who were playing live. Dances were popular at the hall in Eskasoni from the 1940s until 1962, when Winston Fitzgerald played the last regular dance there; the area also had a regular Scottish concert and picnics were held in nearby communities. House parties were also popular, and Prosper hosted one at his home following each concert, this, in time, becoming as well established as the concerts themselves. He preferred playing in listening contexts rather than for dances, a reputation and ability that won him the Maritime Fiddle Championship in the 1960s, and led to his being featured in the films *Down Home* with Shetland fiddler Aly Bain (Channel 4, 1985) and *The Magic Fiddle* (Flying Fox Films, 1991). His music is featured on the Rounder album *Traditional Fiddle Music of Cape Breton Volume 3: Bras d'Or House* (2008) and on a Musicworks recording (No. 24), *The Canadian New Music Periodical* complied by Gordon Monahan (1985); *Fiddler* Magazine included a feature on him in its "Cape Breton Edition" in 2000. He composed a number of tunes including "Bessie's Reel," which was published in the CBFA's *Newsletter*. A former chief of Eskasoni and the spiritual prayer leader of the Mi'kmaw grand council, he spent much of his life researching and teaching Mi'kmaw language, prayers and hymns. In 2015 his contribution to Cape Breton fiddle music was acknowledged at a special concert during Celtic Colours. [**Caplan 1985; MacDonald 2000; MacGillivray 1981;** *Fiddler* **Magazine 2000**].

pub. The public house as a communal drinking establishment does not have a long history in Cape Breton; indeed in rural Cape Breton the few pubs that exist have opened since ca. 2000 (e.g., the Red Shoe in Mabou); an exception to this is in the Acadian community of Chéticamp, for example, where the matinee as a distinct type of performance platform for Cape Breton fiddlers was established at the Doryman Tavern in the 1970s. These continue to be a popular event for musicians and attract substantial audiences. Sydney has the largest proliferation of pubs that have had regular fiddle music in this format since the 1990s; at that time the main pub venues included The Old Sydney Pub, the Bonnie Prince, The County Line, Ziggy's and Daniel's; today the popular pub music venues in the city include Governors and The Old Triangle, part of a Nova Scotia franchise of Irish pubs. Rollie's Wharf in North Sydney hosted the island's only sessions for a number of years, but this has recently closed down; the session has relocated to the Blue Mist Dining Room and Lounge in Bras d'Or. Elsewhere on the island the Red Shoe Pub in Mabou is a popular music venue as is the Ceilidh Pub at the CMIC in Judique, while the Folk and Frolic Pub and Grill has recently opened in Iona, hosting regular music events. *See* **pig-'n-whistle.**

pump organ. The pump organ (referred to elsewhere in Canada as the reed organ or parlour organ) predates the piano in Cape Breton and was used to provide a bagpipe-like drone (and some simple block chords) behind the fiddle music from the early 1900s on. Pump organs were installed in most churches and were also available through the Eaton's and Sears-Roebuck catalogues in the early 1900s. The instruments featured at dances and other events during the early years of the 20th century, often being transported from home to venue by wagon or sleigh, as they were scarce. But by the 1930s the piano began taking over as the accompanying instrument of choice and the pump organ was only occasionally used after that, most memorably by Mary MacDonald who wedged chosen keys with matchsticks and pumped the organ with her feet while playing the fiddle. Many piano players, including Marie MacLellan, started out playing on the organ. Examples of this fiddle-pump organ sound have been recorded by Rounder with Mary Maggie Varnier and Gordon MacLean featuring on *Traditional Fiddle Music of Cape Breton* volumes 3 and 4: *Bras d'Or House* (2008) and *MacKinnon's Brook* (2008). [**Kelly 1991; MacGillivray 1988; MacDonald 2014; McDonald 2012, 2013**].

puirt-a-beul. (singular: *port-a-beul*). A form of mouth music involving rhymes in Gaelic set to dance tunes. Several tunes have been taught to generations of Cape Breton fiddlers using *puirt-a-beul*; they have also been used for dancing to in the absence of an instrument. Although very few tunes are known to have entered the tradition specifically as *puirt-a-beul* (one example is "The Bird's Nest"), there are many instances of tunes that have accompanied *puirt-a-beul*. Examples of such tunes have been compiled by Jackie Dunn in a 1991 paper *"Tha Bias na Gaidhlig air a h-Uile Fhidhleir"* (The Sound of Gaelic is in the Fiddler's Music) including 25 slow airs, 15 marches, 35 strathspeys, 28 reels, and 10 jigs. Among the most popular of such tunes are: "Tullochgorm," "Christie Campbell," "Calum Crubach," "Bog an Lochan," "Muilean Dubh" (strathspeys) and "Caber Feidh" (reel). Further substantial research on the *puirt-a-beul* tradition in Cape Breton has been carried out by Heather Sparling and her book on the subject – *Reeling Roosters and Dancing Ducks: Celtic Mouth Music* – was published in 2014. [**Sparling 2014**].

Q

R

quadrille. A 19th-century French dance that came to inform popular social dance; in Cape Breton the quadrille was introduced via Boston and became the basis for the square sets which are still danced there.

quickstep. An international-style ballroom dance that evolved in England from various other dances such as the foxtrot, Charleston, shag, Peabody and the one-step. "Quick" military marches (as distinct from "slow" and "parade" marches) were used for this dance form and several examples of such quickstep marches are found in the Cape Breton repertoire, although not always referred to as such. Although typically in duple (2/4) or quadruple (4/4) metre in some early Scottish collections – for example, that of Robert MacIntosh – there are some jigs (in 6/8) called quicksteps. Fiddlers such as Winston Fitzgerald, John Campbell, Jerry Holland and Bill Lamey have all recorded quickstep tunes, many of them likely sourced from printed collections such as Kerr's.

radio. Significant in the Cape Breton narrative – given the association with Guglielmo Marconi (1874-1937), who carried out many of his early experiments at Table Head and Glace Bay (from which the world's first radio message to cross the Atlantic from North America was sent in 1902) – radio played, and continues to play, an important role in the fiddle-music tradition. Indeed, since the 1990s there has been a perception among many music-industry promoters and audience members that the lion's share of airplay is directed to those within the Celtic genre. Historically, it was through radio that fiddlers were first given regular opportunities to experience the music of other players from outside of their immediate communities. Live fiddle performances became a significant part of much of the early programming and particular slots became known as designated fiddle slots; stories abound in Cape Breton lore about families gathering round the radio at set times during the week to listen to these performances.

For those pursuing semi-professional careers in the 1940s and 1950s, radio was hugely important in promoting themselves and, specifically, advertising their upcoming dances; Dan Joe MacInnis, Winston Fitzgerald and Bill Lamey were regulars on the radio in this context. Stars of the fiddle community began to emerge based on their association with radio, among these Tena Campbell, who was one of the first female fiddlers to gain a significant reputation based on her involvement with the popular *Cottar's Saturday Night* program, which was produced by CJCB Radio and broadcast nationally on an early incarnation of the CBCn. Many fiddlers were encouraged to use the association with radio in their branding of themselves (e.g., Winston Fitzgerald and his Radio Entertainers; Jimmie MacLellan and the Cosy Cottars [named after the popular show] and Joe Murphy and His Radio Swing Band). During those decades corporate-sponsored programs

LIZ DOHERTY

were popular including those supported by the MacDonald's Tobacco Company and Eastern Bakeries.

role. Even when the focus shifted from live broadcast performances toward the almost exclusive use of commercial recordings from the 1960s onward, radio continued to play a significant role in the Cape Breton fiddle tradition, particularly through the revival years of the 1970s. Outside of industrial Cape Breton, CJFX, the Antigonish-based radio station, was a prominent supporter of the fiddle music following its launch in 1943. Gus MacKinnon's *Scottish Strings* (from 1968-1981) played an important role in keeping Cape Breton fiddle music present on the airwaves, at one point being the only presenter in North America broadcasting this music. Ray "Mac" MacDonald, who presented the *Ceilidh* show on CJFX from the 1980s until his retirement in 1999, also played a significant role in maintaining the profile of Cape Breton fiddle music. During the 1970s and 1980s CBC producers such as Brian Sutcliffe, were responsible for positioning radio as an accessible medium through which aspiring professional musicians might further their career (e.g., in shows such as *Talent Cape Breton*). Sutcliff was also involved in the production of shows such as *Archie Neil's Cape Breton,* which attempted to capture the natural environment for Cape Breton music through simulating a ceilidh.

Fiddle music, positioned alongside the Gaelic language, found a further platform in programs such as *Failte is Furan* (on CHER) and on *Island Echoes* (CBC). In an effort to develop its own music industry in light of British- and American-music invasions of the mid-20th century, the Canadian Radio and Telecommunications Commission introduced Canadian content regulations (1970), wherein a percentage of all radio music programming had to be Canadian. While singer-songwriters and other contemporary artists enjoyed an increase in airplay, this did not have an immediate impact on the fiddle tradition; indeed, local stations such as CJFX had already been promoting a high level of Canadian content in its programming, much of it local fiddle

music. Over the years, however, the Cape Breton fiddle tradition has certainly benefitted from the CanCon arrangement. In terms of fiddle style and repertoire, much material was disseminated over the radio. As recently as the 1980s, young players learned much of their repertoire from radio, recording fiddle music played mostly on CJFX, on portable cassette recorders. Among the Cape Breton diaspora, particularly in Boston, radio station such as WVOM, also played an important role. Furthermore, radio was a significant factor in raising the profile, and subsequently contributing to the popularity of, Cape Breton fiddle music in other regions such as Newfoundland and PEI. As well as enabling live performances and offering airtime for commercial recordings, some radio stations carried out significant amounts of recording over the years, either live in studio (e.g., at CJFX, where there were excellent facilities) or in the field at various concerts, festivals and other events. These have generated substantial libraries, which have in some instances been archived and shared with institutions such as the Beaton Institute, the Nova Scotia Provincial Archives, the CMIC, and the St. FX archives.

Today, radio continues to have a presence within the fiddle-playing community and a small number of shows are recognized for their on-going support of the local tradition. A number of radio stations, including both national and independent, privately own stations, both in Cape Breton and elsewhere in the Maritimes, have contributed to the Cape Breton fiddle tradition since the 1930s. Among these are CBC, including CBI in Sydney, CJFX in Antigonish, CJCB in Sydney, 101.5 The Hawk in Port Hawkesbury, The Coast 89.7 in Glace Bay, CKJM in Chéticamp and CFCY in Charlottetown, PEI. Programs promoting Cape Breton fiddle music today include *Island Echoes* presented by Wendy Bergfeldt (CBC), *Celtic Serenade* hosted by Donnie Campbell (CJCB) and *Highland Fling* hosted by Bob MacEachern (The Hawk). The hosts and producers of these radio programs often inspire great audience loyalty. Donnie Campbell's *Celtic Serenade* routinely attracts ratings in excess of a "thirty share," or roughly one-third of Cape Breton's total listening audience. Hosts such as Ray "Mac" MacDonald of CJFX Radio and Brian Sutcliffe have been honoured at community dinners and awards ceremonies from such diverse groups as chambers of commerce, museum boards and music-industry associations. With the advent of the Internet, most Celtic-focused radio shows attract an international audience who listen either in real time or, increasingly, in podcasts. These listeners are often expatriate Cape Bretoners, but an increasing number are tourists and Celtic-music enthusiasts who may have visited the island for the various summer festivals or the fall season's Celtic Colours. Two on-line radio stations, CapeBretonLive.com and East Coast Kitchen Party have also been involved in promoting Cape Breton fiddle music. (*with* WB) [**Nunn 1984; Harper 2002; Graham 2006; MacInnes 1997; also broadcasting-history.ca**] *See* **Cape Breton Live; CBC; CHER; CJCB; CJFX; CKJM; Coast, The; East Coast Kitchen Party; Hawk, The.**

Randall, Janine. *See* **Muise family of Boston.**

Rankin Family, The. A family band from Mabou, Cape Breton, that rose to national and international prominence during the 1990s as leading figures in the Celtic music boom of that era. Most of the 12 children born to Alex J. "Buddy" and Kathleen (Wright) Rankin were musically inclined and the band evolved from performances given by various family members at local events. While the first formal line-up included Geraldine (1958-2007), Genevieve, David, John Morris (1959-2000) and Raylene (1960-2012), in the 1970s, younger family members – Jimmy, Cookie and Heather – joined later as some of the older siblings moved away from home. *The Rankin Family* album was released independently and in cassette format in 1989, followed by *Fare Thee Well Love* in 1990. Featuring Jimmy, John Morris, Raylene, Cookie and Heather these recordings included original songs and tunes alongside traditional Gaelic songs, mouth music and fiddle tunes. Distributed nationally by an independent company, Soundwright, the band was further introduced to a new audience through an appearance on the CBC-TV variety show *On the Road Again* in 1989 and a CBC-TV special that same year; this led to the band being picked up by a major label, EMI, in 1992. Renamed The Rankins in 1998, the group was among the most prominent acts of the decade, bringing Cape Breton music into the mainstream and winning multiple ECMAs, six Juno Awards, four SOCAN Awards, three Canadian Country Music Awards and two Big Country Music Awards. The band toured internationally and continued to release recordings such as *North Country* (1993); a limited-edition 5-song release, *Grey Dusk of Eve* (1995), which featured a duet with Liam Ó Maonlaí of Ireland's Hothouse Flowers, *Endless Seasons* (1995) and a greatest-hits album in 1996, *The Rankin Family Collection*. While their live show incorporated choreographed step-dance routines and twin-fiddle features (with John Morris and Howie MacDonald), the band's sound was evolving more in the direction of contemporary folk/roots and including more original than traditional material. Raylene left the group in 1998 following the birth of her son, and after one final album (*Uprooted,* 1998) and a collaboration with The Chieftains on their *Tears of Stone* album (1999) they made the decision to disband in order to pursue independent interests. The three sisters, as well as pursuing individual projects recorded and toured together, released a Christmas album (*Do you Hear–Christmas,* 1997) and were the focus of a TV special, *Home for Christmas* (Bravo!); they also pursued a business venture together opening the Red Shoe pub in Mabou in 2004 which has become a popular live-music venue in Inverness County. Jimmy Rankin continued with a career as a singer-songwriter and has released four solo albums: *Song Dog* (2001), *Handmade* (2003), *Edge of Day* (2007), *Forget About the World* (2011) and *Back Road Paradise* (2014), while John Morris continued to compose and perform as a fiddle and piano player, based in Judique, Cape Breton; he died in a car accident in Cape Breton in 2000, only months after the group had retired. In 2003 the compilation album *Souvenir: 1989-1998* was released and, in 2006, the Rankins reunited with

LIZ DOHERTY

John Morris's daughter Molly (singer-songwriter and fiddler) added to the group. In 2007, on the anniversary of John Morris's death (January 16th), the album *Reunion* was released, and in 2009 the Rankin Family released their seventh studio album, *These Are the Moments*; both were promoted by cross-country tours. In 2012, Raylene died after a long battle with cancer. *See* **Rankin, John Morris.**

Rankin, Fr. John Angus. (1918-1995). Piano, massed fiddle group director. Inverness, Broad Cove Banks and Glendale, Inverness County. Fr. Rankin's contribution to the Cape Breton fiddle tradition has been as a cultural activist in which the revival of the 1970s was a major achievement. Born to parents Daniel C. and Sarah (Beaton) Rankin, he was raised from the age of 7 by his grand-uncle and grand-aunt. He first heard the fiddle through players such as his uncle, Alex Beaton, the local milkman "Curly" Sandy Beaton and family friend Sandy MacLean. In Broad Cove Banks he met a new community of musicians, including many of the Beaton family from Mabou Coal Mines, and numerous Gaelic singers. Known as "Black" Angus, he was ordained a priest in 1946 and was appointed curate at Boisdale from 1946 to 1948, then dean of men at St. FX, and, in 1958, was appointed parish priest at St. Mary's, Glendale, and Trinity Mission, Whycocomagh. A key coordinator of the CBFA in the early 1970s (at that time named the Committee for Cape Breton Fiddlers) he was one of the organizers of the first Glendale Fiddle Festival (1973). At this, Fr. Rankin directed the massed fiddle group, his task to create a homogeneous sound from a large number of players of different styles and abilities. He acted as emcee for many concerts and events, often with Archie Neil Chisholm. In 1983 he was awarded an honorary doctorate by St. FX, and in 1988 the CBFA held a tribute ceilidh for him at Port Hawkesbury. The former Glebe House in Glendale was named in his honour as "The Fr. John Angus Rankin Cultural Centre" when it opened in 1997. [**MacGillivray 1988**]. *See* **Father John Angus Rankin Cultural Centre.**

Fr. John Angus Rankin with Donald Angus Beaton on fiddle. Courtesy of Mark Wilson.

Rankin, John Morris. (1959-2000). Fiddle, piano, composer. Mabou and Hillsdale, Cape Breton. Born to parents Alex J. "Buddy" and Kathleen (Wright) Rankin, John Morris grew up in a musical family with most of his eleven siblings being musically inclined. Highlighted on the *Vanishing Cape Breton Fiddler* documentary of 1971 as one of the few young people playing fiddle music at the time, he went on to achieve international prominence as part of The Rankin Family band which released numerous albums and received many awards and accolades. As a piano player John Morris was influential in shaping the Cape Breton accompaniment style, while as a fiddle player his sound reflected elements of older, localized practices associated with the Mabou Coal Mines area. As a composer, he contributed a number of tunes to the repertoire that are now standards of

Jack Daniel's Reel

John Morris Rankin, 1959-2000

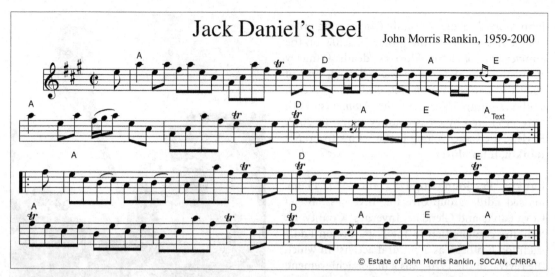

the tradition, including "Molly Rankin's," "Jack Daniel's" and "Hull's Reel." His tunes have been recorded not only by Cape Breton artists but also internationally by such as Hamish Moore, the Tanahill Weavers and Fiddlesticks. While he was mainly involved with The Rankins, John Morris occasionally performed in Cape Breton with Howie MacDonald and Dave MacIsaac and was one of the contingent of Cape Bretoners who participated in the 1993 Éigse na Laoi Festival at University College, Cork, Ireland. His daughter, Molly, is a singer-songwriter who has performed with the Rankins and, most recently, as part of the Toronto-based band Alvvays. **[MacGillivray 1981].**

Rankin, Mairi. (1978-). Fiddle, piano, step dancer, composer, teacher. Mabou and Vancouver. Her mother, Effie Rankin, a native of North Uist, Scotland, is a well-known advocate for the Gaelic language and her father, Daniel, a retired educator, is involved in local choirs and square dances. Mairi attended group fiddle classes with Stan Chapman from the age of 12, and was further encouraged by Kenneth Joseph MacDonald, a neighbour who visited regularly and played tunes which she would record and later learn by ear. Inspired by such as Natalie MacMaster, Buddy MacMaster, The Rankin Family and Howie MacDonald, Mairi went on to develop a full-time music career; since 2009 she has been a member of the group The Outside Track, which has players from Ireland and Scotland as well as Cape Breton; she is also a founding member of Beòlach. In other projects she has liaised with Wendy MacIsaac, Mac Morin, Mary Jane Lamond, Adrian Dolan, Jenny Ritter, Tim Readman, The Rankin Sisters, The Unusual Suspects, Bruce Guthro, Natalie MacMaster, Cullin and Spirit of the Dance, as well as acting with the Eastern Front Theatre group in Nova Scotia in an adaptation of Alistair MacLeod's *Island*, for which she also provided the music score. Her recordings include two CDs with Beòlach (*Beòlach*, 2001; *Variations*, 2004), three with The Outside Track (*Curious Things given Wings*, 2010; *Flash Company*, 2012; *Light up the Dark*, 2014) and a solo album, *First Hand* (2001). She has also appeared on Raylene Rankin's *Lambs in Spring* (2004), The Rankin Family's *Reunion* (2007) and on several compilations such as *Cape Breton Lullabies*, *Failte–A Cape Breton Welcome* and those from Celtic Colours. Her image has been used in Nova Scotia Tourism advertising, adding to a diverse career that includes teaching workshops and classes at festivals and contributing to university programs.

rant. Named from a Germanic word meaning to frolic, romp or revel, this tune-type is common in the Northumberland area of England where it has

LIZ DOHERTY

an associated dance which uses "set" steps; one well-known tune of this type is the pre-1800 "The Morpeth Rant"; rants were also prevalent in 18th-century Scotland. The word rant often appears in the titles of tunes which – depending on rhythm and accent – might be interpreted as either strathspeys or reels; this is the case in Cape Breton. As they were found in the 18th century, the rant, or double rant, typically involved parts of 4 bars; the time signature is 2/2 and the rhythmic pattern involving 2 sixteenth-notes plus an eighth-note (interpreted in Cape Breton as a "cut") is a feature.

Rawlins Cross. A Celtic rock group formed in Newfoundland in 1988 featuring Cape Breton bagpiper and whistle player, Ian McKinnon, and named after a busy street intersection in St. John's. The band started as a trio named "Open Road," which included McKinnon along with Newfoundland brothers Dave and Geoff Panting on guitar/mandolin and accordion/keyboards respectively. It expanded to include bass and drums and, in the early 1990s, PEI singer Joey Kitson joined. The band founded its own label and business company (GroundSwell), and benefited from Warner Music's 1990s interest in East Coast music, signing with them in 1993. Following a first CD and accompanying video in 1989 (*A Turn of the Wheel*), Rawlins Cross went on to release *Crossing the Border* (1992), *Reel 'n' Roll* (1993) and *Living River* (1995). The band issued a collection of their instrumental pieces with *Celtic Instrumentals* in 1997, which included their signature pipes/whistle "MacPherson's Lament." In the same year, they recorded *Make it on Time*, then, in 2008, *Rawlins Cross: Anthology*, followed by *Heart Head Hands* in 2010. The band is seen as holding on to a distinct identity—linked to the prominence of the bagpipes—while negotiating popular acclaim and a balance of fusion elements. [**MacDonald 2010**].

RCA. The Radio Corporation of America, established in New York in 1919. It became associated with The Victor Talking Machine Co. in 1925, and in 1929 acquired the Victor label to become "RCA Victor," a leading recording company. In 1986 it became part of the Bertelsmann conglomerate, but RCA Records (along with Columbia and Epic) remains a flagship recording label of Sony. RCA is the second-oldest recording company in U.S. history, but its Canadian unit (Berliner Gramophone Canada) is Sony's oldest label in Canada, being one of two record companies there to survive the Depression (the other is Universal Music). In 1968 John Allan Cameron recorded *Here Comes John Allan Cameron* with this label, the first multi-track recording by a Cape Breton artist. *See* **recording industry.**

recording. The practice of capturing, storing and reproducing sound. This developed with the aid of various technologies from the late 1800s and fundamentally transformed music experience and practice. Prior to these developments, music was shared aurally (by ear), graphically (by note or other visual representation) and, where music boxes and player pianos were involved, through mechanical simulation. The stages of development of recording technologies for mass or domestic consumption are (a) wax cylinder, (b) 78-rpm discs, (c) 45-rpm and 33 1/3-rpm vinyl discs, (d) tape (reel to reel), (e) cassette tape, (f) CD, (g) digital. While there is Irish and Scottish music on cylinders, there is no evidence of any Cape Breton players on such recordings.

The first commercially recorded Cape Breton fiddle music appeared on 78-rpm records in the U.S. in 1928 when "Big" Dan Hughie MacEachern and Charlie MacKinnon recorded as part of the Columbia Scotch Band and the Caledonia Scotch Band for the Columbia record label. Approximately 150 recordings for 78-rpm records featuring Cape Breton fiddlers were created between 1928 and 1957 by the artists Alcide Aucoin, Colin J. Boyd, Dan J. Campbell, Angus Chisholm, Winston Fitzgerald, Alick Gillis, Wilfred Gillis, Angus Allan Gillis, Bill Lamey, Joe MacLean, Dan R. MacDonald, Hugh A. MacDonald, "Big" Dan Hughie MacEachern, Johnny Wilmot, Joe Murphy, Jimmie MacLellan, Donald MacLellan, Charlie MacKinnon, "Little" Jack MacDonald and Dan Joe MacInnis. A number of groups of players also recorded for this format including The Columbia Scotch Band, The Caledonia Scotch

Band, The Inverness Serenaders, The Five Mac-Donald Fiddlers and the MacLellan Trio; indeed, the majority of the recordings feature not just the fiddle-piano duo, but rather the practice was to include additional accompanying instruments and, as might be expected in the cosmopolitan urban environments of the U.S., where many of these recordings were made, there was often an Irish music presence in terms of artists or influence (e.g., the "Irish dance band" formula). Common too was the practice of two fiddlers playing in duet. While the fiddle player and piano player were generally identified by name on the disc's label, often the other musicians were not. Typically, the 78s featured two groups of tunes, one on each side; where a band or group was involved it was common to feature a solo artist (with accompaniment) on the other side (e.g., Alcide Aucoin is featured on the "B" side of The Inverness Serenaders 78). Cape Breton fiddle 78s were released on various labels in the U.S. initially and later in Canada. These included Columbia, Decca, Celtic, Brunswick, Rodeo and Mac.

The LP (long-playing record, 33 1/3 rpm) became the standard medium for recorded music in the 1950s until around 1985 when the CD took over. Around 400 LPs of Cape Breton fiddle music were recorded on various labels until the 1990s. Winston Fitzgerald was the first Canadian to have his music recorded in this format when he released an album on the Rodeo label in 1953. On the LP, fiddlers could now record significantly more tune selections, and the reduced speed of the disc spin meant that the tempo was closer to that of a natural performance. Vinyl discs were more robust than 78s and as such were easily packaged for shipping, therefore having increased distribution potential. Unlike the 78s, the LPs were packaged in a sleeve that provided the opportunity for liner notes and photographs to be included, but some companies that recorded Cape Breton fiddlers

(such as Rodeo) were slow to do this. Compilation LPs also became a feature of the Cape Breton fiddle recording industry, typically involving reissues of previously released material; Cape Breton artists also began to be featured on such anthology recordings with other fiddlers from across Canada. 45-rpm discs were mostly found in the pop market. Only one example appears in Cape Breton fiddle music – Winston Fitzgerald's *A Selection of New Jigs, Reels, Strathspeys, Hornpipes and Waltzes* (Banff; later reissued on Celtic and Rodeo).

Domestic tape machines (e.g., Webcors and Reveres) came on to the market in the 1950s and remained popular up until the 1970s, facilitating informal recording in Cape Breton, typically in private, house-party or session settings. This was done not only in Cape Breton itself, but even more so in Cape Breton communities in Boston and Detroit. The practice was for a recorder to be set up which would capture the whole night's proceedings, requiring no more skill than someone remembering to change the tape as required. Substantial volumes of material were documented in this way and it became common for the tapes to be shared around the community, thus providing a valuable transmission resource. With the introduction of cassettes in 1963, and following the production of cheaper and more compact machines later in that decade, interest in reel-to-reel recording virtually vanished in a short time. The compact cassette was introduced by Philips ca. 1963 and by 1984 caused audio-cassette sales to exceed those of LPs; major companies typically issued both cassette and LP versions of new albums. Blank tapes were also available for recording purposes and rapidly replaced the reel-to-reel in the home-recording market, becoming hugely important in the dissemination of music during this era. There are ca. 50 commercially recorded cassettes of Cape Breton fiddle music; some players released albums in both LP and cassette format while others used only cassette. According to Ian McKinnon's research, by the late 1980s cassettes were outselling vinyl by a ratio of 2- or 3-to-1 in Cape Breton; they remained popular up until the mid-1990s, not least on account of all motor vehicles prior to ca. 1996 being fitted with built-in cassette players. Cassettes played an important role in the process of taping tunes from the radio, which was a common practice particularly during the 1980s; for the young players emerging at that time (post-revival) this practice (the taping, learning and sharing of material from the radio) was significant in much the same way as the sharing of tune books has been in earlier decades. Compact discs (CDs) use digital technology instead of the analog recording method used from Edison's time through LPs to cassettes. This was introduced in Japan in 1982. To date there are ca. 200 albums of Cape Breton fiddle music on CDs, and many compilations; this is the standard medium used by artists today. In 2015 only a small number of players have as yet embraced the digital download market. [**McKinnon 1989**].

recording industry. (a) Canada. In Canada this has always been closely allied to the major American and European recording companies although many notable contributions were made by Canadian companies or Canadian branches of the larger internationals. From the turn of the 20th century local companies began to appear across Canada, among them Celtic Records established by Bernie MacIsaac in Antigonish in 1933. By 1960 the broadcasting industry could not meet the demand for material with Canadian content so, in 1962, the Canadian Talent Library was formed to produce recordings by Canadians; CAPAC and CAB set up a similar project in 1963. Following a public hearing process organized by the CRTC (Canadian Radio and Television Commission), the MAPL system, created by Stan Klees (co-creator of the Juno Awards), was adopted in 1971 to define and identify Canadian content in music for the purposes of fulfilling the percentage quota of Canadian music broadcast on Canadian

CAPE BRETON SCOTCH RECORDS

TO BE ON SALE AT

BILL LAMEY'S DANCE

186 CHESTNUT HILL AVENUE
BRIGHTON, MASS.
(Saturday, April 27th)

LATEST RECORDINGS BY

Winston Fitzgerald   Joe MacLean
Dan R. MacDonald   Angus Chisholm
Donald and Theresa MacLellan

Bag Pipes   Galic Songs
And A
Scottish Galic Record For Beginners

ALSO SOLD AT
Murdock MacPhail's
Barber Shop
173 BLUE HILL AVE.
ROXBURY, MASS.

Courtesy of The MacInnes Collection.

radio.

(b) Cape Breton fiddle music and the recording industry. This association dates to the late 1920s and has had periods of growth and decline, fluctuations in markets which have variously been local, diasporic and international, and changing patterns of engagement with established record companies which have been ousted by a locally-based cottage industry approach. Research by Ian McKinnon estimates that between 1928 and 1987 more than 300 commercial recordings featuring Cape Breton fiddlers had been released on some 40 labels; today that number is ca. 1,000. A key resource for Cape Breton recordings (from the LP format onwards) is Alan Snyder's webpage cbfiddle.com. In the early days, the impetus for the artist was not monetary recompense; rather recordings offered fiddlers an opportunity to advertise their live performances and, as an added bonus, afforded them greater recognition among their peers. Although Cape Breton fiddlers did collectively turn their backs on the recording industry for a time in the 1960s, by the mid-1970s it had become apparent that having a recording that could be played on air was important, since the era of live music on radio was in decline. Confidence in the recording industry was encouraged by a new approach in which the entrepreneurial spirit of the fiddlers was sparked, initially in partnership with an existing record company (Rounder records in the U.S.). By the 1980s, recording in Cape Breton had also developed into a thriving cottage industry, with fiddlers and their families maintaining ownership of most elements of the process; as a result the Cape Breton tradition statistically produced more saleable recordings per artist than did any other related tradition where the industry was dominated by bigger companies, which focused on a small number of artists. Trends established during that era continue today; Cape Breton fiddlers often record their first album at a very young age and they individually produce a high number of recordings. Since the market might be limited to the local dance and concert circuit, the pressure was on to deliver a new product at least every two years. As cultural tourism to Cape Breton has increased (providing a new customer base), as off-island opportunities to perform have increased, and as international distribution (via websites) has improved, this 2-year new-album trend has relaxed somewhat. **[McKinnon 1989].**

impact on music. The recording industry has affected the Cape Breton tradition in that, as is the case in other traditions, recordings contribute to the standardization of repertoire, style and performance practice. Further, the packaging of the recordings over some 90 years gives an insight into perceptions of identity held by the Cape Breton fiddler and those who marketed them. Cape Breton fiddlers were initially marketed as "Scottish" fiddlers in the early 20th century, then "Cape Breton Scottish" fiddlers in the 1940s-1960s, and "Cape Breton" fiddlers in the 1970s. In the 1990s the "Celtic" label was used (although more so in the context of events and support organizations and to describe the wider fiddle community

than for individual players); more recently the term "Gaelic" has been appropriated by the Cape Breton fiddle community. Through album titles, designations and artwork, a great deal is revealed about such important extra-musical elements of the tradition as a changing sense of identity, as well as mapping trends in music choices. The inclusion of Cape Breton in national and provincial awards systems has served to improve visibility and create opportunities for fiddlers as their artistic contributions gained parity of esteem with other artists from across Canada. Once a symbol of artistic achievement, recordings are now valued as commercial products which can be marketed automatically from performer websites.

role of the U.S. recording industry. The first records of Cape Breton fiddle music were issued in the north-eastern U.S. in 1928 by the New York Columbia Record Co. as part of their Scottish series. Fiddlers "Big" Dan Hughie MacEachern and Charlie MacKinnon, who were living in the U.S. at the time, were recorded as members of bands led by Irish-American piano player, Dan Sullivan, The Caledonia Scotch Band and the Columbia Scotch Band. Aimed at the Scottish ethnic market in the North America, the formula for these was similar to the Boston Irish dance bands of the day. Antigonish fiddler Colin J. Boyd recorded three 78s that were grouped with the Irish series in the late 1920s; two 78s by Colin J. Boyd were released in the U.S. on the Brunswick label's "Songs from Dixie" series; The Inverness Serenaders recorded for Decca in Boston in the early 1930s, as did individuals Colin J. Boyd, Dan J. Campbell, Angus Chisholm, Angus Allan Gillis and Hugh A. MacDonald; several of the records issued during the 1950s were re-releases from the Celtic label. While many of the larger companies curtailed their folk-music recordings during the 1940s, some smaller ones – such as Copley – emerged which, although primarily concerned with Irish music, also recorded some Scottish and Canadian performers including Dan R. MacDonald. It is the work of Mark Wilson with Rounder, however, which marks the next significant activity in Cape Breton fiddle music: that of being recorded by an American company. Wilson began with Joe Cormier and John Campbell in 1974 and 1976 respectively, and Rounder's Cape Breton catalogue expanded, representing, for the most part, the music of the older players. An intended "7000 Series" of Cape Breton and Canadian fiddle generated only a small number of LPs, and these found a home in Rounder's North American Traditions series. This engagement with the Cape Breton fiddle community in the early 1970s marks the end of a hiatus in commercial recordings that had been the case from the mid-1960s. Cape Breton fiddlers, disillusioned with the actual recording process, and often with the final product, and enjoying little or no financial reward, effectively abandoned the industry and were content to confine their sharing of music to what was captured informally on home recordings at various ceilidhs and events. It should be noted, however, that in some instances the record companies allegedly experienced challenges in building professional relationships with individual fiddlers which led to the dissolution of such partnerships. In any case, Rounder offered an alternative in which the record company and the artists had equal vested interests and ownership of the entire project. This allowed the fiddler – or another individual recommended by them – to contribute to the (typically extensive) liner notes and acknowledgements, something that was regarded as extremely important to the Cape Breton fiddler but which had previously not been done. The recordings were carried out in as close to a natural environment as possible (often in the fiddler's own home) and, for the first time, the process of mixing was introduced, providing an opportunity for the fiddler to contribute to the final sound and, most significantly, to decide against production if they were not satisfied.

Furthermore, Rounder's approach instilled an entrepreneurial spirit in the musicians; fiddlers learned new and innovative ways to engage in the business of recording their music. For instance, the artist was given the opportunity to purchase the final product for sale locally, something that not only cemented their involvement in the project but which also realized a greater financial return. Ultimately, the Rounder experience sowed the seed for a modest but viable industry to be established based around the Cape Breton fiddler, one that often involved whole families. Not all of the Cape Breton players reported satisfactory relationships with Rounder, and vice versa. However, the Rounder connection remains and Mark Wilson (most often in collaboration with a Cape Breton facilitator such as Morgan MacQuarrie) continues to produce quality material from the region. The Shanachie label, now in New Jersey, released re-mastered recordings in the 1970s, featuring some of the legends of the Cape Breton fiddle tradition such as Angus Chisholm, Bill Lamey and Colin J. Boyd. More recently, Smithsonian Folkways Recordings supported 2 recordings produced by folklorist, Burt Feintuch, *The Heart of Cape Breton* (2002) and *Cape Breton Fiddle and Piano Music: The Beaton Family of Mabou* (2004).

role of Canada in the industry. Colin J. Boyd from Antigonish is recognized as the pioneer of Scottish violin recordings in Canada, having recorded the first known such disc for the Brunswick label in 1932, but the first local record company to produce Cape Breton fiddle recordings was Celtic records of Antigonish in 1933. Encouraged to generate a local product which could be sold along with the spring-wound phonographs he stocked, Celtic's proprietor, Bernie MacIsaac, made two recording trips to Montréal with Dan J. Campbell, Angus Chisholm and Angus Allan Gillis on fiddle, and Mrs. W. J. (Bess Sidall) MacDonald on piano; they recorded 20 selections that were subsequently released on a series of 78s. In 1960, MacIsaac sold Celtic to George Taylor's Rodeo Records; Rodeo issued some newly recorded material and re-released older material from catalogues acquired from Celtic and Banff. Rodeo produced some 34 78s, 15 LPs and 23 anthology recordings of Cape Breton fiddle music out of an overall catalogue of ca. 350 releases. The label has some shortcomings, such as the absence of LP liner notes, and the fact that piano accompanists (often female) were rarely acknowledged. Taylor however recognized the promotional opportunities of recording, and encouraged musicians who played on radio to brand themselves accordingly, such as Winston "Scotty" Fitzgerald and His Radio Entertainers. At the time John Allan Cameron came to prominence in the early 1960s, the music industry in Canada, including in the Maritime region itself, was not particularly interested in the musicians of Cape Breton. However, this changed during the 1970s when the CBC became involved; in fact it was through engagement with CBC that Cape Breton fiddlers were first encouraged to properly register their copyrighted material in order to be fully recompensed for their work. During the boom of the 1990s, the Rankin Family was the first Cape Breton act to sign with a major label, EMI. Other major Canadian record labels then sought out similar calibre musicians on the East Coast, and each of them signed East Coast performers: The Barra MacNeils (Polygram), Ashley MacIsaac (Universal/A&M), Natalie MacMaster (Warner). Local independent labels also signed with major labels for marketing and distribution as well as some artist development. GroundSwell Records, for example, signed a distribution deal with Warner Music Canada; Halifax-based distribution company, Atlantica Music, signed a national distribution deal with EMI and formed a new EMI-sponsored label, Latitude Records, to find and promote local artists. However, many of these high-profile partnerships were short-lived and some are considered to have compromised the artistic integrity of the musicians along the way. Today the Cape Breton recording industry consists largely of artist-owned, small labels, with only a few of the bigger performers maintaining their connections with the major labels.

recording on Cape Breton Island. Almost from the outset Cape Breton musicians were dissatisfied with elements of the recording industry. In dealing with those companies they felt compromised, and the recording process itself was often uncomfortable for them, with many fiddlers reporting having to spend hours playing the same tune over and over before a final take was authorized. Typically, they had little or no artistic input to the decision-making process; often they were unhappy about the visual aspect of the packaging which, in the early days, might be standard Nova Scotia tourist bureau images, unrelated to the fiddlers or their communities, and without contextual information or acknowledgements; often no artist other than the fiddler was mentioned by name. Generally there was little or no financial gain for the fiddlers; indeed, if material was reissued at a later date they may never have been informed of it. Inevitably, conflicts arose. By the late 1950s, the majority of better-known fiddlers turned away from the record companies and opted to have their music recorded informally and disseminated through the network of domestic home recordings. From that time, most of the recordings produced specifically for the Cape Breton market have been produced by the fiddlers themselves. The first foray into independent record production was by Winston Fitzgerald with the Mac Label launched as a joint venture with Lloyd Taylor of CJCB in Sydney. Although it was never fully developed, it was significant in that it marked the beginning of a move toward fiddlers assuming control of their own music.

While Rounder was fostering a culture of ownership and entrepreneurship within the fiddle community in the 1970s, Sandy MacIntyre, a Cape Breton fiddler based in Toronto in 1974, introduced a new concept by being the first fiddler to record, release and distribute his own album. Dealing with five companies in total from inception to distribution (all of which were available to him in the urban environment) he sold some 6,000 albums, a significant achievement. MacIntyre was happy to share his advice and experience with his fellow Cape Breton musicians and by the time Dave Miller opened Inter-Media Services in Halifax in the mid-1970s there was a community of musicians keen to engage his services. Miller offered a compromise between the record company and the entirely self-directed recording project; he had a good quality mobile recording studio and could travel to the homes of those wishing to record, thus bypassing the studio experience; he offered a package which included the cost of production, pressing (outsourced to World Records, Ontario), cover art and delivery of the final product. Musicians such as Winnie Chafe, Doug MacPhee, Carl MacKenzie, Kinnon Beaton and the Sons of Skye all worked with Inter-Media Services producing recordings in the 1970s. Later, Kinnon Beaton was the first to recognize that a modular approach to the process could be adopted and that Miller could provide simply the recording services, allowing the artist to assume even further controls over all of the other elements. For fiddlers recording from the early 1980s onward this became the preference; often family members contributed to the process through such as distribution, supplying local stores such as Sam the Record Man, McKnight's and Charlie's Down Home Music Store, chains such as Zellers and Woolco and seasonally operated tourist outlets, typically on a sale or return basis. Many of the artists and their family members demonstrated a sharp business sense. While during the boom of the 1990s when the outside world "discovered" Cape Breton a number of artists were drawn toward a new high level of music-industry engagement, it is the artist-owned approach that dominates the Cape Breton tradition today. Music recording is a streamlined, professional industry with various supports and structures that allow fiddlers to avail of funding, business training, networking and showcasing opportunities. Virtually every Cape Breton fiddler who is involved at any level of professional activity is registered with the appropriate bodies; many have their own publishing companies/record labels. A small number of top-quality studios have opened up in Cape Breton, such as Lakewind Sound and Soundpark, that have negated the need (typical of the 1990s) to book studio time in Halifax. Typically, the pressing and packaging are done off-island but the distribution continues to be the responsibility of the artists themselves.

international aspects. Cape Breton music has, on a small number of occasions, attracted the interest of international record companies. Topic is an English-based company which, through the connections of Scottish Gaelic scholars and broadcasters John Shaw and Rosemary (Hutchinson) McCormack who were living in Cape Breton, was convinced to record two LPs in 1978: *The Music of Cape Breton,* Volumes 1 and 2. University College, Cork, Ireland's hosting of the 1993 Éigse na Laoi festival focused on the music of Cape Breton Island and resulted in the record label, Nimbus, recording and subsequently releasing an album in 1994. Until the early 1990s, however, it had been difficult to access Cape Breton recordings in Scotland or Ireland, with the exception of those produced by Topic and by the Toronto-based Brownrigg. Gradually, as Cape Breton fiddlers began to travel more frequently to participate in festivals such as Celtic Connections and to teach at schools such as Sabhal Mòr Ostaig, recordings became more accessible; they are, of course, even more accessible today through various on-line sites such as Cranford publications as well as artists' own websites. Still though, there are occasional locally produced recordings that are difficult to access off-island. *See* **home recordings. [Herdman 2010; McKinnon 1989].**

Red Shoe, The. A seasonal pub, restaurant and music venue in Mabou, Inverness County, named after the first tune composed by Dan R. MacDonald, first published in Gordon MacQuarrie's 1940 collection. It was restored under new ownership in 1998 before being sold to the Rankin sisters in 2004. One of the very few pubs in Inverness County, and a most popular venue, it hosts fiddle music daily during the summer season.

reduced key signature. A practice common since the time of the earliest printed collections as a means of indicating scales or modes, it involves the most economic use of accidentals possible. A key signature in itself does not determine a key as being major, minor or modal (this rather becomes apparent through the playing of the melodic line). Thus, in a modal tune, rather than using the standard key signature associated with the tonic note of the tune and adding accidentals throughout to indicate the mode, an alternative is to adjust the key signature in order to eliminate the need for accidentals throughout the tune. This results in the tune appearing less cluttered on the printed page and thus easier to read. A number of the books published by Cranford employ this approach.

reel. The most prominent tune-type in the Cape Breton fiddle repertoire it also has an associated solo step dance. While there is evidence to suggest that the reel originated in France as the *haye* in the early 1500s, it is documented as being played as a "reill" in Scotland in 1590; from there it travelled to Ireland in the 18th century. In cut time, the reel is played at a lively tempo, although each individual player has his/her own preferences in this regard. Reels consist largely of even eighth-note patterns; in the Cape Breton interpretation beats 1 and 3 of each bar are emphasized (through playing the notes in a slightly uneven manner, through bowing, and in the accompanying foot-tapping pattern). Many tunes of this type have been composed by Cape Breton musicians; occasionally hornpipe tunes are interpreted as reels. In Cape Breton the reel is played for solo and square dancing as well as in listening and presentational contexts.

Regal-Zonophone. Regal was a British low-priced record label owned by Columbia Phonograph Co. General, London and then by the Columbia Gramophone Co. Ltd from 1914 to 1931. Its material varied greatly and came from the U.S., Britain and Europe. With the EMI merger of 1931 Regal came to be part of HMV's Zonophone (1932) and the result was Regal-Zonophone, which continued to 1949 and was revived by EMI in the 1960s and again in 1980 for a few rock items. One 78-rpm record by Colin J. Boyd was released on this label in 1941. *See* **recording industry.**

repertoire. The complete body of tunes in a specific genre, style or geographical area, in this instance, the Cape Breton fiddle tradition. The repertoire represents the type and choice of tune permitted or accepted within the tradition and reflects the function or functions of the music at any given time. The collective Cape Breton fiddle repertoire is made up of the individual repertoires of all of the fiddlers and other relevant individual musicians and composers. While many of them share a common body of tunes – what may be considered the core repertoire or the canon – each individual's own repertoire derived from this body of tunes may vary in size, as well as in type, provenance and age of tunes, all of which reflect choices that have been made by that individual.

Repertoire (both the individual one and, by extension, the collective one) is not static but changes (expands, retracts, diversifies) continually over time.

size and make-up. Prior to the 1920s, the typical Cape Breton fiddler's repertoire was local, mainly of Scottish Highland provenance (from fiddle, vocal and piping sources both aural and literate) and largely orally transmitted; strathspeys, reels and marches were the prominent tune types. Various additions were made over time (as Cape Breton players engaged with such as the bagpipe tradition and non-Scottish traditions); some of these were embraced only fleetingly while others became embedded in the tradition. Dancing has probably been the most crucial factor in shaping the repertoire over the years. Certain group and solo dances (e.g., "Seann Triubhas," "Flowers of Edinburgh," "Jacky Tar," "Irish Washerwoman") had specific tunes which accompanied them. While these dances eventually disappeared, the tunes themselves were often maintained, although sometimes utilized in a different context (for example, hornpipes played as reels). When square-sets, in the form of quadrilles, lancers, Saratoga lancers and the Caledonians, were introduced to Cape Breton around 1890-1900 they required an extension of the repertoire, and so jigs – often Irish in origin – were added. Polkas made an appearance around the turn of the 20th century, initially associated with the new square sets, although their presence in this regard was short-lived. In the 1920s the waltz was introduced specifically to accommodate a new and popular couple dance. Airs, popularized in an instrumental capacity (as opposed to their original, Gaelic language song format) by such as "Little" Jack MacDonald, remained inconspicuous until the 1970s, although players such as Bill Lamey and Angus Chisholm occasionally recorded some and Dan Hughie MacEachern composed fine examples; Winston Fitzgerald was known for his rendering of both Scottish and Irish song airs.

The repertoire experienced a boom throughout the 1940s and 1950s as Dan R. MacDonald and other scholarly fiddlers were afforded increased access to written sources, particularly those from Scotland, through their international travels. This was a period of great experimentation and expansion in repertoire. Today, opportunities to experience and experiment with other musics continue to present themselves as young Cape Breton fiddlers travel the world to perform, have access to unlimited resources via the Internet, and engage with international artists as they visit Cape Breton to perform at events such as Celtic Colours. While the repertoire continues to expand and diversify, however, much of this is within the framework of tune types that have already been accepted into the tradition. Experimentation now takes place more on the level of style, tonality, technique, groupings and presentation rather than in the introduction of new tune types. It is impossible to estimate the number of tunes that currently constitute the Cape Breton fiddle-music repertoire, but it is clear that, from the early decades of the 20th century onward, it has been continuously expanding and diversifying, both in its source material and content. Today's Cape Breton fiddler is likely to have a repertoire that may contain several hundred tunes. Particularly, since the 1970s, the fashion for playing long, extended medleys or groups of tunes became popular at dances, requiring fiddlers to have large volumes of tunes at their disposal. The unspoken rule since that time has been that a fiddler does not repeat a tune over the course of an evening playing for a square dance, for example; prior to this, the opposite was true and it was not uncommon for fiddlers to repeat a tune several times during a night's music-making.

individual choices. An individual fiddler's repertoire does much to define them within the tradition. In the past, the distinction between dance and listening players was underlined by the type of repertoire an individual assembled. Certain players are often associated with particular tunes or with particular tune types; Buddy Mac-Master, for example, is generally acknowledged as being a supreme jig player, Theresa MacLellan is known for excelling at pipe marches, "Little" Jack MacDonald was known for his playing of airs. Some players, by choice, do not include certain tune types in their personal repertories; others are particularly noted for their ability to source old or unusual tunes and to bring these to the attention of the wider fiddle community, while others, particularly those who were first recorded commercially, have been responsible for elevating particular tunes and/or medleys to "classic" status. As with most folk-music traditions the Cape Breton repertoire has its "standards," regarded as being central to the tradition – its canon. Within the Cape Breton fiddle tradition these standards may be older or more recent tunes, traditional or locally composed tunes; indeed the Cape Breton fiddle repertoire includes a substantial body of locally composed material. It is important to note, however, as in all folk music traditions, these standards change over time in a cyclical fashion – appearing, disappearing, re-appearing. While the Cape Breton fiddle tradition is conservative in the area of tune type it has been, and continues to be, quite flexible in terms of the style of the tunes acceptable within a given tune type (i.e., range, scale, note density, etc.). There has been an appreciable change to the style of the repertoire over the past century, therefore, as fiddlers have moved away from an exclusively Highland Scottish repertoire to one that is increasingly eclectic.

tune types. Within a repertoire, tunes are defined as being of a particular type based on metre, tempo, structure, accent and, in some instances, function. Thus distinct tune types are identified by labels such as strathspey, march, reel, jig, etc., each with its own set of defining characteristics. Individual tunes then are aligned to the overarching tune-type criteria, yet distinct from all other tunes of that type in the interpretation of that criteria and in terms of melodic and/or harmonic shape; individual tunes are assigned individual titles. Incidentally, Cape Breton musicians are generally credited with having a strong facility for remembering and acknowledging tune titles, particularly those scholarly fiddlers who had a passionate interest in the published tune collections.

The tune types that dominate the Cape Breton fiddle repertoire are reel, jig and strathspey (dance); less common are the (slow) strathspey, march, air, hornpipe, clog, waltz. While a variety of other tune types are found (e.g., polka, schottische, breakdown, quickstep, two-step, slip-jig, rant, fling, barn dance, slide, marching air), their presence is limited. Since they are not associated with a specific function (i.e., to accompany dance) they tend to be played in isolation (e.g., Winston Fitzgerald playing a medley of polkas), or preceding a more standard group arrangement (e.g., Dan R. MacDonald playing "King of the Fairies," an Irish barn dance, before a reel). *See* **under terms.**

tune conversion. Within the Cape Breton tradition, as in many others, a practice found on occasion is that of converting tunes of one type into another. As Cape Breton players began to experiment with unfamiliar tune types accessed through published sources, altering the metre, rhythm or tempo of such tunes meant that they could be adapted and used for local dances (or simply for listening to). While strathspey and reel versions of a single tune are most common other examples such as playing a hornpipe as a reel or a rant as a strathspey are also found. [**Doherty 1996; Dunlay and Greenberg 1996; Graham 2006**]. *See* **composing.**

research. While Cape Breton fiddle music has been collected and documented in various ways since the 1920s it did not become the subject of ethnomusicological interest until the 1970s. By the end of 2014 some 20 postgraduate level dissertations (6 of them PhDs) have been awarded at Universities in Cape Breton, Nova Scotia, Newfoundland, the rest of Canada, the U.S. and Ireland. These have covered topics related to the history and evolution of the fiddle music and dance traditions, issues of authenticity, identity, transmission, commercialism as well as socioeconomic and contextual issues. The work of other researchers in disciplines such as Gaelic language, song and story; English-language folk song; piping and other ethnographic, anthropological, folklore and historical subject areas often intersects with the fiddle-music tradition; as such, these bodies of work have provided important contributions to the Cape Breton fiddle narrative. A number of undergraduate papers have also been developed on aspects of the tradition. In addition, independent scholars have published material on the fiddle-music tradition presented in such as text books, tune books, magazine articles and album liner notes.

academic dissertations. The first two academic works involving Cape Breton fiddle music were Earl V. Spielman's PhD thesis, "Traditional North American Fiddling: A Methodology for the Historical and Comparative Analytical Style of Study of Instrumental Music Traditions," (1975) and Sheldon MacInnes's MA thesis on the Cape Breton community in Windsor; Virginia Garrison produced the first PhD focused in its entirety on the fiddle tradition in 1985 (Wisconsin-Madison). During the 1980s, Memorial University of Newfoundland's Folklore Department began to yield some output related to Cape Breton including Cape Breton piper Ian McKinnon's thesis "Fiddling to Fortune" (1989). Kate Dunlay's academic research at Indiana University during the 1980s informed the book *Celtic Music of Cape Breton Island* (1986). The 1980s also saw the beginnings of academic interest in the dance tradition with Barbara Le Blanc producing an MA thesis on the church and dance in Chéticamp through Laval University (1986). During the 1990s academic output came from Ireland with Liz Doherty's PhD dissertation (1996). Since the turn of the 21st century there has been a marked increase in academic activity related to fiddle and dance in dissertations produced by such as Bergfeldt-Munro (Can),

Cape Breton fiddle student-performers in the 1980s. Courtesy of the MacInnes Collection.

Dorchak (U.S.), Graham (NS), Hayes (Can), Hennessey (Can), Herdman (Can), Lavengood (U.S.), MacDonald, J. (Can), MacDonald, R. (Can), McGann (U.S.), Melin (Ire), Thompson (NS); as such the scholarly focus continues from both insider and outsider perspectives. Cape Breton music (history/research and/or practical) is now also offered regularly at a number of institutions in the Maritimes and internationally and consequently much worthy material has been generated by undergraduate students and emerging scholars in these regions. *See* **individual entries; select bibliography.**

revival. The fiddle revival of the 1970s came about as a reaction to the CBC-TV documentary *The Vanishing Cape Breton Fiddler* (1971), which suggested that the tradition was not being handed down to younger generations and as such, was in danger of disappearing. In response, the entire existing fiddle community was mobilized, a fiddle festival organized and staged in Glendale in 1973. This was the era in which a Cape Breton music voice was crystallized and articulated; formal classes in fiddle were also established and within a short time substantial numbers of young players were emerging. It was, in fact, this generation of players who were positioned to benefit from the post-*Riverdance* Celtic boom of the 1990s. This also coincided with Cape Breton having been "discovered" by contemporary Scottish fiddlers and pipers. Consequently, increased performance opportunities in Scotland and resulting reciprocal visits to Cape Breton led to Cape Breton music securing parity of esteem with the other Celtic music traditions on the international stage. [**Feintuch 2006; Graham 2006; Lavengood 2008**].

Rhodes, Frank. (1931-). Dance research. Born in Wakefield, England, he began collecting Scottish dances with dance collector and historian Tom Flett. On a visit to Cape Breton in 1957 he interviewed a number of dancers, the first to do so in Cape Breton. Material generated from this fieldwork trip was published as "Dancing in Cape Breton Island, Nova Scotia," as an appendix, to J. F. and T. M. Flett's 1964 *Traditional Dancing in*

Scotland. In 1996 Rhodes's article "Step-Dancing in Cape Breton Island, Nova Scotia," was published as an appendix to another of the Flett's books, *Traditional Step-Dancing in Scotland* (1996).

Roach, Jason. (1983-). Piano. Chéticamp. He began playing piano at the age of 5 and was introduced to the Cape Breton style at 13, further expanding his musical studies with a Bachelor of Music degree from St. FX. He plays regularly with fiddler Gillian Head and is a member of the bands Sprag Session, Còig and the Beaton Sisters Band; he has recorded with each of these and is also featured on other albums including one by piano legend, Maybelle Chisholm MacQueen, *Pure Celtic Hearts* (2001). Having received the Frank "Big Sampie" Sampson Award in 2007, he released his own album that year.

Rocky Shore. A band named after a tune by Paul Cranford it has himself, Sarah Beck and Otis Tomas on fiddles, David "Papper" Papazian on whistle, concertina and fiddle, Deanie Cox on guitar and vocals and Paul MacDonald on guitar. They have been influenced by the music and music practices of a number of traditions, including Irish, and many of the new compositions they perform have come from the band members. This group has also been influential in promoting the concept of the session as a performance context in Cape Breton.

Rodeo Records Ltd. A record label founded originally in Montréal in 1949 by Scotsman George Taylor and Quality Records distributor, Don Johnson. By 1953 Taylor had assumed control, and three years later Rodeo moved to Halifax where it carried country, folk and some classical music. It was supplemented by the formation in 1953 of the Banff label and by the acquisition in 1960 of Bernie MacIsaac's Antigonish-based Celtic label; other labels it absorbed over the years included Europa, Melbourne, Campus and Caprice. Taylor also took over three music publishing companies—Banff Music, Jasper Music (both BMI Canada affiliates) and Melbourne (a CAPAC affiliate). Rodeo produced some 350 LPs and several

78s; more than 30 of its 78s and 16 LPs featured Cape Breton artists such as The Five MacDonald Fiddlers, Dan Joe MacInnis, Joe MacLean, Dan R. MacDonald, Joe Murphy, Johnny Wilmot, Angus Chisholm and Winston Fitzgerald. LPs, in particular, often contained material previously released by the artists on the Celtic label. A number of anthology recordings featuring Cape Breton fiddlers were released on the Rodeo-Banff label; Winston Fitzgerald released two LPs through it.

Rodeo impacted on the Cape Breton tradition in many ways, including 10-inch 33 1/3 LPs in the early 1950s; the first Canadian musician to have his music released on this format was Winston "Scotty" Fitzgerald with *Canada's Outstanding Scottish Fiddler* in 1953. Rodeo maximized the promotional value of its records by referencing the radio performances of the artists and so the fiddler's back-up bands came to be branded accordingly (e.g., Winston "Scotty" Fitzgerald and his Radio Entertainers and Joe Murphy and His Radio Swing Band). Rodeo LPs generally have no liner notes and are not always accurate in the tune information provided. Documentation held by the Beaton Institute shows considerable written correspondence between George Taylor and Cape Breton fiddlers about issues relating to inaccuracies, royalties and the recognition (or, indeed, lack of) afforded the (often female) piano accompanists. In 1962 Taylor left the Maritimes for Montréal and his recording of Cape Breton fiddle music ceased. But reissues of previously released material appeared on the Rodeo label for a number of years. In 1984 Rodeo was sold to Frank Swain of Holborne Distributing Co. Ltd. of Aurora, Ontario. *See* **recording industry.**

Rogers, Eddie. (1941-). Fiddle, teacher. Antigonish, NS, and Reserve Mines, Cape Breton. He was inspired to play fiddle by players he heard on CJFX Radio, especially Winston Fitzgerald, Joe MacLean and Angus Chisholm. While he refers to himself as a kitchen fiddler he has nevertheless played a significant role as a teacher both in Cape Breton and in Guysborough, NS. He has for many years being one of the musical directors of the CBFA.

Roland, Jennifer. (1978-). Fiddle, composer, step dance. Alder Point, Cape Breton County. The youngest of ten children she grew up in Cape Breton's Northside surrounded by music; her father was a fiddle player and there were many ceilidhs at the home. Starting out on piano and taking step dance lessons she took up the fiddle at the age of nine, and was taught by Kyle MacNeil. In 1997, having received the Tic Butler Memorial Award, she released her debut album, *Dedication*. This was followed by *Wings* (2001) and *For Each New Day* (2006) – both of which earned her ECMA nominations in the Instrumental Recording of the Year category. She has toured internationally across Europe, the Arctic, Canada and the U.S. including residences at Dollywood Pigeon Forge, Tennessee (2009), and at Silver Dollar City in Branson, Missouri (2010). These days she is more locally based and operates her own school of music and dance. She performs often at the Louisbourg Playhouse as part of various seasonal productions and has performed at Celtic Colours with her band that includes Jason Kempt (piano), Keith Mullins (percussion), Lyndon MacKenzie (guitar) and Mark MacIntyre (bass).

roll. Although a similar decorative technique appears in some early-18th-century Scottish collections, the roll is most likely borrowed from the Irish tradition; it has not been universally adopted in Cape Breton. The roll has two forms: (a) the long roll, and (b) the short roll, both used as embellishment to the melodic line. It was likely introduced to Cape Breton by Johnny Wilmot, himself regarded as a master of this technique, especially the long roll; others such as Jerry Holland, Dougie MacDonald, Natalie MacMaster, Kyle MacNeil, Brenda Stubbert and Paul Cranford frequently use the roll (long and short as appropriate) in their playing of Irish jigs, reels and hornpipes, and of locally composed music (but not in Scottish tunes).

(a) **long roll.** This is a 5-note ornament used to decorate a dotted 1/4-note. The main melody note is sounded 3 times (as 3 1/8-notes) with an upper grace note separating the first 2 of these and a lower grace note separating the second two. The upper grace note may be 1 or 2 degrees above the main melody note while the lower note is always the pitch immediately below. In performance, the first melody note is lengthened and the remaining notes shortened in order to accommodate this. In Ireland, depending on the individual fiddler's style, the long roll may be articulated in a single bow stroke, or by changing bow direction after the first melody note. The Cape Breton practice leans more toward the former option.

(b) **short roll.** A truncated version of the long roll used to decorate a quarter-note. Here the main melody note is sounded twice (as 2 eighth-notes) with an upper grace note preceding the first melody note and a lower grace note separating the 2 melody notes. The shape is identical to that of the longer roll but with the first iteration of the melody note being absent. In Cape Breton, this type of ornament is referred to by some such as Paul Cranford as a "turn" and it was heard among fiddlers before the long roll became popular, often found in reel playing.

Rollie's Wharf, North Sydney. From 2000-2013, this was the venue each Thursday night throughout the year for Cape Breton's only Irish-style session. The format was for a regular host fiddler and piano player to be joined by other musicians, most of whom were fiddlers. Jean MacNeil was resident pianist for some time, and the regular fiddlers included Paul Cranford and Sarah Beck. Musicians formed a circle around the upright piano located in the middle of the restaurant, and step dancing would take place generally in the central space. The session was started by Larry Parks as a normal type of Cape Breton pub gig; however, at the suggestion of Cranford and Jerry Holland, David Papazian tried the session format he had experienced in Montréal. A considerable reputation was established, rendering the event also a tourist attraction. The session relocated to an alternative venue in North Sydney in 2013 when Rollie's closed down; currently this is the Blue Mist Dining Room and Lounge in Bras d'Or.

Rounder Records. An American record company started in in Somerville, MA, in 1971 by a collective of enthusiasts that included Ken Irwin, Bill Nowlin and Marion Leighton; it was one of a number of folk record companies established as a consequence of the folk revival movement. Mark Wilson, a student and amateur folk musician approached Rounder with the idea of recording some Cape Breton fiddlers who were based in Boston at the time, out of which the first albums of Joe Cormier and John Campbell were released in 1974 and 1976 respectively. These mark the end of Cape Breton fiddlers' absence from the commercial recording industry (which had been due to factors such as frustrations – on both sides – with the business arrangements as well as an increasing pressure on fiddlers to adopt a Don Messer-type style and approach). Since the early 1960s, very few recordings of Cape Breton fiddle music were released with the exception of anthologies of previously released material; instead, a vibrant culture of taping and sharing tapes developed, and fiddlers disseminated their music in this manner. In order to address this, Wilson's strategy was to carefully select local players and liaise with them in a more musician-centred way, including them in every step of the process. Thus the end product was something they could call their own, and for which they were paid acceptable financial advances and royalties. The focus was about recording in an environment in which the players were at ease, and so many of the albums were recorded in Cape Breton, in fiddlers' homes. Since Wilson was himself an academic, he wished to properly contextualize the music, and so included historic images, new photography, as well as lengthy liner notes which were typically based on interviews with, or commentary from, the musicians themselves. Rounder's "7000 Series" of Cape Breton and Canadian fiddle music was developed with a view to marketing it among enthusiasts of Irish fiddle-music in the U.S.; 8 Cape Breton fiddle LPs were released as part of this series. Tensions

escalated, however, between the record company and some individual musicians over money issues surrounding the practice Rounder had initiated of selling artist copies to musicians, which they could then sell on at live performances; despite a number of planned projects being considered it effectively became impossible for Rounder to continue to support recording in Cape Breton and so Mark Wilson's work there was suspended. It was the 1990s when he revisited the idea of recording again in Cape Breton and worked to rebuild bridges. In 2010 Rounder was sold to Concord Records; some of the Cape Breton recordings from its catalogue have been released by Rod Stradling on Musical Traditions. A broad representation of Cape Breton's fiddlers is found on the Rounder label (e.g., the MacLellan family, John Campbell, Joe Cormier, Winnie Chafe) and some of the most iconic Cape Breton albums – such as *The Beatons of Mabou* – were released on this label. After 1999, the Cape Breton CDs were released under Rounder's *North American Traditions* Series.

North American Traditions series (NAT). Since the 1970s, Rounder's NAT series documented folk-music traditions in Canada and the northern U.S., primarily featuring the playing of older musicians who might not otherwise have come to attention beyond their immediate communities. Whenever feasible, these were recorded in as close to a natural environment as possible, and care was taken to contextualize the performances and to provide players' biographies. Thus, the North American Traditions series deliberately eschewed the use of the term "folk," and as a result has been able to provide an authentic portrait of the condition of North American traditional music. The Cape Breton catalogue within this series includes recordings of individual fiddle players such as Jerry Holland, Buddy MacMaster, Joe Peter MacLean, Alex Francis MacKay, Theresa Morrison, Willie Kennedy, Morgan MacQuarrie; in addition it includes four compilation volumes. Titled *Traditional Fiddle Music of Cape Breton,* these introduce a variety of musicians and are themed variously by geography or style. Vol. 1, *Mabou Coal Mines,* features Gregory Campbell,

Alex Francis MacKay, Rannie MacLellan, Johnnie MacLeod, Fr. Angus Morris. Vol. 2, *The Rover's Return,* has John A. Gillis, Willie Kennedy, Allan MacDonald, Francis MacDonald, John MacDougall, Gordon MacLean, Morgan MacQuarrie. Vol. 3, *Bras d'Or House,* presents such as Carl MacKenzie, Joe Peter MacLean, Wilfred Prosper, Fr. Francis Cameron and Kenneth MacLeod. Vol. 4, *MacKinnon's Brook,* includes Stan Chapman, Joe Cormier, Jerry Holland, Willie Kennedy, John L. MacDonald, Donald MacLellan, Theresa MacLellan, Buddy MacMaster, Doug MacPhee, Morgan MacQuarrie, Gordon MacLean and Mary Margaret Vanier. In his negotiation of the insider/outsider issues generated where there were suspicions of the recording industry and also in order to enable the most authentic recording environment possible Wilson's starting point was to identify key local collaborators to work with his as facilitators. In Cape Breton, fiddler Morgan MacQuarrie has been indispensable to the process. All of the NATs recordings have extensive biographical notes extracted from interviews with the musicians and thus place the music in historical and contemporary contexts. Wilson has retained ownership of all of the Cape Breton recordings and plans are current underway to have the materials posted non-commercially on a website managed by the Southern Folklife Collection at the University of North Carolina. *See* **recording industry.**

Royal Canadian Legion, The ("The Legion"). A Canadian veterans' organization founded in Winnipeg in 1925 as the Canadian Legion, its members include former military, Royal Canadian Mounted Police, provincial and municipal police, Royal Canadian Air, Army and Sea Cadets, direct relatives of members and also affiliated members; it expanded after the Second World War and, in 1969, received a royal charter. It has 24 branches in Cape Breton; some of these have provided, and continue to provide, popular venues for square dances, notably the Ashby Legion in Sydney.

Ruckert, George. (1941-). Researcher, fiddle. Connecticut and Maine. An ethnomusicologist who co-founded a California college dedicated to his mentor, Indian sarod master Ali Akbar Khan (1922-2009), he performed and taught sarod in the U.S., Canada, India and Europe, composed for orchestra, film and dance productions and published several books on the classical music of North India. In 1992, while teaching at Massachusetts Institute of Technology, he became interested in Cape Breton fiddle. He attended the Ceilidh Trail School of Celtic Music in Inverness and continued his studies with fiddler, John Campbell, with whom he worked on producing the 2009 publication, *John Campbell–A Cape Breton Legacy.*

S

Sabhal Mòr Ostaig. Part of the University of the Highlands and Islands of Scotland, Sabhal Mòr Ostaig, located on the Sleat peninsula on the Isle of Skye was founded in 1973 and is a significant education provider for Gaelic language and associated culture. Scottish fiddle player Alasdair Fraser taught summer courses at the college since the 1980s and when he became interested in Cape Breton music he invited Buddy MacMaster to join him as a teacher there. MacMaster and Harvey Beaton made their first visit in 1992; while Cape Breton step dance had previously been taught in Scotland (by Mary Janet MacDonald at the Barra Féis in 1983) this marked the first time that Cape Breton fiddle music was taught in Scotland.

Savoy Theatre, The. Marketed as "Cape Breton's Entertainment Showplace," this 761-seat auditorium on Commercial Street, Glace Bay was built in the 1920s as an opulent Victorian-style venue for live performances of all kinds, from theatre to boxing. It eventually became a cinema but in the 1970s it was bought by the city with Federal and Provincial funding. Destroyed by fire in 1991 it was fully restored and re-opened in 1993. The Savoy has presented emerging Cape Breton talent as well as established local, national and international acts, and has hosted such as Symphony Nova Scotia, Natalie MacMaster, Bruce Guthro, and Island Voices, and has been a key location for Celtic Colours. As a venue it has various performance, studio and hospitality spaces that render it useful as a cultural centre for a variety of programs and services.

scale. A sequence of notes that may be configured in different ways to create different types of scales. These include such as major, minor, modal, harmonic, enharmonic, chromatic, whole tone, etc. Modal scales, or modes, are relevant to Cape Breton music, as they dominated the tonality of its tunes up until the mid-20th century; these remain in evidence today, although an increasing number of tunes in clearly defined major and, less commonly, minor keys are found in the contemporary fiddlers' repertoires. Gapped scales, in which certain notes of the scales are omitted (thus creating a reduced melodic spectrum) were especially associated with bagpipe music, and are still found within the repertoire – most often the 5-note Pentatonic and the 6-note hexatonic scales – although fewer new tunes using these are being composed. Within Cape Breton, the most common scale used is the major scale (Ionian mode); the minor scale – using the flat 3rd and 6th and raised 7th – rarely appeared in Cape Breton until very recently, and is still mostly confined to tunes adopted from other traditions. Tunes in the Dorian mode (using a flat 3rd and 7th), however, are very common; the Aeolian mode or natural minor (using a flat 3rd, 6th and 7th) may also be found. Cape Breton fiddlers have developed a practice of constructing extended groups of tunes built around a single tonal area and refer, colloquially, to a group of tunes as being "on" a specific tonic, "on A" or "on D," for instance. Once this tonic note is established, the tunes of the group may involve any number of scales or modes; indeed choices made with regard to the juxtaposition of these is a major factor in shaping the dynamic of a set. **[Dunlay and Greenberg 1996]** *See* **modes; reduced key signatures.**

scholarly fiddlers. A term introduced by Frances MacEachen in *Am Bràighe* (1993) to best describe those fiddlers who, from ca. 1940, became fixated on the printed collections which had become relatively accessible from Scotland and elsewhere, and who ordered and amassed substantial libraries of these. Such players studied them carefully, shared and critiqued them, and the subsequent expansion of the repertoire (in terms of numbers and variety of tunes) was accompanied by a robust knowledge of their origins. Fiddlers such as Bill Lamey, Dan Joe MacInnis, Joe MacLean and Buddy MacMaster were among those known for such scholarly interest; Doug MacPhee, piano player, is another musician this way inclined.

schoolhouse dances. In the days before community or parish halls were built, schoolhouses – often with just a single room – were used also as a communal space for local people to gather together for dances.

schottische. A European round dance and associated tune in 2/4 time that originated in Bavaria in the mid-19th century and was known in England as the "German polka." The "Highland schottische" was introduced in 1855 as the "Balmoral schottische," and James Scott Skinner published one of these in *The Elgin Collection* in 1884; on the same page is a tune of his called "Glenlivet" which he describes as "strathspey" or "Highland schottische" and similar examples of this ambiguity are seen in other published Scottish collections. In Cape Breton the schottische has only appeared occasionally under this name in the playing of a few fiddlers; however it is common instead for schottisches to be played simply as strathspeys.

Scojen Music Productions and Publishing Ltd. This was established in 1988 by composer and multi-instrumentalist Scott Macmillan with Jennyfer Brickenden as a facility to compose scores on the latest music publishing and sequencing programs. Its creative studio is used for production on recordings, publishing and commercial work for film, television and radio. Scojen's library holds Macmillan's works, all of which are commercially available, including his recordings and tune book.

scordatura. *See* **high bass.**

Scotch measure (Scots measure). A tune-type associated with what was most likely a couple dance popular on the London stage in the 1750s. The earliest recorded use of the term is in the Blaikie MS from the late 1600s ("MacLean's Scots Measure"), and its first appearance in print was ca. 1700 in Playford's *Collection of Original Scotch Tunes (Full of the Highland Humours)*. In the period before the hornpipe had established itself as a distinct category, Scotch measures did appear in a number of Scottish collections, such as *The MacGlashan Collection*, that had made their way to Cape Breton. There is some evidence of the Scotch measure being danced to in Cape Breton, with Rhodes suggesting that the Four-handed and Eight-handed reels were danced to tunes of this kind. Such tunes are still found in Cape Breton, played as a reel/hornpipe (e.g., "The Flowers of Edinburgh"), as a march (e.g., "MacLachlan's Scotch Measure") or as a strathspey ("The East Neuk of Fife"). In 2/2 metre, the Scotch measure has distinctive rhythmic pattern in that measures made up of eight notes alternate with measures featuring quarter notes, most typically the first 3 being on the same pitch creating a pom-pom-pom pattern; the use of anacrusis (upbeat) is also a regular feature.

Scotia Sun, The. A weekly newspaper which began publishing in Port Hawkesbury in 1970, an amalgamation of *The Canzo Breeze* and *The Inverness County Bulletin*. Proprietor Marcie MacQuarrie had fiddling and piping in his background and was interested in his area's Scottish heritage; this led to him employing the services of John Gibson, a scholar recently arrived from Scotland. *The Vanishing Cape Breton Fiddler* documentary moved them to interview fiddlers, and between September 1972 and June 1973 they published 28 biographies as a "Scottish Fiddlers" series. Academic in research quality, they were written in a prose style, mostly by Gibson, but some others by Frank MacInnis and Joey Beaton. An inventory of the fiddlers covered is as follows: (1) Dan R. MacDonald, (2) John Morris Rankin, (3) Theresa MacLellan, (4) Kinnon Beaton, (5) Buddy MacMaster, (6) Sandy MacLean, (7) Alex Francis MacKay, (8) John Campbell, (9) Colin J. Boyd, (10) Hugh A. MacDonald, (11) Angus Allan Gillis, (12) Donald Angus Beaton, (13) Carl MacKenzie, (14) Fr. Angus Morris, (15) John MacDougall, (16) Dan Hughie MacEachern, (17) Donnie MacDonald, (18) Don Campbell, (19) Raymond Ellis, (20) John Alex MacLellan, (21) John Donald Cameron, (22) Morgan MacQuarrie, (23) Cameron Chisholm, (24) Jerry Holland, (25) Johnny Archie MacDonald, (26) Angus Chisholm, (27) Joe Cormier, (28)

Arthur Muise (although incorrectly numbered as 27). The series served indirectly to promote the first fiddlers' festival in Glendale, as locals valued seeing their local heroes in print: circulation peaked with each fiddler biography. In the 1970s and 1980s dozens of articles covered the Glendale Festivals and other traditional music subjects.

Scotland. The history of Cape Breton Fiddle music is inextricably linked to Scotland, specifically in the 18th and 19th centuries and which includes the era known as "the golden age" of Scottish fiddle music. Scots, mostly from the Highlands and Islands, emigrating to North America and settling in Cape Breton transported much of their culture with them; conditions in their new home enabled them to maintain aspects of this culture, creating what was in effect what ethnomusicologist Bruno Nettl has termed a "marginal survival" (1976). Fuelled by nostalgia, and by a yearning to hold on to the familiar and the past, old traditions and practices were thus maintained in Cape Breton while back in the homeland of Scotland they evolved and changed. However, while this is the narrative typically crafted and propagated, there is an alternative viewpoint that might reasonably be considered: Scottish fiddle music, as it existed in Cape Breton was, in fact, from the outset, subjected to change by experiences specific to its location. This escalated through the early years of the 20th century as, gradually, a distinct Cape Breton sound emerged, one which was rooted strongly in the past, but was shaped by its current environment. What was once a Scottish tradition sustained on the periphery (in geographic terms and in relation to Scotland) emerged with a new identity shaped by its diasporic conditions; as such, a new voice in Scottish music was born. Sporadic connections were maintained with Scotland through occasional visits and exchanges involving performance, research and documentary work carried out by the BBC and other media; and correspondence channels had also been opened up with music collectors and sellers by Cape Breton musicians stationed in Scotland during the Second World War, but it was not until the late 1980s

that a significant movement began to reintroduce Cape Breton music to Scottish audiences. This movement was spear-headed by Scottish fiddler Alasdair Fraser and later, with a focus on the bagpipe and step dance traditions, by Hamish and Maggie Moore. The message was that Cape Breton music represented Scotland's past and should be celebrated as such. This thesis initially met with some resistance from contemporary exponents of Scottish music who rejected Cape Breton's music being held up as an example of a continuous tradition transmitted from the 18th century; those grounded in Highland Scottish styles and practices, who had embraced neither James Scott Skinner's style nor the musically-literate practices of the strathspey and reel societies, felt particularly offended by the suggestion that these Canadian musicians were the saviours of Scottish music since they themselves had been nurturing their own tradition all along. Furthermore, they pointed out that the very distinctive piano style and a significant portion of the repertoire that had been composed in Cape Breton did not have any place in Scotland's past anyway. But those whose ideal was to "bring the music back home" to Scotland from Cape Breton chose not to present the full story and to take into account the accretions made to Cape Breton's music from outside the Scottish experience; the reality was that this was not a "preserved" Scottish tradition but, rather, one which, although rooted in Scotland, had over time evolved into something quite new and distinct.

The Fraser-Moore emphasis held sway, however, until gradually (as Cape Bretoners began to present themselves in Scotland) a truer picture emerged: here were a people, fiercely proud of their Scottish heritage yet equally aware of, and proud of, their Cape Breton identity and its musical manifestation. Exchange opportunities increased during the 1990s through this speculative and exciting debate, and Cape Breton music and dance came to be shared and explored in Scottish performance and teaching environments. On mainland Scotland since 1994, Celtic Connections has provided performance platforms for many

Cape Breton musicians, as have other festivals and events such as at Sabhal Mòr Ostaig, Ceòlas, Blas, The Scots Fiddle Festival and NAFCo. Reciprocal visits to Cape Breton have also been made possible through Celtic Colours that have seen numerous Scottish musicians perform, and create new collaborations and networks. Today the level of exchange between Cape Breton and Scotland is vibrant and positive, based on a mutual recognition of a shared history – commonalities and differences alike.

exodus. In the century following the mid-1700s, there was a mass exodus from the Scottish Highlands and Islands of Scotland. This migration resulted initially in the transplanting of these people to various centres across North America, primarily North Carolina, Prince Edward Island, Glengarry County, Nova Scotia and Cape Breton Island. Later resettlement of these emigrants brought them to New York City and other North American urban centres, to Newfoundland, Australia and New Zealand. Generally the population movement from the Highlands and Islands of Scotland is considered in two principal phases. The first was chiefly directed toward North Carolina (with some to Nova Scotia), the second toward Cape Breton Island (ca. 1773-1850).

political impetus. At one level, this "epidemical fury of emigration," as it was described by Samuel Johnson, was a matter of choice, through an increase in awareness of the prospects available. On another level, however, emigration was the direct consequence of a series of socioeconomic catastrophes. A sequence of events such as the capture of Baleine, the Darien Expedition (or the "Disaster" as it came to be known), and the Glencoe Massacres, contributed toward an escalating anti-English sentiment in Scotland; the Union of the Governments of England and Scotland in 1707 marked the end of Scotland's political independence. The anti-English attitude manifested itself in support for the Jacobite cause, realized in periodic uprisings from 1709 where an unsuccessful attempt was made to place James (The Pretender) on the throne, through to 1745, in support of The Young Pretender (Bonnie Prince Charlie), until the final vanquishing at Culloden Moor on April 16th, 1746. This defeat activated developments that gradually debased the patriarchal clan system—the quintessence of Highland society—leading to its eventual breakdown, and the subsequent emigration of many of its members to North America. By the 1770s, the bonds of kinship, devotion and service (which had been the sinews of the old society) had been largely severed. The annexation of estates to the crown and deprivation of the rights of heritable jurisdiction immediately set landholding and agriculture off in a new direction. Estates were administered by government commissioners; even when the majority of chiefs had recovered their lands, by 1784 they chose to act as landlords *in absentia,* thus severing what was left of clan alliances. The role of the tacksman (the middle man between a chief and his clansmen) was abolished; subsequently many of these, dissatisfied with their reduced role in society, chose to emigrate themselves, and to encourage others to do the same. For the tenants, dramatic increases in rents were used to encourage depopulation in order to manipulate the Highlands for sheep farming; this had drastic consequences. The amalgamation of small holdings into large sheep farms could only be achieved by the eviction of tenants—the notorious Highland Clearances; replacement of the original Highland tenants with Lowland farmers added insult to injury. Prohibition of indigenous dress, and regulations banning the use of firearms (and with this the pastime of hunting) added to the list of circumstances that drove many to seek refuge in the New World. Aspirations toward political and religious freedom were also factors. According to Charles Dunn, "the lure of real or fancied advantages in the New World did just as much as the disadvantages of the old to induce the Highlanders to leave Scotland" (1991). Eyewitness accounts circulated by those who had served overseas with the British army added to the discontent. So too did published information such as that available in Gaelic periodicals and handbooks like *Ceann-Iuil an Fhir-Imrich do dh'America mu Thuath* (Guide for the Emigrant to North America) by Rob MacDougall. The crisis of confidence in the home place was aggravated too by the undermining action of enticing sales pitches made by shipping company agents – often with the collaboration of landlords who were determined to shift their tenants – which did much to lure the Highlanders away from their native soil. The Outer Hebrides and other west coastal areas had been able to curb their flow of emigration due to a successful kelp industry, but the kelp bubble was burst in the 1820s when the British Government removed import restrictions on competing sources, and so emigration became a necessity once more.

Maritimes settlement. Pictou, Nova Scotia was settled by immigrant Europeans from as early as 1703, and Prince Edward Island from 1769. Pragmatic and chance decisions could dictate where people landed, and an overflow from ships such as the *Alexander* (1772) and the *Hector* (1773), saw the first Scottish settlers (excluding those who had settled briefly at Baleine much earlier) travelling across the Gut of Canso from the Nova Scotian mainland or from Prince Edward Island. These pioneers made their way along the west coast, settling in Judique and Mabou for instance. The first known settler of Inverness County is reputed to be Michael MacDonald, "Sea Captain and Poet of Uist," who arrived in 1775 from Prince Edward Island. The trend for moving around the Maritimes continued; the 1818 Census shows that 25 families had come from Prince Edward Island and 40 from Nova Scotia. Likewise these early years saw arrivals from timber ships bound for the Miramichi, Pictou or Québec. Passengers often chose to alight at Ship Harbour (Port Hawkesbury) or Plaster Cove (Port Hastings) before moving on to settle along the Coast of Inverness County. Although no records were maintained at the Port of Sydney until the 1820s, the direct flood of emigration from the Highlands and Islands can be seen to have begun in earnest as early as 1802 with the arrival in Sydney Harbour of a ship carrying some 300 emigrants. According to *Mabou Pioneers* (1977) many of the original settlers to that area arrived in 1816, largely from the Braes of Lochaber, Moidart, Morar and other areas of the west coast and islands. Smaller numbers had settled in the Baddeck area, River Inhabitants, the Gut of Canso and Little Bras d'Or districts. As ships began including Sydney as a port of call, settlement figures on the eastern side of the island increased. Settlers claimed land in the Framboise-Loch Lomond district in the early years of the 19th century, while the area around Catalone-Mira River-Sydney was populated ca. 1828. Corresponding with the collapse of the kelp industry, the 1820s showed an increase in immigrants from the islands and coastal areas, 1828 reaching the highest point with 2,413 new arrivals landing in Sydney. Throughout the 1830s, the figures dropped but increased dramatically between 1839-1842 with an estimated 1,278 immigrants arriving in 1842. The flow ceased in the mid-1840s at which point it was estimated that of Cape Breton population of ca. 38,000 Scots were unquestionably the majority.

Patterns of settlement were often dictated by the clannish inclinations of the Scottish Highlanders who tended to form clusters based on family groups and with others who shared their religion and dialect. Thus the area around the Mira River is dominated by folk from Uist, Grand Narrows by Barra folk, Baddeck by Skye folk, St. Ann's by Lewis and Harris folk, and Inverness County by folk from Mull, Rum, Tiree, Lochaber, Knoydart and the mainland. Such large numbers of emigrants scattered all over the island created a Highland Scottish presence, which is reflected today in place names such as Glencoe, Inverness, and Iona, and through the family names which have been handed down over several generations of Scots in Cape Breton. Genealogy continues to be an important part of the Highland consciousness in Cape Breton and the standard enquiry upon meeting someone new for many generations starts with the question, "who's your father?" [**Bumstead 1982; Campbell and MacLean 1974; Doherty 1996; MacDonald 1977; Prebble 1961, 1963, 1966; Sawyers 2013**]

The golden age of Scottish Fiddle Music. Scotland experienced what has become known as the "golden age" of fiddling ca. 1780-1820. This was spearheaded by a number of individuals of Highland origin, typically Gaelic-speaking fiddler-composers such as Neil Gow, Nathaniel Gow, William Marshall, Robert Mackintosh, Daniel Dow, Alexander Cummings and Alexander McGlashan, all of whom contributed to a substantial body of published tune collections. Besides being traditional musicians, many of these were also involved in more genteel music circles, since the divide between the folk and European Art musician was not yet rigidly defined. Three collections focus to varying degrees on the music of rural locales. Daniel Dow, ca. 1776, edited a *Collection of Ancient Scots Music,* which has been described as a unique source of Gaelic and Scots song tunes including some by visiting Irish harpers. The dance music repertoire is alluded to in an appendix to the Reverend Patrick McDonald's *Collection of Highland Vocal Airs* (1781), although it appears that the majority of tunes included here are in fact pipe tunes. Another relevant collection of tunes and Gaelic songs (without words) was published by Captain Simon Fraser in 1816 – *Airs and Melodies Peculiar to the Highlands of Scotland and Isles.* The focus of these published collections on pipe music and Gaelic songs along with fiddle music suggest the popularity of all these idioms within the Highland tradition. This supports Bruford and Munro's assertion (1973) that the Highland fiddle style and repertoire were strongly influenced by both the bagpipe and the *puirt-a-beul* traditions. Their attempt to reconstruct an image of the Highland fiddle tradition relies heavily on comparisons between these, as well as considering the style of more contemporary fiddlers from the area. Ironically, they point to Cape Breton as the most viable source representing the old Highland fiddle sound. [**Alburger 1983; Bruford and Munro 1973; Purser 1992**].

transplanting the culture. Just as there is evidence of an active fiddle tradition heavily influenced by piping and aligned with the Gaelic language in the Highlands prior to and during the period of emigration to Cape Breton, there is also evidence to suggest that this same tradition

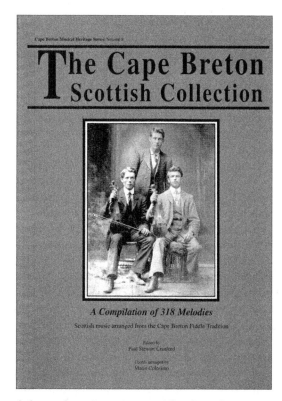

did travel to Cape Breton. The first clues come from accounts, both poetic and otherwise, of music on the emigrant ships themselves. The bard Dòmhnall Gobha (Donald Chisholm) (1735-1810) who emigrated to Nova Scotia in 1803 composed a poem entitled "N uair theid *Flori* 'na h-Eideadh" (When the *Flori* is Rigged), commemorating the ocean crossing in which he refers to dancing to music on board the ship. References to the bagpipe and its music making the journey are to be found in *The Highland Settler* and Sherwood (1973) who states: "As the *Hector* people came ashore the Indians moved back, and when piper Fraser blew up his pipes, and the wailing sound echoed over the waters and against the trees, the Indians took to the woods." Information pertaining to the presence of music among the pioneer settlers may also be culled from similar sources; certainly the number of references to early fiddlers and pipers presented in such as the *CBF* is convincing. [**Mac-Donnell 1982**].

changes in Scottish music. In Scotland there was a shift in geographic location with the music centre moving from the Highlands-Edinburgh axis to Aberdeen and the north-east. Central to the music developments during this period was the renowned James Scott Skinner (1843-1927), the first figurehead in Scots fiddling after the demise of Gow and Marshall a generation or more earlier. Skinner's career has been described as presenting "a virtual history of the development of the Scottish fiddler from untutored player to concert performer" (Alburger 1983). A virtuoso musician, schooled in both the traditional and classical idioms (as were others before him), Skinner introduced new standards of style and technical ability, most significantly through freeing the music from the restrictions imposed upon it by the requirements of the dance. He was also a prolific composer with several published collections to his credit. His influence on the subsequent development of Scottish fiddle music was also due, in no small part, to the fact that he was also the first fiddler to have his music recorded (initially on wax cylinders) thus making it accessible to a wider public. Alongside Skinner, a number of other factors were in operation, all of which were serving to alter irrevocably the face of Scottish music. Technological developments in this industry – recordings, radio and television – were to have a massive additional effect on disseminating a new standard that was dictated chiefly by Skinner himself. The coupling of the upright piano with the fiddle had ramifications for the music sound too, while the accordion, first introduced ca. 1850, quickly gained a foothold, posing a serious threat to the reign of the fiddle, eventually superseding it in importance in parts of Scotland. Furthermore, 1881 saw the establishment of the first of the Strathspey and Reel Societies, in Edinburgh. This was followed by others such as the Highland Strathspey and Reel Society formed in 1903. In 1898 William C. Honeyman published his *Strathspey, Reel and Hornpipe Tutor* which aimed to provide a standard resource from which players of the same level of ability could perform using identical bowing. Standards were also set by the Royal Scottish Country Dance Society formed in 1923. This period (ca. 1850-1920) also saw the birth of some of the later greats of Scottish fiddling such as Hector MacAndrew (1903-1980) and Bill Hardie (1916-1995). By the late 1920s, the music sound, practices, and aesthetics of traditional music in Scotland were considerably different from those during the 18th and early 19th centuries. Meanwhile, the earliest recorded music in Cape Breton supports the theory that there, in fact, elements of the old 18th-century fiddle tradition sounds and practices had not only survived but continued to be practised at that time; equally, however, the piano accompaniments on those same recordings underline the reality that, already, an evolution of sound and practice was, in fact, underway.

"discovering" Cape Breton. Performances of Cape Breton fiddle music in Scotland have been documented at least since the time of the Second World War, when fiddlers such as Dan R. MacDonald spent several months of service there and were often broadcast on the BBC. In the 1960s Bill Lamey was the first Cape Breton fiddler to formally perform in Scotland, and over the next decade there were several opportunities for Cape Bretoners to travel and play. In 1973, the Cape Breton Gaelic Society organized a visit to Scotland which included fiddlers Dan Joe MacInnis and Paddy LeBlanc while, in 1975, a performance by Cape Breton fiddlers at Edinburgh Castle received significant attention media attention. The Cape Breton folk band Sons of Skye toured Scotland as did the Cape Breton Symphony Fiddlers; all were among the increasing numbers of Cape Bretoners to be recorded for the BBC. Cape Breton and Scottish fiddlers also came in contact across Canada and in the U.S. where Cape Breton communities had been established; James Scott Skinner had adjudicated contests in Boston in which Cape Breton fiddlers successfully competed in 1926; decades later Ron Gonnella, the noted Scottish fiddler, met and befriended several Cape Breton fiddlers in Toronto. While Scottish musicians, music enthusiasts and Gaelic speakers and scholars living in Cape Breton maintained links between the two countries, and visits by musi-

(L-r) Sandy MacIntyre, Winston Fitzgerald, Ron Gonnella, Doug MacPhee, Dan Joe MacInnis. Courtesy of The MacInnes Collection.

cians to events such as the Gaelic Mòd or to the outdoor summer concerts happened on occasion, it was only in the 1980s that the historical music connection between the two regions was reignited through performances in Cape Breton by Scottish groups such as Na h-Òganaich, Capercaille and other bands and individual artists of that calibre. A chance encounter between Scottish fiddler Alasdair Fraser and Buddy MacMaster led to Fraser's "discovery" of Cape Breton fiddle music and to his enthusiastic campaign to make Scotland aware of this preserved (as he presented it) archaic Scottish fiddle sound. Hamish Moore and Maggie Moore became equally passionate in their respective discoveries of the Gaelic bagpipe tradition and the step dance tradition also in the 1980s. Both Fraser and Moore established opportunities for Cape Breton music to be heard and taught in Scotland from the 1990s: Fraser at his Sabhal Mór Ostaig Fiddle School in Skye, and Moore at his Ceòlas summer school on South Uist. Both musicians also engaged with the music as practitioners themselves, releasing the albums *The Driven Bow* in 1988 (Fraser) and *Dannsa' Air An Drochaid* (Stepping on the Bridge) in 1994 (Moore). Around that time other Scottish musicians such as Marie Campbell spent time studying Cape Breton music and Glenuig piper Dr. Angus MacDonald lived in St. Peter's for a number of years. Celtic Connections (started in 1994) and its sister festival, Celtic

Colours, continue to provide opportunities for musicians to perform and collaborate, as do many other events across Scotland, Shetland, Orkney and the Western Isles. Bands such as the Outside Track and Dàimh feature players from both Scotland and Cape Breton; Scottish band Runrig features Cape Breton singer, Bruce Guthro. Balnain House, "The Home of Highland Music" at Inverness, Scotland, included a "Canada Room" that featured an audio-visual exhibition on the music of Cape Breton until 2000. [**Doherty 1996, 2006**].

Scots snap (Scotch snap). This is the quintessential rhythmic characteristic of Scottish music. It is achieved by playing a sixteenth note (on the beat) followed by a dotted eighth note, this creating a "short-long" effect. It is particularly associated with (but not confined to) strathspey playing, and is executed using two separate bow strokes, with the bow often being lifted off the strings upon sounding the second of the two notes. In Scotland, the snap is typically interpreted in a very pointed fashion, but in Cape Breton it tends to be played in a more relaxed manner, though still clearly distinguishable as a specific rhythmic motif. While in the hands of older Cape Breton players the dotted nature of the snaps is often smoothed out considerably so that the music swings rather than jerks, there has been a change of approach since the mid-20th century with a growing tendency to define this figure somewhat more sharply. Older players will often introduce Scotch snaps into reel playing, but the younger players are more inclined to reserve them for the strathspey.

Scotsville. The location for a regular Tuesday night dance held through the summer months; it is organized by Dale Gillis and features various fiddlers in rotation.

***Scottish and Cape Breton Fiddle Music in New Hampshire for Violin/Mandolin and Guitar: Arranged and Edited by Jason C. Little* (1984).** When Jason Little heard fiddler Harvey Tolman play Cape Breton music at contra and square dances in

Nelson, New Hampshire, he was inspired to learn to accompany Tolman on guitar and mandolin. At age 24 – after 8 years of study – he decided to share what he had learned by publishing a tune book. This book includes Scottish tunes played in Cape Breton, tunes composed by Cape Bretoners, two of Little's own compositions and a jig by Tolman. In his introduction, Little explains that the piano has traditionally provided accompaniment to this kind of music whereas the potential of the guitar and mandolin haven't been equally explored. Twenty-two of the tunes are arranged with guitar accompaniment (block chord diagrams or written-out arpeggiated chords and sometimes bass runs, all with suggested fingerings). The melody lines alone of an additional 12 tunes are provided, and 2 jigs have written-out mandolin accompaniment. The 36 tunes include 17 reels, 7 jigs, 6 strathspeys, 4 airs, and 2 marches. The original 1984 edition is 42 pages in a landscape-oriented format, whereas the 1984 revised edition (Fiddlecase Books) is 25 pages in standard 8.5 x 11 inch format. A cassette recording of the tunes by Harvey Tolman and Jason Little was also released.

Scottish Country Dance. (a) A social, longways dance form introduced to Cape Breton by the Gaelic College in the 1940s, as part of its campaign to foreground contemporary iterations of Scottish culture. (b) Associated dance tunes which include such as reels and strathspeys and performed often by Scottish Country Dance bands, an ensemble type found in mainland Nova Scotia and across Canada but not in Cape Breton.

Scottish Strings. A popular CJFX radio show started with Gus MacKinnon as host, it ran from 1968-1981 and, particularly in its early years, included much live music. Frank MacInnis co-hosted the show for a time.

Scumalash. A band that began life as The MacDonald Family band in 1977 when Lloyd and Winnie MacDonald from Ironville on fiddle and piano played with some of their children – Paul (guitar), Shawn (fiddle) and Ann and Sandy (step

dance) – at such festivals as Glendale, Rollo Bay in PEI and the 1981 Cape Breton fiddle festival held in Halifax. By 1987 the name Scumalash had been established and the line-up extended to include younger siblings Dan and Marty; the instrumentation now included cello, tin whistle and bodhrán. The band featured at festivals and events in Canada, mainland Europe, Ireland, Wales, Scotland and England where they performed at the Sidmouth International Festival in 2004. Their self-titled album (released in 1992 on cassette; re-issued in 2004 on CD) with Doug MacPhee on piano as a guest performer represents their commitment to the traditional sound and repertoire of Cape Breton and also reveals a strong interest in Irish and Shetland music; indeed this recording is the first in Cape Breton to include Shetland tunes.While individual commitments by members of the group meant that they did not perform often for several years, Scumalash did reunite briefly to perform with *The Magic of Ireland* show, a Toronto-based production that toured Cape Breton and for which Dan MacDonald was musical director; their last band performance was at the Goderich festival in Ontario in 2009, where Lloyd and Winnie were presented with the Tradition Bearer Award in recognition of their efforts nurturing traditional music in the family. *See* **MacDonald family of Ironville.**

session. (a) The term "house session" is occasionally used in Cape Breton to refer to a (usually planned) social gathering in a home setting involving musicians and a select audience where the music is performed, discussed and often recorded for private use. (b) A more recent addition to the performance contexts typical of the Cape Breton ceilidh scene is the Irish-style session, a gathering of musicians which may happen in a private home or in a public space, and which specifically involves ensemble playing. This relaxed and informal format is bound, however, by certain, often unspoken, conventions that must be adhered to in order to be successful. This format was introduced in Cape Breton from the early 1980s onward by musicians who had moved to the island from other parts of Canada and who had previously experienced Irish music sessions elsewhere. A typical feature of this type of event is that the level of musicianship varies, and most players make an effort to ensure that each individual has a chance to be involved by leading groups of tunes that everyone might know, or by offering the less-experienced players an opportunity to suggest or to start a tune that they can play. The session in Cape Breton follows many of the conventions that are typical of an Irish-style session, but the local Cape Breton stamp is the dominance of the fiddle situated around the piano (upright or electric); the repertoire is also typically Cape Breton, with local step dance or a square set occasionally being included; singing is rarely included. In Ireland, the common environment for the session is the pub, whereas, in Cape Breton, the public spaces available include larger pub-eateries and community halls. These larger physical spaces present different challenges in coordinating a public ceilidh in terms of spatial layout and proximity of the musicians to one another and in the positioning – and ultimately engaging with – the other, non-musicians present.

The session in Cape Breton developed with the collective support and participation of a small number of mostly Northside-based Cape Breton musicians who were interested in Irish music. Mostly from the 1980s, house parties in which they were involved became a hybrid of the typical Cape Breton ceilidh (where fiddlers took turns to play) and the Irish session (where the focus is on the collective performance). Celtic Colours later provided another platform for the session to become embedded as a performance context. Visiting artists from Ireland, Scotland and the U.S. commandeered the "green room" area backstage at the festival club night after night and shared tunes in a communal, participatory environment; gradually they were joined by Cape Breton musicians, and the piano became the hub of the gathering. The first Cape Breton session to be formally organized was that established at Rollie's Wharf in North Sydney; since October 2013 it has moved around various premises in the Northside area; the current home is the Blue Mist Dining Room and Lounge in Bras d'Or. Sessions have also started happening in other venues such as the Red Shoe in Mabou, Creignish Recreation Centre, the Public House in Inverness and at the CMIC in Judique as well as at venues in Sydney such as Governors. The amplified session, popular in some city venues in Ireland since the 1990s, and in some Irish-exile areas abroad since the 1970s, which caters to the needs of the audience rather than musicians, has not yet taken off in Cape Breton; the existing matinee event no doubt satisfactorily fulfils this function. *See* **ceilidh; house session; house party.**

setting. The melodic and rhythmic outline of a tune decided upon by an individual fiddler as his/her personal version of that tune. This is often achieved following extensive consultation with various sources (printed and/or aural); ultimately it is dictated by the personal choice of the musician, exercised within the confines of accepted idiomatic boundaries. In the Cape Breton fiddle tradition the setting, once decided upon, becomes, for that fiddler, a fixed entity. While in performance, elements of style such as left-hand embellishments may be added (the flavour), the basic melodic and rhythmic contour is not changeable; this relates to Cape Breton aesthetic values of correctness. Thus, in Cape Breton, settings of tunes are given considerable attention. Some players, for example Winston Fitzgerald, developed a reputation for their ability to create excellent settings of tunes; many of these became common or standard settings which were adopted by others. However, multiple settings of a single tune may exist simultaneously.

Seudan. A Scottish-based, all-Highland pipes band that is made up of Calum MacCrimmon, Fin Moore, Angus Nicolson, Allan MacDonald (all from Scotland) and Angus MacKenzie from Cape Breton; Cape Breton piano player Mac Morin has also recorded with them. Their remarkable feature is that each plays pipes modelled on The Black Set of Kintail, a 1785 instrument held in The Inverness Museum that has been faithfully reproduced by Perthshire pipe maker, Hamish Moore.

Their music is drawn from the Gaelic song and old community dance-piping traditions of Cape Breton and the Hebrides.

Shanachie. One of the largest independent record labels in the world, Shanachie was founded in 1972 in the Bronx, New York City, by Richard Nevins and fiddle player, Dan Collins; now in Newton, New Jersey, it operates as The Shanachie Entertainment Corporation. It started out with a wholly Irish and Irish-American mandate, but the label now includes a range of genres such as Latin American, Gospel, Soul, Country, Ska, Reggae, Jazz and Blues. Three LPs of re-mastered 78 recordings of Cape Breton fiddlers appeared on the label in the late 1970s: *The Early Recordings of Angus Chisholm–Legendary Performances of Traditional Scottish Fiddling* (1978), Colin J. Boyd's *Pioneer Scottish Fiddler* (1979) and Bill Lamey's *Classic Recordings of Scottish Fiddling*, Shanachie (1979). *See* **recording industry.**

Shaw, Kristen. (1993-). Fiddle, guitar, step dance. Margaree Valley and Pleasant Bay, Cape Breton. She was taught by her father, fiddler Kelly Shaw, who in turn was taught by John MacDougall, and was supported in her music development by organizations which gave her other learning and performing opportunities including a school fiddle club run by Lawrence Cameron, the CBFA and the CFM's Mabou Musical Mentorship program, where she had the chance to meet with and learn from some of the older stylists of the Cape Breton fiddle tradition. She can be heard on a CD accompanying *The ABC's of Cape Breton*, an illustrated children's book written by Nicole Shaw and Lindsay Shaw Poirier (2009); on this she plays *Martin's Favourite Fiddle Set* which included tunes composed by she and her father: "Skylar Rose's Strathspey," "My Cape Breton Home" strathspey, "The Glengarry Fiddlers" reel, and "Lindsay Shaw Poirier's reel." Her debut self-titled CD was released in 2014.

Shears, Barry. (1956-). Highland bagpipe, teacher and researcher. Glace Bay, Cape Breton, Halifax, NS, and British Columbia. Encouraged by his father, a fan of pipe music, and his mother, a Gaelic speaker, Barry Shears started taking lessons on the bagpipes at the age of 12 from Angus MacIntyre, Glace Bay, a retired coal miner and member of a well-known Cape Breton piping family, whose musical roots were in South Uist, Scotland, the family having immigrated to Cape Breton around 1826. MacIntyre introduced him to the music and playing techniques practised by other players on the island; later, Shears was encouraged to play in the more modern Scottish style, especially in competitions. Though he was a successful competitor, a workplace accident halted this and he turned to performing, research and teaching, becoming Reserve Army Pipe Major in 1980 in Ottawa, ON. He sought out the handful of old pipers who had first-hand knowledge of the old style of piping in Cape Breton and mainland Nova Scotia who were still alive in the 1980s. In doing so, he discovered an almost lost tradition of step dance piping perpetuated by individuals who had been regarded as community pipers and dance musicians. This practice of step dancing to pipers had been virtually unheard of among the contemporary step dance community and so, recognizing the wealth of material and the fragility of it, Shears began to record the stories of the older pipers as part of his Master of Arts in Atlantic Canada Studies (2003-2005, Saint Mary's University). This resulted in a collection of more than 70 hours of interviews and performances. The picture that emerged was one of a piping tradition that had given way, over the course of the 20th century, to the more popular fiddle music in places such as Inverness County, Iona, Washabuck and Ingonish. Shears has published four books – *Dance to the Piper: The Highland Bagpipe in Nova Scotia* (CBU Press, 2008), The *Gathering of the Clans Collection, Volume Two* (2001), *The Cape Breton Collection of Bagpipe Music, A collection of Bagpipe Music from Cape Breton Island and Abroad* (1995) and *The Gathering of the Clans Collection, Volume One* (1990). He has also written numerous articles and work on further publications is in progress. He has recorded on CD and for television and film and has a busy teaching portfolio especially in the U.S. *See* **bagpipe.**

shows. Variety show productions for both local and visiting audiences that showcase talent from Cape Breton, including fiddle music and dance, have been popular in Cape Breton since the 1970s. The first mass-entertainment-style performance around Cape Breton identity was *The Rise and Follies of Cape Breton.* Staged in Sydney in 1977, 1980, 1981 and 1985, this was inspired by Harry and Liz Boardmore who, through their theatre activities at Xavier College in the mid-1960s, had formed the belief that quality indigenous, live theatre could be developed in Cape Breton. *The Rise and Follies* was produced in a popular theatrical revue format in which traditional music, song and dance were combined with original sketches. Since then, a number of other such shows have been developed which showcase Cape Breton fiddle and step dance traditions, one of the earliest being the live *Ceilidh* series hosted by Winnie Chafe at the Savoy Theatre in Glace Bay from 1977-1986. The longest running of these was the *Cape Breton Summertime Revue* (1986-1998), founded by Leon Dubinsky, Max MacDonald, Stephen MacDonald, Maynard Morrison and Luke Wintermans. The *Revue* alternated fiddle music and vocals in both contemporary folk and country styles with comedic sketches. Many of Cape Breton's best known artists were engaged with the *Revue* at an early stage of their professional careers among them Rita MacNeil, the Rankin sisters (Cookie and Heather), Matt Minglewood, Bruce Guthro and Gordie Sampson. The Cape Breton fiddle tradition and associated step dance was always presented as a core element of this production, with numerous fiddle players involved over the years including Marcel Doucet, Natalie MacMaster, Tara Lynne Touesnard, Krista Touesnard, Wendy MacIsaac, Lisa MacIsaac and Howie MacDonald. Typically the show would have an extended residency in Sydney during the summer season; later it toured Cape Breton Island and eventually developed into a national touring production. In 2015, the concept was revisited as

Cast of the *Cape Breton Summertime Revue*, Marcel Doucet on fiddle, ca. 1988. Photo by Warren Gordon. 96-696-27364. Beaton Institute, CBU.

The Cape Breton Summertime Revue–The Next Generation. Other shows of this nature that have included Cape Breton fiddle music and step dance have been developed at venues such as the Louisbourg Playhouse (e.g., *Spirit of the Island, Lyrics and Laughter* and *Getting Dark Again*) and in smaller communities such as Mabou (*Mabou Jig*); Howie MacDonald produced and performed in *Howie's Celtic Brew* (2000-2001) and *Canadian Loonie* in 2002; Bob Quinn's *Cape Breton Smile* launched in 2014. A number of Gaelic-themed shows have also been produced including that developed to showcase Cape Breton culture and talent such as that presented at Expo '86 in Vancouver; in 2015 *Brigh*, directed by Tracey Dares MacNeil, showcased young talent from the Mabou area.

single jig. *See* **slide.**

Skinner, James Scott. (1843-1927). Scottish violinist and composer who was highly influential in developing fiddle music in Scotland into an art form for listening to, and away from the dance. The first major figure to emerge following the "golden age," he was responsible for the shift from the Highlands and Islands to Aberdeenshire in the northeast of Scotland as the centre for fiddle music developments in the late 19th-early-20th centuries. He informed his playing of traditional music with techniques and stylings from his classical training; his own compositions indicate his preferences for keys which previously were less common among traditional players (B flat, E flat etc.), often extending into the higher positions and utilizing many challenging techniques; he was also a fan of the variation as a form, where a single tune might be fully explored and developed to considerable complexity. In Cape Breton, Skinner's publications (e.g., *The Scottish Violinist*, 1900) were among the book collections amassed in the mid-20th century resulting in many of his tunes becoming popular among Cape Breton fiddlers. For the most part, however, fiddlers adopted the melodies only and did not attempt Skinner's stylings; one of the few exceptions to this is Dwayne Côté who does emulate elements of Skinner's style; also, a small number of other fiddle players (and pianists such as Dougie MacPhee) play some of the multi-variation Skinner tunes, such as "Tullochgorm," as an exhibition piece in their repertoires. Skinner encountered Cape Breton fiddlers while adjudicating a contest in Boston not long before his death and clearly looked on them favourably.

Skye Collection, The. The Skye Collection of the Best Reels and Strathspeys Extant, Embracing Over 400 Tunes Collected from all the Best Sources, Compiled and Arranged for Violin and Piano by Keith Norman MacDonald. Published originally in Edinburgh in 1887, and in an incomplete format in 1948, this collection was a favourite in Cape Breton, regarded as a supreme source of 18th- and 19th-century material. Many of the major fiddlers such as Angus Chisholm, Bill Lamey, Dan J. Campbell, Angus Allan Gillis and Mary Hughie MacDonald used it extensively, some of them having personal copies; Joe MacLean was known to have a copy of the second edition. Indeed, many would argue that this is the collection that defines the repertoire of those Cape Breton fiddlers of the mid-20th century. Both editions were out of print for several decades until 1979 when a new printing with all the tunes from the first edition was published by Paul Cranford. That edition remains

in print by its current publisher, Scott's Highland Services. Its 206 pages carry a foreword and the original preface from 1887, an indexed contents list which names all the tunes from the previous editions and Gaelic titles also. The tunes are grouped according to type, and numerically there are 234 strathspeys, 258 reels, 47 solos, 11 each of country-dances and hornpipes, and 10 jigs (571 tunes in total). The original sources of the tunes are acknowledged as Marshall, the Gows, Daniel and Donald Dow, Davies' *Caledonian Repository*, Lowe, Skinner, Stewart Robertson's *The Inverness Collection* (2 volumes), J. T. Sureness, Peter Milne, Cameron, Kerr, and pipe collections by Ross, Gunn and Glen; other tunes in the collection are "traditional" and common on the Isle of Skye. Some of the classic tunes from the Cape Breton repertoire are contained in this collection such as "Miss Lyall," "Stumpie," "Tullochgorm" and "Deil among the Tailors." *See* **tune books.**

Slàinte Mhath. Formed in 1995, this band enjoyed a presence on the international scene, performing at many of the most prestigious festivals including the Cambridge Folk Festival (England), Celtic Connections (Scotland) and the Tønder Festival (Denmark). Its members were Ryan and Boyd MacNeil from Sydney Mines (whose older siblings are The Barra MacNeils), Brian Talbot from Sydney and Lisa Gallant from Little Bras d'Or; Bruce MacPhee from New Brunswick was the original piper replaced later by John MacPhee from PEI; for a short time the band was joined by singer, Stephanie Hardy. Collectively, with their influences including Cape Breton, Scottish, Irish and Acadian styles, experience in the piping and pipe band field, and connections to indie rock band Slowcoaster, Slàinte Mhath inevitably produced a distinctive new sound that set them apart from other Cape Breton groups. To acoustic instruments from the wider Celtic world (fiddle, piano, highland bagpipes, border pipes, Uilleann pipes, mandolin, guitar, flute, bodhrán, percussion) they added drumbeats, hooks and sub-bass lines, intertwining traditional and contemporary instrumental tunes with elements of dance, funk and electronic music, producing a sound that attracted a young, international audience. A debut self-titled album was released in 1998, followed in 2002 by *Va*. In 2002 they were nominated for the BBC Folk Awards in the "Horizon" category, the first East Coast act ever to receive such recognition. They disbanded in 2005.

slide. Specific left-hand fingering techniques (a), (b) and (c) a tune-type, part of the jig family. **(a)** The slide is achieved by sliding the finger upward along a string from a position below that needed to achieve a particular note. In Cape Breton it first appeared in the rendering of airs by "Little" Jack MacDonald and was later adapted into dance tune performances, though only ever in rare instances. It was not until the 1980s, and influenced by Irish players, that fiddlers such as Dougie MacDonald and Natalie MacMaster made it a regular feature of their styles. **(b)** The fingered slide is a term coined by David Greenberg and first used in the *DunGreen Collection* (1996). It refers to a type of scalar ornament whereby the player arrives at a melody note via 2 grace notes, on 2 consecutive pitches and executed, along with the melody note, in a single bow-stroke. The melody note is often emphasized further by the application of vibrato, thus softening the scalar effect. It is associated in particular with the playing of Winston Fitzgerald and Jerry Holland. **(c)** Part of the jig family, the slide (also referred to as the single jig) is in 12/8 time and characterized by a marked quarter note to eighth note movement. This distinguishes it from the standard jig (sometimes called double jig) that has more regular eighth note movement. While, unlike as in Ireland, there is no specific dance associated with the slide, these tunes do appear occasionally in Cape Breton identified as a discrete tune type; Paul Cranford's *Lighthouse Collection* contains examples. More typically, however, slides are played in combination with other jigs. Indeed, the quintessential Cape Breton jig may be considered a hybrid between a double jig and a slide featuring alternating passages of quarter note to eighth note movement and regular eighth notes. The compositions of Donald Angus

Beaton in particular reveal the closeness between these two tune types in Cape Breton.

slip-jig. The most distinctive of the jig family in that is it in 9/8 metre. Although tunes in 9/8 did exist in older Scottish fiddle and bagpipe collections the slip-jig is a relatively new addition to the Cape Breton repertoire and only a few examples yet exist. Unlike as in Ireland where the slip-jig is a common dance, there is no dance equivalent in Cape Breton. To date, slip-jigs in Cape Breton tend to be added to the start of jig medleys in listening or presentational contexts; tunes of this type are played by such as Derrick and Melody Cameron, Jason Roach and Mac Morin; Paul Cranford, in his *Lighthouse Collection*, contributes two newly composed examples.

slur. Also known as a "tie," a slur involves the playing of two or more consecutive notes in a single bow stroke to create a smooth effect. It is indicated in printed sources by a curved symbol. Variations of the slur occur: **(a) straight slur.** A slur pattern involving two pitches on an up-bow, but which is distinct from a regular slur, and also from a double-up-bow pattern (which marks the end of one music idea and the start of another). The straight slur involves detaching the two pitches by decreasing the bow pressure through slightly lifting the bow after the first note is sounded; the second note is thereby given a strong accent. The straight slur is found mostly in reels and in printed sources it is indicated by a straight line following the direction of the melody, a convention invented by Scott Skinner. An extension of it, found in strathspeys and involving three consecutive pitches, is the pattern known as the up-driven bow. **(b) loop**. The loop is a symbol used in some notated sources to indicate a slurred pattern in which 2 notes of the same pitch are slurred or tied together, with the second one being given additional emphasis by applying extra pressure to, but not lifting, the bow. Named by James Scott Skinner, the loop, which in effect implies a type of "driven" bow, may occur on either an up-bow or a down-bow and is most often found at the end of a phrase, allowing the metrical pulse to be maintained over the course of a long note. The effect is also associated with a cutting pattern common in Cape Breton and labelled in the 1996 *DunGreen Collection* as the "strathspey treble." In that, where the treble is attached to the previous note of the melody with a slur, the second note on the same pitch (i.e., the first note of the treble itself) is emphasized by added accent on the bow. **[Dunlay and Greenberg 1996].** *See* **bowing style; cut; up-driven bow.**

Smith, Cheryl. (1971-). Drumkit, graphic design, Executive Director of CMIC. Born in Montréal, QC, she was drawn to the drums, as her father, Joe Smith, was a professional drummer who played with the 1960s band The Beau Marks. He and her uncle, Bob Plamondon (who played trumpet with many jazz musicians, including Oscar Peterson) encouraged her to play and she was introduced to a range of different styles and players such as Buddy Rich, the jazz drummer and band leader, who was a huge inspiration to her. She started playing at age 12 with some guidance from her father and playing along to recordings. She later played rock music and did some touring in the early 1990s with an all-female rock band, Moonshadow. Irish music was popular in her home and in the pubs around Montréal; playing this led her to discover Cape Breton fiddle music. After she began working for Natalie MacMaster as a graphic designer, she moved to Cape Breton in 2000 where she had the chance to perform with many up-and-coming young artists. Inspired by local Cape Breton drummer, Matt Foulds, she began using brushes on the snare to accompany traditional fiddle music and has gone on to tour and record with many Cape Breton musicians including Troy MacGillivray, Jimmy Rankin, Andrea Beaton, Kendra MacGillivray and Natalie MacMaster. She is the producer of an online radio show *Cape Breton Live,* two recordings from which have been released (*Cape Breton Live: Take 01* (2006) and *Cape Breton Live: Take 02* (2008)). Through her graphic design business, Out Front Productions, she works with many local and international musicians designing CD artwork and websites; this work has earned her many accolades including "Graphic Designer of the Year" from the ECMA in 2005 and 2006. In 2013, Smith was appointed Executive Director at the Celtic Music Interpretive Centre in Judique.

Smithsonian Folkways Recordings. The non-profit record label of the Smithsonian Institution, the national museum of the United States. Folkways Records and Service Co. was incorporated in 1948 in New York City by Moses Asch (1905-1986) and Marian Distler (1919-1964) with the ambition of documenting "the entire world of sound." Over 2,000 albums were released on the label including traditional, ethnic and contemporary music from around the world, spoken word, poetry, instruction and natural sounds. Folkways was one of the first record companies to concern itself with the "world music" concept; it was also the label that signed many of the artists central to the U.S. folk revival of the 1960s. As such, it grew to become one of the world's most influential record companies. The Smithsonian Institution acquired Folkways in 1987, re-naming it Smithsonian Folkways Recordings, which has maintained and built upon the objectives of the original company. Two Cape Breton recordings feature in its catalogue: *The Heart of Cape Breton* (2002) featuring various artists in live performance settings and *Cape Breton Fiddle and Piano Music: The Beaton Family of Mabou* (2004), both of which were produced by American folklorist, Burt Feintuch.

Smith-MacDonald, Dara. (1981-). Fiddle. Antigonish, NS, and Port Hawkesbury, Cape Breton. Born and raised on the mainland her parents are both originally from Inverness; she began playing the fiddle at the age of 12 and is now a regular performer at concerts, dances and ceilidhs. She teaches music at Dalbrae Academy in Mabou and teaches fiddle at the Gaelic College, as well as privately at home in Port Hawkesbury and via Skype. In 2011 she released her debut CD, *Connections.*

SOCAN. The Society of Composers, Authors and Music Publishers of Canada. Formed in 1990, but with predecessors in Canada since 1925, this society administers performing rights in music works on behalf of Canadian composers, authors and publishers who are its members, as well as affiliated societies representing foreign composers, authors and publishers. It collects licence fees, as set by the Copyright Board of Canada, from anyone playing or broadcasting live or recorded music, and distributes these as royalties to the copyright owners; it also collects and pays royalties due to members of affiliated international Performing Rights Organizations (PROs). SOCAN pays royalties to Canadian music creators and publishers when their music is performed in other countries, by virtue of reciprocal agreements with them. SOCAN administers and protects the performance rights only of its members. Royalties are applied across a variety of music uses: concerts, radio, satellite radio, television and cable, cinema, ringtones and private copying. SOCAN was created from the merger of the two earlier Canadian performing rights societies: The Composers, Authors and Publishers Association of Canada (CAPAC) and the Performing Rights Organization of Canada (PROCAN). Virtually all of the Cape Breton fiddlers who have been involved in tune composition since the late 1970s are registered members.

social. A term used widely up until the 1950s to include various social gatherings that often featured fiddle music and dancing. While at times these were freestanding events, they might also be integrated into the wider programming of a parish picnic. Socials often had a specific theme, such as "a pie social" or "a box social"; the latter in fact became popular in parts of Northern Ireland, where it was known as "the Canadian Box Social." For the box social, the women prepared unmarked boxes with picnic food and drinks; these were put on display anonymously and potential male suitors bid on them and shared the contents with the woman who had prepared it. Although pairing off was the ultimate objective of the box socials, music and dance were also important.

societies. From the mid-18th century onward, several societies devoted to the traditions and culture of Scotland emerged in Nova Scotia and in Cape Breton; some of these hosted competitive events in the form of Highland Games; others aligned themselves with the Gaelic language or had religious affiliations (e.g. the Scottish Catholic Society). None of them had a mandate specifically related to the fiddle tradition; however, the Gaelic societies in Cape Breton in particular did play a role in supporting the fiddle community and it was at the invite of such groups that some fiddlers made their first visit to Scotland.

Sommers Smith, Sally. (1953-). Fiddle, lecturer. Wisconsin, Minnesota, Illinois and Kennebunk, ME. A professor at Boston University and Wellesley College, she lectures primarily in Irish music. Her interest in Cape Breton fiddle music dates back to the early 1990s when she first heard the music of Jerry Holland. Cape Breton fiddle music became part of her academic research, particularly on changes in style and repertoire in Cape Breton and in areas where people from Cape Breton have settled, such as Boston; she has published a number of articles on the subject. Her current research uses statistical models to track the growth of preference in the broad traditional music community for tunes by Cape Breton composers.

song. Songs and singing are a part of the cultural life of many of the ethnic groups for which Cape Breton is home. Song in Cape Breton, as it connects and intersects with the fiddle music tradition, historically and contemporaneously, involves both Gaelic song and English-language song. While Cape Breton fiddle music and dance traditions have been communally claimed across a variety of community groups, the vocal traditions tend to remain separated by ethnicity, typically a consequence of language; country music, however, and Irish pub-style ballads, have seemed to infiltrate many of the ethnic groups. Song was very much intertwined with fiddle music (and other cultural elements such as storytelling, piping and dancing) in performance contexts such as the ceilidh; while in certain instances this connection remains today, over the course of the 20th century the two did find many opportunities to separate.

(a) Gaelic song. A rich tradition of Gaelic song traversed the Atlantic Ocean with the immigrants from Highland Scotland in the 18th and 19th centuries and was perpetuated via the oral tradition for generations. This is testified to in the revelation that 60% of the oral material gathered as part of the 1980s Gaelic Folklore Project across Nova Scotia's Gaelic-speaking communities was in the form of song. The fate of Gaelic song has largely mirrored the decline and revival of the spoken language. In general the tradition has been well documented, and a substantial corpus of songs published, including material that originated in Scotland as well as new material created in Nova Scotia. Cape Breton's Gaelic song repertoire falls into three broad categories: (i) songs brought to the New World by Highland and Island immigrants (ii) songs subsequently composed in Nova Scotia and (iii) songs learned from publications and from early commercial recordings. Historically, poetry and song were, in Cape Breton as in Gaelic Scotland, often considered to be one and the same thing and the repertoire includes many of the rich and poetically complex "big" songs composed by master poets or bards both in Scotland and in Cape Breton. Song was an important way of documenting life, and stories of emigration, settlement, love, loss were captured by the song-makers; sea songs, comic songs, elegies, satirical and heroic songs all featured. Even though the Gaelic song repertoire is predominantly secular, Gaelic psalm-singing involving a "precentor" delivering a line of chant and answered by the congregation responding in unison, was still being practised until the 1970s in churches in Glace Bay, Sydney, Whitney Pier and in Victoria and Richmond counties, as well as in the Cape Breton diaspora community in Boston. Particularly popular in secular practices were work songs, characterized by rhythms and a verse-chorus structure that allowed for easy participation by all involved helping lighten the task

in hand. Milling songs, originally sung by women as they repeatedly beat freshly-woven cloth against a wooden table in order to shrink it and prepare it for dyeing, were such an example; these have retained their presence as the focus of Milling Frolics which, although no longer functional (in terms of the practical preparation of cloth), nor only done by women, have become popular as participatory events for language learning and in cultural tourism. Other group performances were not uncommon throughout the 20th century; the North Shore Singers (alternatively known as The Millers), for example, was a group of between 4-12 singers, both male and female which appeared at Canadian and U.S. folk festivals and events such as the International Folk Council gathering in Québec in 1961; they also featured on various commercial recordings. The introduction of the Mòd to Cape Breton in the 1950s inspired the formation of a small number of choirs and choral groups; among these were Coisir an Eilein and the Mira Chorus which were collectives of individual voices rather than arranged choirs. A form of mouth music in which the instrumental dance tunes are performed vocally, with humorous and often nonsensical words is also found in Cape Breton: *puirt-a-beul* are fully formed entities, as opposed to the more extemporized vocal form of jigging, which involves mainly nonsense syllables. *Puirt-a-beul* played an important role in the transmission of the fiddle music (as did jigging) and have enjoyed renewed popularity in recent times as an accessible access point into the language in particular, as well as being the focus of recent scholarship (Sparling 2000, 2014).

contexts. In the past, music, song, dance and storytelling were enjoyed in shared performance spaces across Cape Breton. Performances generally involved participation by most of the people congregated who would share their skills as appropriate. Some individuals excelled across a number of art forms; many of the renowned Cape Breton bards, for example, were also among the noted fiddle players. Gaelic song was indeed the focus for collectors in the 1930s, but by the 1960s, exponents of this song tradition could

Wendy MacIsaac and Mary Jane Lamond. Photo by Riley Smith.

be heard on commercially released albums and were performing outside Cape Breton. In the 1980s, singers joined fiddlers and step dancers in the Cape Breton Gaelic Show, a showcase of the island's combined Gaelic music expressions, most notably over two weeks at Expo '86 in Vancouver. In the 1990s Gaelic song became part of the performance packages of better-known bands such as The Rankin Family and The Barra MacNeils; Gaelic song was foregrounded in other, more locally based music acts such as Dàl Riada and later, to significant international acclaim, through the collaboration of Mary Jane Lamond with fiddler Ashley MacIsaac on "Sleepy Maggie"; through Lamond's continued work the Gaelic singer has eventually came to have parity of esteem with other Cape Breton artists on the international stage. [**Campbell 1990; Campbell and Collinson 1981; Conn 2011; Sparling 2000, 2005, 2014**].

(b) English language song. Cape Breton is arguably as well known for its singers and singer-songwriters as it is for its fiddle players, and names such as the Rankin family, Rita MacNeil, John Allan Cameron, Gordie Sampson and Bruce Guthro are recognized internationally. The earliest English-language songs in Cape Breton were sea shanties and ballads, many of them from the Irish tradition. Song was a popular vehicle for protest among the coal and steel workers, and many local and international compositions appeared in the 1920s newspaper, the *Maritime Labour Herald*; this repertoire has been the focus of a recent project initiated by the Centre for Cape Breton Studies, resulting in the development of a dedicated website: protestsongs.ca. English language song has intersected with fiddle music since the 1940s when fiddle players, cognizant of the changing tastes of audiences, developed instrumental versions of songs in order to expand their repertoires to suit the performance of round dances such as waltzes. Fiddle players began to play backup for singers too as new performance opportunities presented themselves. The spontaneous creativity involved in playing back-up for a singer appealed to the creativity of particular fiddlers only, perhaps because it encouraged the opposite of the standard correctness required of the Cape Breton fiddler; many showed great versatility in this skill. Dance bands or "orchestras" presented popular song and fiddle tunes side-by-side in round and square dances in the 1950s. The songs typically represented American country or mainstream genres that had gained popularity as first radio and then television became more widespread. Song contests promoted by foundling local TV stations such as CJCB encouraged, for the first time, local songwriting; the emphasis was very much on marrying new texts with existing melodies and one of its first exponents was Charlie MacKinnon. Folk singers and singing have been steadily growing in popularity from the 1960s, but although the ballad band or folk group as a product of the U.S.-led urban folk revival was popular in Cape Breton (such as expatriate Irish bands like Ryan's Fancy, Barley Bree and The Clancy Brothers and Tommy Makem), local examples were less common. The Sons of Skye emerged in the 1970s as such a folk band. Solo artists were successful and John Allan Cameron became an internationally acclaimed leader within the folk scene, interspersing his delivery of traditional and newly composed folk songs with Scottish and Cape Breton fiddle tunes played on 12-string guitar; later, the Cape Breton Symphony Fiddlers would present the fiddle music on his TV shows while he concentrated on singing and presentation roles. While in Scotland and Ireland there was—and still is—a clear distinction

between "folk" and "traditional" performers, in Cape Breton the precedent set by the earlier dance bands and continued by Cameron allowed for a greater connectedness between the two idioms. *The Rise and Follies* show in 1977 consolidated this, bringing the urban folk singer and the rural fiddler together in the one performance space and engendering a level of understanding and interaction between them that contributed to a very specific Cape Breton performance identity. Encouraged by the fact that royalties were paid to songwriters for their new music and lyrics, a new approach was fostered and song-writing in Cape Breton developed in this context. Since the new *Follies* material was local in content, what emerged was the model of traditional fiddle music juxtaposed with contemporary folk songs. Bands such as the Barra MacNeils and the Rankins followed this template, showcasing local compositions by such as Allister MacGillivray, Leon Dubinsky and Kenzie MacNeil alongside traditional tunes and Gaelic song. The Cape Breton-centric view generated by much of the subsequent material often assumes anthem-like status among Cape Breton audiences at home and in the diaspora; while this may be a challenge for international audiences in certain places, the coincidence of traditional tunes and urban folk in performance contexts continues to be a hallmark of Cape Breton. Younger bands such as The Cottars have continued the model; so too has the folk singer-songwriter/fiddle player duo, a popular combination since the 1990s when the pub matinee became a regular performance venue. Such duos were both aesthetically pleasing to Cape Breton audiences and economically viable. Singer-songwriter Buddy MacDonald frequently paired up with a young Natalie MacMaster during that decade; more recently he has joined forces with Baddeck fiddler, Rachel Davis; J. P. Cormier is a versatile musician who is equally at home as a guitarist, singer-songwriter and fiddle player and juxtaposes both in a typical performance. Cape Breton continues to boast a thriving culture of singer-songwriters and overlap with the fiddle music does take place in specific circumstances; interestingly, however, while some bands from the

Buddy MacDonald. Photo by Murd Smith. Courtesy of Celtic Colours International Festival.

region, such as The Barra MacNeils, The Rankins and The Cottars, and some fiddler-led bands, such as that of Ashley MacIsaac, include singers (and indeed have been a platform for both Gaelic song and local compositions), the majority of such acts (including contemporary examples) include no vocals. **[Creighton 1966, 1994; MacKinnon 2009; McDonald 2012; McDonald and Sparling 2010].**

Sons of Skye. One of Cape Breton's first folk groups, it was formed in 1974, inspired by the Scottish group and National Mòd gold-medal winners, Na h-Òganaich, who had visited Cape Breton in 1973. Sheldon MacInnes from Big Pond (bagpipes, whistles, vocals, step dance) was keen to explore an alternative soundscape to the pervasive fiddle and piano of Cape Breton, one in which instrumental and vocal music might comfortably co-exist; this was something that he felt would reflect the diversity of the actual music experience enjoyed in Cape Breton homes and local communities. He teamed up with Malcolm (Malcie) MacPhee from St. Peter's (guitar, voice), Clifford Morais from Big Pond (fiddle) and, later, by Blanche (Morais) Sophocleus (guitar, vocals). The band saw itself as presenting what was, at that time in Cape Breton, a fresh new sound, albeit one that had already been popularized in Scotland and Ireland. With an emphasis on vocals, their songs in English, Gaelic and French included both traditional material and their own compositions

The Sons of Skye. Photograph from The Mac-Innes Collection.

such as "Joe Neil," named after the renowned Big Pond Gaelic speaker and storyteller. Their instrumental selections similarly included a mix of old and new material, ranging from Cape Breton favourites such as "Miss Lyall," to "Lindsey-Calum," composed by MacPhee. Morais' performances highlighted a New Brunswick/French and Irish flavour in fiddle playing that was not typical of Cape Breton. Semi-professional, the band organized its schedule around annual appearances at the Big Pond Festival and other summer events in Cape Breton such as the Whycocomagh Summer Festival. They also played in Newfoundland (1975), PEI (1979), Antigonish (1980-1981) and Halifax (1979); in 1982 they toured Nova Scotia in a tourism promotion, *Old Home Summer*. Several radio and TV appearances increased their visibility; in 1978, on CBC's *Up Home Tonight* they accompanied the step dancing of Joe Rankin of Mabou; they also had regular appearance on local CBC Gaelic shows *Island Echoes* and *Talent Cape Breton*. The Sons of Skye were broadcast on CBC Sydney's *New Year's Eve Live* ceilidh in 1976-1977 and 1980-1981. In 1979 they toured Scotland as part of a Cape Breton contingent that included Buddy MacMaster, Carl MacKenzie, Doug MacPhee, Rev. Allan MacMillan and Gaelic storyteller/singer, Joe Neil MacNeil. There the musicians played concerts, school performances, radio and TV spots and in the National Mòd competition (the first Cape Bretoners to do this), and one of their concerts in Inverness was broad-

cast by the BBC on New Year's Day, 1980. They released one LP, *Both Sides of the Water*, in 1981 with its hallmark mix of old and new, Scottish, Irish and French instrumentals and vocals; this was re-released in CD format in 2013. In 2014 the band reunited for a one-off gig at the Big Pond Summer Festival. [**MacInnes 1997**].

Soundpark Studios. Designed and built in Sydney by multi-award winning music producer and recording engineer Jamie Foulds, it opened in 2005. Having considerable experience working as a musician, producer and engineer in other studios in the region his ambition in creating Soundpark was to come up with a creative space, a musician-friendly recording studio – and with great coffee! Artists who have recorded there include: The Barra MacNeils, Andrea Beaton, Natalie Mac-Master, J. P. Cormier, The Rankin Family, Mary Jane Lamond, Pius MacIsaac, Troy MacGillivray, Glenn Graham, John Allan Cameron.

Southwest Margaree. The location of a regular Friday night square dance held at St. Joseph's Parish during the summer season. [**Addison 2001**].

Sparling, Heather. (1972-). Researcher, flute, dance. Toronto and Sydney. Currently Associate Professor of Ethnomusicology at Cape Breton University, she began research into Cape Breton Gaelic song in 1998 after interviews with both a native Gaelic speaker from Scotland and a fluent Gaelic learner from Toronto yielded completely contrasting perspectives on *puirt-a-beul*. She visited Cape Breton initially on short field trips, but relocated to Sydney in 2005 and became a Gaelic teacher in the local community, using song in her classes. Her MA and PhD research at York University dealt with Gaelic traditions: "Puirt-a-Beul: An Ethnographic Study of Mouth Music in Cape Breton, Nova Scotia" (MA, 2000); "Song Genres, Cultural Capital and Social Distinctions in Gaelic Cape Breton" (PhD, 2006). She published *Reeling Roosters and Dancing Ducks: Celtic Mouth Music* in 2014 (CBU Press). While Gaelic song and its interconnections with minority language revitalization remain her primary area of interest, she has more recently worked on a project on Atlantic Canadian "disaster" songs with Professor Joe Scanlon and Dr. Del Muise of Carleton University (disastersongs.ca), and is currently involved in a cross-Canada dance research project. She is also Editor of *MUSICultures*, the semi-annual peer-reviewed journal of the Canadian Society for Traditional Music (successor to *Canadian Journal for Traditional Music/La Revue de musique folklorique canadienne* [1996-2009] and its predecessor *Canadian Folk Music Journal* [1988-1996]). She is the Tier 2 Canada Research Chair in Musical Traditions (2013-2015).

Special Seven, The. A performing group of young fiddlers, most of them one-time students of Stan Chapman in the 1980s, which followed on from previous groups, The Next Generation and Highland Classics.

spell off. The practice of relieving the main fiddler at a dance whereby another fiddler would play for a square set thus allowing him/her to take a short break. "Spelling off" a fiddler was also an opportunity for emerging players to gain experience in playing at a dance without the pressure of having to perform for the whole night; some of the more established players would often give a younger place such an opportunity out of generosity rather than a need to take a break.

Spielman, Earl V. (1942-2005). A music scholar, music producer, video producer, conductor and orchestral arranger based in Nashville, he worked as a forensic musicologist dealing with copyright disputes. Raised in New York and, having studied music at Oberlin College, he received a PhD in musicology from the University of Wisconsin-Madison in 1975; his dissertation, "Traditional North American Fiddling: A Methodology for the Historical and Comparative Analytical Style of Study of Instrumental Music Traditions" touches on the Cape Breton fiddle tradition, the first such academic work to do so. For this his informants were John Allan Cameron, Dan R. MacDonald and Buddy MacMaster. He also published a paper

in 1972, "The Fiddling Traditions of Cape Breton and Texas: A Study in Parallels and Contrasts" (*The Yearbook for Inter-American Musical Research*, vol. 8).

Sprag Session. Formerly The Colin Grant Band, Sprag Session is a self-styled "trad-funk fusion band" that explores traditional and contemporary Cape Breton, Scottish and Irish repertoire and motifs. It has Colin Grant (fiddle), Jason Roach (piano), Darren McMullen (mandolin, guitar, banjo), Colin Clarke (drums) and Donnie Calabrese (bass). The five are from a range of backgrounds including Scottish and Acadian, and bring experience from classical music to rock. Their soundscapes and experimentation are similar to the work of Slàinte Mhath in Cape Breton and internationally by bands such as Kila, Horslips and Moving Hearts (Ireland) and Shooglenifty, Wolfstone and the Treacherous Orchestra (Scotland). Their first, self-titled album was released in 2012.

square dance. (a) a form of social dance choreography, and (b) a social dance occasion. *See* **dance.**

St. Ann's. *See* **Colaside na Gàidhlig / Gaelic College of Arts and Crafts.**

St. Francis Xavier University (St. FX) is located in Antigonish, Nova Scotia. Originally founded as Arichat College, a Roman Catholic Diocesan educational institution, in 1853 it moved to Antigonish, and became established as St. Francis Xavier College in1855. In 1866 it was given university status and awarded its first degrees in 1868; in 1897, it became the first co-educational Catholic university in North America to grant degrees to women. St. FX is associated with The Antigonish Movement which was led by a group of priests and educators, including Father Moses Coady, Father Jimmy Tompkins and Rev. Hugh MacPherson and A. B. MacDonald from a base at the Extension Department in 1928. This liberal Catholic movement focused on improving the social and economic circumstances of small rural communities in the Maritimes through such as adult education and the founding of co-operatives such as the Credit

Union; the Coady International Institute at St FX has engaged in community development globally since 1959. Today St. FX has a student population of around 5,000 mostly undergraduates, and offers courses in arts, science, business and information systems. Graduates are distinguished by their "X-rings" the distinctive emblem of the University.

Celtic Studies Department. In terms of music, St. FX has a high reputation for it's Jazz Studies degree which has been taught since 1977; a small number of Cape Breton fiddlers have graduated from this program. Cape Breton fiddle music is featured under Celtic Studies; while this has as its core the languages, literatures, and histories of Celtic-speaking peoples the program does extend into related areas such as archaeology, art, literature, folklore, religion, dance, immigration and ethnic studies as well as music. Gaelic was first taught at St. FX in 1891 by Father D. A. MacAdam, a major advocate of Gaelic; he also organized the student Celtic Society from 1893 to 1900. Others teaching Gaelic in the early 20th century there were Rev. Dr. Alexander Maclean Sinclair, a Presbyterian minister and renowned Gaelic scholar, Fr. MacPherson and Angus L. Macdonald who was Premier of Nova Scotia from 1945 to 1954; during his time in that role he advocated for a Celtic Studies department at St FX and in 1958 Major C. I. N. MacLeod from the Isle of Lewis, Scotland was employed to progress this and establish the Department of Celtic Studies. Sister Margaret MacDonell became the next Chair of the department; she established the Cape Breton Gaelic Folklore Project which enabled Dr. John Shaw to collect, through tape recording, examples of folklore from Gaelic speakers throughout Cape Breton. In 1983 MacDonnell secured funds to establish the Sister Saint Veronica (Mary Macdonald) Chair in Gaelic Studies; Dr. Kenneth E. Nilsen (1947-2012) became the first holder of the Chair in 1984. Staff numbers in the Celtic Department have grown since then, enabling an expansion in the number of courses being delivered, including an honours program in Celtic Studies; staff have included Catriona NicIomhair Parsons, a native of the Isle of Lewis (from 1993-2008); Michael Linkletter currently holds the Ben Alder Chair in Celtic Studies. Visiting faculty have included such as Gearóid Ó hAllmhuráin, scholar and musician from Co. Clare, Ireland.

resources. St. FX has a substantial collection of materials relating to Scottish Gaelic including manuscripts, monographs, newspapers, rare books, and recordings such as those made of Duncan Angus MacRae in Glengarry in 1914, by John Lorne Campbell in Nova Scotia in 1937, and the Cape Breton Gaelic Folklore Collection by John Shaw from 1977 to 1982. Housed in the Angus L. Macdonald Library on the St. FX campus much of the material has been digitized and is available online at the *Struth nan Gàidheal* / Gael Stream website: http://gaelstream.stfx.ca/.

St. FX. Celtic Music Society. A significant part of the St. FX experience is the vibrant student social scene and the Celtic Music Society is part of this. Formed in the 1980s this is a student-run organization and has hosted various fiddle music events in a number of locations around Antigonish over the years.

strathspey. (a)A solo step dance and (b) a popular tune type. **(a)** The strathspey dance, extemporized or choreographed, has been retained in Cape Breton to the present day, and is always followed by the reel, with the transition from one to the other marked by an increase in tempo and anticipation, and is achieved seamlessly. Strathspeys are also danced in the formation known as the Scotch Four.

(b) As a popular tune type in the Cape Breton fiddler's repertoire (the largest tune type group following reels and jigs) it is found in both dance, listening and presentational contexts where it is almost always followed by a reel. A slow variant of the strathspey also exists, found in listening contexts only; this generally segues into the dance strathspey as part of a larger medley or group configuration. The name is associated with the course of the river Spey (strath meaning valley) that drains the Scottish Highlands northward, and as a tune the strathspey came to prominence in the 18th century; while it has widely been considered

Calum Crubach

strathspey

traditional
arr: P.S.C

an indigenous form, some scholars postulate that it is, rather, "a Gaelic response to contemporary social dance developments" (Newton 2014). The term came into use first in the 17th century in the context of a "strathspey minuet" and then as a style of dancing the reel during the 18th century, first appearing in the Menzies MS (ca. 1749) in relation to "The Montgomerie's Rant," described as "a strathspey reele." It first appeared in print in James Oswald's *Caledonian Pocket Companion*, vol. iii, in 1751, then in Robert Bremner's *Collection of Scots Reels or Country Dances* ca. 1760; the first title page to include the term was in Daniel Dow's 1775 publication. The term also appeared in relation to various existing tunes – e.g., strathspey minuet, strathspey waltz and strathspey quadrille – thus suggesting it referred to a style rather than a tune type, but eventually it established itself as a discrete tune type.

The strathspey is in common time and has a tempo slower than that of the reel. It is characterized by consistent use of dotted rhythms – both long-short and short-long – the latter known as "the Scots snap." In Scotland, many strathspeys composed from the 19th century onward are further marked by runs of triplets at the end of parts. In Cape Breton the strathspey has been retained as a staple of the repertoire, fundamentally associated with dance, but utilized in the same manner even when dance is not part of the performance context. The dotted rhythms, while prominent and pervasive, are articulated in a less pointed

fashion than is the practice in Scotland. Each individual beat is marked by a strong foot tap (generally using the flat of the whole foot or the heel). In performance, the strathspey generates the sensation of an increasing sense of propulsion with the tempo gradually accelerating through the last turn (and perhaps earlier than this) toward the point of release as the strathspey transitions into a reel. Cape Breton dancers and audiences alike are finely attuned to this moment as the crux of the medley, and they respond accordingly by clapping, whooping, calling out praise and such. The "slow strathspey" was introduced during the mid-20th century as a slower, more lyrical version of the dance strathspey, while maintaining much of the dotted rhythmic features. Although most Cape Breton fiddlers include a substantial number of strathspeys in their repertoires some have recordings that feature few or no strathspeys. This is trend is evident in the most contemporary releases – perhaps because the strathspey is (arguably) the least familiar of the tune types to the non-Cape Breton audiences which these fiddlers are targeting commercially. [**Newton 2015**]

structure of Cape Breton music. An individual piece of music in the Cape Breton fiddlers' repertoire is called a "tune" as distinct from a "song" that has associated lyrics. Typically, a tune consists of 2 parts, each of which has 8 bars, referred to as simply "first part" and "second part," or "A" and "B turn." Each 8-bar part is generally repeated before the second part is played, thus creating a 32-bar round or iteration in AABB format. Exceptions are "single" tunes where the parts are played once only and not repeated, leading to a 16-bar round (AB); only rarely in Cape Breton are longer tunes involving multiple parts of more than 32 bars found (e.g., AABBCCDD). Even in these instances, however, the same 8-bar structure applies. In Cape Breton, a full tune iteration is known as a "turn" or, occasionally as a "round"; step dancers will often request a specific number of turns/rounds of a strathspey to be played before the reel in a performance context, indicating that this terminology has a shared understanding. Typically, the first part of the tune will be in the lower register while the second part is melodically distinct, being largely in the higher register. Within each tune, the individual 8-bar sections (in both the A and B sections) can be further divided into 4 phrases of 2 bars each, a simple structure that is adhered to, irrespective of the tune type. The melodic material generally follows a simple formula where the idea is stated, responded to, stated again and closed off. This formula, which underpins the entire repertoire of tunes, lends itself favourably to the aural transmission process, since by understanding the tune in terms of 2-bar phrases, the ear can easily identify where material is repeated and the tune can be logically pieced together. In performance, an extended group or medley of tunes is assembled which may, or may not, include a number of different tune-types depending on the context. *See* **groups.**

Stubbert family of Point Aconi. A family from Cape Breton's Northside area known for its fiddle playing, step dancing and composing, the Stubberts are also often associated with the Irish music tradition in Cape Breton. **Robert Stubbert** (1923-2008) was born to parents Peter and Margaret (MacQueen) Stubbert who were both musicians themselves. He was influenced by fiddle players Jack Walker and John R. Fraser and later by Joe Confiant who introduced him to Irish tunes and stylings. Others of his brothers also played, Lauchie (1926-1988) who lived in Alder Point,

a noted fiddler, while Earl and Emerson played fiddles, mandolins and guitars. Robert married Regina (Roland) Stubbert, a piano player and step dancer. Of their children, Brenda became a well-known fiddler and composer while Byron and Wilbert also played. The Stubbert home was frequented by fiddlers such as Johnny Wilmot, Joe Confiant and Winston Fitzgerald; other local fiddlers such as Johnny Walker and John R. Fraser would also visit and play tunes. Robert Stubbert is recognized for making a contribution to the Irish music of the Northside and was a significant influence on fiddlers such as Kyle MacNeil. [**MacGillivray 1981**].

Stubbert, Brenda. (1959-). Fiddle, piano, step dance, composer, teacher. One of the very few females of her generation in Cape Breton to pursue fiddle playing in public and as a career, she step danced from a young age and started taking piano lessons at seven; she was 10 when she turned to the fiddle just before the modern revival took place. By the mid-1970s she was one of the young players featured at concerts and events across the island with her peer group of Jerry Holland, Donny LeBlanc, Howie MacDonald, Kinnon Beaton, John Morris Rankin and Dave MacIsaac. She was with a group of fiddlers who performed for Queen Elizabeth II in Halifax in 1976, and was part of the group that performed the "Cape Breton Concerto" in New York in 1982. Brenda Stubbert has 7 albums: *Tamerack'er Down* (1987); *House Sessions* (1992); *In Jig Time* (1994); *Some Tasty Tunes* (1999); *Music All Around* (2003); *Different Strokes with Different Folks* (2011); and *Endless Memories (2008),* which won the East Coast Music Award for Roots/Traditional Solo Recording of the Year in 2009. A composer, her tunes have been published in two collections as part of the Cape Breton Heritage Series: *Brenda Stubbert's Collection of Fiddle Tunes* (1994) and *Brenda Stubbert–The Second Collection* (2007). She has recorded a number of these tunes, as have others such as Buddy MacMaster, Natalie MacMaster and Carl MacKenzie. "Brenda Stubbert's," a reel composed in her honour by Jerry Holland, has become a popular session tune in

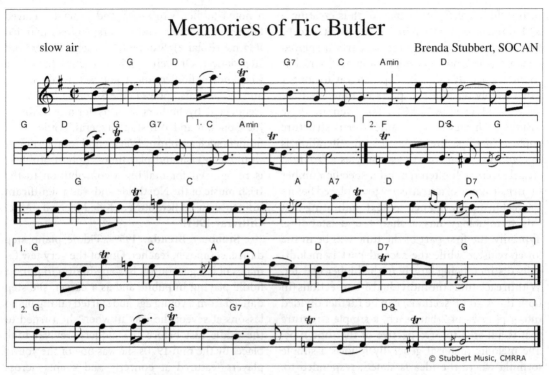

Memories of Tic Butler

slow air

Brenda Stubbert, SOCAN

© Stubbert Music, CMRRA

Cape Breton, Irish and Scottish musics. Stubbert works exclusively by ear and has never used music notation. She has taught fiddle at the Ceilidh Trail School of Celtic Music and at the Gaelic College, as well as at workshops internationally. Performing as a fiddler and piano player she has toured with other Cape Breton musicians participating in events such as Celtic Connections in Glasgow, NAFCo in Aberdeen, and Éigse na Laoi in Cork, Ireland, in 1993. At times labelled as an Irish-style fiddler, this is something of a misnomer, for while Irish tunes do feature in her repertoire, and she does occasionally simulate particular ornaments such as rolls, her style is Northside Cape Breton where Scottish and Irish styles intersect, creating a distinct voice within the Cape Breton tradition. Brenda's daughter, Tracey is a step dancer. [**MacGillivray 1981**].

— ≈ —

Brenda Stubbert's Collection of Fiddle Tunes. 131 traditional and original melodies. Published in 1994 and edited by Paul Cranford,

this is Volume 2 of the *Cape Breton Musical Heritage Series: Contemporary Performer.* Its 56 pages, which include images by Carol Kennedy, has tunes presented as (a) strathspeys and reels, hornpipes, marches and slow airs, and (b) jigs. Within these categories tunes are individually numbered, arranged by key, and with an alphabetic index. There are 50 jigs (including two in 12/8) and 49 reels, 12 marches, 11 strathspeys, 6 hornpipes, 1 clog, 2 airs and 1 slow strathspey. Pipe tunes feature here, notably among the reels and marches; 75 of the tunes are composed by Brenda herself including the well-known "Rannie MacLellan's reel"; 19 are by other composers – ranging from 18th-19th-century Scottish (Robert MacIntosh, William Marshall, James Walker, James Scott Skinner) to more contemporary Shetland (Aly Bain), Irish (Francie Byrne, Finbar Dwyer), Irish American (Liz Carroll), American (Frank Ferrell) and Cape Breton itself (Wilfred Burke, Paul Cranford, Winston Fitzgerald, Piper Alex MacDonald,

Sandy MacLean, Rannie MacLellan, Lauchie Stubbert, Robert Stubbert, Otis Tomas, Johnny Wilmot). The balance of the music is traditional Scottish, Irish and Cape Breton. An introduction, acknowledgements, explanation of terminology, comment on keys and scales, list of composers, discography of Stubbert's recordings and selected tune notes provide useful contextual information.

— ≈ —

Brenda Stubbert–The Second Collection. A Totally New Compilation of Traditional and Original Melodies (complete with piano chords arranged by Melissa Emmons and Brenda Stubbert). A tune-book published in 2007, edited by Paul Cranford, this is Volume 6 of the *Cape Breton Musical Heritage Series: Contemporary Performer.* Its 80 pages have 161 tunes presented in 3 sections as (a) marches, strathspeys and reels, (b) jigs, and (c) waltzes, laments, slow airs and piano solo. Within these categories, tunes have an alphabetical index and are numbered and arranged according to key. There are 72 reels, 40 jigs (including one in 9/8 and two in 12/8), 22 strathspeys, 13 marches, 9 slow airs and 1 each clog, hornpipe, waltz, lament and piano solo (the latter, effectively, an air with melody and bass). While all of these represent Brenda Stubbert's repertoire at the time, the sources are varied. Some are newly composed Cape Breton tunes, many of them by Brenda herself; there are traditional and contemporary Scottish, Irish and Shetland tunes from fiddlers and other instrumentalists including a number of tunes from the bagpipe repertoire. Also included are tunes by 18th- and 19th-century composers such as George S. MacLennan, William Ross, James Scott Skinner, Simon Fraser, John McColl, William Martin, Nathaniel Gow, J. Abercrombie, Joseph Lowe, James Morrison, Daniel Dow, James Stewart Robertson, J. MacKenzie and James Fraser. More recent compositions included are by Tommy Basker, Donald Carrigan, Maybelle Chisholm, Cameron Chisholm, Tommy

Coen, Ronnie Cooper, Paul Cranford, Joe Doucette, Gordon Duncan, Frank Ferrell, Jerry Holland, Dan R. MacDonald, Gordon MacLean, John MacLean, Rannie MacLellan, David Papazian, Larry Parks, Paddy O'Brien, John Morris Rankin, Dave Richardson, Jimmy Shand, Robert Stubbert and Otis Tomas. 60 of Stubbert's own compositions are also included, and variations (sometimes in extended form) are also suggested for certain tunes; this renders the volume a veritable who's-who sampler of quite contemporary Cape Breton and Irish composition. Contextual information on the music and some playing instruction are provided in notes that also illuminate individual tunes.

— ≈ —

style. The term refers to the complete set of characteristics that identify a music's or a musician's particular sound. Collectively, shared elements of style among a cohort of players – for instance, Cape Breton fiddlers – contribute to the wider definition of a local or regional style, in this instance a Cape Breton style, which is distinct from other styles such as Scottish, Irish or Down East. An individual style may be thought of as the realization of the greater generic style which, while incorporating the stylistic universals of the idiom, also shows personal discrepancies (i.e., an interpretation of the generic style). Conversely, the starting point for consideration might be the individual style, and the macro or generic style may be viewed as the result of combined individual styles, where sufficient commonalities are achieved in order to justify a collective categorization.

defining style. Style is defined in relation to the elements recognized by the practitioners of a music as being crucial to the creation and identification of its "sound." These are the elements referred to in making qualitative judgements of performance; choices are made as to how and when these are used, ultimately shaping the style and, crucially, also permitting distinction between individuals even when a broad set of common conventions are in place. These variables, and choices made in regard to their implementation, are the defining factors in shaping any given style.

Several overarching features shape the Cape Breton sound and style and make it clearly distinguishable from other related fiddle traditions, but these are broad generalizations within which there is considerable flexibility and difference from player to player and at any given time. While many combinations of musicians and instruments were created (as circumstances and availability dictated), the fiddle and piano emerged over the course of the 20th century as the core of the Cape Breton sound, a pairing which was often the basis of bigger ensembles. The piano in its own right also played a key role in shaping the fiddle sound over the years as it evolved into the established partner of the fiddle; as the piano's style became increasingly busy, the fiddle style adapted to compensate for this and stylistic elements in tone, intonation, tempo, bowing, left-hand embellishments, articulation, phrasing, drive and technical ability were reimagined accordingly. The association between fiddle music and dance has informed both the presentational, listening and dance contexts for Cape Breton music resulting not only in a specific set of needs as regards tune choice, but also in terms of style affecting choices of tempo, articulation, accentuation, ornamentation and drive. The relatively strict approach to the interpretation of the melodic line, particular settings, and to the conventions implied in playing a tune "correctly," paired with the flexibility afforded individual flavour, all contribute to identifying the style of the Cape Breton fiddler.

local styles. Cape Breton music and culture might easily be mapped over the decades to show the geographic areas in which the fiddle – or other instruments, song or dance – were prominent from the time of the first settlers. The first documented clusters of fiddle players were in Inverness County, including (but not confined to) the Mabou Coal Mines area. By the second half of the 19th century, Mabou Coal Mines had consistent and significant numbers of fiddlers, many of whom had emerged as influential "masters." There, a set of stylistic criteria was consistently employed, and there was a distinct repertoire,

influenced by the dance. The Mabou Coal Mines style was largely perpetuated by the extended Beaton family but, also in Inverness County, other communities such as Broad Cove Marsh, Mabou, Glenora and Glenville had clusters of fiddle players from the 1850s-1890s; South West Margaree was also known for fiddle players during this era, mainly the Gillis family, as was Meat Cove, further north. In Victoria County, the parishes of Christmas Island and Cooper's Pond had their own fiddle clusters, much of them contained within particular families. A case study of the Iona area conducted by the Highland Village and published in *Naidheachd a'Chlachain/The Village News*, identifies 17 discrete communities within that area, and names individuals who contributed to the music, song and dance from the first known settlers to more recent times. Of these, some communities are revealed as strongholds of Gaelic song, bagpiping and, later, accordion; only 4 show no indication of the fiddle being present; others such as Cain's Mountain, Gillis Point and, in particular, Washabuck, show strong interest in the instrument. In Cape Breton County, Johnstown and Terra Nova were known for fiddlers (although never in substantial numbers nor over extended periods of time), or for fiddlers who stayed in those communities long enough to create the impression of a local style. Many other pockets of style existed around the island; in Bras d'Or, for example, the intersection of Acadian and Irish musics led to the development of a distinctive sound and repertoire.

evolution of a Cape Breton style. This varied, mosaic soundscape was further influenced (likely from the outset and, increasingly so, as time progressed) by a myriad of other elements. Travelling fiddlers, for example, were among the first to share new tunes and techniques (acquired on the island or on their travels in North America) among geographically dispersed fiddle communities; pipers, particularly those involved in the military, influenced the fiddlers' repertoire and style; the advent of the gramophone, radio and, later, television offered further opportunities for exposure to other influences; as roads and transport facilities improved, musicians themselves began to travel beyond their immediate communities to picnics, concerts and dances. While industrial Cape Breton was a melting pot of cultures, even after an influx of other immigrants in the early 1900s, Catholic Scottish Gaels were the primary ethnocultural group working the mines; their cultural components such as the music were still a source of pride among the miners and steel workers (who maintained connections with their friends and families in rural Cape Breton) in this urban setting and added to a strengthening culture in that area. Establishment of a strong co-operative movement on the island also capitalized upon, and helped to foster, cooperation and community-mindedness among island residents. These factors helped to construct the regional cultural identity of the island. Post Second World War, the sense of an island-wide fiddle community was well established and certain fiddlers had a dance circuit that criss-crossed the island and brought them to Cape Breton communities in Boston and Detroit. "Scholarly" fiddlers shared and critiqued newly acquired tune books; newly composed tunes were hand-written and mailed to certain fiddlers around the island whose renditions would ensure their acceptance into the canon and "star" fiddlers emerged, setting new standards and establishing new directions for the fiddle sound. Of paramount important, however, was the individual sound of each player. The 1970s revival further consolidated the sense of a coherent Cape Breton fiddle sound and identity; thus, while individual voices continued to be critical reference points, the notion of localized, community clusters of style was no longer significantly in evidence. This is not to suggest that a singular sound dominated at this point; on the contrary much individual discrepancy was evident. But rather than being geographically situated, this could now be distinguished based on chronology (old vs. new), ethnic origin (e.g., Acadian, Irish), and function or context (dance vs. listening-to players). This resonated across the island as well as further afield, among the displaced Cape Breton communities across Canada and in the U.S. It might be argued that it was as a result of the 1970s revival (which saw significant changes to the Cape Breton tradition, most relevant, perhaps a clearly articulated sense of identity and ownership of the music) that the notion of local, community styles or regionalism disappeared, as the focus shifted to presenting Cape Breton fiddle music as a convincing, robust, cohesive tradition. From the 1990s onward the consolidation of a discrete fiddle music identity ensued; homogeneity in terms of style was increasingly supported as the Cape Breton fiddle style was successfully integrated into the global Celtic music world. In the early 21st century, the concern for some is that Cape Breton music will lose its individual identity as a dominant pan-Celtic style takes over here as elsewhere; the recent trend of branding the music as Gaelic seems to be, to some degree, a response to this and an effort to reclaim and foreground a bone fide heritage. At the very crux of the issue surrounding the large-scale embracing of an homogenous sound and practice is the very real threat to what was, for generations, the very life-blood of the Cape Breton fiddle tradition: the individual discrepancies that gave each player his/her own unique voice in the tradition. Of course younger players experiment by pushing the boundaries of their inherited style as they become influenced by sounds and practices from elsewhere; many have, in previous generations, crossed the un-verbalized yet clearly recognized line beyond what is regarded as authentic Cape Breton into new territory. Such experiments (more or less standard practice in all musics), despite causing heated debates when they occur are, however, generally considered as contributing to the dynamic of a tradition if those driving it are fully aware of and have been grounded in that tradition and are aware of where the boundaries of integrity lie. It is only when players are not fully versed in that tradition (in this instance, Cape Breton) that this becomes problematic, as they do not have a solo aesthetic sense or point of reference to return to. (*With* GG, PMD). **[Bickerton 2013; Doherty 1996; Dunlay and Greenberg 1996; Frank 1986; Graham 2006].**

Sullivan, Dan. (1875-1948). An American piano player and entrepreneur of Irish descent who led numerous ensembles, among them The Columbia Scotch Band and The Caledonia Scotch Band, both of which had Cape Breton fiddlers "Big" Dan Hughie MacEachern and Charlie MacKinnon along with banjo and percussion. He was married to Ella Grant from Nova Scotia who had connections with many prominent musicians in the Antigonish area. Sullivan's influence on the evolution of the Cape Breton piano style has never been fully explored and recent research has suggested that this is likely to be more significant than has previously been acknowledged. *See* **Caledonia Scotch Band; Columbia Scotch Band.**

Sutcliffe, Brian. (1934-). Radio producer and host. Halifax and Dartmouth, NS. His career in radio started in 1971 with CBC Cape Breton, and although he started presenting a current affairs show by 1974 he had become the key figure involved in the recording of local musicians for radio. Bert Wilson, the manager of CBC Cape Breton, was keen to support Cape Breton talent and enabled Sutcliffe to develop this remit. Twice a year Sutcliffe and his team held auditions for musicians, many of them fiddlers, to identify existing and emerging talent; they then held more than one hundred recording sessions each year and broadcast the material on shows such as *Talent Cape Breton* and *Island Echoes.* In the 1980s Sutcliffe produced *Archie Neil's Cape Breton,* which aired for 4 seasons; he also produced 4 New Year's Eve shows that were broadcast nationally. He worked at CBC Cape Breton until 1988 when his position was cut. He was relocated to the CBC in Halifax where he enjoyed a second career as the host of the popular *Weekend Mornings* show, emerging as a recognized radio star in this own right. He retired in 1998 and took up fiddle lessons. *See* **CBC.**

Sydney Scottish Violins. A fiddle group based in the Sydney area started up by Sandy MacInnis and later led by piano player, Lila Hashem. Originally intended as an alternative to the CBFA, primarily for reasons of geography, its membership included, in their later years, such as fiddlers Joe MacLean and Dan Joe MacInnis.

T

Tamarac Records and Publishing. A record label set up in 1996 to record and produce the artistic work of Scott Macmillan and his collaborations with featured guests. It recorded *The Minnie Sessions, Volume 1*, which had Scott Macmillan with Brian Doyle, Doris Mason, Rodney MacDonald and Jon Goodman; volumes 2 and 3 were issued in 2014 with performers such as Jimmy Rankin, Lennie Gallant, Jerry Holland, Bernard Felix, Lisa MacIsaac and Janet Munson.

teaching. While teachers of fiddle music have been recognized within Cape Breton from the 19th century, the teaching of Cape Breton fiddle music in formal group classes did not happen until the 1970s, a product of the revival of interest in the fiddle tradition. Since then opportunities to learn the musical style and repertoire are available in many formats, including one-to-one classes, groups, summer schools and workshops, not only in Cape Breton, but internationally and on-line. Many Cape Breton fiddlers engage in teaching to greater or lesser extents to supplement their performing career. Teaching methods and approaches vary from teacher to teacher; music literacy skills are mostly (but not always) taught; target outcomes are solely performance related and, (although it was not always the case), competition and exams play little ot no role for those learning to play in the Cape Breton style.

approach. In Cape Breton, as in other folk traditions, the practice of teaching fiddle music was, and continues to be, primarily aural, where the emphasis is mostly on learning by ear; however, music notation – specifically as a source of repertoire – has long played an important role. Since the establishment of group teaching as a means of passing on the fiddle music, various forms of notation (standard staff notation, tablature, alphabetic) have also been used as a pedagogic tool. For most, however, learning to play the fiddle was based on self-motivation; it involved careful listening to other players at ceilidhs and dances or to others jigging the tunes orally, followed by efforts to replicate that sound based on trial and error. Tales abound in Cape Breton of younger children sneaking the fiddle off the wall or out of its case to practice in secret; occasionally a family member might offer some guidance; but learning to play was more typically a solo endeavour. There is evidence of peripatetic teachers – travelling or itinerant pipers and fiddlers – dating back to the 19th century; such individuals were often musically literate, many of them having spent time away from Cape Breton where they had access to formal music tuition; typically they moved from community to community, staying with families and teaching younger members to play and to read music. Trained music teachers – locally acknowledged as "professors" – also ran music classes from at least the 1800s; these were mostly based in urban centres and they would offer tuition primarily in classical music, although a number also taught Cape Breton music, some in rural areas. Often those learning to play the violin would have attended such classes, learning classical music techniques and applying these, later, to their practice of Cape Breton fiddle tunes. The Gaelic College offered music and dance tuition from the 1930s; however, in its early years it focused primarily on competition piping and Highland and Scottish country dance, and fiddle was not included until much later. It was, indeed, *The Vanishing Cape Breton Fiddler* documentary (1971) that indirectly led to the formation of group classes for fiddle; these were often organized by

Buddy MacMaster teaching at The Ceilidh Trail School of Celtic Music. Courtesy of Janine Randall.

and supported by the local clergy (who provided fiddles in some instances) or by the newly formed CCB (a precursor to today's CBFA), which subsidized the teachers. John MacDougall and Stan Chapman were among the first to teach these classes; with no real precedent, they were charged with developing their own teaching methods. Much of Chapman's early work in this regard has been documented in a PhD dissertation by Virginia Garrison (1985). By the 1980s, fiddle classes were well established at the Gaelic College and other teaching programs and music schools emerged across the island; Cape Breton fiddlers were also being invited to deliver workshops, first in North America, later in Europe, at various festivals and fiddle camps. Today, the majority of Cape Breton fiddlers (and piano players) feel confident in offering instruction and many maintain a busy teaching schedule, some year round, others just in the summer months. Classes are offered privately by a small number of tutors (among them music teachers from the U.S. who have settled in Cape Breton and embraced the local music traditions, e.g., Marianne Jewell (1948-2014) from Milwaukee, WI, and Melissa Emmons from Lawrence, MA). While courses such as those at the Gaelic College remain popular, occasional workshops and events such as the Buddy MacMaster Fiddle School, which takes place during Celtic Colours, are also found. At third level, fiddle music is also taught as part of a program offered at CBU (and has been since the 1970s); Stan Chapman and Kyle MacNeil are the fiddle teachers on the faculty. Despite the plethora of opportunities now available for young people to learn, a recent concern emerging is that fewer locals are in fact taking up the fiddle; in 2015 Féis Cheap Breatuinn was introduced as an initiative to engage youths in music and other elements of culture; education is an element of this. Ironically, Cape Breton fiddle music today is being embraced by fiddle students the world over; besides increased access to workshops with fiddlers (in person at events worldwide or via Skype) it is entirely possible to learn Cape Breton tunes and the style without ever visiting the island. However, few resources have been de-

Stan Chapman, one of Cape Breton's foremost fiddle teachers. Photo by Victor Maurice Faubert.

veloped for teaching Cape Breton fiddle; fiddlers Francis MacDonald and Natalie MacMaster have released the only fiddle tutorial videos/DVDs to date; Tracey Dares has done similar for piano; the Gaelic College is launching a new online instruction initiative in 2015. Of course, as is the case in most traditions, much of the integrity of a performance is connected to the context, and for that, nothing can replace experiential learning. **[Garrison 1985; Graham 2006].**

teams. Fiddle duos have held a long and popular position in Cape Breton's music history. Initially a means of adding volume (in pre-amplification days) the pairing of fiddles became a core part of the earliest band formations; in some instances this was expanded out to 3 or more fiddles. While the practice became less common in listening settings in the mid-20th century, it was maintained for longer in dance contexts. As the music industry encroached on Cape Breton, the opportunity for star players to emerge led to a focus on the solo fiddle; this was further cemented by changes in the style which supported cleaner, more precise playing, something more easily achieved in a fiddle-piano combination. However, the twin, fiddle concept has never quite disappeared and in more recent times it has become a popular option in presentational performance settings and the core of a number of current band line-ups. *See* **bands.**

television. The Canadian Broadcasting Corporation opened Canada's first TV stations in 1952, beginning with CBFT out of Montréal and CBLT in Toronto. Customer affordability was an issue initially as receivers were expensive and reception could be poor or absent in rural areas where electrification was still incomplete even by the 1960s. Yet TV rapidly became a big part of Canadian life and attracted significant investment. The first station to broadcast in Nova Scotia was CJCB-TV on October 9, 1954, with CBC following on December 20 of that year. ATV (now CTV Atlantic) came on air in 1961. A number of community stations have also been established (TELILE, formerly CIMC-TV out of Isle Madame, now based in Arichat, Nova Scotia, and CHNE-TV in Chéticamp) as well as an online TV channel, www.livestream.com/capebretonlive.tv, which streams much of the Celtic Colours festival.

impact. The arrival of television in the second half of the 20th century affected the Cape Breton fiddle music tradition in many ways. While it did, to a degree, draw audiences – particularly young people – away from live music events there were many positive aspects to its impact. Besides creating opportunities for having their music broadcast to new and substantial-sized audiences, CBC, for instance, played a significant role in professionalizing the Cape Breton fiddle community, to the advantage of its members. Previous negative experiences in dealing with record companies had left many fiddlers disillusioned with the music business. However, by insisting on signed contracts and respecting copyright, publishing, performance and broadcasting laws, CBC effectively forced Cape Breton fiddlers to get their houses in order by registering themselves and their music with the relevant agencies; in return they were appropriately compensated for their involvement in any CBC production; the first instance of this formalization happened in relation to the CBC *Ceilidh* show of the early 1970s. That network contributed generally to the awareness of the Scottish tradition in Canada, much of which related to Nova Scotia and Cape Breton. It was responsible for the watershed *Vanishing Cape Breton Fiddle*r documentary of the early 1970s that was the catalyst for sparking a revival in the fiddle tradition. There was also an impact on the style and repertoire as increasingly the spontaneous live programming of the 1950s evolved by the 1970s into highly choreographed, carefully rehearsed and edited productions, all with strict time limits imposed. Cape Breton fiddle ensembles such as that associated with the *Ceilidh* show emerged, as did the Cape Breton Symphony, a group that continued to have a performing and recording career for a number of decades. TV also contributed to the creation and rise of looked-up-to or "star" performers; the TV special – typically a show focusing on a single artist, with invited guests – played a major role in this. Often through transatlantic partnerships between broadcasters, television has also contributed to the raising of the profile of the Cape Breton fiddle tradition in general and to individual players. Cape Breton musicians have been promoted on the New York WLIW21 network, in Scotland on BBC and the Gaelic station BBC Alba, and in Ireland on RTÉ and TG4. Since the 1970s, Scottish radio and TV have produced documentaries filmed in Cape Breton. More recently, Cape Bretoners have been recorded for broadcast at events in Scotland such as Celtic Connections that is filmed annually by the BBC, or have been invited to participate in documentaries being filmed there and in Ireland. **[MacNeil and Wolfe 1982; Thompson 2003, 2006; Graham 2006; MacInnes 1997]** *See* **CJCB-TV; CBC-TV; CTV.**

tempo. The speed at which a tune is played. In Cape Breton this is considered (in synchrony with other aspects of performance practice) to contribute to the lift or drive of the music, the whole combination being referred to as timing. However, tempo may also be considered in isolation and has been the focus of much discussion with regard to its role in the changing sound of the Cape Breton fiddle. It is generally considered that the tempo of the music has increased over the decades; distinction between slower and faster tempos is often synonymous with older and newer styles respectively; typically, younger players are chastised for their inclination toward faster tempos. This habit (incidentally one that is not confined to Cape Breton) has often been challenged, however, and scholars such as Dunlay and Greenberg (1996) and Graham (2006) have provided analyses to contradict such generalized assumptions. Nevertheless, a noticeable increase in tempo choices can be observed in recordings from the 1940s and 1950s; Angus Chisholm's playing in particular (typically for listening to rather than for dancing to) created a new marker in terms of accepted tempos. Other factors, such as changes to the requirements for the local dance practices and the separation of music and dance through the establishment of distinct listening platforms for the music, also played a part in allowing fiddlers to experiment with tempo; this was less feasible when music was tied completely to the dance. Increased exposure to related music traditions also played a part in encouraging players to alter tempo and, at home, the participation of other ethnic groups brought in new interpretive elements, including a preference for faster tempos. A frequently quoted comment in Cape Breton music circles is one by Dan R. MacDonald, which draws a parallel between musical tempo and driving a car: "if it's played too fast, you miss the scenery," this suggesting that with excessive tempo the nuances of expression (and listeners' interpretation) are compromised. However, choices in tempo remain a matter of personal taste and are shaped by the contexts and conditions of an individual fiddler's experience.

tempo acceleration within a tune group. A characteristic of Cape Breton fiddle music is the gradual increase in tempo within a single group of tunes, as it moves through tune types such as the air, march, strathspey and reel. The energy of the tune group is propelled to a degree by the gradual increase in tempo; the point of transition from strathspey into the reel is a climactic one and is achieved by a gradual acceleration in tempo throughout the strathspey, becoming more marked in the final bars before the release into the reel; the point at which the strathspey changes into the reel is essentially a subtle one although the greater the tempo change involved, the more conspicuous the change of tune type will be. Typically at this point the reel tempo is stabilized over the course of a few bars, although some players like to allow the reel to continue to accelerate through the remainder of the medley or group. **[Doherty 1996; Dunlay and Greenberg 1996; Graham 2006].** *See* **timing**.

Thompson, Marie. (1954-). Freelance TV director (CBC), researcher. Ottawa, ON, and Halifax, NS. Thompson approached the Cape Breton fiddle tradition with a specific interest in the CBC's role there during the 1970s fiddle revival. Her MA thesis, "The Fall and Rise of the Cape Breton Fiddler: 1955-1982," was done in 2003 at Saint Mary's University; she has published further on this topic and has also produced two CBC-TV documentaries leading from her research: *The Fate of the Fiddle* (2000) and *The Wakeup Call* (2001). Her work with CBC occasionally brings her back in contact with the Cape Breton fiddle tradition, for instance, in 2011 when she produced *The Fiddle Tree* documentary piece on the Otis Tomas project for *Land and Sea*.

Tic Butler Memorial Award, The. Established in 1996 in memory of "Tic" Trotsky Butler (1919-1995), guitar player and singer who, with his wife, Emily, was known for his love of music and the hospitality he extended to local Cape Breton and visiting artists. A few months after his death a memorial concert was staged in Centre 200 by

Fr. Greg MacLeod and Brookes Diamond. Titled *A Grand Ceilidh–A Celebration of the Life of Tic Butler,* it was hosted by Denis Ryan and Donnie Campbell with music directors for the event Richard Burke and Fred Lavery. Among the many featured acts were The Barra MacNeils, Cookie, Heather and Raylene Rankin, Tommy Makem, Natalie MacMaster, The Men of the Deeps and Howie MacDonald; the concert also featured a reunion of folk group, Ryan's Fancy. Proceeds were used to set up a trust out of which the following year's award was established, offering $1,000 annually to a Cape Breton artist. Recipients have included: Marc Boudreau (1996); Jennifer Roland (1997); Michelle Boudreau Sampson (1998); Beatrice MacNeil (1999); Kimberley Fraser (2000); Colin Watson (2001); The Cottars (2001); John Allan Cameron (2005); Donnie Campbell (2006); Rachel Davis (fiddle, 2007). The award was discontinued after 2007.

time signature. A convention used to specify the number of beats per bar and the type of beats involved. In notated music the time signature appears at the beginning of the piece, immediately following the key signature. This is in the form of a symbol (such as "C") or stacked numerals (such as 3/4). In Cape Breton fiddle music the most used time signatures are simple forms such as (2/4, 3/4, 4/4, 2/2) and compound (6/8, 9/8, 12/8) forms.

timing. A general term used in Cape Breton to denote both tempo (the speed at which a tune is played) and the related components of metre, phrasing, accent and articulation (i.e., the complex infra-rhythmic structure which generates swing, lift or drive within the fiddle music). Good timing is aspired to by all Cape Breton fiddlers, and is one of the criteria most commonly referred to in the appraisal of an individual's style. Certain players have been noted over the years for having especially good timing, among them Duncan MacQuarrie, Joe MacLean, Winston Fitzgerald and Buddy MacMaster. [**Dunlay and Greenberg 1996; Graham 2006**]. *See* **drive; tempo.**

Tomas, Otis. Luthier, fiddle, composer. Goose Cove, Cape Breton. Originally from New York state, he has made Cape Breton his home since the 1970s, one of a small number of Americans to do so around that time. As a luthier he specializes in individually crafted violins and guitars; he has also made mandolins, harps and various other stringed instruments totalling more than 600 to date. Local fiddlers including Brenda Stubbert, Dougie MacDonald and Paul Cranford play Otis Tomas fiddles, although his instruments can be heard around the world. Tomas is also a fiddle player and prolific composer of tunes, some of which – such as "The New Land" (waltz) – have become popular in the Cape Breton repertoire. His project, *The Fiddletree,* brought together his skills as an instrument maker, tune maker and player, and resulted in a published book and CD; it was the focus of a number of performances at Celtic Colours in 2011. In 2013, another recording emerging from the project, *The Unfathomable Menagerie,* was released. Tomas, along with his wife, Deanie Cox, is a member of the group, Rocky Shore. [**Caplan 1991**].

— ∽ —

Fiddletree Collection, The: Fiddle Tunes Composed by Otis A. Tomas. A 2001 collection that is the precursor to the extended *Fiddletree* project. Presented with two tunes per page and photographs of instruments which were made by Tomas from a single tree – "the fiddle tree." It has 104 pieces, most of them reels, but with jigs, airs, hornpipes, waltzes, polkas and what is referred to as a slip-reel. Tunes are alphabetically indexed and identified by type, and all include chords.

— ∽ —

Fiddletree, The. A 2011 monograph by luthier Otis A. Tomas that has 34 tune transcriptions among its 178 pages of text and photographs (by Carol Kennedy); a CD carries the performed melodies. This work is the outcome of a unique project – *The Fiddletree* – which documents the transformation by Tomas of a single maple tree into an ensemble of music instruments: fiddle, viola, cello, guitar, harp and mandolin, all of which feature on the accompanying CD played by an international collective of musicians performing new music composed by Tomas. The tunes—Carolan-style airs, waltzes, march and reels—are presented in 14 groups or sets, most of them arranged for 2 to 6 parts, with chords. Many of the tunes had been published before as single-line melodies in *The Fiddletree Collection* (2001).

— ≈ —

Topic Records. The world's oldest independent record company, it was started in England in 1939 by the Marxist Workers' Music Association, with the aim of releasing gramophone records of historical and social interest. The label began issuing revivalist folk music in 1951 and skiffle and American music in the middle of that decade on account of these forms representing the art of the working classes and of poor, marginalized or otherwise disadvantaged members of British society; by the mid-1960s, Topic was established as *the* revivalist recording label in Britain and Ireland. Tony Engle took over as music director in 1973 and, by the 1980s, a noticeable shift had taken place in favour of English performers, folk and traditional, an emphasis that continues today. Topic's engagement with Cape Breton dates to the late 1970s when two LPs were produced by John Shaw (a Scottish Gaelic scholar then based in Cape Breton), Rosemary Hutchinson (later McCormack) (Gaelic speaker and broadcaster, also based in Cape Breton at the time) and Tony Engle himself. Entitled *The Music of Cape Breton,* volume 1 (1978) focused on the Gaelic tradition and included a small number of instrumentals among the Gaelic song selections. Musicians included Mike MacDougall (fiddle), Dan Joe MacInnis (fiddle), Alex Francis MacKay (fiddle), Joe Burke (harmonica), Charlie Dobbin (mandolin) and Alex MacNeil (mandolin); the singers were Mrs. Rod MacLean, Lauchie MacLellan, Tommy MacDonald, Malcolm Angus MacLeod and the North Shore Singers. Volume 2 presented the *Cape Breton Scottish Fiddle Tradition* (1978) and

included John Willie Campbell, Mary MacDonald, Mike MacDougall, Dan Joe MacInnis, George MacInnis, Alex Francis MacKay, John Neil MacLean and Theresa MacLellan on fiddles with various accompanists on piano.

Toronto. While Boston was the main émigré destination for Cape Bretoners in the early decades of the 20th century, by the 1950s it was more common to head west to Toronto. Cape Breton dances were organized there by Angus MacKinnon on an occasional basis, generally held in an old school house with John L. MacDonald of Foot Cape often the fiddle player. In the early 1960s MacDonald initiated a regular dance in Toronto in partnership with Bill MacDonald, a fiddle player from Middle River; they rented a hall and hired a piano player, Kay Jamieson, to accompany them. These dances were held on Saturday nights and were attended by upwards of 200 hundred expatriate Cape Bretoners. Bill MacDonald then established his own Friday night dance, but the Saturday nights continued with music by John L. MacDonald and Sandy MacIntyre. Together they continued the dances for more than a decade, doing all the organizing and management, plus playing individually and as a team. Liberty Hall was the long-standing venue, and a prompter was always involved; later they moved the dance to St. Mary's Hall, sometimes featuring Donald Angus Beaton, Winston Fitzgerald, Angus Chisholm and Cameron Chisholm. Johnny "Washabuck" MacLean and his wife were other prominent figures on the Toronto Cape Breton scene, organizing dances, hosting parties and extending generous hospitality to new arrivals from home to the city; they also recorded much of the music performed at their home and were part of the robust home-tape network, sharing this material among fiddlers and enthusiasts. Sandy MacIntyre, a prominent teacher of Cape Breton fiddle music in the city, took an active part in forming the Scottish Social Club in Toronto, which held down-east dances bringing Cape Breton fiddlers in to play.

House parties or ceilidhs were an important part of the Cape Breton community's social life in Toronto and though no money was involved, many noteworthy players were keen to participate. For instance, when Doug MacPhee arrived in 1955 he developed a music partnership with Donald MacLellan and together they often played for many hours at the MacLellan home and or at that of Glen and Vera Shaw from Prince Edward Island. Other Cape Bretoners who were prominent on the house party scene in the city included Johnny Wilmot (who moved there in 1959), and Kay Beaton (a piano player from Foot Cape who, having a young family, was not hugely active but who, before MacPhee's arrival, was one of the few piano players there). Ontario had many Cape Breton players at that time, among them Johnny "Washabuck" MacLean, and "Little" Jack MacDonald, and a well-known party character, Hughie "Shorty" MacDonald. While, unlike as in Boston, the Cape Breton scene in Toronto was quite contained, players did engage with some Scottish musicians living in the area, such as the violin player, Ron Gonnella. Today Cape Breton music is still found in the city and Sandy MacIntyre continues to play and teach there; the vibrant session scene finds Cape Breton fiddle music presented alongside Irish music.

Touesnard sisters. Born to parents Adrian and Tena (Mombourquette) Touesnard, Tara Lynne, Krista Lea and Rhonda were raised in River Bourgeois, Richmond County, Cape Breton. They were taught fiddle in their younger years by Winnie Chafe, whose mix of classical and Cape Breton music cultivated in them an interest in many styles and traditions and a versatility that was manifest in their individual performance interests.

Touesnard, Tara Lynne. (1972-1994). Fiddle, step dance. A member of various classical quartets and orchestras, she played a lot of down-east music and was a member of a Scottish country dance band in Wolfville, where she was pursuing a music degree at Acadia University; she also competed in various contests, winning the Maritime Fiddle Championship on four occasions and being invited to take part in the Canadian Grand Masters Fiddle Contest in Ottawa. She joined the cast of the *Cape Breton Summertime Revue* in 1993, where she demonstrated her ability to play tunes and step dance at the same time, and to improvise backup for songs. She recorded her first album, *Heritage*, in 1988, followed by *Fiddle Fingers* in 1990 and *Bowing the Strings* in 1992. She was the recipient of many community, academic and provincial awards, including a Cultural Life Award from the Cultural Federation of Nova Scotia (1991), and first prize in the traditional category of the national Give Me A Song contest, sponsored by *Today's Generation* magazine and Roland Canada (1991). She won the Terry Fox Achievement Award in November 1990 and was subsequently featured on the YTV show *Canada's Best* in 1991. Tara Lynne died in a car accident in 1994 while on her way to perform on a morning TV show. Her family released a CD, *Let's Never Say Farewell: Tara Lynne Touesnard* (2004), which has tracks from her previous albums, musical tributes from the cast of the *Summertime Revue*, and performances by her sister Krista and her brother-in-law, Denis Lanctot, who composed the air "For the Love of Tara." Her memorial in music initiatives include an annual Thanksgiving weekend concert in River Bourgeois, The Tara Lynne Touesnard Memorial Award which is offered annually to student musicians by the Maritime Fiddlers' Association, and the Tara Lynne Touesnard Memorial Bursary in Music, which is awarded annually to a music student at Acadia University. In her home area she was honoured too in the year following her death by the renaming of the River Bourgeois Community Hall as The Tara Lynne Community Center.

Touesnard, Krista Lea. (1976-) Fiddle. A member of the cast of the *Cape Breton Summertime Revue* (1993-1995) Krista has been living in New Brunswick since 1994 after attending University there. She has released a solo CD (*A Little Taste of 'er,* 1999), recorded with the band Brollachan, and and is featured on several compilation albums with the *Summertime Revue*. Previously the director of the Violin Studio in Fredericton, she currently works as a music specialist in the school system there; a group of her students,

Celtic Discovery, has toured Scotland, Ireland, France, Cape Breton and Quebce. Touesnard performs as a solo artist and with piano player, Kyle MacDonald, originally from Troy, Cape Breton.

transmission. The passing on of the music traditions through performance, teaching, observation and other methods such as recording and broadcasting. *See* **teaching.**

travelling fiddlers. Travelling, wandering or itinerant fiddle players, also referred to locally as "knockabouts," have been part of the Cape Breton tradition up until the 21st century and have made a significant contribution in many ways. Typically bachelors and with no regular employment, the musicians would spend anything from a few days to an entire winter with a family; their presence often prompted music activities such as house parties, ceilidhs and dances. Often the visiting musician took on the role of music tutor, teaching young family members. Music literacy skills were also taught by many of these travelling players, and many new tunes were composed by them, often as a means of thanking their hosts. Much repertoire was disseminated across the island by these musicians, particularly in the earlier part of the 20th century, as they were the only ones travelling great distances and experiencing music as it was being practised in different areas of Cape Breton and beyond. While it is easy perhaps to view the travelling players in a somewhat romantic light, it is important to note that they were not necessarily fully embraced by the community at all times. Some of the important names are Donald John "The Tailor" Beaton of Mabou, Allan MacFarlane (piper/fiddler) who stayed in the Margaree area, Joe LeBlanc, who was from Margaree Forks but travelled Down North regularly, Angus MacDonald from Margaree Harbour whose "route" took him only about 10 miles from home, "Little" Jack MacDonald who stayed with John Archie MacDonald and his family in Detroit and Jimmy MacInnis of Big Pond who stayed with the Chisholms of Margaree Forks for a year at one point. Others included Ronald Gillis from Marga-

ree, Johnny "MacVarish" MacDonald from Broad Cove Marsh; Gordon MacQuarrie, Ned MacKinnon, Vincent A. MacLellan, Archie Gwinn, Peter MacPhee, Simon Cremo and James D. Gillis (pipes and fiddle). Perhaps the most legendary of the travelling fiddlers was Dan R. MacDonald, the noted tune composer, while Sandy Boyd, a piper who greatly impacted on the fiddle music, also lived this lifestyle.

tributes and Testimonials. *See* **awards.**

triplet. Three consecutive notes, played within the value of a quarter note which may be bowed (a) in a single slur to create a smooth effect or (b) separately, with varied emphasis, to add rhythmic interest.

tune books. The published tune books relevant to the Cape Breton repertoire are (a) Cape Breton fiddle and piano books (b) Scottish fiddle and bagpipes books and (c) Irish, Canadian and American books. Today, although fewer hard-copy tune collections are consulted by the younger fiddlers (who are more likely to use online resources such as www.thesession.org), they remain an important part of the Cape Breton fiddle-music story.

(a) **Cape Breton books**. While a 2/4 bagpipe march composed by Cape Bretoner Archie A. Beaton of Mabou Coal Mines, "The Charlottetown (Cape Breton) Caledonia Club" was published in Davis Glen's *Collection of Highland Bagpipe Music, Book 7*, in Edinburgh, Scotland ca. 1905, and another march, "The New Year," by Malcolm H. Gillis published in Book 11 of that series in 1908, it was not until 1940 that Cape Breton fiddle tunes were published. This happened in a dedicated collection – *The Cape Breton Collection of Scottish Melodies for the Violin* – issued by Gordon MacQuarrie; it contained 152 compositions by MacQuarrie himself and other fiddlers and pipers. It was several decades before the next Cape Breton fiddle publication came about, although the intervening years are marked by an exponential growth of interest in Scottish tune-books. It was in 1975 when the first volume of the music of Dan Hughie MacEachern was issued; from 1980 on, there was a significant rise in this activity, which continued steadily over the next decades. In total, some 40 Cape Breton tune-book collections have been published to date by both fiddlers and piano players; more than half have been published by the artists themselves, sometimes through a publishing company which they have set up (e.g., Scojen, Trolleymac, August MusicWorks, DunGreen); others have been published posthumously either privately by a fiddler-composer's family (e.g., the MacEacherns), a family publishing company (e.g., Cameron Music Sales, publishing Dan R. Mac Donald's material) or a family friend (e.g., Mike Farrell's publication of Jimmie MacLellan's music). Kinnon Beaton, with 4 published tune collections to his credit, has the most substantial output to date for one musician. The focus on self and local publishing very much reflects the position of Cape Breton fiddlers regarding ownership of their material. Other publishers who have been involved are from Nova Scotia (Casket Printing and Publishing, Antigonish), Upper Canada but with a connection to Cape Breton (e.g., Brownrigg) or the U.S., including music publishing giant Mel Bay, who published both the Natalie MacMaster and the John Campbell collections. The latter two collections, along with another by Jason Little, represent the few instances where outsiders to the Cape Breton tradition have been responsible for compiling and editing its music. Cranford Publications has brought out several Cape Breton fiddle collections to date as well as disseminating some of the volumes self-published by other artists through its mail-order catalogue (Silver Apple News) and its website, and publishing other relevant material such as Scottish and Irish collections. The majority of the more recent publications acknowledge the importance of accompaniment in Cape Breton and provide chords; a small number specifically indicate accompaniment for guitar rather than for piano. In addition, the majority of books (although by no means all of them) are linked to a particular recording/recordings by the author/artist. *See* **under individual authors; Select Bibliography.**

Traditional Celtic
VIOLIN MUSIC
of
CAPE BRETON

139 transcriptions
complete with
historical and musicological annotations
and descriptions of the performance practice

by Kate Dunlay and David Greenberg

The DunGreen Collection

(b) Scottish books. These have a variety of approaches and instrumental foci which contribute much to understanding preference, taste, initiative and opportunity in the assembly of Cape Breton tune repertoire. This group of collections concerns both music for the fiddle and music for bagpipes.

fiddle music. Notated manuscript collections (e.g., by David Young, George Skene) and printed collections emanating from London (e.g., by Playford, John Young) were part of the music landscape in Scotland by the early 18th century. But after 1726 the music publishing business expanded greatly in Scotland with volumes generally compiled by semi-professional, musician-composers who were well versed in both classical and folk fiddling styles. In 1743 James Oswald began publication of a series of 12 books, *The Caledonian Pocket Companion*, which contains the first documented evidence of a strathspey reel. Then Robert Bremner, between 1757 and 1761, published *A Collection of Scots Reels or Country Dances (With a Bass for the Violoncello or Harp-*

sichord) in fourteen 8-page sections, the earliest Scottish publication to concentrate on dance music. The next wave of activity saw tune composers come to the fore in publishing material, among them Daniel Dow, Alexander MacGlashan, John Riddell, Robert MacIntosh, William Marshall, Neil Gow and his many sons. In the 19th century, a new generation of collectors and/or composers included Simon Fraser, Charles Grant, William Christie, Joseph Lowe and Alexander Walker; these were followed by Peter Milne and James Scott Skinner, all of whom produced a substantial body of material. This was followed by a trend for republishing collections of tunes no longer in print (e.g., by John Glen, James Kerr, Keith Norman MacDonald and James Stewart Robertson). In Cape Breton it is known that the *Skye Collection* was being used in Inverness County by 1920; fiddler, Ned MacKinnon (1876-1926) of Christmas Island used James Scott Skinner's books.

Further deductive information is found in the 1930s, in that recordings by the Inverness Serenaders, Angus Chisholm, Dan J. Campbell and Angus Allan Gillis included repertoire likely gleaned from printed sources. After the 1940s things are clearer for, following the connections made by Dan R. MacDonald in Scotland, Scottish books were mailed across the Atlantic. *The Skye Collection* was one of the most sought after of the Scottish collections and 6 copies are known to have arrived in Cape Breton in a single shipment; fiddler Mary Hughie MacDonald was known to have had a section, but not all of, the *Skye*; it was later reproduced in Cape Breton (1979) and enjoyed a level of sale which was testimony to the high regard in which it was already held among the music community. Other Scottish books reprinted by Cranford and eagerly bought include Captain Simon Fraser's 1816 *The Airs and Melodies Peculiar to the Highlands of Scotland and the Isles* (reprinted 1982 and 1986) and Alexander Walker's 1866 *A Collection of Scottish Strathspeys, Reels, Marches &c.* (reprinted 1991). Other Scottish collections popular in Cape Breton included those of James Scott Skinner, especially *The Scottish Violinist* (1900), the *Kerr's Collections*

(1-4) and various publications by the Gows and by William Marshall. Books such as those by Mozart Allan, Angus Cumming, John Glen, J. Murdoch Henderson and Alexander MacGlashan were also popular, as was the 1960s edition of *The Athole Collection* and volumes from the 1970s and 1980s by Ron Gonnella, James Hunter, David Johnson and Alastair Hardie. No more recent Scottish music publications appear to have infiltrated the Cape Breton tradition to any significant degree. In 2013, Paul Cranford published *The Cape Breton Scottish Collection*, Volume 8 of *The Cape Breton Musical Heritage* Series, which is comprised exclusively of older Scottish tunes that have informed the Cape Breton fiddler's repertoire.

— ≈ —

Cape Breton Scottish Collection. A Compilation of 318 Melodies; Scottish Music Arranged from the Cape Breton Fiddle Tradition. Published in 2013 and edited by Paul Cranford, this has 128 pages of Scottish tunes from 18th- and 19th-century published collections; they are presented in settings generated in performance by Cape Breton fiddlers. It is music from these old printed sources which has, from the 1940s onward, contributed to a body of music which is regarded as defining the Cape Breton sound. Thus the book is dedicated by its editor to "all the generous Cape Bretoners who have assisted my study of older Scottish music especially to Doug MacPhee who for the past 36 years has guided me to the best sources." The *Scottish Collection*' is 38% traditional material, with the rebalance by known composers. The latter vary in the scale of their output, and consequently in their personal impact on the forging of a music tradition. Among them, from the 18th century are Neil Gow (17 tunes), Daniel Dow (9), Robert Petrie (8), Malcolm MacDonald (6), John Riddell (5), John MacGlashan (3), and one each by John Anderson, John and Peter Bowie, Isaac Cooper, Andrew, George Jenkins, Lucy Johnstone and J. MacDonald. In the 1800s, James Scott

Skinner is most prolific—26 tunes—with Simon Fraser (12), Nathaniel Gow (10), Joseph Lowe (9) and Duncan MacIntyre (6); five each are from William Christie, Peter Milne and William Shepherd; four from Charles Grant; three from Duncan McKerracher, and Alexander Deas; two from William Morrison, Robert Baillie, Williamson Blyth. Neil Gow Jr., Alexander MacKay, Donald Grant, Alexander Given and Edwin Christie; and single tunes from A. W. Doig, Frank Gilruth, William Hardie, James Henry, Alexander Laybourn, William MacDonald, James McQueen, A. Menzies, Archibald Morrison, Mrs. Robertson of Ladykirk, John Smith, Captain L. Stewart, Charles Stewart, Miss Magdalena Stirling, Alexander, James Warden and James Watt. The six 20th-century tunes are from J. Murdoch Henderson. Among all of these, just 3 are by women, reflecting the phenomenal change in fiddle uptake and composition patterns today: Lucy Johnstone in the 1700s, Mrs. Robertson of Ladykirk and Miss Magdalena, Stirling, in the 1800s. Much information is supplied on the music, which is set out in sections: "The Evolution of Strathspeys and Reels," "Airs, Marches, Strathspeys and Reels" and a "Jig" section. Overall there are 119 reels, 34 6/8 jigs, 19 strathspeys, 19 slow strathspeys, 14 slow airs, 8 "marching airs," 6 hornpipes, 4 marches and 1 slip jig, quickstep, schottische and song air, in addition to two tunes which fall between strathspey and reel. One tune – "My Ain Kind Dearie O" – is noted in both standard and scordatura tunings. Tunes are grouped by key, with chords by pianist Mario Colosimo. Much material valuable to players' communication from the stage is given too, such as a section on "Memory and Key Change," on "Sources" and "Composers." Each tune is numbered and alphabetically indexed.

— ∾ —

bagpipe music. The Highland bagpipe has played a significant part in the Cape Breton fiddle narrative with many musicians demonstrating proficiency on both instruments and the sharing of tunes in both directions. Collections of pipe tunes were among the earliest printed sources to arrive in Cape Breton and, particularly during the 1940s and 1950s, those who sought Scottish tune collections were as likely to purchase a pipe book as a fiddle book. Winston Fitzgerald, for instance, had bagpipe publications such as those by, J. Wilson, William Ross and James Robertson as well as the Glen Collection and *The Glendaruel*. Joe MacLean's books included the Ross Collection, College of Piping publications and parts of several books of bagpipe music. Other piping collections popular among the fiddle music community were *The Scots Guard* (Books 1 and 2), the *Edcath* and the *Logan* collections.

— ∾ —

Cape Breton Highland Collection. A Compilation of 228 Melodies; Scottish Pipe Music in Cape Breton's Fiddle Tradition. Published in 2015 and edited by Paul Stewart Cranford; chords arranged by Mario Colosimo. This is volume 9 of the Cranford Publications' *Cape Breton Musical Heritage Series*. In the preface Cranford gives a short history of the connection between the fiddle music and piping in 19th-century Cape Breton; sharing of tunes between both instruments was common and indeed many individuals played both pipes and fiddle. Pipers too played an important role in introducing music literacy to the fiddle players, with many pipers learning this skill in the military. The preface continues with a guide to using the collection for both pipers and fiddlers and a number of examples illustrating the methodology of the editor. The tunes are arranged into three sections: (i) 2/4 marches, strathspeys and reels, (ii) jigs and 6/8 marches, and (iii) polkas and hornpipes. Marches are the predominant tune type (67), followed by reels (62) and jigs (52). There are 35 strathspeys, 5 polkas, 4 hornpipes and 3 6/8 marches. A small number of less common tunes are included such as slip-jigs; there are some airs or marching airs and some tunes where optional interpretations are given (e.g., jig or quickstep and march or quickstep). The tunes are grouped according to key. The composers index lists those whose tunes are included; there is also an alphabetical tune index listing all tunes in the collection plus piping tunes that appear in other Cranford publications. Information concerning the source of individual tunes is found throughout the collection. Tunes are given with suggested chords; some stylistic suggestions are also made such as fourth-finger markings; variations are also outlined in certain tunes. The collection also includes a number of photographs of historical significance.

$- \approx -$

(c) Irish, Canadian and American tune book collections. Increased access to published collections from traditions beyond the Cape Breton-Scottish axis has led to the infiltration of a wide variety of tunes into the repertoire. The origin of these sources varies from Ireland to Shetland to American and Canadian old-time traditions. Important among these have been Irish music collections such as Captain Francis O'Neill's *The Music of Ireland* (1903) and *The Dance Music of Ireland* (1907), which arrived in Cape Breton in the early 20th century via Irish America. Other Irish collections found in Cape Breton include those of P. W. Joyce (1909), Francis Roche (1911) and later publications such as those by Ed Reavey and Jerry O'Brien. Popular Canadian books included those published by Allen Ward (1956), Ned Landry (1959), Andy de Jarles (1959), Don Messer (1981) and Graham Townsend (1971). American collections include David Brody's *The Fiddler's Fakebook* (1983), R. P. Christenson's *The Old-Time Fiddler's Repertoire* (1973) Peter Kennedy's *The Fiddler's Tune-Book* (1951), Hazel G. Kinscella's *Folk Songs and Fiddle Tunes of the USA* (1959) and Miles Krassen's *Appalachian Fiddle* (1973). *Ryan's Mammoth Collection/Cole's One Thousand Fiddle Tunes* (1883/1940), an eclectic collection of Irish, English, German and American tunes, was also popular. Visits by fiddlers from the Shetland

Islands to Cape Breton prompted an interest in tunes from that region, following which collections by Ronald Cooper and Tom Anderson, among others were introduced. Cape Breton fiddlers' compositions have been included in generic collections also, such as in Ed Whitcomb's *Canadian Fiddle Music*, Vols. 1 and 2 (1990, 2001). *See* **collecting; note reading; tune books.**

tuning. In Cape Breton the fiddle strings are typically tuned to G,DAE' as is standard violin practice. However, in the past, various alternative tunings might be employed, known as scordatura.

"In tune" or "out of tune"? As regards standard G,DAE' tuning there have been shifts in practice and perception over the course of the 20th century. Equal temperament (where the spaces between the notes are equal whole-tones and semi-tones throughout the scale, as on the piano) has been more the standard only from the mid-20th century on. This came about as the piano gradually became an equal partner with the fiddle in creating the Cape Breton sound: its accompaniment became busier, leading to the fiddle sound being made cleaner, thinner, with fewer discords, dissonances and drones which would clash with the piano's precision. Consciously pioneered by Winston Fitzgerald and Angus Chisholm – for different reasons – this cleaner sound included a reassessment of intonation, aligning the fiddle to the equal temperament of the piano, and thus setting a new standard. Subsequent generations therefore have a Western-standard, clear perception of something being in tune or out of tune. A concession is made for older players however, for their "out of tune-ness" was an inherent part of their handed-down style and, far from being sub-standard, was actually the product of conscious choices connected with, for example, the natural scale used in bagpipe tunings; Cape Breton fiddlers were, in fact, playing to a different set of values in tuning compared to the classical violinist or today's contemporary fiddler. This shift in attitudes to tuning over time is shared with other traditions. In Ireland, for example, Richard Henebry in 1903 postulated that Irish music was

based on a small number of unique scales or modes, as distinct from the modern tempered scale. Tuning, and perceptions thereon within the Donegal fiddle tradition, is currently the topic of a PhD dissertation at Ulster University, Northern Ireland, by fiddler, Aidan O'Donnell. [**Doherty 1996; Dunlay and Greenberg 1996; Graham 2006**]. *See* **intonation; neutral notes.**

tuning room. A 20th-century Cape Breton term for the industry-standard, multi-purpose dressing and/or catering room backstage at concerts where musicians and other artists prepared for their performance and from which they entered the stage. A less formal benefit of the tuning room was that it provided the artists with a private venue to congregate, socialize and often share a few tunes, away from the eyes of the audience. Typically, refreshments are provided and often a piano (previously acoustic, now electric) is in place. Often great music emerged from the tuning room to the extent that it was, at times, a hardship for artists to have to go on stage; this was particularly the case during the heyday of the outdoor concerts from the 1970s. Today, Green Room is the more common title for this important zone; that at the late-night Festival Club at Celtic Colours continues the tradition of being a supreme venue for music-making—a true musicians' space.

two-step. A 2/4 time, polka-like social dance-form and associated tune-type popular in the first half of the 20th century; it was rarely played by Cape Breton fiddlers, but was catered for by the other musicians who played for round dances while sharing the stage with fiddlers who played for square dances. *The Cape Breton Fiddlers Collection* (2007) carries one of these—"Jacinta's Two Step"—composed by Jacinta MacKinnon.

U

UCCB. University College of Cape Breton. *See* **Cape Breton University.**

Uilleann pipes. *See* **bagpipes.**

unison. *See* **double stop; doubling.**

University College, Cork (UCC). In 1993 University College Cork, Ireland, hosted a festival of Cape Breton music. It was organized by Liz Doherty (who had begun doctoral research on Cape Breton music in 1991), traditional music lecturer Mícheál Ó Súilleabháin, and the UCC Irish Traditional Music Society. The festival was one of a 5-part series of events under the banner of Éigse na Laoi, which included *Fiddlesticks–Music from Donegal and Shetland* (1991), *Dear Old Erin's Isle–Irish Music in America* (1992), *Across the Water–Irish Music in England* (1994) and *The Gathering* (1995). These festivals were each recorded by Nimbus Records and released as a series of CD albums, one of which is *Music from Cape Breton Island* (1995) with 15 live tracks and extensive liner notes. The festival took place over 5 days on the UCC campus and in various city locations; it included concerts, workshops and a ceilidh in Cork City Hall that featured the visiting Cape Breton musicians and dancers with Irish musicians who included such as Seán Maguire and Donal Lunny. At this, hundreds of dancers alternated Irish set dances with Cape Breton sets that had been taught at workshops over the previous days. The Cape Breton artists in the program were Harvey Beaton, Hilda Chiasson, Dwayne Côté, Tracey Dares, Goiridh Dòmhnullach, Jerry Holland, Dougie MacDonald, Howie MacDonald, Jamie MacInnis, Dave MacIsaac, Carl MacKenzie, Buddy MacMaster, Natalie MacMaster, Paul Mac-Neil, John Morris Rankin, Brenda Stubbert. In addition, a large group of Cape Bretoners, as well as a number of the Boston-Cape Breton community, attended. This event was significant in that it was the first such extensive showcase of Cape

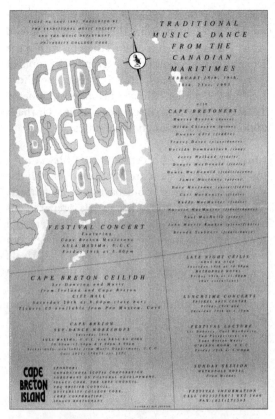

Breton music in Ireland and indeed, predated such as Celtic Connections and the normalising of regular international performance opportunities.

Up Home Tonight. A television series involving Cape Breton fiddle music, it was conceived and written by its host and music director Gordon Stobbe and produced by Barry Bramhill. It ran for 8 seasons on CTV from 1982 until 1989 when, despite high ratings, it was cancelled. The show followed a format that had previously been successful on radio, using a set that replicated the informal kitchen or house party. *Up Home Tonight* became one of the most popular shows on Maritime television, and was also carried by other stations in Canada. The musicians were from Nova Scotia, New Brunswick and PEI, with well-known artists from Ontario and the U.S. also taking part; Cape Breton performers included such as The Rankins, The Barra MacNeils, Natalie

MacMaster, Buddy Mac Master, Ashley MacIsaac, J. P. Cormier, Dave MacIsaac, Eddy Poirier, Howie MacDonald, Jerry Holland, the Pellerin brothers and the Warner Sisters. *See* **CTV; television.**

up-driven bow. A four-note bowing pattern associated with the playing of Scotland's Neil Gow that is commonly used in Cape Breton, particularly in strathspeys. It involves a sixteenth-to-dotted eighth note and a dotted eighth note-to-sixteenth note with notes 2 and 3 usually being on the same pitch. Over the 4 notes a down-bow followed by 3 up-bows is used. Each of the up-bows is separated, the first 2 by lifting the bow and the second and third by stopping the bow, although maintaining contact with the strings. Additional pressure is applied to the second of the up-bows to emphasize the rhythm and add the driven effect; the third note is also driven and played in a staccato fashion, so that the complete pattern is quite distinct within the melodic line. In *The DunGreen Collection* (1996) the up-driven bow is interpreted and annotated as the combination of 2 shorter bowed patterns, the loop and the straight slur. While a prominent feature of older styles, this bowing pattern, though still used, is less common today. A further interpretation of the up-driven bow known as flying spicatto involves playing the three up-bows in an exaggerated, detached fashion. [**Dunlay and Greenberg 1996**]. *See* **bowing style.**

V

Vanishing Cape Breton Fiddler, The (*VCBF*). A television documentary produced by CBC in the early 1970s, intended by its creators as a lament for a tradition they perceived to be in decline. Although local lore suggests that the documentary was inflammatory, a more measured view (as taken by Marie Thompson in her academic writings on the topic (2003, 2006)) is that the message was specific, local and well informed; in any case, it generated an unexpected response from within the fiddle community, resulting in a revitalization of the music that has shaped the path of Cape Breton fiddle music for subsequent generations. The brainchild of freelance broadcaster, Ron MacInnis, who acted as writer/commentator on what was, in fact, his first TV documentary; it was produced and directed by Charlie Reynolds, and filmed by a small crew on location in Cape Breton during late July and August, 1971. While it appears that some members of the fiddle community had opted not to be interviewed for the show, fiddler-composer Dan R. MacDonald was a prominent figure and his involvement lent considerable weight to it. *The Vanishing Cape Breton Fiddler* simply stated, and sought to prove, that few young people were learning to play the instrument in Cape Breton and thus the tradition was in imminent danger of disappearing. The idea had previously been explored in radio format for CBC's *Maritime Magazine* show; however, the medium of TV appeared more powerful, although the program did not attract any notable attention ahead of its broadcast; indeed there is no evidence of any advance promotion. It was aired, likely on CJCB-Channel 4, the CBC affiliate in Sydney, between Christmas and New Year, 1971-1972; it was rebroadcast nationally later that year. The documentary did not provoke an immediate outcry; rather, a small but powerful reaction was ignited creating a movement that gained momentum over several months. The view of a number of individuals, among them Frank MacInnis and Fr.

Eugene Morris, was that it had been inaccurately represented, that the Cape Breton fiddle tradition was not in danger of vanishing but was alive and well. Various conversations and larger meetings led to plans being developed for a fiddlers' festival to prove such points, and in 1973 the first such event was hosted in Glendale, Inverness County. With Ron MacInnis in the audience, the highlight of the two-day event was the massed fiddle finale featuring more than 100 Cape Breton fiddlers. As part of the revival movement that had been ignited since the broadcast a number of classes offering tuition in fiddle music had been established and several younger players were included in that line-up – further testimony to the message that the fiddle music was in safe hands for the future. Both the formation of the Committee for Cape Breton Fiddle (which later became the CBFA), which organized the Glendale fiddle festivals, and the development of classes for fiddle music, and later step dance, were direct, measurable outcomes of the response to the *VCBF*. Ron MacInnis, aware of the impact the *VCBF* had made, later produced stage shows about Cape Breton fiddle history, with reference to the 1970s revival sparked by his documentary. CBC also produced further documentaries about the *VCBF*: *Gzowski and Co.*, which featured Ron MacInnis and his efforts in the 1980s to mount a stage show with the CBFA, and a 10-minute documentary in 2001, *Country Canada–The Fate of the Fiddle*; this was expanded in 2002 to a half-hour show *The Wakeup Call*. The producer of the latter, Marie Thompson, wrote her Master's thesis on the topic – "The Fall and Rise of the Cape Breton Fiddler, 1955-1982" (St. Mary's University 2003) – and published further on the subject. In October 2002, Celtic Colours included in its program a show titled *The Thriving Cape Breton Fiddler*, celebrating the growth of the tradition in the wake of the *VCBF* documentary; in 2008 the festival included a show, *Salute to the Cape Breton Fiddler*, documenting the contemporary status of Cape Breton fiddle music and highlighting recent work which Ron MacInnis, a board member of the festival at that time, has done in relation to this. A new documentary project, currently in production, is what MacIn-nis has titled *The Return of the "Vanishing" Cape Breton Fiddler*. This he considers a celebration of the 40-year volunteer effort that brought about revival and ultimately generated a robust industry around the fiddle music; in particular, he is reviewing what he perceives as the positive effects that the revival has had on families and communities across Cape Breton. [**MacInnis in Cranford, 2007; Thompson 2003, 2006**]. *See* **Cape Breton Fiddler's Association; CBC; Glendale Fiddle Festivals; Ron MacInnis; television.**

variation. (a) Melodic and rhythmic changes made to the basic tune and part of the creative process of establishing settings of such tunes. (b) A practice found on occasion in Cape Breton music in which fixed variations are added to existing tunes. Such pieces as "The High Road to Linton," "The Drunken Landlady," "Miss Flora MacDonald" and "The Drover Boy" all have extra parts added to the original version that are essentially variations. Fiddlers such as Dan R. MacDonald added variations to both traditional tunes – such as "Miss MacLeod's Reel" – and to his own compositions, mostly jigs. These extended tunes then often become the standard adopted setting. Published tune books, notably those by Cranford, often include variation options for individual tunes. *See* **setting.**

Varnier, Mary Maggie (Smith). Piano. Deepdale and Inverness, Inverness County, Cape Breton. Along with Jessie Maggie MacLellan and Lila MacIsaac (later MacDonald, 1900-1985), she was one of a small number of piano players – mostly female – who were active in the Inverness County area in the early 20th century. Her father was a fiddle player and she also learnt much from Peter MacPhee, an itinerant fiddler who often stayed with the Smith family during the winter months. She went on to be the accompanist for 10 years in Kenloch for older fiddlers such as Malcolm Beaton, Angus Allan Gillis, Dan J. Campbell and Sandy MacLean, and also played with John Alex MacLennan in S.W. Margaree, and occasionally with Archie Neil Chisholm. From time to time she played with Angus Chisholm at house parties

LIZ DOHERTY

and travelled to Boston where she played with Bill Lamey. In her later years Varnier played often with John MacDougall and Willie Kennedy. She is featured on the North American Series album *Traditional Fiddle Music of Cape Breton: MacKinnon's Brook* (2008), where she accompanies Willie Kennedy and Morgan MacQuarrie, both on fiddles. Her piano playing is of an older style and features a basic left-hand accompaniment and a more expressive right hand, which often carried the melody along with the fiddle.

Venetian Gardens. A venue located on the waterfront in Sydney, it was developed by Florino Byron (formerly Biron), who was born in Possagno, near Venice, Italy, in 1900 and emigrated to Glace Bay in the early 1920s. Following a 5-year sabbatical in Italy in the 1930s he opened the Minto Hotel in Charlotte Street, Sydney, later bought the Sydney Hotel, and in 1948 he began construction of the four-storey Venetian Gardens. With a round roof and double-thick walls, this unique dance hall was adorned with star-shaped lights and a huge mural of Venice, creating a romantic atmosphere. It catered to a range of activities including big bands like the Emilio Pace and the Gib Whitney orchestras, but one night each week was dedicated to square dancing with Joe Murphy or Winston Fitzgerald and his Orchestra as regulars during the late 1950s and early 1960s. The building was destroyed by fire in 1964. [**Spada 1969**].

vibrato. A technique achieved through the forward and backward rocking of the finger on any stopped note on the violin. It is metred by the rate of the rocking motion and the extent of pitch variation involved; the resulting pitch oscillation – the vibrato – is used to enhance expression. While it has come to define the tone of much classical string playing, in Cape Breton it is used in the original Baroque manner as an occasional effect or embellishment. Introduced there around the 1940s, and associated initially with the playing of airs only, it was the 1970s before it became widely recognized and began to be used in the dance-music repertoire as a means of adding colour and

accent to selected notes. Buddy MacMaster and Jerry Holland use the technique to great effect on exposed longer notes, particularly in jigs and, to a lesser degree, in reels. Winnie Chafe, Kyle MacNeil and Colin Grant are fiddlers who use vibrato to a large degree (although never consistently in the classical fashion) and in a controlled, even and wider manner than most others in Cape Breton who opt for faster, narrower cycles. Here the distinction between the classically trained and non-classically trained (in terms of instrument hold and, hence, the extent to which the left hand is positioned to create vibrato, as well as delivery) is evident. The embellishment referred to as the "warble" involves an element of vibrato in its execution. *See* **warble**.

Victoria Standard, The. Based in Baddeck this bi-weekly newspaper, currently in publication for more than 20 years, focuses on Victoria County but also looks beyond. *The Standard* is important in music for its contributions by Paul Cranford who publishes tunes in it every two weeks; more than 500 tunes, representing many local composers, have been published in it to date.

violin. The term used to denote the bowed, stringed instrument – more commonly referred to today as the "fiddle" – the instrument is the standard violin, the mainstay of the symphony orchestra and classical music since the 17th century. The violin has had various precursors but the modern-day violin emerged in Italy in the early 1500s; early inventors are suggested as Giovan Giaboca dalla Corno and Zanetto Montichiaro; however, the first noted maker was Andrea Armati (1525-1611), founder of the famous school of violin-making in Cremona.

instrument. Made up of more than 80 parts, the violin's distinct shape includes 2 sound holes ("f" holes) carved out of the front, a bridge which supports the 4 strings, and a peg box which houses the tuning pegs; internally a sound post is positioned between the front and back of the instrument to support pressure on the belly and help determine the sound quality.

The strings are typically tuned to G, D A E', but sometimes, particularly in the past, in other ways (cross-tuning or scordatura); this alters both the volume and quality of the sound produced. The violin's sound is created when a bow, strung with tensioned horsehair, is moved across the strings between the bridge and the fingerboard. Violins today come equipped with a chinrest, to the left of the tailpiece; individual players may or may not choose to add a shoulder rest, attached to the back of the instrument for extra support and to free the left hand in order to better achieve higher position work (something that is a necessity for some classical but not traditional players).

hold. Using a chinrest, the violin is supported between the neck and shoulder; this standard position is, for the most part, adopted by Cape Breton players but, particularly in the past, alternative approaches – such as holding it against the chest, holding it vertically or tilting it upward – were seen. Typically, the violin is held on the left side of the body and the bow in the right hand, but as in all musics, in Cape Breton, there are a number of left-handed players who either simply switch sides, so the instrument is on the left and the bow on the right, or who switch sides *and* reverse the order of the strings. *See* **bow; fiddle; left-handed players.**

violin makers. There is much anecdotal evidence that fiddles were brought to Cape Breton with the early settlers but little supporting evidence. However, much information about instruments used from the early 20th century is to be found in *The Cape Breton Fiddler* (MacGillivray 1981). Starter instruments were available at this time for purchase in certain stores around the island (e.g., McNutt's in Inverness); mail-order was another option via such as the Sear's and Eaton's catalogues, and players often made their own instruments when starting out (Lee Cremo tells of a fiddle he played which was constructed from baseball bat timber and the flat wood of a coffee table) and a few fiddlers used tin fiddles. A number of violin makers have become established in Cape Breton, among them Otis Tomas and Clay Carmichael.

W

Waipu. The site, on New Zealand's North Island, of a significant Presbyterian settlement from St. Ann's, Cape Breton. Rev. Norman McLeod (1780-1866), a Presbyterian minister from Assynt, Scotland, had led his people from the Highlands of Scotland to Pictou, Nova Scotia, and then to Cape Breton in 1820 only to leave there in the 1850s, initially bound for Australia. The first of five ships arrived in Waipu in 1853 and records suggest that between 800 and 1,200 people made the journey. Today in Waipu there are a number of memorials documenting the history of the settlement of this Gaelic community there and its links to Cape Breton. The site vacated by McLeod in St. Ann's became the home of the Gaelic College. **[Lamb 1992; Sawyers 2013].**

Walker Collection, Alexander, The. Published in Scotland (1866) as *A Collection of Strathspeys, Reels, Marches &c.,* this is the work of fiddler-composer Alexander Walker (1837-ca. 1893), a native of Aberdeenshire and a gardener by trade who immigrated to America in 1870. The collection contains 196 of his original compositions, one of them a collaboration with James Scott Skinner, and more than 40 of them circulated in the Cape Breton fiddlers' repertoire during the 20th century. The collection has 84 strathspeys, 79 reels, 8 each of jigs and airs, 7 each of hornpipes and marches, and 1 each of quickstep, waltz and country dance. A revised edition of the book – subtitled *Newly typeset edition based on the 1866 original* and including "some melodic variation from Cape Breton fiddlers" – was published by Cranford in Cape Breton in 1991, and reprinted with further revisions in 1997. Based on an original edition owned by fiddler Joe MacLean, this edition omits the bass lines, presenting just the melody (and some variations) while maintaining the original sequence, alphabetically by key. The 72 pages have an introduction by Paul Cranford, a preface, a contents list of tunes numbered 1-196, an alphabetical index of titles, and melodic notation of all pieces with the tune-type indicated. Cranford notes that Walker's compositions show a "challenging and balanced original repertoire ... in all the common keys and using all the traditional structures." He observes too that "Walker had a less chromatic style of composing than Skinner ... more akin to 20th century Cape Breton music" and suggests that many of the tunes would suit the high-bass tunings practiced by Cape Breton fiddlers. More than 40 of Walker's tunes circulated in the Cape Breton fiddlers' repertoire in the 20th century. *See* **tune books.**

Wallace, Beattie (Boutilier). (1915-1979). Piano. Amherst, NS, and Coxheath, Cape Breton. Born to parents Albert Boutilier (ca. 1885-1973) and Gertie Boutilier (later Turnball) she came from a long line of musicians. Her paternal grandfather and great-grandfather were fiddle players as was her father who, with his brothers (all of them award-winning step dancers, singers and piano or fiddle players), had immigrated to Canada from the Irish province of Ulster. Beattie's mother played piano, autoharp and mouth organ and was her husband, Albert's, regular accompanist at dances. Beattie's brother Bud was a fiddler and mouth-organ player and her aunt Lillian Boutilier also played fiddle. By age 8 Beattie was taking piano lessons in Sydney and practiced chording to her father's playing, sometimes with her mother on piano as well. The Boutilier family home had 2 pianos – one bought specially for Beattie by her grandfather – and was a popular venue for music. Many local fiddlers called regularly, among them Johnny Wilmot, Charlie Campbell, Joe MacLean, Angus Chisholm and Winston Fitzgerald. Beattie played her first dance with her aunt Lillian when she was about 9, and as a teenager she played regularly in Boutilier's Orchestra along with her mother on autoharp and her father on fiddle. They played round and square dances, mostly at venues such as The Fire Fly in Seven Mile Bridge and The Cave Park Inn in Westmount. She became a regular performer in the fiddle-music community

in Sydney, and played with many of the fiddlers there including Prof. James MacDonald. In the late 1930s and early 1940s she played with Tena Campbell on the radio show *Cottar's Saturday Night,* and during the war years was Campbell's accompanist at dances in East Bay. In 1947 she became a regular member of Winston Fitzgerald's Radio Entertainers ensemble along with Estwood Davidson on guitar. Beattie Wallace had a well-grounded knowledge of harmonies and, guided by Fitzgerald, she and Davidson worked out coordinated accompaniments for the fiddle tunes, leading to a slick, polished sound and a unified sense of ensemble that was special in Cape Breton at that time. For round and square dances this core ensemble was joined by other musicians and collectively known as The Winston Fitzgerald Orchestra. Wallace also played with Fitzgerald and Davidson 6 nights a week for regular dances in the Ashby Legion and Venetian Gardens in Sydney as well as in halls in Whycocomagh and Inverness. They also performed on radio, on such as the MacDonald Tobacco Company's sponsored show each Saturday. She also played on all of Fitzgerald's recordings, and one of his 78s has a medley titled "Mrs. Shoes," after a tune Dan R. MacDonald had composed for her, "Beattie Wallace's Red Shoes." In later years she played with such as Joe Cormier, Dan R. MacDonald, Mike Fitzgerald and the Eastern Aires at the Ashby Legion (Sydney) and Sandy MacInnis's in Valley Mills. **[Caplan 1989; MacGillivray 1988]**.

waltz. A 3/4-metre dance and associated tune-type that first appeared in Europe at the end of the 18th century, likely derived from an old German tune type, the Ländler. As a fashion, the waltz swept across Europe and America, despite being opposed as morally improper; instrumental versions of the tune-type were also popularized. The waltz has a rhythmic accent on beat one of each bar creating a regular ONE-two-three, ONE-two-three accentual pattern, which is further emphasized by the harmony (actual or implied); this is generally based around one chord per bar, with the full chord articulated in beat one and blocks

The New Land

waltz

Otis Tomas

© Otis Tomas, SOCAN, www.fiddletree.com

of the chord on the other two beats. The waltz was introduced to Cape Breton in the 1920s, since when it has enjoyed mixed fortunes, depending on favour for the dance; it was especially popular in the 1940s-1960s at round and square dances. The fiddler only played for square dances as part of the evening's proceedings while the music for the round dances (including the waltz) was provided by either gramophone recordings or by a singer or other instrumentalist such as a saxophonist, suggesting that not many tunes of this type were known by the fiddling community. Winston Fitzgerald was the first fiddle player to begin experimenting with the waltz to any significant degree, and became known for his repertoire of such tunes, many based on songs that were Irish in origin. He played these with both his regular piano and guitar accompanists (Beattie Wallace and Estwood Davidson) and with his big band or orchestra. Today, virtually all Cape Breton fiddlers have waltzes in their repertoires; since the early 1990s it has become common for fiddlers to be fluent in providing backup for singers and many waltz-metre vocals are part of the standard repertoire. A body of locally composed tunes has also been made in the idiom, some of the more popular being Jerry Holland's "My Cape Breton Home" and Otis Tomas's "The New Land."

warble. A term introduced to the Cape Breton context by Kate Dunlay (1986, 1996) to refer to a particular type of finger ornament used by Cape Breton fiddlers. The warble involves the execution of a double grace note as an indistinct mordent. The rocking motion of the finger used to achieve vibrato is combined with the releasing of pressure on that finger so that the upper and lower spectrum of pitches achieved by the oscillation are actually sounded, albeit imprecisely. The warble is most often used to ornament long notes that are realized through employing the second finger, although it can occur in other situations. The warble is a particular favourite of older players such as Willie Kennedy, Mary MacDonald and Buddy MacMaster, and of old-style players like John Morris Rankin. However, the pitch oscillation involved is not conducive to today's preferred precision and so is heard less among contemporary Cape Breton fiddlers. [**Dunlay and Greenberg 1996; Dunlay with Reich 1986**]. *See* **grace note; vibrato.**

Warner sisters. *See* **Cameron, Melody.**

Washabuck Connection, The. A young, all-female group showcasing triple fiddle, piano and choreographed step-dance routines that was popular during the 1990s on the local summer concert circuit. Its members were Bhreagh MacDonald, Jill MacLean and Martia MacLean on fiddles and Susan MacLean on piano, all from or connected to the Washabuck area and whose families included many noted musicians, including Michael Anthony MacLean who was grandfather to 3 of the girls. They began working together in 1991 when they were aged between 11 and 14 years old, while taking courses at the Gaelic College; their first public performance was the following year at Iona's Highland Village Day. In subsequent years the group played at many summer concerts on the island, including at Big Pond, St. Ann's and Ben Eoin. Education and relocation caused the group to disband, but several of them continue to play and teach music and step dance in different parts of Nova Scotia.

weddings. For the early settlers, a wedding was an opportunity for great celebration by the entire community. While there is no evidence to suggest that music featured as part of the actual ceremony, music and dancing were central to the associated social gathering. The wedding reception, dance or "time," which was often held at the home of the parents of one of the couple would last from early evening to early morning the following day, and, occasionally might extend over a couple of days. The music was provided by a fiddler or piper (depending on who was available locally). Sometimes a single player alternated on both instruments; sometimes musicians played in pairs (fiddle and pipes or two fiddles); typically, other musicians in attendance would take turns to "spell off" the house fiddler. The importance of the musician's role was highlighted in some communities where it was customary for the bride to present the first drink to the musician before the dancing began; however, by the 1950s these various rituals had largely been forgotten. Historically, certain tunes were associated with parts of the proceedings; "The Old Time Wedding Reels," retained as part of the fiddle-music canon, are reminiscent of this. During the 19th and early 20th centuries, weddings were typically held during the winter months since spring and summer were the busiest

seasons for farmers. By mid-20th century this had changed, and weddings came to be held during the summer months, to coincide with the vacation home of those Cape Bretoners "from away." In many instances the festivities continued to be held at the home of one of the married couple's parents, often with a makeshift stage erected outside the house for the occasion. Gradually, however, the receptions moved into church or community halls, and this is the norm today. The day after the wedding (and sometimes over a few days) often involves a ceilidh in the family home of either of the couple. Fiddle music is not the only music at a typical wedding reception but, depending on the preferences of the couple, it may sit, to a greater or lesser degree, alongside rock, pop, folk and country music. Since the 1990s, fiddle music may be presented as part of the music of the actual wedding ceremony, but outside of families who are musicians themselves this is not a widespread practice. [**Rhodes 1985; MacGillivray 1988**].

West Mabou Square Dance. A unique "family" square dance held in West Mabou each Saturday night, it is the only event of its kind to be held year-round (weather permitting). Hosted by the West Mabou Sports Club, this no-liquor dance has been running since the early 1990s (following a few dances held there in the 1980s when John Campbell was the resident fiddler). Organized as a fundraiser by Margie and Jimmy MacInnis, Neil Beaton played for the inaugural dance with Stephanie Wills on piano. While it was common practice at the time for a resident fiddler to play all the dances held at a particular venue, the West Mabou dances started a new trend by inviting different fiddle players to perform each week. This has allowed them to feature most of the island's top players, to host special multiple-fiddle events on occasion, and to offer emerging young players experience in dance playing. Many photographs of these musicians are exhibited on the walls of the West Mabou Hall, which accommodates ca. 250, although double this number have attended some of the dances played by the more popular fiddlers. An outside deck was added to increase capacity, but dancers prefer the hall interior, highlighting the reality that the connection between the dancer and the musician is an intrinsic part of the experience. A special celebration of the West Mabou Square dances was held in 2015 in recognition of the significance of this event in maintaining Cape Breton's culture and traditions. **[Feintuch 2010]**.

whip-bow technique. A term coined by David Greenberg and introduced in *The DunGreen Collection* (1996), it refers to a bowing technique that is used to highlight the metrical impulse of specific parts of a tune. It generally relates to repeated rhythmic motifs involving a dotted note in a long-short pattern (such as in strathspeys or at the point of transition between a strathspey and reel). The technique refers to the way in which these notes are connected, most particularly to the elasticity of the connection between them: the dotted note is elongated using the down-bow, while the shorter note or "whip" comes in between on the up-bow (Greenberg gives the analogy of a runner band being stretched and then rebounding). **[Dunlay and Greenberg 1996]**.

wild note. This occurs where one melody note is substituted by another, typically more dissonant alternative, and generally involves a fourth-finger note replacing a third-finger note. The wild note, which is found in reels, is usually in a rhythmically-weak position, never on the strong beat. A characteristic of the Mabou Coal Mines style of playing, the wild note may represent a fiddler's more dissonant interpretation of a consonant melodic line or, in locally composed material, it may be conceived of as an integral part of the basic melody line; however, in practice it is not uncommon, particularly among contemporary players, to replace a wild note with the implied consonant melody note (perhaps with the wild note relegated to grace-note status). "Molly Rankin's," in which a wild note was deliberately inserted in the melodic line by the composer (John Morris Rankin), is an example where this frequently happens. The term itself was coined by Kate Dunlay and David

The wild-note in "Molly Rankin's Reel"; often players, missing the subtlety of this, play an A' instead of B' (the wild note) as intended by the composer.

Greenberg in *The DunGreen Collection* (1996) and was previously not used by the players themselves to describe this technique. **[Doherty 1996; Dunlay and Greenberg 1996]**.

Wills, Stephanie. Fiddle, piano, step dance, teacher. Creignish and Sydney. Inspired by the legend of her grandmother, fiddler Tina "Jim Angus" MacDougall of Creignish Mountain, Stephanie was taught fiddle by Stan Chapman in the 1980s. As part of the first group of young fiddlers to be taught fiddle in a structured class setting (something that was activated in response to the *VCBF* documentary), she was presented with many performance opportunities from the outset as part of student groups alongside Wendy MacIsaac, Natalie MacMaster, Jackie Dunn and others. She has also performed in the past with the *Cape Breton Summertime Revue* and *Cape Breton Gold*. Her piano and fiddle playing are featured on recordings by Brenda Stubbert and Wendy MacIsaac, including on the *Fiddler Magazine* DVD release *Carrying on the Traditions: Cape Breton Scottish Fiddling Today* (1996). Her single fiddle recording, *Tradition*, was released in 1994. Her fiddle style displays a cross section of influences, such as Theresa MacLellan, Donald Angus Beaton and Howie MacDonald, and she is particularly noted as being a popular dance player. Having taught at the Gaelic College for many years, more recently she has taught from her home in Sydney.

Wilmot, John (Johnny). (1916-1993). Fiddle, composer. Mabou, Centreville, Toronto, and Glace Bay. From the age of three he lived with his maternal grandparents, the Fortunes, in Centreville, near Sydney Mines. Originally from Bras d'Or, the family, although of French descent, had married into the Irish community; "Old" Henry Fortune was noted for having a distinctive Irish style and repertoire that he passed on to his nephews George, Jack and Joe Confiant, all fiddlers in the Irish style. Johnny's mother, although not a player herself, favoured Irish music and had a collection of recordings of Irish and Irish-American musicians such as Michael Coleman, James Morrison, Paddy Killoran, O'Leary's Irish Minstrels, Dan Sullivan's Shamrock Band, the Flanagan Brothers and the Hanafin Brothers, which she had acquired from the U.S. Johnny started to play fiddle as a teenager and at an early stage mastered note reading. He played his first picnic in Frenchvale with Joe Confiant, also on fiddle, and John Willie Morrison from Sydney Mines on piano. He formed a band with Sonny Slade, Elizabeth (Northen) Finnell and Roy Romeo, and played many dances in communities such as Boisdale and Johnstown. In 1936 he moved to Glace Bay and joined forces with Art Munroe on guitar and Mildred Leadbeater, Margaret MacPhee or Catherine Ann (MacDonald) McSween on piano. During the early 1950s, "Johnny Wilmot and His Irish Serenaders" played a regular live radio broadcast from CJCB Sydney that became one of the longest-running shows of his time. He also made three trips to Boston, where he was welcomed by both the Cape Breton and the Irish communities and played with musicians such as Irish fiddler Paddy Cronin and accordionist Joe Derrane. He performed on WMEX and WVON radio and at venues such as the Greenville Cafe and later, Joe MacPherson's Irish Tavern in Roxbury. From 1959 he lived in Toronto and became a regular performer at events organized by the Cape Breton community there until he returned to Cape Breton in 1976. He composed a number of tunes, among them the well-known "Hughie Shorty's Reel," which became a favourite in Cape Breton and Ireland alike. Remastered tracks from his 78s and LPs were presented in CD and cassette form: *Another Side of Cape Breton* (Breton Books 1994); he is also featured on a number of anthology recordings. Among those accompanying him on his albums are Tommy Basker (harmonica), Margaret MacPhee, (piano) Chris Langan (tin whistle and uilleann pipes), Bill Legere (bass), Bill

MacDonald (guitar) and John Angus Kennedy (guitar). Wilmot's unique sound straddled Scottish, Irish and Cape Breton styles. His repertoire reflected his interests in each of these traditions and was a mix of Cape Breton standards and other tunes he gleaned from books such as Kerr's and O'Neill's, and from recordings, most of which were Irish (including what were considered unusual tune-types in Cape Breton, such as barn dances) but also French and American old-time tunes. He was intrigued by the creative process in the playing of Irish fiddle players, in particular, Michael Coleman: "I slowed that fellow down, many's the time, and I played him too to see if I could learn his tunes. Play and play and play and play. Every time I put him on he'd be doing something else" (Caplan 1985). While he challenged himself to introduce Coleman's type of spontaneous variation into his interpretation of Irish tunes, in his renditions of Cape Breton and Scottish tunes he adhered to the local aesthetic values concerning correctness and his settings were thus considered authentic. His bowing showed evidence of the Sligo technique, with long, slurred passages being a notable feature; his timing was regarded as solid and suitable for dancing to, and he was considered a lively player, although his tempo was not fast. He had good command of the bow and his use of the bowed cut as a type of embellishment was clearly articulated. Johnny Wilmot was an influential player, particularly for those fiddlers, such as Jerry Holland and Brenda Stubbert, who shared his interest in Irish music. [**Caplan 2006; MacGillivray 1981**].

Wilson, Mark. (1947-). Guitar, banjo, fiddle. Oregon and Pittsburgh. A Harvard graduate who is currently professor of philosophy at the University of Pittsburgh, his involvement with Cape Breton music came through Rounder Records, engaged in as a hobby and a passion rather than as a profession. This makes his output of almost 30 recordings of Cape Breton fiddle music, each accompanied by extensive liner notes, all the more remarkable. Wilson's ambitions were to get as much homegrown North American folk music

Dan R. MacDonald (left) with Mark Wilson of Rounder Records. Courtesy of Mark Wilson.

recorded in tolerable fidelity as possible before it vanished, to bring wider recognition to those he recognized as great musicians while they were still alive, and to ensure that the artists were fully involved in all aspects of the recording process. As such, his interests stretched from Kentucky and the Ozarks, West Virginia and the Midwest to Cape Breton and other Maritime areas. He became involved in the then new-Rounder Record label while he was in graduate school in 1973. He encountered Cape Breton fiddle music initially through the recordings of Winston Fitzgerald and was subsequently introduced to Joe Cormier (who became the subject of his first Cape Breton recording) by New Brunswick fiddler, Gerry Robichaud. Because of issues between the record company and individual Cape Breton musicians, Wilson was unable to pursue his recording of Cape Breton music after 1977 until the 1990s, when he

began a fresh round of recordings. He began with a new CD by Joe Cormier and the publication of an unreleased recording by Joe MacLean, which had been started many years earlier. Wilson's primary (though not exclusive) focus was on older players; his modus operandi was to identify and work with existing experts in the field. Through Theresa Morrison he became acquainted with Cape Breton fiddler Morgan MacQuarrie, with whom he worked in close partnership on most of the subsequent Cape Breton releases; other occasional collaborators were Frank Ferrel and Burt Feintuch. These pointed him to, and introduced him to, potential recording artists, and they often facilitated the recording sessions that were held in various locations in Cape Breton. Fiddlers he recorded included Joe Cormier, Winnie Chafe, Jerry Holland, Theresa and Marie MacLellan, John Campbell, Carl MacKenzie, Donald Angus and Kinnon Beaton, Joe MacLean, Theresa Morrison, Willie Kennedy, Donald MacLellan, Joe Peter MacLean, Morgan MacQuarrie, John L. MacDonald, Buddy MacMaster and Alex Francis MacKay; Doug MacPhee on piano was also recorded. From this material he produced, for example, *The Beatons of Mabou* (1978), one of the most significant and influential Cape Breton recordings; most of the Cape Breton recordings have found a home in Rounders' North American traditions series. His most recent work is this regard is a series of 4 compilation albums titled *Traditional Fiddle Music of Cape Breton*. As with all his recordings, besides drawing out representative repertoires, Wilson also interviews each fiddler extensively in order to have them describe, in their own words, their lives in music. This contextual narrative, supplemented by essays on aspects of the tradition by various Cape Breton scholars, provides a rich insight into the Cape Breton fiddle tradition, past and present; these liner notes (some of them independently available online at mustrad.org.uk) represent an important contribution to the Cape Breton cultural record. The author of *Wandering Significance* (2006), he is currently working on a publication and website about the full range of his folk music recordings, with scholar Norm Cohen. *See* **Rounder Records.**

Windsor. *See* **Detroit; Diaspora; out-migration.**

women. The subject of female musicians and their contribution to Cape Breton culture is no less topical than in other genres, with dynamic changes having taken place in the area of gender balance since the early 20th century and the rise of feminism. Cape Breton society in its geographic isolation was by no means a leader in this movement, but some of the principal concepts nevertheless have come to be applied in its social system. Traditionally in Cape Breton the fiddle was very much associated with the male population. In MacGillivray's *The Cape Breton Fiddler* (1981) only 7 of the 93 biographies are of women players. However, the "Partial Directory of Cape Breton Violinists" appended to this publication yields some 20 extra names, suggesting that a greater number of females were indeed active as fiddle players, yet they were not considered significant nor prominent enough for them to have been included in the main narrative. As has been revealed by research in many traditions, it is the positioning of women in the private domain (i.e., in the home and before a family audience) that has often led to the perception (highlighted by publications, which focus on the male-dominated public domain representations of the culture), that women have not been significant contributors to the tradition; further, it is suggested that their contribution was limited to specific aspects of the culture, those that were sustainable within the home environment and that might be incorporated into their caring or work roles. Women did emerge, over the course of the 20th century, into the public tradition; between the 1920s and the late 1960s women came to prominence, in most cases, as piano accompanists to the male fiddlers. This is borne out in the publication *A Cape Breton Ceilidh* (MacGillivray, 1988), where almost three-quarters of the 200 piano players listed are female. Since the revival period of the 1970s onward, the roles of men and women in Cape Breton music have become less separate;

Students of Kyle MacNeil perform at the CBFA concert at the Gaelic College, 2013. (L-r) McKayla MacNeil, (St. Peter's), Maria Howatson (Little Bras d'Or), Katya Koral-O'Dwyer (Albert Bridge), Chantal Chafe (Sydney) and Maggie MacLeod (Grand Mira). Photo by Victor Maurice Faubert.

today, many of the prominent fiddle players are female and, conversely, piano accompanists are often male. Dancers today may be either male or female, although in the past were, at different times, predominantly either one. In teaching contexts, women are today the dominant gender; and in recordings over the past 2 decades female fiddle players are well represented.

the home environment. Cape Breton women played an important role in the transmission of music, encouraging their children to play even when they were not instrumentalists themselves. Songs in the Gaelic language were a natural part of everyday life, particularly for the women who sang as they worked. Many of these songs made the transfer from vocal to instrumental piece (voice to fiddle), and often it is a woman who is acknowledged as being the source. Women have often been noted for their jigging of tunes and for *puirt-a-beul* that at times might be danced to, and often were the source of repertoire for the fiddlers. Maggie Ann Cameron Beaton – grandmother to Natalie MacMaster and Dawn and Margie Beaton – was a well-known jigger as were other women such as Lloyd MacDonald's aunt Lizzie MacDonald; Archie Neil Chisholm credited his mother with providing much of the early material that he and his brother Angus shared in their fiddle

Tena Campbell, ca. 1938. 78-1209-2595. Beaton Institute, Cape Breton University.

repertoires. Many of these women were indeed credited with having astonishing aural skills and music memories, and could retain tunes correctly upon hearing them once at a dance. Other women played an active role in passing on music-literacy skills to the male fiddlers. Trained in music at school or through church music activities, they were able to share the basics of note reading when the demand for this escalated from the 1940s onward. Fiddlers such as Danny Beaton, Johnny Ranald Beaton and Dan J. Campbell have respectively acknowledged a mother, a wife and a sister as contributing to the accuracy of their playing, having introduced them to the rudiments of notation. Buddy MacMaster learned to read music with the help of piano player Mildred Leadbeater in Antigonish; Wilfred Prosper acknowledges the

nuns in Eskasoni as being important in teaching music notation skills to the Mi'kmaw community there, and in Chéticamp the Sisters of Notre Dame also fulfilled this function. A few women fiddle players were known for taking a central role in passing the music on within their own families, among these Cassie MacIntyre (mother of Sandy MacIntyre) and Katie Anne Cameron (mother of John Donald and John Allan Cameron), who taught their children to play. While the general understanding is that both girls and boys were afforded the opportunity to pick up the fiddle in a family, the decision to pursue or abandon this in public at a later stage was as a result of gender-determined social conditioning. Some females, who did play in public as teenagers and young women, retired from public performances once they had families of their own, something that was not uncommon in other traditions; in some cases these female players resumed their public music lives once their families had been reared.

the public domain. The first female Cape Breton fiddlers to gain significant public recognition were Tena Campbell, who was a regular performer on CJCB radio in the 1930s on shows such as *Cottar's Saturday Night,* and Mary "Hughie" MacDonald when she started playing at picnics around Inverness County. During the Second World War, more women musicians had a higher public profile since many of the men who had previously provided the music were serving in the military; Veronica MacKinnon, for instance, played frequently for dances in the Iona area at this time, while Tena Campbell became the resident fiddler at dances in East Bay. Cape Breton women also featured on some of the early recordings of Cape Breton fiddle music in the role of accompanist (e.g., Betty Maillet and Bess Sidall MacDonald). However, it was the 1970s before the first commercial recordings of female Cape Breton fiddlers appeared; Theresa MacLellan (with the MacLellan Trio) and Winnie Chafe both recorded, while Mary MacDonald appeared on Topic's Cape Breton LP. Also in the 1970s Cape Breton, MacLellan and Chafe both appeared on the CBC-TV show, *Ceilidh,* as part of the regular house band. Brenda Stubbert and Margaret Chisholm were among the next generation of females to emerge on the scene just ahead of the 1970s revival; once fiddle classes opened up it became common for young girls and women to be prominent on the scene.

piano. With the introduction of first the pump organ and then the piano into Cape Breton fiddle music, from the turn of the 20th century, women's music interests seemed almost unanimously to be tied to it. Originally this appears as an extension of the male/female role with the fiddle – the dominant instrument – being played by the male, and the piano or accompanying instrument by the female; many such duos emerged, further underlining this status quo, among them various husband-and-wife and brother-sister combinations. However, on many of the early recordings the piano player is not even mentioned by name, something which some of those involved were sufficiently incensed about to complain the record companies. Whether this was a matter of gender discrimination or more a matter of foregrounding the fiddle is a matter for debate. Piano accompaniment has enjoyed an elevation in status over the course of the 20th century into the 21st, and indeed it is considered that the sound is not Cape Breton without it. Among those who have made a significant imprint on the evolution of the style are many female players including Mary Jessie MacDonald, Margaret MacPhee, Marie MacLellan, Maybelle Chisholm MacQueen, Betty-Lou Beaton, Hilda Chiasson and Tracey Dares MacNeil.

more recent developments. The dissolution of gender distinctions within the Cape Breton fiddle tradition has been a very recent phenomenon. The establishment of formal classes in fiddle playing did much to encourage the participation of both genders in much the same way as it allowed the music to move outside the confines of home environments. Certainly the genders are much more balanced than in the past as regards numbers of females playing the fiddle; incidentally, there are probably fewer female piano players today than in the past. Today, women are positioned

Andrea Beaton. Scott McIntyre Photography.

alongside men in virtually every aspect of the music tradition. A number play professionally; others on a more part-time basis while managing other careers. Many are teachers of fiddle music, piano or step dance. Cape Breton women also rank among some of the most prolific and popular composers, with Brenda Stubbert and Andrea Beaton both having published collections of their tunes, and the *Cape Breton Fiddlers Association Collection* including a significant number of compositions by female composers. Each year, since its inception, Celtic Colours has celebrated the contribution of Cape Breton's female performers in a dedicated women's concert, where they share the stage with prominent female players from other genres. And, as is also typical, women play various key administrative and organizational roles in various aspects of the music industry as it intersects with the Cape Breton fiddle tradition. In terms of scholarly research and in print women have made a significant contribution (e.g., Kate Dunlay, Jackie Dunn MacIsaac, Heather Sparling, Wendy Bergfeldt, Frances MacEachen). [**Doherty 1996; Graham 2006; MacGillivray 1981, 1988**].

Wukitsch, Paul. Fiddle. Schenectady, NY, and Boisdale, Cape Breton. Introduced to Scottish music initially by George Wilson in New England, Wukitsch was one of a number of Americans to make Cape Breton their home in the late 1970s, drawn there by the music and the culture. Settling in Boisdale he became involved in the local music scene befriending fiddlers such as Johnny Wilmot and Wilfred Prosper. He later joined Joe Peter MacLean and Janet Cameron in forming The Boisdale Trio; this ensemble is featured on the LP, *Joe MacLean: Back of Boisdale* (Rounder, 2005). Influenced by Johnny Wilmot, he developed a repertoire and style that reflected the Irish tradition of Cape Breton's Northside area. He is featured on the Rounder album *Traditional Fiddle Music of Cape Breton: Bras d'Or House* (2008). **[Wilson and MacLean 2008].**

X

X. A symbol used in some published collections such as the *DunGreen Collection* (1996) to indicate a specific bowed ornament where the pitch of the note is obscured and the bow instead makes a percussive sound. While a dot used above or below the note in such sources indicates that, although the note is short, the pitch of the note can still be heard, an X means that the pitch of the note is obscured and the bow is makes a percussive sound. **[Dunlay and Greenberg 1996].**

Y

Young, Adam. (1980-). Piano, accordion, tin whistle. Sydney, Cape Breton. Born to parents Doug and Freda Young, he started taking classical music lessons in piano at age 5 with various tutors for more than a decade. Inspired by his cousin, Tracey Dares MacNeil (in particular, one performance with Dares and Tara Lynne Touesnard), as a teenager he diversified from his classical training and began accompanying fiddlers among his peers such as Colin Grant, Troy MacGillivray, Kimberley Fraser and Ian MacDougall. He performs locally, often for tourism events, with various younger players such as Anita MacDonald and Jason MacDonald (in The Goin's On), Meaghan Grant-Bennett, Michelle Hollohan, Eric Angus Whyte and Jason MacDonald (in the show *Lyrics and Laughter*) and, occasionally, Dara Smith-MacDonald, Rachel Davis and Chrissy Crowley. He has recorded with various musicians including fiddlers Colin Grant (*Colin Grant*, 2006; *Fun for the Whole Family*, 2010) and Dara Smith-MacDonald (*Connections*, 2011).

Z

Ziggy's. A pub and restaurant (Ziggy's Pub and Grill) in the Sydney area that often hosts Saturday afternoon fiddle matinees.

SELECT BIBLIOGRAPHY

REFERENCE MATERIALS

Bibliographies and Reference Works

Beisswenger, Drew. *North American Fiddle Music: A Research and Information Guide*. New York: Routledge, 2011.

Dunlay, Kate. Encyclopaedia Britannica *Encyclopaedia Britannica 2009 Ultimate Reference Suite* (2009). s.v. "Cape Breton Island."

——— . "Snapshot: The Celtic Revival in Cape Breton." In vol. 3 of *The Garland Encyclopedia of World Music: The United States and Canada*, 1127-1131. Ed. Ellen Koskoff. New York: Garland Pub., 2001.

———. *The Grove Dictionary of American Music*, 2nd ed. (2013), s.vv. "MacIsaac, Ashley," "MacMaster, Natalie," "Rankin Family, The."

Doherty, Liz. "Cape Breton Island." In *The Companion to Irish Traditional Music*, 101-105. 2nd ed. Ed. Fintan Vallely. Cork: Cork University Press, 2011. First published 2009.

Feintuch, Burt. "Cape Breton Music in Boston, Massachusetts." In vol. 3 of *American Musical Traditions: British Isles Music*. Ed. Jeff Todd Titon and Bob Carlin. New York: Schirmer Reference, 2002.

Historica Canada. *The Canadian Encyclopedia*. Toronto: Historica Canada, 2013. thecanadianencyclopedia.ca. Includes The Encyclopedia of Music in Canada.

Keillor, Elaine, Timothy James Archambault and John Medicine Horse Kelly. *Encyclopedia of Native American Music of North America*, 2013. Wesport, CT: Greenwood Publishing Group.

Marco, Guy A. *Encyclopedia of Recorded Sound in the United States*. NY and London: Garland Reference Library of Humanities,1993.

McGann, Clifford. "Canadian Maritimers" in *The Encyclopedia of New England*. Eds. Burt Feintuch and David H. Watters. New Haven: Yale University Press, 2005.

Tennyson, Brian Douglas. *Cape Bretoniana—An Annotated Bibliography*. Toronto: University of Toronto Press in association with the Beaton Institute, Sydney, 2005.

University of Toronto/Université Laval. *Dictionary of Canadian Biography/Dictionnaire biographique du Canada*. Toronto: University of Toronto and the Université Laval, 2003-2015. biographi.ca

Online Sources

Readers should presume the www. prefix

acadian-explorations.ca. Information on Acadian traditions including much on dance by Barbara Le Blanc.

acadianfiddle.com. A compendium of Acadian fiddlers created by Louis and Devon Léger.

androchaid.ca An Drochaid Eadarainn (the bridge between us) is an online resource developed by Highland Village for sharing Gaelic expression through the medium of the Gaelic language.

beatoninstitute.com. Website of the Beaton Institute at Cape Breton University; includes the digital archive which is in the process of being populated with Cape Breton music audio and visual material. Also includes the virtual exhibit: Music – Cape Breton's Diversity in Unity which includes the Gaelic song tradition.

cainntmomhathar.com. A learning resource developed by the Nova Scotia Highland Village Museum based on video recordings of fluent speakers using everyday, idiomatic Gaelic.

capebretonfiddlers.com The website of the Cape Breton Fiddlers' Association.

capebretonsmagazine.com. On-line archive of Cape Breton's Magazine; 74 issues.

cbfiddle.com. Alan Snyder's index of Cape Breton fiddle recordings; an extensive discography of Cape Breton fiddle music including album covers and tune excerpts.

cranfordpublications.com. Online store, tune archive and newsletter about Cape Breton music; also Irish and Scottish.

celticmusiccentre.com. The Celtic Music Interpretive Centre in Judique; the site includes an online store and a database of musicians' biographies. Also includes Cape Breton Live which offers online streaming of shows on a subscription basis.

davidgreenberg.ca. Baroque violinist and Cape Breton fiddle player; short papers on aspects of performance style and practice.

gaeliccollege.edu. Website of *Colaisde na Gàidhlig*/The Gaelic College; includes information on education opportunities and events, biographies of individual musicians and videos of select performers.

gaelstream.stfx.ca. A comprehensive digital resource of material from St. FX relating predominantly to Nova Scotia's Gaelic tradition.

novascotia.ca/archives. Online resource of the provincial archives based in Halifax.

newcommonground.org. Bill Aucoin's website aiming to archive the past and present music of Cape Breton Island.

tunearch.org. The Traditional Tune Archive of North American, British and Irish traditional instrumental music with annotation, formerly known as The Fiddler's Companion; by Andrew Kuntz and Valerio Pelliccioni.

rreid.net. Cape Breton piano players are the focus on this website, by hobbyist Roger Lane Reid.

virtualmuseum.ca/virtual-exhibits/exhibit/ceilidh-air-cheap-breatunn/. Created by Highland Village Museum/*An Clachan Gàidhealach* and part of Canada's virtual museum project this gives an insight into a Cape Breton Ceilidh.

Discography and Film

Beaton, Donald Angus. *Donald Angus Beaton–His Life and Music: A Music Documentary.* CMIC, 2009. DVD.

Cormier, J.P. *J.P. Cormier: The Man and his Music.* NS: Seabright Productions, 2005. (BRAVO TV)

Creighton, Helen (featuring Mary Jane Lamond). *A Sigh and A Wish*. Canada: National Film Board, 2001.

Cremo, Lee. *Arm of Gold*. Edwin Communications, 1986.

Cormier, Joe. *New England Fiddles*. Folkstreams.net, 1983.

Donovan, Kenneth. *The Irish to Cape Breton, 1713-1900*. Sydney, NS: Irish Benevolent Society, 1990.

Fitzgerald, Winston and John Allan Cameron. *Celtic Spirit*. Canada: National Film Board, 1978.

Fraser, Willie F. *God Bless Your Feet*. Canada: Red Liquorice Films, 2004. DVD

MacDonald, Howie. *Ceilidh Gone Wild*. DVD.

MacMaster, Buddy. *Buddy MacMaster Live in Concert*. NS: Seabright Productions, 2001. (BRAVO TV)

MacMaster, Buddy. *Buddy MacMaster: The Master of the Cape Breton Fiddle*. NS: Seabright Productions, 1993.

MacMaster, Buddy. *The Best of Buddy MacMaster*. NS: Seabright Productions

Tomas, Otis et.al. *Cape Breton Fiddles*. CBC: *Land and Sea*, 2011.

Various. *A Tribute to Ray "Mac" MacDonald*. NS: The Beaton Institute. 1999.

Various. *And they Danced*. Genuine Pictures (BRAVO TV), 2006.

Various. *Cape Breton Island, Volume 1*. NS: Seabright Productions, 1994.

Various. *Cape Breton Island, Volume 2*. NS: Seabright Productions, 1997.

Various. *Carrying on the Traditions: Cape Breton Scottish Fiddling Today*. *Fiddler Magazine* 1996. VHS.

Various. *Celtic Tides – A Musical Odyssey*. Documentary film, Hallyway Productions Inc.; Companion video byPutumayo World Music. 1998. VHS.

Various. *From the Heart: Three Maritime Folk Musicians – Scottish, Acadian and Mi'kmaq*. Sydney: Folkus Atlantic Video Production, 1995.

Various. *Highland Legacy: The Music of Cape Breton*. Halifax: Nova Scotia Tourism, Culture and Heritage, 2006. DVD

Various. *Music in the Blood*. NS: Seabright Productions, 1999. (BRAVO TV)

Various. *Peoples of the Maritimes: The Gaels of Cape Breton*. National Film Board, 1947.

Various. *The Beauty of the Dance* (Video). MacInnes, S. (ed.). Beaton Institute, Cape Breton University, 2000.

Various. *The Blood is Strong*. Grampian TV for Channel 4, 1988. VHS.

Various. *The Magic Fiddle*. U.K.: Flying Fix Films, 1991.

Various. *The Pipes the Pipes are Calling*. NS: Seabright Productions, 1996.

Various. *The Vanishing Cape Breton Fiddler*. Canada: CBC, 1971.

Various. *New Scotland*. Canada: National Film Board, 1943.

Various. *Down Home with Aly Bain in North America* (Cape Breton and Québec). Scotland, UK. A Pelicula Film, Channel 4 TV (TV Broadcast only), 1985.

Newspapers, Magazines, Periodicals

A number of early regional newspapers have been digitized and may be found at novascotia.ca/archives/

Am Bràighe. Edited by Frances and Ron MacEachen this quarterly magazine was published from 1993–2003 and focused on Cape Breton Gaelic culture, including fiddle music. Digitized as part of the Gaelstream project at St. F.X.

Cape Breton Post. Daily newspaper based in Sydney.

Cape Breton's Magazine. Edited by Ron Caplan and published from 1972-1998. Now available online.

Casket, The. Weekly newspaper founded in 1852, continuing today.

Celtic Life International. Formerly *The Clansman,* a bi-monthly magazine launched in the mid-1990s, and later *Celtic Heritage Magazine,* it's focus has expanded from Nova Scotia-Scotland to the wider 'Celtic' world; available in print and online.

Chronicle Herald, The. In 2014 a daily Cape Breton edition of this Halifax-based newspaper was launched.

Fiddler Magazine. Published in Los Altos, CA this magazine founded in 1994 continues today; editor Mary Larsen Holland. Regular content on Cape Breton fiddle music and a number of special editions dedicated to this tradition e.g. Cape Breton 2000.

Inverness Oran/Oran Inbhir Nis. Weekly newspaper started in 1976 and continuing today. An important local source of information about fiddle music events.

Mac-Talla (The Echo). Gaelic newspaper founded in Sydney in 1892 by Jonathan G. MacKinnon; continued until 19904.

Mosgladh / Awakening. Monthly Gaelic newspaper published by the Scottish Catholic Society in Sydney; the first several issues (from 1922) are followed by a gap of five years (1923 to 1928) before publication resumed. Published mostly in English, with a few Gaelic translations of prayers, Gaelic songs, and some Gaelic stories.

Participaper of Inverness County. Periodical magazine published by the Municipality of Inverness since 1979; provided free of charge to every household in the county; available online.

Scotia Sun. Published in Port Hawkesbury from 1970; this weekly newspaper carried an important series of articles mostly by John Gibson on local fiddlers as part of the revival.

Spirit of the Times, The. Published in Sydney from 1841-'46 by J.D. Kuhn.

Victoria Standard. Bi-weekly newspaper published in Baddeck since the 1990s; regular music content.

Reports

Davidson, Lyle Tilley. *Music Industry Survey: Assessment of the Nova Scotia Music Industry.* Halifax: Music Industry of Nova Scotia, 1999.

Kennedy, Mike. *Gaelic Nova Scotia: An Economic, Cultural and Social Impact Study.* Nova Scotia Curatorial Report No. 97. Halifax, NS: Nova Scotia Museum, 2002.

Music Nova Scotia. *The 2007b Nova Scotia Music Sector Strategy.* Halifax, NS: Music Nova Scotia, 2007.

Cape Breton Tune Collections and Tutorials

Beaton, Andrea. *Tunes from the Albums.* Cape Breton: Privately published, 2008.

Beaton, Donald Angus. *Donald Angus Beaton's Cape Breton Scottish Violin Music.* ed. Kinnon Beaton. Cape Breton: privately published, 1987.

Beaton, Joseph. *Mabou Music.* Antigonish, NS: Casket Printing and Publishing, 1980.

———. *Tunes and Ties: Music from Mabou, Cape Breton.* Antigonish, NS: Privately published, 1997.

Beaton, Kinnon. *105 Original Fiddle Tunes by Cape Breton Fiddler/Composer Kinnon Beaton.* Cape Breton: Privately published , 2010.

———. *Beaton's Collection of Cape Breton Scottish Violin Music. Volume 1. 100 Compositions by Kinnon Beaton.* Port Hawkesbury: Privately published, 1984.

———. *Cape Breton Fiddler Kinnon Beaton's 100 Original Fiddle Tunes.* Cape Breton: Privately published, 2003.

———. *The Beaton Collection: Over 600 Cape Breton Fiddle Tunes.* Cape Breton: Privately published, 2000.

Bogrreen, Jørn. *Right to the Helm- Cape Breton Square Dances: A Collection of Square Sets.* Jyllinge, Denmark: privately published, 2002. (4th ed., 2012)

Briand, Elmer. *Fiddle Tunes: A Collection of Elmer Briand's Musical Compositions, Cape Breton Style.* Toronto: George LeFort, 1980.

Campbell, John: A Cape Breton Legacy. Transcribed by George Ruckert. MO: Mel Bay Publications, Inc., 2009.

Cape Breton Fiddlers' Association, The. *The Cape Breton Fiddlers Collection.* Cape Breton Musical Heritage Series, vol. 7. Englishtown, Cape Breton: Cranford Publications, 2007.

Celtic Colours and Paul Cranford (Ed.). *The Celtic Colours Collection.* Englishtown: Cranford Publications, 2011.

Chafe, Patricia. *Bits and Pieces: A Collection of Original Music by Pat Chafe.* Glace Bay: August Musicworks, 2009.

Cranford, Paul. *Lighthouse Collection of Newly Composed Fiddle Tunes: Original Melodies in the Cape Breton, Irish and Scottish Tradition.* Cape Breton Musical Heritage Series: Volume 3 edn. Englishtown, Cape Breton: Cranford Publications, 1996.

———. *The Cape Breton Scottish Collection.* Cape Breton Musical Heritage Series: Volume 8 edn. Englishtown: Cranford Publications, 2013.

———. *The Cape Breton Highland Collection. Cape Breton Musical Heritage Series*: Volume 9 edn. Englishtown: Cranford Publications, 2015.

Dares, Tracey. *A' Chording to the Tunes: A Cape Breton Piano Accompaniment Lesson.* NS: Crooked Lake Music, 1997.

Dunlay, Kate and David Greenberg. *Traditional Celtic Violin Music of Cape Breton Toronto: the Dun-Green Collection.* NS: DunGreen Music, 1996.

Dunlay, Kate with David Reich. *Traditional Celtic Music of Cape Breton Island.* Harrisville: Fiddlecase books, 1986.

Ellis, Raymond. *Cape Breton Fiddle Tunes: A Collection of Original Compositions*. Cape Breton: Privately published, 2008.

Farrell, Mike. *Cape Breton Medleys: Scottish Violin Music by Jimmie MacLellan*. Westport, Ontario: privately published, 1992

Ferrel, Frank. *Boston Fiddle: The Dudley Street Tradition*. Mel Bay Publications Inc., 1999.

Fitzgerald, Winston. *Winston Fitzgerald: A Collection of Fiddle Tunes*. ed. Paul Cranford. Cape Breton Musical Heritage Series: Volume 4 edn. Englishtown, Cape Breton: Cranford Publications, 1997.

Graham, Glenn. *The Glenn Graham Collection of Cape Breton Violin Music*. Halifax: Privately published, 2000.

Holland, Jerry. *Jerry Holland's Collection of Fiddle Tunes*. First edition 1988. (2nd ed. revised and expanded 1992; 3rd ed. 1995; 4th ed. 2000). Cape Breton Musical Heritage Series, Volume 1. Englishtown, Cape Breton: Cranford Publications, 2000.

———. *Jerry Holland: The Second Collection*. Ed. Paul Cranford. Cape Breton Musical Heritage Series, Volume 5. Englishtown, Cape Breton: Cranford Publications, 2000.

Le Blanc, Barbara. 1986. *Inverness County Dance Project*. Ottawa: Museum of Man.

———. *Tous ensemble: Guide pour enseigner les danses traditionnelles acadiennes/All Join Hands: Guide to Teach Traditional Acadian Dance*. Halifax: Dance Nova Scotia, 2004.

Le Blanc, Barbara with Mary Janet MacDonald, Betty Matheson, Dianne Milligan and Dolena Roach. 1992. *No Less, No More, Just Four on the Floor: A Guide to Teaching Traditional Cape Breton Square Sets for Public Schools*. Halifax: Dance Nova Scotia. 1994? 4th edition.

Little, Jason C. *Scottish and Cape Breton Fiddle Music in New Hampshire for Violin/Mandolin and Guitar*. Fiddlecase Books, 1984.

MacDonald, Dan R. *The Heather Hill Collection: The Music of Dan R. MacDonald*. Ed. John Donald Cameron. Port Hawkesbury: Cameron Music Sales, 2000. (first published 1985 Brownrigg: Toronto).

———. *The Trip to Windsor Collection: The Music of Dan R. MacDonald*. Volume 2. Ed. John Donald Cameron. Port Hawkesbury, Cape Breton: Cameron Music Sales. 1994.

MacDonald, Cassie and Maggie. Tunes. Halifax: Privately published, 2011.

MacDonald, Dougie. *Cape Breton Fiddler Dougie MacDonald: Fiddle Tunes*. Mabou: Mabou Communications, 1993.

MacDonald, Francis. *Cape Breton Fiddling: Instructional Video for Beginners*. Inverness: Dongael Video Productions, 1993.

MacDonald, J. Francis and Rod MacDonald. *A Collection of Cape Breton Violin Music Consisting of Original, Traditional and Favorite Tunes Selected and Arranged by J. Francis MacDonald and Rod MacDonald*. NS: Cape West Music. 2006.

MacDonald, Mary Janet. *One Step at a Time*. Instructional Step Dance Video. NS: Port Hood, 1992.

———. *A Family Tradition, A Cape Breton Step dancing Instructional Video with Mary Janet MacDonald*. St. George's Bay, Antigonish: Seabright Productions, 2002 (DVD), 1999 (Video).

MacEachern, Dan Hughie. *MacEachern's Collection—Cape Breton Scottish Music for the Violin. Volume 1*. Queensville: Dan Hugh MacEachern, 1975.

———. *MacEachern's Collection: The Music of Dan Hughie MacEachern, Vol. 11*. Antigonish, NS: Margaret Dunn, 1993.

MacGillivray, Troy. 2008. *Fiddle Tunes*. Antigonish, NS: Trolleymac Music. PDF.

MacIntyre, Sandy and Leigh Cline. *Cape Breton Style Fiddle Sets with Guitar Tablature*. MO: Mel Bay Pub. Inc., 2011.

MacMaster, Natalie. *A Fiddle Lesson with Natalie MacMaster* (Video, DVD). NS: Homespun Tapes, no date.

———. *Mel Bay Presents Natalie MacMaster's Cape Breton Island Fiddle*. Transcribed by Stacey Phillips. MO: Mel Bay Pub. Inc., 2001.

Macmillan, Scott. *Scoobie Tunes, A Family Fiddle Frenzy: Cape Breton Fiddle Tunes composed by Scott Macmillan*. Halifax, NS: ScoJen Music Pub., 1996.

MacNeil, Jean. *Spring in your Step – Cape Breton Step dance Instruction from Beginner to Intermediate* (Video). Sydney Mines: Cape Breton Steps, 2005.

MacQuarrie, Gordon. *The Cape Breton Collection of Scottish Melodies for the Violin*. Medford, Massachussets: Joseph Beaton, 1940.

Rankin, L. "Introduction to Traditional Step dancing: A Quick Lesson for Children and Adults." *Gaelic Cape Breton: 1996 Visitors Supplement*. Mabou: Cape Breton, Sandy Pub.: 5,1996.

Ruckert, George. *John Campbell—A Cape Breton Legacy*. St. Louis: Mel Bay Publications, Inc., 2009.

Stubbert, Brenda. *Brenda Stubbert's Collection of Fiddle Tunes*. Cape Breton Musical Heritage Series: Volume 2 edn. Englishtown, Cape Breton Island: Cranford Publications, 1994.

———.*Brenda Stubbert: The Second Collection*. Cape Breton Musical Heritage Series: Volume 6 edn. Englishtown, Cape Breton: Cranford Publications, 2008.

Tomas, Otis. *The Fiddletree Collection: Fiddle Tunes Composed Otis A. Tomas*. Privately published, 2001.

———. *The Fiddletree*. Book and CD edition. Privately published, 2011.

Various. *The Celtic Colours Collection*. Ed. Paul Cape Breton Musical Heritage Series: Volume 8 edn. Englishtown, Cape Breton: Cranford Publications, 2011.

BOOKS, DISSERTATIONS, ARTICLES, LINER NOTES

Addison, E. L. "The Perception and Value of Dance Halls in Inverness County, Cape Breton." BA thesis, Trent University, 2001.

Akenson, D. H. *Between Two Revolutions: Islandmagee, County Antrim, 1798-1920*. Gazelle Book Series, 1979.

Alburger, Mary Ann. *Scottish Fiddlers and their Music*. London: Victor Gollanz, 1983.

Ballantyne, Pat. 'Closer to the floor: Reflections on Cape Breton step dance', in *Driving the bow: Fiddle and dance studies from around the North Atlantic 2 (2008)*. Eds. Ian Russell and Mary Anne Alburger. Abderdeen: Elphinstone Institute, University of Aberdeen: 135-143.

Beaton, Harvey. "Dannsa." *Mac-Talla (Gaeltalk Communications, Mabou)* 1, no. 1 (May 1998): 11.

Bennett, Margaret. "Step-Dancing: Why We Must Learn from Past Mistakes." *West Highland Free Press*, October 14, 1994.

Bennett, Margaret. *The Last Stronghold: Scottish Gaelic Traditions in Newfoundland*. St. John's, NL: Breakwater Books, 1989.

Bergfeldt-Munro, Wendy. "Tuned In: radio, Ritual and Resistance, Cape Breton's Traditional Music, 1973-1998." MA thesis. Athabasca: AB, 2015.

Bickerton, James P. "Building Regions in the Maritimes." In *Governing: Essays in Honour of Donald J. Savoie*, 260-290. Ed. James Bickerton and B. Guy Peters. Montréal: McGill-Queens University Press, 2013.

———. *Nova Scotia, Ottawa, and the Politics of Regional Development*. Toronto: University of Toronto Press, 1990.

Borggreen, Jørn."Square Dance on Cape Breton I-III." *Newsletter from Danish-Cape Breton Society*, 2006.

Boulton, Laura. *The Music Hunter: The Autobiography of a Career*. New York: Doubleday, 1969.

Brewer, John D. *Ethnography: Understanding Social Research*. Ed. Alan Bryman. UK: Open University Press. 2000.

Bruford, Alan and A. Munro. *The Fiddle in the Highlands*. Inverness, NS: An Comunn Gaidhealach, 1973.

Bruford, Alan. Vol. 57 of *Tales until Dawn. Sgeul gu Latha*. Dublin: An Cumann Le Béaloideas Éireann/ The Folklore of Ireland Society, 1989.

Bumstead, J. M. *The People's Clearance: Highland Emigration to British North America, 1770-1815*. Edinburgh, UK: Edinburgh University Press & and Winnipeg, MB: University of Manitoba Press, 1982.

Burrill, Gary. *Away: Maritimers in Massachusetts, Ontario, and Alberta: An Oral History of Leaving Home*. Montréal: McGill-Queen's University Press, 1992.

Campbell, D. and R. A. MacLean. *Beyond the Atlantic Roar—A Study of the Nova Scotia Scots*. Toronto: McClelland and Stewart, 1974.

Campbell, J. L. "Scottish Gaelic in Canada. *American Speech* 11, no. 2 (April 1936): 128-36.

Campbell, J. L. *Songs Remembered in Exile: Traditional Gaelic Songs from Nova Scotia Recorded in Cape Breton and Antigonish County in 1937 with an Account of the Causes of Hebridean Emigration, 1790-1835*. Aberdeen University Press: Aberdeen, 1990.

Campbell, J. L. and Francis Collinson. *Hebridean Folksongs, A Collection of Waulking Songs by Donald MacCormick*. Oxford: Clarendon Press,1969.

———. Hebridean Folksongs, II, Waulking Songs from Barra, South Uist, Eriskay and Benbecula. Oxford: Clarendon Press, 1977.

———. *Hebridean Folksong*. Vol. 3. Oxford: Clarendon Press, 1981.

Campbell, J. L., and Margaret Fay Shaw. "Canadian Folk Song Collections." *Journal of the International Folk Music Council* 14 (1962): 174.

Campbell, John L. and Trevor H. Hall. *Strange Things: The Story of Fr. Allan McDonald, Ada Goodrich Freer, and the Society for Physical Research's Enquiry into Highland Second Sight*. Edinburgh: Birlinn, 2006.

Campey, L. H. *After the Hector: The Scottish Pioneers of Nova Scotia and Cape Breton 1773-1852*. Toronto: Natural Heritage Books, 2004.

Caplan, Ron and R. A. Grace. *Acadian Lives in Cape Breton Island*. Wreck Cove, NS: Breton Books, 2004.

Caplan, Ron. *Down North*. Toronto: Doubleday, 1980.

———. *Talking Cape Breton Music: Conversations with People Who Love and Make the Music*. Wreck Cove, NS: Breton Books, 2006.

Chisholm, Anselme. *Chéticamp: History and Acadian Traditions*. St. John's, NL: Breakwater Books, 1986.

Clancy, Liam. *The Mountain of the Women: Memoirs of an Irish Troubadour*. New York: Doubleday, 2002.

Collinson, F. *The Traditional and National Music of Scotland*. London: Routledge & Kegan Paul, 1966.

Conn, Stephanie. "Fitting between Present and Past: Memory and Social Interaction in Cape Breton Gaelic Singing." *Ethnomusicology Forum* 21, no. 3 (December 2012.): 354-73.

———. "*Carn Mor de Chlachan Beaga*/A Large Cairn from Small Stones: Multivocality and Memory in Cape Breton Gaelic Singing." PhD dissertation, University of Toronto, 2011.

Corbin, C. and J. A. Rolls. *The Centre of the World at the Edge of a Continent*. Sydney, NS: University College of Cape Breton Press, 1996.

Cormier, Sam. "The Dances Down Home, Joe Cormier." Liner notes to *Scottish Violin Music from Cape Breton*. Rounder, 2001. CD. First issued 1974.

Cowell, Sidney Robertson. "The Connection between the Precenting of Psalms on Cape Breton Island and in the Colonial New England Churches." *Journal of the International Folk Music Council* 14 (1962): 155-6.

Craig, David. *On the Crofters' Trail: In Search of the Clearance Highlanders*. London: Jonathan Cape, 1990. Reprinted Reading, UK: Cox and Wyman, 1992.

Creighton, Helen and Calum MacLeod. *Gaelic Songs in Nova Scotia*. National Museum of Man Bulletin, Ottawa, 1964.

Creighton, Helen and Doreen Senior. *Twelve Folksongs from Nova Scotia*. London: Novello, 1940.

———. *Traditional Songs from Nova Scotia*. Toronto: Ryerson University Press 1950.

Creighton, Helen. *Maritime Folk Songs*. Toronto: Ryerson University Press,1972. First published 1962.

———. *Songs and Ballads from Nova Scotia*. Toronto and Vancouver: Dent, 1932. Reprinted New York: Dover, 1966.

———. *A Folk Tale Journey through the Maritimes*. Breton Books, 1994.

Croft, Clary. *Helen Creighton: Canada's First Lady of Folklore*. Halifax: Nimbus Pub., 1999.

Cusick Hazeltin, Elizabeth. "The Water's Width: Community Media's Relation to Place, Community and Identity in the Isle of Skye in Scotland and Cape Breton Island in Nova Scotia." Undergraduate thesis, University of North Carolina, 2011.

Dembling, Jonathan. "Joe Jimmy Alec Visits the Mod and Escapes Unscathed: The Nova Scotia Gaelic Revivals." MA thesis, Saint Mary's University, 1997.

———. "The Gaelic Revival in Nova Scotia." *Proceedings of the Harvard Celtic Colloquium* 18/19 (1998): 11-33.

———. "You Play It as You Would Sing It: Cape Breton, Scottishness, and the Means of Cultural Production." In *Transatlantic Scots,* 180-97. Ed. C. Ray. Tuscaloosa, USA: University of Alabama Press, 2005.

Denzin, N. *The Research Act*. Chicago: Aldine, 1970.

Dickson, Joshua. *When Piping was Strong: Tradition, Change and the Bagpipe in South Uist*. Edinburgh: John Donald Publishers, 2006.

Divine, T. M. *To the Ends of the Earth: Scotland's Global Diaspora, 1750-2010*. London: Allen Lane, 2011.

Doherty, Elizabeth Anne. "The Paradox of the Periphery—Evolution of the Cape Breton Fiddle Tradition c. 1928-1995." PhD dissertation, University of Limerick, 1996.

Doherty, Liz. *The Music of Cape Breton: An Irish Perspective*. Cork, Ireland: The Irish Traditional Music Society, University College Cork, 1994.

———. Liner notes to *Music from Cape Breton Island*. Nimbus, 1995. Compact disc.

———. "Bringing it all Back Home? Issues Surrounding Cape Breton Fiddle Music in Scotland" in *Play It Like It Is: Fiddle and Dance Studies from Around the North Atlantic* 1 (2006): 102-109. Eds. Ian Russell and Mary Anne Alburger. Aberdeen: The Elphinstone Institute.

Donaldson, E. A. *The Scottish Highland Games in America*. New York: Firebird Press, 1999.

Donovan, Ken. "After Midnight We Danced until Daylight: Music, Song and Dance in Cape Breton, 1713-1758." *Acadiensis* 32, no. 1 (2002): 3-28.

———, ed. *Cape Breton at 200: Historical Essays in Honour of the Island's Bicentennial 1785-1985*. Sydney, NS: University College of Cape Breton Press, 1985.

———. *The Island: New Perspectives in Cape Breton History 1703-1990*. Sydney, NS: Acadiensis Press, University College of Cape Breton Press, 2002.

Dorchak, G. J. "Fiddling with Tradition: The Question of Authenticity within Cape Breton Fiddle Music." MA thesis, Syracuse University, 2006.

———. "The Formation of Authenticity within Folk Tradition: A Case Study of Cape Breton Fiddling." *Driving the Bow: Fiddle and Dance Studies from Around the North Atlantic* 2 (2008): 153-165. Ed. Ian Russell and Mary Anne Alburger Aberdeen: The Elphinstone Institute.

———. "Rhetorical Cycels: Music, Rhetorical Effect and Tradition." In The Effects of Rhetoric, and the Rhetoric of Effects: Past, Present, Future. Eds. Amos Kiewe and Davis W. Houck. Columbia: University of South Carolina Press, 2015.

———. "The Exported Cape Breton Fiddler: A Hermeneutic Study of the Meaning of Cape Breton Fiddle Music Outside Cape Breton." *Crossing Over: Fiddle and Dance Studies from Around the North Atlantic* 3 (2010): 250-259. Ed. Ian Russell and Anna Kearney Guigné. Aberdeen: The Elphinstone Institute.

Ducharme, Mary Anne. *Archie Neil: A Triumph of a Life!* Wreck Cove, NS: Breton Books, 1992.

Dunkly, Nancy. "Studies in the Scottish Gaelic Folk-song Tradition in Canada." PhD dissertation, Harvard University, 1984.

Dunlay, Kate and David Reich. *Celtic Music of Cape Breton Island.* Harrisville: Fiddlecase Books, 1986.

Dunlay, Kate. "A Cape Breton Primer: Canada's Old World Music." *Sing Out!* 34, no. 4 (1989): 24-32.

———. "Musings on Cape Breton Fiddle versus Irish." In "Cape Breton Edition," special issue, *Fiddler Magazine*, 2000.

———. "The Playing of Traditional Scottish Dance Music: Old and New World Styles and Practices." In *Celtic Languages and Celtic Peoples: Proceedings of the Second North American Congress of Celtic Studies*, 173-191. Ed. C. J. Byrne, M. Harry and P. O Siadhail. Halifax, NS: D'Arcy McGee Chair of Irish Studies, St. Mary's University, 1992

———. "Timeline of Cape Breton Fiddling." In "Cape Breton Edition," special issue, *Fiddler Magazine*, 2000.

Dunlay, Kathleen E. (Kate). "Traditional Celtic Fiddle Music of Cape Breton." MA thesis, Indiana University, 1986.

Dunn, C. W. *Highland Settler: A Portrait of the Scottish Gael in Cape Breton and Eastern Nova Scotia.* NS: Breton Books, 1991 (Original edition Toronto: University of Toronto Press, 1953).

Dunn, J. A. "*Tha blas na gaidhlig air a h-uile fidhleir* (The Sound of Gaelic is in the Fiddler's Music): An Investigation of the Possible Influence the Scottish Gaelic Language has had on the Fiddling Style of Cape Breton." Undergraduate thesis, St. Francis Xavier University, 1991.

Emmerson, G. S. *Rantin' Pipe and Tremblin' String: A History of Scottish Dance Music.* London: J.M. Dent and Sons, 1971.

Falzett, Tiber. "*Seinn na píobadh 's an t-seann nós*: Bagpipe Traditions in Gaelic Cape Breton." *An Rubha*, Winter 2008/2009: 18-9.

———. "*Brìgh 'chiùil*: Vernacular Ear-Learned Piping in Cape Breton and South Uist Explored through *Seanchas*-based Narratives." *Scottish Studies* 35 (2010): 59-91.

Farnham, C. H. "Cape Breton Folk." *Harpers New Monthly*, 1886.

Feintuch, Burt. Longing for Community." In "Communities of Practice: Traditional Music and Dance," special issue, *Western Folklore* 60, no. 2/3 (2001): 149-61.

———. Liner notes to *The Heart of Cape Breton: Fiddle Music Recorded Live along the Ceilidh Trail.* Smithsonian Folkways Recording, 2002. CD.

———. "The Conditions for Cape Breton Fiddle Music: The Social and Economic Setting of a Regional Soundscape." *Ethnomusicology* 48, no. 1 (2004.): 73-104.

———. Liner notes to *Cape Breton Fiddle and Piano Music: The Beaton Family of Mabou.* Smithsonian Folkways Recording, 2004. CD.

———. "Revivals on the Edge: Northumberland and Cape Breton: A Keynote." *Yearbook for Traditional Music* 38 (2006): 1-17.

———.Music on the Margins: Fiddle Music in Cape Breton." *Play It Like It Is: Fiddle and Dance Studies from Around the North Atlantic* 1 (2008): 110-120.

———. A Week on the Ceilidh Trail." In *Northeast Folklore: Essays in Honor of Edward D. Ives*. Ed. Paulina MacDougall and David Taylor. Toronto: Northeast Folklore Society, 2002.

Feintuch, Burt and G. Samson. *In the Blood: Cape Breton Conversations on Culture*. Logan, UT: Utah State University Press and Syney: Cape Breton University Press, 2010.

Fergusson, Donald A. *Fad Air Falbh As Innse Gall: Beyond the Hebrides, Including the Cape Breton Collection*. Halifax: privately published, 1977.

Fleming, Ian. *Rock, Rhythm and Reels: Canada's East Coast Musicians on Stage*. PEI: Gynergy Books/Ragweed Press,1997.

Frank, David. "The Industrial Folksong in Cape Breton." *Canadian Folklore Canadien* 8, no. 1-2 (1986): 21-42.

Garrison, Virginia Hope. "Traditional and Non-traditional Teaching and Learning Practices in Folk Music: An Ethnographic Field Study of Cape Breton Fiddling." PhD dissertation, University of Wisconsin-Madison, 1985.

Gedutis, Susan. *See You at the Hall: Boston's Golden Era of Irish Music and Dance*. New England: Northeastern University Press, 2004.

Geertz, Clifford "Thick Description: Toward an Interpretive Theory of Culture". In *The Interpretation of Cultures: Selected Essays*. New York: Basic Books, 1973.

Gibson, John G. "Traditional Gaelic Bagpiping, 1745-1945." PhD dissertation, University of Edinburgh, 2002.

———. *Old and New World Highland Bagpiping*. Montréal: McGill-Queen's University Press, 2002.

———. *Traditional Gaelic Bagpiping, 1745-1945*. Montréal: McGill-Queen's University Press, 2000.

Gibson, John and J. Beaton. "The Role of the Parish Priest in Maintaining Ethnic Tradition in Eastern Nova Scotia." ." In *Highland Heritage*. NS: Port Hastings, 1977.

Gillis, Rannie. *Travels in the Celtic World*. Halifax, NS: Nimbus, 1994.

Graham, Glenn. "Cape Breton Fiddle Music: The Making and Maintenance of a Tradition." MA thesis, Saint Mary's University, 2004.

———. *The Cape Breton Fiddle: Making and Maintaining Tradition*. Sydney, NS: Cape Breton University Press, 2006.

Gurstein, Michael. "Fiddlers on the Wire: Music, Electronic Commerce, and Local Economic Development on a Virtual Cape Breton Island." In *Doing Business on the Internet: Opportunities and Pitfalls*, 193-207. Ed. F. Sudweeks and C. T. Romm. Berlin: Springer Verlag, 1999.

Hamilton, Diane. Liner notes to *Nova Scotia Folk Music from Cape Breton*. Elektra, 1954. LP.

Harper, M. and M. E. Vance, eds. *Myth, Migration and the Making of Memory: Scotia and Nova Scotia c. 1700-1990*. Edinburgh: John Donald Publishers, 1999.

Hayes, Ian. "Festival Fieldwork and the Participant Observer: Celtic Colours, Custom, and the Carnivalesque."*Canadian Folk Music* 46, No. 2 (Summer 2012): 29-33.

———. "You have to Strike a Balance between Sharing and Charging: Cape Breton Fiddling and Intellectual Property Rights." *Ethnologies* 33, no. 2 (2011): 181-201.

———."How Traditional Do You Want to Sound? Deconstructing Notions of Traditionalism in Cape Breton Fiddling." *Eighth International Small Islands Culture Conference Refereed Proceedings*, 2012. http://sicri-network.org/archives/isic8/ (accessed July 2, 2014).

———. "Our Fiddles Sound Big. That's the Way I Think It Should Be: Cape Breton Fiddling and Amplification Practices." *MUSICultures* 39, no. 2 (2012): 161-80.

———.'It's a balancing act. That's the secret to making this music fit in today': Negotiating Professional and Vernacular Boundaries in the Cape Breton Fiddling Tradition." PhD dissertation, Memorial University of Newfoundland, 2015.

Heaney, Seamus. *Opened Ground: Poems 1966-1996*. London: Faber and Faber, 1998.

Hennessy, J. J. "Fiddle Grooves: Identity, Representation, and the Sound of Cape Breton Fiddle Music in Popular Culture." PhD dissertation, University of Toronto, 2008.

Herdman, Jessica. "'Old style' Cape Breton Fiddling: Narrative, Interstices, Dancing." In vol. 3 of *Crossing over: Fiddle and Dance Studies from Around the North Atlantic*, 148-155. Eds. Ian Russell and Anna Kearney Guigné. Aberdeen: The Elphinstone Institute, University of Aberdeen, 2010.

———. "The Cape Breton Fiddling Narrative: Innovation, Preservation, Dancing." MA thesis, University of British Columbia, 2008.

Higgins, Benjamin. "Entrepreneurship and Economic Development: The Case of Cape Breton." In *the Maritime Provinces: Looking to the Future*, 125-156. Ed. Donald J. Savoie and Benjamin Higgins. Moncton, NB: Canadian Institute for Research on Regional Development, 1993.

Hogg, Elaine Ingalls. *When Cape Breton Joined Canada*. Halifax: Nimbus, 2005.

Hornby, James. "The Fiddle on the Island: Fiddling Tradition on Prince Edward Island." PhD dissertation, Memorial University of Newfoundland, 1983.

Hornby, Jim. "The Great Fiddling Contests of 1926." *The Island Magazine* 7 (1979): 25-30.

Hornsby, S. J. *Nineteenth-Century Cape Breton: A Historical Geography*. Montréal and Kingston: McGill-Queen's University Press, 1992.

Hunter, James. *A Dance Called America: The Scottish Highlands, The United States and Canada*. Edinburgh: Mainstream Publishing. 1995.

Hunter, James. *The Fiddle Music of Scotland*. Edinburgh: Chambers, 1979.

Ivakhiv, Adrian. "Colouring Cape Breton 'Celtic': Topographies of Culture and Identity in Cape Breton Island." *Ethnologies* 27, no. 2 (2005): 107-136.

Johnson, David. "Regional Development as the Work of Prometheus: Enterprise Cape Breton Corporation, A Critical Analysis." In *Doing Development Differently: Regional Development on the Atlantic Periphery*, 150-171. Ed. Susan Hodgett, David Johnson and Stephen A. Royle. Sydney, NS: Cape Breton University Press, 2007.

Johnston, A. A. Vol. 1 of *A History of the Catholic Church in Eastern Nova Scotia, 1611-1827*. Antigonish, NS: St. FX Press, 1960.

Kelly, James. "A Sociographic Study of Gaelic in Cape Breton, Nova Scotia." MA thesis, Concordia University, 1980.

Kelly, Wayne. *Downright Upright: A History of the Canadian Piano Industry*. Toronto: Natural Heritage, 1991.

Kerman, Joseph. *Musicology*. Fontana Masterguides, ed. Frank Kermode. London: Fontana Press/Collins, 1985.

Lamb, James B. *The Celtic Crusade: The Story of A. W. R. MacKenzie and the Gaelic College*. Hantsport, NS: Lancelot Press, 1992.

———. *A Place Apart: The Cape Breton Story*. Sydney, NS: Steel Town Pub., 1998.

Landin, Anne. *Guthan Prìseil: Guthan agus Òrain Gàidheil Cheap Breatainn/Precious Voices: Voices and Songs of the Cape Breton Gael*. Sydney, NS: Centre for Cape Breton Studies, Cape Breton University, 2009.

Lavengood, Kathleen Elizabeth. "A Journey through Time and Tradition: Laura Boulton's Discovery of Cape Breton Fiddler Sandy MacLean." *Resound* 22, no. 3-4 (2003): 1-6.

———. "Transnational Communities through Global Tourism: Experiencing Celtic Culture through Music Practice on Cape Breton Island, Nova Scotia." PhD dissertation, Indiana University, 2008.

Laxer, J. *The Acadians—In Search of a Homeland*. 2nd ed. Toronto: Anchor Canada, 2007.

Le Blanc, Barbara. "L'Église et la Danse." In *Patrimoine folklorique des Franco-Américains*, 115-126. Ed. Claire Quintal. Québec: Le Conseil de la Vie Française en Amérique du Nord, 1986.

———. "To Dance or Not to Dance: The Case of Church and Group Social Control in Chéticamp, Cape Breton Island, Nova Scotia." MA thesis, Université Laval, 1986.

———. "Simonne Voyer: Following her Bliss." *Dance Collection Danse: The News, Toronto* 38 (1994): 3-5.

———. "Changing Places: Dance, Society and Gender." In *Undisciplined Women, Tradition and Culture in Canada*, 101-113. Ed. Pauline Greenhill and Diane Tye. Montréal: McGill-Queens University Press, 1997.

———. "Survol impressioniste de la danse traditionnelle et sociale dans une communauté acadienne. In *L'acadie au féminin: Un regard multidisciplinaire sur les Acadiennes et les Cadiennes.*, 161-181. Ed. Maurice Basque et al. Moncton, NB: Chaire d'études acadiennes, l'Université de Moncton, 2000.

Le Blanc, Barbara and Laura Sadowsky. "La survivance par la chanson et la danse." In *Patrimoine folklorique des franco-américains*, 105-114. Ed. Claire Quintal. Québec: Le Conseil de la Vie Française en Amérique du Nord, 1986.

Le Blanc, Barbara, Laura Sadowsky, and Tess LeBlanc. "Aperçu de la danse acadienne traditionnelle." *La Société Historique Acadienne: Les Cahiers* 21, no. 1 (1990): 2-21.

Linkletter, Michael. "*Bu dual dha sin* (That was his birthright): Gaelic Scholar Alexander MacLean Sinclair (1840-1924)." PhD dissertation, Harvard University, 2006.

———. "The Alexander MacLean Sinclair Papers in NSARM." *Scotia: Interdisciplinary Journal of Scottish Studies* 27 (2003).

Lotz, Jim and Pat Lotz. *Cape Breton Island*. Vancouver: Douglas David and Charles, 1974.

MacDonald, A. D. Vol. 1 of *Mabou Pioneers: A Genealogical Tracing of Some Pioneer Families who Settled in Mabou and District*. Antigonish, NS: Formac Pub., no date.

MacDonald, G. *The Highlanders of Waipu or Echoes of 1745: A Scottish Odyssey*. Dunedin, New Zealand: Coulls Somerville Wilkie, 1928.

MacDonald, Jennifer Marie. "Devil on the Fiddle: The Musical and Social Ramifications of Genre Transformation in Cape Breton Music." MA thesis, McGill University, 2006.

MacDonald, Martha Jane. "Group Identity in Social Gatherings: Traditions and Community on the Iona Peninsula, Cape Breton." MA thesis, Memorial University of Newfoundland, 1986.

———. "The Cape Breton Ceilidh." *Culture & Tradition* 12 (1988): 76-85.

MacDonald, Paul M. "The Cape Breton Piano Style." http://www.cranfordpub.com/articles/cape_breton_piano.htm (accessed March 1 2014).

———. "Irish Music in Cape Breton." In *The Irish in Cape Breton*, 119-129. Ed. A. A. MacKenzie. Wreck Cove, NS: Breton Books, 1999.

———. Liner notes to *Alex Francis MacKay: A Lifelong Home*. Rounder Records Corps., CD, 1997.

———. Liner notes to *Celtic Mouth Music, Musical Expeditions CD*. Ellipsis Arts, 1997.

———. Liner notes to *Here Comes John Allan Cameron*. Stephen MacDonald Productions. CD, 2012.

———. "The Cape Breton Piano Style – A Timeline." In Celtic Colours International Festival Programme, 2014.

———. "Wilfred Prosper: A Mi'kmaq Fiddler." In *Fiddler Magazine: Cape Breton Edition 2000*. Ed. Mary Larsen Holland. North Sydney, NS: 2000, 27-30.

MacDonald, Paul, Patricia Lamey Hart and Mary Elizabeth Lamey. Liner notes to *Bill Lamey: Full Circle from Cape Breton to Boston and Back – Classic House Sessions of Traditional Cape Breton Music 1956-1977*. Rounder records Corps., CD, 2000.

MacDonald, Robert. "Music from the Dead: The Tune Making of John MacDougall." MSc dissertation. Utah State University, 2009.

MacDonald, Sandy. Rawlins Cross: A Brief History. http://wwww.rawlinscross.com (accessed Jun 15 2015)

MacDonald, Sherry Mulley. *Cape Breton: The Pride of an Island*. Sydney, NS: New Deal Development, 2007.

MacDonnell, Margaret. *The Emigrant Experience*. Toronto: University of Toronto Press, 1982.

MacDougall, J. L. *History of Inverness County, Nova Scotia*. Ontario: Mika Publishing,1922.

MacGill-Fhinnein [MacLennan], Gordon. "*Canuint Ghaidhlig de Chuid Contae Inbhir nis, Ceap Breatainn, Albainn Nua, Ceanada*." PhD dissertation, National University of Ireland, 1974.

MacGillivray, Allister. *The Cape Breton Fiddler*. Sydney, NS: College of Cape Breton Press, 1981.

———. *A Cape Breton Ceilidh*. Cape Breton: Sea-Cape Music, 1988.

———. *Original: The Cape Breton Fiddler*. 2nd ed. Marion Bridge, NS: Sea-Cape Music, 1997.

MacInnes, Sheldon. "Cape Bretoners in Windsor: A Folk Society in an Urban Setting." MA thesis, Merrill-Palmer Institute, 1977.

———. "Cape Breton Step-dance: An Irish or Scottish Tradition?" *Éisge na Laoi, Cork, Festival programme* 1993. http://www.siliconglen.com/celtfaq/3_2.html (accessed July 20 2015).

———."Stepdancing: *Gach taobh dhe'n uisge*"/Both sides of the water. In *The Centre of the World at the Edge of a Continent*, 111-118. Ed. C. Corbin and J. A. Rolls. Sydney, NS: University College of Cape Breton Press, 1996.

———. *Buddy MacMaster: The Judique Fiddler*. Lawrencetown Beach, NS: Pottersfield Press, 2007.

———. *A Journey in Celtic Music: Cape Breton Style*. Sydney, NS: University College of Cape Breton Press, 1997.

MacInnis, Frank. "Response to *The Vanishing Cape Breton Fiddler*." In *The Cape Breton Fiddlers Collection*. Ed. Paul Cranford. Englishtown, Cape Breton: Cranford Publications, 2007.

MacInnis, J. J. "Scottish Music in Cape Breton, Nova Scotia: Violin Players I Have Met." In *Eilean Cheap Breatann*, Canadian-American Gael Vol. 1 1943/44.

———."Scottish Music in Cape Breton, Nova Scotia: Violin Players I Have Met." In *Eilean Cheap Breatann*, Canadian-American Gael Vol. 2 1948.

MacIsaac, Ashley and F. Condron. *Fiddling with Disaster: Clearing the Past*. Toronto: Warwick Music Pub., 2007.

MacKay, Donald. *Scotland Farewell: The People of the Hector*. Toronto: McGraw-Hill Ryerson, 1980.

MacKay, Ian. "Tartanism Triumphant: The Construction of Scottishness in Nova Scotia 1933-1954." *Acadiensis* 21, no. 2 (1992): 5-47.

MacKenzie Campbell, P.J. *Highland Community on the Bras d'Or*. NS: Casket Printing and Publishing Co. Ltd. 1978.

MacKenzie, A. A. *The Irish in Cape Breton*. Wreck Cove, NS: Breton Books, 1999.

MacKenzie, Archibald J. *The MacKenzie's History of Christmas Island and Parish*. Sudbury, ON: MacKenzie Rothe, 1984. First published 1926.

MacKenzie, Hugh A. and Rod C. Mac Neil. *Mar a b'àbhaist 's a' Ghleann/As it was in the Glen: Gaelic Songs and Traditions from Cape Breton*. NS: Sìol Cultural Enterprises, 2012.

MacKinnon, Richard. "Protest Song and Verse in Cape Breton Island." *Ethnologies* 30, no. 2 (2008): 33-71.

MacKinnon, Richard. "Victorian Parlour Instrument Meets the Celtic Fiddle: The Dynamics of the Cape Breton Piano Style." In *Discovering Cape Breton Folklore*, 30-43. Ed. R. MacKinnon. Sydney, NS: Cape Breton University Press, 2009.

MacLean, M. *The People of Glengarry, Highlanders in Transition, 1745-1820*. Montréal: McGill-Queen's University, 1991.

MacLean, R. A. *A State of Mind: The Scots in Nova Scotia*. Hantsport, NS: Lancelot Press, 1992.

MacLean, Vincent, W. *These were my People: Washabuck, An Anecdotal History*. Sydney: Cape Breton University Press, 2014.

MacMaster, Natalie and Eileen MacNamara. *Natalie MacMaster's Cape Breton Aire: The Story of a Musical Life and Place*. Photographs by Eric Roth. Ontario: MacMaster Music, 2010.

MacMillan, A. J. *To the Hills of Boisdale: A Short History and a Genealogical tracing of the Pioneer Families of Boisdale, Cape Breton and the Surrounding Areas*. Sydney: Music Hill Publications, 1986.

MacNeil, Bill and M. Wolfe. *Signing on: The Birth of Radio in Canada*. Toronto: Doubleday, 1982.

MacNeil, Hector. "Work and Language in a Cape Breton Gaelic Community." MA thesis, St. Francis Xavier University, 1988.

MacNeil, J. N. and J. W. Shaw. *Tales until Dawn—The World of a Cape Breton Gaelic Story-Teller*. Montréal: McGill-Queen's University Press and Edinburgh University Press, 1987.

MacNeil, Vincent. "A Study of Gaelic Language & Culture in Cape Breton's Barra Gaidhealtachd." MA thesis, Mount Saint Vincent University, 2008.

MacOdrum, Murdock Maxwell. "Survival of the English and Scottish Popular Ballad in Nova Scotia: A Study of Folksong in Canada." MA thesis, McGill University, 1924.

Mahalik, Dave with photography by Murdock Smith. *Ten Nights without Sleep: Cape Breton's Celtic Colours Festival*. Wreck Cover, NS: Breton Books, 2011.

McDavid, J. "The Fiddle Burning Priest of Mabou." *Ethnologies* 30, no. 2 (2008): 115-136.

McDonald, Chris. "John Allan Cameron: The Godfather of Cape Breton's Celtic Music." *Canadian Folk Music* 46, no. 1 (2012): 1-6.

McDonald, Chris and Heather Sparling. "Interpretations of Tradition: From Gaelic Song to Celtic Pop." *Journal of Popular Music Studies* 22 no. 3 (2010): 309-28.

McGann, Joseph Clifford. "Dan R. MacDonald: Individual Creativity in the Cape Breton Fiddle Tradition." MA thesis, Memorial University of Newfoundland, 2003.

McGuigan, Peter T. *Irish. Peoples of the Maritimes*. Ed. Bridglal Pachai. Tantallon, NS: Four East Pub., 1991.

McKinnon, Ian Francis. "Fiddling to Fortune: The Role of Commercial Recordings made by Cape Breton Fiddlers in the Fiddle Music Tradition of Cape Breton Island." MA thesis, Memorial University of Newfoundland, 1989.

McPherson, Flora. *Watchman Against the World: The Remarkable Journey of Norman MacLeod and his People from Scotland to Cape Breton Island to New Zealand*. Wreck Cove, NS: Breton Books, 1993.

Melhuish, Martin. *Celtic Tides: Traditional Music in a New Age*. Kingston, ON: Quarry Press Inc., 1998.

Melin, Mats. "Gendered Movements in Cape Breton Step dancing." In *Proceedings of the 26th Symposium of the ICTM Study Group on Ethnochoreology, 2010*, 37-47. Translated by E. I. Dunin, D. Stavelova, D. Gremlicova, and Z. Vejvoda, Z. Prague: ICTM, 2012.

———. "Improvising within a Genre Framework." Paper presented at the Dance Research Forum Ireland's 3rd International Conference, Firkin Crane, Cork, Ireland, 24-27 June, 2010.

———. "Local, Global, and Diasporic Interaction in the Cape Breton Dance Tradition." In vol. 4 of *Routes and Roots: Fiddle and dance Studies from Around the North Atlantic*, 132-144. Eds. Ian Russell and Chris Goertzen. Aberdeen: The Elphinstone Institute, University of Aberdeen, 2012.

———. "Observations of Communication between Dancer and Musician in the Cape Breton Community." In *Proceedings of the Dance Research Forum Ireland*, 119-126. Translated by S. A. Phelan. Dublin: Dance Research Forum Ireland 2009, 2008.

———. "'Putting the Dirt Back in': An Investigation of Step dancing in Scotland." In vol. 3 of *Crossing over: Fiddle and Dance Studies from Around the North Atlantic*, 215-227. Eds. Ian Russell and Anna Kearney Guigné. Aberdeen: The Elphinstone Institute, 2010.

———. "Exploring the Percussive Routes and Shared Commonalities in Cape Breton Step Dancing." PhD dissertation, University of Limerick, 2012.

———. "Step dancing in Cape Breton and Scotland: Contrasting Contexts and Creative Processes." In "Atlantic Roots and Routes," ed. Heather Sparling, Kati Szego, and Frances Wilkinson, special issue, *MUSICultures* 40, no. 1 (2013).

———. "Visual Learning in the 21st Century: Cape Breton Step Dance on the Small Screen and as a Learning Tool in the Dance Class." *Canadian Folk Music* 46, no. 4 (2013): 1-6.

———. *One with the Music: Cape Breton Step Dance Tradition and Transmission.* Cape Breton University Press, 2015.

Moore, Maggie. *Scottish Step Dancing.* Edinburgh: Scottish Arts Council, 1995.

Morgan, R. J. *Early Cape Breton: From Founding to Famine, 1784-1851: Essays, Talks and Conversations.* Canada: Breton Books, 2000.

———. *Rise Again! The Story of Cape Breton Island, Vol. 1.* Toronto: Breton Books, 2008.

———. *Rise Again! The Story of Cape Breton Island from 1900 to Today, Vol. 2.* Toronto: Breton Books, 2009.

Morrison, Alex and Ted Slaney. *The Breed of Manly Men: The History of the Cape Breton Highlanders.* Toronto, ON: Canadian Institute of Strategic Studies and Sydney, NS: Cape Breton Highlanders Association, 1994.

Murray, L. "Step Dancing Makes Its Return Journey across the Atlantic." *West Highland Free Press,* August 5, 1994.

Neil, MacNeil. *The Highland Heart in Nova Scotia.* Antigonish, NS: Formac Pub. Company, 1971.

Nettl, Bruno and Helen Myers. *Folk Music in the United States: An Introduction.* Detroit: Wayne State University.,1976.

Newton, Michael. "The Macs Meet the 'Micmacs': Scottish Gaelic First Encounter Narratives from Nova Scotia." *Journal of Irish and Scottish Studies* 5, no. 1 (2011): 67-96.

———. Celts in the Americas. Sydney: Cape Breton University Press, 2013.

———. "The Origins of the Strathspey: A Rebuttal." https://virtualgael.wordpress.com , 2014. (accessed July 4 2014).

———. *Seanchaidh na Coille/The Memory-Keeper of the Forest.* Cape Breton University Press, 2015.

Nilsen, Kenneth E. "The Priest in the Gaelic Folklore of Nova Scotia." *Béaloideas* 64/65 (1996): 171-194.

———. "The Nova Scotia Gael in Boston." *Proceedings of the Harvard Celtic Colloquium* 6 (1986): 83-100.

O'Connell, Bridget. "Examining the Fiddle Styles of Newfoundland." *Irish Journal of Newfoundland and Labrador Research* (2009): 91-114.

O'Connell, Bridget. "A Comparative Study of Newfoundland and Irish Fiddle Styles." *Canadian Studies in Europe* 7 (2007): 89-111.

Osborne, Evelyn. "'I've Been Playing the Fiddle Wrong All These Years!' The Intersections between Cape Breton Radio Play and French-Newfoundland Musicians." Paper presented at the Acadian Celtic Crossroads Conference, Cape Breton University, Sydney, NS, October 12, 2013.

Osborne, Evelyn. "Fiddling with Technology: The Influence of Media on Traditional Newfoundland Musicians." *Newfoundland and Labrador Studies* 22, no. 1 (2007): 187-204.

Parette, Henri-Dominique. *Acadians: Peoples of the Maritimes*. Ed. Bridglal Pachai. Tantallon, NS: Four East Pub., 1991.

Parsons, Catrìona Nic Ìomhair. "Comparison of Scottish and Cape Breton Variants of the same Waulking Song." *Éigse: A Journal of Irish Studies* 34 (2004): 171-92.

Pease, Thomas H. "Gaelic Music of Cape Breton Island: The Last Fifteen Years." *Notes* 63, no. 2 (2006): 401-417.

Perlman, Ken. *The Fiddle Music of Prince Edward Island: Celtic and Acadian tunes in Living Tradition*. Pacific, MO: Mel Bay Publications, Inc., 1996.

———. *Couldn't Have a Wedding without the Fiddler: The Stry of Traditional Fiddling on Prince Edward Island*. Tennessee: University of Tennessee Press, 2015.

Pierce, Jennifer Ewing. "Toward a Poetics of Transubstantiation: The Performance of Cape Breton Music and Dance." *The Drama Review (TDR): A Journal of Performance Studies* 52, no. 3 (2008): 44-60.

Porter, James. "Introduction: Locating Celtic Music (and Song)." In "Locating Celtic Music (and Song)," special issue, *Western Folklore* 57, no. 4 (Autumn 1998): 205-224.

Prebble, John. *Glencoe*. London: Penguin Books, 1966.

———. *The Highland Clearances*. London: Penguin Books, 1963.

———. *Culloden*. London: Penguin Books, 1961.

Punch, Terence M. *Erin's Sons: Irish Arrivals in Atlantic Canada 1751-1858*, vol. 111. NS: Genealogical Publishing Company, 2009.

Purser, John. *Scotland's Music: A History of the Traditional and Classical Music of Scotland from Early Times to the Present Day*. Edinburgh: Mainstream Pub., 1992.

Rankin, D. J. "Reverend Kenneth J. MacDonald." *CCHA Report* 12 (1944-45): 109-116.

Reid, J. M. "Stepdancing Did Not Die Out in Scotland." *West Highland Free Press*. August 12, 1994.

Rhodes, Frank. "Dancing in Cape Breton Island, Nova Scotia." In *Traditional Dancing in Scotland*, 267-285. Ed. J. F. Flett and T. M. Flett. London: Routledge and Kegan Paul, 1985.

———. "Step-dancing in Cape Breton Island, Nova Scotia." In *Traditional Step-dancing in Scotland*, 185-211. Ed. J. F. Flett and T. M. Flett. Edinburgh: Scottish Cultural Press, 1996.

Robinson, Ann E. "The Piping Tradition in Cape Breton." MA thesis, St. Francis Xavier University, 1986.

Ross, Sally and Alphonse Deveau. *The Acadians of Nova Scotia Past and Present*. Halifax, NS: Nimbus Pub., 1992.

Ruckert, George. "John Campbell and the Cape Breton Fiddle Tradition." In *"Driving the Bow: Fiddle and Dance Studies from Around the North Atlantic* 2 (2008): 144-152. Eds. Ian Russell and Mary Anne Alburger. Aberdeen: the Elphinstone Institute.

Sawyers, June Skinner. *Bearing the People Away: The Portable Highland Clearances Companion*. Sydney, NS: Cape Breton University Press, 2013.

Shaw, John William. "A Cape Breton Gaelic Story-teller." PhD dissertation, Harvard University, 1982.

Shaw, John, Fr. John Angus Rankin and Bill Lamey. Liner notes to vol. 2 of *The Music of Cape Breton: Cape Breton Scottish Fiddle Tradition*. Topic, 1978. LP.

Shears, Barry. *The Cape Breton Collection of Bagpipe Music*. Halifax, NS: Bounty Press, 1995.

———.*The Gathering of the Clans Collection*. 2nd ed. Halifax, NS: Bounty Press, 2001.

———. *Dance to the Piper: The Highland Bagpipe in Nova Scotia*. Sydney, NS: Cape Breton University Press, 2008.

Sherwood, R.H. "Landing of the Hector." In *The Nova Scotia Historical Quarterly* Vol. 3 no. 2, June 1973.

Smith, Gordon C. "Lee Cremo: Narrative about a Micmac Fiddler." In *Canadian Music: Issues of Hegemony and Identity*, 541-556. Ed. Beverley Diamond and Robert Witmer. Toronto: Canadian Scholar's Press, 1994.

Smith, Jesse. "Realising the Music of Michael Coleman." MA thesis. Dundalk Institute of Technology, Ireland, 2008.

Spada, A. V. *The Italians in Canada*. Ottawa: Riviera Printers and publishers, 1969.

Sparling, Heather. "Mitigating or Marketing Culture? Promoting Mouth Music in Cape Breton, Nova Scotia." *Canadian Journal for Traditional Music/Revue De Musique Folklorique Canadienne* 27 (1999): 1-9.

———. "Turn that Bagpipe Up to 11, or What Happens To Ritual After 100 Decibels." Abstract. *Music Bulletin* 33, no. 1 (1999).

———. 2000. "*Puirt-a-beul*: An Ethnographic Study of Mouth Music in Cape Breton." MA thesis, York University.

———. Music is Language and Language is Music: Language Attitudes and Musical Choices in Cape Breton, Nova Scotia." *Ethnologies* 25, no. 2 (2003): 145-71.

———. "Song Genres, Cultural Capital and Social Distinctions in Gaelic Cape Breton." PhD dissertation, York University, 2005.

———. "Transmission Processes in Cape Breton Gaelic Song Culture." In *Folk Music, Traditional Music, Ethnomusicology: Canadian Perspectives, Past and Present*, 13-26. Ed. Anna Hoefnagels and Gordon E. Smith. Newcastle: Cambridge Scholars Pub., 2007.

———. "One Foot on Either Side of the Chasm: Mary Jane Lamond's Gaelic Language Choice." *Shima: The International Journal of Research into Island Cultures* 1, no. 1 (2007): 28-42.

———. "Categorically Speaking: Towards a Theory of (Musical) Genre in Cape Breton Gaelic Culture." *Ethnomusicology* 52, no. 3 (2008): 401-25.

———. "Grist for the Tourist Mill: Tourists in Gaelic Milling Frolics in Cape Breton, Nova Scotia." In *Refereed Papers from the Third International Small Islands Culture Conference*, 94-100. Ed. I. Novaczek. Sydney: Small Islands Cultures Research Initiative, 2008.

———. "Cape Breton Island: Living in the Past? Gaelic Language, Song, and Competition." In *Island Songs: A Global Repertoire*, 49-63. Ed. G. Baldacchino. Lanham: Scarecrow Press, 2011.

———. *Reeling Roosters and Dancing Ducks: Celtic Mouth Music*. Cape Breton University Press, 2014.

Speck, F. G. "Some Micmac Tales from Cape Breton Island." *The Journal of American Folklore* 28, no. 107 (January-March 1915): 59-69.

Spielman, Earl V. "The Fiddling Traditions of Cape Breton and Texas: A Study in Parallels and Contrasts." *Anuario Interamericano De Investigacion Musical* 8 (1972): 39-48.

———. "Traditional North American Fiddling: A Methodology for the Historical and Comparative Analytical Style of Study of Instrumental Music Traditions." PhD dissertation, University of Wisconsin-Madison, 1975.

Stanford Reid, W. *The Scottish Tradition in Canada: A History of Canada's Peoples*. Toronto: McClelland and Stewart, 1988.

Stanley, Laurie. *The Well-Watered Garden: The Presbyterian Church in Cape Breton, 1798-1860*. Sydney, NS: University College of Cape Breton Press, 1983.

Sullivan, Cheryl. *Ar dileab 's ar dochas: Fifty Years of the Nova Scotia Highland Village*. Nova Scotia Highland Village Society: 2000

Tennyson, Brian. *Impressions of Cape Breton*. Sydney, NS: University College of Cape Breton Press, 1986.

Thompson, Marie. "The Fall and Rise of the Cape Breton Fiddler: 1955-1982." MA thesis, Saint Mary's University, 2003.

———. "The Myth of the Vanishing Cape Breton Fiddler: The Role of a CBC Film in the Cape Breton Fiddle Revival." *Acadiensis* 35, no. 2 (2006): 5-26.

Thurgood, Ranald. "Storytelling on the Gabarus-Framboise Coast of Cape Breton: Oral/Narrative Repertoire Analysis of a Folk Community." PhD dissertation, Memorial University of Newfoundland, 2000.

Trevor-Roper, Hugh. "The Invention of Tradition: The Highland Tradition of Scotland." In *The Invention of Tradition*, 15-42. Ed. E. Hobsbawm and T. Ranger. Cambridge: Cambridge University Press, 1983.

Turino, Thomas. *Music as Social Life: The Politic of Participation*. Chicago: University of Chicago Press, 2008.

Vallely, Fintan. *Tuned Out–Traditional Music and Identity in Northern Ireland*. Ireland: Cork University Press, 2008.

———. "The Making of a Lifelong Companion: An Editor's Memoir." In *New Hibernia Review/Iris Éireannach Nua*, 4 (2) (Summer).

Vernon, C. W. *Cape Breton, Canada at the Beginning of the Twentieth Century*. Toronto: National Pub., 1903.

Voyer, Simonne. "La Danse Traditionnelle dans l'Est du Canada." Québec: Université Laval, 1986.

Wallis. W. D. and R. S. Wallis. *The Micmac Indians of Eastern Canada*. Minneapolis: University of Minnesota Press, 1954.

Williams, Scott. *Pipers of Nova Scotia: Biographical Sketches, 1773 to 2000*. Antigonish, NS: Scott Williams Pub., 2000.

Wilson, Mark. Liner notes to *Traditional Music of Cape Breton, Volume 1: Mabou Coal Mines*. Rounder records Corp., CD, 2002.

———. Liner notes to *Traditional Music of Cape Breton, Volume 2: The Rover's Return*. Rounder records Corp., CD, 2002.

———. Liner notes to *Willie Kennedy: Cape Breton Violin*. Rounder records Corp., CD, 2002.

———. Liner notes to *Alex Francis MacKay: Gaelic in the Bow*. Rounder Records Corp., CD, 2005.

———. Liner notes to *Joe Peter MacLean: Back of Boisdale*. Rounder Records Corp., CD, 2005.

———. Liner notes to John L. MacDonald: Formerly of Foot Cape. Rounder records Corp., CD, 2005.

———. Liner notes to *Theresa Morrison: Laments and Merry Melodies*. Rounder Records Corp., CD, 1999.

Wilson, Mark and Kate Dunlay. Liner notes to *Traditional Music of Cape Breton, Volume 4; MacKinnon's Brook*. Rounder Records Corp., CD, 2008.

Wilson, Mark and Vince MacLean. Liner notes to *Traditional Music of Cape Breton, Volume 3; Bras d'Or House*. Rounder Records Corp., CD, 2008.

Woods, Bret D. "Bakhtin and Genre: Musical-Social Interaction at the Cape Breton Milling Frolic." PhD dissertation, Florida State University, 2011.

Zinck, John R. *East Coast Ceilidh: A Look at Atlantic Canada's Music Scene*. Halifax, NS: Nimbus Publishing, 1999.

INDEX

The Index is an alphabetical listing of musicians and other stakeholders in the tradition whose contribution is noted throughout *The Companion*, but not in an individual (or a family) article.

Page numbers refer to the print edition.

MacLellan, Angus 267
MacLellan, Archie Dan 51
MacLellan, Charlie 58, 185
MacLellan, Charles 248
MacLellan, Dan Allan 186
MacLellan, Donald Allan 58
MacLellan, Donald Allan "Red John" 309
MacLellan, Flora 56
MacLellan, Jessie Maggie 184, 303, 380
MacLellan, Joe 58
MacLellan, John Alex 58
MacLellan, Johnnie 266
MacLellan, Lauchie 103
MacLellan, Malcolm 266
MacLellan, Neil Francis 123
MacLellan, Roddie 58
MacLellan, Wilfred 58
MacLennan, Angus 91
MacLennan, Danny 91
MacLennan, Dr. Gordon 102
MacLennan, John Alex 380
MacLennan, John A. "Wild Archie" 97, 123
MacLennan, Kelly (Warner) 57
MacLeod, CIN 103, 357
MacLeod, Fr. Colonel 40, 94, 240, 268
MacLeod, Cynthia 179
MacLeod, Fr. Greg 369
MacLeod, John 60
MacLeod, Johnnie 334
MacLeod, Maggie 389
MacLeod, Norman 201
MacLeod, Rev. Norman 382
MacLeod, Phyllis 262
MacLeod, Robert 61
MacLeod, Rory 268
MacMaster, Minnie 39, 51, 128, 183, 271
MacMaster, Vincent 269
MacMillan, Fr. Allan J. 79, 94, 355
MacMillan, John 41
MacMullen, Joseph 123
MacMullin, Annie 20
MacMullin, Rod 86
MacMullin MacNeil, John Alex 53
MacNab, Mary Isdale 128
MacNeil, Alex 370
MacNeil, Ann (MacDonald) 139, 217-18

MacNeil, Archie A. 40, 68, 253
MacNeil, Dave 46
MacNeil, Donald Anthony 164
MacNeil, Hector 43
MacNeil, Hughie C. 8
MacNeil, "Black Jack" 219
MacNeil, Jack 259, 277
MacNeil, Jackie 44, 246
MacNeil, Jerry 54
MacNeil, Joe 68, 119
MacNeil, Joe Neil 79, 188, 355
MacNeil, John Alex "The Fiddler" 259, 262
MacNeil, John Angus 211
MacNeil, John S. 259
MacNeil, Kenzie 354
MacNeil, Marion 24
MacNeil, Mary 67
MacNeil, McKayla 68, 389
MacNeil, Mike 53, 157
MacNeil, Myrna 24
MacNeil, Paul 22, 24, 73, 182, 276, 298-99, 378
MacNeil, Peter 80
MacNeil, Rita 30, 41, 43, 52, 162, 252, 272, 282, 347, 353
MacNeil, Fr. Rory 32, 265
MacNeil, Rosemary 24
MacNeil, Ryan J. 18, 42, 84
MacNeil, Seumas 22
MacNeil, Stanley 89
MacNeil, Steve 67
MacPhee, Billy 264, 285
MacPhee, Bruce 348
MacPhee, Cyril 198
MacPhee, Danny 279
MacPhee, Henry 277
MacPhee, Ian 68
MacPhee, John 348
MacPhee, Malcolm (Malcie) 198, 245, 354
MacPhee, Peter 32, 59, 68, 191, 254, 279, 372
MacPhee, Wendell 53
MacPherson, A. Martin 221
MacPherson, Angus 221
MacPherson, Courtney 8, 233
MacPherson, Joe 46, 387
MacPherson, John Alick 201
MacPherson, Judge Hugh J. 66

CPSIA information can be obtained
at www.ICGtesting.com
Printed in the USA
LVOW03s1744031115

460931LV00017B/597/P

9 781772 060249